Plato's *Sophist*

Martin Heidegger

Plato's *Sophist*

Translated by
Richard Rojcewicz
and
André Schuwer

INDIANA
University Press
Bloomington & Indianapolis

Publication of this work was supported by funding
from Inter Nationes, Bonn.

This book is a publication of

Indiana University Press
601 North Morton Street
Bloomington, Indiana 47404-3797 USA

http://iupress.indiana.edu

Telephone orders 800-842-6796
Fax orders 812-855-7931
Orders by e-mail iuporder@indiana.edu

Published in German as *Platon: Sophistes*

First Indiana University Press paperback edition 2003

The paper used in this publication meets the minimum requirements of American National Standard for Information Sciences—Permanence of Paper for Printed Library Materials, ANSI Z39.48-1984.

Library of Congress Cataloging-in-Publication Data

Heidegger, Martin, 1889–1976.
[Platon, Sophistes. English]
Plato's Sophist / Martin Heidegger ; translated by Richard Rojcewicz and André Schuwer.
p. cm.—(Studies in Continental thought)
Reconstructs Martin Heidegger's lecture course at the University of Marburg, winter semester, 1924–1925.
Includes bibliographical references.
ISBN 978-0-253-33222-6 (cloth : alk. paper)
1. Plato. Sophist. 2. Logic. 3. Meaning (Philosophy)
4. Aristotle I. Title. II. Series.
B384.H4513 1997
184—dc20 96-32709

ISBN 978-0-253-21629-8 (pbk.)

4 5 6 7 13 12 11

Contents

MAIN PART

Plato's Research into Being
Interpretation of the Sophist

Preliminary Remarks

INTRODUCTION

The Prelude to the Dialogue
*(*Sophist *216a–219a)*

SECTION TWO

Ontological Discussion
The Being of Non-beings (Sophist *236e–264b)*

Introduction
(236e–237a)

Translators' Foreword

This book is a translation of *Platon: Sophistes*, which was published in 1992 as volume 19 of Heidegger's *Gesamtausgabe* (Collected Works). The text is a reconstruction of the author's lecture course delivered under the same title at the University of Marburg in the winter semester 1924–25. The course was devoted to an interpretation of both Plato, especially his late dialogue, the *Sophist*, and Aristotle, especially Book VI of the *Nicomachean Ethics*. It is one of Heidegger's major works, because of its intrinsic importance as an interpretation of ancient philosophy and also on account of its relation to *Being and Time*.

The first page of Heidegger's *magnum opus*, *Being and Time*, immediately following the table of contents, quotes a passage from Plato which Heidegger uses as a motto for the entire work. Heidegger himself later stressed that this quotation was not intended to serve as a mere decoration.[1] Thus it is, on the contrary, intrinsically connected to the matter at issue in *Being and Time*; it names the central, unifying matter at issue in *Being and Time*, which can then be seen as a single protracted meditation revolving around this one sentence from Plato. The sentence occurs at the heart of the *Sophist*. Furthermore, Heidegger chose it as the motto precisely at the time he was both delivering these lectures on that dialogue, in 1925, and composing *Being and Time*, which was published in 1927 but was substantially complete when presented to Husserl in manuscript form the year before, at a gathering in the Black Forest to celebrate Husserl's sixty-seventh birthday (whence the place and date on the dedication page: *Todtnauberg i. Bad. Schwarzwald zum 8. April 1926*). Thus *Being and Time* is closely connected to this lecture course, both temporally and thematically. They are both meditations on the matters at issue in the *Sophist* and shed light on each other. In one of the senses in which *Being and Time* is a repetition, it is a repetition of this lecture course. It is not a *mere* repetition, naturally, and the difference is that in these lectures Heidegger stays closer to the text of Plato and approaches the problematic in Platonic terms, while in the repetition he engages in the ontological problem by taking a more thematically determined route, namely, the path of a hermeneutical analysis of Dasein (human

1. Martin Heidegger, *Kant und das Problem der Metaphysik*, hrsg. F.-W. von Herrmann (GA 3), Frankfurt: Klostermann, 1991, p. 239. English translations: of the 1973 edition by Richard Taft, *Kant and the Problem of Metaphysics*, Bloomington: Indiana University Press, 1990, p. 163; and of the 1950 edition by James Churchill, *Kant and the Problem of Metaphysics*, Bloomington: Indiana University Press, p. 248.

being insofar as it is the place where Being reveals itself). These lectures then show what Heidegger always claimed, namely, that the hermeneutic of Dasein has its roots in the philosophical tradition and is not a viewpoint foisted dogmatically on the problem of Being.

Heidegger devoted the first part of his lecture course on the *Sophist* to a preparation for reading Plato. This part, amounting to a full-length treatise in itself, is an interpretation of Aristotle. It is one of Heidegger's major interpretations of Aristotle and his only extended commentary on Book VI (the discussion of the so-called intellectual virtues) of the *Nicomachean Ethics*. Heidegger uses Aristotle to approach Plato, rather than the other way around, which would be chronologically correct, because of his view that as a principle of hermeneutics we must go from the clear to the obscure. For Heidegger, Aristotle is the only path to Plato, because Aristotle prepares the ground for our understanding of Plato's ontological research, specifically by making explicit what is only implicit in Plato, namely, the link between truth (understood as disclosedness) and Being.

The actual interpretation of the *Sophist* is unique among Heidegger's works in being so extensively devoted to a single dialogue. Heidegger slowly and painstakingly interprets the text, practically line by line. The interpretation is quintessential Heidegger, displaying his trademark original approach to Greek philosophy, one which created such a sensation among his students. The contemporary reader is invited to participate in Heidegger's venture, as were the original auditors of his courses, and can now see what caused the sensation and make his or her own judgment on it.

The theme of Plato's *Sophist*, mirrored in a remarkable number of ways—for instance in the seemingly extraneous search for the definition of the sophist—is the relation of Being and non-being, and the central concern is to challenge Parmenides' view that non-beings in no way are. Heidegger's interpretation of this dialogue lies, accordingly, at the center of his own thinking, for these are fundamental themes of his philosophy as well: Being in distinction to beings, to non-beings, to falsity, to appearance. For Heidegger, and, as he shows, for Plato too, these are not simple oppositions; instead, they have something in common. This commonality or δύναμις κοινωνίας ("potential for sharing") is a thread of Ariadne to the entire ontological problematic, and Heidegger nowhere focuses on it as intensely as he does here.

In form, the book is practically a running commentary; Greek citation and Heidegger's interpretation leapfrog one another down every page. In almost all cases, Heidegger himself translates the citations or at least translates those portions he wishes to draw out, although these translations are often paraphrases and are not always put in quotation marks. Readers with little or no knowledge of Greek can then be confident that they are following the main train of thought. In addition to these citations, almost every sentence in the book incorporates isolated Greek terms and phrases Heidegger often does not render into German. For these, I have prepared an extensive glossary, which can be found at the end of the book. This glossary can hardly substitute for Heidegger's nuanced understanding of the concepts of Greek philosophy as this understanding emerges in the course of the lectures. I offer it merely to provide a general orientation. Its use, of course, does presuppose some familiarity with ancient Greek, since not every form of the words on the list could be included.

Instead of a glossary of German terms, I have, when I thought it necessary to indicate that the translation misses some nuance, interpolated the German words directly into the text, placing them within square brackets ([ ]). These brackets have been reserved throughout the book for translators' insertions, and all footnotes stemming from the translators are marked "Trans." For the convenience of those wishing to correlate our translation with the original, the German pagination is given in the running heads.

My collaborator, mentor, and friend, André Schuwer, passed away before this translation was complete. He was a Franciscan friar who chose as his personal device the Biblical ideal: *Esto perfectus*. I could almost hear him reprove me with that as I carried on this work, which I dedicate to his memory.

Richard Rojcewicz
Point Park College
Pittsburgh

Plato's *Sophist*

In memoriam
Paul Natorp

A lecture course on Plato today in Marburg is obliged to call up the memory of Paul Natorp, who passed away during the recent holidays. His last activity as a teacher at our university was a seminar on Plato in the previous summer semester. These exercises were for him a new approach to a revision of his work on "Plato's Theory of Ideas."[1] This book has had a decisive influence on the Plato scholarship of the last twenty years. The outstanding feature of the work is the level of philosophical understanding it strives for and actually carries out with unprecedented narrow focus. This "narrowness" is not meant as a reproach; on the contrary, it indicates just how intensely penetrating the book is. It provided a sharp awareness of the fact that a thorough acquaintance with the material is not sufficient for a genuine understanding and that the latter cannot be realized by means of average philosophical information, randomly acquired. The best testimonial to the work is the fact that it met with opposition, i.e., it compelled reflection. But its level of understanding has not been equaled.

The history of the origin of the book is telling. Natorp wanted to work out a text, with commentary, of the single dialogue *Parmenides*, and the book presents the preparation for it. The hermeneutic situation, or rather its foundation, was marked by Kant and the Marburg School, i.e., by epistemology and theory of science. In accord with his basic philosophical orientation, Natorp considered the history of Greek philosophy in the perspective and within the limits of the epistemologically oriented Neo-Kantianism of the Marburg School. Accordingly, he took a critical position against Aristotle, who represented realism, as well as against the appropriation of Aristotle in the Middle Ages, which was dogmatism. Yet this by no means derived from an inadequate knowledge of Aristotle. On the contrary, Natorp anticipated results we are attaining only today. Natorp's studies on Greek philosophy are the following: *"Thema und Disposition der aristotelischen Metaphysik,"* 1888; *"Aristoteles: Metaphysik K 1–8,"* 1888; *"Aristoteles und die Eleaten,"* 1890; *"Die ethischen Fragmente des Demokrit, Text und*

1. P. Natorp, *Platos Ideenlehre: Eine Einführung in den Idealismus*, Leipzig, 1903. Zweite, durchges. und um einen metakritischen Anhang (Logos-Psyche-Eros, pp. 457–513) vermehrte Ausgabe, Leipzig, 1921.

Untersuchungen," 1893; *"Forschungen zur Geschichte des Erkenntnisproblems im Altertum,"* 1884.[2]

Furthermore, the hermeneutic situation was marked by the fact that, within the compass of Neo-Kantianism, Natorp raised on the basis of the philosophy of Kant the most acute questioning with regard to a universal science of consciousness. His special position and his special merit within the Marburg School consist in the fact that he raised the question of psychology within Neo-Kantianism for the first time, i.e., the question of how it might be possible to integrate into philosophy the natural scientific psychology then prevailing. His works in this field are the following: *"Einleitung in die Psychologie nach kritischer Methode,"* 1888; *"Allgemeine Psychologie nach kritischer Methode,"* 1912.[3] He took his orientation from Descartes, whose epistemology he had written about: *"Descartes' Erkenntnistheorie,"* 1882.[4]

Natorp raised in his psychology the problem of consciousness, i.e., he questioned the method by which consciousness itself comes into question as the foundation of philosophical research. The question of consciousness as the foundation of philosophy was then, as we said, essentially dominated by the natural scientific mode of questioning; at the same time, however, it was given direction by Brentano's *Psychologie vom empirischen Standpunkt*.[5] The new edition of Natorp's *Psychologie*, which appeared in 1912,[6] is especially valuable on account of the two critical appendices, in which he comes to terms with the philosophical investigations of his contemporaries.

Natorp was the one who was best prepared to discuss Husserl. This is demonstrated by his works *"Zur Frage der logischen Methode,"*[7] 1901, where he takes up Husserl's *Logische Untersuchungen, Erster Band: Prolegomena zur*

2. P. Natorp, *"Thema und Disposition der aristotelischen Metaphysik,"* in *Philosophische Monatshefte*, Bd. 24, 1888, Teil I, pp. 37–65; Teil II, pp. 540–574.

P. Natorp, *"Ueber Aristoteles' Metaphysik, K 1–8, 1065a26,"* in *Archiv für Geschichte der Philosophie*, Bd. I, Heft 2, 1888, pp. 178–193.

P. Natorp, *"Aristoteles und die Eleaten,"* in *Philosophische Monatshefte*, Bd. 26, 1890, Teil I, pp. 1–16; Teil II, pp. 147–169.

P. Natorp, *Die Ethika des Demokritos. Text und Untersuchungen*, Marburg, 1893.

P. Natorp, *Forschungen zur Geschichte des Erkenntnisproblems im Altertum: Protagoras, Demokrit, Epikur und die Skepsis*, Berlin, 1884.

3. P. Natorp, *Einleitung in die Psychologie nach kritischer Methode*, Freiburg i. Br., 1888.

P. Natorp, *Allgemeine Psychologie nach kritischer Methode. Erstes Buch: Objekt und Methode der Psychologie*, Tübingen, 1912.

4. P. Natorp, *Descartes' Erkenntnißtheorie: Eine Studie zur Vorgeschichte des Kriticismus*, Marburg, 1882.

5. F. Brentano, *Psychologie vom empirischen Standpunkt. In zwei Bänden.* Band I, Leipzig, 1874.

F. Brentano, *Von der Klassifikation der psychischen Phänomene. Neue, durch Nachträge stark vermehrte Ausgabe der betreffenden Kapitel der Psychologie vom empirischen Standpunkt*, Leipzig, 1911.

6. Cf. note 3, second listing.

7. P. Natorp, *"Zur Frage der logischen Methode. Mit Beziehung auf Edm. Husserls 'Prolegomena zur reinen Logik' (Logische Untersuchungen, Teil 1),"* in *Kantstudien*, 6, H. 2/3, 1901, pp. 270–283.

reinen Logik, and furthermore by his "*Husserls Ideen zu einer reinen Phänomenologie*,"[8] which was published in 1914 and again in 1918, where he treats Husserl's *Ideen*. Natorp's instigations were determinative for Husserl himself.

The expanse of Natorp's field of work is visible in the following. As a rule, the Marburg School was oriented toward epistemology. For Natorp, however, essentially different themes were alive in the background: social philosophy and pedagogy and, ultimately, the philosophy of religion as well, which latter was the concern of his first publication and of his very last days. Thus his first publication, his first work[9] as a doctor of philosophy, concerned the relation of theoretical and practical knowledge with respect to the foundation of a non-empirical reality. There followed the time of his work with Cohen. To appreciate Natorp's scientific merit, we must locate his work back into the last two decades of the nineteenth century; at that time everyone did not yet have a philosophical interest. That today we can go beyond Kant is possible only because we were first forced back to him by the Marburg School. The mission of the Marburg School was on the one hand to uphold and resume the tradition and on the other hand to cultivate the rigor of conceptual thought. At the same time, we must locate the scientific work of the Marburg School, e.g., Cohen's *Theorie der Erfahrung*,[10] back into its era, when Brentano wrote his *Psychologie vom empirischen Standpunkt* and Dilthey his *Das Leben Schleiermachers*.[11] It was starting from these three books and standpoints that more recent philosophy, contemporary philosophy, developed. It is the peculiar characteristic of the Marburg School to have attained the most acute questioning and to have developed the keenest conceptualization. We do not wish to come to a decision here on the question of its truth or falsity. Perhaps that is even a mistaken question.

Natorp was one of the few and one of the first, indeed perhaps the only one among German professors, who more than ten years ago understood what the young people of Germany wanted when in the fall of 1913 they gathered at Hohen Meißner and pledged to form their lives out of inner truthfulness and self-responsibility. Many of these best have fallen. But whoever has eyes to see knows that today our Dasein is slowly being transposed upon new foundations and that young people have their part

8. P. Natorp, "*Husserls Ideen zu einer reinen Phänomenologie*," in *Die Geisteswissenschaften*, Jahrg. 1, 1913–14, pp. 420–426, 448–451; reprinted in *Logos*, Bd. VII, 1917–18, H. 3, pp. 224–246.

9. P. Natorp, "Über das Verhältniß des theoretischen und praktischen Erkennens zur Begründung einer nichtempirischen Realität. Mit Bezug auf: W. Herrmann, Die Religion im Verhältniß zum Welterkennen und zur Sittlichkeit," in *Zeitschrift für Philosophie und philosophische Kritik*, Jg. 79, 1881, pp. 242–259.

10. H. Cohen, *Kants Theorie der Erfahrung*, Berlin, 1871; 2., neubearbeitete Auflage, Berlin, 1885.

11. W. Dilthey, *Leben Schleiermachers*. Erster Band, Berlin, 1870.

to play in this task. Natorp understood them, and so they are the best ones to preserve his memory. It is difficult for us to take up the heritage of his spirit and to work with the same impartiality and thoroughness. Even in the last weeks of his life he was attacked very sharply and most unjustly. His response was, "I will keep silent." He could keep silent; he was one of those men with whom one could walk in silence. The thoroughness and expanse of his real knowledge can no longer be found today. His genuine understanding of Greek philosophy taught him that even today there is still no cause to be especially proud of the progress of philosophy.

PRELIMINARY CONSIDERATIONS

§1. The necessity of a double preparation for interpreting the Platonic dialogues.

Our lectures will make it their task to interpret two of Plato's late dialogues.[1] The reason for restricting the interpretation to these two dialogues is that their thematic content requires an especially penetrating understanding. The appropriation of the issues we are about to broach must be carried out in such a way that they are brought home to us constantly anew. Being and non-being, truth and semblance, knowledge and opinion, concept and assertion, value and non-value, are basic concepts, ones which everyone understands at first hearing, as it were. We feel they are obvious; there is nothing further to be determined about them. The interpretation of the two dialogues is to make us familiar with what these concepts really mean. A double preparation will be required:

1.) an orientation concerning how such peculiar objects as Being and non-being, truth and semblance, become visible at all: where things like that are to be sought in the first place, in order then to be able to deal with them;

2.) a preparation in the sense that we grasp in the right way the past which we encounter in Plato, so that we do not interpret into it arbitrary viewpoints and foist upon it arbitrary considerations.

The double preparation thus comprises an orientation concerning, on the one hand, the character of the objects to be dealt with and, on the other hand, the ground out of which we attain the historical past.

As to the first, we can let a consideration of the method and aim of phenomenology serve as the preparation. This consideration should be taken merely as an initial brief indication. It is indeed our intention, in the course of the lectures and within a discussion of the concepts, to introduce ourselves gradually into this kind of research—precisely by taking up the matters at issue themselves.

a) Philosophical-phenomenological preparation. Method and aim of phenomenology.

The expression "phenomenology" is easily the most appropriate to make clear what is involved here. Phenomenology means φαινόμενον: that which

1. Heidegger is referring to the dialogues *Sophist* and *Philebus*. In this course only the interpretation of the *Sophist* was actually worked out.

shows itself, and λέγειν: to speak about. As so determined, however, phenomenology could be identified with any given science. Even botany describes what shows itself. The phenomenological way of consideration is distinguished by the determinate respect in which it posits the beings that show themselves and in which it pursues them. The primary respect is the question of the Being of these beings. We shall henceforth call what shows itself the "phenomenon." This expression must not be confused with what is denoted by "appearance" or "semblance." "Phenomena" designates beings as they show themselves in the various possibilities of their becoming disclosed. This type of consideration, which is at bottom an obvious one, is not a mere technical device but is alive in every originally philosophizing work. Thus we can learn it precisely from the simple and original considerations of the Greeks. In the present era, the phenomenological mode of thought was adopted explicitly for the first time in Husserl's *Logical Investigations*. These investigations have as their theme specific phenomena out of the domain of what we call consciousness or lived experience. They describe specific types of lived experience, acts of knowledge, of judgment; they question how these really appear, how their structure is to be determined. That consciousness and lived experience were the first themes is founded in the times, i.e., in history. Of importance here was descriptive psychology and, above all, Dilthey. In order to establish something about knowledge, about the various acts of lived experience, etc., one must understand how these phenomena appear. That entails a whole chain of difficulties. Yet what is most difficult to master here resides in the fact that all these regions already trail behind themselves a rich history of research, with the consequence that their objects cannot be approached freely but instead come into view in each case through already determined perspectives and modes of questioning. Hence the necessity of constant criticism and cross-checking. The Platonic dialogues, in the life of speech and counter-speech, are particularly suited to carry out such criticism and cross-checking. We will not discuss the further course of development of the phenomenological movement in philosophy. What is decisive is that phenomenology has once again made it possible, in the field of philosophy, to raise questions, and to answer them, scientifically. Whether phenomenology solves all the questions of philosophy is not yet decided thereby. If it understands itself and the times correctly, it will restrict itself at the outset to the work of bringing into view for the first time the matters at issue and providing an understanding of them.

Now an introduction into phenomenology does not take place by reading phenomenological literature and noting what is established therein. What is required is not a knowledge of positions and opinions. In that way phenomenology would be misunderstood from the very outset. Rather, concrete work on the matters themselves must be the way to gain an understanding of phenomenology. It would be idle to go back over phenomenological trends and issues; instead, what counts is to bring oneself into position to see phenomenologically in the very work of discussing the matters at issue. Once an understanding of these is gained, then phenomenology may very well disappear. Our lectures do not intend to train you to be phenomenologists; on the contrary, the authentic task of a lecture course in philosophy at a university is to lead you to an inner understanding of scientific questioning within your own respective fields. Only in this way is the question of science and life brought to a decision, namely by first learning the movement of scientific work and, thereby, the true inner sense of scientific existence.

Let us now proceed to the second point of our preparation, namely the correct grasp of the historical past we encounter in Plato.

b) Historiographical-hermeneutical preparation. The basic principle of hermeneutics: from the clear into the obscure. From Aristotle to Plato.

This past, to which our lectures are seeking access, is nothing detached from us, lying far away. On the contrary, we are this past itself. And we are it not insofar as we explicitly cultivate the tradition and become friends of classical antiquity, but, instead, our philosophy and science live on these foundations, i.e., those of Greek philosophy, and do so to such an extent that we are no longer conscious of it: the foundations have become obvious. Precisely in what we no longer see, in what has become an everyday matter, something is at work that was once the object of the greatest spiritual exertions ever undertaken in Western history. The goal of our interpretation of the Platonic dialogues is to take what has become obvious and make it transparent in these foundations. To understand history cannot mean anything else than to understand ourselves—not in the sense that we might establish various things about ourselves, but that we experience what we *ought* to be. To appropriate a past means to come to know oneself as indebted to that past. The authentic possibility to *be* history itself resides in this, that philosophy discover it is guilty of an omission, a neglect, if it believes it can begin anew, make things easy for itself, and let itself be stirred by just any random philosopher. But if this is true, i.e., if history means something such as this for spiritual existence, the difficulty of the task of understanding the past is increased. If we wish to penetrate into the actual philosophical work of Plato we must be guaranteed that right from the start we are taking the correct path of access. But that would mean coming across something that precisely does not simply lie there before us. Therefore, we need a guiding line. Previously it was usual to interpret the Platonic philosophy by proceeding from Socrates and the Presocratics to Plato. We wish to strike out in the opposite direction, from Aristotle back to Plato. This way is not unprecedented. It follows the old principle of hermeneutics, namely that interpretation should proceed from the clear into the obscure. We will presuppose that Aristotle understood Plato. Even those who have only a rough acquaintance with Aristotle will see from the level of his work that it is no bold assertion to maintain that Aristotle understood Plato. No more than it is to say in general on the question of understanding that the later ones always understand their predecessors better than the predecessors understood themselves. Precisely here lies the element of creative research, that in what is most decisive this research does not understand itself. If we wish to penetrate into the Platonic philosophy, we will do so with Aristotle as the guiding line. That implies no value judgment on Plato. What Aristotle said is what Plato placed at his disposal, only it is said more radically and developed more scientifically. Aristotle should thus prepare us for Plato, point us in the direction of the characteristic questioning of the two Platonic dialogues *Sophist* and *Philebus*. And this preparation will consist in the question of λόγος as ἀληθεύειν in the various domains of ὄν and ἀεί as well as of the ἐνδέχεται ἄλλως.[2]

Now because Aristotle was not followed by anyone greater, we are forced to leap into his own philosophical work in order to gain an orientation. Our lectures can indicate this orientation only in a schematic way and within the limits of basic questions.

Plato will be cited following the edition of Henricus Stephanus of 1519; in all modern editions the numbers of these pages and columns are included. We will restrict our interpretation to the two dialogues *Sophist* and *Philebus*.[3] In order to clarify more difficult questions we will refer to the dialogue *Parmenides* for ontology and *Theaetetus* for the phenomenology of cognition.

c) First indication of the theme of the *Sophist*. The sophist. The philosopher. The Being of beings.

In the *Sophist*, Plato considers human Dasein in one of its most extreme possibilities, namely philosophical existence. Specifically, Plato shows indirectly what the philosopher is by displaying what the sophist is. And he does not show this by setting up an empty program, i.e., by saying what one would have to do to be a philosopher, but he shows it by actually philosophizing. For one can say concretely what the sophist is as the au-

2. Aristotle, *Nic. Eth.* VI, 2, 1139a6ff., and 3, 1139b20ff.
3. See p. 5, note 1.

thentic non-philosopher only by actually living in philosophy. Thus it happens that this dialogue manifests a peculiar intertwining. Precisely on the path of a reflection on the Being of beings, Plato attains the correct ground for interpreting the sophist in his Being. Accordingly, our first orientation toward Aristotle will focus on what he says about beings and Being.

§2. *Orientation toward Plato's* Sophist, *with Aristotle as point of departure.*

a) The theme: the Being of beings.

At first, beings are taken wholly indeterminately, and specifically as the beings of the world in which Dasein is and as the beings which are themselves Dasein. These beings are at first disclosed only within a certain circuit. Man lives in his surrounding world, which is disclosed only within certain limits. Out of this natural orientation in his world, something like science arises for him, which is an articulation of Dasein's world, and of Dasein itself, in determinate respects. Yet what is most proximally there is not yet known in the sense of a cognition; instead, consciousness has a determined view about it, a δόξα, which perceives the world as it for the most part appears and shows itself, δοκεῖ. In this way certain views are initially formed in natural Dasein, opinions about life and its meaning. Both the sophist and the orator move in them. Yet insofar as scientific research gets underway from this natural Dasein, it must precisely penetrate through these opinions, these preliminary determinations, seek a way to the matters themselves, so that these become more determinate, and on that basis gain the appropriate concepts. For everyday Dasein this is not an obvious course to pursue, and it is difficult for everyday Dasein to capture beings in their Being—even for a people like the Greeks, whose daily life revolved around language. The *Sophist*—and every dialogue—shows Plato underway. They show him breaking through truisms and coming to a genuine understanding of the phenomena; and at the same time they manifest where Plato had to stand still and could not penetrate.

In order to be able to watch Plato at work and to repeat this work correctly, the proper standpoint is needed. We will look for information from Aristotle about which beings he himself, and hence Plato and the Greeks, had in view and what were for them the ways of access to these beings. In this fashion we put ourselves, following Aristotle, into the correct attitude, the correct way of seeing, for an inquiry into beings and their Being. Only if we have a first orientation about that do we make it possible to transpose ourselves into the correct manner of considering a Platonic dialogue and, once having been transposed, to follow it in each of its steps. The interpretation has no other task than to discuss the dialogue still once more as originally as possible.

b) The way of access: knowledge and truth. Ἀλήθεια.

Usually knowledge refers to a way of access and a way of relating which disclose beings as such and such and take possession of what is thus disclosed. The knowledge that discloses beings is "true." Knowledge which has grasped beings expresses itself and settles itself in a proposition, an assertion. We call such an assertion a truth. The concept of truth, i.e., the phenomenon of truth, as it has been determined by the Greeks, will hence provide information about what knowledge is for the Greeks and what it is "in its relation" to beings. For presumably the Greeks have conceptually analyzed the concept of "truth" as a "property" of knowledge and have done so with regard to the knowledge that was alive in their Dasein. We do not want to survey the history of Greek logic but are seeking instead an orientation at the place within Greek logic where the determination of truth reached its culmination, i.e., in Aristotle.

From the tradition of logic, as it is still alive today, we know that truth is determined explicitly with reference to Aristotle. Aristotle was the first to emphasize: truth is a judgment; the determinations true or false primarily apply to judgments. Truth is "judgmental truth." We will see later to what extent this determination is in a sense correct, though superficial: on the basis of "judgmental truth" the phenomenon of truth will be discussed and founded.

§3. *First characteristic of* ἀλήθεια.

a) The meaning of the word ἀλήθεια. Ἀλήθεια and Dasein.

The Greeks have a characteristic expression for truth: ἀλήθεια. The α is an α-privative. Thus they have a negative expression for something we understand positively. "Truth" has for the Greeks the same negative sense as has, e.g., our "imperfection." This expression is not purely and simply negative but is negative in a particular way. That which we designate as imperfect does not have nothing at all to do with perfection; on the contrary, it is precisely oriented toward it: in relation to perfection it is not all that it could be. This type of negation is a quite peculiar one. It is often hidden in words and meanings: an example is the word "blind," which is also a negative expression. Blind means not to be able to see; but only that which can see can be blind. Only what can speak can be silent. Hence the imperfect is that which has in its Being a definite orientation toward perfection. "Imperfect" means that that of which it is predicated does not have the perfection it could have, should have, and is desired to have. With regard to perfection something is lacking, something has been taken away, stolen from it—*privare*, as the α-"privative" says. Truth, which for us is something positive, is for the Greeks negative as ἀλήθεια; and falsehood, which for us is something negative, is positively expressed by them as ψεῦδος. Ἀλήθεια means: to be hidden no longer, to be uncovered. This privative expression indicates that the Greeks had some understanding of the fact that the uncoveredness of the world must be wrested, that it is initially and for the most part not available. The world is primarily, if not completely, concealed; disclosive knowledge does not at first thrust itself forward; the world is disclosed only in the immediate circle of the surrounding world, insofar as natural needs require. And precisely that which in natural consciousness was, within certain limits, perhaps originally disclosed becomes largely covered up again and distorted by speech. Opinions rigidify themselves in concepts and propositions; they become truisms which are repeated over and over, with the consequence that what was originally disclosed comes to be covered up again. Thus everyday Dasein moves in a double coveredness: initially in mere ignorance and then in a much more dangerous coveredness, insofar as idle talk turns what has been uncovered into untruth. With regard to this double coveredness, a philosophy faces the tasks, on the one hand, of breaking through for the first time to the matters themselves (the positive task) and, on the other hand, of taking up at the same time the battle against idle talk. Both of these intentions are the genuine impulses of the spiritual work of Socrates, Plato, and Aristotle. Their struggle against rhetoric and sophistry bears witness to it. The transparency of Greek philosophy was hence not acquired in the so-called serenity of Greek Dasein, as if it was bestowed on the Greeks in their sleep. A closer consideration of their work shows precisely what exertion was required to cut through idle talk and penetrate to Being itself. And that means that we must not expect to get hold of the matters themselves with less effort, especially since we are burdened by a rich and intricate tradition.

Unconcealedness is a determination of beings—insofar as they are encountered. Ἀλήθεια does not belong to Being in the sense that Being could not be without unconcealedness. For nature is there at hand even before it is disclosed. Ἀλήθεια is a peculiar character of the Being of beings insofar as beings stand in relation to a regard aimed at them, to a disclosure circumspecting them, to a knowing. On the other hand, the ἀληθές is certainly both in ὄν and is a character of Being itself, and specifically insofar as Being = presence and the latter is appropriated in λόγος and "is" in it.

Disclosure, however, in relation to which there is ἀλήθεια, is itself a mode of Being, and indeed not of the beings which are first disclosed—those of the world—but, instead, of the beings we call human Dasein. Insofar as disclosure and knowledge have for the Greeks the goal of ἀλήθεια, the Greeks designate them as ἀληθεύειν, i.e., designate them in terms of what is achieved in them, ἀλήθεια. We do not intend to translate this word, ἀληθεύειν. It means to be disclosing, to remove the world from concealedness and coveredness. And that is a mode of Being of human Dasein.

It appears first of all in speaking, in speaking with one another, in λέγειν.

b) Ἀλήθεια and language (λόγος). Ἀλήθεια as a mode of Being of man (ζῷον λόγον ἔχον) or as a mode of life (ψυχή).

Thus ἀληθεύειν shows itself most immediately in λέγειν. Λέγειν ("to speak") is what most basically constitutes human Dasein. In speaking, Dasein expresses itself—by speaking about something, about the world. This λέγειν was for the Greeks so preponderant and such an everyday affair that they acquired their definition of man in relation to, and on the basis of, this phenomenon and thereby determined man as ζῷον λόγον ἔχον. Connected with this definition is that of man as the being which calculates, ἀριθμεῖν. Calculating does not here mean counting but to count *on* something, to be designing; it is only on the basis of this original sense of calculating that number developed.

Aristotle determined λόγος (which later on was called *enuntiatio* and judgment), in its basic function, as ἀπόφανσις, as ἀποφαίνεσθαι, as δηλοῦν. The modes in which it is carried out are κατάφασις and ἀπόφασις, affirmation and denial, which were later designated as positive and negative judgments. Even ἀπόφασις, the denial of a determination, is an uncovering which lets something be seen. For I can only deny a thing a determination insofar as I exhibit that thing. In all these modes of speaking, speech, φάναι, is a mode of the Being of life. As vocalization, speaking is not mere noise, ψόφος, but is a ψόφος σημαντικός, a noise that signifies something; it is φωνή and ἑρμηνεία: ἡ δὲ φωνὴ ψόφος τίς ἐστιν ἐμψύχου (*De An.* B, 8, 420b5ff.). "The φωνή is a noise that pertains essentially only to a living being." Only animals can produce sounds. The ψυχή is the οὐσία ζωῆς, it constitutes the proper Being of something alive. Aristotle determines the essence of the soul ontologically in the same book of the *De Anima:* ἡ ψυχή ἐστιν ἐντελέχεια ἡ πρώτη σώματος φυσικοῦ δυνάμει ζωὴν ἔχοντος (B, 1, 412a27ff.). "The soul is what constitutes the proper presence of a living being, of a being which, according to possibility, is alive." In this definition, life is simultaneously defined as movement. We are used to attributing movement to the phenomenon of life. But movement is not understood here merely as motion from a place, local motion, but as any sort of movement, i.e., as μεταβολή, as the coming to presence of some alteration. Thus every πρᾶξις, every νοεῖν, is a movement.

Speaking is hence φωνή, a vocalizing which contains a ἑρμηνεία, i.e., which says something understandable about the world. And as this vocalizing, speaking is a mode of Being of what is alive, a mode of the ψυχή. Aristotle conceives this mode of Being as ἀληθεύειν. In this way, human life in its Being, ψυχή, is speaking, interpreting, i.e., it is a carrying out of ἀληθεύειν. Aristotle did not only, in the *De Anima,* found this state of affairs ontologically, but, for the first time and before all else, he saw and interpreted on that ground the multiplicity of the phenomena, the multiplicity of the various possibilities of ἀληθεύειν. The interpretation is accomplished in the sixth book of *Nicomachean Ethics,* chapters 2–6, 1138b35ff.

Accordingly, let us proceed to our interpretation of the sixth book of the *Nicomachean Ethics.* We will also refer to other writings of Aristotle.

INTRODUCTORY PART

The Securing of ἀλήθεια as the Ground of Plato's Research into Being
Interpretations of Aristotle: *Nicomachean Ethics* Book VI and Book X, Chapters 6–8; *Metaphysics* Book I, Chapters 1–2

Chapter One

Preparatory Survey of the Modes of ἀληθεύειν (ἐπιστήμη, τέχνη, φρόνησις, σοφία, νοῦς) (*Nic. Eth.* VI, 2–6)

§4. *The meaning of* ἀληθεύειν *in Aristotle for Plato's research into Being.*

a) The five modes of ἀληθεύειν (*Nic. Eth.* VI, 3). Ἀληθεύειν as ground of research into Being. Ἀλήθεια as the determination of the Being of Dasein (ἀληθεύει ἡ ψυχή).

Aristotle introduces the actual investigation (VI, 3, 1139b15ff.) with a programmatic enumeration of the modes of ἀληθεύειν: ἔστω δὴ οἷς ἀληθεύει ἡ ψυχὴ τῷ καταφάναι ἢ ἀποφάναι, πέντε τὸν ἀριθμόν· ταῦτα δ'ἐστὶν τέχνη ἐπιστήμη φρόνησις σοφία νοῦς· ὑπολήψει γὰρ καὶ δόξῃ ἐνδέχεται διαψεύδεσθαι. "Hence there are five ways human Dasein discloses beings in affirmation and denial. And these are: know-how (in taking care, manipulating, producing), science, circumspection (insight), understanding, and perceptual discernment." As an appendix, Aristotle adds ὑπόληψις, to deem, to take something as something, and δόξα, view, opinion. These two modes of ἀληθεύειν characterize human Dasein in its ἐνδέχεται: ἐνδέχεται διαψεύδεσθαι; insofar as human Dasein moves in them, "it can be deceived." Δόξα is not false without further ado; it *can* be false, it can distort beings, it can thrust itself ahead of them. Now all these diverse modes of ἀληθεύειν stand connected to λόγος; all, with the exception of νοῦς, are here μετὰ λόγου; there is no circumspection, no understanding, which would not be a speaking. Τέχνη is know-how in taking care, manipulating, and producing, which can develop in different degrees, as for example with the shoemaker and the tailor; it is not the manipulating and producing itself but is a mode of knowledge, precisely the know-how which guides the ποίησις. Ἐπιστήμη is the title for what we call science. Φρόνησις is circumspection (insight), σοφία is genuine understanding, and νοῦς is a discernment that discerns by way of perception. Νοεῖν had emerged already at the decisive beginning of Greek philosophy, where the destiny of Greek and Western philosophy was decided, namely in Parmenides: discerning and what is discerned are the same.

If we apply ourselves to what Aristotle says about the modes of disclosure, then we acquire:

1. an orientation regarding the possible ways open to Greek Dasein to experience and interrogate the beings of the world,

2. a preview of the diverse regions of Being which are disclosed in the various modes of ἀληθεύειν as well as a preview of the characteristic determinations of their Being, and

3. a first understanding of the limits within which Greek research moved.

With this threefold acquisition we will secure the ground on which Plato moved in his research into the Being of beings as world and into the Being of beings as human Dasein, the Being of philosophically scientific existence. We will be brought into position to participate in the possible ways of Plato's research into Being.

Before Aristotle enumerated the modes of ἀληθεύειν, he said: ἀληθεύει ἡ ψυχή. Truth is hence a character of beings, insofar as they are encountered; but in an authentic sense it is nevertheless a determination of the Being of human Dasein itself. For all of Dasein's strivings toward knowledge must maintain themselves against the concealedness of beings, which is of a threefold character: 1.) ignorance, 2.) prevailing opinion, 3.) error. Hence it is human Dasein that is properly true; it is in the truth—if we do translate ἀλήθεια as "truth." To be true, to be in the truth, as a determination of Dasein, means: to have at its disposal, as unconcealed, the beings with which Dasein cultivates an association. What Aristotle conceives in a more precise way was already seen by Plato: ἡ ἐπ' ἀλήθειαν ὁρμωμένη ψυχή (cf. *Sophist* 228c1f.),[1] the soul sets itself by itself on the way toward truth, toward beings insofar as they are unconcealed. On the other hand, it is said of the οἱ πολλοί: τῶν πραγμάτων τῆς ἀληθείας ἀφεστῶτας (*Sophist* 234c4f.), "they are still far from the unconcealedness of things." We see thereby that we will find in Plato the same orientation as Aristotle's. We have to presuppose in them one and the same position with regard to the basic questions of Dasein. Hence the soul, the Being of man, is, taken strictly, what is in the truth.[2]

If we hold fast to the meaning of truth as unconcealedness or uncovered-

1. Hereafter, when the Greek quotations deviate from the original text, on account of Heidegger's pedagogically oriented lecture style, the citation will be marked with a "cf."

2. See the appendix.

ness, then it becomes clear that truth means the same as compliance *[Sachlichkeit]*, understood as a comportment of Dasein to the world and to itself in which beings are present in conformity with the way they are *[der Sache nach]*. This is objectivity correctly understood. The original sense of this concept of truth does not yet include objectivity as universal validity, universal binding force. That has nothing to do with truth. Something can very well have universal validity and be binding universally and still not be true. Most prejudices and things taken as obvious have such universal validity and yet are characterized by the fact that they distort beings. Conversely, something can indeed be true which is not binding for everyone but only for a single individual. At the same time, in this concept of truth, truth as uncovering, it is not yet prejudged that genuine uncovering has to be by necessity theoretical knowledge or a determinate possibility of theoretical knowledge—for example, science or mathematics, as if mathematics, as the most rigorous science, would be the most true, and only what approximates the ideal of evidence proper to mathematics would ultimately be true. Truth, unconcealedness, uncoveredness, conforms rather to beings themselves and not to a determinate concept of scientificity. That is the intention of the Greek concept of truth. On the other hand, it is precisely this Greek interpretation of truth which has led to the fact that the genuine ideal of knowledge appears in theoretical knowledge and that all knowledge receives its orientation from the theoretical. We cannot now pursue further how that came about; we merely wish to clarify the root of its possibility.

b) The history of the concept of truth.

Ἀληθές means literally "uncovered." It is primarily things, the πράγματα, that are uncovered. Τὸ πρᾶγμα ἀληθές. This uncoveredness does not apply to things insofar as they are, but insofar as they are encountered, insofar as they are objects of concern. Accordingly, uncoveredness is a specific accomplishment of Dasein, which has its Being in the soul: ἀληθεύει ἡ ψυχή. Now the most immediate kind of uncovering is speaking about things. That is, the determination of life, a determination which can be conceived as λόγος, primarily takes over the function of ἀληθεύειν. Ἀληθεύει ὁ λόγος, and precisely λόγος as λέγειν. Insofar now as each λόγος is a self-expression and a communication, λόγος acquires at once the meaning of the λεγόμενον. Hence λόγος means on the one hand speaking, λέγειν, and then also the spoken, λεγόμενον. And insofar as it is λόγος which ἀληθεύει, λόγος qua λεγόμενον is ἀληθής. But strictly taken this is not the case. Nevertheless insofar as speaking is a pronouncement and in the proposition acquires a proper existence, so that knowledge is preserved therein, even the λόγος as λεγόμενον can be called ἀληθής. This λόγος qua λεγόμενον is precisely the common way truth is present. In ordinary conversation one adheres to what is said, and, in hearing what is said, real knowledge is not necessarily achieved every time. That is, to understand a proposition, I do not necessarily have to repeat it in each of its steps. Some days ago it rained, I can say, without presentifying to myself the rain, etc. I can repeat propositions and understand them without having an original relation to the beings of which I am speaking. In this peculiar confusion, all propositions are repeated and are thereby understood. The propositions acquire a special existence; we take direction from them, they become correct, so-called truths, without the original function of ἀληθεύειν being carried out. We participate in the propositions, with our fellows, and repeat them uncritically. In this way λέγειν acquires a peculiar detachment from the πράγματα. We persist in idle talk. This way of speaking about things has a peculiar binding character, to which we adhere inasmuch as we want to find our orientation in the world and are not able to appropriate everything originally.

It is this λόγος which subsequent considerations—those that had lost the original position—viewed as what is true or false. It was known that the detached proposition could be true or false. And insofar as such a detached proposition is taken as true without knowing whether it is actually true, the question arises: in what does the truth of this proposition consist? How can a proposition, a judgment, which is a determination of something in the soul, correspond with the things? And if one takes the ψυχή as subject and takes λόγος and λέγειν as lived experiences, the problem arises: how can subjective lived experiences correspond with the object? Truth consists then in the correspondence of the judgment with the object.

A certain line of thinking would say: such a concept of truth, which determines truth as the correspondence of the soul, the subject, with the object, is nonsense. For I must have already known the matter in question in order to be able to say that it corresponds with the judgment. I must have already known the objective in order to measure the subjective up to it. The truth of "having already known" is thus presupposed for the truth of knowing. And since that is nonsensical, this theory of truth cannot be maintained.

In the most recent epistemology, a further step is taken. To know is to judge, judging is affirming and denying, affirming is acknowledging, what is acknowledged is a value, a value is present as an ought, and thus the object of knowledge is actually an ought. This theory is possible only if one adheres to the factual carrying out of the judgment as affirmation and, on that basis, without concerning oneself with the being in its Being, attempts to determine what the object of this acknowledgment is. And since the object of knowing is a value, truth is a value. This structure is extended to all regions of Being, so that ultimately one can say: God is a value.

This history of the concept of truth is not accidental but is grounded in Dasein itself, insofar as Dasein moves in the common everyday sort of knowledge, in λόγος, and lapses into a fallenness into the world, into the λεγόμενον. While λόγος thus becomes a mere λεγόμενον, it is no longer understood that the "problem" lies in λόγος itself and in its mode of Being. But we could have already learned, precisely from Aristotle and Plato, that this spoken λόγος is the most extrinsic. Now is not the occasion to enter more thoroughly into this characteristic history of the fallenness of truth.

Let us retain the following: what is ἀληθές is the πρᾶγμα; ἀληθεύειν is a determination of the Being of life; it is especially attributed to λόγος; Aristotle distinguishes primarily the five ways of ἀληθεύειν just mentioned; he distinguishes them with respect to λέγειν; they are μετὰ λόγου. The μετά does not mean that speech is an arbitrary annex to the modes of ἀληθεύειν; on the contrary, μετά—which is related to τὸ μέσον, the mean—signifies that in these modes, right at their heart, lies λέγειν. Knowing or considering is always a speaking, whether vocalized or not. All disclosive comportment, not only everyday finding one's way about, but also scientific knowledge, is carried out in speech. Λέγειν primarily takes over the function of ἀληθεύειν. This λέγειν is for the Greeks the basic determination of man: ζῷον λόγον ἔχον. And thus Aristotle achieves, precisely in connection with this determination of man, i.e., in the field of the λόγον ἔχον and with respect to it, the first articulation of the five modes of ἀληθεύειν.

§5. *The first articulation of the five modes of* ἀληθεύειν (Nic. Eth. *VI, 2).*

a) The two basic modes of λόγον ἔχον: ἐπιστημονικόν and λογιστικόν.

ὑποκείσθω δύο τὰ λόγον ἔχοντα (*Nic. Eth.* VI, 2, 1139a6): "Let this underlie our consideration: there are two basic modes of λόγον ἔχον." These are (1139a11f):

1.) the ἐπιστημονικόν: that which can go to develop knowledge; that λόγος which contributes to the development of knowledge, and

2.) the λογιστικόν: that which can go to develop βουλεύεσθαι, circumspective consideration, deliberation; that λόγος which contributes to the development of deliberation.

It is with regard to these that Aristotle distinguishes the modes of ἀληθεύειν mentioned above:

1. ἐπιστημονικόν: ἐπιστήμη, σοφία

2. λογιστικόν: τέχνη, φρόνησις

It seems at first that νοῦς is not included here. Yet it must be noted that νοεῖν is present in all four modes of ἀληθεύειν; they are determinate modes in which νοεῖν can be carried out; they are διανοεῖν.

The distinction between the ἐπιστημονικόν and the λογιστικόν is made in reference to *what* is disclosed in such speech and discourse; it is taken from the beings themselves, the beings appropriated in the ἀληθεύειν. The ἐπιστημονικόν is that, ᾧ θεωροῦμεν τὰ τοιαῦτα τῶν ὄντων ὅσων αἱ ἀρχαὶ μὴ ἐνδέχονται ἄλλως ἔχειν (a6ff.); it is that "with which we regard beings whose ἀρχαί cannot be otherwise," beings which have the character of ἀΐδιον (b23), of being eternal. The λογιστικόν is that, ᾧ θεωροῦμεν, with which we regard beings that ἐνδεχόμενον ἄλλως ἔχειν (cf. 1140a1), "that can also be otherwise." These are beings τέχνη and φρόνησις deal with. Τέχνη has to do with things which first have to be made and which are not yet what they will be. Φρόνησις makes the situation accessible; and the circumstances are always different in every action. On the other hand, ἐπιστήμη and σοφία concern that which always already was, that which man does not first produce.

This initial and most primitive ontological distinction does not arise primarily in a philosophical consideration but is a distinction of natural Dasein itself; it is not invented but lies in the horizon in which the ἀληθεύειν of natural Dasein moves. In its natural mode of Being, Dasein busies itself with the things that are the objects of its own production and of its immediate everyday concerns. This entire surrounding world is not walled off but is only a determinate portion of the world itself. Home and courtyard have their Being under heaven, under the sun, which traverses its course daily, which regularly appears and disappears. This world of nature, which is always as it is, is in a certain sense the background from which what can be other and different stands out. This distinction is an entirely original one. Therefore it is wrong to say that there are two regions of Being, two fields, as it were, which are set beside one another in theoretical knowledge. Rather, this distinction articulates the *world;* it is its first general ontological articulation.

That is why Aristotle says immediately with reference to the principle of the distinction between the ἐπιστημονικόν and the λογιστικόν: the distinction must take its orientation from the beings. πρὸς γὰρ τὰ τῷ γένει ἕτερα καὶ τῶν τῆς ψυχῆς μορίων ἕτερον τῷ γένει τὸ πρὸς ἑκάτερον πεφυκός, εἴπερ καθ' ὁμοιότητά τινα καὶ οἰκειότητα ἡ γνῶσις ὑπάρχει αὐτοῖς (1139a8ff.). I translate starting from the end: "If indeed to these two parts of the soul (the two modes of ἀληθεύειν of the human ψυχή, i.e., the ἐπιστημονικόν and the λογιστικόν) is to be ordered the familiarity with the things (γνῶσις, which is not theoretical knowledge but in a quite broad sense any sort of ἀληθεύειν) and precisely in the sense of a certain appropriateness to the beings, in such a way that these two modes of ἀληθεύειν are as it were at home with the beings they uncover, then, following the differentiation of the beings, each mode of comportment of the soul (of uncovering) must also be different, as regards the structure of its Being, according to its respective beings."

b) Task and first outline of the investigation.

Aristotle now interrogates these two basic modes of disclosure, the ἐπιστημονικόν and the λογιστικόν, more precisely: which one would be the μάλιστα ἀληθεύειν, which one most takes beings out of concealment? ληπτέον ἄρα ἑκατέρου τούτων τίς ἡ βελτίστη ἕξις (a15f.): with regard to each we are to discern what is its βελτίστη ἕξις, its most genuine possibility to uncover beings as they are and to preserve them as uncovered, i.e., to be toward them as dwelling with them. For the ἐπιστημονικόν, this highest possibility lies in σοφία; for the λογιστικόν, in φρόνησις. Thus there are distinctions and levels of the disclosive access and preservation; the ways in which the world is uncovered for Dasein are not all indifferently on the same plane. The disclosedness of Dasein, insofar as Dasein does possess the possibility of disclosing the world and itself, is not always one and the same. Now Aristotle's more precise analysis does not proceed from the highest modes of ἀληθεύειν but from the modes which are most immediately visible in Dasein, i.e., ἐπιστήμη (chapter 3) and τέχνη (chapter 4). And as Aristotle proceeds he demonstrates that these are not the highest. Thereby Aristotle appropriates the customary understanding of the modes of ἀληθεύειν. Thus it is not a matter of invented concepts of knowledge and know-how, but instead Aristotle only seeks to grasp and to grasp ever more sharply what these ordinarily mean. Furthermore, the type of consideration Aristotle carries out in his analysis of the five modes of ἀληθεύειν is the one that was already alive in the fundamental distinction he drew: it takes its orientation from the actual beings which are disclosed in the respective mode of ἀληθεύειν.

§6. The determination of the essence of ἐπιστήμη *(*Nic. Eth. *VI, 3).*

Aristotle begins his more precise consideration with ἐπιστήμη. Ἐπιστήμη has an ordinary, rather broad sense in which the word means much the same as τέχνη or any sort of know-how. Ἐπιστήμη has this sense for

Aristotle too. But here ἐπιστήμη has the quite sharply defined sense of scientific knowledge. Aristotle introduces the analysis of ἐπιστήμη with the remark: δεῖ ἀκριβολογεῖσθαι καὶ μὴ ἀκολουθεῖν ταῖς ὁμοιότησιν (VI, 3, 1139b18f.): "The task is to regard this phenomenon (ἐπιστήμη) itself in the sharpest way and not simply to illustrate it on the basis of something else," i.e., on the basis of that which it is not or is also. The general guiding line Aristotle uses to orient his analysis of the phenomena of ἐπιστήμη, τέχνη, etc. is a double question: 1.) what is the character of the beings which the mode of ἀληθεύειν uncovers, and 2.) does the respective mode of ἀληθεύειν also disclose the ἀρχή of those beings? Thus the guiding line for the analysis of ἐπιστήμη is: 1.) the question of the beings uncovered by ἐπιστήμη, and 2.) the question of the ἀρχή. Why that double question is posed is not, at this point, immediately understandable.

a) The object of ἐπιστήμη: beings that always are (ἀίδιον). Ἐπιστήμη as ἕξις of ἀληθεύειν. The interpretation of Being on the basis of time (ἀίδιον, ἀεί, αἰών).

The question of the ἐπιστητόν must be taken up first. ὑπολαμβάνομεν, ὃ ἐπιστάμεθα, μὴ ἐνδέχεσθαι ἄλλως ἔχειν (b20ff.). "We say of that which we know that it cannot be otherwise," it must always be as it is. Aristotle thus begins with the way beings are understood when they are known in the most proper sense of knowledge. In that sense of knowledge, there resides ὃ ἐπιστάμεθα, "that which we know," of which we say: it is so. I am informed about it, I know already. And that implies: it is always so. Ἐπιστήμη thus relates to beings which always are. Only what always is can be known. That which can be otherwise is not known in the strict sense. For if that which can be otherwise, ἔξω τοῦ θεωρεῖν γένηται (b21f.), "comes to stand outside of knowledge," i.e., if I am not actually present to it at the moment, it may change during that interval. I, however, continue in my former view of it. If it has indeed changed, then my view has now become false. In opposition to this, knowing is characterized by the fact that even ἔξω τοῦ θεωρεῖν, outside of my present actual regard, I still always continue to know the beings that I know. For the beings which are the object of knowledge always are. And that means that if they are known, this knowledge, as ἀληθεύειν, always is. To know is hence to have uncovered; to know is to preserve the uncoveredness of what is known. It is a positionality toward the beings of the world which has at its disposal the outward look of beings. Ἐπιστήμη is a ἕξις of ἀληθεύειν (b31). In this the outward look of beings is preserved. The beings known in this way can never be concealed; and they can never become other while in hiddenness, such that then knowledge would no longer be knowledge. Therefore these beings can γενέσθαι ἔξω τοῦ θεωρεῖν, can disappear from what is presently actually perceived and *still be known*. Therefore knowledge does not need to be constantly carried out, I do not have to look constantly at the known beings. On the contrary, the knowing is a tarrying being-present to beings, a disposition toward their uncoveredness, even if I do not stand before them. My knowledge is secure because these beings always are. I do not have to return to them again and again. Hence I have no knowledge of beings which can be otherwise—and that is the reason for saying that what is historical cannot be known in a proper sense. This mode of the ἀληθεύειν of ἐπιστήμη is a wholly determinate one, for the Greeks surely the one which grounds the possibility of science. The entire further development of science and today's theory of science take their orientation from this concept of knowledge.

This concept is not deduced but is intuited on the basis of the full phenomenon of knowing. Precisely there we find that knowing is a preserving of the uncoveredness of beings, ones which are independent of it and yet are at its disposal. The knowable, however, which I have at my disposal, must necessarily be as it is; it must always be so; it is the being that always is so, that which did not become, that which never was not and never will not be; it is constantly so; it is a being in the most proper sense.

Now that is remarkable: beings are determined with regard to their Being by a moment of *time*. The everlasting characterizes beings with regard to their Being. The ὄντα are ἀΐδια (b23f.). Ἀΐδιον belongs to the same stem as ἀεί and αἰών. καὶ γὰρ τὸ ἀεὶ συνεχές (*Phys*. Θ, 6, 259a16f.). Ἀεί, "always, everlasting," is "that which coheres in itself, that which is never interrupted." Αἰών means the same as lifetime, understood as full presence: τὸν ἅπαντα αἰῶνα (*De Caelo* A, 9, 279b22). Every living being has its αἰών, its determinate time of presence. Αἰών expresses the full measure of presence, of which a living being disposes. In a broader sense, αἰών signifies the duration of the world in general, and indeed according to Aristotle the world is eternal; it did not come into being and is imperishable. The existence of what is alive as well as of the world as a whole is hence determined as αἰών. And the οὐρανός determines for the living thing its αἰών, its presence. Furthermore, the ἀΐδια are πρότερα τῇ οὐσίᾳ τῶν φθαρτῶν (*Met*. Θ, 8, 1050b7): "what always is is, with regard to presence, earlier than what is perishable," earlier than what once came into being and hence was once not present. Therefore καὶ ἐξ ἀρχῆς καὶ τὰ ἀΐδια (cf. 1051a19f.), the ἀΐδια are what form the beginning for all other beings. They are therefore that which properly is. For what the Greeks mean by Being is presence, being in the present. Therefore that which always dwells in the now is most properly a being and is the ἀρχή, the origin, of the rest of beings. All determinations of beings can be led back, if necessary, to an everlasting being and are intelligible on that basis.

On the other hand, Aristotle stresses: τὰ ἀεὶ ὄντα, ᾗ ἀεὶ ὄντα, οὐκ ἔστιν ἐν χρόνῳ (*Phys.* Δ, 12, 221b3ff.). "That which always is, insofar as it always is, is not in time." οὐδὲ πάσχει οὐδὲν ὑπὸ τοῦ χρόνου (ibid.), "it suffers nothing from time," it is unchangeable. And yet Aristotle also maintains that precisely the heavens are eternal, αἰών, and specifically eternal in the sense of *sempiternitas,* not in the sense of *aeternitas.* Here in *Physics* Δ, 12, on the contrary, he says that the ἀεὶ ὄντα are not in time. Nevertheless, Aristotle provides a precise clarification of what he understands by "in time." To be in time means τὸ μετρεῖσθαι τὸ εἶναι ὑπὸ τοῦ χρόνου (cf. b5), "to be *measured* by time with regard to Being." Aristotle hence does not have some sort of arbitrary and average concept of "in time." Instead, everything measured by time is in time. But something is measured by time insofar as its nows are determined: now and now in succession. But as to what always is, what is constantly in the now—its nows are numberless, limitless, ἄπειρον. Because the infinite nows of the ἀΐδιον are not measurable, the ἀΐδιον, the eternal, is not in time. But that does not make it "supertemporal" in our sense. What is not in time is for Aristotle still temporal, i.e., it is determined on the basis of time—just as the ἀΐδιον, which is not in time, is determined by the ἄπειρον of the nows.

We have to hold fast to what is distinctive here, namely, that beings are interpreted as to their Being on the basis of time. The beings of ἐπιστήμη are the ἀεὶ ὄν. This is the first determination of the ἐπιστητόν.

b) The position of the ἀρχή in ἐπιστήμη (*Nic. Eth.* VI, 3; *Post. An.* I, 1). The teachability of ἐπιστήμη. Ἀπόδειξις and ἐπαγωγή. The presupposition of the ἀρχή.

The second determination of the ἐπιστητόν is found first in the *Nicomachean Ethics* VI, 6: the ἐπιστητόν is ἀποδεικτόν (1140b35). Here (VI, 3) that is expressed as follows: ἐπιστήμη is διδακτή (139b25–35), "teachable"; the ἐπιστητόν, the knowable as such, is μαθητόν (b25f.), learnable. It pertains to knowledge that one can teach it, i.e., impart it, communicate it. This is a constitutive determination of knowledge, and not only of knowledge but of τέχνη as well.[1] In particular, scientific knowledge is ἐπιστήμη μαθηματική. And the μαθηματικαὶ τῶν ἐπιστημῶν (71a3), mathematics, is teachable in a quite preeminent sense. This teachability makes clear what is involved in knowledge. Knowledge is a positionality toward beings which has their uncoveredness available without being constantly present to them. Knowledge is teachable, i.e., it is communicable, without there having to take place an uncovering in the proper sense.

1. Cf., on the following, *Post. An.* I, 1, 71a2ff.

Furthermore, the λόγοι are teachable and learnable. Aristotle is thinking here primarily of natural speech, where there are two types of speaking. When orators speak publicly in court or in the senate they appeal to the common understanding of things which is shared by everyone. Such speaking adduces no scientific proofs but does awaken a conviction among the auditors. This occurs διὰ παραδειγμάτων, by introducing a striking example. δεικνύντες τὸ καθόλου διὰ τὸ δῆλον εἶναι τὸ καθ' ἕκαστον (a8f.): "They show the universal," which is supposed to be binding on others, "through the obviousness of some particular case," i.e., through a definite example. This is one way to produce a conviction in others. This is the way of ἐπαγωγή (a6), which is a simple leading toward something but not an arguing in the proper sense. One can also proceed in such a way that what is binding and universal λαμβάνοντες ὡς παρὰ ξυνιέντων (a7f.), is taken from the natural understanding: i.e., from what all people know and agree upon. One takes into account definite cognitions which the audience possesses, and these are not discussed further. On the basis of these, one tries then to prove to the audience something by means of συλλογισμός (a5). Συλλογισμός and ἐπαγωγή are the two ways to impart to others a knowledge about definite things. The concluding ἐκ προγιγνωσκομένων (cf. a6) "out of what is known at the outset" is the mode in which ἐπιστήμη is communicated. Hence it is possible to impart to someone a particular science without his having seen all the facts himself or being able to see them, provided he possesses the required presuppositions. This μάθησις is developed in the most pure way in mathematics. The axioms of mathematics are such προγιγνωσκόμενα, from which the separate deductions can be carried out, without the need of a genuine understanding of those axioms. The mathematician does not himself discuss the axioms; instead, he merely operates with them. To be sure, modern mathematics contains a theory of axioms. But, as can be observed, mathematicians attempt to treat even the axioms mathematically. They seek to prove the axioms by means of deduction and the theory of relations, hence in a way which itself has its ground in the axioms. This procedure will never elucidate the axioms. To elucidate what is familiar already at the outset is rather a matter of ἐπαγωγή, the mode of clarification proper to straightforward perception. Ἐπαγωγή is hence clearly the beginning, i.e., that which discloses the ἀρχή; *it* is the more original, not ἐπιστήμη. It indeed leads originally to the καθόλου, whereas ἐπιστήμη and συλλογισμός are ἐκ τῶν καθόλου (*Nic. Eth.* VI, 3, 1139b29). In any case, ἐπαγωγή is needed, whether it now simply stands on its own or whether an actual proof results from it. Every ἐπιστήμη is διδασκαλία, i.e., it always presupposes that which it cannot itself elucidate as ἐπιστήμη. It is ἀπόδειξις, it shows something on the basis of that which is already familiar and known. In this way, it always already makes use of an ἐπαγωγή which it itself does not, properly speaking, carry out. For at the very outset it is sufficiently familiar with the "that out of which." Ἐπιστήμη, hence, as ἀπόδειξις, always presupposes something, and what it presupposes is precisely the ἀρχή. This latter is not properly disclosed by the ἐπιστήμη itself.

Therefore, since ἐπιστήμη cannot itself demonstrate that which it presupposes, the ἀληθεύειν of ἐπιστήμη is deficient. It is ill-provided to exhibit beings as such, inasmuch as it does not disclose the ἀρχή. Therefore ἐπιστήμη is not the βελτίστη ἕξις of ἀληθεύειν. It is rather σοφία that is the highest possibility of the ἐπιστημονικόν.

Nevertheless genuine knowledge is always more than a mere cognizance of results. He who has at his disposal merely the συμπεράσματα (cf. b34), i.e., what emerges at the end, and then speaks further, does not possess knowledge. He has ἐπιστήμη only κατὰ συμβεβηκός (*Post. An.* I, 2, 71b10), from the outside; he has it only accidentally, and he is and remains unknowing in any proper sense. Knowledge itself entails having the συλλογισμός at one's disposal, being able to run through the foundational nexus upon which a conclusion depends. Thus ἐπιστήμη is an ἀληθεύειν which does not make beings, and specifically the everlasting beings, genuinely available. For ἐπιστήμη, these beings are precisely still hidden in the ἀρχαί.

At the outset we emphasized that Aristotle pursues his analysis of the phenomena of ἀληθεύειν in two directions: at first he asks about the beings which are to be disclosed; then he raises the question of whether the respective ἀληθεύειν also discloses the ἀρχή of those beings. The second question is always a criterion for determining whether the ἀληθεύειν is a genuine one or not. This double questioning is at work in the case of τέχνη as well. Τέχνη is an ἀληθεύειν within the λογιστικόν. And just as, in the case of the ἐπιστημονικόν, ἐπιστήμη, though the most immediate ἀληθεύειν, was not the genuine ἀληθεύειν, so also in the case of the λογιστικόν, τέχνη, though the most familiar ἀληθεύειν, proves to be an ungenuine form of it. Insofar as τέχνη belongs to the λογιστικόν, it is a disclosing of those beings ὃ ἐνδέχεται ἄλλως ἔχειν (cf. *Nic. Eth.* VI, 4, 1140a1), "which can also be otherwise." But to such beings φρόνησις also relates. Therefore within the ἐνδεχόμενον there is a distinction; it can be a ποιητόν or a πρακτόν, i.e., the theme of a ποίησις, a producing, or of a πρᾶξις, an acting.

c) Πρᾶξις and ποίησις as the first ways of carrying out ἀληθεύειν. Ἐπιστήμη as the autonomous "πρᾶξις" of ἀληθεύειν.

Up to now we have not yet been able to see in ἐπιστήμη a phenomenon which is included more or less explicitly in all modes of ἀληθεύειν. Ἐπιστήμη, insofar as it is a task to be carried out, is itself a πρᾶξις, admittedly one which does not have as its goal some sort of result (the way producing does) but instead simply strives to get hold of beings as ἀληθές. The task and the goal of ἐπιστήμη is thus to know the ἀληθές. Initially and for the most part, however, this knowing is in service to a making. Ἀληθεύειν contributes to the carrying out of a ποίησις or a πρᾶξις.

For ἀληθεύειν is indeed not the only determination of the ψυχή. It is merely a particular possibility (though, to be sure, a constitutive one) of a being which possesses the character of life (ψυχή): namely of that being which is distinguished by the fact that it speaks. Aristotle characterizes quite generally the two basic possibilities of the soul (ψυχή) as κρίνειν and κινεῖν. The αἴσθησις of the animal already has the character of κρίσις; even in αἴσθησις, in the natural act of perceiving, something is set off against something else. The second determination is κινεῖν, "to bestir oneself." To this corresponds the higher determination of the Being of man: πρᾶξις, κινεῖν in the sense of κρίνειν, in the sense of distinguishing things in speech. The ζωή of man is πρακτική μετὰ λόγου.[2] It is characterized by πρᾶξις καὶ ἀλήθεια (cf. *Nic. Eth.* VI, 2, 1139a18), i.e., by πρᾶξις, acting, and by ἀλήθεια, the uncoveredness of Dasein itself as well as of the beings to which Dasein relates in its actions. Both these basic determinations—with regard to the possible ways they may manifest themselves—can be termed: αἴσθησις, νοῦς, ὄρεξις. Thus Aristotle says: the κύρια, the dominant possibilities of every human comportment, are: αἴσθησις, νοῦς, ὄρεξις. τρία δ' ἐστὶν ἐν τῇ ψυχῇ τὰ κύρια πράξεως καὶ ἀληθείας, αἴσθησις νοῦς ὄρεξις (a17ff.).

Every comportment of Dasein is thus determined as πρᾶξις καὶ ἀλήθεια. In the case of ἐπιστήμη, scientific knowledge, the character of the πρᾶξις did not explicitly come out because, in science, knowledge is autonomous and as such it is already πρᾶξις and ὄρεξις. In the case of τέχνη, however, the ἀληθεύειν is that of a ποίησις; τέχνη is a διάνοια ποιητική (a27f.), a thorough thinking about beings that contributes to producing something, to the way in which something is to be made. Therefore in τέχνη, as ποίησις, and in every πρᾶξις, the ἀληθεύειν is a λέγειν which ὁμολόγως ἔχον τῇ ὀρέξει (cf. a30), "which speaks exactly as ὄρεξις desires." It is not a theoretical speculation about beings, but instead it expresses beings in such a way that it provides the correct direction for a proper production of what is to be made. In this way the ἀληθεύειν in τέχνη and φρόνησις is oriented respectively toward ποίησις and πρᾶξις.

2. Cf. *Nic. Eth.*, I, 6, 1098a3ff.

§7. *The analysis of* τέχνη *(*Nic. Eth. *VI, 4).*

a) The object of τέχνη: what is coming into being (ἐσόμενον).

As was the case with ἐπιστήμη, so here too as regards τέχνη the first task is to determine the beings to which it relates. In τέχνη the know-how is directed toward the ποιητόν, toward what is to be first produced and hence is not yet. This implies that the object can also be otherwise; for what is not yet is not always: ἔστιν δὲ τέχνη πᾶσα περὶ γένεσιν (*Nic. Eth.* VI, 4, 1140a10f.). "All know-how," as guiding the production of something, "moves within the circuit of beings which are in the process of becoming, which are on the way to their Being." καὶ τὸ τεχνάζειν καὶ θεωρεῖν ὅπως ἂν γένηταί τι τῶν ἐνδεχομένων καὶ εἶναι καὶ μὴ εἶναι (11ff.). "And τεχνάζειν is specifically a considering," not one that would live for nothing else than the considering, but one that it is oriented to the ὅπως, "to having something occur in such and such a way," i.e., having something be correctly executed. The dealing with a thing which is guided by τέχνη is always a preparation for something. The θεωρεῖν of the τέχνη is by no means speculation but instead guides the dealing with a thing in an orientation toward a "for which" and an "in order to." In this way the beings of τέχνη are in each case ἐσόμενον, something that will come to be.

b) The position of the ἀρχή in τέχνη (*Nic. Eth.* VI, 4; *Met.* VII, 7). The double relation of τέχνη to its ἀρχή. Εἶδος and ἔργον. The παρά-character of the ἔργον.

The second question is the one about the ἀρχή of the beings, i.e., to what extent can τέχνη itself disclose the ἀρχή of the beings it is concerned with. For τέχνη, the ἀρχή is ἐν τῷ ποιοῦντι (a13): that from which the fabrication sets out resides "in the producer himself." If something is to be produced, deliberation is required. Prior to all producing, the for which, the ποιητόν, must be considered. To the producer himself, thus, the ποιητόν is present at the very outset; since he must have made it clear to himself through τεχνάζειν (a11) how the finished work is supposed to look. In this way the εἶδος of what is to be produced, for example the blueprint, is determined prior to the producing. From these plans the producer, e.g., the house builder, proceeds to construct the product itself. The ἀρχή of the beings of τέχνη, the εἶδος, is thus in the ψυχή, ἐν τῷ ποιοῦντι, "in the producer himself." ἀλλὰ μὴ ἐν τῷ ποιουμένῳ (a13f.), but it is not the case that the ἀρχή is in what is to be produced, in the ἔργον, in what is to be made. This is a peculiar state of affairs which has to be elucidated in spite of its obviousness. It becomes most clear in relation to beings which are indeed produced, but which produce *themselves:* the φύσει ὄντα. These produce themselves in such a way that the ἀρχή resides in the producer as well as in the produced. ἐν αὐτοῖς γὰρ ἔχουσι ταῦτα τὴν ἀρχήν (a15f.), "for these have the ἀρχή in themselves." In the case of τέχνη, on the contrary, the ἔργον resides precisely παρά, "beside," the activity; and precisely as ἔργον, as finished work, it is no longer the object of a ποίησις. That the shoes are finished means precisely that the cobbler has delivered them up. Now, insofar as the τέλος constitutes the ἀρχή, in the case of τέχνη the ἀρχή is in a certain sense not available. That shows that τέχνη is not a genuine ἀληθεύειν.

The object of τέχνη is the ποιητόν, the ἔργον, the finished product, which arises through a production and a fabrication. This ἔργον is a ἕνεκά τινος (1139b1), it is "for the sake of something," it has a relation to something else. It is οὐ τέλος ἁπλῶς (b2), "not an end pure and simple." The ἔργον contains in itself a reference to something else; as τέλος it refers away from itself: it is a πρός τι καί τινος (b2f.), it is "for something and for someone." The shoe is made for wearing and is for someone. This double character entails that the ἔργον of the ποίησις is something produced for further use, for man. Τέχνη therefore possesses the ἔργον as an object of its ἀληθεύειν only as long as the ἔργον is not yet finished. As soon as the product is finished, it escapes the dominion of τέχνη: it becomes the object of the use proper to it. Aristotle expresses this precisely: the ἔργον is "παρά" (cf. *Nic. Eth.* I, 1, 1094a4f.). The ἔργον, as soon as it is finished, is παρά, "beside," τέχνη. Τέχνη, therefore, is concerned with beings only insofar as they are in the process of becoming. ἔστιν δὲ τέχνη πᾶσα περὶ γένεσιν (*Nic. Eth.* VI, 4, 1140a10f).

Aristotle distinguishes three possibilities regarding those beings which are determined by becoming: τῶν δὲ γιγνομένων τὰ μὲν φύσει γίγνεται τὰ δὲ τέχνῃ τὰ δὲ ἀπὸ ταὐτομάτου (*Met.* VII, 7, 1032a12ff.). "With regard to what becomes, the first is φύσει (by self-production) another is through τέχνη, another happens by chance." With regard to what happens by chance, Aristotle thinks above all of miscarriages and the like, i.e., that which is properly against nature, but which yet in a certain sense comes from itself, φύσει. The modes of becoming that are not those of nature Aristotle calls ποιήσεις. αἱ δ' ἄλλαι γενέσεις λέγονται ποιήσεις (a26f.). Through such ποίησις, there comes to be ὅσων τὸ εἶδος ἐν τῇ ψυχῇ (b1), "everything whose outward look is in the soul." We must consider this more closely in order to understand to what extent τέχνη in a certain sense has the ἀρχή and in a certain sense does not. For instance, in the case of the τέχνη ἰατρική, health is the εἶδος ἐν τῇ ψυχῇ, and in the case of οἰκοδομική it is the house. If a house is going to be built, then the course of the deliberation—of τέχνη—has basically the following structure: since the house is supposed to look such and such a way, it is necessary that such and such things be on hand. In this exemplary deliberation, there is ἐν τῇ ψυχῇ an ἀληθεύειν, a disclosing—here, b6, νοεῖν—an ἀποφαίνεσθαι, a letting be seen of what is going to be produced. And what is here disclosed in the soul, and is present in it, is the εἶδος of the house, its outward look, its "physiognomy," as that is some day going to stand there and which constitutes the proper presence of the house. All this is anticipated ἐν τῇ ψυχῇ in a προαίρεσις. For, the house which is to be made is indeed not yet there. The expression τὸ εἶδος ἐν τῇ ψυχῇ refers to this anticipation of the εἶδος in the ψυχή. German expresses this well: the outward look is "pre-presentified" *[vergegenwärtigt]*. The house which will some day be present is presentified beforehand as it is going to look. This pre-presentification of the house is a disclosing of the εἶδος ἄνευ ὕλης (cf. b12). The wood, etc., is not yet there. In a certain way, naturally, even the ὕλη is present in the deliberation: the material was taken into consideration while drawing up the plans. But the ὕλη in the expression ἄνευ ὕλης has to be understood in an ontological sense: the ὕλη is not, in the proper sense, present in τέχνη. The ὕλη is genuinely there only insofar as it is the "out of which" of the factually occurring finished house, in its being finished, and constitutes the proper presentness of that house. The ὕλη is τὸ ἔσχατον καθ' αὑτό, what does not first need to be produced but is already available, and indeed in such a way that it is what genuinely brings the ποιούμενον into the present. ἐνυπάρχει γὰρ καὶ γίγνεται αὕτη (b32f.). "For it is the ὕλη which is there throughout and which becomes." In the deliberation, therefore, the ὕλη is not ἐν τῇ ψυχῇ—i.e., insofar as it ἐνυπάρχει, "is there throughout" and insofar as it γίγνεται, properly "becomes," i.e., insofar as it brings something into the present in the proper sense.

The εἶδος as εἶδος ἐν τῇ ψυχῇ is the anticipated presence of the house. And to the extent that a man pre-presentifies it, he carries out the entire execution of the plans while keeping his regard constantly fixed on this εἶδος. τὸ δὴ ποιοῦν καὶ ὅθεν ἄρχεται ἡ κίνησις τοῦ ὑγιαίνειν, ἐὰν μὲν ἀπὸ τέχνης, τὸ εἶδός ἐστι τὸ ἐν τῇ ψυχῇ (b21ff.). "The genuine producer, and that which initiates the movement, is the εἶδος ἐν τῇ ψυχῇ." Hence the εἶδος is the very ἀρχή; it initiates the κίνησις. This κίνησις is first of all that of νόησις, of deliberation, and then the one of ποίησις, of the action which issues from the deliberation. Insofar as the εἶδος in this way, i.e., as ἀρχή of the total movement of the producing, is ἐν τῇ ψυχῇ, the ἀρχή of the ποιητόν is ἐν τῷ ποιοῦντι (*Nic. Eth.* VI, 4, 1140a13), i.e., it is a matter of τέχνη itself. On the other hand, the ποιούμενον, the finished house, is no longer an object of τέχνη. As a finished house, it escapes τέχνη. Now the τέλος, taken in its ontological character, is πέρας. πέρας λέγεται τὸ τέλος ἑκάστου (τοιοῦτον δ' ἐφ' ὃ ἡ κίνησις καὶ ἡ πρᾶξις) (cf. *Met.* V, 17, 1022a4ff.);

furthermore, even the ἀρχή is in a certain sense πέρας; ἡ μὲν ἀρχὴ πέρας τι (cf. a12). Since therefore the τέλος has the same ontological character as the ἀρχή—namely, πέρας—and because in τέχνη the τέλος is precisely not preserved, τέχνη stands in the exact same relation to its beings as ἐπιστήμη does to its.

Because the ἔργον is no longer in the grasp of τέχνη, i.e., because the ἔργον escapes τέχνη, the latter is in a certain sense similar to τύχη, the accidental. τρόπον τινὰ περὶ τὰ αὐτά ἐστιν ἡ τύχη καὶ ἡ τέχνη (*Nic. Eth.* VI, 4, 1040a18): τύχη and τέχνη in a certain sense have to do with the same things. The essential characteristic of the accidental is that what emerges from it is out of its hands. The same occurs in the case of τέχνη: it may be developed in the most minute detail, and yet it does not have at its disposal, with absolute certainty, the success of the work. In the end the ἔργον is out of the hands of τέχνη. Here we see a fundamental deficiency in the ἀληθεύειν which characterizes τέχνη.

c) The εἶδος as ἀρχή of the κίνησις of τέχνη as a whole (*Met.* VII, 7). Νόησις and ποίησις. Τέχνη as ground of the interpretation of Being through the εἶδος.

In τέχνη, the εἶδος comes into play as ἀρχή. In τέχνη the εἶδος ἐν τῇ ψυχῇ is the ἀρχή of the κίνησις, which is first that of νόησις and then that of ποίησις. In Book VII of the *Metaphysics,* chapter 7, Aristotle offers a penetrating presentation of the connection of νόησις and ποίησις, where he illustrates it with the examples of ὑγίεια and οἰκοδομική. He says: ἡ δὲ ὑγίεια ὁ ἐν τῇ ψυχῇ λόγος (1032b5). Health is the λόγος ἐν τῇ ψυχῇ. Λόγος here means λεγόμενον, the spoken. On the other hand, Aristotle says: ἡ δὲ τέχνη λόγος τοῦ ἔργου ὁ ἄνευ ὕλης ἐστίν (*De Partibus Animalium* a, 1, 640a31f.). Λόγος here means λέγειν, pre-presentification in speech. The λόγος qua λεγόμενον, however, is the εἶδος. We have here an echo of the Platonic way of speaking and seeing; for an εἶδος is nothing else than an Idea. Therefore Aristotle can write succinctly: ἡ οἰκοδομικὴ τὸ εἶδος τῆς οἰκίας (cf. *Met.* VII, 7, 1032b13f.). "Architecture is the outward look of the house." Τέχνη is λόγος qua λέγειν of the λεγόμενον, i.e., of the εἶδος. Οἰκοδομική, architecture, discloses and preserves the εἶδος, the outward look of the house. (Let it be noted in passing that this is also decisive for an understanding of the νόησις νοήσεως in *Met.* XII, chapters 9–10. There the question of genuine Being is raised. In chapter 9, that is νοῦς as the θειότατον, as the most genuine Being, to which, however, belong life and duration.) The εἶδος, which is disclosed and preserved in οἰκοδομική, is the ἀρχή of the κίνησις, first the one of νόησις and then the one of ποίησις. Let us pursue this movement more closely, as it occurs in its departure from the εἶδος ἐν τῇ ψυχῇ. γίγνεται δὴ τὸ ὑγιὲς νοήσαντος οὕτως· ἐπειδὴ τοδὶ ὑγίεια, ἀνάγκη, εἰ ὑγιὲς ἔσται, τοδὶ ὑπάρξαι . . . καὶ οὕτως αἰεὶ νοεῖ, ἕως ἂν ἀνάγκῃ εἰς τοῦτο ὃ αὐτὸς δύναται ἔσχατον ποιεῖν (*Met.* VII, 7, 1032b6ff.). "The healthy comes to be by means of the following course of disclosure: since health is such and such, it is necessary, if there is to be something healthy, that such and such be on hand for it. . . . And one goes on to disclose always more and more until what is ultimate is reached, i.e., what one can bring about oneself." This ἔσχατον is also called τὸ τελευταῖον τῆς νοήσεως (cf. b17), "the ultimate of circumspective disclosure." The circumspection of τέχνη reaches what, as the uttermost, is the first to be accomplished, the place where the undertaking can break in. This circumspection does not run through any theoretical steps, but instead it isolates that with which the action, the bringing into being, the ποιεῖν, begins. The νόησις is here a τεχνάζειν (*Nic. Eth.* VI, 4, 1140a11), a disclosure that is "on the lookout" for the ὑπάρχοντα. ἡ ἀπὸ τούτου κίνησις ποίησις (*Met.* VII, 7, 1032b10). "The movement which begins from this ultimate of νόησις is ποίησις." The latter is the properly productive action, whereas the movement of νόησις is a type of elucidation. Νόησις and ποίησις belong together. Their connection constitutes the full movement of the enterprise. συμβαίνει τρόπον τινὰ τὴν ὑγίειαν ἐξ ὑγιείας γίγνεσθαι (b11). "The result is that in a certain sense health comes from health," i.e., from the εἶδος of health ἐν τῇ ψυχῇ. Hence the εἶδος is the ἀρχή of the whole connection of νόησις and ποίησις in τέχνη. Therefore ἡ οἰκοδομικὴ τὸ εἶδος τῆς οἰκίας (cf. b13). "Architecture is the εἶδος of the house."

On the basis of τέχνη, the Being of the house is understood as something *made,* as corresponding to the "outward look." The presence at hand of the house is related, genuinely and uniquely, to the modes of becoming, the modes of production; all other determinations are κατὰ συμβεβηκός. <τὸ κατὰ συμβεβηκὸς> οὐθὲν μέλει τῇ τέχνῃ (*Nic. Eth.* V, 15, 1138b2). "The determinations κατὰ συμβεβηκός are by no means a concern of τέχνη." (Φύσις is also understood in an analogous way: as the process of self-becoming, as the process by which something brings itself from itself into its form and its outward look.) This conception has its ground in the philosophy of Plato. The εἶδος is, as we said, nothing else than a designation of the Platonic Idea. The usual exposition of Plato places the doctrine of the Ideas in the center and takes it as the guiding line for an interpretation of his whole philosophy. We will see to what extent that is a prejudice and to what extent it touches the actual state of affairs. For one who has learned to understand an author it is perhaps not possible to take as a foundation for the interpretation what the author himself designates as the most important. It is precisely where an author keeps silent that one has to begin in order to understand what the author himself designates as the most proper. Without wishing to preempt a discussion of the doctrine of Ideas, let us merely remark that we will understand the genesis, the primary sense, and what is opaque in Plato's Ideas only if we remain oriented toward the place where the εἶδος first steps forth quite naturally, i.e., in which mode of ἀληθεύειν it explicitly emerges. That is the point of departure for understanding why Plato says the Idea is genuine Being. We have seen that the εἶδος is the ἀρχή of the whole connection of νόησις and ποίησις in τέχνη. ἡ οἰκοδομικὴ τὸ εἶδος τῆς οἰκίας. Τέχνη is the ground upon which something like the εἶδος becomes visible in the first place. We have therefore not dealt with τέχνη unadvisedly: in it the εἶδος first becomes present.

Let us represent the first division of the modes of ἀληθεύειν:

1. ἐπιστημονικόν: ἐπιστήμη / σοφία

2. λογιστικόν: τέχνη / φρόνησις

The characterization of the common modes of ἀληθεύειν, ἐπιστήμη and τέχνη, has made ἀληθεύειν itself more clear. These two basic possibilities, of the ἐπιστημονικόν and of the λογιστικόν, are not the highest ones. But we may not assume without further ado that the two other modes have to be the genuine possibility and full development, the ἀρετή, of the ἐπιστημονικόν and of the λογιστικόν. First of all, we care less for such systematics than for the concrete understanding of the phenomena of ἀληθεύειν itself. Ἀληθεύειν always has the meaning of upholding Dasein against degradation by the λεγόμενον, in such a way that Dasein will not be deceived by it.

In the further analyses of the remaining modes of ἀληθεύειν, Aristotle deals first with φρόνησις, circumspection, circumspective insight.

§8. The analysis of φρόνησις *(*Nic. Eth. *VI, 5).*

The analysis of φρόνησις begins by first determining what φρόνησις relates to, in order then to delimit it against each of the previously analyzed modes of ἀληθεύειν, ἐπιστήμη and τέχνη. In the delimitation against ἐπιστήμη, φρόνησις emerges as δόξα, and in the delimitation against τέχνη, as ἀρετή. That constitutes the tight cohesion of chapter 5 of Book VI of the *Nicomachean Ethics,* where Aristotle carries out the analysis of φρόνησις.

a) The object of φρόνησις: Dasein itself. The determination of the τέλος of φρόνησις in delimitation against the τέλος of τέχνη. Its relation to ἀληθεύειν: prior identity in φρόνησις; difference (παρά) in τέχνη.

Aristotle begins by asking what natural Dasein understands by φρόνησις, i.e., which human being is called a φρόνιμος. δοκεῖ δὴ φρονίμου εἶναι τὸ δύνασθαι καλῶς βουλεύσασθαι περὶ τὰ αὑτῷ ἀγαθὰ καὶ συμφέροντα, οὐ κατὰ μέρος, οἷον ποῖα πρὸς ὑγίειαν ἢ πρὸς ἰσχύν, ἀλλὰ ποῖα πρὸς τὸ εὖ ζῆν ὅλως (1140a25ff.). "A φρόνιμος is evidently one who can deliberate well, i.e., appropriately," who is βουλευτικός, and specifically who can deliberate appropriately over "that which is good (full and perfect) and which is, in addition, good αὑτῷ, for him, the deliberator himself . . . " The object of φρόνησις is hence determined as something which can also be otherwise, but from the very outset it has a relation to the deliberator himself. On the other hand, the deliberation of τέχνη relates simply to what contributes to the production of something else, namely, the ἔργον, e.g., a house. The deliberation of φρόνησις, however, relates to this ἔργον insofar as it contributes to the deliberator himself. The ἀληθεύειν of φρόνησις therefore contains a referential direction to the ἀληθεύων himself. Yet we do not designate as a φρόνιμος the one who deliberates in the correct way κατὰ μέρος, i.e., in relation to particular advantages, e.g., health or bodily strength, which promote Dasein in a particular regard. Instead, we call φρόνιμος the one who deliberates in the right way ποῖα πρὸς τὸ εὖ ζῆν ὅλως, regarding "what is conducive to the right mode of Being of Dasein as such and as a whole." The βουλεύεσθαι of the φρόνιμος concerns the Being of Dasein itself, the εὖ ζῆν, i.e., the right and proper way to be Dasein. Accordingly, φρόνησις entails a reference πρὸς τέλος τι σπουδαῖον (1140a29f.), "to that kind of τέλος which bestows seriousness," and specifically ὧν μὴ ἔστιν τέχνη (a30), "in relation to such beings which cannot be the theme of a fabrication or production." The τέλος of φρόνησις is hence not παρά, over and against the Being of the deliberation itself, as is the case with the ἔργον of τέχνη. Rather, in the case of φρόνησις, the object of the deliberation is ζωή itself; the τέλος has the same ontological character as φρόνησις. τῆς μὲν γὰρ ποιήσεως ἕτερον τὸ τέλος, τῆς δὲ πράξεως οὐκ ἂν εἴν· ἔστιν γὰρ αὐτὴ ἡ εὐπραξία τέλος (1140b6ff.). "In the case of ποίησις, the τέλος is something other; but this does not hold for πρᾶξις: the εὐπραξία is itself the τέλος." In the case of φρόνησις, the πρακτόν is of the same ontological character as the ἀληθεύειν itself. And here, presumably, the τέλος is in fact disclosed and preserved; for it is the Being of the deliberator himself. The φρόνιμος is therefore not identical with the τεχνίτης; for the ἀληθεύειν of the τεχνίτης is related to an other order of Being.

βουλεύεται δ' οὐθεὶς περὶ τῶν ἀδυνάτων ἄλλως ἔχειν (1140a31f.); "the βουλευτικός is not one who deliberates about what cannot be otherwise," just as in the case of the τεχνίτης. But the βουλευτικός deliberates οὐδὲ τῶν μὴ ἐνδεχομένων αὐτῷ πρᾶξαι (a32f.); "nor does he deliberate about that which he cannot accomplish himself." In the deliberation of the φρόνιμος, what he has in view is himself and his own acting. Τέχνη, on the contrary, is cleverness, ingenuity, and resource regarding things I myself do not necessarily want to carry out or am able to carry out. The βουλευτικός is hence the one who deliberates with regard to the πρακτόν. The deliberation of φρόνησις is, furthermore, a certain drawing of conclusions: if such and such is supposed to occur, if I am to behave and be in such and such a way, then. . . . Here that from which and in constant consideration of which I deliberate, namely the οὗ ἕνεκα, is different in every case. In this way the deliberating of φρόνησις is a discussing, a λογίζεσθαι, but not an ἀπόδειξις, an ἐπιστήμη. Conversely, the necessary cannot, as such, be a possible object of deliberation. Thus the deliberation of φρόνησις, like that of τέχνη, is related to something which can be otherwise. And, as a deliberation, it again bears a certain resemblance to the one of τέχνη: if I am to act in such and such a way, then this or that must happen. Τέχνη would deliberate as follows: if such and such is to come to be, then this or that must happen. And yet φρόνησις is different from τέχνη; for in the case of τέχνη the πρακτόν is a τέλος which is παρά. Not so in the case of the τέλος of φρόνησις. This τέλος is a ἕξις ἀληθὴς μετὰ λόγου πρακτικὴ περὶ τὰ ἀνθρώπῳ ἀγαθά (cf. 1140b5), "such a disposition of human Dasein, that it has at its disposal its own transparency."[1] The τέλος of φρόνησις is not a πρός τι and not a ἕνεκά τινός; it is the ἄνθρωπος himself. αὐτὴ ἡ εὐπραξία τέλος (b7), the proper Being of man is the τέλος. But this is ζωὴ πρακτικὴ μετὰ λόγου. The τέλος of φρόνησις is a τέλος ἁπλῶς and a οὗ ἕνεκα, a "for the sake of which." Now insofar as Dasein is disclosed as the οὗ ἕνεκα, the "for the sake of which," there is a predelineation of what is for its sake and what has to be procured at any time for its sake. In this way, with Dasein as the οὗ ἕνεκα, there is grasped with one stroke the ἀρχή of the deliberation of φρόνησις. αἱ μὲν γὰρ ἀρχαὶ τῶν πρακτῶν τὸ οὗ ἕνεκα τὰ πρακτά (1140b16f.). These ἀρχαί are Dasein itself; Dasein finds itself disposed, and comports itself to itself, in this or that way. Dasein is the ἀρχή of the deliberation of φρόνησις. And what φρόνησις deliberates about is not what brings πρᾶξις to an end. A result is not constitutive for the Being of an action; only the εὖ, the how, is. The τέλος in φρόνησις is the ἄνθρωπος

1. Editor's paraphrase, in accord with p. 37.

himself. In the case of ποίησις, the τέλος is something other, a worldly being over and against Dasein; not so in the case of πρᾶξις.

Now, to what extent is φρόνησις an ἀληθεύειν?

b) Φρόνησις as ἀ-ληθεύειν. Ἡδονή and λύπη. Σωφροσύνη. Φρόνησις as a struggle against Dasein's inherent tendency to cover itself over. Φρόνησις as non-autonomous ἀληθεύειν in the service of πρᾶξις.

Insofar as man himself is the object of the ἀληθεύειν of φρόνησις, it must be characteristic of man that he is covered up to himself, does not see himself, such that he needs an explicit ἀ-ληθεύειν in order to become transparent to himself. In fact, διαφθείρει καὶ διαστρέφει τὸ ἡδὺ καὶ τὸ λυπηρὸν τὴν ὑπόληψιν (cf. b13f.). "What gives pleasure and what depresses one's disposition can destroy or confuse one's ὑπόληψις." A disposition can cover up man to himself. A person can be concerned with things of minor significance; he can be so wrapped up in himself that he does not genuinely see himself. Therefore he is ever in need of the salvation of φρόνησις. Circumspection regarding himself and insight into himself must again and again be wrested away by man in face of the danger of διαφθείρειν and διαστρέφειν. It is not at all a matter of course that Dasein be disclosed to itself in its proper Being; ἀλήθεια, even here, must be wrested out. And in this way Aristotle, like Plato, assumes a peculiar etymological relation. σωφροσύνη σῴζει τὴν φρόνησιν (cf. b11f.). "Prudence is what saves φρόνησις," preserves it against the possibility of being covered over. Plato determines σωφροσύνη in a similar manner in the *Cratylus:* "σωφροσύνη" δὲ σωτηρία . . . φρονήσεως (411e4f.). But ἡδονή and λύπη threaten only certain modes of ἀληθεύειν. οὐ γὰρ ἅπασαν ὑπόληψιν διαφθείρει οὐδὲ διαστρέφει τὸ ἡδὺ καὶ λυπηρόν . . . , ἀλλὰ τὰς περὶ τὸ πρακτόν (*Nic. Eth.* VI, 5, 1140b13ff.). "For what gives pleasure and what depresses do not destroy or confuse every ὑπόληψις but only the one related to the πρακτόν." Yet insofar as ἡδονή and λύπη are among the basic determinations of man, he is constantly exposed to the danger of covering himself to himself. Φρόνησις, consequently, cannot at all be taken for granted; on the contrary, it is a task, one that must be seized in a προαίρεσις. Φρόνησις thus eminently illustrates the meaning of ἀ-ληθεύειν, i.e., the uncovering of something concealed. Aristotle emphasizes: τῷ δὲ διεφθαρμένῳ δι' ἡδονὴν ἢ λύπην εὐθὺς οὐ φαίνεται ἡ ἀρχή (b17f.). "Dasein can be corrupted by ἡδονή and λύπη." If one of these dominates a man, the result is that οὐ φαίνεται ἡ ἀρχή. The correct οὗ ἕνεκα no longer shows itself; it is thus concealed and must be uncovered through λόγος. In this way, therefore, φρόνησις, as soon as it is achieved, is involved in a constant struggle against a tendency to cover over residing at the heart of Dasein. ἔστι γὰρ ἡ κακία φθαρτικὴ ἀρχῆς (b19f.). "The κακία, the bad disposition, destroys the ἀρχή," i.e., does not allow the correct οὗ ἕνεκα to show itself. Here, in Dasein itself, is precisely where the risk to, and the resistance against, φρόνησις lies. Aristotle can then summarize the determination of φρόνησις as follows: ὥστ' ἀνάγκη τὴν φρόνησιν ἕξιν εἶναι μετὰ λόγου ἀληθῆ περὶ τὰ ἀνθρώπινα ἀγαθὰ πρακτικήν (b20f.). Φρόνησις is a ἕξις of ἀληθεύειν, "a disposition of human Dasein such that in it I have at my disposal my own transparency." For its themes are the ἀνθρώπινα ἀγαθά. And it is a ἕξις of ἀληθεύειν which is πρακτική, "which lives in action." That is why it is εὖ insofar as it comports itself ὁμολόγως to ὄρεξις, or to πρᾶξις,[2] in such a way that the deliberation measures up to the "for the sake of which" of the acting. Φρόνησις itself is hence indeed an ἀληθεύειν, but it is not an autonomous one. It is an ἀληθεύειν in service to πρᾶξις. It is an ἀληθεύειν which makes an action transparent in itself. Insofar as the transparency of a πρᾶξις is constitutive for this πρᾶξις, φρόνησις is co-constitutive for the proper carrying out of the very action. Φρόνησις is an ἀληθεύειν; yet, as we said, it is not an autonomous one but rather one that serves to guide an action.

That is why Aristotle can think φρόνησις by delimiting it against the two other modes of ἀληθεύειν, τέχνη and ἐπιστήμη.

c) The delimitation of φρόνησις versus τέχνη and ἐπιστήμη. Φρόνησις as ἀρετή. Φρόνησις as "unforgettable" conscience. Σοφία as ἀρετὴ τέχνης.

The delimitation is carried out first in opposition to τέχνη. Now although φρόνησις, exactly like τέχνη, is directed to beings that can also be otherwise, yet τέχνη does not possess its ἔργον, while φρόνησις indeed does, and so one might presume that φρόνησις would be the ἀρετή of τέχνη. The ontological character of ἀρετή is τελείωσις; it constitutes the perfection of something, it brings something to completion, specifically something that has the potentiality for it, i.e., can also be without it. The question is thus whether φρόνησις can be the τελείωσις of τέχνη. ἀλλὰ μὴν τέχνης μὲν ἔστιν ἀρετή, φρονήσεως δ'οὐκ ἔστιν (b21f.). "But in truth there is an ἀρετή for τέχνη, a possible τελείωσις; for φρόνησις there is none." For φρόνησις there is no τελείωσις. How are we to understand that for τέχνη an ἀρετή is possible? In the deliberation of know-how there are various degrees of development. Τέχνη can presume things and concede things. Trial and error are proper to

2. Cf. *Nic. Eth.* VI, 2, 1139a2ff.

it. Through τέχνη, one discovers whether something works or not. The more τέχνη risks failure, the more secure it will be in its procedure. It is precisely through failure that certitude is formed. It is precisely the one who is not ingrained in a definite technique, a set routine, but again and again starts anew and cuts through rigid procedure, who acquires the correct possibility of know-how, has at his disposal the proper kind of the ἀληθεύειν that corresponds to τέχνη, and acquires more and more of that kind of uncovering. καὶ ἐν μὲν τέχνῃ ὁ ἑκὼν ἁμαρτάνων αἱρετώτερος (b22f.). The possibility of failure is an advantage belonging to τέχνη itself. It is precisely on the basis of this possibility that τέχνη is τελειωτέρα. This possibility of failure is constitutive for the development of τέχνη. But in the case of φρόνησις, on the contrary, where it is a matter of a deliberation whose theme is the proper Being of Dasein, every mistake is a personal shortcoming. This shortcoming with regard to oneself is not a higher possibility, not the τελείωσις of φρόνησις, but precisely its corruption. Other than failure, the only possibility open to φρόνησις is to genuinely hit the mark. Φρόνησις is not oriented toward trial and error; in moral action I cannot experiment with myself. The deliberation of φρόνησις is ruled by the either-or. Φρόνησις is by its very sense στοχαστική; it has a permanent orientation, it pursues the goal, and specifically the μεσότης. With φρόνησις, unlike τέχνη, there is no more or less, no "this as well as that," but only the seriousness of the definite decision, success or failure, either-or. Insofar as φρόνησις is στοχαστική, it is impossible for it to be more complete. Thus it has no ἀρετή but is in itself ἀρετή. In this way, the very mode of the carrying out of ἀληθεύειν is different in the case of φρόνησις from the one of τέχνη, although both, in terms of their objects, are concerned with beings which can also be otherwise. Thereby we have gained a delimitation. Φρόνησις cannot be the ἀρετή of τέχνη—because of its very mode of carrying out ἀληθεύειν, quite apart from the fact that the object of τέχνη is a ποιητόν, whereas the object of φρόνησις is a πρακτόν. Thus it is clear that φρόνησις is an ἀρετή but is not a τέχνη: δῆλον οὖν ὅτι ἀρετή τίς ἐστιν καὶ οὐ τέχνη (b24f.). And because φρόνησις is directed at once to the ἀρχή and the τέλος and preserves both, it is the βελτίστη ἕξις of the ἀληθεύειν that corresponds to those beings which can also be otherwise.

How then does φρόνησις relate to ἐπιστήμη? The λόγον ἔχον is divided into two basic possibilities: the λογιστικόν and the ἐπιστημονικόν. Since φρόνησις is not the ἀρετή of τέχνη, the question arises whether it can be the ἀρετή for ἐπιστήμη, for the ἐπιστημονικόν. Now it does indeed appear that φρόνησις is the ἀρετή of ἐπιστήμη, admittedly of an early stage of ἐπιστήμη. Within knowledge there is in fact a mode of disclosure which, precisely as in the case of φρόνησις, relates to beings which can also be otherwise: δόξα. ἥ τε γὰρ δόξα περὶ τὸ ἐνδεχόμενον ἄλλως ἔχειν καὶ ἡ φρόνησις (b27f.). Δόξα possesses in a certain sense the character of simple knowledge; it is like a "thematic" opinion, a view, which has no impact on any particular action. Natural Dasein has certain views and opinions about the things of everyday life which come to pass and therefore change. And one might think that in fact δόξα, which is not a genuine mode of ἀληθεύειν, has its ἀρετή in φρόνησις. Aristotle thus takes up the possibility that the ground of φρόνησις is δόξα. He does not consider this just for the sake of completeness but, instead, because such opinions have arisen. Aristotle cuts this possibility short, however: ἀλλὰ μὴν οὐδ' ἕξις μετὰ λόγου μόνον (b28). "But φρόνησις is not a ἕξις of ἀληθεύειν, a ἕξις which is autonomous in itself and is only for the sake of a disclosing"; on the contrary, it is a ἕξις of ἀληθεύειν which is πρακτική. Because this pertains to its structure, from the very outset φρόνησις cannot be considered the τελείωσις of δόξα, which indeed aims only at the acquisition of views and opinions. Furthermore, it is to be noted that ἀληθεύειν, as it exists in δόξα, in μάθησις, and in ἐπιστήμη, has a peculiar character of fallenness. What I experience, notice, or have learned, I can forget; in this possibility, ἀληθεύειν is subject to λήθη (where the stem of the verb λανθάνειν lies hidden)—what is disclosed can sink back into concealment. The ability to become forgotten is a specific possibility of that ἀληθεύειν which has the character of θεωρεῖν. For the ἕξις μετὰ λόγου is a ἕξις of ἀληθεύειν into which Dasein places itself explicitly. In the case of φρόνησις things are different. This is manifest in the fact that I can experience, notice, and learn what has already been experienced, noted, and learned, whereas φρόνησις is in each case new. Hence there is no λήθη in relation to φρόνησις: σημεῖον δ' ὅτι λήθη τῆς μὲν τοιαύτης ἕξεως ἔστιν, φρονήσεως δ' οὐκ ἔστιν (b28ff.). As regards φρόνησις, there is no possibility of falling into forgetting. Certainly the explication which Aristotle gives here is very meager. But it is nevertheless clear from the context that we would not be going too far in our interpretation by saying that Aristotle has here come across the phenomenon of conscience. Φρόνησις is nothing other than conscience set into motion, making an action transparent. Conscience cannot be forgotten. But it is quite possible that what is disclosed by conscience can be distorted and allowed to be ineffective through ἡδονή and λύπη, through the passions. Conscience always announces itself. Hence because φρόνησις does not possess the possibility of λήθη, it is not a mode of ἀληθεύειν which one could call theoretical knowledge. Therefore φρόνησις is out of the question as the ἀρετή of ἐπιστήμη or of τέχνη. We will still look more closely at the connection ἐπιστήμη and τέχνη have to the two highest modes of ἀληθεύειν, φρόνησις and σοφία.

What is most striking now is that Aristotle designates σοφία as the ἀρετή of τέχνη (*Nic. Eth.* VI, 7, 1141a12). The highest mode of ἀληθεύειν, philosophical reflection, which according to Aristotle is the highest mode of human existence, is at the same time the ἀρετή of τέχνη. This must seem all the more remarkable in view of the fact that τέχνη has as its theme beings which can also be otherwise, whereas the theme of σοφία is in a preeminent sense what always is.[3]

§9. *The analysis of* σοφία *(*Nic. Eth. *VI, 6–7).*

a) The dia-noetic relation of ἐπιστήμη, φρόνησις, and σοφία to the ἀρχαί (*Nic. Eth.* VI, 6).

In order to understand σοφία we must first remind ourselves of the persistent context of Aristotle's interpretation. He analyzes the various modes of ἀληθεύειν with regard to the ἀρχαί, their disclosure and their preservation. Ἐπιστήμη has its foundation in the ἀρχαί; it uses the ἀρχαί as its axioms, the self-evident principles, from which it draws conclusions. Ἐπιστήμη implicitly co-intends the ἀρχή[1] and τέλος, as well as the εἶδος and ὕλη, of beings. But ἐπιστήμη does not make the ἀρχαί thematic; on the contrary, it only wants to pursue its deliberations following the guiding line of the εἶδος. As for τέχνη, it anticipates only the ἀρχή, the εἶδος; it does not even co-intend the τέλος. But τέχνη does not make the εἶδος thematic; it merely takes its course following the guiding line of the εἶδος, which gives direction to its λογίζεσθαι. In φρόνησις the οὗ ἕνεκα is given and, along with it, the ἀρχή as well, and also the τέλος, the εὐπραξία—for the ἀρχή is the τέλος itself. But here too it is not a matter of a thematic consideration. Ἀρχή and τέλος are not taken up *as* ἀρχή and τέλος. Φρόνησις is not a speculation about the ἀρχή and the τέλος of acting as such; it is not an ethics and not a science, not a ἕξις μετὰ λόγου μόνον (*Nic. Eth.* VI, 5, 1140b28). According to its proper sense, it is what it can be when it is a view of a concrete action and decision. And even σοφία, which ultimately aims at the final principles of beings, is an ἀληθεύειν which does not have the ἀρχαί as its exclusive and proper theme. Rather, its research into the ἀρχή is such only insofar as it looks for the principles of those beings which stand under the principles. τοῦ γὰρ σοφοῦ περὶ ἐνίων ἔχειν ἀπόδειξιν ἐστίν (*Nic. Eth.* VI, 6, 1141a2f.). Hence even σοφία is not the ἀληθεύειν which makes the ἀρχή thematic *as* ἀρχή. εἰ δὴ οἷς ἀληθεύομεν καὶ μηδέποτε διαψευδόμεθα περὶ τὰ μὴ ἐνδεχόμενα ἢ καὶ ἐνδεχόμενα ἄλλως ἔχειν, ἐπιστήμη καὶ φρόνησις

3. See the appendix.

1. Editor's note: in the sense of the ἀρχὴ τῆς κινήσεως. Cf. Aristotle's so-called theory of the four causes, inter alia *Met.* I, 3, 983a24ff.

ἐστιν καὶ σοφία καὶ νοῦς, τούτων δὲ τῶν τριῶν μηδὲν ἐνδέχεται εἶναι (λέγω δὲ τρία φρόνησιν ἐπιστήμην σοφίαν), λείπεται νοῦν εἶναι τῶν ἀρχῶν (a3ff.). "If therefore the ways in which we disclose beings truly and thereby do not distort them (i.e., deceive ourselves) are ἐπιστήμη, φρόνησις, σοφία, and νοῦς, and if the three first mentioned, φρόνησις, ἐπιστήμη, and σοφία, do not properly make the ἀρχαί thematic, then all that remains is that νοῦς is that ἀληθεύειν which discloses the ἀρχαί as ἀρχαί." It is striking that τέχνη is omitted here. Nevertheless, Aristotle is referring here to the modes of ἀληθεύειν in which we have certainty and are not subject to deception, whereas in τέχνη mistakes will be made and the ἁμαρτάνειν is constitutive. Now what about νοῦς?

b) Νοῦς as ἀληθεύειν of the ἀρχαί (*Nic. Eth.* VI, 7). Σοφία as νοῦς καὶ ἐπιστήμη.

Aristotle does not say anything more precise about νοῦς here. What can we learn about it? On the whole, Aristotle has transmitted to us very little about νοῦς; it is the phenomenon which causes him the most difficulty. Perhaps Aristotle did elucidate it as far as was possible within the Greek interpretation of Being. We find a preliminary interpretation already in *Nicomachean Ethics* VI, 6. Here Aristotle reminds us that ἐπιστήμη—just like φρόνησις and σοφία—is μετὰ λόγου (1140b33). We will see that the ἀληθεύειν of νοῦς is in fact ἄνευ λόγου, insofar as λόγος is understood as κατάφασις and ἀπόφασις. Νοῦς as pure νοῦς possesses, if it is to be conceived μετὰ λόγου, an altogether peculiar λόγος which is neither κατάφασις nor ἀπόφασις. In anticipation, it must be said that νοῦς as such is not a possibility of the Being of man. Yet insofar as intending and perceiving are characteristic of human Dasein, νοῦς can still be found in man. Aristotle calls this νοῦς: ὁ καλούμενος τῆς ψυχῆς νοῦς,[2] the "so-called" νοῦς, which means a nongenuine νοῦς. This νοῦς in the human soul is not a νοεῖν, a straightforward seeing, but a διανοεῖν, because the human soul is determined by λόγος. On the basis of λόγος, the assertion of something *as* something, νοεῖν becomes διανοεῖν. Other than νοῦς, there is no mode of ἀληθεύειν which in the proper sense is an ἀληθεύειν of the ἀρχαί.

Because σοφία takes into consideration that for which the ἀρχαί are ἀρχαί, the concrete beings, and then at the same time relates them for the most part to the ἀρχαί, Aristotle is able to characterize σοφία as νοῦς καὶ

2. *De An.* III, 4, 429a22ff: ὁ ἄρα καλούμενος τῆς ψυχῆς νοῦς (λέγω δὲ νοῦν ᾧ διανοεῖται καὶ ὑπολαμβάνει ἡ ψυχή).

ἐπιστήμη, as an ἀληθεύειν which, on the one hand, assumes in a certain sense the ἀληθεύειν of νοῦς and, on the other hand, has the scientific character of ἐπιστήμη. ὥστε εἴη ἂν ἡ σοφία νοῦς καὶ ἐπιστήμη (1141a19f.).

c) The further outline of the investigation. Φρόνησις and σοφία as the highest modes of ἀληθεύειν. The priority of σοφία. The origin of this priority in the natural understanding of Greek Dasein. The phenomenology of Dasein as the method of the investigation. Θεωρία: clarification of the term and history of the concept.

From our preliminary survey of the modes of ἀληθεύειν, we can, without preempting the actual interpretation of the highest modes of ἀληθεύειν, retain three points:

1.) The comparative interpretation of the various modes of ἀληθεύειν makes it clear that ἀληθεύειν is in the end presented here with regard to the disclosure and preservation of the ἀρχαί.

2.) This regard toward the ἀρχαί is then also decisive for the discussion of the two highest modes of ἀληθεύειν, φρόνησις and σοφία.

3.) Accordingly, we will gain a real understanding of the various modes of ἀληθεύειν only if we lay out how it happens that precisely the question of the ἀρχή furnishes the guiding line for establishing and distinguishing the various modes of ἀληθεύειν.

In chapters 6–13 of Book VI of the *Nicomachean Ethics,* the consideration plays out within a focus on the two basic phenomena of φρόνησις and σοφία. The question at issue is which one has a pure and simple priority over the other.

Let us remark incidentally that what Aristotle achieved here, working in the soil of phenomena of such difficult content, i.e., what he discussed under the titles φρόνησις and σοφία, later entered into philosophy under the rubric of practical and theoretical reason. Of course, this newer discussion of the faculties of reason has gone through manifold influences within the history of philosophy and has been saturated with them, so that the original soil is scarcely recognizable without direction from the work of Aristotle. Thus it is not possible to understand φρόνησις and σοφία under the guiding line of the Kantian distinction between practical and theoretical reason.

To anticipate the result, Aristotle establishes:

1.) that σοφία is the other highest possibility of ἀληθεύειν, the second βελτίστη ἕξις, beside φρόνησις, and

2.) that it has a priority over φρόνησις, such that this ἀληθεύειν constitutes a proper possibility, and the genuine possibility, of Dasein: the βίος θεωρητικός, the existence of scientific man.

This result is all the more astonishing if we consider that the theme of σοφία is beings which always are, whereas φρόνησις aims at and makes transparent precisely the ἐνδεχόμενον ἄλλως ἔχειν, the Being of human Dasein.

A searching investigation is required to see why σοφία is nevertheless the highest possibility of ἀληθεύειν, and in particular:

1.) Σοφία is to be worked out in its own structure versus φρόνησις and presented as the genuine mode of ἀληθεύειν, as the highest possibility of the Being of Dasein—whereby φρόνησις will also appear more concretely.

2.) Aristotle does not force this result dogmatically on the Dasein of the Greeks of that time. Aristotle is not seeking something unprecedented and novel; on the contrary, he understands σοφία as the highest possibility of the Being of Dasein on the basis of the Being of Greek Dasein itself. He thinks that which the natural understanding of the life of the Greeks strove for; he thinks this radically and to its end.

3.) By pursuing this rootedness of the priority of σοφία in Dasein we will at the same time come to understand why the ἀρετή of τέχνη is not φρόνησις but is precisely σοφία as the ἀρετή of ἐπιστήμη, as ἀκριβεστάτη τῶν ἐπιστημῶν (cf. *Nic. Eth.* VI, 7, 1141a17), as the "most rigorous of all sciences."

We will begin with the second point and will see that σοφία was the highest possibility of Greek Dasein and that Aristotle was the first to clarify it as such on the basis of the natural everyday Dasein of the Greeks.

Concerning the method of our interpretation here, as well as of our lecture course in general, let us note that it is grounded in a phenomenology of Dasein, one which we cannot now expound explicitly. Here we can carry out only a brief methodological deliberation. Indeed, methodological speculations make little sense if no specific issue backs them up. We want to pursue our concrete interpretation first and postpone "questions of method." To be sure, the latter then become more than the phrase suggests; that is, they themselves then become actual research into the matter at issue. Thus, methodologically, the interpretation does not proceed to draw in previously unnoticed texts and passages from Aristotle—after all, he has been at our disposal for 2,000 years—but instead the preparation for the interpretation already contains a rich hermeneutic. That is not to imply that the interpretation will be carried out in a roundabout way, uncritical of other standpoints. The presupposition for the interpretation is thus that Dasein be thematic, and if the interpretation interprets something "into" Aristotle, it does so merely to attain and to understand what is genuinely taking place in him. It is one thing to approach a philosophical system from various disciplines, and it is something else to make the issues sharper and the intentions more explicit and not to remain back behind them.

Σοφία is carried out in pure knowledge, pure seeing, θεωρεῖν—in the βίος θεωρητικός. The word θεωρεῖν was already known prior to Aristotle. But Aristotle himself coined the term θεωρητικός. The word θεωρεῖν, θεωρία, comes from θεωρός, which is composed of θέα, "look," "sight," and ὁράω, "to see." Θέα, "sight," which allows the look of something to be seen, is similar in meaning to εἶδος. Θεωρός then means the one who looks upon something as it shows itself, who sees what is given to see. The θεωρός is the one who goes to the festival, the one who is present *as a spectator* at the great dramas and festivals—whence our word "theater." The word θεωρία expresses "seeing" in a twofold way. The history of the meaning of this expression cannot be exhibited here in more detail. Let us only refer to the fact that in the time immediately prior to Plotinus, in the second and third centuries, θεωρία was so interpreted that one could say: in θέω- resides the stem θεῖον, θεός; θεωρεῖν thus means: to look upon the divine. This is a specific Greek etymology, given, for example, by Alexander Aphrodisius. We have here a re-interpretation, which has its ground in certain statements of Aristotle, though it does not touch the genuine meaning of the word. The Latin translation of θεωρία is *speculatio,* which means pure onlooking; "speculative" thus means the same as "theoretical." The word θεωρία then played a large role in theology, where it was opposed to ἀλληγορία: θεωρία is that consideration which lays out the historiographical facts, just as they are, prior to all ἀλληγορία; θεωρία becomes identical with ἱστορία. Finally it becomes identical with biblical theology and with theology pure and simple. Later the translation of θεωρία as *theologia speculativa* presents the precise opposite of exegetical theology. That is one of those peculiar accidents which very often arise in the history of meanings.

We will now attempt a concrete understanding of σοφία. Aristotle has dealt searchingly with σοφία in: 1.) *Nicomachean Ethics,* Book VI, chapters 6–13; 2.) *Nicomachean Ethics* X, chapters 6–10 (in conjunction with εὐδαιμονία); and 3.) *Metaphysics,* Book I, chapters 1–2. We already stressed that Aristotle did not invent the conception of σοφία as the ultimate possibility of Dasein but only made it explicit out of the natural understanding of Greek Dasein itself. We want first to travel this path with Aristotle and to see how a tendency to σοφία and the preliminary stages of it are prepared in Greek Dasein itself. This consideration of the preliminary history of σοφία within natural Dasein is carried out in Aristotle's *Metaphysics* I, 1–2.[3]

3. See the appendix.

Chapter Two

The Genesis of σοφία within Natural Greek Dasein (αἴσθησις, ἐμπειρία, τέχνη, ἐπιστήμη, σοφία) (*Met.* I, 1–2)

§10. Introductory characterization of the investigation. Its guiding line: the self-expression of Dasein itself. Its course: the five levels of εἰδέναι. *Its goal:* σοφία *as* μάλιστα ἀληθεύειν.

The first book of the *Metaphysics* is supposed to be an early work. But it refers to the *Ethics*,[1] which has been proven to be late; that would contradict the supposition just mentioned. Of course, the reference to the *Ethics* may also be a later insertion. I consider a chronology of the writings of Aristotle impossible. Werner Jaeger calls *Metaphysics* I a grand "improvisation."[2] At I, 3, 983a33 there is a reference to the *Physics;* here (*Met.* I, 3) the theory of the αἰτία is clearly elaborated;[3] therefore the "unsettling reference" (*Met.* I, 1, 981b25) to the Ἠθικά should be taken out. But this is in truth no reason; especially since at bottom nothing different is said there. If we think of the confusion which still is present in Plato regarding the fundamental concepts of τέχνη, ἐπιστήμη, σοφία, and φρόνησις, as well as regarding their relations, and compare this to the clearly superior presentation by Aristotle in *Metaphysics* I, 1, 2, then we may not speak of an "improvisation," even if it is called "grand." In Aristotle the fundamental concepts are already wholly clear at the very outset, assuming this first book of the *Metaphysics* actually is early. The first two chapters of *Metaphysics* I are conceived wholly within the same horizon as the one of Book VI of the *Nicomachean Ethics*. Admittedly, ἀληθεύειν is not as such explicit; this is shown at *Metaphysics* I, 1, 981b5ff., where, instead of ἀληθεύειν, Aristotle says λόγον ἔχειν, αἰτίας γνωρίζειν, and finally in general "to know the ἀρχή." Σοφία is hence to be determined as a mode of λόγον ἔχειν. That concurs with the determination of Dasein itself, i.e., of man as λόγον ἔχον.

What is the first and most original phenomenon of natural Dasein that one could call a preliminary stage of σοφία? When we raise such questions, we must begin by asking about a guiding line. The guiding line for Aristotle is to get "information" from Dasein itself, i.e., from what Dasein, which is

1. *Met.* I, 1, 981b25f.

2. W. Jaeger, *Aristoteles: Grundlegung einer Geschichte seiner Entwicklung*, Berlin, 1923. 2. Aufl., Berlin, 1955, p. 178.

3. *Met.* I, 3, 983a24f.

self-expressive, means when it uses terms like σοφία and σοφός. Here Aristotle has two things in mind. On the one hand, everyday employment of these expressions must betray the understanding natural Dasein has of them. Admittedly, they are not, for everyday Dasein, rigorous scientific concepts—since, in general, a first self-expression, as first, is undetermined and never a univocally fixed concept. Yet this does not preclude the possibility that Dasein's understanding is here on a secure path. As is the case with all everyday speech, with the expressions in question Dasein moves in the indeterminateness of the "more or less"; one does not speak about σοφός but about μᾶλλον and ἧττον σοφός; one cannot give definitions, but one knows this is σοφώτερον than that. Such a comparative mode of speech is characteristic of everyday language, and the question is only to grasp it and to hear out of it what the μάλιστα of this μᾶλλον is. Aristotle pursues this method in *Metaphysics* I, 1. In addition, Aristotle takes an orientation from what Dasein says directly and explicitly about the σοφός. He follows this method in I, 2.

Aristotle takes his first orientation from the comparative mode of speech characteristic of everyday language. There various levels of understanding manifest themselves; these occur in natural Dasein itself and are familiar. In the μᾶλλον and ἧττον there is a tendency toward the μάλιστα, and τέχνη is already μᾶλλον σοφός than ἐμπειρία. The τελείωσις hence points in the direction of ἐπιστήμη and θεωρεῖν. Aristotle demonstrates that his interpretation of σοφία and θεωρεῖν is nothing else than Dasein's own interpretation, made clear and raised in self-understanding.

Aristotle articulates five different levels of understanding to be found in natural Dasein, namely the levels of:

1.) κοιναὶ αἴσθησεις (*Met.* I, 1, 981b14), the common orientation toward the world;

2.) ἐμπειρία (usually translated as "experience" *[Erfahrung]*), getting used to *[Eingefahrensein]* a particular operation;

3.) τέχνη, or the τεχνίτης or the χειροτέχνης, the laborer, who works with his hands, following the guideline of the determinate orientation of τέχνη;

4.) the ἀρχιτέκτων, the architect, who does not himself work on the building, does not put his hands to it, but who simply moves in the domain of applicable knowledge and whose main task lies in drawing the plan and contemplating the εἶδος—an activity which is still a ποίησις, since it aims at the fabrication of the house;

5.) simple θεωρεῖν, onlooking and exposing, where it is no longer a matter of χρῆσις.

In each case these levels manifest a μᾶλλον of σοφόν in relation to the previous one. In enumerating the levels of understanding, I began with the

Dasein of man. Aristotle also proposes, prior to that, the life of animals, who already have "a little experience."[4]

Θεωρεῖν is the way σοφία is carried out, a mode of Being of human Dasein, a mode which includes a so-called διαγωγή: lingering, leisure, idleness. Διαγωγή as idleness means not acting, not accomplishing anything: no ποίησις whatsoever. Insofar as θεωρεῖν is determined by διαγωγή, it is not ποίησις but a mere onlooking, a lingering with the object. This characteristic of θεωρεῖν, and consequently of the mode of Being of σοφία, expresses more acutely what Plato often said, e.g., in the *Sophist* at 254a8f: ὁ δέ γε φιλόσοφος, τῇ τοῦ ὄντος ἀεὶ διὰ λογισμῶν προσκείμενος ἰδέᾳ. The philosopher "lies with," is constantly occupied with, a looking upon beings, and specifically in such a way that in this looking upon beings he speaks about them and pursues an understanding of them. Thus in Plato the same scientific attitude is alive which Aristotle later made explicit; it is just that in Plato it is not yet ontologically-theoretically founded.

If σοφία is to be delimited over and against φρόνησις, then the γένεσις of the comportment of σοφία must be elucidated. By means of this consideration of the γένεσις of σοφία we will gain at the same time the horizon for understanding the fact that σοφία is simultaneously the ἀρετή of both τέχνη and ἐπιστήμη. It must hence appear why τέχνη, which genuinely aims at a ποίησις, presents, on the basis of its most proper structure, an early stage of σοφία. Aristotle remarks explicitly: οὐθὲν ἄλλο σημαίνοντες τὴν σοφίαν ἢ ὅτι ἀρετὴ τέχνης ἐστίν (*Nic. Eth.* VI, 7, 1141a11f.). "Genuine understanding, σοφία, is the consummation, ἀρετή, τελείωσις, of the know-how employed to construct something." At the same time Aristotle says: ὥστε δῆλον ὅτι ἡ ἀκριβεστάτη ἂν τῶν ἐπιστημῶν εἴη ἡ σοφία (a16). "Σοφία is the most rigorous of the sciences." Ἀ-κριβής has the same form as ἀ-ληθής, α-privative and κρυπτόν: "unconcealed," whereby Aristotle is referring to a character of knowledge as uncovering. Because σοφία is the most rigorous science, i.e., the one which uncovers beings most genuinely, Aristotle can say: δεῖ ἄρα τὸν σοφὸν μὴ μόνον τὰ ἐκ τῶν ἀρχῶν εἰδέναι, ἀλλὰ καὶ περὶ τὰς ἀρχὰς ἀληθεύειν. ὥστε εἴη ἂν ἡ σοφία νοῦς καὶ ἐπιστήμη, ὥσπερ κεφαλὴν ἔχουσα ἐπιστήμη τῶν τιμιωτάτων (a17ff.). "The σοφός must not only know beings on the basis of the ἀρχαί, but he must also uncover them within the circuit of the ἀρχαί, so that σοφία is νοῦς καὶ ἐπιστήμη and is, as it were, the pinnacle, the ἐπιστήμη of the τιμιώτατα." Because σοφία is the most rigorous science, it pursues the τιμιώτατα, the most desirable objects of knowledge, namely what always is, ἀεί, in such a way that it

4. *Met.* I, 1, 980b26f.

thereby uncovers the ἀρχαί. That is why it is the pinnacle, occupies the first place, and has the μάλιστα ἀληθεύειν.

The task is now to understand, on the basis of Dasein itself, the γένεσις of this highest possibility of human Dasein. As regards method, let us make the following remark.[5] Ἀληθεύειν is a mode of Being of Dasein, and specifically insofar as Dasein comports itself to a being, to the world, or to itself. The being which in the Greek understanding is genuine Being is the world, the ἀεί. Because an occupation with something is determined in its Being by the "through which," the modes of Being of Dasein must be interpreted on the basis of Dasein's comportment to the respective objects.

§11. *The first three levels of* εἰδέναι: αἴσθησις, ἐμπειρία, τέχνη *(*Met. *I, 1).*

a) Αἴσθησις. The priority of ὁρᾶν. Ἀκούειν as a condition of learning. Μνήμη and φρόνησις.

We know from our previous considerations that what is at issue in σοφία is only an orientation of Dasein toward uncoveredness and visibility. Because σοφία is determined as pure θεωρεῖν, Aristotle proceeds in the first sentence of the *Metaphysics* from this Dasein: πάντες ἄνθρωποι τοῦ εἰδέναι ὀρέγονται φύσει (*Met.* I, 1, 980a1f.). "All human beings have an inherent striving to see." "Seeing," perception in the broadest sense, is part of Dasein; indeed still more: Dasein includes an ὄρεξις, a being out to see, a being out to get acquainted with things. σημεῖον δ' ἡ τῶν αἰσθήσεων ἀγάπησις (a1f.). "A sign of this is the predilection we have for looking, for sense perception." In connection with εἰδέναι, as that to which human Dasein aspires, Aristotle places a priority on one mode of αἴσθησις above all others, namely *seeing*. We prefer seeing, ὁρᾶν, to all the other senses. The governing point of view here is the possibility of experiencing something about the world through a particular sense, i.e., the extent to which the beings of the world are disclosed through that sense. αἴτιον δ' ὅτι μάλιστα ποιεῖ γνωρίζειν ἡμᾶς αὕτη τῶν αἰσθήσεων καὶ πολλὰς δηλοῖ διαφοράς (a26f.). Δηλοῦν here means to let be seen, to make manifest. Seeing is thus preeminent among the senses in that "it lets many differences be seen"; seeing provides the greatest possibility of differentiating the things in their manifoldness and orienting oneself within them. This privileged position of ὁρᾶν is all the more remarkable in view of Aristotle's emphasis (b23) that ἀκούειν is the highest αἴσθησις. But that is not a contradiction. Hearing is basic to the

5. Cf. the comments on method on p. 43.

constitution of man, the one who speaks. Hearing, along with speaking, pertains to man's very possibility. Because man can hear, he can learn. Both senses, hearing and seeing, have, in different ways, a privilege: hearing makes possible communication, understanding others; seeing has the privilege of being the primary disclosure of the world, so that what has been seen can be spoken of and appropriated more completely in λόγος.

Aristotle determines definitively the being of man with the following anticipatory characterization: τὸ δὲ τῶν ἀνθρώπων γένος <ζῇ> καὶ τέχνῃ καὶ λογισμοῖς (b27ff.). This determination of the Being of man shows that the γένεσις of σοφία in the *Metaphysics* coincides perfectly with that given in the *Nicomachean Ethics*. "The human race (i.e., the strain of beings that are characterized as living) lives τέχνῃ καὶ λογισμοῖς." Here are united the two modes of λόγον ἔχον familiar to us from the *Nicomachean Ethics:* the ἐπιστημονικόν and the λογιστικόν. And this characterization of the Being of man implies that man has at his disposal a higher mode of orientation than animals. This orientation itself has various levels. φύσει μὲν οὖν αἴσθησιν ἔχοντα γίγνεται τὰ ζῷα, ἐκ δὲ ταύτης τοῖς μὲν αὐτῶν οὐκ ἐγγίγνεται μνήμη, τοῖς δ' ἐγγίγνεται (a27ff.). Animals have for the most part mere αἴσθησις, though many also have μνήμη, "retention." Μνήμη does not here mean memory but rather the ability to think of something in the widest sense; this μνήμη does not require λόγος or νοεῖν. καὶ διὰ τοῦτο ταῦτα φρονιμώτερα καὶ μαθητικώτερα τῶν μὴ δυναμένων μνημονεύειν ἐστί (b1f.). On the basis of this capacity to retain, living beings have a certain φρόνησις, i.e., φρόνησις in a broader sense, a particular certainty in their orientation. Those animals that can hear have at the same time the possibility of learning in a certain sense; one can train them. Μνήμη, the one that, understood in this quite broad form, is already in animals, plays a fundamental role in the development of τέχνη as a mode of orientation of man. In quite definite ways αἰσθάνεσθαι develops into ἐμπειρία: ἐκ μνήμης.

b) Ἐμπειρία. The referential connection: as soon as-then. Its temporal character.

γίγνεται δ' ἐκ τῆς μνήμης ἐμπειρία τοῖς ἀνθρώποις· αἱ γὰρ πολλαὶ μνῆμαι τοῦ αὐτοῦ πράγματος μιᾶς ἐμπειρίας δύναμιν ἀποτελοῦσιν (b28ff.) "In man, there arises from μνήμη an ἐμπειρία; many μνῆμαι (of the same state of affairs) develop the possibility of a single ἐμπειρία, a single procedure." What is essential in ἐμπειρία is the retaining present of a determined connection of occurrences in a single affair. Aristotle later (981a7ff) introduces an example of ἐμπειρία from medicine, which we may take up now. If everyday experience devises a determinate remedy for a poor state of health, for a particular bodily state of man, then these remedies are at first unaccompanied by any real insight into the effective connection of the remedy with that which it is supposed to cure. What is understood is only that there is some connection or other, which we must designate as a connection of the presence of determinate occurrences. Schematically, this connection can be formulated in the following way: as soon as such and such a state sets in, then such and such a remedy must be applied; as soon as this, then that. There is no insight into what the state is, what the remedy is, or how the condition is cured; it is simply a matter of relieving the ailment. You see without further ado that this connection is a temporal one, and indeed at first a purely temporal one: as soon as . . . , then . . . . It is a matter here of a peculiar connection in the temporal Being of Dasein. Dasein's making present, which is expressed in the "now," appears here as the "as soon as:" as soon as . . . , then . . . .

This connection can in the course of time develop into an experience. πλῆθος γὰρ χρόνου ποιεῖ τὴν ἐμπειρίαν (*Nic. Eth.* VI, 8, 1142a15f.). Then Dasein has at its disposal a determinate orientation. What is brought to the fore in ἐμπειρία is simply this connection of the as soon as-then. I cannot here enter further into the structure of this connection. I call this "as soon as-then" (as soon as such and such is present, then such and such must be provided, made present as well) the connection of presentification. In αἴσθησις, the first self-orientation of Dasein, the circumstances and things are accidental, in each case precisely as they offer themselves. Over and against the accidental and arbitrary, trial and error, ἐμπειρία already has a definite certainty. The "as soon as this, then that," the determinate connection, is already made explicit as determinate. Thus ἐμπειρία already has a μία ὑπόληψις present: ἔχει ὑπόληψιν (cf. *Met.* I, 1, 981a7). Dasein is familiar with the connection and has an opinion about it. But Dasein is still without insight into the connection as such; there is here no insight into the what, because Dasein is still wholly concerned with results. Thus we have here a quite primitive presentification. Yet, even so, ἐμπειρία already has a priority over mere perception. Within the focus on mere results, ἐμπειρία is indeed already a δύναμις, a first oriented disposition toward something or other. For over and against the multiplicity of αἴσθησις, Dasein has at its disposal in ἐμπειρία the unity of a determinate and concrete connection. Thus ἐμπειρία as δύναμις is a determinate predelineation of comportment, and specifically in accordance with the respective occurrence or lack of something or other. In ἐμπειρία there is a certain readiness for such and such happenings and circumstances, as they can occur. This readiness is a being-oriented, which is certain but which still contains no insight. The "more," which comes into view in ἐμπειρία, is described by Aristotle as follows: οἱ γὰρ ἔμπειροι περὶ ἕκαστα κρίνουσιν ὀρθῶς τὰ ἔργα, καὶ δι' ὧν ἢ πῶς ἐπιτελεῖται συνιᾶσιν, καὶ ποῖα ποίοις συνᾴδει· τοῖς δ' ἀπείροις ἀγαπητὸν τὸ μὴ διαλανθάνειν εἰ εὖ ἢ κακῶς πεποίηται τὸ ἔργον[1] (*Nic. Eth.* X, 10, 1181a19ff.). "Those who have got used to a certain procedure can decide περὶ ἕκαστα, about the particulars, about every step, and have an understanding of how the ἔργα are to be carried out, which qualities are connected with which, and which concrete connections there are. The ἄπειροι, who indeed also have a knowledge of the work, must be satisfied that to them it is not entirely hidden (διαλανθάνειν: λανθάνειν—ἀ-ληθές!) whether the results are good or not."[2] They have a judgment only about the bare result. To the ἔμπειρος even the εἶδος is no longer hidden. Although this transparency does lie in ἐμπειρία, the concrete connection as such still does not come into view. From this ἐμπειρία, τέχνη can develop.

c) Τέχνη. The modifications of the referential connection. The extraction of the εἶδος. If-then. Because-therefore. Τέχνη and ἐμπειρία. Καθόλου and καθ' ἕκαστον.

γίγνεται δὲ τέχνη ὅταν ἐκ πολλῶν τῆς ἐμπειρίας ἐννοημάτων μία καθόλου γένηται περὶ τῶν ὁμοίων ὑπόληψις (*Met.* I, 1, 981a5ff.). "Τέχνη arises when there is . . . one ὑπόληψις, a determinate opinion, whose object is the καθόλου." In ἐμπειρία, certainty exists regarding the referential connection. If the ἐμπειρία is consolidated, then out of a repeated looking at the matter in question a ὑπόληψις μία καθόλου develops. Through the many single cases to which Dasein comports itself in ἐμπειρία in the mode of the "as soon as this, then that," and through repetition, constantly comporting itself to them in the mode of the "as soon as this, then that," what is one and the same and consequently the very "what" are extracted and understood (ἐννοεῖσθαι). Beyond the purely temporal connection, the "what" is disclosed. The εἶδος ἀφορίζεται (cf. a10), "the εἶδος is extracted," and the matter is now understood κατ' εἶδος ἕν, in view of one outward look that persists and constantly recurs. What was given in ἐμπειρία in a wholly provisional understanding is thereby modified: the "as soon as-then" becomes the "if such and such, then so and so," the "if-then." This neutral "if" has from the first a quite remarkable meaning: it does not denote a mere "as soon as" but already a certain "because." If (and that means, in a certain sense, *because*) such and such appears, then I have to take these or those steps. In this way, therefore, a more genuine understanding modifies the referential connection. And the understanding becomes more genuine insofar as the outward look of the matter in question is extracted. The understanding is then no longer founded in a pre-pre-

1. Susemihl: ἔργων; obviously a typographical mistake.
2. This paraphrasing translation occurs in the notes taken by H. Jonas, F. Schalk, and H. Weiß.

sentification of the connection effective in practice, in a retention of the order of succession, but in an actual presentation of the outward look of the thing itself which is to be treated in some way or other. Therefore we say that he who disposes of τέχνη is σοφώτερος, more of a σοφός, than someone who has recourse only to ἐμπειρία: καὶ σοφωτέρους τοὺς τεχνίτας τῶν ἐμπείρων ὑπολαμβάνομεν (a25f.). The new phenomenon, which makes it possible to speak of τέχνη as σοφωτέρα over and against ἐμπειρία, lies on the path of seeing, not of the carrying out in practice. The latter remains untouched. In fact, it can even as such turn out better in ἐμπειρία than in τέχνη: πρὸς μὲν οὖν τὸ πράττειν ἐμπειρία τέχνης οὐδὲν δοκεῖ διαφέρειν, ἀλλὰ καὶ μᾶλλον ἐπιτυγχάνοντας ὁρῶμεν τοὺς ἐμπείρους τῶν ἄνευ τῆς ἐμπειρίας λόγον ἐχόντων (a12ff.). "It seems that with regard to carrying something out in practice, nothing distinguishes ἐμπειρία from τέχνη; indeed we even see that the ones who dispose of ἐμπειρία reach the goal better than those who, without ἐμπειρία have only the λόγος," i.e., have at their disposal, as uncovered, the outward look, the structural connections within the production. The one who has got used to the right way of doing something, who has put his hand to the task, has for the most part, as regards results, a priority over the one who merely has at his disposal greater understanding. αἴτιον δ' ὅτι ἡ μὲν ἐμπειρία τῶν καθ' ἕκαστόν ἐστι γνῶσις ἡ δὲ τέχνη τῶν καθόλου, αἱ δὲ πράξεις καὶ αἱ γενέσεις πᾶσαι περὶ τὸ καθ' ἕκαστόν εἰσιν (a15ff.). "The reason resides in this, that τέχνη, by its very sense, is concerned with the καθόλου," the outward look which recurs in all the single cases, whereas the meaning of πρᾶξις is, e.g., healing, i.e., making this particular determinate sick person healthy. Πρᾶξις is concerned with the καθ' ἕκαστον. (Here we touch upon concepts, the καθόλου and the καθ' ἕκαστον, which are very important for grasping the distinction between σοφία and φρόνησις. We will still have to consider these concepts more precisely. Their meaning coincides with the ἀεί ὄν and the ἐνδεχόμενον ἄλλως ἔχειν.) Thus the one who disposes of ἐμπειρία has for the most part, as far as results are concerned, a priority over someone who disposes only of the λόγος. Indeed the latter person often fails precisely in practice. And yet, in spite of this shortcoming or failure, τέχνη or the τεχνίτης receives a priority: namely, as being σοφώτερος. The σοφία therefore is not in this case a matter of greater skill (which derives from trial and error) but of a greater power in looking disclosively upon that to which the practice refers. The μᾶλλον has to do with a "more" of insightful understanding, a "more" of autonomous, simply disclosive looking. Τέχνη has its τελείωσις in εἰδέναι. To that extent, ἐμπειρία has a drawback versus τέχνη in that what its object is remains hidden to it: the εἶδος is still συγκεχυμένον.[3] On the other hand, in τέχνη the "what" of

3. Cf. *Phys.* I, 1, 184a21f., and Heidegger's interpretation on p. 59ff.

its object is given. Τέχνη goes back behind the referential connection of the as soon as-then to the because-therefore. The if-then can thus pass over into the because-therefore. But the as soon as-then is still alive even here; in the because-therefore it is elucidated and transparent. Yet the temporal characters only step into the background, they do not disappear. And in the because-therefore, as disclosed in τέχνη, the connection between ground and consequence is already predelineated. That which in the referential connection is primarily αἴτιον, due to something, motive for something, becomes more and more the ἀρχή. The "why" is then no longer that which leads to results but simply that which discloses beings. The whence-connection in the structure of beings, and thus beings themselves, become disclosed and understood more and more. In the tendency toward simple disclosive looking at beings with regard to their ἀρχή resides the σοφώτερον. Hence in τέχνη σοφία is predelineated.

In our interpretation the following relations are becoming visible. In ἐμπειρία the referential connection of the as soon as-then is given, and it expresses a providing of something that is made present, a producing. To the extent that ἐμπειρία is sustained, this connection gets modified into the "as soon as such and such, then *always* so and so," which for its part is modified, in repetition, into the if-then, the because-therefore. Thereby the what-connection is extracted as such. That which is presentified in the presentification of the referential connection is given in each case in its εἶδος and specifically within the referential connection itself. For in τέχνη that which is at issue becomes understandable according to its outward look, in such a way that the foundation of the relation can be read off from this concrete connection. Ultimately, the presentification of the referential connection of the as soon as-then, or of the as soon as-then always, is preparatory for the disclosure of beings out of their ἀρχή. The ἀρχή is indeed the whence and is always already there. Thus the presentification of this connection is in the last analysis preparatory for making beings disposable in their presence (οὐσία), in a disclosive return to that which is already there, the ἀρχή.

This structure is not explicit in Aristotle. But we have to say in general that an interpretation must go beyond what can be found in the text at first glance. This is not interpreting something into it; it is rather a matter of disclosing what was present to the Greeks though unexplicit. If in doing so we go beyond what a primitive understanding sees at first glance, then there resides here a certain danger that we might attribute to Aristotle and the Greeks too much. But closer knowledge will see that they precisely merit this "too much." When an exact reckoning is at issue then it must be said that if one has previously gone beyond the text, the only course left is to make reductions. Such reckoning suffices provided that by its means what alone is there becomes more understandable. And such a hermeneutic is precisely at stake here. If we as a matter of principle orient the Greek concept of Being to time, then this is not a mere haphazard idea but has a quite determined foundation. When we take up Plato our reasons will become clearer.

We now have to come to a closer understanding of both the εἶδος, i.e., the καθόλου, and, concurrently, the counter-concept of the καθ' ἕκαστον.

§12. *Excursus:* καθόλου *and* καθ' ἕκαστον. *The way of philosophy (especially:* Met. *V, 26;* Top. *VI, 4;* Phys. *I, 1).*[1]

The term καθόλου is composed out of κατά and ὅλον. The concept of ὅλον will be our path to a closer elucidation of the Being of the καθόλου. Aristotle provides an orientation toward the ὅλον in *Metaphysics* V, 26. There he understands the καθόλου as a determinate mode of the ὅλον.

a) The manifold meanings of ὅλον. Καθόλου as ὅλον λεγόμενον (*Met.* V, 26).

The ὅλον is understood in many ways:

1.) ὅλον λέγεται οὗ τε μηθὲν ἄπεστι μέρος ἐξ ὧν λέγεται ὅλον φύσει (1023b26f.). "A ὅλον is something in which nothing is absent, in which no part, no relevant piece, is missing." Positively formulated, the ὅλον is the full presence of the being in all that pertains to its Being. Our expression "completeness" *[Vollständigkeit]* renders it very well; the being is com-plete, i.e., in its "full" state *[in seinem vollen Stand]*. It should be noted that Aristotle claims this same definition of ὅλον for the τέλειον as well. τέλειον λέγεται ἓν μὲν οὗ μὴ ἔστιν ἔξω τι λαβεῖν μηδὲ ἓν μόριον (*Met.* V, 26, 1023b27f.). "The τέλειον is in the first place that in which not even a single piece is missing." The ὅλον thus means first of all the full presence of the pieces that make up the finished state of a being.

2.) (ὅλον λέγεται) καὶ τὸ περιέχον τὰ περιεχόμενα ὥστε ἕν τι εἶναι ἐκεῖνα (*Met.* V, 26, 1023b27f.) The ὅλον is the comprehensive, in such a way that the things comprehended form something like a one. We have no corresponding expression for this second sense of ὅλον; "whole" *[das "Ganze"]* will not do. This second sense is determined in two ways. The ὅλον is περιέχον (b28f.), comprehensive:

1. There is no record of this excursus (pp. 54–62) in Heidegger's manuscript. The editor offers it based on the lecture notes of H. Jonas, F. Schalk, and H. Weiß.

a) ἢ γὰρ ὡς ἕκαστον ἕν, "either in the sense that everything to be comprehended is one"

b) ἢ ὡς ἐκ τούτων τὸ ἕν, "or in the sense that the one is composed out of what is comprehended." In the latter instance, the ἕκαστα first constitute the ἕν, whereas in the case of a), every single thing is for itself the ὅλον.

An example of a) is the καθόλου: τὸ μὲν γὰρ καθόλου καὶ τὸ ὅλως λεγόμενον ὡς ὅλον τι ὄν, οὕτως ἐστὶ καθόλου ὡς πολλὰ περιέχον τῷ κατηγορεῖσθαι καθ' ἑκάστου καὶ ἓν ἅπαντα εἶναι ὡς ἕκαστον, οἷον ἄνθρωπον, ἵππον, θεόν, διότι ἅπαντα ζῷα (b29ff.). The καθόλου is a περιέχον in such a way that every ἕκαστον is itself this ὅλον. Thus, e.g., animate being is a ὅλον; man, horse, god are ἕκαστα. And animate being unifies these ἕκαστα into a united whole in such a fashion that every single one of them is, as such, animate being. We have not yet seen, however, what makes possible this peculiar character that, of many single things, each of them, as a single one, is the whole. This is possible only τῷ κατηγορεῖσθαι καθ' ἑκάστου "by the fact that the ὅλον is predicated of each ἕκαστον." This determination is already indicated in the word καθόλου itself, insofar as the κατά refers to λέγειν as κατάφασις. The καθόλου belongs to Dasein insofar as Dasein is disclosive in the mode of λέγειν. The καθόλου is a ὅλον λεγόμενον, a ὅλον, a wholeness, which shows itself only in λέγειν. It is a ὅλον characterized by the fact that its Being is determined by accessibility in λόγος. How the καθόλου is a whole in relation to its unity can be seen only in κατηγορεῖσθαι. The καθόλου comprehends the singulars in such a way that every singular is as such ὅλον; ἄνθρωπος, ἵππος, θεός are in each case for themselves ζῷα. The Being of this wholeness has its ground in λέγεσθαι. The καθόλου is a ὅλον περιέχον λεγόμενον. Among the various kinds of ὅλον, the ὅλον as καθόλου has a preeminent position insofar as λέγειν functions in it.

The second type of the ὅλον περιέχον is given, b), in whatever is denoted as συνεχές: τὸ δὲ συνεχὲς καὶ πεπερασμένον, ὅταν ἕν τι ἐκ πλειόνων ᾖ, ἐνυπαρχόντων μάλιστα μὲν δυνάμει, εἰ δὲ μή, ἐνεργείᾳ (b32ff). A line, e.g., is a ὅλον, and specifically in such a way that it consists ἐκ πλειόνων, i.e., ἐκ στιγμῶν, out of single points. Here not every single point is the ὅλον, the line, but all points together first constitute the ἕν; only together do they make the line. For the most part, the ἐνυπάρχοντα are only there δυνάμει. In the perception of a line the single points do not as a rule stand out explicitly; the pieces stand out only δυνάμει. But if not, then they are there ἐνεργείᾳ.

Prior to this meaning of ὅλον in the sense of συνεχές there is the primarily ontological meaning according to which the ὅλον is identical with the τέλειον, completeness. The full appurtenance of the determinations which constitute a being, the completeness, is the ὅλον in a primarily ontological sense. Thus we have seen up to now the following meanings of ὅλον: 1.) ὅλον as completeness. 2.) as the comprehensive: a) in the sense of the general, καθόλου, b) in the sense of continuous connection, συνεχές, in which the parts which are the ἐνυπάρχοντα exist either δυνάμει or ἐνεργείᾳ.

There is still a third kind of ὅλον: 3.) the totality, πᾶν. ἔτι τοῦ ποσοῦ ἔχοντος δὲ ἀρχὴν καὶ μέσον καὶ ἔσχατον, ὅσων μὲν ποιεῖ ἡ θέσις διαφοράν, πᾶν λέγεται, ὅσων δὲ ποιεῖ, ὅλον (1024a1ff.). The ὅλον in the sense of the comprehensive and the continuous, insofar as it is considered as to its quantity, is: a) a πᾶν, a totality, a sum. The sum of the points is something other than the whole line. What comes into play here is the notion of multitude, in which the order, θέσις, of the parts that make up the whole is arbitrary; no point as point has a priority over any other. b) But there can also be a whole in which the θέσις of the parts is not indifferent. ὅσων δὲ ἡ θέσις ποιεῖ διαφοράν, ὅλον λέγεται (cf. a2). That is then called ὅλον, whole. c) Or again, there can also be something which is at the same time πᾶν *and* ὅλον. ἔστι δὲ ταῦτα ὅσων ἡ μὲν φύσις ἡ αὐτὴ μένει τῇ μεταθέσει, ἡ δὲ μορφὴ οὔ, οἷον κηρὸς καὶ ἱμάτιον (a3ff). "This is the case where the φύσις in a μετάθεσις, in a change of the order of the parts, remains the same, but the μορφή, the outward look, the Gestalt, does not." This latter changes. A dress, e.g., is indeed a ὅλον, a whole. The μορφή of the dress can, nevertheless, through a μετάθεσις of the parts—by being folded, draped, or worn differently—change. Throughout this μετάθεσις it remains identical with itself, the φύσις remains the same, the ὅλον is preserved; but the μορφή changes: ὅλον *and* πᾶν. d) The ultimate determination of the πᾶν is that determination of wholeness which is also claimed for number. καὶ ἀριθμὸς πᾶν μὲν λέγεται, ὅλος δ' ἀριθμὸς οὐ λέγεται (cf. a7f.). The ἀριθμός, that which is counted, the sum, is called πᾶν, totality, but not ὅλον, whole. e) And finally it is called πάντα, "all things collected," but not the whole. πᾶσαι αὗται αἱ μονάδες, "these collected units." πάντα δὲ λέγεται ἐφ' οἷς τὸ πᾶν ὡς ἐφ' ἑνί, ἐπὶ τούτοις τὸ πάντα ὡς ἐπὶ διῃρημένοις· πᾶς οὗτος ὁ ἀριθμός, πᾶσαι αὗται αἱ μονάδες (a8ff.). "Whereas τὸ πᾶν, the totality, is used in order to signify the unit, so τὰ πάντα, the collected, denotes the separate parts, this total number, these collected 'ones.'"

This consideration is in Aristotle of fundamental significance for the structure of beings and for the λόγος which uncovers beings in their structure. And it is also the basis for the distinction between the καθόλου and the καθ' ἕκαστον. This distinction resides in the mode of access to the beings and at the same time in the degree of the uncoveredness (ἀλήθεια) of the beings.

b) The mode of access as *distingens* between καθ' ἕκαστον and καθόλου. Αἴσθησις and λόγος. Πρὸς ἡμᾶς γνωριμώτερον and ἁπλῶς γνωριμώτερον. The way of philosophy (according to *Top.* VI, 4 and *Met.* VII, 3): from καθ' ἕκαστον to καθόλου.

The καθόλου is a determinate ὅλον; its distinctive feature derives from the fact that its Being is determined by accessibility in λόγος: it is a ὅλον λεγόμενον. The καθόλου can never be uncovered by an αἴσθησις, which is limited to mere visual appearance. In order to grasp the καθόλου I have to *speak*, address something *as* something. In this distinction between λόγος and αἴσθησις we also find the distinction between the καθόλου and the καθ' ἕκαστον. The καθ' ἕκαστον is a being as it initially presents itself, i.e., in αἴσθησις. The καθόλου is something which shows itself first and only in λέγειν. This distinction touches the fundamental question of the manner and the levels in which beings are accessible in their proper Being. Dasein can be disclosive according to two extreme possibilities. These are predelineated by the distinction we just mentioned: καθ' ἕκαστον and καθόλου. It is striking that in the expression καθ' ἕκαστον the κατά takes the accusative, and in the other case the genitive. With the accusative, κατά usually signifies stretching beyond something, whereas κατά with the genitive expresses the explicit grasp of that beyond which the comportment stretches itself. Κατά with the genitive occurs, e.g., in the expression τοξεύειν κατά τινος, to shoot *at* someone with a bow, i.e., to shoot down at someone from a tree. The ὅλον in the καθόλου is hence, according to the genitive construction, characterized by the fact that it shows itself only insofar as it becomes an explicit theme; whereas in αἴσθησις the καθ' ἕκαστον shows itself of itself, without becoming an explicit theme.

This distinctive feature of the καθόλου versus the καθ' ἕκαστον is also captured in the distinction between the ἁπλῶς γνωριμώτερον and the πρὸς ἡμᾶς γνωριμώτερον:

1.) πρὸς ἡμᾶς γνωριμώτερον, i.e., ἡμῖν γνωριμώτερον, in relation to us, those beings are better known and more familiar which are disclosed in our immediate comportment. And these are precisely the καθ' ἕκαστον, which show themselves in αἴσθησις. Beings in their proper Being, that which in beings is always already there and out of which everything further is determined—that is at first concealed to us.

2.) ἁπλῶς γνωριμώτερον, simply, without relation to us, with regard to beings on their own, what is more known is that which is simply there in beings, in such a way that it gives all other determinations their presence. And that is the καθόλου, that which is accessible primarily through λόγος or νοῦς, whereas the καθ' ἕκαστον initially and for the most part falls under αἴσθησις.

ἁπλῶς μὲν οὖν γνωριμώτερον τὸ πρότερον τοῦ ὑστέρου, οἷον στιγμὴ γραμμῆς καὶ γραμμὴ ἐπιπέδου καὶ ἐπίπεδον στερεοῦ, καθάπερ καὶ μονὰς ἀριθμοῦ· πρότερον γὰρ καὶ ἀρχὴ παντὸς ἀριθμοῦ. ὁμοίως δὲ καὶ στοιχεῖον συλλαβῆς. ἡμῖν δ' ἀνάπαλιν ἐνίοτε συμβαίνει· μάλιστα γὰρ τὸ στερεὸν ὑπὸ τὴν αἴσθησιν πίπτει <τοῦ ἐπιπέδου>, τὸ δ' ἐπίπεδον μᾶλλον τῆς γραμμῆς, γραμμὴ δὲ σημείου μᾶλλον. <διὸ μᾶλλον> οἱ πολλοὶ γὰρ τὰ τοιαῦτα προγνωρίζουσιν· τὰ μὲν γὰρ τῆς τυχούσης, τὰ δ' ἀκριβοῦς καὶ περιττῆς διανοίας καταμαθεῖν ἐστιν (*Top.* VI, 4, 141b5ff.). To us, ἡμῖν, in our immediate comportment, what is initially familiar is the στερεόν, or the σῶμα, the physical body as a human body. It is only in a progressive return to the ἀρχή that we disclose ἐπίπεδον, γραμμή, στιγμή, surface, line, point. The point is then the ἀρχή. Likewise in the case of the ἀριθμός, a determinate number, it is only in a similar return that the μονάς, the unit, is disclosed as ἀρχή. Thus, whereas ἁπλῶς, simply, seen in terms of beings themselves, the στιγμή or μονάς is the ἀρχή, as related to us things are reversed. The naive person does not see points and does not know that lines consist of points. Οἱ πολλοί, people as they are at first and for the most part, know bodies, i.e., what first strikes the eyes and what can be experienced by merely looking. There is no need for any special arrangements of reflection in order to see things in their wholeness.

According to this distinction, even the scope of αἴσθησις is different from that of λόγος. With regard to ἀληθεύειν, αἴσθησις remains behind λόγος and νοῦς. τὰ δ' ἑκάστοις γνώριμα καὶ πρῶτα πολλάκις ἠρέμα ἐστὶ γνώριμα, καὶ μικρὸν ἢ οὐδὲν ἔχει τοῦ ὄντος. ἀλλ' ὅμως ἐκ τῶν φαύλως μὲν γνωστῶν, αὑτῷ δὲ γνωστῶν, τὰ ὅλως γνωστὰ γνῶναι πειρατέον, μεταβαίνοντας, ὥσπερ εἴρηται, διὰ τούτων αὐτῶν (*Met.* VII, 3, 1029b8ff.). "What is familiar to anyone whatever and is given to him in the first place is often imprecise (not brought out, though it is seen) and it has little or nothing of the being about it." It is certainly the case that in αἴσθησις the πολλοί have seen the world, but what is given in αἴσθησις contains little or nothing of beings. This peculiar mode of expression shows that for Aristotle a determinate sense of Being guides all his discussions about beings. At the same time it is clear that beings, even if given in the most immediate onlooking, are nevertheless still not ἀλήθεια, beings as uncovered, and that it is precisely ἀλήθεια which is the concern of philosophy. That does not mean we are to speculate about the "truth"; the identification of ὄν and ἀλήθεια will be clear only if we gain clarity about ἀλήθεια. Furthermore: "but nevertheless," although in αἴσθησις "something uncovered as straightforwardly familiar" is present, one must depart from it. For what is thus uncovered, although straightforward, is yet "familiar to someone himself," i.e., it is the ground at his disposal.[2] One must depart from

2. Cf. p. 68.

what is thus uncovered, even if it is straightforwardly uncovered; one must appropriate this ground explicitly and not leap beyond it to a reality which is simply fabricated by a theory, i.e., to a superbeing, as Plato has done. It will not do to take as μὴ ὄν that which is at first familiar and which is straightforwardly uncovered, but instead one must take one's departure from it and, μεταβαίνων, "running through it, through that which is straightforwardly uncovered, see what is simply and properly known." Plato, on the other hand, happened to gain a certain sense of Being—to be sure, not one as radical as that to be found later in Aristotle—and it then "occurred" to him to express this Being as a being, such that he had to posit genuine beings as non-beings. Aristotle saw through this peculiar error perfectly, which was quite an accomplishment for a Greek, nearly beyond our power to imagine.

One must fasten onto precisely the καθ' ἕκαστον of αἴσθησις and admit it as the first factual state of beings. Even Aristotle was successful here only within certain limits, and in spite of his tendency to radicality he did not press on into the ultimate originality of the Being of the world. There is a possible interpretation which even endeavors to see the beings of the world detached from the Greek concept of Being. That, however, will not happen in these lectures. The way on which beings are uncovered in their most proper Being thus proceeds from the καθ' ἕκαστον and passes through it (μεταβαίνων), to the καθόλου. The καθ' ἕκαστον is indeed the πρὸς ἡμᾶς γνωριμώτερον; it shows itself in αἴσθησις, whereas the καθόλου first manifests itself in λόγος. *De An.* B, 5: τῶν καθ' ἕκαστον ἡ κατ' ἐνέργειαν αἴσθησις, ἡ δ' ἐπιστήμη τῶν καθόλου (417b22f.).

This characterization of the way would be without further difficulty—apart from the difficulty the καθόλου itself raises not only for Plato but also for Aristotle—if the foregoing interpretation of Aristotle, according to which the πρὸς ἡμᾶς γνωριμώτερον is the καθ' ἕκαστον, did not seem to contradict the methodological principles Aristotle laid down in the introduction to the *Physics*, that is to say in the introduction to an investigation whose task is precisely to make beings accessible in their Being.

c) The way of philosophy (*Phys.* I, 1). From the καθόλου to the καθ' ἕκαστον. Resolution of the supposed contradiction between *Topics* VI, 4 and *Physics* I, 1.

In the introduction to the *Physics*, Aristotle emphasizes that the way we must take leads from the καθόλου to the καθ' ἕκαστον: διὸ ἐκ τῶν καθόλου εἰς τὰ καθ' ἕκαστα δεῖ προιέναι (*Phys.* I, 1, 184a23f.). Thus here the way to proceed is precisely the reverse of the way characterized up to now—which is obviously a contradiction. If it could be demonstrated that this is indeed no contradiction, then we would thereby also gain a more precise elucidation of the καθόλου and the καθ' ἕκαστον. For these concepts are not material ones, i.e., ones that fit certain definite beings and not others. Now the difficulty is enhanced still further by the fact that the reflections preceding the statement we just quoted are in harmony with what we had been saying. πέφυκε δὲ ἐκ τῶν γνωριμωτέρων ἡμῖν ἡ ὁδὸς καὶ σαφεστέρων ἐπὶ τὰ σαφέστερα τῇ φύσει καὶ γνωριμώτερα (a16f.). For us, according to our φύσις, our Dasein, the way is such that it is determined by αἴσθησις: it proceeds ἐκ τῶν γνωριμωτέρων ἡμῖν, "from what is more familiar to us," ἐπὶ τὰ τῇ φύσει γνωριμώτερα, "to what is, according to its own nature, more knowable." This formulation intensifies the opposition to the *Topics:* οὐ γὰρ ταὐτὰ ἡμῖν τε γνώριμα καὶ ἁπλῶς (a18). "For what is familiar to us is not the same as what is knowable in itself." After this reflection, a closer description of the προιέναι begins. ἔστι δ' ἡμῖν πρῶτον δῆλα καὶ σαφῆ τὰ συγκεχυμένα μᾶλλον (a21f.). "For us what is δῆλον is initially what is still rather mingled together," what is unseparated. To take the example in the *Topics,* a body primarily presents itself as something mingled together: surface, line, and point are given only as unseparated out. We handle physical things, and in doing so we perceive first of all only the physical body as a whole. ὕστερον δ' ἐκ τούτων γίνεται γνώριμα τὰ στοιχεῖα καὶ αἱ ἀρχαὶ διαιροῦσι ταῦτα (a22ff.). Out of this συγκεχυμένως δῆλον, "the στοιχεῖα, the elements, become known later," i.e., the surface, line, and point, "as well as the ἀρχαί, the starting places," whence the physical body, according to the constitution of its Being, comes into being: the point. What is intermingled is separated out "by our taking it apart." Such διαιρεῖν is the basic function of λόγος; in discourse, λόγος takes things apart. The συγκεχυμένα, the inter-mingled, the inter-flowing, is characterized by Aristotle in the same first chapter of the *Physics* as ἀδιορίστως (184b2), "what is not yet delimited." The ἀρχαί are still hidden; only the whole is seen. Hence the συγκεχυμένα have to be taken apart in λόγος, and from being indistinct they thereby become delimited, such that the limit of the individual determinations is fixed and what is given first as συγκεχυμένως can be grasped in a ὁρισμός (b12). Hence upon closer inspection it is manifest that with the συγκεχυμένα the constitutive pieces of the being are meant from the outset, i.e., the ἀρχαί, and they will be made prominent by the appropriate consideration. When Aristotle claims that a being is given συγκεχυμένως, he means that it has already been interrogated in view of an ἀρχή. When we presentify a physical body in immediate perception, its ἀρχαί are not explicitly given; but they are indeed there, undisclosed, in αἴσθησις. This agrees with what we have seen in *Metaphysics* VII, 3:[3] beings, as far as they are given in αἴσθησις, i.e., as immediately known to us,

3. Cf. p. 58.

contain little or nothing of these beings. For the being is still not yet there, since the ἀρχαί, though in a certain sense present, are intermingled. Their presence is not uncovered and grasped as such. Accordingly, the ἀρχαί—or what is identical to them, the καθόλου—are themselves still hidden in their structure. The μέρη are not yet disclosed; they are not yet taken apart in διαίρεσις. Thus we can understand how Aristotle can write: τὸ γὰρ ὅλον κατὰ τὴν αἴσθησιν γνωριμώτερον (a24f.). "As regards perception, the whole is more familiar." I see at first the whole body; and this ὅλον contains in itself, as a possibility, the περιεχόμενα.

In the sense of the καθόλου, the ὅλον has, as is now evident, a double meaning; it means.

1.) the ὅλον λεγόμενον in the sense just made explicit: the ὅλον which shows itself only in λέγειν in such a way that in being addressed everything comprehended, every καθ' ἕκαστον, itself shows itself as the whole; ἄνθρωπος, ἵππος, and θεός are in each case ζῷα.

2.) The καθόλου means at the same time that every ζῷον as such possesses an inherent structure. The καθόλου includes in itself—apart from the individual cases which it comprehends—determinate structural moments, which in αἴσθησις are not expressly given at first. The καθόλου is initially present συγκεχυμένως.

Hence the assertion of *Physics* I, 1 (184a23f.) does not at all contradict what was said previously in the *Topics*. On the contrary, it makes the latter still more explicit: the way proceeds from the unarticulated καθόλου to the articulated καθ' ἕκαστον, such that every single μέρος becomes visible. And even the καθ' ἕκαστον now becomes visible for the first time in its functional significance; the καθ' ἕκαστον does not refer here to a determinate realm of beings but to the mode of Being: articulated versus not articulated. Thus the καθ' ἕκαστον means: 1.) that which first stands out in αἴσθησις, 2.) the moments which stand out purely and simply, ones which reside in the καθόλου itself.

This is all consonant with the tenor of the treatment carried out in Aristotle's *Physics*. The latter is from the very outset ἀρχή-research; at issue is a grasping of the ἀρχαί. For ἐπιστήμη is always ἐπιστήμη of the καθόλου; and ἐπιστήμη proceeds from the unarticulated καθόλου to the articulated in such a way that its μέρη are brought into the open in the ὁρισμός. The methodological principle Aristotle formulated in *Physics* I, 1 expresses this precisely: ἐκ τῶν καθόλου εἰς τὰ καθ' ἕκαστα δεῖ προιέναι. In this principle, which seems to be wholly formal, Aristotle grasps at the same time the meaning of the movement of the history of the question of the Being of φύσις, i.e., the history which preceded his own research and which he set forth in the first book of the *Physics*. When the philosophers raised questions about the givenness of the world, they saw immediately what was given immediately, and they saw it in such a way that it was unarticulated. This applies above all to the Eleatics, who saw immediately nothing but Being. Aristotle brings forward here a phrase of Parmenides: ἓν τὰ πάντα (*Phys.* I, 2, 185a22). Being is everywhere Being; everything that is is Being, is present, is there. In relation to the task Aristotle imposed on himself, namely to find a manifold of ἀρχαί, i.e., the structure of this ἕν, for him the Eleatic philosophers presented the ἕν in such a way that this basic structure was still συγκεχυμένως and not yet brought to the fore. Others who were not even that far advanced took a determinate being as the ἀρχή and applied it to the whole: e.g., Thales water and Anaximander air.[4] What immediately offered itself to them they saw as permeating beings, and they posited it as ἀρχή. Aristotle had this history of ἀρχή-research in mind when he formulated, at the beginning of the *Physics*, the proposition just mentioned: ἐκ τῶν καθόλου εἰς τὰ καθ' ἕκαστα.

In this way, what Aristotle says can even be understood positively: καὶ τοῦτο ἔργον ἐστίν, ὥσπερ ἐν ταῖς πράξεσι τὸ ποιῆσαι ἐκ τῶν ἑκάστῳ ἀγαθῶν τὰ ὅλως ἀγαθὰ ἑκάστῳ ἀγαθά, οὕτως ἐκ τῶν αὑτῷ γνωριμωτέρων τὰ τῇ φύσει γνώριμα αὑτῷ γνώριμα (*Met.* VII, 3, 1029b5ff.). This task is the same as in the case of action: "Just as in action it is important to proceed from what is in the individual case good for someone and pass through this good to the ὅλως ἀγαθόν, in such a way that in bringing about the ὅλως ἀγαθόν at the same time the ἕκαστον ἀγαθόν is carried out, likewise in the case of knowledge, one must proceed from what is immediately most familiar for a single individual and pass through this to the τῇ φύσει or ὅλως γνώριμον, in order to go back in turn from that to the αὑτῷ γνώριμον in such a way that the latter will become transparent from the former." Hence it is necessary to press on, from what is in a single case initially most familiar, to the ἀρχή and to appropriate the ἀρχή in such a way that from this appropriation there takes place a genuine appropriation of the καθ' ἕκαστον and so that the transparency of the procedure itself is gained and the καθ' ἕκαστον is understood on the basis of the ἀρχή.

From this we may finally understand what it means that the καθόλου is the proper theme of τέχνη and of ἐπιστήμη.

§13. Continuation: τέχνη *and* ἐπιστήμη *(*Met. *I, 1). The tendency residing in* τέχνη *toward an "autonomous"* ἐπιστήμη*. The further development of* ἐπιστήμη.

In contradistinction to the ἔμπειρος, the τεχνίτης is the one who ἄνευ τῆς ἐμπειρίας ἔχει τὸν λόγον (cf. *Met.* I, 1, 981a21), "who, without being used

4. Cf. *Phys.* I, 2, 184b17f.

to any particular procedure, knows the εἶδος." He is the one who καθόλου γνωρίζει (cf. a2f.) the being in question, "knows the being in its generality," but who thereby τὸ ἐν τούτῳ καθ' ἕκαστον ἀγνοεῖ (cf. a22), "is unfamiliar with what in each case the being is for itself," the being which in this ὅλον is a ἕν among others. For τέχνη, thus, what is decisive is paying heed, watching, i.e., disclosure. Therefore Aristotle can say: <ἀρχιτέκτονες> τὰς αἰτίας τῶν ποιουμένων ἴσασιν (981b1f.), "The architects know the causes of what is to be built." The following is thus manifest at the same time: the αἰτία, or the καθόλου, are initially not the theme of a mere onlooking. They indeed stand out as εἶδος, but not in such a way as to be the *theme* of a special investigation. The knowledge of the αἰτία is initially present only in connection with the fabricating itself; i.e., the αἰτία are present initially only as the because-therefore of such and such a procedure. The εἶδος is at first present only in τέχνη itself. But because in τέχνη the εἶδος is precisely already made prominent, therefore μᾶλλον εἰδέναι (a31f.), "to know more," is attributed to the τεχνῖται, and they are held to be σοφώτεροι than the mere ἔμπειροι. The μᾶλλον is hence attributed to them κατὰ τὸ λόγον ἔχειν (b6), with regard to the development of a discourse about just what is the object of the concernful dealing or the fabricating, i.e., with regard to disclosure. Within the fabricating, the λέγειν becomes more and more autonomous, and the naturally most immediate Dasein interprets it as σοφώτερον. Furthermore, one who λόγον ἔχων can make something understandable in the way it comes into its Being, how the whole fits together; he knows what it is composed of and what it contributes to, how thereby something becomes present as disposable just as it is. In this way, he can provide information about beings in regard to their origin, δύναται διδάσκειν (cf. b7f.). Therefore the naturally most immediate Dasein is of the opinion that τὴν τέχνην τῆς ἐμπειρίας μᾶλλον ἐπιστήμην εἶναι (cf. b8f.). Τέχνη, hence, because it possesses the λόγος and can provide information about beings in regard to their origin, is taken to be μᾶλλον ἐπιστήμην than ἐμπειρία. In this way, within the γένεσις of σοφία, τέχνη draws near to ἐπιστήμη; it is even designated as ἐπιστήμη.

Hence what is called ἐπιστήμη is: 1.) τέχνη; 2.) the highest science, σοφία, in its determination as νοῦς καὶ ἐπιστήμη (*Nic. Eth.* VI, 7, 1141a19f.).

Here the first sense, according to which ἐπιστήμη means the same as τέχνη, is the everyday one. In this everyday use, the concept of ἐπιστήμη occupies a peculiar mid-position. Specifically, τέχνη is designated as ἐπιστήμη insofar as, in distinction to ἐμπειρία, it already extracts the εἶδος. But this does not yet properly determine what constitutes the distinguishing character of ἐπιστήμη. Τέχνη is ἐπιστήμη, although it is properly a ἕξις ποιητική and therefore aims at ποίησις. At the same time, however, it is a ἕξις μετὰ λόγου ἀληθοῦς (*Nic. Eth.* VI, 4, 1140a10). In τέχνη, ἐπιστήμη is most properly harnessed to an intention to fabricate. But τέχνη also contains a tendency to liberate itself from handling things and to become an autonomous ἐπιστήμη. And insofar as this tendency resides in τέχνη, immediate natural Dasein credits it with being σοφώτερον.

On the other hand, τῶν αἰσθήσεων οὐδεμίαν ἡγούμεθα εἶναι σοφίαν (*Met.* I, 1, 981b10), immediate and natural Dasein does not at all attribute to αἴσθησις the character of σοφία, καίτοι κυριώταταί γ'εἰσὶν αὗται τῶν καθ' ἕκαστα γνώσεις (b11), although αἴσθησις is the mode of ἀληθεύειν in which the καθ' ἕκαστον, the particular case, is accessible as such. Therefore, precisely in the field of πρᾶξις, where the καθ' ἕκαστον is at issue, αἴσθησις is a κύριον over νοῦς and ὄρεξις. Indeed, Aristotle later (*Nic. Eth.* VI, 9, 1142a23ff.) even identifies αἴσθησις in a certain way with φρόνησις. Nevertheless, ἀλλ' οὐ λέγουσι τὸ διὰ τί περὶ οὐδενός (*Met.* I, 1, 981b11f.), the αἰσθήσεις do not provide the "why" of anything given and shown in them. Therefore natural Dasein does not attribute to the αἰσθήσεις the character of σοφία.

On the other hand, as has been said, there is in τέχνη itself a tendency to set itself free from handling things and to become an autonomous ἐπιστήμη. That this tendency resides in Dasein itself is evident for Aristotle in the fact that a τεχνίτης, he who, as we say, "dis-covers" something, is admired. τὸν ὁποιανοῦν εὑρόντα τέχνην παρὰ τὰς κοινὰς αἰσθήσεις θαυμάζεσθαι ὑπὸ τῶν ἀνθρώπων μὴ μόνον διὰ τὸ χρήσιμον εἶναί τι τῶν εὑρεθέντων ἀλλ' ὡς σοφὸν καὶ διαφέροντα τῶν ἄλλων (b13ff.). "The τεχνίτης, he who, beyond what everyone sees, 'dis-covers' something, is admired," i.e., he is respected as one who distinguishes himself, who makes something that other people would not be capable of, yet precisely "not because what he invents might be very useful" but because he advances the grasp of beings, no matter whether what he discovers is great or small: i.e., because he is σοφώτερος. His discovering goes beyond the immediate possibilities in the power of Dasein. In this way, the admiration dispensed by everyday Dasein demonstrates that in Dasein itself there lives a special appreciation of dis-covery. Dasein is itself directed toward discovering beings and toward that by itself, μὴ πρὸς χρῆσιν (b19f.), "apart from all usefulness," as Aristotle emphasizes. Thereby we can understand this, too, that the less τεχνάζειν and ἐπιστήμη are oriented πρὸς τἀναγκαῖα and πρὸς διαγωγήν (b18), toward the urgencies of life or toward amusements, the more Dasein addresses those who carry them out as σοφώτεροι.

The development of ἐπιστήμη now continues.[1] As soon as the τέχναι and ἐπιστῆμαι were found which are required πρὸς τὰ ἀναγκαῖα, for the necessities of life, and πρὸς τὴν ἡδονήν, for recreation and pleasure, Dasein

1. Cf. *Met.* I, 1, 981b20ff.

could, unburdened by these necessities, dedicate itself wholly to contemplation. Therefore the first sciences, e.g., mathematics, originated in Egypt, because the priests had the time to do nothing but observe. If thus there is indeed in Dasein a tendency to disclosure, yet an autonomous disclosure for its own sake is genuinely possible only where Dasein is free from concern over the ἀναγκαῖα. In such σχολάζειν there occurs a leap from the tendency to fabricate; σχολάζειν is a matter of abstaining from all concern over the ἀναγκαῖα in order to linger in mere onlooking and disclosure. The more mere onlooking and disclosure come into their own, the more visible becomes the why—the διὰ τί or the αἰτία—and ultimately more and more clear becomes the "from out of which," τὸ διὰ τί πρῶτον (*Met.* I, 3, 983a29) or τὰ ἐξ ἀρχῆς αἴτια (cf. a24)—the ἀρχή.

We now have in αἴσθησις and ἐπιστήμη two end-stations, without our having genuinely understood σοφία. That possibility which first goes beyond the merely momentary disclosedness of αἴσθησις, making beings more explicitly accessible, is retention: μνήμη. Retaining present, as a mode of access to beings, maintains itself up to σοφία, in which the presentifying relates explicitly to the ἀρχαί.

§14. Σοφία *(*Met. *I, 2). The four essential moments of* σοφία *(*πάντα, χαλεπώτατα, ἀκριβέστατα, αὑτῆς ἕνεκεν*). Clarifying reduction of the first three essential moments to the* μάλιστα καθόλου.

We must now ask what is σοφία; i.e., who is the σοφός himself? Aristotle confronts this question in *Metaphysics* I, 2. The determination is not made dogmatically; instead, Aristotle returns again to natural and most immediate Dasein. εἰ δὴ λάβοι τις τὰς ὑπολήψεις ἃς ἔχομεν περὶ τοῦ σοφοῦ, τάχ'ἂν ἐκ τούτου φανερὸν γένοιτο μᾶλλον (982a6ff.). The task is to take up and select the opinions *we*—κοινωνία—already possess, i.e., the interpretations of the σοφός in natural everyday Dasein, and to make this preliminary conception of σοφία more explicit and so make the interpretation found in natural Dasein more transparent. Aristotle enumerates four moments in which this interpretation characterizes Dasein's first understanding of the σοφός.

1.) πρῶτον μὲν ἐπίστασθαι πάντα τὸν σοφὸν ὡς ἐνδέχεται, μὴ καθ' ἕκαστον ἔχοντα ἐπιστήμην αὐτῶν (982a8ff.). The wise one is conspicuous in the first place as the one "who knows πάντα, everything altogether," who in a peculiar sense understands everything, "without, however, having a knowledge which looks upon the καθ' ἕκαστον, every single thing separately," i.e., without having special knowledge of every possible subject matter. Nevertheless, when one speaks with him on any subject, he understands everything, and his understanding is genuine. It is noteworthy that πάντα in natural speech means the whole in the sense of the totality, the sum. The σοφός understands τὰ πάντα, the totality, the sum, without, however, having acquired knowledge καθ' ἕκαστον, from the particulars. He understands the sum without having run through every single unit. In this way, knowledge of the πάντα, accompanied by an obvious lack of knowledge of the particulars, is enigmatic.

2.) τὸν τὰ χαλεπὰ γνῶναι δυνάμενον καὶ μὴ ῥᾴδια ἀνθρώπῳ γιγνώσκειν, τοῦτον σοφόν (a10ff.). The σοφός is the one who is able to disclose that which is difficult to disclose, i.e., that which is not easily disclosed by man in his immediate existence, by the πολλοί. What the σοφός can disclose is hence not only concealed but difficult to unconceal, and that because it does not readily reveal itself to the most immediate everyday Dasein, i.e., it does not reveal itself in the common easy way.

3.) τὸν ἀκριβέστερον καὶ τὸν διδασκαλικώτερον τῶν αἰτιῶν σοφώτερον εἶναι περὶ πᾶσαν ἐπιστήμην (a12ff.). In every "science" and τέχνη, the σοφός is "more profound"; he goes more to the foundations of things. That is why he is better able to teach, to instruct; he can make things clear and can more genuinely explain how things are. The reason is that he does not see things in their immediate aspect but in their genuine whence and why.

4.) τῶν ἐπιστημῶν δὲ τὴν αὑτῆς ἕνεκεν καὶ τοῦ εἰδέναι χάριν αἱρετὴν οὖσαν μᾶλλον εἶναι σοφίαν ἢ τὴν τῶν ἀποβαινόντων ἕνεκεν (a14ff.). Σοφία is a kind of ἐπιστήμη accomplished simply for its own sake. That is, in σοφία the disclosure of what is disclosed is accomplished merely for its own sake and not with a view to what could possibly result from it, i.e., its practical applicability. Σοφία is the ἐπιστήμη that is determined solely by the pure tendency toward seeing, and it is carried out simply τοῦ εἰδέναι χάριν, in order to see and, in seeing, to know. As such, σοφία guides, leads, and predelineates.

Aristotle discusses in detail these four moments in which everyday Dasein expresses its opinions about the σοφός and σοφία. We may say in anticipation that all four moments have in view a disclosure that concerns the first origins of beings purely as such. This means, conversely, that the idea of σοφία as concerned with the αἰτία as such and specifically with τὰ ἐξ ἀρχῆς, i.e., the ἀρχαί, makes explicit what Dasein strives for implicitly and without clarity.

1.) To what extent does the σοφός understand "everything"? τὸ μὲν πάντα ἐπίστασθαι τῷ μάλιστα ἔχοντι τὴν καθόλου ἐπιστήμην ἀναγκαῖον ὑπάρχειν (a21f.). The σοφός knows "everything" because he, more than any other, has at his disposal the disclosure of the "general." Because σοφία is an εἰδέναι καθόλου, the σοφός necessarily understands πάντα. We need to note that immediate understanding conceives the whole as a sum total, and for it therefore this understanding of "everything" is very enigmatic, since a knowledge of the particulars is lacking in this "whole." Aristotle clarifies this πάντα as a ὅλον in the sense of the καθόλου; for πάντα he substitutes ὅλον. So he does not mean that the σοφός sees the whole as the sum of all the particulars; instead, the σοφός understands what every particular, along with the others, is *ultimately*. So it is clear that the πάντα, which the σοφός has at his disposal, is grounded in the ὅλον as the καθόλου. That is the genuine πᾶν, the whole, which the σοφός aims at. In such an understanding of "everything," what matters is the καθόλου, which is a ὅλον λεγόμενον; i.e., what matters is a preeminent λεγόμενον: λόγον ἔχειν. That is why Aristotle says: ἀνάγεται γὰρ τὸ διὰ τί εἰς τὸν λόγον ἔσχατον (*Met.* I, 3, 983a28). In σοφία what matters is that the why, the αἴτιον, be reduced to the most ultimate λόγος, to the most ultimate expression of beings in their Being. The disclosure of the καθόλου does not require one to run through each and every particular as such in explicit knowledge, and the καθόλου is not simply the sum of the particulars. Its peculiar feature is that it is a whole without a registration of each case as such. And nevertheless, or precisely for that reason, each case is understood in its genuine presence. The ground for this is the fact that at the very outset the σοφός leaps ahead to the genuine whole, whence he takes his orientation for the discussion of every concrete singular. Therefore he can genuinely partake in these discussions, despite having no specialized knowledge. In this way Aristotle reduces the common talk about the πάντα ἐπίστασθαι to the ὅλον as καθόλου.

2.) The reduction of the πάντα to the καθόλου immediately clarifies why the everyday interpretation claims that the σοφός aims at what is χαλεπόν, difficult, to know. χαλεπώτατα ταῦτα γνωρίζειν τοῖς ἀνθρώποις, τὰ μάλιστα καθόλου· πορρωτάτω γὰρ τῶν αἰσθήσεών ἐστιν (*Met.* I, 2, 982a24f.). What the σοφός knows is difficult, "because it is the most general of all." And "that is the farthest removed from what shows itself to immediate vision," where everyday considerations dwell. Αἴσθησις is, for the πολλοί, the most immediate dwelling place and mode of disclosure; αἴσθησις presents no difficulties, everyone moves in it, and one person can procure for another this everyday orientation or can assist him with it. The φύσις of man comprises a certain predilection for what is immediately given in αἴσθησις; this is the ἀγάπησις τῶν αἰσθήσεων (cf. *Met.* I, 1, 980a21). And especially if the orientation toward the necessity of making things falls away, if everyday Dasein is exempted from this orientation, if the onlooking becomes free, precisely then does Dasein lose itself all the more in the outward appearance of the world, but in such a way that Dasein remains always in αἴσθησις. Over and against this easy and obvious movement in immediate vision, an advancement beyond it to what genuinely is becomes difficult. This difficulty does not reside in the matters at issue but in Dasein itself, in a peculiar mode of Being of Dasein, that of the immediate. Dasein, as it immediately is, has its present in the now, in the world; it has a tendency to adhere to the immediate. Σοφία, however, is concerned with advancing into what remains covered in immediate Dasein, into the μάλιστα καθόλου, and this advancement occurs *in opposition to* immediate vision. Σοφία hence is concerned with a disclosure which proceeds as a counter-movement in relation to immediate Dasein. Σοφία is a counter-tendency against immediate Dasein and its tendency to remain caught up in immediate appearances. As such, σοφία is difficult for Dasein. And that is the only reason the matters with which σοφία is concerned are "difficult" with respect to their ἀληθεύειν. For now, the following must be noted: in relation to αἴσθησις, to be σοφώτερον, i.e., σοφία, is a μᾶλλον εἰδέναι, a μᾶλλον ἐπαίειν (cf. 981a24f.). Σοφία arises in a counter-movement against αἴσθησις. Nevertheless, σοφία does not thereby exclude αἴσθησις but merely takes it as a point of departure; αἴσθησις provides the ground, in such a way that the consideration no longer remains in its field.[1] Αἴσθησις is a κύριον (cf. *Met.* I, 1, 981b11; *Nic. Eth.* VI, 2, 1139a18),[2] something which belongs to Dasein in general, but not something by which beings themselves can be seen as beings.

3.) ἀκριβέσταται δὲ τῶν ἐπιστημῶν αἳ μάλιστα τῶν πρώτων εἰσιν (*Met.* I, 2, 982a25f.). It is distinctive of σοφία to be ἀκριβεστάτη, not because the σοφοί display special acumen but because the theme of σοφία is what most of all touches the foundations of beings in their Being. The ἀκριβέστατον is, most basically, the μάλιστα τῶν πρώτων, "what most presses on to the first 'out of which.'" These "first things," the first determinations of beings, are, as the most original, not only simple in themselves but require the greatest acuity to be grasped in their multiplicity, because they are the fewest. A peculiar character of the ἀρχαί consists in this, that they are limited in number. And in their limited number they are transparent in their relations among themselves. In the first Book of the *Physics*, chapter 2ff., Aristotle shows that there must be more than one ἀρχή but that the number of the ἀρχαί is determined by a limit, πέρας. Therefore a ὁρίζεσθαι must delimit how many there are, whether two, or three, etc. Aristotle shows why there can be no more than three or four. And only because the ἀρχαί are limited is a determination of beings in their Being possible and guaranteed, and the same applies to an addressing of beings as a ὁρίζεσθαι and a ὁρισμός, and, consequently, to science as ultimately valid knowledge.

Aristotle illustrates the rigor of science with the examples of μαθηματική,

1. Cf. p. 58.
2. Cf. p. 27.

ἀριθμητική and γεωμετρία (982a28). Those disciplines are more rigorous and more fundamental which proceed from fewer ἀρχαί, which hence posit fewer original determinations in the beings which are their theme. αἱ γὰρ ἐξ ἐλαττόνων ἀκριβέστεραι τῶν ἐκ προσθέσεως λεγομένων, οἷον ἀριθμητικὴ γεωμετρίας (982a26f.). Arithmetic is in this way distinguished from geometry. Arithmetic has fewer ἀρχαί than geometry. In the case of geometry, a πρόσθεσις, something additional, takes place as regards the ἀρχαί. In order to understand this we need a brief general orientation regarding Aristotle's conception of mathematics. We will provide that in an excursus, which will serve at the same time as a preparation for our interpretation of Plato.

§15. Excursus: General orientation regarding the essence of mathematics according to Aristotle.

We want to proceed so as to present the basic issues: a) in μαθηματική in general and, b) in ἀριθμητική and γεωμετρία.

a) Fundamental issues in mathematics in general (*Phys.* II, 2). Χωρίζειν as the basic act of mathematics. Critique of the χωρισμός in Plato's theory of Ideas.

The μαθηματικαὶ ἐπιστῆμαι have as their theme τὰ ἐξ ἀφαιρέσεως, that which shows itself by being withdrawn from something and specifically from what is immediately given. The μαθηματικά are extracted from the φυσικὰ ὄντα, from what immediately shows itself.[1] Hence Aristotle says: ὁ μαθηματικὸς χωρίζει (cf. *Phys.* II, 2, 193b31ff.). Χωρίζειν, separating, is connected with χώρα, place; place belongs to beings themselves. The μαθηματικός takes something away from its own place. ἄτοπον δὲ καὶ τὸ τόπον ἅμα τοῖς στερεοῖς καὶ τοῖς μαθηματικοῖς ποιῆσαι (ὁ μὲν γὰρ τόπος τῶν καθ' ἕκαστον ἴδιος, διὸ χωριστὰ τόπῳ, τὰ δὲ μαθηματικὰ οὐ ποῦ), καὶ τὸ εἰπεῖν μὲν ὅτι ποῦ ἔσται, τί δέ ἐστιν ὁ τόπος, μή (*Met.* XIV, 5, 1092a17ff.). What is peculiar is that the mathematical is not in a place: οὐκ ἐν τόπῳ. Taken in terms of modern concepts, this has the ring of a paradox, especially since τόπος is still translated as "space." But only a σῶμα φυσικόν has a τόπος, a location, a place. This χωρίζειν, which we will encounter in Plato's theory of the χωρισμός of the Ideas, where Plato indeed explicitly assigns to the Ideas a τόπος, namely the οὐρανός, this χωρίζειν is for Aristotle the way in which the mathematical itself becomes objective.

1. Cf. *Met.* XI, 3, 1061a28f; *De Caelo* III, 1, 299a15ff; *Met.* XIII, 3; *Met.* XII, 8, 1073b6ff.

Aristotle analyzes these things in *Physics* II, 2. The mathematical objects, e.g., στερεόν and γραμμή, can to be sure also be considered as φυσικά; the natural man sees a surface as πέρας, as the limit of a body. Versus this, the mathematician considers the mathematical objects purely in themselves, ἀλλ' οὐχ ᾗ φυσικοῦ σώματος πέρας ἕκαστον (193b32), i.e., "not insofar as these (e.g., a line or a surface) are the πέρας, limit (termination), of a natural body." Aristotle's negative delineation of the mathematical here—namely, that it is *not* the πέρας of a φυσικὸν σῶμα—means nothing other than that the mathematical is not being considered as a "location." Insofar as the φυσικὰ ὄντα are κινούμενα, i.e., insofar as motility is a basic determination of their Being, the mathematical can be considered initially as appertaining to beings that move. The mathematical as such is removed from things characterized by motion. χωριστὰ γὰρ τῇ νοήσει κινήσεώς ἐστι (b34), the mathematical, e.g., a point, is "extracted from beings insofar as they move," i.e., insofar as they change, turn around, increase and decrease. And specifically the mathematical is χωριστὰ τῇ νοήσει, "discerned," extracted simply in a particular mode of consideration. Κίνησις itself, however, is initially and for the most part κίνησις κατὰ τόπον, change of location. τῆς κινήσεως ἡ κοινὴ μάλιστα καὶ κυριωτάτη κατὰ τόπον ἐστίν, ἣν καλοῦμεν φοράν (*Phys.* IV, 1, 208a31f.). The most general motion is local motion, which presents itself in the revolution of the heavens. The mathematician extracts something from the φυσικὸν σῶμα, but οὐδὲν διαφέρει (*Phys.* II, 3, 193b34f.), "this makes no difference"; this extracting changes nothing of the objective content of that which remains as the theme of the mathematician. It does not turn into something else; the "what" of the πέρας is simply taken for itself, as it appears. It is simply taken as it presents itself in its content as limit. οὐδὲ γίνεται ψεῦδος χωριζόντων (b35). "In extracting, the mathematician cannot be subject to any mistake," i.e., he does not take something which is actually not given to be what is showing itself. If the mathematician simply adheres to his special theme, he is never in danger that that will present itself to him as something other than it is. It is indeed here nothing other than what has been extracted. Beings are not distorted for the mathematician through χωρίζειν; on the contrary, he moves in a field in which something determinate may be disclosed. Thus with this χωρισμός everything is in order.

λανθάνουσι δὲ τοῦτο ποιοῦντες καὶ οἱ τὰς ἰδέας λέγοντες (b35ff.). Those who discuss the Ideas, and disclose them in λόγος, proceed this way as well: χωρίζοντες, "they extract." It is just that they themselves λανθάνουσι, "are covered over," as regards what they are doing and how they are doing it; they are not transparent to themselves in their procedure, neither as to its limits nor its distinctions. Λανθάνουσι, "they remain concealed while they do this," concealed precisely to themselves. (This is a characteristic usage of the term λανθάνειν. Conversely, there is then also an ἀλήθεια pertaining to Dasein itself.) Those who speak of the Ideas are not themselves clear about which possibilities χωρισμός harbors. Χωρισμός has a justifiable sense in mathematics, but not where it is a matter of determining the ἀρχαί of *beings*. τὰ γὰρ φυσικὰ χωρίζουσιν ἧττον ὄντα χωριστὰ τῶν μαθηματικῶν (193b36f.). Such a one "posits the φύσει ὄντα (i.e., the ἀρχαί pertaining to these as such) for themselves, in a separate place, but they are even less to be removed from their place." For the φύσει ὄντα are κινούμενα; in every category of physical beings there resides a determinate relation to motion. In his Ideas, as ἀρχαί, however, the man in question leaves out precisely the κίνησις which is the basic character of the φύσει ὄντα, with the result that he makes of these ἀρχαί genuine beings, among which finally even κίνησις itself becomes one. Yet it is possible to determine the ἀρχαί of the moving φύσει ὄντα in such a way that the ἀρχαί are not taken as divorced from motion and, furthermore, such that κίνησις itself is not taken as an Idea and hence as χωριστόν. In the ἀρχαί the κινούμενον ᾗ κινούμενον must be co-perceived and hence must basically be something else as well, namely the τόπος itself whereby Being and presence are determined.

Let this suffice as an initial orientation concerning the mathematician in opposition to the physicist and at the same time as an indication of the connection of the mathematical χωρίζειν with the one Plato himself promulgates as the determination of the method of grasping the Ideas. We will see later why the Ideas were brought into connection with mathematics. Let us now ask how, within mathematics, geometry differs from arithmetic.

b) The distinction between geometry and arithmetic. The increasing "abstraction" from the φύσει ὄν: στιγμή = οὐσία θετός; μονάς = οὐσία ἄθετος.

Geometry has more ἀρχαί than does arithmetic. The objects of geometry are λαμβανόμενα ἐκ προσθέσεως (cf. *Post. An.* I, 27, 87a35f.), "they are gained from what is determined additionally, through θέσις." Πρόσθεσις does not simply mean "supplement." What is the character of this πρόσθεσις in geometry? λέγω δ' ἐκ προσθέσεως, οἷον μονὰς οὐσία ἄθετος, στιγμὴ δὲ οὐσία θετός· ταύτην ἐκ προσθέσεως (87a35ff.). Aristotle distinguishes the basic elements of geometry from those of arithmetic. The basic element of arithmetic is μονάς, the unit; the basic element of geometry is στιγμή, the point. Μονάς, the unit—related to μόνον, "unique," "alone"—is what simply remains, μένειν, what is "alone," "for itself." In the case of the point, a θέσις is added. τὸ δὲ μηδαμῇ διαιρετὸν κατὰ τὸ ποσὸν στιγμὴ καὶ μονάς, ἡ μὲν ἄθετος μονὰς ἡ δὲ θετὸς στιγμή (*Met.* V, 6, 1016b29f.). "What is in no way divisible according to quantity are the point and the μονάς; the latter, however, is without θέσις, the point with θέσις."[2] Then how are the two basic objects of mathematics to be distinguished? μονὰς οὐσία ἄθετος, στιγμὴ δὲ οὐσία θετός· ταύτην ἐκ προσθέσεως (*Post. An.* I, 27, 87a36).

Both are οὐσία, something that is for itself. The στιγμή, however, over and against the μονάς, is marked by a πρόσθεσις; in the στιγμή there resides a θέσις in a preeminent sense. What is the meaning of this θέσις which characterizes the point in opposition to the μονάς? A thorough elucidation of this nexus would have to take up the question of place and space. Here I can only indicate what is necessary to make understandable the distinction of the ἀκριβές within the disciplines of mathematics.

Θέσις has the same character as ἕξις, διάθεσις. Ἕξις = to find oneself in a definite situation, to have something in oneself, to retain, and in retaining to be directed toward something. Θέσις = orientation, situation; it has the character of being oriented toward something. ἔστι δὲ καὶ τὰ τοιαῦτα τῶν πρός τι οἷον ἕξις, διάθεσις, . . . θέσις (*Cat.* 7, 6b2f.). According to its categorial determination, θέσις is τῶν πρός τι, "it belongs to what is πρός τι." Every θέσις is a θέσις τινός (cf. b6).

α) Τόπος and θέσις (according to *Phys.* V, 1–5). The absolute determinateness (φύσει) of τόπος, the relative determinateness (πρὸς ἡμᾶς) of θέσις. The essence of τόπος: limit (πέρας) and possibility (δύναμις) of the proper Being of a being.

We need to clarify briefly the distinction between θέσις and τόπος. Aristotle emphasizes that the mathematical objects are οὐκ ἐν τόπῳ (cf. *Met.* XIV, 5, 1092a19f.), "not anyplace."[3] The modern concept of space must not at all be allowed to intrude here. Aristotle determines τόπος at first in an apparently quite naive way. ὅτι μὲν οὖν ἔστι τι ὁ τόπος, δοκεῖ δῆλον εἶναι ἐκ τῆς ἀντιμεταστάσεως· ὅπου γάρ ἐστι νῦν ὕδωρ, ἐνταῦθα ἐξελθόντος ὥσπερ ἐξ ἀγγείου πάλιν ἀὴρ ἐκεῖ ἔνεστιν· ὅτε δὲ τὸν αὐτὸν τόπον τοῦτον ἄλλο τι τῶν σωμάτων κατέχει, τοῦτο δὴ τῶν ἐγγινομένων καὶ μεταβαλλόντων ἕτερον πάντων εἶναι δοκεῖ· ἐν ᾧ γὰρ ἀήρ ἐστι νῦν, ὕδωρ ἐν τούτῳ πρότερον ἦν, ὥστε δῆλον ὡς ἦν ὁ τόπος τι καὶ ἡ χώρα ἕτερον ἀμφοῖν, εἰς ἣν καὶ ἐξ ἧς μετέβαλον (*Phys.* IV, 1, 208b1ff.). Τόπος must itself be something. If there formerly was water in a container and if now there is air in it, then the τόπος is something other than that which fills it. The place *was* already, ἦν, i.e., before specifically water or air was in it. The ἦν does not mean that the τόπος would be something separated, separated from what is in it; the place is simply something other than the two things which have been exchanged

2. Cf. *De An.* I, 4, 409a6ff.
3. Cf. p. 69.

in it. Aristotle proceeds at once to the characteristic determination of place: ἔχει τινὰ δύναμιν (b10f.), "place has a certain power" (translating in the usual way). Δύναμις is here understood in a quite strictly ontological sense; δύναμις implies that the place pertains to the being itself, the place constitutes precisely the possibility of the proper presence of the being in question. This possibility, like every possibility, is prescribed in a determinate direction: every being has *its* place. The δύναμις of the τόπος pertains to beings themselves as such. φέρεται γὰρ ἕκαστον εἰς αὐτοῦ τόπον μὴ κωλυόμενον, τὸ μὲν ἄνω τὸ δὲ κάτω (b11f.). Fire, πῦρ, as such, has its place ἄνω; earth, γῆ, as such has its place κάτω (cf. b19f.). The light possesses in its Being a prescription to its place, above; the heavy to its place, below. And that is not arbitrary but φύσει (b18). These assertions of Aristotle's are self-evident, and we may not permit mathematical-physical determinations to intrude. The heavy goes below, the light above. Fire has its determined location; i.e., the τόπος of fire pertains to its very Being. In the same way, what is light belongs above; if it is not above, then, as long as it is not impeded, it will go up. Each being possesses in its Being a prescription toward a determinate location or place. *The place is constitutive of the presence of the being.* Every being is carried, φέρεται, to its place, εἰς τὸν αὐτοῦ τόπον, τὸ μὲν ἄνω, τὸ δὲ κάτω, "the one above, the other below." This consideration of τόπος is carried out in *Physics* IV, chapters 1–5.

Aristotle designates ἄνω and κάτω as μέρη or εἴδη of place. Μέρος has here a quite broad meaning: character, moment, determination. ταῦτα δ' ἐστὶ τόπου μέρη καὶ εἴδη, τὸ ἄνω καὶ κάτω καὶ αἱ λοιπαὶ τῶν ἕξ διαστάσεων (*Phys.* IV, 1, 208b12ff.). The outward look of a place is determined according to these possibilities: above-below, front-back, right-left. These are the six διαστάσεις into which beings can be dissected. Aristotle emphasizes expressly: ἔστι δὲ τὰ τοιαῦτα οὐ μόνον πρὸς ἡμᾶς, τὸ ἄνω καὶ κάτω καὶ δεξιὸν καὶ ἀριστερόν (b14f.), "these things, above and below, right and left, are not just in relation to us," relative to the particular orientation we happen to take up. ἡμῖν μὲν γὰρ οὐκ ἀεὶ τὸ αὐτό, "admittedly, for us the above and the below are not always the same," they do not properly exist, ἀλλὰ κατὰ τὴν θέσιν, ὅπως ἂν στραφῶμεν, γίνεται (b15f.), "but instead they correspond to a θέσις, to the way we happen to stand and turn at any time." Here θέσις is introduced in opposition to τόπος as such. Hence there are determinations of τόπος which in a certain sense are *absolute* within the world; along with these, however, there is also the possibility that much changes: what is above for one person may be below for another. This change is one of θέσις, is dependent on how we place ourselves, on our particular stance. Therefore one and the same thing is often to the right and to the left at the same time. ἐν δὲ τῇ φύσει διώρισται χωρὶς ἕκαστον (b18f.). "On the other hand, in nature itself (i.e., considering things simply in their

Being) everything is for itself positioned in its own place." οὐ γὰρ ὅ τι ἔτυχέν ἐστι τὸ ἄνω, ἀλλ' ὅπου φέρεται τὸ πῦρ καὶ τὸ κοῦφον ὁμοίως δὲ καὶ τὸ κάτω οὐχ ὅ τι ἔτυχεν, ἀλλ' ὅπου τὰ ἔχοντα βάρος καὶ τὰ γεηρά (b19ff.). "For 'above' is not something arbitrary, but is that toward which fire and what is light are carried; likewise 'below' is nothing arbitrary but that toward which the heavy and earthy are carried." That is the way it is—and here is the comprehensive characterization—ὡς οὐ τῇ θέσει διαφέροντα μόνον ἀλλὰ καὶ τῇ δυνάμει (208b21f.), "because these places are not differentiated merely through a θέσις—πρὸς ἡμᾶς (b24)—but on the contrary τῇ δυνάμει." This δυνάμει means that the place is the possibility of the proper presence of the being which belongs to it and in fact so much so that the direction to its own place, to the place were it belongs, appertains to the very Being of the being, which being is indeed always itself δυνάμει.

We now want to bring more clarity to our discussion of τόπος. πρῶτον μὲν οὖν δεῖ κατανοῆσαι ὅτι οὐκ ἂν ἐζητεῖτο ὁ τόπος, εἰ μὴ κίνησίς τις ἦν ἡ κατὰ τόπον (*Phys.* IV, 4, 211a12ff.). It can occur to us that there is such a thing as place only because we encounter the αἰσθητά as moved, only because there is in general such a thing as motion. In a change of location, place as such gets set in relief; it can be occupied by something else. οὐ γὰρ πᾶν ἐν τόπῳ, ἀλλὰ τὸ κινητὸν σῶμα (*Phys.* IV, 5, 212b28f.), only what is κινητόν, moveable, is in a place. διὰ γὰρ τοῦτο καὶ τὸν οὐρανὸν μάλιστ' οἰόμεθα ἐν τόπῳ, ὅτι ἀεὶ ἐν κινήσει (*Phys.* IV, 4, 211a13f.). "Therefore we believe that the heavens are most in a place, because they are constantly in motion." Nevertheless, further consideration will show that the heavens are not in a place. ὁ δ' οὐρανός οὔ που ὅλος οὐδ' ἔν τινι τόπῳ ἐστίν, εἴ γε μηδὲν αὐτὸν περιέχει σῶμα (cf. *Phys.* IV, 5, 212b8ff.). Instead, the heavens are themselves the place for all beings which stand below them.

Place is then designated more precisely: ἀξιοῦμεν δὴ τὸν τόπον εἶναι πρῶτον μὲν περιέχον ἐκεῖνο οὗ τόπος ἐστί, καὶ μηδὲν τοῦ πράγματος (*Phys.* IV, 4, 210b34f.). εἰ τοίνυν μηδὲν τῶν τριῶν ὁ τόπος ἐστί, μήτε τὸ εἶδος μήτε ἡ ὕλη μήτε διάστημά τι . . . , ἀνάγκη τὸν τόπον εἶναι . . . τὸ πέρας τοῦ περιέχοντος σώματος (212a2ff.). Place is the limit of the περιέχον, that which encloses a body, not the limit of the body itself, but that which the limit of the body comes up against, in such a way, specifically, that there is between these two limits no interspace, no διάστημα. This peculiar determination of place, as the limit of what encircles the body, is understandable only if one maintains that the world is oriented absolutely, that there are preeminent places as such: the absolute above, the heavens, and then the μέσον, the middle of the heavens, and an absolute below, the earth, which is immersed in water. Aristotle himself concedes: δοκεῖ δὲ μέγα τι εἶναι καὶ χαλεπὸν ληφθῆναι ὁ τόπος διά τε τὸ παρεμφαίνεσθαι τὴν ὕλην καὶ τὴν μορφήν, καὶ διὰ τὸ ἐν ἠρεμοῦντι τῷ περιέχοντι γίνεσθαι τὴν μετάστασιν τοῦ φερομένου (212a7ff.). "It seems that it is something great and very difficult to grasp place for what it is, because along with it there always is given the body, in what it is made of and in its outward look, its form," so that one is tempted to take the extension of the material or the limit of the form as the place. And, further, it is difficult to see place as such, because the μετάστασις of what is in motion comes to pass in each case in such a way that the place itself does not thereby move. And what is in motion has a privilege with regard to perceptibility.

In summary, a first understanding of the concept of place can be acquired if we keep in mind that place has a δύναμις: ἔχει τινὰ δύναμιν.[4] Place is the possibility of the correct appurtenance of a being. The correct appurtenance refers to that presence which belongs to beings as such according to their objective constitution. It belongs to fire to be above, to the earth to be below. The beings of the world, as "nature" in the largest sense, have their place. Place belongs in each case to the being itself and constitutes the possibility of the proper presence of the being there where it appertains. This possibility is not intended as empty conceptual (logical) possibility, as arbitrariness, such that it would be left freely to the body to be here or there, but instead the δύναμις is a possibility which is determinately prescribed and which always harbors in itself a direction. This determinateness of δύναμις belongs to the τόπος itself. Δύναμις is understood as an ontological basic category. The possibility is itself a being. Place is something belonging to beings as such, their capacity to be present, a possibility which is constitutive of their Being. The place is the ability a being has to be there, in such a way that, in being there, it is properly present.

β) The genesis of geometry and arithmetic from τόπος. The acquisition of geometrical objects by extraction of the πέρατα (τόπος) of the φύσει ὄντα. The determination of their site (θέσις). *Analysis situs*. Μονάς: οὐσία ἄθετος.

Geometrical objects can serve to clarify the distinction between τόπος and θέσις. If we abstract from the peculiar mode of being of τόπος, a mode which is determined φύσει, and retain simply the multiplicity of possible sites, the moments of orientation, we are then in a position to understand how the specifically geometrical objects are constituted. What is extracted from the αἰσθητά and becomes then the θετόν, the posited, is the moment of place, such that the extracted geometrical element is no longer in its place. Indeed the moments of place, which ἀφαίρεσις withdraws from the σῶμα, extracts from it, are the πέρατα of a physical body; but insofar as

4. Cf. p. 73.

they are extracted from it they are understood mathematically and no longer as limits of the physical body. Instead, through the θέσις, they acquire an autonomy over and against the physical body. The geometrical objects are indeed not in a place; nevertheless, I can determine in them an above and a below, a right and a left. In a square, e.g., I can determine the sides: above, below, right, left. I still have here the possibility of a determination of the θέσις, the possibility of an *analysis situs,* i.e., of drawing out differentiations in the sites as such, although the geometrical objects themselves, in what they are, do not possess these determinations. Geometrical objects can always be oriented in accord with a θέσις. Every geometrical point, every element, line, and surface is fixed through a θέσις. Every geometrical object is an οὐσία θετός.[5] This θέσις does not have to be a determination, but it pertains to one. On the other hand, the unit, the μονάς, does not bear in itself this orientation; it is οὐσία ἄθετος. In mathematics, the θέσις survives only in geometry, because geometry has a greater proximity to the αἰσθητόν than does arithmetic.

The geometrical consists of a manifold of basic elements—point, line, etc.—which are the πέρατα for the higher geometrical figures. But it is not the case that the higher figures are *put together* out of such limits. Aristotle emphasizes that a line will never arise out of points (*Phys.* VI, 1, 231a24ff.), a surface will never arise out of a line, nor a body out of a surface. For between any two points there is again and again a γραμμή, etc. This sets Aristotle in the sharpest opposition to Plato. Indeed, the points are the ἀρχαί of the geometrical, yet not in such a way that the higher geometrical figures would be constructed out of their summation. One cannot proceed from the στιγμή to the σῶμα. One cannot put a line together out of points. For in each case there is something lying in between, something that cannot itself be constituted out of the preceding elements. This betrays the fact that in the οὐσία θετός there is certainly posited a manifold of elements, but, beyond that, a determinate kind of connection is required, a determinate kind of unity of the manifold. In the realm of arithmetic the same holds. For Aristotle, the μονάς, the unit, is itself not yet number; instead, the first number is the number two.[6] Since the μονάς, in distinction to the elements of geometry, does not bear a θέσις, the mode of connection in each realm of objectivities is very different. The mode of connection of an arithmetical whole, of a number, is different than that of a geometrical whole, than a connection of points. Number and geometrical figures are in themselves in each case a manifold. The "fold" is the mode of connection of the manifold. We will understand the distinction between στιγμή and μονάς only if we

5. Cf. p. 71f.
6. Cf. *Met.* V, 6, 1016b18, 1016b15, and 1021a13; *Phys.* IV, 12, 220a17ff.

grasp in each of these the respective essence of the structure of that mode of manifoldness. What is the essence of the mode of manifoldness of points, lines, etc.? What is the essence of the mode of manifoldness of number?

γ) The structure of the connection of the manifold in geometry and arithmetic; συνεχές and ἐφεξῆς.

Our consideration will set forth from the point. We have indicated that geometrical objects still have a certain kinship with what is in αἰσθάνεσθαι. Everything in αἰσθάνεσθαι possesses μέγεθος; everything perceivable has extension. Extension, as understood here, will come to be known as continuousness. Since everything perceivable has extension, μέγεθος, it is an οὐκ ἀδιαίρετον. τὸ αἰσθητὸν πᾶν ἐστι μέγεθος καὶ οὐκ ἔστιν ἀδιαίρετον αἰσθητόν (*De Sensu* VII, 449a20). This peculiar structure of the αἰσθητόν is preserved in the geometrical, insofar as the geometrical, too, is continuous, συνεχές. The point presents only the ultimate and most extreme limit of the continuous. For τὸ δὲ πάντῃ <ἀδιαίρετον> καὶ θέσιν ἔχον στιγμή (*Met.* V, 6, 1016b25f.), "That which cannot be resolved further, in any regard, and specifically that which has a θέσις, an orientation as to site, is the point." Conversely, the γραμμή is μοναχῇ διαιρετόν (cf. b26f.), that which is resolvable as to one dimension; the surface, ἐπίπεδον, is διχῇ διαιρετόν (cf. b27), that which is doubly resolvable; and the body, σῶμα, is πάντῃ καὶ τριχῇ διαιρετόν (b27), that which is divisible trebly, i.e., in each dimension. The question is what Aristotle understands by this peculiar form of connection we call the continuous. Characteristically, Aristotle acquires the determination of continuousness not, as one might suppose, within the compass of his reflections on geometry but within those on physics. It is there that he faces the task of explicating the primary phenomena of co-presence, and specifically of worldly co-presence, that of the φύσει ὄντα: *Physics*, V, chapter 3. I will present, quite succinctly, the definitions of the phenomena of co-presence in order that you may see how the συνεχές is constituted and how the mode of manifoldness within number is related to it. You will then also see to what extent the geometrical has a πρόσθεσις, i.e., to what extent there is more co-posited in it than in number.

αα) The phenomena of co-presence as regards φύσει ὄντα (*Phys.* V, 3).

1.) Aristotle lists, as the first phenomenon of co-presence, i.e., of objects being with and being related to one another, specifically as regards the φύσει ὄντα, the ἅμα, the "concurrent," which is not to be understood here in a temporal sense, but which rather concerns place. What is concurrent is what is in *one* place. We must be on our guard not to take these determinations as self-evident and primitive. The fundamental value of these analyses resides in the fact that Aristotle, in opposition to every sort of theoretical construction, took as his point of departure what is immediately visible. Ἅμα is then that which is in one place.

2.) χωρίς, "the separate," is that which is in another place. Here the determination of place must be held fast.

3.) ἅπτεσθαι, "the touching," ὧν τὰ ἄκρα ἅμα (226a23) "occurs in that whose ends, extremities, are (now the first moment recurs) in one place," whose ends occupy the same place.

4.) μεταξύ, "the intermediate," is that which εἰς ὃ πέφυκε πρότερον ἀφικνεῖσθαι τὸ μεταβάλλον (226b23f.), "that at which a changing being, one whose change is in accord with its Being, first arrives, i.e., arrives at earlier." It is that which something, in changing, passes through, that to which something changes prior to arriving at the ἔσχατον of its continuous change.[7] We can obtain a rough idea of what Aristotle means if we take a quite primitive example: for a boat moving in a stream, the stream (the μεταξύ, the medium, within which the motion occurs) is distinguished by the fact that it least of all leaves something out; it retains its integrity.

5.) ἐφεξῆς, "the successive." Here the μεταξύ is taken up again. The successive as such is connected with what it follows in this way, that there is nothing intermediate between them which τῶν ἐν ταὐτῷ γένει (227a1), "which is of the same ontological lineage," i.e., the same as the beings themselves which are in order one after another. Ἐφεξῆς, "in succession," are, e.g., the houses on a street. That which is between them is not something of the same ontological character as that which makes up the series. But something *else* can very well be between them.

6.) ἐχόμενον, "the self-possessed," "the self-coherent." The ἐφεξῆς here recurs. Ἐχόμενον, "the self-consistent," is an ἐφεξῆς, a "one after the other," but of such a kind that it is determined by the ἅπτεσθαι. ἐχόμενον δὲ ὃ ἂν ἐφεξῆς ὂν ἅπτηται (227a6) "What is coherent is that whose successive parts are in touch with one another." The ἐχόμενον is determined by such a

7. μεταξὺ δὲ εἰς ὃ πέφυκε πρότερον ἀφικνεῖσθαι τὸ μεταβάλλον ἢ εἰς ὃ ἔσχατον μεταβάλλει κατὰ φύσιν συνεχῶς μεταβάλλον (226b23ff). "The intermediate is that at which something in motion by nature can arrive prior to arriving at its final state, provided the motion is natural and continuous." The word πρότερον at 226b24 is controversial. Πρότερον can be found in the parallel passage in *Met.* XI, 1068b28, as well as in *Themistii in physica paraphrasis,* 172. In the codices such as *Simplicii in physicorum libris commentaria* 871, 20, the word πρῶτον occurs. Heidegger seems to have incorporated both words. H. Weiß remarks in a footnote (as formulated by the editor): "In the text of Bekker (*Aristotelis opera edidit Academia Regio Borussica (ex recensione I. Bekkeri*) Berlin 1831–1870) the word is πρῶτον. Πρότερον might very well be a conjecture. Yet if one accepts πρῶτον, then b24 (ἢ εἰς ὃ ἔσχατον μεταβάλλει) becomes unintelligible. The ἢ ('than') must be related to the word πρότερον ('earlier'), πρότερον-ἢ ('earlier-than')." A similar annotation can be found in the transcript of H. Jonas. Thus: "The intermediate is that at which a changing being arrives prior to arriving at the state it will ultimately change into." The Latin translation of the Bekker edition also reads *prius-quam.*

succession, one in which the ends are in the same place; i.e., the objects of the series abut one another, touch each other in their extremities.

7.) συνεχές, *continuum*, is a very complicated form, since it presupposes the other determinations, although for αἴσθησις it is what is primarily given. τὸ συνεχὲς ἔστι ὅπερ ἐχόμενόν τι (cf. a10). The συνεχές is an ἐχόμενον, and specifically ὅπερ. Ὅπερ is an expression which recurs in quite fundamental ontological investigations.[8] The συνεχές is a ὅπερ ἐχόμενον, "it is already at the very outset, quite certainly, an ἐχόμενον"; hence there is here in each case nothing between. The συνεχές is an ἐχόμενον even more originally than the ἐχόμενον itself; the ἐχόμενον is only the immediate aspect of an ἔχεσθαι. The συνεχές is still more originally an ἐχόμενον because it is this still more, i.e., it is still more with regard to the mode of its ἔχειν: it is a συνεχόμενον: λέγω δ' εἶναι συνεχὲς ὅταν ταὐτὸ γένηται καὶ ἓν τὸ ἑκατέρου πέρας οἷς ἅπτονται (a11f.). The συνεχές occurs when the limit of the one that touches the other is one and the same limit. In the case of συνεχές not only do the limits of the one house strike the limits of the other, but this happens in such a way that the limits of the one house are identical with those of the other: ταὐτὸ καὶ ἕν.

These are the determinations of co-presence. The συνεχές is the structure that makes up the principle of μέγεθος, a structure which characterizes every extension.

After the description of these determinations, Aristotle considers their relations. The ἐφεξῆς has a special distinction: φανερὸν δὲ καὶ ὅτι πρῶτον τὸ ἐφεξῆς ἐστιν (a17f.). "It is evident that the ἐφεξῆς is first as regards constitution." ἐν προτέροις τῷ λόγῳ (a19f.). "In all speech it is already co-intended and said," i.e., expressed in an unexpressed way. τὸ μὲν γὰρ ἁπτόμενον ἐφεξῆς ἀνάγκη εἶναι, τὸ δ' ἐφεξῆς οὐ πᾶν ἅπτεσθαι (a18f.). The ἁπτόμενον, that whose ends touch in a determinate connection, and whose ends, in the mode of such touching, are side by side, is already in itself, as bearing such touching, a succession. Everything whose ends touch is ἐφεξῆς. But not every ἐφεξῆς has to be one in which the ends touch. Therefore the ἐφεξῆς is first.

On the basis of this consideration, Aristotle shows to what extent μονάς and στιγμή cannot be the same. For the mode of their connection is different.

ββ) The structures of connection in the geometrical and the arithmetical: συνεχές and ἐφεξῆς.

εἰ ἔστι στιγμὴ καὶ μονάς, οὐχ οἷόν τε εἶναι μονάδα καὶ στιγμὴν τὸ αὐτό· ταῖς μὲν γὰρ ὑπάρχει τὸ ἅπτεσθαι, ταῖς δὲ μονάσιν τὸ ἐφεξῆς, καὶ τῶν μὲν

8. The transcripts of H. Weiß and H. Jonas add in brackets: time, metaphysics. Heidegger had indeed given in the lecture a brief reference.

ἐνδέχεται εἶναί τι μεταξύ (πᾶσα γὰρ γραμμὴ μεταξὺ στιγμῶν), τῶν δ' οὐκ ἀνάγκη· οὐδὲν γὰρ μεταξὺ δυάδος καὶ μονάδος (cf. a27ff.). To points there pertains the ἅπτεσθαι, touching, and indeed the ἐχόμενον in the preeminent sense of the συνεχές. To the μονάδες, the units, there pertains, however, only the ἐφεξῆς. The mode of connection of the geometrical, of points, is characterized by the συνεχές, the series of numbers by the ἐφεξῆς, where no touching is necessary. The structure of the connection is in the latter case more simple, as compared to the continuum. With points there can always be something in between; between two points there is always an extension which is more or less large. But that is not necessary in the case of the ἐφεξῆς. Here, therefore, another connection obtains. For there is nothing between unity and twoness. Hence it is clear that the being together of the basic elements in the geometrical has the character of the ἅπτεσθαι or of the συνεχές; the being together of numbers has the character of the ἐφεξῆς, of the one after another. Thus in considering geometrical figures we must add something which according to its structure co-posits more elements than ἐφεξῆς does. Such elements, which are constitutive for the συνεχές, are μέγεθος, πρός τι, θέσις, τόπος, ἅμα, ὑπομένον. The ὑπομένον, "from the very outset to be permanently there," pertains to that which is determined by θέσις.[9] Therefore the geometrical is not as original as the arithmetical.

Note here that for Aristotle the primary determination of number, insofar as it goes back to the μονάς as the ἀρχή, has a still more original connection with the constitution of beings themselves, insofar as it pertains equally to the determination of the Being of every being that it "is" and that it is "one": every ὄν is a ἕν. With this, the ἀριθμός in the largest sense (ἀριθμός stands here for the ἕν) acquires for the structure of beings in general a more fundamental significance as an ontological determination. At the same time it enters into a connection with λόγος, insofar as beings in their ultimate determinations become accessible only in a preeminent λόγος, in νόησις, whereas the geometrical structures are grasped in mere αἴσθησις. Αἴσθησις is where geometrical considerations must stop, στήσεται, where they rest. In arithmetic, on the other hand, λόγος, νοεῖν, is operative, which refrains from every θέσις, from every intuitable dimension and orientation.

Contemporary mathematics is broaching once again the question of the continuum. This is a return to Aristotelian thoughts, insofar as mathematicians are learning to understand that the continuum is not resolvable analytically but that one has to come to understand it as something pregiven, prior to the question of an analytic penetration. The mathematician Hermann Weyl has done work in this direction, and it has been fruitful

9. Cf. *Cat.*, chapter 6, 5a27f.

above all for the fundamental problems of mathematical physics.[10] He arrived at this understanding of the continuum in connection with the theory of relativity in contemporary physics, for which, in opposition to the astronomical geometry that resulted from the impetus Newton gave to modern physics, the notion of field is normative. Physical Being is determined by the field. This course of development lets us hope that physicists might perhaps in time, with the help of philosophy, come to understand what Aristotle understood by motion, abandon the old prejudices, and no longer maintain that the Aristotelian concept of motion is primitive and that motion is to be defined simply by velocity, which is of course one characteristic of motion. Perhaps in time the Aristotelian concept of motion will be appreciated even more radically. I make this reference in order to indicate how much Aristotle, free of all precipitous theory, arrived at facts natural scientific geometry is striving for today, though from the opposite direction.

Aristotle displays, in his *Categories*, keen insight into the consequences of the conception of the continuum for the determination of number. The genuineness of this work has been controversial in the history of philosophy. I consider it to be authentic; no disciple could write like that. In chapter 6, Aristotle provides the fundamental differentiation of ποσόν.[11]

γγ) Consequences for the connecting of the manifold in geometry and arithmetic (*Cat.*, 6).

τοῦ δὲ ποσοῦ τὸ μέν ἐστι διωρισμένον, τὸ δὲ συνεχές· καὶ τὸ μὲν ἐκ θέσιν ἐχόντων πρὸς ἄλληλα τῶν ἐν αὐτοῖς μορίων συνέστηκε, τὸ δὲ οὐκ ἐξ ἐχόντων θέσιν (4b20ff.). Quantity is different in the συνεχές, that which coheres in itself, and in the διωρισμένον, that which is in itself delimited against other things in such a way that each moment of the plurality is delimited against the others. The parts of the συνεχές relate to each other insofar as they are θέσιν ἔχοντα; what is posited in this θέσις is nothing else than the continuum itself. This basic phenomenon is the ontological condition for the possibility of something like extension, μέγεθος: site and orientation are such that from one point there can be a continuous progression to the others; only in this way is motion understandable. In the other way of possessing ποσόν, the διωρισμένον, the parts relate to one another such that they are οὐκ ἐξ ἐχόντων θέσιν μορίων (b22); ἔστι δὲ διωρισμένον μὲν οἷον ἀριθμὸς καὶ λόγος, συνεχὲς δὲ γραμμή, ἐπιφάνεια, σῶμα, ἔτι δὲ

10. H. Weyl, *Raum—Zeit—Materie. Vorlesungen über allgemeine Relativitätstheorie.* Berlin 1918; 5., umgearb. Aufl., Berlin, 1923.

11. Heidegger's manuscript only contains references to the passages without any remarks on their interpretation. The editor offers the following interpretation (up to page 83) on the basis of the transcriptions of H. Jonas, F. Schalk, and H. Weiß.

παρὰ ταῦτα χρόνος καὶ τόπος (ibid. ff.). The διωρισμένον includes, e.g., ἀριθμός and λόγος; the συνεχές includes, e.g., line, surface, body, and, furthermore, χρόνος and τόπος. Insofar as the διωρισμένον consists of parts which are οὐ θέσιν ἔχοντα, whereas the συνεχές consists of parts which are θέσιν ἔχοντα, there is then also a difference in the way the elements of the number series and those of the continuum are connected into unity.

What is the mode of connection of units such as those that belong to the series of numbers? τῶν μὲν γὰρ τοῦ ἀριθμοῦ μορίω οὐδείς ἐστι κοινὸς ὅρος, πρὸς ὃν συνάπτει τὰ μόρια αὐτοῦ· οἷον τὰ πέντε εἰ ἔστι τῶν δέκα μόριον, πρὸς οὐδένα κοινὸν ὅρον συνάπτει τὰ πέντε καὶ τὰ πέντε, ἀλλὰ διώρισται (b25ff.). The parts of a number have no common ὅρος, no common delimitation in the sense that through the ὅρος, which is identical here with the καθόλου, each of the parts would be determined proportionally. For example, in the case of 10, the two μόρια, 5 and 5, have no κοινὸς ὅρος; each is for itself, διωρισμένον, each is distinct. Likewise, 7 + 3 indeed make 10, but 7 does not have a relation, in the sense of the καθόλου or the κοινόν (b28f.), to 10 or 3. There exists here a peculiar relation, such that the μόρια cannot be connected together, συνάπτεσθαι. οὐδ' ὅλως ἂν ἔχοις ἐπ' ἀριθμοῦ λαβεῖν κοινὸν ὅρον τῶν μορίων, ἀλλ' ἀεὶ διώρισται· ὥστε ὁ μὲν ἀριθμὸς τῶν διωρισμένων ἐστίν (b29ff.). There is therefore for the manifold of numbers no such κοινόν at all, in relation to which every particular number would be something like an instance, and number itself would be the καθόλου. There is no question here of generalization, to speak in modern terms. Number is not a genus for the particular numbers. This is admittedly only a negative result, but it is still a pressing ahead to the peculiar sort of connection residing in the number series.

Aristotle carries out the same analysis in the case of λόγος; the same mode of connectedness resides there. ὡσαύτως δὲ καὶ ὁ λόγος τῶν διωρισμένων ἐστίν· (ὅτι μὲν γὰρ ποσόν ἐστιν ὁ λόγος φανερόν· καταμετρεῖται γὰρ συλλαβῇ μακρᾷ καὶ βραχείᾳ· λέγω δὲ αὐτὸν τὸν μετὰ φωνῆς λόγον γιγνόμενον)· πρὸς οὐδένα γὰρ κοινὸν ὅρον αὐτοῦ τὰ μόρια συνάπτει· οὐ γὰρ ἔστι κοινὸς ὅρος πρὸς ὃν αἱ συλλαβαὶ συνάπτουσιν, ἀλλ' ἑκάστη διώρισται αὐτὴ καθ' αὑτήν (b32ff.). Λόγος is taken here as a μετὰ θωνῆς γιγνόμενος, as vocalization, which is articulated in single syllables as its στοιχεῖα. Aristotle and Plato are fond of the example of λόγος for the question of that peculiar unity of a manifold which is not continuous but in which each part is autonomous instead. Thus λόγος in the sense of vocalization is a ποσόν, whose individual parts are absolutely delimited against one another. Each syllable is autonomously opposed to the others. There is no syllable in general, which would represent what all syllables have in common—however, this does not apply to a point, which is indeed like all other points.

Thus a line has another mode of unity: ἡ δὲ γραμμὴ συνεχές ἐστιν· ἔστι γὰρ λαβεῖν κοινὸν ὅρον πρὸς ὃν τὰ μόρια αὐτῆς συνάπτει, στιγμήν· καὶ τῆς ἐπιφανείας γραμμήν (5a1ff.). The line, as continuous, has another mode of unity. That is, one can extract from the line, from the continuous, something with regard to which each part of the line can be called a part in the same sense, namely the point. But it must be noted that these extracted points do not together constitute the line. No point is distinct from any other. What is remarkable for the possibility of this κοινὸς ὅρος resides in the fact that the line is more than a multiplicity of points, that it, namely, has a θέσις. On the other hand, in the case of the manifold of the series of numbers, there is no θέσις, so that this series is determined only by the ἐφεξῆς. Now, insofar as the co-positing of a θέσις is not required for the grasping of mere succession as the mode of connection of numbers, then, viewed in terms of the grasping as such, in terms of νοεῖν, number is ontologically prior. That is, number characterizes a being which is still free from an orientation toward beings which have the character of the continuum and ultimately are in each case an αἰσθητόν. Therefore number enters into an original connection, if one interrogates the structure of beings as the structure of something in general. And this is the reason the radical ontological reflection of Plato begins with number. Number is more original; therefore every determination of beings carried out with number, in the broadest sense, as the guiding line is closer to the ultimate ἀρχαί of ὄν.

When Aristotle brings up the distinction between geometry and arithmetic in *Metaphysics* I, chapter 2,[12] his concern is simply to show that within the ἐπιστῆμαι there are gradations of rigor. But he does not claim that arithmetic would be the most original science of beings in their Being. On the contrary, Aristotle shows precisely that the genuine ἀρχή of number, the unit or oneness, is no longer a number, and with that a still more original discipline is predelineated, a discipline which studies the basic constitution of beings: σοφία.

§16. Continuation: σοφία *(*Met. *I, 2, part 1). The fourth essential moment of* σοφία*: the autonomy of its* ἀληθεύειν *(*ἑαυτῆς ἕνεκεν. μὴ πρὸς χρῆσιν*).*

The fourth and last moment of σοφία is its autonomy in itself. Aristotle demonstrates it in a twofold way: first, on the basis of what is thematic in σοφία; second, on the basis of the comportment of Dasein itself.

12. 982a28.

a) What is thematic in σοφία. The ἀγαθόν as τέλος and ultimate οὗ ἕνεκα; as αἴτιον and ἀρχή; as object of pure θεωρεῖν.

τὸ δ' εἰδέναι καὶ τὸ ἐπίστασθαι αὐτῶν ἕνεκα μάλισθ' ὑπάρχει τῇ τοῦ μάλιστ' ἐπιστητοῦ ἐπιστήμῃ (982a30ff.). "Seeing and knowing for their own sake reside most of all in that ἐπιστήμη whose theme is the μάλιστα ἐπιστητόν." This μάλιστα ἐπιστητόν, which most of all turns knowledge into something genuinely formative, is what is grasped when it is a matter of acquiring the ultimate orientations in beings and when it is a matter of seeing why such and such should happen. This ultimate why, i.e., this ultimate "for the sake of which," οὗ ἕνεκα, is, as τέλος, always an ἀγαθόν (*Met.* I, 3, 983a31f.). The ἀγαθόν, however, is a matter of the ἀρχικωτάτη among the ἐπιστῆμαι and τέχναι, insofar as the ἀρχικωτάτη is the one that γνωρίζουσα τίνος ἕνεκέν ἐστι πρακτέον ἕκαστον (982b5f.), "provides insight about that for the sake of which each single thing is to be accomplished precisely in such and such a way." Accordingly, σοφία, insofar as it is the μάλιστα ἐπιστήμη, and as such provides insight about the μάλιστα ἀγαθόν, the ὅλως τὸ ἄριστον ἐν τῇ φύσει πάσῃ (cf. 982b7), is the ἀρχικωτάτη among all ἐπιστῆμαι and τέχναι in general. Hence it is the one that is no longer guided but instead is itself explicitly or inexplicitly the guide. Thus it is autonomous. Σοφία asks about the ἄριστον, the highest good, in relation to which every other τέχνη and ἐπιστήμη must be oriented. To that extent σοφία is ἀρχικωτάτη, guiding and autonomous.

With this characterization of σοφία as aiming at an ἀγαθόν, Aristotle comes in questionable proximity to another relation to beings: πρᾶξις. For πρᾶξις is oriented precisely toward the for the sake of which. Thus if σοφία aims at the ἀγαθόν, then it seems that it is ultimately a πρᾶξις, whereas the preceding has shown precisely that it is free of χρῆσις and is a pure θεωρεῖν. Thus the difficulty is that we have here a comportment of Dasein which, on the one hand, relates to something determined as ἀγαθόν, yet, on the other hand, it is not supposed to be πρᾶξις but θεωρεῖν.

The difficulty can be resolved by recalling what Aristotle emphasized: "The ἀγαθόν, too, is one of the causes." καὶ γὰρ τἀγαθὸν ἓν τῶν αἰτίων ἐστίν (cf. 982b10f.). Now the basic character of an αἴτιον consists in being the ἀρχή, the ultimate, out of which something is understood: μάλιστα δ' ἐπιστητὰ τὰ πρῶτα καὶ τὰ αἴτια (982b2). Already ἐμπειρία and τέχνη asked about the αἴτιον. But what is most important is not simply that for Aristotle the ἀγαθόν is an αἴτιον but that he succeeded in showing for the first time that the ἀγαθόν is nothing else than an ontological character of beings: it applies to those beings which are determined by a τέλος. To the extent that a being reaches its τέλος and is complete, it is as it is meant to be, εὖ. The ἀγαθόν has at first no relation to πρᾶξις at all; instead, it is a determination of beings insofar as they are finished, com-plete. A being that always is does not at all first need to be produced; it is always already constantly there as finished. Insofar as Aristotle understands the ἀγαθόν as τέλος—being finished—and counts the τέλος among the other causes, like ὕλη, εἶδος, and ἀρχὴ κινέσεως,[1] he achieves for the first time a fundamental ontological understanding of the ἀγαθόν. If we take the ἀγαθόν as value, then this is all nonsense. The proper meaning of the ἀγαθόν is rather this:

ἀγαθόν
|
τέλος
|
πέρας
|
ἀρχή τοῦ ὄντος.

We must hold fast to this genuine sense of the ἀγαθόν as long as our concern is to understand the expression ἀγαθόν as a properly *philosophical* term.

We are thus led to the following circumstance, namely, that insofar as the ἀγαθόν is not primarily related to πρᾶξις but instead is understood as a basic constitution of beings in themselves, the possibility is predelineated that the ἀγαθόν as ἀρχή is precisely the object of a θεωρεῖν, indeed that exactly with regard to a being as ἀεὶ ὄν, as everlasting being—in relation to which I can take no action—the correct comportment is θεωρία. This possibility is predelineated by the interpretation of the ἀγαθόν as πέρας. How Aristotle interprets this we will see in the following session.[2]

We have now merely gained the following possibility: although the ἀγαθόν is oriented toward πρᾶξις, yet, on the basis of the fundamental ontological understanding of the ἀγαθόν, a way is open to see that there is a comportment which, as theoretical, presents the correct relation to the ἀγαθόν. Thus Aristotle can say that σοφία, within which he sees this θεωρεῖν, is a quite peculiar φρόνησις, a τοιαύτη φρόνησις (982b24). It is not φρόνησις as we know it in relation to beings which can be otherwise, in relation to the objects of our action; it is a φρόνησις which is indeed directed to an ἀγαθόν, but an ἀγαθόν that is not πρακτόν. Aristotle's designation of σοφία as a τοιαύτη φρόνησις manifests at the same time an orientation against Plato, who did not attain a very discriminating understanding of these phenomena. When Aristotle speaks of σοφία as φρόνησις, he is indi-

1. *Met.* I, 3, 983a26ff.

2. This announcement occurs in the thirteenth session (November 24, 1924). The "following session" is the fourteenth (November 25, 1924). It contains, however, no corresponding explication.

cating thereby that he sees in σοφία (as Plato did in φρόνησις) the highest mode of ἀληθεύειν and in general man's highest comportment, the highest possibility of human existence.

Thus far we know, on the basis of the γένεσις of σοφία, that it more and more renounces practical goals. But that σοφία is μὴ πρὸς χρῆσιν[3] is a determination which is given only negatively and only concomitantly, with regard to something else. It does not yet determine σοφία itself. But now it must be shown positively that σοφία is predelineated in Dasein itself in accord with the very possibility of Dasein; i.e., it is the development of a primary possibility of the Being of Dasein itself. Thereby the autonomy of σοφία first becomes ontologically understandable and the discussion of it in relation to φρόνησις is planted in the proper soil. The task is to demonstrate the possibility that, first, φρόνησις no longer has as its theme the ζωή as πρακτόν but that, second, as ἀληθεύειν it is precisely a mode of Being of the ζωή.

b) The origin of σοφία in Dasein itself. Θαυμάζειν and ἀπορεῖν as origin of philosophy. The tendency in Dasein itself toward pure θεωρεῖν.

The root of an autonomous sheer onlooking upon the world already lies in primitive and everyday Dasein. Aristotle shows that σοφία is unconcerned with ποίησις and πρᾶξις not just by accident and subsequently, but that it is so primordially and originally. ὅτι δ' οὐ ποιητική, δῆλον καὶ ἐκ τῶν πρώτων φιλοσοφησάντων. διὰ γὰρ τὸ θαυμάζειν οἱ ἄνθρωποι καὶ νῦν καὶ τὸ πρῶτον ἤρξαντο φιλοσοφεῖν, ἐξ ἀρχῆς μὲν τὰ πρόχειρα τῶν ἀπόρων θαυμάσαντες, εἶτα κατὰ μικρὸν οὕτω προϊόντες καὶ περὶ τῶν μειζόνων διαπορήσαντες, οἷον περί τε τῶν τῆς σελήνης παθημάτων καὶ τῶν περὶ τὸν ἥλιον <καὶ περὶ ἄστρων> καὶ περὶ τῆς τοῦ παντὸς γενέσεως (*Met.* I, 2, 982b10ff.). The fact that σοφία, from the very beginning, constitutes an autonomous mode of Being of Dasein, juxtaposed to ποίησις, can be seen on the basis of two primary moments in which Dasein may be actualized: 1.) θαυμάζειν and 2.) διαπορεῖν.[4]

1.) Σοφία arises from θαυμάζεσθαι, which is attained very early in natural Dasein. θαυμάζει εἰ οὕτως ἔχει (cf. 983a13f.). "Wonder is about something encountered, whether it really is" as it shows itself. θαυμαστὸν γὰρ εἶναι δοκεῖ πᾶσιν, εἴ τι τῷ ἐλαχίστῳ μὴ μετρεῖται (a16f.). "For everyone, it is a matter of wonder when something is supposed to be unmeasurable by means of what is smallest," i.e., more generally, when something cannot be

3. *Met.* I, 2, 982b24f: δι' οὐδεμίαν χρείαν ἑτέραν.

4. See the appendix.

made intelligible by means of what is most known and at one's disposal. Μετρεῖν, to take measure, to determine, is the mode in which Dasein makes something intelligible. Μέτρον and ἀριθμός belong in the same realm as λόγος, namely the realm of ἀληθεύειν.[5] The θαυμαστόν is that which is awry. "Here something is awry." The astonishing, the wondrous, is constituted in relation to an onlooking insofar as the understanding at one's disposal does not suffice for this encountered state of affairs. The understanding is shocked by what shows itself. Wondering originally begins simply with what is plain and obvious, τὰ πρόχειρα (982b13), "what lies right at hand." Subsequently, the consideration gradually widens, so that one is also wondering about greater things, which were at first taken as self-evident: about the πάθη of the moon, what happens to the moon, about the remarkable fact that the moon changes, and similarly about what happens to the sun, and finally about the genesis of beings as a whole, whether they are as they show themselves.

2.) Aristotle now interprets wonder as an original phenomenon of Dasein and thereby shows that in wonder there is operative a tendency toward θεωρεῖν; Dasein from the very outset possesses a tendency toward sheer onlooking and understanding. In this connection, Aristotle employs an expression familiar to the philosophy of his time: ἀπορεῖν. Ἄπορος means "without passage," one cannot get through. Πόρος originally referred to the passage through a stream at a shallow place. Ἀπορία is a consideration of the world that does not get through; it does not find a way. The immediately familiar αἰτία, the available means of explication, do not suffice. The mode of running through by explication is blocked. Things are distorted, in their genuine outward look as well as in their immediate appearance. Notice how ἀπορία corresponds perfectly to the meaning of ἀληθεύειν and to the conception of Dasein we are already acquainted with: the beings of the world are at first occluded and Dasein does not get through. In this sense of ἀληθεύειν, whose first form of execution is λόγος, there corresponds:

	ἀπορεῖν				λέγειν
ἀπορία				λόγος	
	ἀπορούμενον				λεγόμενον

5. Cf. p. 12f.

This ἀπορεῖν, if it is expressly carried out, indicates that one does not know the matter which he cannot get through. ὁ δ' ἀπορῶν οἴεται ἀγνοεῖν (cf. 982b17f.). "The one who does not get through and finds no way out," and establishes that the matter at issue is occluded to him, "is convinced that he is not yet genuinely familiar with the matter," that he still does not know it. Yet insofar as one becomes transparent to oneself precisely in this conviction of being unable to get through, so that one continues the διαπορεῖν and makes the attempt to get through, there then resides in such ἀπορεῖν and διαπορεῖν a desire to get through, a φεύγειν τὴν ἄγνοιαν and a διώκειν τὸ ἐπίστασθαι διὰ τὸ εἰδέναι: ὥστ' εἴπερ διὰ τὸ φεύγειν τὴν ἄγνοιαν ἐφιλοσόφησαν, φανερὸν ὅτι διὰ τὸ εἰδέναι τὸ ἐπίστασθαι ἐδίωκον καὶ οὐ χρέσεώς τινος ἕνεκεν (b19ff.). The one who continues the ἀπορεῖν and διαπορεῖν and attempts to get through reveals in such endeavors that he is flying in the face of ἄγνοια, ignorance, coveredness, and is pursuing ἐπίστασθαι, knowledge, having beings present in their uncoveredness. Thus what the Greeks call ἀπορία characterizes the peculiar intermediate position of Dasein itself over and against the world. It characterizes a peculiar being underway of Dasein: in a certain sense knowing beings and yet not getting through. The ἀπορεῖν in itself, however, does not have any sort of autonomous and positive meaning but only has the functional sense of the correct pursuit of the knowledge of beings themselves. Δια-πορεῖν, the interrogating that presses forward, means to find something no longer obvious (where the "obvious" is what is intelligible on the basis of some perfectly accidental understanding) and to endeavor to extract an understanding from the matter itself instead. The positive steps in διαπορεῖν are nothing else than the presentifying of the determinate matter at issue. The way and the direction of the ἀπορεῖν depart from the familiar surroundings and proceed toward the world and specifically in such a way that the ἀπορεῖν does not concern what is encountered accidentally and happens to be striking but rather includes the sense that Dasein sets itself on the path where what is striking is what was always already there. Where such ἀπορεῖν occurs, there takes place this setting oneself on the way, this being underway toward. Thus the ἀπορεῖν, or the διαπορεῖν, becomes a phenomenon in the natural consideration of the world as well as in explicitly scientific research, which shows to what extent Dasein in itself aims at an uncovering of beings simply for the sake of uncovering. Thereby we procure the ultimate determination of σοφία and see at the same time that θεωρεῖν is a completely autonomous comportment of Dasein, not related to anything else whatsoever.

§17. *Summary:*[1] *The modes of* ἀληθεύειν *as modifications of self-orienting Dasein.*

We have gained an insight into Dasein insofar as in it various modes of ἀληθεύειν initially occur in such a way that they are not delimited against one another and thus that the expressions τέχνη, ἐπιστήμη, φρόνησις, and σοφία are ambiguous. The development of this ambiguity is not arbitrary. And a real overcoming of this ambiguity cannot occur simply by putting dogmatic definitions up against it and making these modes of comportment fixed. The ambiguity will be overcome only when its motives are visible, i.e., when it becomes understood why these various expressions are employed with this ambiguity.

Dasein discloses its immediate surrounding world: it *orients* itself in its world without the individual modes of self-orientation becoming explicit. Insofar as this self-orientation is a taking cognizance and a deliberating concerned with producing, it is of the character of τέχνη. Insofar as this know-how is nevertheless a knowing and makes its appearance explicitly as knowing, the same state can be conceived as ἐπιστήμη. But it does not yet have to be science at all. Insofar as the self-orientation is concerned with a πρακτόν which is dealt with for one's own use, αὑτῷ, for one's self, this self-orienting is φρόνησις in the broadest sense, as it is proper to the ζῷα. Whether what is discovered in such orienting is the ποιητόν of a πρᾶξις or not does not matter at all. Insofar as the self-orienting is concerned explicitly with the αἴτιον and becomes real understanding for its own sake, these same modes of self-orienting—τέχνη, ἐπιστήμη, φρόνησις—can also be conceived as σοφία. That is the basic way Dasein itself uses these expressions. We must make this fundamentally clear in order to see that the γένεσις into explicit modes of existence is accomplished precisely on the basis of Dasein itself.

It has been shown that Dasein aims at σοφία merely διὰ τὸ εἰδέναι and not χρήσεώς τινος ἕνεκεν (b20f.), that θεωρεῖν is a completely autonomous comportment of Dasein, not related to anything else. In this way σοφία manifests a possibility of existence in which Dasein discloses itself as free, as completely delivered over to itself. ὥσπερ ἄνθρωπός φαμεν ἐλεύθερος ὁ ἑαυτοῦ ἕνεκα καὶ μὴ ἄλλου ὤν, οὕτω καὶ αὕτη, μόνη ἐλευθέρα οὖσα τῶν ἐπιστημῶν· μόνη γὰρ αὐτὴ ἑαυτῆς ἕνεκέν ἐστιν (b25ff.). And thus the question arises whether such a possibility of existence is at all within the reach of human Dasein, since, after all, the ζωή of man is δούλη (b29), i.e., since the life of man, his Being in the world, is in a certain sense to be a slave of circumstances and of everyday importunities. It seems therefore

1. Title in Heidegger's manuscript.

that insofar as human Dasein is a slave, the possibility of an autonomous comportment in pure θεωρία must remain denied it, that consequently σοφία cannot be a possible κτῆσις (b29) for man. The question arises whether σοφία can be a κτῆσις ἀνθρώπου. This question, which arises here concerning κτῆσις, is the same as the one which arose in the *Nicomachean Ethics* concerning ἕξις: i.e., whether σοφία is a possible ἕξις of human Dasein.

Only after the clarification of this question will we be sufficiently prepared to decide whether it is φρόνησις, which as such has human Dasein for the goal of its uncovering, or σοφία that is the highest mode of uncovering. We will have to examine on what basis Aristotle decided about the mode of Being of φρόνησις in opposition to the mode of Being of σοφία as possibilities of human Dasein. This determination will make understandable at the same time the sense in which there can be a science such as ethics with regard to human life, insofar as ethics deals with the ἦθος, the Being of man, which can also be otherwise. The question is to what extent there can be a science of something like that, if indeed science proper is concerned with beings which always are.

Chapter Three

The Question of the Priority of φρόνησις or σοφία as the Highest Mode of ἀληθεύειν (*Met.* I, 2, part 2; *Nic. Eth.* VI, 7–10, X, 6–7)

§18. The divinity of σοφία *and the questionableness of* σοφία *as a possibility of man (*Met. *I, 2, part 2).* Σοφία *as constant dwelling with the* ἀεί*. Human Dasein as "slave" (*δούλη*) of* ἀναγκαῖα *and* ἄλλως ἔχοντα*. The priority of* σοφία *with respect to* ἀληθεύειν*.*

The question is whether σοφία can be a κτῆσις and ἕξις of man. Aristotle first raises this question by quoting Greek poetry.[1] This citation says that σοφία is a θεῖον. Aristotle shows this explicitly in the *Nicomachean Ethics* (X, 7, 1177b26ff.). Here, in the *Metaphysics,* Book I, 2, only natural Dasein expresses itself, and what it says is that the θεός alone would have the possibility of καθ' αὑτὸν ἐπιστήμη (b31f.), i.e., of σοφία. It is reserved for the gods alone. What possibilities are the gods otherwise supposed to have? But, further, the poets say that the gods are jealous with regard to man, that they begrudge man σοφία. But, Aristotle says, let us not give too much weight to such claims of poets, because, as even a proverb has it, they mostly deceive.[2] The gods cannot be jealous at all, and this is not because they are too good to be jealous, but because the mode of existence of the θεῖον excludes all πάθη, all affects. On the other hand, there is no higher kind of knowledge than σοφία. Aristotle shows this by saying cautiously that perhaps a god would most of all actually have σοφία and therefore one could justly speak of σοφία as a θεῖον; and a further reason would be that the object of σοφία is everlasting being,[3] θεῖον. Aristotle initially lets the question stand at this point. Note that Aristotle, in ascribing σοφία to the θεῖον, is not asserting the proposition absolutely, and that for him σοφία is not a θεῖον factually but only potentially. He concludes the consideration by remarking that ἀναγκαιότεραι μὲν οὖν πᾶσαι ταύτης, ἀμείνων δ' οὐδεμία (983a10f.), "for Dasein, all modes of knowing, in the broadest sense,

1. 982b31: Θεὸς ἂν μόνος τοῦτ' ἔχοι γέρας. "Only a god is supposed to have this privilege." Semonides, Fragment 3, 5; in *Anthologia lyrica sive lyricorum Graecorum veterum praeter Pindarum. Reliquiae potiores. Post Theodorum Bergkium quartum edidit Eduardus Hiller. Exemplar emendavit atque novis fragmentis auxit O. Crusius,* Leipzig, 1913.

2. πολλὰ ψεύδονται ἀοιδοί (*Met.* I, 2, 983a4), "The poets lie a great deal."

3. Cf. *Nic. Eth.* VI, 7, 1141a24.

are more necessary and more pressing than σοφία, but none is better." With regard to ἀληθεύειν, the uncovering of beings, σοφία has the priority.

Over and against this rather popular discussion of σοφία and its relation to man, Aristotle himself has a much more original understanding of the entire question. It is precisely the treatment of these difficulties that leads him to show how σοφία is the highest possibility for man. In order to clear the way for indicating this briefly, we must hold fast to the following. Σοφία is, according to its idea: τῶν ἐξ ἀρχῆς αἰτίων ἐπιστήμη (cf. *Met.* I, 3, 983a24f.). As far as the question of the being of ἀληθεύειν, i.e., the mode of Being of Dasein, is concerned, this idea entails: 1.) complete autonomy in itself, and 2.) a relation to genuine beings in their Being, a dwelling with them. This idea requires one to be posited freely on oneself in having beings in themselves present. That raises the question of whether σοφία can be a κτῆσις and ἕξις of man. For human Dasein is δούλη; it is delivered over to ἀναγκαῖα, which are ἄλλως ἔχοντα; it is forced to dwell with such ἀναγκαῖα and ἄλλως ἔχοντα. Man cannot constantly dwell among the τιμιώτατα; for man, this autonomous mode of Being, forever attending to the τιμιώτατα, is unthinkable.

This question receives its keenness when one considers that σοφία is a θεῖον. Aristotle's characterization of σοφία as a θεῖον is purely ontological in intention; metaphysics is not theology. Σοφία is an ἐπιστήμη, one that is θειοτάτη. And it is so in a twofold way: 1.) it is κτῆσις of a θεός, and 2.) it makes thematic τὰ θεῖα. This is a very early anticipation of Aristotle's metaphysics.[4] Insofar as σοφία is 1.) κτῆσις of a θεός, i.e., insofar as the comportment in it is divine, it is νοῦς, νοεῖν, νόησις; and insofar as 2.) σοφία is τῶν θείων, i.e., insofar as it has as its object the θεῖον, it is νοήσεως. Hence 1.) as κτῆσις of a θεός, σοφία is νόησις; and 2.) as making τὰ θεῖα thematic, σοφία is νοήσεως. We will not now look more closely into this.

According to our investigations thus far, the θεῖον in σοφία is presented in the following way: insofar as σοφία 1.) has the θεῖον as its object, to that extent it has as its object the ἀεί; and insofar as 2.) the θεῖον is in it as a mode of comportment, it is a pure and simple onlooking, sheer θεωρεῖν. The comportment of σοφία is in keeping with its object. It tarries constantly with what is everlasting. Its distinguishing mark is that, as θεωρεῖν, it constantly dwells on that which always is. Hence the idea of this mode of existence resides in a constant actual presence to the ἀεί. Nevertheless, Aristotle emphasizes[5] that human existence cannot sustain this comportment throughout the whole time of its life. The way of man's temporality makes it impossible for him to attend constantly to the ἀεί. Man needs

4. *Met.* XII, 7.
5. *Nic. Eth.* X, 7, 1177b26ff., in connection with X, 6, 1176b33f.

recreation and relaxation from θεωρεῖν. These nexuses in a certain way underlie Aristotle's reflections in *Metaphysics,* I, 2, without his explicitly entering into them. But this much is clear, that, in its Being, the comportment of Dasein to the ἀεί, if it is to be in keeping with the ἀεί, must *always* be a θεωρεῖν. That is in a certain sense possible, and in a certain sense impossible.

But this does not dispose of the task of delimitating σοφία over and against φρόνησις. For φρόνησις in itself claims to be the highest mode of human knowledge.

§19. Φρόνησις as the proper possibility of man, and the rejection of φρόνησις as "σοφία" (Nic. Eth. VI, 7, part 2). The gravity of φρόνησις. The ἀκρότατον ἀγαθὸν ἀνθρώπινον as object of φρόνησις. The ἄριστον ἐν τῷ κόσμῳ as object of σοφία. Predelineation of ontological superiority as criterion of the priority of σοφία.

Φρόνησις in itself claims, as we said, to be the highest mode of human knowledge, namely insofar as one can say that it is the gravest of all knowledge, since it is concerned with human existence itself; it is the σπουδαιοτάτη (cf. 1141a21f.). Σοφία may indeed deal with the τιμιώτατα (cf. b3), the highest beings; but these beings are not ones that concern man in his existence. What concerns man is Dasein itself, the ἀκρότατον ἀγαθὸν ἀνθρώπινον, namely εὐδαιμονία. And for this, φρόνησις provides direction. Φρόνησις is supposed to render Dasein transparent in the accomplishment of those actions which lead man to the εὖ ζῆν. If, accordingly, φρόνησις is the gravest and most decisive knowledge, then that science which moves within the field of φρόνησις will be the highest. And insofar as no man is alone, insofar as people are together, πολιτική (*Nic. Eth.* VI, 7, 1141a21) is the highest science. Accordingly, πολιτικὴ ἐπιστήμη is genuine σοφία, and the πολιτικός is the true φιλόσοφος; that is the conception of Plato.

Nevertheless, one can ask whether this determination of φρόνησις in relation to σοφία is legitimate. Notice what Aristotle brings to the arena: the ἀγαθόν, as ἀγαθόν of human Dasein, as εὐδαιμονία, is indeed an ἀκρότατον ἀγαθόν; it is that in which human Dasein attains its completion. But it is still an ἀνθρώπινον ἀγαθόν, a determination of the Being of *man,* and as such is ἕτερον in opposition to the ἀγαθόν which, e.g., is that of a fish. According to the Being of the respective being, the ἀγαθόν, too, as τέλος, is in each case different. Furthermore, even the ἀγαθόν of individual human beings, in their possibility as Dasein, can in each case be different. Insofar as the ἀγαθόν can in each case be different, we have in this ἀγαθόν an ontological determination of beings which can also be otherwise, not of ones that are ἀεί. The Dasein of man is not something ordained to be ἀεί, whereas the λευκόν or the εὐθύ is τὸ αὐτὸ ἀεί (a24), "always identical." These are ontological determinations which always are what they are; therefore they are σοφόν, an object of σοφία. If we say that σοφία is concerned with such beings, ones which are αὐτῷ ὠφέλιμον, then there would be many σοφίαι, one for man, one for animals, etc. The identification of φρόνησις and σοφία would be legitimate, provided man is ἄριστον τῶν ἐν τῷ κόσμῳ (a21f.), i.e., provided he is, "of all the beings in the world, a being in the most proper sense." The question whether φρόνησις itself is σοφία must in principle be oriented toward beings which are the concern of both φρόνησις and σοφία; it must be oriented toward the ἀκρότατον ἀγαθόν. εἰ δ' ὅτι βέλτιστον ἄνθρωπος τῶν ἄλλων ζῴων, οὐδὲν διαφέρει (a33f.). "That man, compared to other living things, is the βέλτιστον does not matter in the least." For there are still other, much more divine beings ἐν τῷ κόσμῳ than human Dasein. καὶ γὰρ ἀνθρώπου ἄλλα πολὺ θειότερα τὴν φύσιν (a34f.). There are still θειότερα τὴν φύσιν—φύσις means here the same as οὐσία—there are beings other than human Dasein which are still more properly present, considered in terms of their mode of presence. Θεῖον denotes here simply the higher mode of Being of a being. It has nothing to do with religion or God or Aristotle's religiosity. As an expression for the higher mode of Being, θειότερον has a purely and formally ontological sense. This becomes clear from what Aristotle offers as evidence for the "more divine" Being: φανερώτατα ἐξ ὧν ὁ κόσμος συνέστηκεν (cf. b1f.), of all the things which make up the "world," that which is the most revealed and wholly uncovered: οὐρανός, ἥλιος, σελήνη, etc. To prove that Aristotle considered the sun a god might very well be difficult. ἐκ δὴ τῶν εἰρημένων δῆλον ὅτι ἡ σοφία ἐστὶν καὶ ἐπιστήμη καὶ νοῦς τῶν τιμιωτάτων τῇ φύσει (b2f.). Φύσις here means the same as οὐσία. Σοφία concerns the τιμιώτατα τῇ φύσει, i.e., that which, with regard to its mode of being present, has the priority and hence is what is most properly present. For Aristotle and the Greeks, as well as for the tradition, beings in the proper sense are what exists always, what is constantly already there. The Greeks made this clear to themselves; today it is simply believed. On the other hand, human Dasein, if it is an ἄριστον, is still not an ἄριστον ἁπλῶς, i.e. φύσει, but only an ἄριστον πρὸς ἡμᾶς. Human Dasein is not ἀεί, always; the Being of man arises and passes away; it has its determinate time, its αἰών.

Now we can begin to see where lies the basis for the privilege of σοφία over φρόνησις. Σοφία has the priority in relation to beings in themselves, insofar as the beings with which it is concerned have for the Greeks ontological priority. Beings come into view on the basis of what in themselves they always already are.

Aristotle concludes the presentation of σοφία, at 1141b3ff., with a revised enumeration of the qualities which characterize the autonomy of σοφία and their independent genesis in Dasein. Nevertheless the two modes of ἀληθεύειν, φρόνησις and σοφία, are distinguished not only in terms of their objects but also in their own proper structure. To see this, we need a closer examination of the structure of φρόνησις itself.

§20. *More radical conception of* φρόνησις[1] (Nic. Eth. *VI, 8–9).*

a) Φρόνησις as πρακτικὴ ἕξις[2] (*Nic. Eth.* VI, 8).

In order to see to what extent φρόνησις and σοφία are distinct in their structure, it is important to note that φρόνησις is an ἀληθεύειν, but one that is in itself related to πρᾶξις. "In itself" means the πρᾶξις is not something which lies next to it, which comes afterward, like the ἔργον in the case of τέχνη, but instead each step of the ἀληθεύειν of φρόνησις is oriented toward the πρακτόν. Accordingly, the mode of carrying out ἀληθεύειν in φρόνησις is different than the one in σοφία. Aristotle has explicated this connection in the last chapters of the sixth book of the *Nicomachean Ethics,* beginning with chapter 8.

In this chapter, Aristotle shows that φρόνησις is a πρακτικὴ ἕξις. For that which φρόνησις discloses is the πρακτὸν ἀγαθόν (1141b12). Thereby, the specific ἕξις-character of φρόνησις is the εὖ βουλεύεσθαι (b10). ὁ δ' ἁπλῶς εὔβουλος ὁ τοῦ ἀρίστου ἀνθρώπῳ τῶν πρακτῶν στοχαστικὸς κατὰ τὸν λογισμόν (b12ff.). "The one who simply deliberates appropriately (whose deliberation and circumspection into the τέλος pertain to the end and the finished product) is the one who uncovers the ἄριστον ἀνθρώπῳ, what is in itself best for man," and, specifically, the ἄριστον τῶν πρακτῶν, "what is best among the possible πρακτά." This is what bestows on man the εὐδαιμονία that is man's οὗ ἕνεκα. Such disclosure of the ἄριστον ἀνθρώπῳ τῶν πρακτῶν is the power of the ἁπλῶς εὔβουλος because he is στοχαστικός, because he can "hit the mark," and specifically κατὰ τὸν λογισμόν, "in deliberating on and discussing" human Dasein in the concrete possibilities of its Being. οὐδ' ἐστὶν ἡ φρόνησις τῶν καθόλου μόνον (b14f.). Such disclosure of the ἄριστον, however, is not exclusively concerned to bring out in an altogether simple way, as it were, the outward look of the immediate mode of human Dasein; as such, the task of φρόνησις would not only be unaccomplished but would be fundamentally misun-

1. Title based on Heidegger. The manuscript says: "To take φρόνησις itself more radically."
2. Title in Heidegger's manuscript.

derstood. The ἀληθεύειν of φρόνησις as such δεῖ καὶ τὰ καθ' ἕκαστα γνωρίζειν (b15) "must also disclose the concrete individual possibilities of the Being of Dasein." πρακτικὴ γάρ, ἡ δὲ πρᾶξις περὶ τὰ καθ' ἕκαστα (b16). That is, the disclosure of φρόνησις is ὁμολόγως ὀρέξει,[3] it is carried out with a constant regard toward the situation of the acting being, of the one who is deciding here and now. On this basis, the meaning of the ἀγαθόν for human Dasein and the mode of dealing with it in λέγειν are determined not just incidentally but according to their most proper sense: this ἀγαθόν is an ἀκρότατον. Φρόνησις is not a ἕξις μετὰ λόγου μόνον (*Nic. Eth.* VI, 5, 1140b28), it is not a mere discussing that proceeds for its own sake, but instead, already in every word, in every saying it utters, it speaks of the πρακτόν and for the sake of the πρακτόν. ἡ δὲ φρόνησις πρακτική· ὥστε δεῖ ἄμφω ἔχειν, ἢ ταύτην μᾶλλον (ibid., 8, 1141b21f.). "Φρόνησις must have both": ἀληθεύειν and πρᾶξις, "or, rather, the latter still more." Φρόνησις dwells in πρᾶξις still more than in λόγος. What is decisive in φρόνησις is πρᾶξις. In φρόνησις, the πρᾶξις is ἀρχή and τέλος. In foresight toward a determinate action, φρόνησις is carried out, and in the action itself it comes to its end.

εἴη δ' ἄν τις καὶ ἐνταῦθα ἀρχιτεκτονική (b22f.). And also here within the πρακτική there may exist a certain order of connection, a leading and a guiding. Insofar as the ἄνθρωπος is the ζῷον πολιτικόν, πρᾶξις is to be understood as a mode of being with others; and insofar as this is the τέλος, φρόνησις is of the character of the πολιτική.[4]

Hence what is decisive for φρόνησις is πρᾶξις. This gives rise to an essential distinction between φρόνησις and ἐπιστήμη, one which concerns their genesis. Aristotle shows this in chapter 9.

b) The mode of origin of φρόνησις and ἐπιστήμη (*Nic. Eth.* VI, 9). Φρόνησις: ἐξ ἐμπειρίας (life experience). Mathematics: δι' ἀφαιρέσεως.

Φρόνησις requires χρόνος. Life experience is needed for the possibility of correct decisions but not for ἐπιστήμη. Thus it can happen that young people are already able to discover important things. Aristotle refers here to the mathematician, and Pascal would be an example for us. Mathematics is an autonomous σχολάζειν.[5] γεωμετρικοὶ μὲν νέοι καὶ μαθηματικοὶ γίνονται καὶ σοφοὶ τὰ τοιαῦτα (1142a12f.). Precisely in mathematics quite young people can already do research autonomously and in this regard can

3. Cf. *Nic. Eth.* VI, 2, 1139a29ff.: τοῦ δὲ πρακτικοῦ καὶ διανοητικοῦ ἡ ἀλήθεια ὁμολόγως ἔχουσα τῇ ὀρέξει τῇ ὀρθῇ.
4. Heidegger did not elaborate further.
5. Cf. *Met.* I, 1, 981b20ff.

become σοφοί. The reason is that for mathematics no γνῶσις of the καθ' ἕκαστα is required, and that can only be gained in ἐμπειρία, in life experience. νέος δὲ ἔμπειρος οὐκ ἔστιν (a15). "Young people are not experienced in the factual conditions of human Dasein itself." πλῆθος γὰρ χρόνου ποιεῖ τὴν ἐμπειρίαν (a15f.). "Only through much time (through the many nows of the 'as soon as-then') is life experience possible." This is reserved for the maturity of old age. In this way, πλῆθος χρόνου, much time, is required for φρόνησις. Since it is τῶν καθ' ἕκαστα (a14), φρόνησις is in need of life experience. Therefore φρόνησις is not properly an affair of young people. Young people can, on the other hand, as has been said, be σοφοὶ τὰ τοιαῦτα, σοφοί with regard to mathematics. But there is a distinction between mathematical and philosophical knowledge. Quite young people can have mathematical knowledge but not philosophical knowledge. ἢ ὅτι τὰ μὲν δι' ἀφαιρέσεώς ἐστιν, τῶν δ' αἱ ἀρχαὶ ἐξ ἐμπειρίας (a18f.). "For mathematics is a knowledge which comes to pass by abstracting from beings"; i.e., that which is abstracted from, looked away from, namely concrete existence, is not further considered and determined. What is attended to is only the τί of the πέρας, γραμμή, ἐπίπεδον, etc. Mathematics does not have to concern itself with concrete existence in order to carry out the ἀφαίρεσις. On the other hand, for σοφία it is necessary that the σοφός, or the φυσικός, insofar as he is one who genuinely understands, gain ἐξ ἐμπειρίας that which he is trying to attain. It would be a misunderstanding to translate ἐξ ἐμπειρίας as "induction," as if what is at issue here were a matter of the generalization of single cases. Instead, ἐξ ἐμπειρίας is opposed to ἀφαίρεσις. And what is in this fashion opposed to ἀφαίρεσις is precisely the exposition of the ultimate ontological foundations of the concrete beings themselves. This requires that one presentify the beings themselves in order to see their outward look, their εἶδος, and to draw from them their ἀρχαί. But this calls for the knowledge and domination of the manifold of beings, and this manifold can be appropriated only in the course of time. Accordingly, even with regard to the mode of its origin, φρόνησις is different from ἐπιστήμη.

What we have worked out up to now are merely preliminary distinctions. We will attain the essential distinctions only if we recall the guiding line employed for differentiating the various modes of ἀληθεύειν. Aristotle oriented the consideration in two directions: 1.) what sort of beings are disclosed, are they ἀεί or ἐνδεχόμενον ἄλλως ἔχειν, and 2.) to what extent can these beings be disclosed and preserved in their ἀρχή.

In the meantime, what an ἀρχή as such is has become more transparent. The ἀρχή is that which already is, that from out of which every being is properly what it is. It is telling that, as regards every being which can also be otherwise, the ἀρχή—the always already—of φρόνησις is anticipated in a προ-αίρεσις.

The question is to what extent the various modes of ἀληθεύειν succeed in disclosing and preserving the being in its ἀρχή, i.e., to what extent they succeed in grasping the being in its proper Being and at the same time, as ἕξις, succeed in holding fast to it. Aristotle discussed these matters first of all in regard to ἐπιστήμη and τέχνη. Τέχνη anticipates in the εἶδος the ἀρχή, the τέλος, but it does not succeed in grasping it in the ἔργον. Even in ἐπιστήμη, no genuine grasping of the ἀρχή takes place. What then is the case regarding the disclosure and preservation of the ἀρχή in φρόνησις and σοφία?

§21. Exposition of the further tasks: the relation of φρόνησις *and of* σοφία *to the* ἀρχαί. Σοφία: νοῦς καὶ ἐπιστήμη. *The task of the clarification of the* βουλεύεσθαι *of the mode of carrying out* φρόνησις.

We have seen that σοφία is in a certain sense ἐπιστήμη; it makes use of the ἀρχαί. But it is also νοῦς. It is νοῦς καὶ ἐπιστήμη (1141a19f.). It is precisely νοῦς which, in the proper sense, aims at the ἀρχαί and discloses them. Now σοφία is not pure νοεῖν. The νοεῖν operative in σοφία is carried out by man within speech; σοφία is μετὰ λόγου (*Nic. Eth.* VI, 6, 1140b31ff.). At the same time, σοφία is not sheer διαλέγεσθαι but is in a certain sense νοεῖν. The νοεῖν of νοῦς itself, however, would be ἄνευ λόγου.

How do these connections lie in φρόνησις? Can φρόνησις disclose and preserve the ἀρχή of the beings at which it aims? The analysis of the beings which are thematic in φρόνησις will be difficult because φρόνησις itself also belongs in a certain manner to those beings which are its theme. For the object of φρόνησις is πρᾶξις, the ζωή of man, human Dasein itself. To action itself pertains deliberation, the becoming transparent of the acting itself. The transparency is not a mode of onlooking which considers disinterestedly how the action could appear. Φρόνησις is included in its own theme; it itself occurs among the beings it is supposed to disclose. This is how the difficulty of the analyses of the beings which are thematic in φρόνησις is first given, and it is not easy to presentify correctly the phenomenon of φρόνησις at one stroke. It will be shown that φρόνησις, too, is νοῦς and νοεῖν and is a genuine disclosure of the ἀρχή. Since, however, the theme of φρόνησις is πρᾶξις, beings which can be otherwise, and since, accordingly, even the ἀρχαί are ones that can be otherwise, the comportment to these beings will have a completely different structure than the comportment to the ἀεί in σοφία. Insofar as both, φρόνησις and σοφία, each in its own way, are νοῦς, Aristotle recognizes each of them as a βελτίστη ἕξις. Since both are placed on the same level, it will be all the more difficult to decide to what extent the one has a priority over the other.

Up to now we have clarified the character of the ἀληθεύειν of φρόνησις in such a way that we have come to understand that φρόνησις is a ἕξις πρακτική. What it discloses is from the very outset intended with regard to its being relevant to action. The mode of carrying out the disclosive appropriation of the πρακτόν is βουλεύεσθαι, circumspective self-debate. This βουλεύεσθαι is μετὰ λόγου and therefore is a λογίζεσθαι, a discussing. Insofar as βουλεύεσθαι is the way to carry out φρόνησις, the structure of the βουλεύεσθαι must make visible how φρόνησις grasps the ἀρχαί of the beings which are thematic in it, the ἀρχαί of human ζωή. Aristotle carries out the consideration by first asking what is correct βουλεύεσθαι. How does εὐβουλία look? δεῖ δὲ λαβεῖν καὶ περὶ εὐβουλίας τί ἐστιν (*Nic. Eth.* VI, 10, 1142a32f.). With the structure of the εὐβουλία, i.e., with this mode of carrying out φρόνησις, the character of φρόνησις as ἀληθεύειν first becomes visible and this even, and precisely, with regard to the disclosing of the ἀρχή. The second basic question will be: How does φρόνησις relate to νοῦς itself, if it, like σοφία, discloses the ἀρχή, i.e., has the character of νοῦς? From this point of departure we can understand νοῦς. The understanding of νοῦς on the basis of σοφία and φρόνησις is, in my view, the only way to gain a preliminary insight into the difficult phenomenon of νοῦς.

§22. Εὐβουλία *as the mode of carrying out* φρόνησις (Nic. Eth. *VI, 10).*

The mode of carrying out φρόνησις is βουλεύεσθαι, which itself is a λογίζεσθαι, a discussion. To that extent φρόνησις is a ἕξις μετὰ λόγου. The disclosure of φρόνησις is carried out μετὰ λόγου, in speech, in the discussion of something. It must be noted that λόγος, as it is in question here, is to be grasped as the asserting of something about something, as λέγειν τι κατά τινος. Insofar as something is asserted of a being within an intention to disclose it in this asserting, a διαίρεσις already resides there. Insofar as I assert something about something, the asserting has taken apart the being spoken of. Everything that is a theme of λόγος is, as such, a διαιρετόν. On the other hand, a being, insofar as it is given only καθόλου, as a whole, in the way we encounter it immediately, is συγκεχυμένον, intermingled, "poured together."[1] To assert means to articulate what is spoken about. It is only on the basis of such διαίρεσις that σύνθεσις follows, the σύνθεσις which is proper to λόγος. Λόγος is diairetic-synthetic. If now, on the other hand, φρόνησις is supposed to be a βελτίστη ἕξις, then it must grasp the ἀρχή of the beings which are its theme. An ἀρχή, however, especially if it

1. *Phys.* I, 1, 184a21ff. Cf. p. 60f.

is an ultimate, final ἀρχή, is itself no longer something we can speak of as something. The appropriate speaking of an ἀρχή cannot be carried out by λόγος, insofar as the latter is a διαίρεσις. An ἀρχή can only be grasped for itself and not as something else. The ἀρχή is an ἀδιαίρετον, something whose Being resists being taken apart. Accordingly, φρόνησις includes the possibility of a sheer grasp of the ἀρχή as such, i.e., a mode of disclosure transcending λόγος. Insofar as φρόνησις is a βελτίστη ἕξις, it must be more than mere λόγος. That corresponds precisely to the position in which we left σοφία. Σοφία is concerned with the ἀρχαί as such; thus there is alive in it something like pure νοεῖν. For an ἀρχή, which is an ἀδιαίρετον, is not disclosed in λέγειν but in νοεῖν.[2] The question arises whether, in analogy with the way σοφία is νοῦς καὶ ἐπιστήμη, so also φρόνησις might include the possibility, beyond the λέγειν and λογίζεσθαι and yet in connection with them, of uncovering the ἀρχή as such and holding fast to it, i.e., whether there is in φρόνησις, too, something like a pure νοεῖν, a pure perceiving.

a) The structure of the βουλεύεσθαι.

α) Structural analysis of action. The constitutive moments of action. Ἀρχή and τέλος of action. Εὐπραξία and εὐβουλία.

Our consideration will begin by presentifying the beings disclosed in φρόνησις. We cannot say: the beings *thematic* in φρόνησις, as long as to be thematic means to be the object of a theoretical consideration. Φρόνησις has properly no theme, since it does not as such have in view the beings it discloses. The being disclosed by φρόνησις is πρᾶξις. In this resides human Dasein. For human Dasein is determined as πρακτική, or—to make the determination more complete—the ζωή of man is determined as ζωὴ πρακτικὴ μετὰ λόγου (cf. *Nic. Eth.* I, 7, 1098a3f.).

In the case of a definite action, the question immediately arises as to that *of which* it is the action. Every action is action in relation to a determinate "of which." Since the ζωὴ πρακτική moves in each case within a definite surrounding world, this action is carried out under determined circumstances. These circumstances characterize the *situation* in which Dasein at any time finds itself. Thus action itself is characterized by various moments:[3]

1.) that of which it is the action (ὅ),

2.) that which must be taken up as ways and means and must already

2. Cf. *Met.* IX, 10.
3. *Nic. Eth.* VI, 10, 1142b23ff.

be available in order to act (δι' οὗ). For example, in order to please another with a gift, the object in question must be available.

3.) the objects in question must be used in a determinate way (πώς); they must in general stand within a determinate possibility of use, such that I can freely dispose of them in my orientation toward what I intend in my action.

4.) every action is carried out at a determinate time (ὅτε), and finally

5.) insofar as Dasein is determined as being with others, every action is carried out vis-à-vis one or another definite person.

In this way, Dasein, as acting in each case now, is determined by its situation in the largest sense. This situation is in every case different. The circumstances, the givens, the times, and the people vary. The meaning of the action itself, i.e., precisely what I want to do, varies as well.

This entire context of acting Dasein, in its full situation, is to be disclosed by φρόνησις. It is precisely the achievement of φρόνησις to disclose the respective Dasein as acting now in the full situation within which it acts and in which it is in each case different. Φρόνησις, however, is not at all like spectating the situation and the action; it is not an inventorization in the sense of a disinterested constatation, it is not a *study* of the situation in which I find myself. Even the moment of interest does not capture the sense of φρόνησις. But discussion does itself belong to the action in the full sense. From the ἀρχή on, from what I want to do, from my decision to act, all the way up to the completed action itself, φρόνησις belongs intrinsically to the acting. In every step of the action, φρόνησις is co-constitutive. That means therefore that φρόνησις must make the action transparent from its ἀρχή up to its τέλος. For the action is a being that can in each case be otherwise; correspondingly, φρόνησις is co-present, such that it co-constitutes the πρᾶξις itself.

The ἀρχή of the action is the οὗ ἕνεκα, the "for the sake of which"; this οὗ ἕνεκα is at the beginning of the action the προαιρετόν, that which I anticipate in my choice. I am now supposed to make such and such happen for this or that person in such and such a way. In this προαίρεσις what is anticipated is nothing else than the action itself. The ἀρχή with which φρόνησις has to do is the action itself. And the τέλος which is taken into consideration in φρόνησις is the action itself, namely the action carried out. We have here in φρόνησις a comportment analogous to that of τέχνη, insofar as the τεχνίτης in a certain manner anticipates the εἶδος of the house. But in the case of τέχνη the τέλος is not the architect himself; the τέλος is for the architect himself and as such παρά. As architect, he precisely does not have the τέλος at his disposal. The τέλος as ἔργον falls outside of τέχνη. On the other hand, in φρόνησις the action itself is anticipated; and the τέλος of the action is nothing else than the action itself, to which φρόνησις belongs as προαίρεσις. This entire connection from the ἀρχή up to the τέλος is nothing else than the full Being of the action itself. This full Being of the action is supposed to be uncovered through φρόνησις.

If we now follow the structure of φρόνησις from its first beginning, this is the connection: the action, as that in favor of which I have resolved, is indeed anticipated; but in the anticipation, in the ἀρχή, the circumstances are characteristically not given, nor is that which belongs to the carrying out of the action. Rather, precisely out of the constant regard toward that which I have resolved, the situation should become transparent. From the point of view of the προαιρετόν, the concrete situation of the action is still a ζητούμενον, it is covered over. In *Metaphysics* VII, chapter 13, Aristotle calls the ζητούμενον a λανθάνον (1041a32); that which is sought is still hidden. Therefore the task is to uncover, on the basis of a regard toward the ἀρχή of the action, the concrete situation, which is at first hidden, and in that way to make the action itself transparent. This uncovering of the hidden, in the sense of making transparent the action itself, is an affair of φρόνησις.

But now the τέλος of the action is the action itself, and specifically it is the εὐπραξία. The concern is not that something should come to pass in general, but instead the concern is that the action comes to pass in the correct way, so that it attains its end in what it can be. Now insofar as φρόνησις belongs co-constitutively to πρᾶξις, φρόνησις, too, must have, in being carried out, the character of the εὖ. The how of the deliberation, λογίζεσθαι, is determined by the character of the action itself. This λογίζεσθαι, the discussing and thorough deliberation, which is the path on which φρόνησις discloses the situation of the action, is also called βουλεύεσθαι. This βουλεύεσθαι is the way φρόνησις is carried out. Accordingly, the βουλεύεσθαι must have the character of the εὖ; if the τέλος of the πρᾶξις is indeed to be the εὐπραξία, the βουλεύεσθαι must be characterized by εὐβουλία. As εὐβουλία, φρόνησις is genuinely what it is. The question of the structure of φρόνησις is hence concentrated on the question of what εὐβουλία is, i.e., the correct deliberation on action, from its ἀρχή to its τέλος, its last reach.

β) Εὐβουλία as genuine φρόνησις. The correctness (ὀρθότης) of the εὐβουλία. The resolution (βουλή). The βουλεύεσθαι as συλλογίζεσθαι. The ὀρθὸς λόγος.

This βουλεύεσθαι is not a considering in the sense of a mere description of something present but instead is a considering of something sought, something not yet present, something still to be uncovered. τὸ γὰρ βουλεύεσθαι ζητεῖν τι ἐστίν (*Nic. Eth.* VI, 10, 1142a31f.). The character of the ζητεῖν must be kept in mind from the very outset. The ζητεῖν does not move as blind trial and error but is a being underway which from the very outset has an orientation: 1.) whence, i.e., from the ἀρχή, and 2.) whither, i.e., toward the τέλος. These are merely two different determinations of the one πρᾶξις itself. In the constant looking upon the ἀρχή, the discussion and thorough deliberation about the situation are a movement toward the τέλος. The τέλος is the action itself, the action as achieved, carried out. This implies that the βουλεύεσθαι has a direction; it is in itself directed upon something, and specifically such that in a certain sense from the very beginning the orientation is constantly toward the anticipated, the action. Βουλεύεσθαι as such includes the structural moment of directedness. Insofar as the βουλεύεσθαι is to be directed εὖ (in the right way), the εὖ belongs to the carrying out of the βουλεύεσθαι itself. The being directed in the right way—εὖ—is the correctness, ὀρθότης, of the acting, which in a certain sense maintains the direction which is predelineated by the ἀρχή and the τέλος of the acting: δῆλον ὅτι ὀρθότης τίς ἡ εὐβουλία ἐστίν (1142b8f.). The elaborated correctness of the concrete action is the ὀρθότης βουλῆς. βουλή is the decision, the resolution. ἀλλ' ὀρθότης τίς ἐστιν ἡ εὐβουλία βουλῆς (b16). The elaboration of the concrete situation aims at making available the correct resoluteness as the transparency of the action. And insofar as this resoluteness is in fact appropriated and carried out, i.e., insofar as I am resolved, the action is present in its final possibility. The directed disclosure of the full situation terminates in genuine resoluteness toward something, venturing upon the action itself.

This βουλεύεσθαι, the thorough deliberation, is carried out as λογίζεσθαι in such a way that a nexus of speaking is alive, a speaking-together, συλλογίζεσθαι, συλλογισμός, extrinsically called "conclusion."[4] Every course of demonstration has a consequent, συμπέρασμα. The consequent of the βουλεύεσθαι is the action itself; it is not some sort of proposition or cognition but is the bursting forth of the acting person as such. This shows how in φρόνησις the ἔργον is also included and for its part belongs to the Being of the acting person. On the basis of this foundational structure we can now understand what has constantly been so difficult to interpret, namely the expression ὀρθὸς λόγος.[5] This concept has generated a veritable history of nonsense. From what I have said you will understand without further ado what is at issue here. Λόγος means discussion, not reason. Ὀρθός is nothing else than ὀρθότης βουλῆς, the correctness which has its structure in the peculiar character of the directedness of φρόνησις. This directedness rests on the fact that in the case of πρᾶξις the λόγος belongs

4. *Nic. Eth.* VI, 13, 1144a31ff.: οἱ γὰρ συλλογισμοὶ τῶν πρακτῶν ἀρχὴν ἔχοντές εἰσιν, ἐπειδὴ τοιόνδε τὸ τέλος καὶ τὸ ἄριστον.
5. Inter alia, *Nic. Eth.* VI, 1, 1138b29.

intrinsically to the action; the λόγος is ὁμολόγως τῇ ὀρέξει.[6] The προαίρεσις is in itself διανοητική; i.e., διάνοια is in itself προαιρετική. Διανοητικὴ προαίρεσις and προαιρετικὴ διάνοια[7] designate the same phenomenon, namely action transparent to itself.

I have characterized for you thus far only the general structure of εὐβουλία as the way φρόνησις is carried out. We must now pursue this structure more closely as well as the way Aristotle, purely phenomenologically, works his way to it. Aristotle elaborates the structure of εὐβουλία in such a manner that he makes it visible in delimitation against other possible modes of disclosure. This is the method he usually favors.

b) Delimitation of εὐβουλία against other modes of ἀληθεύειν. Knowledge (ἐπιστήμη), sureness of aim (εὐστοχία), presence of mind (ἀγχίνοια), opinion (δόξα).

What then is εὐβουλία? First of all, is it perhaps something like ἐπιστήμη? Does it have the character of knowledge? ἐπιστήμη μὲν δὴ οὐκ ἔστιν (οὐ γὰρ ζητοῦσι περὶ ὧν ἴσασιν, ἡ δ' εὐβουλία βουλή τις, ὁ δὲ βουλευόμενος ζητεῖ καὶ λογίζεται) (a34ff.). Εὐβουλία cannot be an ἐπιστήμη, because ἐπιστήμη means knowledge. In knowing, I have a determinate being, as already uncovered, present to me. In ἐπιστήμη the ζητεῖν comes to an end. In knowledge, there is no seeking; instead, there is an already having found. Accordingly, εὐβουλία cannot be interpreted as ἐπιστήμη.

Secondly, we might wonder whether εὐβουλία is something like εὐστοχία, sureness of aim, the possibility of correct deliberation in the sense of a quality many people have as regards action, namely to hit instinctively the decisive circumstance and the correct moment: the sureness of instinct. ἀλλὰ μὴν οὐδ' εὐστοχία. ἄνευ τε γὰρ λόγου καὶ ταχύ τι ἡ εὐστοχία, βουλεύονται δὲ πολὺν χρόνον, καὶ φασὶ πράττειν μὲν δεῖν ταχὺ τὰ βουλευθέντα, βουλεύεσθαι δὲ βραδέως (b2ff.). Εὐβουλία cannot be εὐστοχία. For εὐβουλία requires λόγος, actual discussion. In instinctual certitude, I simply act, without genuine discussion. Furthermore, in εὐστοχία, the acting is characterized by the ταχύ; it happens in an instant. On the other hand, βουλεύεσθαι needs πολὺν χρόνον. Versus precipitous action, correct deliberation takes time. Εὐβουλία is deliberating well and slowly and acting resolutely, but it is not deliberating in such a way that everything is left to the future. Insofar as εὐστοχία lacks the moment of

6. *Nic. Eth.* VI, 2, 1139a29ff.: τοῦ δὲ πρακτικοῦ καὶ διανοητικοῦ ἡ ἀλήθεια ὁμολόγως ἔχουσα τῇ ὀρέξει τῇ ὀρθῇ.

7. b4f.: ἢ ὀρεκτικὸς νοῦς ἡ προαίρεσις ἢ ὄρεξις διανοητική.

λόγος and the moment of the πολὺς χρόνος, it cannot be considered εὐβουλία.

The third phenomenon is ἀγχίνοια (b5), a νοεῖν which is ἀγχί, close by something, and which we might translate as "presence of mind," the ability to survey a situation quickly. ἔστιν δὲ εὐστοχία τις ἡ ἀγχίνοια (b6). Ἀγχίνοια has a certain affinity with εὐστοχία, although ἀγχίνοια expresses more the momentary, the capacity to survey a situation in an instant, whereas instinctual certitude consists more in proceeding with certainty by examining things step by step. Ἀγχίνοια is out of the question as an interpretation of εὐβουλία.

The fourth phenomenon against which εὐβουλία is to be delimited is δόξα, precisely because δόξα, being of an opinion, in fact has in its structure an ὀρθότης. An opinion is directed to something. In the opinion I have, I maintain that something is such and such. Opinion, according to its very sense, contains an orientation toward beings as they would show themselves to a correct investigation and examination. Insofar as δόξα has an ὀρθότης, one might think that εὐβουλία is a δοξάζειν. This is impossible, however. οὐδὲ δὴ δόξα ἡ εὐβουλία οὐδεμία. . . . δόξης δ' ὀρθότης ἀλήθεια (1142b6ff.). "Εὐβουλία cannot be a δόξα, because the ὀρθότης of δόξα is directed to ἀλήθεια," whereas εὐβουλία is directed to βουλή, being resolved. Εὐβουλία is not directed toward truth or falsity but primarily and exclusively toward being resolved. Furthermore, δόξα is constituted in such a remarkable fashion that, although it does indeed have an ὀρθότης, it is still not a ζητεῖν. καὶ γὰρ ἡ δόξα οὐ ζήτησις ἀλλὰ φάσις τις ἤδη, ὁ δὲ βουλευόμενος, ἐάν τε εὖ ἐάν τε κακῶς βουλεύηται, ζητεῖ τι καὶ λογίζεται (b13ff.). Δόξα is not a seeking but instead is something one *has*. In having an opinion there resides already a certain φάσις: I am of the opinion *that* such and such is the case. I am not seeking. Finally, δόξα is indeed concerned with what can also be otherwise, the συγκείμενον, and to that extent it is, like βουλεύεσθαι, a λέγειν, an asserting of something about something, a διανοεῖν, a taking apart. Because it is such a separating λόγος, δόξα can, it seems, be true or false. In fact, however, it is neither true nor false but is instead *directed* to the ἀληθές. Likewise, βουλεύεσθαι, too, can be one or the other: it can be κακῶς or εὖ; it can fail, ἁμαρτάνειν, or hit the mark. What is essential, however, is that βουλεύεσθαι is in general directed to something, and precisely not to the ἀληθές but, as we said, to the βουλή, the being resolved. Nor is this ὀρθότης the one of ἐπιστήμη. For ἐπιστήμη has no ὀρθότης at all, just as it also has no ἁμαρτία. It is rather an already complete ἕξις; it is not merely underway to something.

Through this delimitation, Aristotle makes visible the phenomenon of εὐβουλία. The four different possibilities against which it is delimited have not been conceived apriori; on the contrary, they emerge, in considering the phenomenon of εὐβουλία, out of the affinity of the phenomena themselves. Yet, what, within εὐβουλία, the ὀρθότης itself is remains to be clarified.

c) The ὀρθότης of εὐβουλία. Being persistently directed to the ἀγαθόν.

ἐπεὶ δ' ἡ ὀρθότης πλεοναχῶς, δῆλον ὅτι οὐ πᾶσα (b17f.). There are different conceptions of the ὀρθότης; not every one of them, however, touches the ὀρθότης of εὐβουλία. Thus the task arises of determining in what precise sense the ὀρθότης of εὐβουλία *is* ὀρθότης. Aristotle characterizes it in its various moments by means of a delimitation against the different conceptions. ὁ γὰρ ἀκρατὴς καὶ ὁ φαῦλος οὗ προτίθεται τυχεῖν ἐκ τοῦ λογισμοῦ τεύξεται, ὥστε ὀρθῶς ἔσται βεβουλευμένος, κακὸν δὲ μέγα εἰληφώς (b18ff.). Someone who is driven by passions or who is in a bad mood can be resolved toward something κακόν. Then the ἀρχή of the action, the goal anticipated in the προαίρεσις, is κακόν, and thus the whole action is misguided. Nevertheless, while aiming at this κακόν the discussion of the concrete situation may be a εὖ λογίζεσθαι and correspond precisely to the κακόν posited in the resolution. Then the βουλεύεσθαι is indeed ὀρθῶς, it measures up completely to the ὀρθότης βουλῆς. Nevertheless, the τέλος, the end of such a deliberation, namely, the action itself, is κακόν, and is this although nothing can be objected against the φρόνησις itself as regards the mode in which it has formally been carried out. Yet the ὀρθότης of εὐβουλία is supposed to go precisely toward constituting the ἀγαθόν of an action. Thus the ὀρθότης of the βουλεύεσθαι whose τέλος is the κακόν cannot be considered the ὀρθότης of εὐβουλία.

Conversely, it may be that the τέλος is a genuine ἀγαθόν but that the deliberation is inappropriate, that the συλλογισμός is ψευδής, one in which I am deceived. ἀλλ' ἔστιν καὶ τούτου ψευδεῖ συλλογισμῷ τυχεῖν, καὶ ὃ μὲν δεῖ ποιῆσαι τυχεῖν, δι' οὗ δὲ οὔ, ἀλλὰ ψευδῆ τὸν μέσον ὅρον εἶναι· ὥστε οὐδ' αὕτη πω εὐβουλία, καθ' ἣν οὗ δεῖ μὲν τυγχάνει, οὐ μέντοι δι' οὗ ἔδει (b22ff.). Thus it may be that the συλλογισμός or the μέσος ὅρος is ψευδής, that it distorts the circumstances, the means, and the ways, that it does not provide me with them as they should be in relation to the προαιρετόν. Accordingly, it is part of εὐβουλία not only to posit the τέλος as ἀγαθόν but to be ἀγαθόν in each of its steps. In every step the εὐβουλία must be directed in such a way that it has the ἀγαθόν in view and discusses all the circumstances and occasions with regard to it. The ὀρθότης of εὐβουλία can be considered only as ἀγαθοῦ τευκτική. ἡ γὰρ τοιαύτη ὀρθότης βουλῆς εὐβουλία, ἡ ἀγαθοῦ τευκτική (b21f.). Even time as such, whether one deliberates long or briefly, is not a distinguishing mark of the ὀρθότης of εὐβουλία; what matters is simply that the time of the action be ἀγαθόν. Insofar as the ὀρθότης εὐβουλίας is ἀγαθοῦ τευκτική in each of its steps, it is ὀρθότης ἡ κατὰ τὸ ὠφέλιμον, καὶ οὗ δεῖ καὶ ὡς καὶ ὅτε (b27f.). It is correctness with regard to what matters for the carrying out of the προαιρετὸν ἀγαθόν, which is more precisely determined as: 1.) οὗ δεῖ, 2.) ὥς, and 3.) ὅτε, i.e., what it needs, how it is used, and when. All these moments must have the character of ἀγαθόν. ἔτι ἔστιν καὶ ἁπλῶς εὖ βεβουλεῦσθαι καὶ πρός τι τέλος. ἡ μὲν δὴ ἁπλῶς ἡ πρὸς τὸ τέλος τὸ ἁπλῶς κατορθοῦσα, τὶς δὲ ἡ πρός τι τέλος (b28f.). Εὐβουλία itself can be carried out either as a discussion which is related straightforwardly to the ἀγαθόν or as a discussion that is πρός τι τέλος, i.e., related to a determinate τέλος, thus to a τέλος which again is πρός τι, related to another one.

Aristotle concludes by determining εὐβουλία in this way: εἰ δὴ τῶν φρονίμων τὸ εὖ βεβουλεῦσθαι, ἡ εὐβουλία εἴη ἂν ὀρθότης ἡ κατὰ τὸ συμφέρον πρὸς τὸ τέλος, οὗ ἡ φρόνησις ἀληθὴς ὑπόληψις ἐστίν (b31ff.). "Εὐβουλία is correctness in relation to what contributes to the end," i.e., contributes to the way of bringing an action to its end. The τέλος itself is for its part anticipated in φρόνησις. Φρόνησις is ὑπόληψις ἀληθὴς τοῦ τέλους. Ὑπόληψις is related to ὑπολαμβάνειν, to anticipate, grasp in advance. Ὑπό is often used in fundamental concepts: e.g., ὑποκείμενον (translated in Latin as *sub-stantia*), ὑπομένον, ὑπάρχον. These are expressions which indicate that something is already there at the outset: ὑποκείμενον, the substratum; ὑπομένον, that which always remains there; ὑπάρχον, that which is already there from the very outset in such a way that it dominates. Ὑπάρχειν applies to the Being of the ἀρχή. Φρόνησις is ὑπόληψις ἀληθὴς τοῦ τέλους, "that which from the very outset grasps the τέλος" in such a way that this τέλος is ὑπό, in advance of everything, already there. And εὐβουλία, insofar as it is ὀρθότης ἡ κατὰ τὸ συμφέρον πρὸς τὸ τέλος, is nothing else than the concrete mode of carrying out φρόνησις.

Φρόνησις itself, however, insofar as it is a constitutive moment of πρᾶξις, is explicitly related to beings that can also be otherwise. Every possible object of an action is a being that has the character of momentariness, specifically in the sense of the ἔσχατον. The πρακτόν is ultimately an ἔσχατον. We have to understand more precisely what is meant by saying that φρόνησις must be familiar with the ἔσχατα. It will turn out that they are matters for νοῦς.

§23. Φρόνησις *and* νοῦς[1] (Nic. Eth. *VI, 12)*.

a) Νοῦς in σοφία and in φρόνησις. The double direction of νοῦς. Σοφία: νοῦς → πρῶτα; φρόνησις: νοῦς → ἔσχατα. The practical syllogism. Practical νοῦς as αἴσθησις.

ἔστιν δὲ τῶν καθ' ἕκαστα καὶ τῶν ἐσχάτων ἅπαντα τὰ πρακτά· καὶ γὰρ τὸν φρόνιμον δεῖ γινώσκειν αὐτά (*Nic. Eth.* VI, 12, 1143a32ff.). Ἔσχατον literally means the outermost limit, and here more precisely it refers to the outermost limit of λογίζεσθαι, hence that in which discussion comes to an end, where in a certain sense it stands still. In Book VII of his *Metaphysics*, within a determination of ποίησις in the broadest sense, which includes πρᾶξις, Aristotle offers a brief illustration of the ἔσχατον, and we can carry it over without further ado to πρᾶξις. He describes there a deliberation within τέχνη, the διανοεῖν of the ἰατρός. γίγνεται δὴ τὸ ὑγιὲς νοήσαντος οὕτως· ἐπειδὴ τοδὶ ὑγίεια, ἀνάγκη, εἰ ὑγιὲς ἔσται, τοδὶ ὑπάρξαι, οἷον ὁμαλότητα, εἰ δὲ τοῦτο, θερμότητα· καὶ οὕτως ἀεὶ νοεῖ, ἕως ἂν ἀγάγῃ εἰς τοῦτο ὃ αὐτὸς δύναται ἔσχατον ποιεῖν. εἶτα ἤδη ἡ ἀπὸ τούτου κίνησις ποίησις καλεῖται, ἡ ἐπὶ τὸ ὑγιαίνειν (*Met.* VII, 7, 1032b5ff.). "Since such and such is the healthy state of a man or of an organ in question, then, insofar as the man or the organ is to become healthy, this and that must be present at the outset; and if this and that must be at hand, then so must these others, etc. And in this way the ἰατρός keeps on deliberating until he leads the deliberation and himself to that which he himself can do as the outermost, i.e., to the point at which he can intervene with a treatment."[2] The ἔσχατον is that moment of the Being of concrete beings with which the intervention of the doctor begins, and, conversely, it is that at which the deliberation and discussion come to a standstill. Then the further procedure will only be ποίησις, the treatment itself. The ἔσχατον is the outermost limit of the deliberation and in that way is the presentifying of the state of affairs with which the action begins.

We have seen that Aristotle calls even the πρακτά ἔσχατα. How are these ἔσχατα themselves grasped in the deliberation of φρόνησις? To what extent does there reside in φρόνησις, as a λογίζεσθαι, a grasping of beings, one which, as a grasping, transcends λόγος? To what extent is there in φρόνησις νοῦς, νοεῖν? Aristotle brings out this phenomenon by means of a comparison with σοφία. καὶ ὁ νοῦς τῶν ἐσχάτων ἐπ' ἀμφότερα· καὶ γὰρ τῶν πρώτων ὅρων καὶ τῶν ἐσχάτων νοῦς ἐστι καὶ οὐ λόγος (*Nic. Eth.* VI, 12, 1143a35ff.). The straightforward discernment of the ἔσχατα is possible

1. Title in Heidegger's manuscript.
2. Heidegger's paraphrasing translation.

from two sides; νοῦς can, in a double direction, grasp what is outermost. Νοῦς is related to the πρῶτοι ὅροι, to the first demarcations, to the ἀρχαί pure and simple, to the ultimate elements of that which always is, as well as to the outermost in the sense of the momentary individual this-there. The latter is no longer a matter for discourse but instead is grasped simply in νοεῖν.

Aristotle then determines both these possibilities more precisely: καὶ ὁ μὲν κατὰ τὰς ἀποδείξεις τῶν ἀκινήτων ὅρων καὶ πρώτων, ὁ δ' ἐν ταῖς πρακτικαῖς τοῦ ἐσχάτου καὶ ἐνδεχομένου καὶ τῆς ἑτέρας προτάσεως (1143b1ff.). This is the first possibility: νοεῖν concerns the last outcomes of ἀπόδειξις, the theoretical demonstration of the ἀκίνητα, of beings which are not in motion. Here nothing else is meant than the ἀρχαί, which are objects of σοφία. The other possibility is the counter direction to this νοεῖν. The text has been transmitted: ἐν ταῖς πρακτικαῖς, with ἀποδείξεσιν understood. Victorius writes instead: ἐν τοῖς πρακτικοῖς, with λόγοις understood.[3] Within these πρακτικοὶ λόγοι there is also a νοεῖν. And here the νοεῖν is concerned with the ἔσχατον. Ἔσχατον is the counter-concept to what was called πρῶτον in the case of ἀπόδειξις. To the ἀκινητόν, the ἀεί, corresponds the ἐνδεχόμενον. The straightforward grasping in νοεῖν relates here to an ἔσχατον which at every moment is always different.

And the grasping in νοεῖν relates, as Aristotle says, "to the other premise," ἑτέρα πρότασις (cf. b3). "Premise," πρότασις, is here understood in a broad sense as that which is posited in advance, that which stands before the consequent. Such προτάσεις do not only occur in the ἀποδείξεις of the ἐπιστῆμαι. For example, in public rhetoric the προτάσεις are the ἔνδοξα, the opinions which have prestige. Keep in mind that in this context, demonstration, in the sense of the ἐπιστῆμαι, as well as λογίζεσθαι, in the sense of circumspective discussion, have the structure of συλλογισμός. Βουλεύεσθαι is placed structurally in a συλλογισμός. Φρόνησις begins with a προαίρεσις: for the sake of this, for the sake of an ἀγαθόν (whichever one it may be), such and such is to be done. That is the first premise. And now the circumstances and the situation of the action are such and such. That is the second premise. The consequent is: hence I will act in such and such a way. The first premise concerns the grasping of the οὗ ἕνεκα, which is an ἐνδεχόμενον. The second premise concerns the finding of the ἔσχατον, the outermost point, at which the λογίζεσθαι comes to a halt. Now Aristotle says: τούτων οὖν ἔχειν δεῖ αἴσθησιν, αὕτη δ' ἐστὶ νοῦς (1143b5). "What is needed now is αἴσθησις, straightforward perception." In the deliberation

3. Susemihl, whose edition Heidegger cites, refers in his critical apparatus to the "*codices Victori*" for the reading ἐν τοῖς πρακτικοῖς. Victorius himself, however, in his edition of 1584 (*Petri Victorii commentarii in X libros Aristotelis De Moribus ad Nicomachum. Florentiae ex officina iunctarum 1584.*), has in the main text ἐν ταῖς πρακτικαῖς.

over the situation in which I am to act, I finally touch upon the straightforward grasping of the determinate states of affairs on hand, the determinate circumstances, and the determinate time. All deliberating ends in an αἴσθησις. This straightforward perceiving within φρόνησις is νοῦς. Aristotle explicates the character of this αἴσθησις in the same book of the *Nicomachean Ethics*, chapter 9.

b) Practical νοῦς and αἴσθησις (*Nic. Eth.* VI, 9, III, 5). Αἴσθησις as the grasping of the ἔσχατα. Comparison with ἀνάλυσις in geometry. Modes of αἴσθησις. Geometrical and practical αἴσθησις.

ὁ μὲν γὰρ νοῦς τῶν ὅρων, ὧν οὐκ ἔστιν λόγος, ἡ δὲ τοῦ ἐσχάτου, οὗ οὐκ ἔστιν ἐπιστήμη ἀλλ' αἴσθησις, οὐχ' ἡ τῶν ἰδίων, ἀλλ' οἵᾳ αἰσθανόμεθα ὅτι τὸ ἐν τοῖς μαθηματικοῖς ἔσχατον τρίγωνον· στήσεται γὰρ κἀκεῖ (*Nic. Eth.* VI, 9, 1142a25ff.). In φρόνησις, the states of affairs are grasped purely, as they show themselves. Such grasping is a matter of perception, αἴσθησις. This perception, however, does not relate to the specific objects of perceiving in the strictest sense, to the ἴδια of αἴσθησις. In Book II, chapter 6, of the *De Anima*, Aristotle explains what these ἴδια αἰσθητά are: λέγω δ' ἴδιον μὲν ὃ μὴ ἐνδέχεται ἑτέρᾳ αἰσθήσει αἰσθάνεσθαι καὶ περὶ ὃ μὴ ἐνδέχεται ἀπατηθῆναι (418a11f.). The ἴδια αἰσθητά are the objects that correspond respectively to seeing, hearing, smelling, etc. The ἴδιον of seeing is color, of hearing tone, etc. These ἴδια are ἀεὶ ἀληθῆ for the corresponding αἰσθήσεις. Aristotle distinguishes these ἴδια αἰσθητά from the κοινὰ αἰσθητά. The latter are κοινὰ πάσαις (a19), objects of perception which are common to all αἰσθήσεις, as, e.g., σχῆμα and μέγεθος, which can be perceived by various αἰσθήσεις.

Concerning now φρόνησις and the straightforward grasping of the ἔσχατον, where πρᾶξις intervenes, there it is a matter not of such an αἴσθησις, i.e., one which is τῶν ἰδίων, but of αἴσθησις in the broadest sense of the word, as it is commonly given in everyday existence. In αἴσθησις I see states of affairs as a whole, whole streets, houses, trees, people, and precisely in such a way that this αἴσθησις at the same time has the character of a simple constatation. It is a matter of an αἴσθησις such as the one with whose help we perceive ὅτι τὸ ἐν τοῖς μαθηματικοῖς ἔσχατον τρίγωνον (*Nic. Eth.* VI, 9, 1142a28f.), an αἴσθησις such as the one which, for example, plays a fundamental role in geometry, where it grasps the ἔσχατον of geometry: τρίγωνον. It must be noted here that in Greek geometry the triangle is the ultimate, most elementary plane figure, which emerges out of the polygon by means of a διαγράφειν, "writing through." Διαγράφειν analyzes the polygons until they are taken apart in simple triangles, in such a way that the triangles are the ἔσχατα where the διαιρεῖν stops. In αἴσθησις, as it occurs in geometry, I see the triangle at one stroke as the most original element, which cannot itself be resolved again into more elementary figures.

Just as in geometry an αἰσθάνεσθαι provides the ἔσχατον, so also in φρόνησις. It is essential thus that in this αἴσθησις something shows itself straightforwardly, purely and simply. Aristotle emphasizes that with this sort of coming to an end of the consideration, the deliberation στήσεται (a29), "stands still"; it goes no further. This αἴσθησις is here in φρόνησις, as in geometry, a stopping in which it is only and essentially a matter of putting oneself in opposition to something, allowing it to be encountered simply and purely. Such νοεῖν is a matter of a simple presentifying of something, so that it speaks purely out of itself and no longer requires discourse or a demonstration on our part. Here it can still be said: φαίνεται, the things show themselves in this way. The only possibility here is to look on and, in looking, to grasp.

Aristotle describes this nexus still more extensively in *Nicomachean Ethics* III, 5, 1112b11ff.[4] There he returns to the content of geometry, to the διάγραμμα. Aristotle proceeds from deliberation: one does not deliberate about the τέλος, but instead the τέλος is the object of a decision. The object of the deliberation is συμφέρον πρὸς τὸ τέλος, that which is pertinent to the correct bringing to an end of what has been decided. βουλευόμεθα δ' οὐ περὶ τῶν τελῶν ἀλλὰ περὶ τῶν πρὸς τὰ τέλη. οὔτε γὰρ ἰατρὸς βουλεύεται εἰ ὑγιάσει, οὔτε ῥήτωρ εἰ πείσει, οὔτε πολιτικὸς εἰ εὐνομίαν ποιήσει, οὐδὲ τῶν λοιπῶν οὐδεὶς περὶ τοῦ τέλους (b11ff.). A doctor does not deliberate about whether he is going to heal; on the contrary, that belongs to the meaning of his existence itself, because as a doctor he has already resolved in favor of healing. Just as little does the orator deliberate about whether he should convince; for that lies in the very sense of his existence. ἀλλὰ θέμενοι τέλος τι πῶς καὶ διὰ τίνων ἔσται σκοποῦσιν (b15f.). The τέλος is thus a τέλος τεθέν; the end is posited and held fast. In their deliberating the doctor or orator do not have this in view but instead the πῶς καὶ διὰ τίνων, the how and the ways and means. And they look around, in each case within the concrete situation of their acting, until ἕως ἂν ἔλθωσιν ἐπὶ τὸ πρῶτον αἴτιον, ὃ ἐν τῇ εὑρέσει ἔσχατον ἐστίν (b18ff.), until their consideration touches the first αἴτιον whence they can intervene, that which, in the uncovering of the whole state of affairs, is the outermost of the deliberation. ὁ γὰρ βουλευόμενος ἔοικεν ζητεῖν καὶ ἀναλύειν τὸν εἰρημένον τρόπον ὥσπερ διάγραμμα . . . , καὶ τὸ ἔσχατον ἐν τῇ ἀναλύσει πρῶτον εἶναι ἐν τῇ γενέσει (b20ff.). The ἔσχατον of the ἀνάλυσις is what

4. Cf. in addition 1113a2ff.

is first for ποίησις, i.e., where the ποίησις, the genuine becoming, begins. This passage in the *Nicomachean Ethics* is thus of importance because Aristotle does not speak there of ποίησις but explicitly of πρᾶξις in the strict sense.[5]

This αἴσθησις at which the deliberation comes to a standstill is a pre-eminent one. It must be distinguished from the αἴσθησις in mathematics. ἀλλ' αὕτη μᾶλλον αἴσθησις ἢ φρόνησις, ἐκείνης δὲ ἄλλο εἶδος (*Nic. Eth.* VI, 9, 1142a29f.). The geometrical αἴσθησις, in which I see the ultimate figural element, the triangle, is μᾶλλον αἴσθησις, more of pure perception, more of pure grasping than the αἴσθησις of φρόνησις. In geometry it is a sheer matter of pure onlooking and constatating. The αἴσθησις of φρόνησις has a different character. For φρόνησις is, in its very sense, still πρακτική, even in αἴσθησις. The αἴσθησις of φρόνησις is hence, as φρόνησις, related to the πρακτά. It is, specifically, an ultimate inspection of the states of affairs, but this inspection is in φρόνησις not a mere inspection but a circumspection. In other words, it is guided by the ὀρθότης and hence is directed to the τέλος, the εὐπραξία, so that the objects grasped in it have the character of the συμφέρον.

c) Φρόνησις and σοφία as opposite highest modes of ἀληθεύειν (= νοῦς). Ἀεί and the moment. Prospect: νοῦς and διαλέγεσθαι. Aristotle and Plato.

Φρόνησις has become visible in this fundamental structural moment, namely that in it there is accomplished something like a pure perceiving, one that no longer falls within the domain of λόγος. Insofar as this pure perceiving concerns the ἔσχατον, it is αἴσθησις. Insofar as this αἴσθησις, however, is not dedicated to the ἴδια but is nevertheless a simple perceiving, it is νοῦς. Therefore Aristotle can say: ἀντίκειται μὲν δὴ τῷ νῷ (1142a25); φρόνησις obviously resides opposite to νοῦς, provided νοῦς is understood as the νοῦς in σοφία, the one that aims at the ἀρχαί. Φρόνησις is, structurally, identical with σοφία; it is an ἀληθεύειν ἄνευ λόγου. That is what φρόνησις and σοφία have in common. But the pure grasping in the case of φρόνησις lies on the opposite side. We have here two possibilities of νοῦς: νοῦς in the most extreme concretion and νοῦς in the most extreme καθόλου, in the most general universality. The νοῦς of φρόνησις aims at the most extreme in the sense of the ἔσχατον pure and simple. Φρόνησις is the inspection of the this here now, the inspection of the concrete momentariness of the transient situation. As αἴσθησις, it is a look of an eye in the blink of an eye, a momentary look at what is momentarily concrete, which

5. Versus the corresponding analyses of ποίησις in *Met.* VII, 7, 1032bff. Cf. p. 108ff.

as such can always be otherwise. On the other hand, the νοεῖν in σοφία is a looking upon that which is ἀεί, that which is always present in sameness. Time (the momentary and the eternal) here functions to discriminate between the νοεῖν in φρόνησις and the one in σοφία. In this way it becomes clear that φρόνησις, as well as σοφία, on the basis of the fact that they both harbor νοεῖν, are possibilities in which beings, according to the basic modes of their Being, are ultimately disclosed and become graspable ἐπ' ἀμφότερα (*Nic. Eth.* VI, 12, 1143a35f.), "from both sides" up to their ἀρχαί. On the basis of their being related to the ἀρχαί, φρόνησις and σοφία are the highest possibilities of the disclosure of beings themselves. Insofar as they are modes of Dasein, they constitute its mode of Being: σοφία is Dasein's positionality toward the beings of the world in the full sense. Φρόνησις is Dasein's positionality toward the beings which are themselves Dasein. With this, however, the question arises precisely as to the meaning of Being which provides the guiding line, on the basis of which Aristotle reaches the point that he can attribute to σοφία a priority over φρόνησις.[6]

We have now clarified the phenomenon of ἀληθεύειν,[7] specifically as a possibility of human Dasein and as determining human Dasein in its Being. The goal of this reflection was to prepare us for the interpretation of a Platonic dialogue, to transpose us into the proper attitude to genuinely grasp the deliberation as it is carried out there and to sympathetically carry it out ourselves, step by step. Only if we acquire this attitude will we be guaranteed of seeing the things spoken of. A dialogue is carried out in διαλέγεσθαι. We will grasp more precisely how this διαλέγεσθαι, seen from the viewpoint of the maturity of Aristotle's philosophical reflections, proves to be a legitimate preliminary stage of philosophizing. In order to demonstrate this, we have to be conveyed ahead of time to a higher stage of philosophizing and understand the dialogue from that point of view, looking back down upon it. Already from this term, διαλέγεσθαι, you can see that what is at issue is λόγος. We will conclude our examination of ἀληθεύειν by bringing the highest and ultimate stage of ἀληθεύειν into connection with the question of the extent and accomplishment of λόγος within a theoretical consideration.

6. See the appendix.

7. Heidegger remarks here in his manuscript that in the meantime six sessions were canceled. (See the editor's epilogue, p. 456.) That is why he begins now with a reflection on the meaning of the Aristotle part of the lecture course.

§24. *The decision on the question of the priority of* φρόνησις *or* σοφία *in favor of* σοφία (Nic. Eth. *VI, 13).*

a) The difficulty of the decision: merits and deficiencies of φρόνησις and σοφία. The question of the relation to human Dasein. The autonomy and non-autonomy of the ἀληθεύειν.

We have reached the point of acknowledging φρόνησις as the mode of disclosure of a determinate being which has the character of being able to be otherwise, namely human Dasein. Φρόνησις has a double possibility for pure disclosure, i.e., for pure and simple perception: 1.) insofar as, in φρόνησις, the ἀγαθόν shows itself purely and simply, φαίνεται (1144a34), i.e., the ἀγαθόν in favor of which I decide in the προαίρεσις, and 2.) in φρόνησις the ἔσχατον of the deliberation shows itself in an αἴσθησις; in a momentary glance I survey the concrete situation of the action, out of which and in favor of which I resolve myself.

Thus, taken as a whole and, above all, seen in connection with the βουλεύεσθαι, φρόνησις proves to be that truth which is related to Dasein itself. One might suppose that, insofar as his own Being, his own existence, is of decisive importance for a man, that truth is the highest which relates to Dasein itself, and therefore φρόνησις is the highest and most decisive mode of disclosure. Yet Aristotle says that σοφία, pure understanding, is, with regard to its ἀληθεύειν (and insofar as ἀληθεύειν characterizes the Being of man), the highest possible mode of human existence. Now if φρόνησις is concerned with the Being of man, yet is not the highest possibility of disclosure, then the difficulty can only reside in this, that φρόνησις is not completely autonomous but instead remains related in its very structure to another mode of human comportment. In fact Aristotle shows that the ἀγαθόν manifests itself in φρόνησις only to an existence which is in itself good, ἀγαθόν. τοῦτο δ' εἰ μὴ τῷ ἀφαθῷ, οὐ φαίνεται (*Nic. Eth.* VI, 13, 1144a34). "The ἀγαθόν does not show itself except to the ἀγαθός." διαστρέφει γὰρ ἡ μοχθηρία καὶ διαψεύδεσθαι ποιεῖ περὶ τὰς πρακτικὰς ἀρχάς (a34f.). Evil disposition or a generally bad constitution can bring it about that the ἀγαθόν presents itself to Dasein as something it is not. ὥστε φανερὸν ὅτι ἀδύνατον φρόνιμον εἶναι μὴ ὄντα ἀγαθόν (a36f.). Hence only someone who is already ἀγαθός can be φρόνιμος. The possibility of the ἀληθεύειν of φρόνησις is bound up with the proviso that the one who carries it out is himself, in his Being, *already* ἀγαθός. Thus there appears, from this side as well, a peculiar appurtenance of φρόνησις to πρᾶξις. There pertains to πρᾶξις not only, as we have seen in the point of departure of our reflection, a certain orientation and guidance; it is not enough for πρᾶξις to be guided by circumspection, the sight of φρόνησις. For it is clear that this sight, the anticipation of the ἀγαθόν, as the mode of carrying out the disclosure, is only possible in an ἀγαθός. Φρόνησις is nothing if it is not carried out in πρᾶξις, and πρᾶξις as such is determined by ἀρετή, by the πρακτόν as ἀγαθόν. Merely possessing the τέλος of an action, merely having φρόνησις at our disposal, does not yet make us πρακτικώτεροι; we are not thereby led to act better morally if we are not already good. εἴπερ ἡ μὲν φρόνησίς ἐστιν περὶ τὰ δίκαια καὶ καλὰ καὶ ἀγαθὰ ἀνθρώπῳ, ταῦτα δ' ἐστὶν ἃ τοῦ ἀγαθοῦ ἐστιν ἀνδρὸς πράττειν, οὐθὲν δὲ πρακτικώτεροι τῷ εἰδέναι αὐτά ἐσμεν, εἴπερ ἕξεις αἱ ἀρεταί εἰσιν (1143b21ff.). The mere self-standing ἀληθεύειν of φρόνησις has no effect on action unless this φρόνησις is carried out by someone who is himself ἀγαθός. Just as οὐθὲν πρακτικώτεροι τῷ ἔχειν τὴν ἰατρικήν ἐσμεν (cf. b26ff.). Just as little as we become more able to act and to intervene just by mastering ἰατρική, just by possessing the art of healing purely theoretically, i.e., if we have not actually learned how to use it by becoming doctors ourselves. The mere having of the orientation and guidance does not place us on the level of Being which genuinely corresponds to the meaning of ἀληθεύειν. Insofar as φρόνησις, with regard to the possibility of its correct execution, depends on being carried out by an ἀγαθός, it is not itself autonomous. Thereby the priority of φρόνησις is shaken, although φρόνησις does indeed relate to human Dasein.

On the other hand, the question still remains: how can σοφία be the highest possibility, since it does not have to do with human Dasein? ἡ μὲν γὰρ σοφία οὐθὲν θεωρεῖ ἐξ ὧν ἔσται εὐδαίμων ἄνθρωπος (οὐδεμιᾶς γάρ ἐστιν γενέσεως) (b18ff.). Σοφία is indeed autonomous but what is thematic in it is the ἀεί, hence that which has nothing at all to do with γένεσις, whereas the Being of human Dasein intrinsically involves γένεσις, πρᾶξις, κίνησις. The pure understanding of the philosopher does not consider whence man could properly come into being. What philosophy considers, according to its very meaning, settles nothing for human existence. This assertion already shows that Aristotle is as far removed as possible from a religious world-view or the like. Thus the following difficulty results:

1.) φρόνησις specifically concerns human Dasein; but because it is dependent on the Being of man as ἀγαθός, it is not autonomous.

2.) On the other hand, σοφία is indeed autonomous, insofar as it is purely concerned with the ἀρχαί; but because it is concerned precisely with the ἀεί, it does not settle anything as regards human Dasein.

At bottom the difficulty consists in this, that both, φρόνησις and σοφία, are not ἕξεις.

This now requires a solution. Aristotle himself solves the difficulty at 1141a1ff.

b) Criteria for the decision. The rank of the ἀληθεύειν as such. The autonomy of the "accomplishment" (ποιεῖν); σοφία as ὑγίεια of the ψυχή. Ontological priority according to the Greek concept of Being.

To understand this important decision with regard to the priority of σοφία over φρόνησις, we must keep in mind that Aristotle transfers the discussion of this entire question back to a purely ontological level. πρῶτον μὲν οὖν λέγομεν ὅτι καθ' αὑτὰς ἀναγκαῖον αἱρετὰς αὐτὰς εἶναι, ἀρετάς γ' οὔσας ἑκατέραν ἑκατέρου τοῦ μορίου, καὶ εἰ μὴ ποιοῦσι μηδὲν μηδετέρα αὐτῶν (1144a1ff.). Aristotle is saying, first of all, that the question about which of the two modes is more decisive is inappropriate as long as we do not consider these modes of Being precisely as modes of Being. As long as we interrogate the ἀρετή only in terms of what it provides and what it can be used for (ποιεῖ), we have not yet arrived at the appropriate question. The appropriate question is whether the mode of Being of the respective ἀληθεύειν is higher or lower. Even if neither of these two could accomplish anything, the question of the genuine character of their ἀρετή would still be necessary. For the ἀρετή is something like a τελείωσις; it is that which brings some being to itself in its most proper Being.[1] In this way, Aristotle places the whole discussion within a purely theoretical consideration.

ἔπειτα καὶ ποιοῦσι μέν (1144a3f.). In that case, however, the same consideration of beings in themselves discovers that φρόνησις and σοφία in fact accomplish something, ποιεῖν, whereby ποιεῖν means to bring out, deliver, bring into being. Precisely this ποιεῖν of φρόνησις and σοφία, seen more closely, provides the foundation for the delimitation and higher position of σοφία over φρόνησις. This ποιεῖν will decide the ontological priority of σοφία.[2] For the principle is: ἡ γὰρ ποιοῦσα ἄρχει καὶ ἐπιτάττει περὶ ἕκαστον (1143b35). "That possibility of human Dasein which in itself ποιεῖ, accomplishes something (which accomplishes something more properly than another one does), dominates and guides all others." Accordingly, if this principle is to be applied here, we must be attentive to discover in σοφία still, in spite of everything we have presented about it hitherto, a ποίησις. Now, Aristotle says that the philosopher's pure considering in fact delivers something, ποιεῖ, and specifically τῷ ἔχεσθαι καὶ τῷ ἐνεργεῖν (cf. 1144a6), "by the very fact of having it and carrying it out," hence not by results but simply by the fact that I live in this θεωρεῖν. This uncovering as such accomplishes something. Aristotle proposes a comparison which can

1. Cf. *Met.* V, 16, 1021b20ff.

2. Heidegger delivered the following comments (up to page 118) extemporaneously. There are only very few indicating remarks in the manuscript. The editor could but rely on the transcripts of H. Jonas, F. Schalk, and H. Weiß.

be understood only if the ground of this comparison is secured in advance. He compares philosophy's theoretical considerations with health: καὶ ποιοῦσι μέν, οὐχ ὡς ἡ ἰατρικὴ δὲ ὑγίειαν, ἀλλ' ὡς ἡ ὑγίεια, οὕτως ἡ σοφία εὐδαιμονίαν (a3ff.). Aristotle is here comparing σοφία with ὑγίεια and φρόνησις with ἰατρική.

ὑγίεια	—	σοφία
ἰατρική	—	φρόνησις

In order to understand the ground of this comparison, we need to consider the example of a man who is a doctor. If a doctor who is sick heals himself on the basis of the knowledge he has as a doctor, then that is a peculiar way to take care of his own Dasein by himself, to make his own Dasein healthy once again. A higher way of being healthy, however, is health itself. The healthy man does not at all need to be skilled in medicine in order to be healthy. He is healthy without further ado, i.e., he is simply what he is. Health is itself a mode of Being which keeps a man in the proper state of his bodily Being. Now the same applies to φρόνησις and σοφία. Φρόνησις leads and guides all human acting, but it is still dependent on something else, namely the action itself. But the θεωρεῖν of σοφία, on the contrary, does not, as is the case with ἰατρική, have a further goal; instead, it is carried out purely as such by the man who lives in it. Θεωρεῖν is a mode of Being in which man attains his highest mode of Being, his proper spiritual health.

There still remains a lacuna, however, in the understanding of the priority of σοφία, although we already understand that σοφία in a certain sense accomplishes something immediately, simply by the fact that it is there, whereas φρόνησις accomplishes something with regard to something other than itself. This structure is clear. Nevertheless, we cannot yet understand to what extent σοφία can be compared to human health, i.e., to what extent the comportment which is nothing but the disclosure of the everlasting constitutes the proper Being of man. We can come to understand it only on the basis of the meaning of the Greek concept of Being. Because precisely that to which σοφία is related is everlasting, and because σοφία is the purest way of comportment to, and of tarrying with, the everlasting, therefore σοφία, as a genuine positionality toward this highest mode of Being, is the highest possibility. The decision on the priority of σοφία is therefore made ultimately on the basis of that to which it relates. Ἐπιστήμη is excluded here since it cannot disclose the ἀρχαί but instead presupposes them. The constant tarrying with what is everlasting is the accomplishment of pure νοεῖν, which Aristotle also compares to αἴσθησις.[3] In this manner we gain

3. Cf. p. 110ff.

a prospect into the basic conception of human Dasein which served as a guideline for Aristotle: human Dasein is properly attained only if it always is what it can be in the highest sense, i.e., when it tarries in the highest degree, as long as possible, and most nearly always, in the pure pondering of what is everlasting. Yet insofar as man is mortal, and insofar as he needs recreation and relaxation in the widest sense, the constant tarrying with what is everlasting, the ultimately appropriate comportment to what always is, is denied him.

We want to conclude our consideration of σοφία by presentifying the same phenomenon as seen from the opposite side. Though σοφία is the highest mode of ἀληθεύειν, it is, on the other hand, still a ἕξις τῆς ψυχῆς, i.e., a ἕξις of the Being of man, and then the question arises as to what extent the possibility of human εὐδαιμονία resides in σοφία. The task is therefore to conceive σοφία and its ἀληθεύειν as a mode of Being of human Dasein. Since for Aristotle σοφία is the highest possibility of human Dasein, he must also see in it εὐδαιμονία.

§25. The priority of σοφία *with regard to* εὐδαιμονία *(*Nic. Eth.* X, 6–7).*

a) The idea of εὐδαιμονία (*Nic. Eth.* X, 6). The ontological meaning of εὐδαιμονία as the fulfilled Being of the ψυχή.

Aristotle takes εὐδαιμονία in a strictly ontological sense, as τέλος. This ontological meaning of εὐδαιμονία must be kept in mind. λοιπὸν περὶ εὐδαιμονίας τύπῳ διελθεῖν, ἐπειδὴ τέλος αὐτὴν τίθεμεν τῶν ἀνθρωπίνων (1176a31ff.). "Of those things that touch the Being of man, we name that which constitutes its finished state εὐδαιμονία." It constitutes the proper Being of human Dasein. This Being amounts to nothing else than presence, pure being present to that which always is. Now εὐδαιμονία, insofar as it constitutes the completeness of this Being, cannot be a mere ἕξις, i.e., a mere possibility at man's disposal, without any opportunity to be actualized. For in that case it could also pertain to somebody who sleeps his whole life away, who lives the life of a plant. Formulated differently, it cannot be an optional capacity which sometimes is awake and sometimes sleeps. On the contrary, εὐδαιμονία, insofar as it concerns the Being of man as its finished state, as the proper Being of man's highest ontological possibilities, must be a Being of man which is at every moment, constantly, what it is. It does not concern a mere possibility of Being but is this possibility in its presence, ἐνέργεια. μᾶλλον εἰς ἐνέργειάν τινα θετέον (1176b1). Accordingly, εὐδαιμονία, as man's proper Being, must be reduced to ἐνέργεια. Ἐνέργεια means nothing else than presence, pure immediate presence at hand. τῶν δ' ἐνεργειῶν αἳ μέν εἰσιν ἀναγκαῖαι καὶ δι' ἕτερα αἱρεταὶ αἳ δὲ καθ' αὑτάς (b2f.). "Of the ἐνέργειαι, some are δι' ἕτερα, because of something else, oriented toward something else, and others are καθ' αὑτάς αἱρεταί, graspable for themselves. καθ' αὑτὰς δ' εἰσὶν αἱρεταὶ ἀφ' ὧν μηδὲν ἐπιζητεῖται παρὰ τὴν ἐνέργειαν (b6f.). "Graspable for themselves are those modes of ἐνέργεια of a living being, those modes of pure presence and pure being at hand, from which nothing additional is pursued and nothing is sought besides the pure and simple presence." Now insofar as εὐδαιμονία is the τέλος, it cannot be an ἐνέργεια which is δι' ἕτερα, oriented toward something else, but can only be an ἐνέργεια which is graspable καθ' αὑτήν. In this way, εὐδαιμονία is complete in itself and is self-sufficient, αὐτάρκης. οὐδενὸς γὰρ ἐνδεὴς ἡ εὐδαιμονία ἀλλ' αὐτάρκης (b5f.). Hence that which constitutes εὐδαιμονία is οὐκ ἐνδεής, not in need of anything else.

Now there are in human Dasein various possibilities of acting which are related among themselves and which have a hierarchy. Εὐδαιμονία, as τέλος pure and simple, is in the purest sense the autonomous presence at hand of the living being in the world. It is the pure presence of the living being with regard to its ultimately actualized possibility of Being. ψυχῆς ἐνέργειά τις κατ' ἀρετὴν τελείαν (*Nic. Eth.* I, 13, 1102a5f.). Therein resides an elevation of the τέλος-character. Κατ' ἀρετὴν τελείαν means properly κατὰ τελείωσιν τελείαν; for the expression ἀρετή already contains the determination of the τελείωσις. Εὐδαιμονία is thus the presence of the finished state of the living being with regard to its highest possibility of Being. It is the τελείωσις of the Being of the being as Being-in.[1]

On the basis of this idea of εὐδαιμονία, Aristotle now (*Nic. Eth.* X, 7) determines the structure of εὐδαιμονία more concretely from seven points of view.

b) The structural moments of εὐδαιμονία and their fulfillment through the θεωρεῖν of σοφία (νοῦς) (*Nic. Eth.* X, 7).

That which brings Dasein into its own most proper Being must:

1.) be the κρατίστη ἕξις (cf. 1177a13), that mode of Being in which man most properly has at his disposal that which he can be. This highest determination of Being is νοῦς.

2.) This highest ontological determination in us, ἐν ἡμῖν, namely νοῦς, the pure ability to perceive beings as such, is related to the γνωστά, with

1. Thus in Heidegger's manuscript.

which I become familiar in pure onlooking; and specifically it is related to a being which is itself κράτιστον, everlasting. καὶ γὰρ ὁ νοῦς <τὸ κράτιστον> τῶν ἐν ἡμιν, καὶ <τὰ κράτιστα> τῶν γνωστῶν, περὶ ἃ ὁ νοῦς (1177a20).

3.) This mode of Being, which satisfies εὐδαιμονία, is συνεχεστάτη (a21), that which most of all coheres in itself, that which is more unbroken than anything else. θεωρεῖν τε γὰρ δυνάμεθα συνεχῶς μᾶλλον ἢ πράτειν ὁτιοῦν (a21f.). Our human mode of Being entails that we are able to live more unbrokenly in the mode of pure onlooking than in the mode of acting. For action, in its very sense, is in each case different: according to circumstances, time, people. The constancy of acting, in the extension of a determined nexus of life, is continually interrupted by new commitments, each of which requires a decision. On the other hand, pure onlooking is in itself a uniform unbroken perseverance, which in its very sense cannot be otherwise. For it is an abiding with beings which in themselves cannot be otherwise. Whereas the beings of πρᾶξις can be different in each case and require a decision at every new moment, the pure considering of what is everlasting perseveres, as it were, in an enduring now. This third moment, the συνεχέστατον, is attributed to the comportment we know as the θεωρεῖν of σοφία.

4.) This θεωρεῖν of σοφία is that ἐνέργεια which is ἡδίστη (a2). Aristotle justifies this assertion in the following way: οἰόμεθά τε δεῖν ἡδονὴν παραμεμῖχθαι τῇ εὐδαιμονίᾳ (a22f.). We believe that in the most proper Being of man there is also mixed a corresponding humor, an affective disposition, namely ἡδονή, enjoyment. It is in general constitutive of the Being of a living being to be disposed in this or that way in relation to that with which and for which the living being exists. This basic constitution, which belongs to life, may not be lacking on the highest level of Being of a living being. The question is which mode of Being confers the purest ἡδονή. ἡδίστη δὲ τῶν κατ'ἀρετὴν ἐνεργειῶν ἡ κατὰ τὴν σοφίαν ὁμολογουμένως ἐστίν (a23f.). Everyone agrees that the purest joy comes from being present to beings κατὰ τὴν σοφίαν, i.e., from pure onlooking. This pure abiding-with, pure presence-to, is in itself the purest disposition in the broadest sense. The purity and stability of this disposition belonging to pure onlooking is again understandable only on the basis of what is thematic in the onlooking, namely what always is. It is not in the least possible for what is everlasting to admit a disturbance, a change, or a confusion in the self-comportment of man as a researcher. Thus it cannot destroy man's disposition from the root up. Man remains, insofar as he attends to this object, in the same disposition. Therefore the abiding with what always is contains the possibility of διαγωγή, the possibility of a pure tarrying, which has nothing of the unrest of seeking. Seeking, for the Greeks, seeks the disclosure of the concealed, of the λανθάνον. Seeking is not yet being in the presence of the unconcealed, whereas the pure tarrying of knowledge, of seeing, of having in view, is an abiding with a being in its unconcealedness. Therefore Aristotle can say of the ancients, insofar as they were genuine philosophers: φιλοσοφήσαντες περὶ τῆς ἀληθείας (*Met.* I, 3, 983b2f.), "they philosophized about truth." This does not mean they philosophized about the concept of truth or the like, but rather that they were friends of the truth, they had decided in favor of the pure disclosure of Being in its unconcealedness.

5.) The fifth moment which is attributed to εὐδαιμονία and which fulfills the θεωρία of σοφία is the αὐτάρκεια, that comportment of man which is dependent only on itself. ἥ τε λεγομένη αὐτάρκεια περὶ τὴν θεωρητικὴν μάλιστ' ἂν εἴη (*Nic. Eth.* X, 7, 1177a27f.) Aristotle emphasizes: τῶν μὲν πρὸς τὸ ζῆν ἀναγκαίων καὶ σοφὸς καὶ δίκαιος καὶ οἱ λοιποὶ δέονται (cf. a28f.). The philosopher, exactly as is the case with every man, requires the necessities of life. He cannot detach himself from them; he can exist only insofar as they are at his disposal. ὁ μὲν δίκαιος δεῖται πρὸς οὓς δικαιοπραγήσει καὶ μεθ' ὧν (a30f.). In addition, "the one who, as judge, wants to act justly needs other people, toward whom and with whom he can act justly." The same applies to one who wants to be prudent, σώφρων, or courageous, ἀνδρεῖος. Not only these, but all possibilities of Being with regard to the πρᾶξις of prephilosophical man are dependent, in their very sense, on being with others. Therefore they cannot be man's proper possibilities of Being, and this is so although they are in each case an ἀγαθὸν καθ' αὑτὸ αἱρετόν. But now our concern is precisely the proper Being and presence of life. We are asking about the radically and ontologically grasped most proper Being, which is itself the ontological basis for the factual concrete existence of man. Thus whereas the possibilities of Being with regard to πρᾶξις are dependent on being with others, the pure onlooking upon what always is is free of this bond. ὁ δὲ σοφὸς καὶ καθ' αὑτὸν ὢν δύναται θεωρεῖν, καὶ ὅσῳ ἂν σοφώτερος ᾖ, μᾶλλον (a32f.). The philosopher, who is concerned purely and exclusively with understanding and disclosing beings, can be who he is only if and precisely if he is καθ' αὑτὸν ὤν, alone with himself. And the more he is with himself and strives only to disclose, the less he is in need of others. βέλτιον δ' ἴσως συνεργοὺς ἔχων, ἀλλ' ὅμως αὐταρκέστατος (a34f.). Perhaps, to be sure, it is still better if he has companions who strive along with him, ones who work with him and who persevere in this attitude with him. But even then he is what he is only if in each case he by himself sees things as they are. Nobody can see things on behalf of someone else, and no one can have things present on account of some other person's disclosure of them. Pure seeing is a matter of the single individual, although precisely he who sees for himself, if he sees the same things as the others, is with the others, in the mode of συμφιλοσοφεῖν, philosophizing together.

6.) Thus the mode of Being of pure onlooking is the only one which can be loved for its own sake. δόξαι τ' ἂν αὐτὴ μόνη δι' αὐτὴν ἀγαπᾶσθαι· οὐδὲν γάρ ἀπ' αὐτῆς γίνεται παρὰ τὸ θεωρῆσαι, ἀπὸ δὲ τῶν πρακτικῶν ἢ πλεῖον ἢ ἔλαττον περιποιούμεθα παρὰ τὴν πρᾶξιν (b1ff.). For in this mode of Being of pure onlooking we do not produce anything else, and we do not look about for anything else, as we do in πρᾶξις, where there is always something else at stake. Hence this mode of Being is then characterized by the fact that it ἐν τῇ σχολῇ ἐστιν (cf. b4), "it is in leisure," i.e., in pure tarrying and in genuine presence-to.

7.) This mode of human Dasein is a genuine one only if it λαβοῦσα μῆκος βίου τέλειον (b24): ἡ τελεία δὴ εὐδαιμονία αὕτη ἂν εἴη ἀνθρώπου, λαβοῦσα μῆκος βίου τέλειον (b24f.). It is a genuine one only "if it has been taken up in a complete course of life," i.e., only if it in fact extends over the whole duration of a human existence, hence only if this mode of comportment does not merely determine human existence occasionally but is continuously carried on as the proper one. For what always is, which is thematic in this comportment, is constantly predelineated in such a way that even the presence of Dasein to it is determined as constant and persevering. Herein resides the peculiar tendency of the accommodation of the temporality of human Dasein to the eternity of the world. The abiding with what is eternal, θεωρεῖν, is not supposed to be arbitrary and occasional but is to be maintained uninterruptedly throughout the duration of life. Therein resides for man a certain possibility of ἀθανατίζειν (1177b33), a mode of Being of man in which he has the highest possibility of not coming to an end. This is the extreme position to which the Greeks carried human Dasein.

Only from this point of view, from the wholly determined and clear domination of the meaning of Being as eternal Being, does the priority of σοφία become understandable. Now it is clear why the pure onlooking settles something for the existence of man and why it is the highest in the Greek sense. Our understanding of the ultimate meaning of human existence for the Greeks depends on our seeing how an ethical consideration was for them from the very outset outside of the points of view we know today from traditional philosophies. For the Greeks the consideration of human existence was oriented purely toward the meaning of Being itself, i.e., toward the extent to which it is possible for human Dasein to be everlasting. The Greeks gathered this meaning of Being, Being as absolute presence, from the Being of the world. Accordingly, one cannot force Greek ethics into the mode of questioning of modern ethics, i.e., into the alternatives of an ethics of consequences or an ethics of intentions. Dasein was simply seen there with regard to its possibility of Being as such, whereby neither intentions nor practical consequences play any role. Even the expression ἦθος corresponds to this conception of the Being of man; ἦθος means comportment, the proper way of Being. If one keeps in mind this point of view, this primarily ontological questioning, one can understand the peculiar fact that σοφία may be compared with ὑγίεια, health. This idea of the Being of man determines in advance the meaning of εὐδαιμονία, which Aristotle defines as ψυχῆς ἐνέργεια κατ' ἀρετὴν τελείαν. The ψυχή is what is proper to a being which is alive. This being that lives is in εὐδαιμονία insofar as it is simply present at hand with regard to its highest possibility of Being. This highest possibility of Being of the living being called man is νοῦς. Νοεῖν, as ἐνέργεια θεωρετική, most satisfies the ἐνέργεια of this living being, its pure simple presence. To this extent, νοεῖν most properly satisfies εὐδαιμονία. Therefore human life in its most proper Being consists in νοῦς. This most proper Being is grasped in a radically ontological way so that it is as such the ontological condition of the factual concrete existence of man.

We must still gain more clarity on the relation νοῦς has to λόγος.

§26. Extent and limit of λόγος.

a) Λόγος and νοῦς. Νοεῖν and διανοεῖν. The grasping of the πρῶτα and ἔσχατα by νοεῖν.

Νοῦς is the highest determination of man, such that it must even be understood as divine; life in νοῦς is a θεῖον (b30f.). Nevertheless, human comportment moves for the most part, and especially at first, not in pure νοεῖν but in διανοεῖν. Because the Being of man is determined as ζῷον λόγον ἔχον, because man speaks, and discourses about the things he sees, pure perceiving is always a discussing. Pure νοεῖν is carried out as θιγεῖν.[1,2] The νοεῖν carried out within a being that has λόγος is a διανοεῖν. In this way there exists a διαφορά between pure νοῦς and νοῦς σύνθετος (cf. b28f.): the νοῦς of man is always carried out in the mode of speaking. The νοῦς of man is not the proper one but is ὁ καλούμενος νοῦς.[3] It must be kept in mind that λόγος is intrinsic to the Being of man and that at first and for the most part discernment is carried out in λόγος: discerning is νοεῖν μετὰ λόγου. And so we find the justification of Aristotle's characterization of the modes of ἀληθεύειν we have spoken of, namely ἐπιστήμη, τέχνη, φρόνησις,

1. Reading θιγεῖν for τιγεῖν, an obvious misprint.—Trans.
2. *Met.* IX, 10, 1051b24.
3. *De An.* III, 9, 432b27.

and σοφία, as ἕξεις μετὰ λόγου.[4] Thorough looking, διανοεῖν, is a speaking, λέγειν. Admittedly, this discernment, insofar as it is to grasp the ἀρχή, must leave λόγος behind. It has to be ἄνευ λόγου in order to have the possibility of grasping an ἀδιαίρετον. The character of λέγειν is indeed to speak of something as something. But what is utterly simple, ἁπλοῦν, is what can no longer be spoken of as something else. Everything ἔσχατον and everything πρῶτον can be grasped properly only if the νοεῖν is not a διανοεῖν but a pure onlooking. Here the disclosure in the mode of the carrying out of λόγος fails and recedes.

That λόγος can recede here is a fact grounded in λόγος itself. For λόγος as λόγος, according to its very sense, is *not* already ordered toward ἀληθεύειν, toward the disclosure of beings, toward truth. Speaking as such does not primarily have the meaning of ἀποφαίνεσθαι, letting beings be seen. On the contrary, only a quite specific λόγος is λόγος ἀποφαντικός. This fundamental state of affairs must be kept in mind in order to understand the basic sense we have to make out of the Greek concept of truth.

b) Λόγος and ἀλήθεια.

α) Λόγος σημαντικός (speech) and λόγος ἀποφαντικός ("judgment") (*De Int.*, chapter 4; *De An.* II, 8).

Hence it is not intrinsic to λόγος to be true, to uncover beings, ἀληθεύειν. Not every λόγος is ἀποφαντικός. But indeed every λόγος is σημαντικός. Aristotle treats this in *De Interpretatione,* chapter 4: ἔστι δὲ λόγος ἅπας μὲν σημαντικός, . . . ἀποφαντικὸς δὲ οὐ πᾶς, ἀλλ' ἐν ᾧ τὸ ἀληθεύειν ἢ ψεύδεσθαι ὑπάρχει (16b33ff.). All speech is as speech σημαντική; σημαίνειν means "to signify." Thus all speech means something, it is understandable. All speech has in itself a ἑρμηνεία, a comprehensibility, as Aristotle shows in the *De Anima.*[5] But to mean something in this way and at the same time to let the thing meant show itself in this meaning, ἀποφαίνεσθαι—that does not occur in all speech. On the contrary, speaking, which is in its very sense σημαντική, becomes ἀποφαντική only if there is present in it either a disclosing, ἀληθεύειν, *or* a distorting, ψεύδεσθαι. For not only to disclose but also to distort is to let be seen, even if disclosing is the proper letting be seen. Hence not all speech contains either ἀληθεύειν or ψεύδεσθαι. Therefore speech, in its very sense, is at first neither true nor false. οὐκ ἐν ἅπασι δὲ ὑπαρχει, οἷον ἡ εὐχὴ λόγος μέν, ἀλλ' οὔτ' ἀληθὴς οὔτε ψευδής (17a3f.). A request, e.g., is neither true nor false. This must be understood in the Greek sense: a request, as a request, does not at first have the sense of letting be seen that which is

4. *Nic. Eth.* VI, 6, 1140b31ff. Cf. p. 40.
5. *De An.* II, 8, 420b5ff. Cf. p. 12f.

requested. Aristotle indicates that the manifold types of speaking which are to be sure comprehensible, i.e., which communicate something and provide an orientation but yet do not let anything be seen, belong to rhetoric and poetry. ῥητορικῆς γὰρ ἢ ποιητικῆς οἰκειοτέρα ἡ σκέψις,—ὁ δὲ ἀποφαντικὸς τῆς νῦν θεωρίας (a5ff.). The λόγος ἀποφαντικός, on the other hand, is the object of the current investigation.

Aristotle says, as we know, that λόγος, speech, is ἀποφαντικός, i.e., it lets something be seen, if a disclosure, ἀληθεύειν, is present in it. Traditional logic, precisely in its appeal to this analysis, had allowed itself to be led astray into a fundamental misunderstanding insofar as it maintained that for Aristotle judgment is the proper bearer of truth. Then, when closer study found investigations in which Aristotle speaks about truth and yet not about judgment, his concept of truth was said to be contradictory.

On the basis of what we have clarified, we want to gain a fundamental understanding of the relation between λόγος and ἀλήθεια. Already now it is clear that Aristotle is not at all primarily referring to judgment but to speech and that speech can show something, be ἀποφαντικός, only if there occurs in it ἀληθεύειν, true disclosure. Speech is not the primary and unique bearer of the ἀληθές; it is something in which the ἀληθές can occur but does not have to occur. Λόγος is not the place where ἀληθεύειν is at home, where it is autochthonous.

β) Rejection of λόγος as the proper place of truth. Νοεῖν as ἀληθεύειν without λόγος. The λόγος ἀποφαντικός as the place of ψεῦδος. The synthetic structure of the λόγος ἀποφαντικός as the condition of ψεῦδος.

Λόγος, insofar as it possesses the structure of ἀποφαίνεσθαι, of the "something as something," is so little the place of truth that it is, rather, quite the reverse, the proper condition of the possibility of falsity. That is, because this λόγος is a showing which lets that about which it speaks be seen *as something*, there remains the possibility that the thing might get distorted through the "as" and that deception would arise. Something can be distorted only if it is grasped in terms of something else. Only when ἀληθεύειν is carried out in the mode of the "as something," only when the "as" is structurally present, can it occur that something is presented as that which it is not. In simple disclosing, in αἴσθησις as in νοεῖν, there is no longer a λέγειν, an addressing of something as something. Therefore no deception is possible there either.

Aristotle now determines more precisely the structure by which λόγος is disclosive: if we remain with κατάφασις—"That is so"—then in this emergence of speech the whole is given without anything standing out in relief. Κατάφασις, insofar as it is a λέγειν τι κατά τινος, implies that the καθ' οὗ λέγεταί τι, that in relation to which something is said, is already present at the very outset and at the very outset is already objectified without anything standing out in relief. Λόγος—e.g., "The table is black"—is carried out in such a way that at the very outset I have in view the whole without anything standing out in relief: black table, a ἕν, an ὄν. Now if this table is to be disclosed as such, if a speaking about it is to let it be seen explicitly, then that will be carried out in an asserting-as. And this asserting-as is carried out for its part in the following way: I have in view the whole table and I articulate what I thus see: table—black; the νοήματα, the perceived, namely table and black, are set in relief and the one attributed to the other: the table as black. This λόγος contains a σύνθεσις of νοήματα, a certain co-positing, a positing together of what is discerned. σύνθεσίς τις ἤδη νοημάτων ὥσπερ ἓν ὄντων (*De An.* III, 6, 430a27f.). I posit the one together with the other, "as if they were one." I posit table together with black, so that they are seen as one. For I already have this one in view at the very outset. But speaking about it first makes what is seen properly visible to me, the table explicitly as black. The pregiven is set in relief in the "as" in such a way that precisely in going through the articulation which breaks it open it is understood and seen as one. The grasping, in the sense of the letting something be seen by means of λόγος, thus has the structure of σύνθεσις. And only where there is such a σύνθεσις, only where the character of the "as" occurs, is there falsity. The distorting of something is possible only in this way, that something else (grey) which presumably could show the being (the table) is posited in place of it. Hence the possibility of distortion requires necessarily a setting in relief, i.e., a co-positing, of something. Falsity, i.e., to assert something as what it is not, occurs only where there is a σύνθεσις. τὸ γὰρ ψεῦδος ἐν συνθέσει ἀεί· καὶ γὰρ ἂν τὸ λευκὸν μὴ λευκόν, τὸ μὴ λευκὸν συνέθηκεν (430b1ff.). "Deception occurs only where there is a σύνθεσις; for even if I speak of the white as not-white, the not-white is thereby co-posited," seen by me together with what is spoken of. One might think that it is a separating that resides in the μή. But, on the contrary, the asserting of the λευκόν as μὴ λευκόν entails precisely a σύνθεσις. Even the presenting of something as what it is *not* includes structurally a σύν, the co-discerning of the one νόημα together with the other, as ἕν.

These phenomenal states of affairs must be kept in mind in order to understand the nonsense rampant in the traditional treatment of λόγος.

γ) Critique of the traditional theory of judgment. Σύνθεσις and διαίρεσις as basic structures of the λόγος ἀποφαντικός in general.

It is commonly said that Aristotle divides judgments into the positive and the negative, into κατάφασις and ἀπόφασις. Affirmation would be the connecting of two representations, σύνθεσις; denial would be their separation, διαίρεσις. The connection and separation of representations are taken to be the respective structures of positive and negative judgments. This is a complete perversion of what Aristotle, in keeping with the phenomena, says. Both κατάφασις and ἀπόφασις have the character of σύνθεσις, and both have the character of διαίρεσις. Σύνθεσις and διαίρεσις are original structures, which, as founding, precede κατάφασις and ἀπόφασις. ἐτι πᾶν τὸ διανοητὸν καὶ νοητὸν ἡ διάνοια ἢ κατάφησιν ἢ ἀπόφησιν· . . . ὅταν μὲν ὡδὶ συνθῇ φᾶσα ἢ ἀποφᾶσα, ἀληθεύει, ὅταν δὲ ὡδί, ψεύδεται (*Met.* IV, 7, 1012a2ff.). "Everything that is the theme of a discerning and a thorough discerning is discerned or perceived by thinking in the mode of affirmation or denial. If thinking puts together what is discerned in one way, affirming or denying (i.e., positing and discerning as νοῦς—and precisely here it becomes clear that κατάφασις *and* ἀπόφασις are ordered into σύνθεσις) then the thinking is true, then it uncovers; if it puts together in another way, then it is false, then it distorts." I cite this passage to confront a common mistake in logic and in the interpretation of Aristotle. It is said that affirmation is σύνθεσις, connecting; denial is διαίρεσις, separating. The quotation above, however, says that both, κατάφασις and ἀπόφασις, letting be seen in affirmation *and* in denial, are σύνθεσις. And this applies not only when the κατάφασις and ἀπόφασις are true but also when they are false. τὸ γὰρ ψεῦδος ἐν συνθέσει ἀεί. καὶ γὰρ ἂν τὸ λευκὸν μὴ λευκόν, τὸ μὴ λευκὸν συνέθηκεν (*De An.* III, 6, 30b1ff.). There is falsity only where there is a σύνθεσις. For even if I speak of what is white as not white, the not white is put together with the white. Every affirmation or denial, whether true or false, is hence at the very outset a σύνθεσις.

And, conversely, both, affirmation and denial, κατάφασις and ἀπόφασις, letting be seen in affirmation and denial, are at the very outset διαίρεσις as well. Aristotle says this with reference to ψεῦδος in the continuation of the passage cited from the *De anima:* ἐνδέχεται δὲ καὶ διαίρεσιν φάναι πάντα (b3f.). Affirmation and denial are likewise to be interpreted as διαίρεσις, taking apart. Taking apart is indeed a mode of carrying out perception, a mode of carrying out νοεῖν, i.e., having the ὄν in view, having the whole in view; it is a preserving letting the whole be seen, a positing of a one with an other.

Σύνθεσις *and* διαίρεσις constitute the full mode of carrying out νοεῖν, and νοεῖν itself, insofar as it is the νοεῖν of the λόγον ἔχον, can be κατάφασις or ἀπόφασις. What is essential to both forms of carrying out νοεῖν, essential to their σύνθεσις and διαίρεσις, is the primarily unitary having in sight of the ὑποκείμενον, that which is spoken about, that which is under discussion. In the σύνθεσις there comes to the fore the moment by which the assertion sees together the one with the other and in this way sees the whole. On the other hand, in the διαίρεσις there resides the moment by which λόγος, because it lets something be seen as something, takes apart (table—black) the whole (black table) at the very outset, yet not in such a way that the νοήματα are placed one next to the other, but ὥσπερ ἓν ὄντων (*De An*. III, 6, 430a28), in such a way that they are seen as a unity. The whole theory of λόγος can be understood by keeping in mind the basic structure of the ἀπόφανσις, of the letting be seen and of seeing. In this fundamental attitude, affirmation and denial are carried out.[6]

Aristotle investigates this structure of σύνθεσις and διαίρεσις, and at the same time the phenomenon of the ἀληθές, in a still much more fundamental context than in *De Anima* III, chapters 6 and 7. I refer specifically to *Metaphysics* VI, chapter 4; IX, chapter 10; and XI, chapter 8, 1065a ff.

δ) The ἀληθές as a character of Being as encountered (*Met*. VI, 2 and 4).

We have shown that being true, disclosure, is a mode of Being of human life and refers first of all to the world.[7] Here a problem arises: what connection is there between beings insofar as they are uncovered and the other characters of Being? For, independently of any theory of knowledge and its prejudices, it is obvious that unconcealedness is in a certain way a character of the Being of beings themselves. It is therefore that Aristotle speaks of ὂν ὡς ἀληθές, of beings insofar as they are unconcealed, and correspondingly of μὴ ὂν ὡς ψεῦδος, and he does so specifically in connection with a fundamental constatation of research into the distinction of the various regards in which Being can be spoken of. These are: 1.) the ὄν of the categories, 2.) the ὂν κατὰ συμβεβηκὸς, 3.) the ὂν δυνάμει and ἐνεργείᾳ, and 4.) the ὂν ὡς ἀληθές.[8] Here the phenomenon of the ἀληθές arises in connection with the question of the basic determinations of beings themselves. Nevertheless, Aristotle says that this ὂν ὡς ἀληθές does not properly belong within the theme of ontology, inasmuch as the character of the ἀληθές does not provide something of beings which would pertain to them as such but only insofar as they are *there*, i.e., insofar as they encounter an uncovering discernment.[9] It is wrong, however, to maintain that this ὂν ὡς ἀληθές would mean something like truth in the sense of the validity of a judgment, simply because Aristotle excludes the ὂν ὡς ἀληθές from his ontological consideration. That is not what Aristotle means. The ὂν ὡς ἀληθές is not a mode of Being that is taken up as a consequence of a mere

6. See the appendix.
7. Cf. pp. 12f. and 16f.
8. *Met*. VI, 2, 1026a33ff.
9. *Met*. VI, 4, 1027b25ff.

factually occurring process of thought. It is rather the Being of the same beings of which the categories are also determinations of their Being. It is just that the categories pertain to beings themselves as beings, whereas the ἀληθές is a character of the Being of beings only insofar as beings are there and present for a grasping. Hence there is no question at all here of logical Being, of the validity or invalidity of judgment. The ὂν ὡς ἀληθές is rather the same beings which also are the theme of ontology: the beings of the world. Closer inspection will discover that Aristotle ultimately assigns even this character, this Being, to ontological research.[10] The ὂν ὡς ἀληθές proves to be a character of Being insofar as Being is encountered. Thereby we will acquire an insight into the dimension of the meaning of truth for Aristotle. It will be shown that truth, unconcealedness, is not at home in λόγος. But if not in λόγος, the positive question arises: where then? From this point we acquire again an orientation toward the central question of the *Sophist*, the question of the Being of ψεῦδος, whether there is such a thing as μὴ ὄν, whether non-being is. Our consideration of the problem of the ἀληθές will be conducted only far enough for us to learn from Aristotle the general orientation of the *Sophist*.[11]

10. *Met.* IX, 10.
11. See the appendix.

TRANSITION[1]

Delineation of the Thematic Field, with ἀληθεύειν as the Point of Departure

§27. What has been accomplished up to now and the future task. What has been accomplished: the acquisition of the point of departure (= ἀληθεύειν). The task: the delineation of the theme, with ἀληθεύειν in Plato (= διαλέγεσθαι) as the point of departure. First indication of the theme: a revolution in the concept of Being; the Being of non-beings (= ψεῦδος).

Our considerations thus far have had the sense of a preparation for understanding a *scientific* dialogue of Plato. I expressly emphasize "a *scientific* dialogue" in order to indicate that not all Platonic dialogues attain this height of scientific research, although all of them in a certain way aim at knowledge. There is no scientific understanding, i.e., historiographical return to Plato, without passage through Aristotle. Aristotle at first blocks, as it were, every access to Plato. This is obvious when we consider that we always issue from the later ones, and it is as ones who are still later that we go back to the earlier ones, and that there is in principle no arbitrariness within the field of philosophical reflection. In a historiographical return to the basic sources of our spiritual existence, we must rather adhere to the inner current of historical development. Choosing a philosophy or a philosopher is never arbitrary. For the rest, it might be permitted to select spiritual hobbies, on the basis of the most diverse motivations, from the history of ideas, examples, and possible existences—hence to deal with history arbitrarily—yet this permission does not apply to philosophical research, if indeed this research is to uncover Dasein in its foundations and if this Dasein *is* history, i.e., if we ourselves are history. In this way the passage through an interpretation of Aristotle, whether explicit or not, is basically something obvious, especially if we consider that Aristotle's own research is nothing else than a more radical apprehension of the same

1. Continuation of the lecture course after the Christmas recess of 1924–25. Heidegger's manuscript contains the titles: "Recapitulation, Introduction" and "Transition."

From this point on, the present text is based not only, as was previously the case, on Heidegger's handwritten manuscript and on the lecture notes of H. Jonas, F. Schalk, and H. Weiß, but, in addition, on a typewritten copy of the stenographic lecture transcript of S. Moser, which begins only after the Christmas recess. This copy was reviewed by Heidegger, authorized, and annotated with marginalia which will be presented in the text separately, marked "AH" (= Heidegger's annotation of the Moser transcript).

problems with which Plato and earlier thinkers had grappled. An interpretation of Plato cannot merely *not* bypass Aristotle, but every such interpretation must legitimize itself in him. Following the principle of hermeneutics, we are proceeding from the clear back into the obscure, i.e., from the distinct, or the relatively developed, back to the confused. "Confused" must not be taken here as a denigration; it means rather that various directions of seeing and questioning intermingle in Plato, not on account of a personal intellectual incapacity but on account of the difficulty of the very problems themselves. The confused and undeveloped can only be understood if guiding lines are available to bring out the immanent intentions. These guidelines cannot be arbitrary philosophical questions, just as little as they can be all the possibilities of a system, in a maximum of superficiality. On the contrary, the fundamental question of Greek philosophical research is the question of Being, the question of the meaning of Being, and characteristically, the question of truth.[1]

In one direction, we are sufficiently prepared, insofar as the foregoing consideration of ἀληθεύειν[2] has allowed us to appropriate the basic position within which the dialogue sees and questions, the way in which the steps of the dialogical treatise themselves run their course. Yet what was to be delineated in this preparation was not only the mode of consideration, the mode of research, but also, equally, the thematic field of this consideration. In the dialogue we will deal with first,[3] this entails a remarkable double character. The *Sophist* questions what a sophist is, with the specific intention of determining what a philosopher is. The sophist is first made visible in the multiplicity of his comportments. From this multiplicity and from its corresponding interpretation, that toward which the sophist comports himself becomes visible as well. The mode of sophistical speaking about, and dealing with, all things makes clear at once what is involved in sophistry.

The comportment of the sophist is, in the broadest sense, τέχνη. I indicated earlier[4] that in Plato the expressions τέχνη, ἐπιστήμη, σοφία, and φρόνησις still partially run together.[5] For Plato, τέχνη has the breadth of meaning the term still manifests in Book I of Aristotle's *Metaphysics:* know-how in the broadest sense and in any comportment whatsoever. Here, as regards sophistry, it is a matter of know-how in speaking about everything there is; that means knowing how to speak about *beings*. In the course of the further characterization, the remarkable determination arises that this know-how is a way of deception regarding that which is spoken of. The

1. See the appendix.
2. AH: Aristotle, *Nic. Eth.* Z, in the preceding first part of the lectures.
3. AH: The plan had been to include the *Philebus*.
4. Cf. p. 45.
5. AH: Cf. *Theaetetus* 207c: τεχνικός as ἐπιστήμων versus mere δοξαστικός.

speech of the sophist presents its object as something which basically, in a more proper consideration, it is not; i.e., what he speaks about is not as he shows it to be. The manifold characterization of the sophist, which is indeed immediately striking, from the very first reading of the dialogue, and which is illustrated again and again from various sides, has the sense of bringing near to us, quite tangibly, the concrete existence of the sophist within the life of the Greeks. But from that, from the ineluctable factual existence of the comportment of the sophist, which indeed was a preeminent force within the spiritual world of the Greeks, from this unquestionably powerful Being of the comportment of the sophist, it becomes clear at the same time that what he comports himself to, what he as a sophist deals with, is involved in deception and trickery. But insofar as deception and trickery are things which basically are not, things which present non-being as being, the Being of non-beings becomes clear on the basis of the very existence of the sophist. Thus the concrete factual Being of the sophist, the very existence of something like a sophist, demonstrates (to be sure only for a consideration standing on a higher level) that non-beings—delusion, trickery—are.

This insight, that non-beings are, signifies at the same time a revolution in terms of the previous conception, in terms of the previous meaning of Being adhered to even by Plato himself. The interpretation of the mode of Being of the sophist ultimately counts as a demonstration of the Being of non-beings. This demonstration is nothing else than a more radical conception of the meaning of Being itself and of the character of the "not" enclosed therein. And that implies a more original appropriation of the theme of philosophical research. This is not merely set up in the sense of a program but is actually carried out in the course of the dialogue by way of an actual concrete elaboration of the question of Being. This more radical grasping and founding of research into Being entails at the same time a more fundamental interpretation of this research itself, i.e., of philosophizing. Thus the path of a thematic consideration of the Being of non-beings leads back to a consideration of a new, more proper, existence, that of the philosopher. It is telling that what is dealt with thereby is not a determinate type of man, a typology of the various sorts of men; instead, concrete research is carried out, from which the meaning of the philosopher will arise on its own, without Plato having to speak explicitly about it. To answer the question of the meaning of sophistical existence is to co-answer, indirectly, the question of the philosopher.

If we now shift the weight of the questioning to the thematic question of the concept of Being and the transformation of the previous concept of Being, then we face the task of appropriating the position of the consideration which makes present and evident for the first time the givenness of non-beings. It is a matter of demonstrating the states of affairs phenomenologically. We will have to inquire: in what way does the Being of non-beings become present and evident? Where and in what way are we to avoid the givenness of non-beings no longer? And we will have to ask: what is the meaning of this way? How are the transformation and development of the concept of Being to be carried out in view of the Being of non-beings? How did Parmenides accomplish a transformation previously? Whence does Plato attain his question of Being? The theme of the consideration is thus beings in their Being; it is a matter of the character of beings insofar as they are beings.

The beings treated in the dialogue are the theme of a speaking, and specifically of a speaking, διαλέγεσθαι, which makes the beings become visible as uncovered. It is therefore that Plato always speaks of ὂν ἀληθινόν; these are beings as uncovered in themselves. We are sufficiently oriented concerning ἀληθεύειν, the mode of access to beings as uncovered.[6] Among the possible ways of ἀληθεύειν, we came to know an eminent one, one uniquely and only concerned with pure uncovering: θεωρεῖν, and specifically the θεωρεῖν of σοφία, which has the sense of making beings visible in their ἀρχαί, i.e., from that which a being always already is in its Being. That is, it makes visible the ὂν ἀληθινόν or the ἀληθές of the ὄν. On the basis of this inner connection between Being and uncoveredness, the Greeks can also say in abbreviated form: philosophy is concerned with ἀλήθεια.[7] Ἀλήθεια means, on the one hand, the pure and simple uncoveredness of something but means, at the same time, in analogy with the meanings of λόγος, the uncovered itself, the uncovered being. The straightforward use of ἀλήθεια expresses nothing else than beings in their Being, beings insofar as they are properly uncovered.[8]

Our treatment of ἀληθεύειν has made clear the mode of access and the manner of considering and disclosing but not the corresponding thematic field: namely, the very research into Being, i.e., the theme of beings as discussed in Aristotle's ontology. This has been indicated only in an insufficient way. It is out of the question here, and would be even if we had at our disposal more than one semester, to exhibit this theme exhaustively, *viz.*, Aristotelian ontology. Only in a quite abbreviated form do we want to procure at the outset an orientation concerning what the dialogue deals with. Specifically, since the thematic field is determinable through the mode of access and the mode of dealing with it, we will take the shortest path to do what we spoke of at the beginning, namely to bring the mode of consideration in the dialogue, the ἀληθεύειν, closer to us in relation to the characteristic way it occurs in Plato, i.e., in relation to διαλέγεσθαι.

6. AH: The first part of this lecture course is an interpretation of Aristotle's *Nicomachean Ethics* Z.

7. *Met.* I, 3, 983b3.

8. See the appendix.

§28. *First characterization of dialectic in Plato.*

a) Διαλέγεσθαι as ἀληθεύειν. Repetition and continuation of what has been established about λόγος: rejection of λόγος as the proper place of truth.[1] Λόγος as the most immediate mode of ἀληθεύειν and as concealing prattle. The basic meaning of "dialectic": breaking through the prattle, tendency toward seeing (νοεῖν).

If we are justified in making an explication of ἀληθεύειν our preparation for understanding the dialogue, and if this is indeed a genuine preparation, then it must be able to elucidate the mode of consideration employed in the dialogue, namely διαλέγεσθαι. What we have determined about ἀληθεύειν must be able to clarify the proper sense of διαλέγεσθαι, the specific comportment of inter-locution that constitutes the dia-logue. And the elucidation of the meaning of διαλέγεσθαι will, at the same time, allow us to understand why in general the dialogue considers that which it does consider precisely by taking the form of a dialogue, and why Plato philosophizes in dialogues. The reason is not the trivial one that Plato was an artist and wanted to present even such matters, whatever they might be called, in a beautiful way. The reason is, rather, an inner need of philosophizing itself, the radical acceptance on Plato's part of the impetus he received from Socrates: to pass from λόγος as prattle, from what is said idly and hastily about all things, through genuine speaking, to a λόγος which, as λόγος ἀληθής, actually says something about that of which it speaks. Διαλέγεσθαι is a passing "through speech," departing from what is idly said, with the goal of arriving at a genuine assertion, a λόγος, about beings themselves. In this sense, διαλέγεσθαι—as it is later called in Plato's *Sophist*—is a διαπορεύεσθαι διὰ τῶν λόγων (cf. 253b10), a running through what is said, precisely so as to show what could be discerned there regarding Being. Accordingly, διαλέγεσθαι, as is the case with λόγος, has the function of disclosing and specifically of disclosing in the mode of discussion. This "speaking-through" begins with what people first say about the matter, passes through this, and is directed to and finds its end in a speaking which genuinely expresses something about the theme, i.e., in a genuine assertion, genuine λόγος.

If we say that λόγος, here as διαλέγεσθαι, is disclosive, and is taken in any case in this facticity, then that means that an ἀληθεύειν belongs to λόγος. Upon closer inspection, we can see that λόγος itself, simply as λόγος, does not constitute without further ado a carrying out of ἀληθεύειν and

1. Cf. §26 b) β), p. 125.

that consequently the uncovering within λόγος is not indigenous to it as λόγος. Λόγος *can* take upon itself the actual performance of a disclosure, but it does not have to. Factually, however, it is precisely λόγος which ordinarily permeates all modes of uncovering, such that all the forms of ἀληθεύειν we saw in Aristotle, with the exception of νοῦς, are determined by the character of the μετὰ λόγου: they are carried out in discourse. Aristotle, however, does not consider more closely this bond between λόγος and ἀληθεύειν. In fact, he gives no more than the indication that all modes of ἀληθεύειν are first and for the most part μετὰ λόγου. Λόγος, addressing something in speech, is our most immediate mode of carrying out ἀληθεύειν, whereas νοῦς, pure perception, is as such not possible for man, the ζῷον λόγον ἔχον. For us, νοεῖν is initially and for the most part διανοεῖν, because our dealing with things is dominated by λόγος.[2]

Λόγος can therefore take upon itself ἀληθεύειν, yet it does not do so on its own but from the νοεῖν and διανοεῖν in each case, i.e., from the respective αἴσθησις. According to its original sense and according to its original facticity as well, λόγος is not disclosive at all but, to speak in an extreme way, is precisely concealing. Λόγος is at first mere prattle, whose facticity is not to let things be seen but instead to develop a peculiar self-satisfaction at adhering to what is idly spoken of. The domination of idle talk precisely closes off beings for the Dasein[3] and brings about a blindness with regard to what is disclosed and what might be disclosive. But if it is λόγος in this facticity as prattle which first permeates Dasein, then the pressing ahead to beings as disclosed must precisely pass through this λόγος. The pressing ahead must be such a speaking that, by means of speeches pro and con, it leads more and more to what is at issue and lets that be seen. Διαλέγεσθαι therefore possesses immanently a tendency toward νοεῖν, seeing. Yet insofar as the consideration remains in λέγειν and as διαλέγεσθαι continues on in thorough discussion, such "speaking through" can indeed relinquish idle talk but cannot do more than *attempt* to press on to the things themselves. Διαλέγεσθαι remains a matter of speeches; it does not arrive at pure νοεῖν. It does not have at its disposal the proper means to attain its genuine end, i.e., to attain θεωρεῖν. Although διαλέγεσθαι does not reach its goal and does not purely and simply disclose beings, as long as it still remains in λέγειν, it need not be a mere game but has a proper function insofar as it cuts through the idle talk, checks the prattle, and in the speeches lays its finger, as it were, on what is at issue. In this way, διαλέγεσθαι presents the things spoken of in a first intimation and in their immediate outward look. That is

2. Thus in Heidegger's manuscript.
3. AH: of man (in place of what is crossed out in the text: and for life).

the fundamental sense of Platonic dialectic.[4] This dialectic possesses an intrinsic tendency toward seeing, disclosing. One will therefore not understand dialectic by distinguishing intuition and thinking and placing dialectic on the side of thinking. Dialectic is not something like a higher level of what is known as thinking, in opposition to so-called mere intuition, but, quite to the contrary, the only meaning and the only intention of dialectic is to prepare and to develop a genuine original intuition, passing through what is merely said.[5] The fact that Plato did not advance far enough so as ultimately to see beings themselves and in a certain sense to overcome dialectic is a deficiency included in his own dialectical procedure, and it determines certain moments of his dialectic, e.g., the much discussed κοινωνία τῶν γενῶν, the association, the keeping company together, of the kinds. These characteristics are not merits and are not determinations of a superior philosophical method but are indications of a fundamental confusion and unclarity, which, as I have already said, is founded in the difficulty of the matters themselves, the difficulty of such first foundational research.

b) Critique of the traditional conception of dialectic. Dialectic: not a technique of thinking but a preliminary stage of νοεῖν. Aristotle's position with regard to dialectic.

The domination of λόγος produces later—as is the case still today—a repercussion, specifically in the "theoretical" in general and in the "logical." The history of philosophy and dialectically-oriented philosophical reflection took from this Platonic dialectic their first ideal and saw in it a superior kind of philosophizing. In connection with this, a wonderful technique of philosophical thinking has been devised, a technique of thinking embodying a dialectical movement to and fro, a method which runs best when it is as unencumbered as possible with substantive knowledge and to which nothing else pertains than an understanding that has become wild and lost in emptiness. What for Plato was an inner need, namely to get at the matters at issue, has here been made into a principle to play with them. Plato's concern in the dialectic runs precisely in the opposite direction, namely to see the ὂν ἀληθινόν, that which is. The obverse of this misunderstanding of the meaning of Platonic dialectic, and perhaps of dialectic in general, is a denigrating judgment on the position of Aristotle as regards dialectic. It has become a commonplace in the history of philosophy that Aristotle no longer understood Plato's dialectic and downgraded it to a mere technique of deductive thinking.[6]

4. AH: Marginal note: in the sense of the original meaning of this philosophizing.
5. AH: Knowledge—cf. *Being and Time*—and intuition. Hegel in the background as well.
6. See the appendix.

Of late it has been emphasized again that Aristotle deprived the word "dialectic" of its high Platonic dignity. Now such a dictum, which indeed does not mean much philosophically, springs from a romantic conception of philosophy. In fact there is some truth to it, but only if the correct foundation is adduced, not if there lurks behind it a romantic regret. Aristotle did deprive dialectic of its dignity, but not because he did not understand it. On the contrary, it was because he understood it more radically, because he saw Plato himself as being underway toward θεωρεῖν in his dialectic, because he succeeded in making real what Plato was striving for. Aristotle saw the immanent limits of dialectic, because he philosophized more radically. This limitation of Platonic dialectic enabled him at the same time to restore to it its relative right. Aristotle could do this, of course, only because he understood the function of λόγος and of διαλέγεσθαι within scientific reflection and within human existence in general. Only on the basis of a positive understanding of the phenomenon of λέγειν within life (as can be found in his *Rhetoric*) did Aristotle acquire the foundation for interpreting λέγεσθαι in a wholly concrete way and thus for seeing διαλέγεσθαι more acutely. Hence Aristotle could not at all downgrade dialectic, since for him it was already, according to its very sense, down below, i.e., a preliminary stage of θεωρεῖν. As such, dialectic is not some sort of crafty operation of thinking but is in its very sense always already a wanting to *see*, insofar as λόγος has precisely the meaning of ἀποφαίνεσθαι, letting be seen. Dialectic is not the art of out-arguing another but has precisely the opposite meaning, namely of bringing one's partner in the argument to open his eyes and see.

Let us now presentify the more precise determination of διαλέγεσθαι, as it occurs in Aristotle and which we have acquired in our interpretation of him, in order to test our interpretation of διαλέγεσθαι and dialectic. We will ask: on what occasions and in what contexts does Aristotle speak of dialectic? This consideration of dialectic in Aristotle will serve at the same time to sum up our preparation for interpreting the Platonic dialogue. This consideration of dialectic in Aristotle will hence bring us finally to the dialogue itself, and so we must hold fast to the designated sequence of steps in our consideration and specifically in order that we retain in view at the same time what is thematic in this διαλέγεσθαι.[7]

In the preceding exposition, in connection with our consideration of ἀληθεύειν, as well as of νοεῖν in the strict sense, we encountered the expression λόγος in its various meanings. If we have good grounds for interpreting λόγος as an assertion about something and as an addressing of something as something, then this interpretation of λόγος and of its

7. See the supplement to p. 137.

fundamental meaning must also be the root out of which the other, derived, meanings of λόγος become intelligible.[8,9] I will now expose these meanings by way of anticipation, since again and again within the Platonic dialogues they occur entirely intermingled and unclarified.

c) The meanings of the expression "λόγος" in Plato.

Plato speaks of λόγος in quite different senses, not arbitrarily, but with an indeterminateness which has a certain foundation in the matters themselves. Λόγος means:

1.) λέγειν,

2.) λεγόμενον, and specifically this meaning of λεγόμενον, "the said," has a double sense: it can mean what is spoken about, hence the content, but also

3.) its being said, its being expressed—so and so has said it—a mode of Being of λόγος which precisely predominates in everyday Dasein, such that, as Aristotle remarks, often simply being said suffices to evoke a πίστις, a conviction, about what is said, without an explicit appropriation of the expressed content or the way of saying it.

These three different meanings display the first variations of the term λόγος. Then

4.) λόγος means the same as εἶδος. This sense is connected to the fact that λόγος can mean λεγόμενον, "the said," and specifically—insofar as λέγειν means ἀποφαίνεσθαι, to let be seen—it can mean that about beings which speech lets be seen, i.e., beings in their outward look, as they show themselves in λόγος as ἀποφαίνεσθαι. Therefore λόγος can often be identified with εἶδος, i.e., Idea. As a further meaning we find

5.) an identification of λόγος with νοῦς, νοεῖν. From what preceded, we know that λόγος is the phenomenon which is taken to be the basic determination of the constitution of the Being of man: man is the living being that speaks. Insofar as this speaking, however, is the mode of carrying out seeing and perceiving, i.e., the mode of carrying out αἴσθησις as well as νοεῖν, λόγος as the basic character of the Being of man becomes at the same time representative for the other determination of the ζωή of man, νοῦς.[10] The circuitous path of this intermingling of phenomena leads eventually

8. AH: Cf. the better presentation of the concept of λόγος in S.S. 31, beginning. Editor's note: i.e., GA II, Bd. 33, *Aristoteles, Metaphysik Θ, 1–3. Von Wesen und Wirklichkeit der Kraft.* Freiburger Vorlesung SS 1931. Edited by H. Hüni, p. 5. [English translation by Walter Brogan and Peter Warnek: *Aristotle's Metaphysics Θ 1–3: On the Essence and Actuality of Force,* Bloomington: Indiana University Press, 1995, p. 2.—Trans.]

9. AH: Cf. *Theaetetus.* Concluding section. 3 meanings of λέγειν.

10. AH: λόγος—*ratio.*

to the translation of λόγος as "reason." But λόγος does not mean reason, and in itself it does not have the meaning of νοεῖν but can only be the mode of carrying out perception itself. This usage requires a clarification of the unexplicit state of affairs lying at its foundation.

6.) Λόγος also means "relation." This meaning becomes intelligible on the basis of the fundamental sense of λέγειν. Λέγειν means λέγειν τι κατά τινος: to address something as something, i.e., in regard to something. In λέγειν there resides a looking out on, a looking from one to another; therefore λόγος also signifies relation. From its sense as an addressing of something as something, the term λόγος receives the derived meaning of relation. On this basis it is also intelligible that λόγος

7.) means ἀνάλογον, "ana-logy," the analogous, the cor-responding, to correspond as a determinate mode of being related.[11,12]

I will limit myself to this range of meaning of λόγος, because these are the ones we encounter predominantly, and specifically such that often several meanings are intended in one. And thus we can also understand how in the dialogue one step of the consideration is the result of another. This would remain obscure if we adhered to a single isolated meaning of λόγος.

And now as a transition to the dialogue itself a short orientation concerning διαλεκτική. Aristotle speaks about dialectic principally in two places: 1.) in connection with the determination of the task of philosophy as the fundamental science of beings (*Met.* IV, 2); and 2.) in the theory of λόγος in the *Topics* and in the treatise about false conclusions, which indeed properly belongs to the *Topics* and is to be considered the last book of the *Topics*. Thus 1.) in connection with σοφία, and 2.) in connection with the theory of λέγειν in the sense of theoretical discourse.[13] A consideration of dialectic in connection with the πρώτη φιλοσοφία, the fundamental science, will at the same time provide us with an opportunity to cast a concrete regard toward the field of ontological research and to form a preliminary concept of the matters at issue in the Greeks' research into Being and how these matters were taken up. Thus far, we have only heard that this research would deal with the ἀρχαί of beings. A short exposition will provide us the outward look of such an ἀρχή. Likewise our consideration of the theory of λέγειν will allow us to understand the concept of the "logical" in connection with the phenomenon of λόγος.

11. AH: λέγειν—to take together in general—to relate.

12. See the appendix.

13. In his lectures Heidegger presented dialectic only in relation to *Met.* IV, 2 (cf. p. 149). From indications in the transcripts of the lectures as well as from a few clues in Heidegger's own manuscript, it is evident that a presentation of dialectic in relation to the *Topics* was also planned. But this was not carried out. See the appendix, Supplements 23 and 26.

§29. *Addendum: The innovation in Plato's* Sophist *with regard to the ground of the Greeks' research into Being.*[1]

a) The double guiding line of the research into Being in Plato's *Sophist:* concrete Dasein (the philosopher, the sophist); λέγειν.

If we consider the dialogue *Sophist* as a whole and proceed from its title, we find on closer inspection a remarkable innovation compared to previous endeavors of Greek philosophy. For now, a determinate mode of existence, namely that of the philosopher, is offered as ground for a discussion of Being and beings. The dialogue has no other goal than to explicate this ground, this concrete mode of Dasein, and thereby to create, as it were, the milieu within which beings can show themselves in their Being. I say that this new foundation for research into the Being of beings is remarkable compared to the starting point of the usual Greek consideration of Being, e.g., compared to the position of Parmenides, where Being is simply determined in correlation with νοεῖν. These are indeed basically the same, insofar as the philosopher is the one who, in a preeminent sense, νοεῖ, perceives, considers, but yet with this difference, that for Parmenides this νοεῖν remains wholly undetermined. He does not say whether it is the νοεῖν of a determinate realm of Being or of beings in general; he speaks of Being only in general and in an undetermined way, and likewise for νοεῖν. The innovation with respect to the research, not with respect to the result, resides in this, that the ground upon which rests the question of the meaning of Being now becomes concrete. The task of the appropriation of the ground becomes more difficult but the result richer. This can be seen in the fact that even non-beings are acknowledged in their Being and in any case are put into question. In both instances, as in general, it is shown that something can be settled about beings with regard to their Being only insofar as the beings are present, or, as we say, insofar as beings can be encountered at all. It is simply a matter of adhering to the beings encountered, in their most immediate and most original way of being encountered, and, within this, of questioning how the beings show themselves. This is the one direction in which the question of the meaning of beings, the question of Being, is raised.

1. We have here the transition from the nineteenth session (Thursday, January 8, 1925) to the twentieth (Friday, January 9). It is an expanded and more definite version of the beginning of the former session (p. 132) and leads directly to the determination of dialectic in Aristotle. On account of its own train of thought, it could not be incorporated into the earlier version. It is here reproduced separately.

The other direction goes immediately together with the first for a more concrete research into Being, insofar as the encountered beings (= the world, in naive ontology) are present to everyday Dasein, which speaks about the world[2] in such a way that discoursing and addressing become at the same time a further guideline orienting the question of Being. That is, how do beings look insofar as they are addressed and spoken of, insofar as they are λεγόμενα? This question about Being, following the guideline of λέγειν, is at the same time the proper origin of logic. "Logic" in the Greek sense has at first nothing at all to do with thinking but instead stands wholly within the task of the question of Being. Thus the *Sophist*—as well as all the other dialogues of Plato grouped around it—is a remarkable turning point between the position of Parmenides and the one of Aristotle, which consummates all these projects of Greek ontology. This meaning of the *Sophist* shows itself, to be sure, only if we grasp it originally enough as regards what it did not settle at all and what from that position could not be settled. Fundamental difficulties remain which this position cannot remove and which are present for us.[3] Hence not only the world as encountered, but also the world insofar as it is spoken of, are given in this double sense as the guiding lines of research into Being.

b) Λόγος as guiding line of Aristotle's research into Being ("onto-logy").

Hence λόγος, discourse about the world and beings, has the role of the guiding line insofar as beings are present in the λεγόμενον. Even where the research into Being, as is the case with Aristotle, goes beyond dialectic, beyond confinement to beings as addressed, toward a pure grasping of the ἀρχαί, toward θεωρεῖν—even there it can be shown that λόγος is still fundamental for the final conception of Being. Even Aristotle, although he overcomes dialectic, still remains oriented toward λόγος in his entire questioning of Being. This state of affairs is the origin of what we today call formal ontology and is taken up into it. Διαλέγεσθαι is a way of asking about beings with regard to their Being, a way in which λόγος is and remains the guiding line. For Aristotle, however, λόγος manifests itself in its peculiar relational structure: λέγειν is always a λέγειν τι κατά τινος. Insofar as λόγος addresses something as something, it is in principle unfit to grasp that which by its very sense cannot be addressed as something else but can only be grasped for itself. Here, in this primary and predominating structure, λόγος, as it were, fails. There remains, if one passes

2. AH: the "is" in simple saying and asserting.
3. See the appendix.

beyond it, only a new idea of λόγος: the λόγος καθ' αὐτό, as Aristotle has shown in chapter 4 of Book VII of the *Metaphysics*.

On the basis of this more precise insight into the structure of λόγος, Aristotle succeeds in characterizing the preliminary status of Platonic dialectic. Aristotle accomplishes this characterization in connection with the mode of research called "first philosophy," which considers beings in their Being. In connection with the exposition of the idea of an original and first science of Being, Aristotle refers even to the dialecticians and sophists, insofar as he says that they too claim to be philosophers.[4] This claim to philosophy means that their knowledge and their interest in knowledge are directed to the whole, the ὅλον, to the ἅπαντα, all beings, and not to a determinate being. In this consideration, Aristotle takes the fact that there are dialecticians and sophists, as inauthentic philosophers, to be proof that philosophy aims at the whole. It indeed aims at the whole, ὅλον, in a quite determined sense: not in the sense that the determinations of the content of all beings whatsoever would be enumerated, and the various sorts of beings would be recounted and the qualities of individual things tallied. On the contrary, philosophy aims at beings insofar as they are and only insofar as they are. Thus it is not concerned, as we would say, with the ontical, with beings themselves in such a way that it becomes utterly engrossed in them, but instead it is concerned with beings in such a manner that it addresses the ὄν *as* ὄν—the ὄν λεγόμενον ᾗ ὄν. Hence it addresses beings in such a way that they are simply addressed with regard to their Being and not according to any other respect. This idea of "onto-logy," of λέγειν, of the addressing of beings with regard to their Being, was exposed for the first time with complete acumen by Aristotle. In this connection he arrives at the delimitation of dialectic and sophistry by opposing them to this idea of a first philosophy. We want to make that clear, quite briefly and more concretely, with the aid of the exposition Aristotle offers in Book IV of the *Metaphysics*.

4. *Met.* IV, 2, 1004b17ff.

*§30. Aristotle on philosophy, dialectic, sophistry (*Met. *IV, 1–2).*[1]

a) The idea of first philosophy. First philosophy as the science of ὂν ᾗ ὄν. Delimitation of first philosophy versus the special sciences. Being as φύσις τις. The ancients' research into the στοιχεῖα. Further structures of Being. First and second philosophy.

The fourth Book of the *Metaphysics* begins, apparently quite dogmatically, with the assertion: Ἔστιν ἐπιστήμη τις ἣ θεωρεῖ τὸ ὂν ᾗ ὂν καὶ τὰ τούτῳ ὑπάρχοντα καθ' αὑτό (chapter 1, 1003a21f.). "There is a science which specifically θεωρεῖ, considers, τὸ ὂν ᾗ ὄν, beings as beings," i.e., beings precisely with regard to their Being, beings hence not as something else, as having this or that property, but simply as beings, insofar as they are. Καὶ τὰ τούτῳ ὑπάρχοντα καθ' αὑτό, and it considers "that which in these beings, namely in beings with regard to their Being, ὑπάρχει, is already there in advance" and which pertains to beings as to their Being, and indeed καθ' αὑτό, "in themselves." There is hence a science which considers the characters of the Being of beings, to put it very succinctly. The traditional interpretation has found a difficulty here, since this proclamation of first philosophy calls it ἐπιστήμη, whereas in fact ἐπιστήμη, in contradistinction to σοφία, is not an original science. For ἐπιστήμη is a theoretical knowledge that presupposes definite principles, axioms, and basic concepts. Strictly taken, then, the very sense of ἐπιστήμη excludes its being able to grasp thematically something original in its very originality. Hence Aristotle should have said here: ἔστι σοφία τις. We can see immediately, however, that this is nonsense. Aristotle means, precisely without concern for terminology, that over and against the concrete specific sciences, there is, as we would say, one "science" which considers, θεωρεῖ, beings in their Being. Thus here ἐπιστήμη has the quite broad sense of θεωρεῖν. We should not press the expression in the sense of an epideictic idea. It is a matter here of a mode of knowledge whose character and type must precisely first be determined. The problem of σοφία corresponds to the ὂν ᾗ ὄν.

Now this science, which considers beings in their Being, αὕτη δ' ἐστὶν οὐδεμιᾷ τῶν ἐν μέρει λεγομένων ἡ αὐτή (a22f.), "is not the same as the others." It does not coincide with any other, i.e., it does not coincide with οὐδεμιᾷ τῶν ἐν μέρει λεγομένων. The usual translation assumes λεγόμενον is related to ἐπιστημῶν. But the context and the final section (1003b17) of the second chapter make it clear that λεγόμενα means the matters them-

1. For the following interpretation of *Met.* IV, 1–2 (pp. 144–148), Heidegger's manuscript contains no notes, only an allusion: *Met.* Γ, 1 and 2. Cf. interpretation.

selves to which the sciences relate. There is hence a manifold of sciences which relate to beings that are "addressed in part," and that means here "addressed by way of cutting off a piece." There are sciences which cut out, from the whole of beings, determined regions and then address those regions purely as delimited in themselves, elaborating them in λέγειν. Every such science has, as we say, its determined region. To the regions of these sciences there corresponds a definite αἴσθησις, an original perception in which the fundamental character of the objects in the region is grasped, either explicitly or not. In geometry, the objects are the relations of space or site, which are not at all given with Being as such; the objects of φυσική are beings insofar as they are in motion. The physicist does not first prove that the beings he makes thematic are in motion; they are seen that way in advance. Every strain, every autonomous region of beings, has a definite αἴσθησις which mediates the access to the primary character of its objects: space, motion, etc. That means that this μία αἴσθησις as regards what is seen is ἐν μέρει, "by way of cutting off a piece," compared to the ὅλον, "the whole." But the science that considers the Being of beings οὐδεμιᾷ ἡ αὐτή, "does not coincide with any of those" that address beings by way of cutting off a piece. This becomes still clearer in the sentence that follows: οὐδεμία γὰρ τῶν ἄλλων ἐπισκοπεῖ καθόλου περὶ τοῦ ὄντος ᾗ ὄν, ἀλλὰ μέρος αὐτοῦ τι ἀποτεμόμεναι περὶ τούτου θεωροῦσι τὸ συμβεβηκός (chapter 1, 1003a23f.). "None of the other sciences consider beings as a whole in their Being, but instead every one cuts out a part of them and aims its consideration at this part," or, more precisely, "at that which is proper to the beings as such which are cut off in this way." Thus, e.g., geometry considers the relations of site themselves.

ἐπεὶ δὲ τὰς ἀρχὰς καὶ τὰς ἀκροτάτας αἰτίας ζητοῦμεν, δῆλον ὡς φύσεώς τινος αὐτὰς ἀναγκαῖον εἶναι καθ' αὑτήν (a26ff.). "Since we are now seeking τὰς ἀρχάς, the starting points, that out of which the Being of beings is what it is," and precisely τὰς ἀκροτάτας αἰτίας, "the highest αἰτία, the first ones, then it is clear that these determinations, the ἀρχαί, are determinations ὡς φύσεώς τινος, of something which is present by means of itself." This last expression is telling, and it elucidates the whole idea of this science of Being in Aristotle. He can indeed say no more than Plato already said, namely that the Being of beings is itself a being; but the Being of beings is precisely something of a quite peculiar sort and cannot be characterized in turn by that which it itself categorially determines. I cannot grasp the Being of beings in turn as a being; I can grasp it only by acquiring immanent determinations for Being itself out of itself. Aristotle therefore saves himself when he says: Being and the manifold of the characters which pertain to Being καθ' αὑτό are ὡς φύσεώς τινος, like something ὡς φύσις τις, "something already present by means of itself." He says φύσις in order to emphasize that these characters of the Being of beings do not pertain to beings merely insofar as they are addressed, but are already there for ἀποφαίνεσθαι, for the showing in λέγειν. Φύσις signifies precisely a being which has the ἀρχή of its Being in itself rather than, as is the case with ποίησις (here is the opposition) by means of human knowledge and production. More precisely, Aristotle applies this expression φύσις τις to the ὄν, to the characters of Being, in order to indicate that they themselves are present as determinations by means of themselves. Furthermore, he points out at a28ff., the ancients, when they inquired into the στοιχεῖα, the elements of beings, offered various answers: water, air, earth, etc. That is, their inquiries did not properly investigate a determinate region of beings, and the ancients did not intend to recount how beings look as to content. On the contrary, they were actually guided by an interest in determining the Being of beings. It is just that the ancients were not yet on the level of a consideration which understands that beings as beings cannot be elucidated on the basis of a determinate region of beings but only by means of Being itself. With this reference to an admittedly imperfect way of questioning the Being of beings, Aristotle desires at the same time, as he always does, to bring his idea of first philosophy and of the science of Being into continuity with the previous tradition of research.

Now this science is one that falls in a preeminent way within the tasks of the philosopher. περὶ τούτων (chapter 2, 1004a32f.), i.e., about the determinations of beings, καὶ τῆς οὐσίας, and above all about οὐσία, it is necessary λόγον ἔχειν, i.e.—if we do not translate this directly—it is necessary to have beings as exhibited in speech. Thus it is necessary to exhibit the Being of beings. καὶ ἔστι τοῦ φιλοσόφου περὶ πάντων δύνασθαι θεωρεῖν (1004a34f.). "And it is the peculiar right and task of the philosopher δύνασθαι, to bear, as the one who knows, the possibility of initiating an investigation περὶ πάντων, about everything." But we realize from what preceded, from our interpretation of the second chapter of *Metaphysics* I,[2] that περὶ πάντων does not refer to everything in the sense of a sum total, but to the whole with regard to its origins.

Aristotle develops further this idea of the original science of Being by pointing out that every being which is what it is is a ἕν. Unity—that every something is *one*—likewise devolves upon this science. That is to say, the ἕν is included in the thematic field of this original science of Being. In addition, further questions belong to this field, such as εἰ ἓν ἑνὶ ἀναντίον (1004b3), "whether there is something which as one is opposed to another one." Ἐναντίον means "over and against," in a certain sense lying in view of the other. And further: τί ἐστι τὸ ἐναντίον (b3f.), what properly is this

2. Cf. p. 65ff.

"against" of the "over and against," and ποσαχῶς λέγεται, in how many ways can one speak of what is over and against ("contrary" is no longer appropriate in this context). Now Aristotle did not simply set up a program for such a science but has himself initiated concrete investigations into the ἓν ἐναντίον in *Metaphysics* V. This inquiry into the structures of the Being of beings as such is what constitutes the fundamental science.

This mode of questioning is formally the same as the one of second philosophy, i.e., of the other philosophies, which consider definite regions of beings with regard to the structure of their Being. These philosophies do not describe beings, e.g., the φύσει ὄντα, but investigate precisely the structure of their Being; they explicate, e.g., the idea of κίνησις. Likewise, this is how they consider, e.g., the field of objects which are characterized by the title of ἀριθμός, number. Aristotle makes a sharp distinction between number and the ἕν: the ἕν still belongs to ὄν, the ἕν is not yet a number. Plato, on the other hand, intermingled these nexuses, which can be seen in the fact that the Ideas themselves are conceived as numbers. Likewise other regions, such as the στερεόν, the solid, solidity (we would say "materiality") have their definite structures; furthermore so do the ἀκίνητον, the unmoved in its unmoveableness, the ἀβαρές, the unheavy, which has no weight, and the heavy. All these beings have, with regard to their Being, ἴδια, peculiar categorial determinations. And in this way there is a science which considers beings as beings. οὕτω καὶ τῷ ὄντι ᾗ ὂν ἔστι τινὰ ἴδια (1004b15f.), "and thus even for beings insofar as they are beings, there are τινὰ ἴδια, determinate structures proper only to them." καὶ ταῦτ' ἐστὶ περὶ ὧν τοῦ φιλοσόφου ἐπισκέψασθαι τ' ἀληθές (b16f.), "and the truth (to translate roughly) of these characters of Being is what the philosopher must investigate"; i.e., put more strictly, he must see these characters in their uncoveredness.

Versus this task of philosophy and of philosophizing, how does the procedure of the dialecticians and the sophists appear?

b) Delimitation of dialectic and sophistry versus first philosophy. The common object of dialectic, sophistry, and philosophy: the "whole." How dialectic and sophistry are distinct from philosophy: philosophy = γνωριστική; dialectic = πειραστική: sophistry = φαινομένη σοφία (εὖ λέγειν).

Οἱ γὰρ διαλεκτικοὶ καὶ σοφισταὶ τὸ αὐτὸ μὲν ὑποδύονται σχῆμα τῷ φιλοσόφῳ (1004b17f.), "the dialecticians and the sophists dress themselves (literally, immerse themselves) in the form of a philosopher." ἡ γὰρ σοφιστικὴ φαινομένη μόνον σοφία ἐστί (b18f.), (this shows that Aristotle knew very well that the science he is speaking of is σοφία) "sophistry φαινομένη μόνον, merely looks like philosophy," καὶ οἱ διαλεκτικοὶ διαλέγονται περὶ ἁπάντων (b19f.), "and the dialecticians make everything the theme of their discussions," i.e., they do not move within a definite region but claim to be able to speak and give answers about everything. This is in exact analogy to the sophists, who in their way of educating claim to educate young people in such a way that they will be able εὖ λέγειν, "to debate and speak well about everything." It is peculiar to both the sophists and the dialecticians κοινὸν δὲ πᾶσι τὸ ὄν ἐστιν (b20), "to have beings as a whole for their theme." περὶ μὲν γὰρ τὸ αὐτὸ γένος στρέφεται ἡ σοφιστικὴ καὶ ἡ διαλεκτικὴ τῇ φιλοσοφίᾳ (b22f.). "Sophistry and dialectics move within the same field of beings as philosophy does," according to their claim. All three, namely the dialectician, the sophist, and the philosopher, claim to deal with the whole.

But this is the distinction: ἀλλὰ διαφέρει τῆς μὲν τῷ τρόπῳ τῆς δυνάμεως (b23f.), "philosophy distinguishes itself from the one, namely from dialectics, τῷ τρόπῳ τῆς δυνάμεως, by the type and the mode of competence." That is to say, there is a distinction regarding the extent to which each is adequate. Dialectics is not as adequate, it is not as adequate for its task as philosophy is. Dialectics is specifically, at b25, πειραστική, or in terms of Aristotle's paraphrase of this expression in the *Topics,* πεῖραν λαβεῖν,[3] "it makes an attempt at something." Dialectics makes an attempt—to do what? To exhibit beings in their Being. Dialectics is on its way to this goal, but it is not adequate. Dialectics is thus distinguished from philosophy proper with regard to the extent of the adequacy or proficiency. Dialectics remains preordained and subordinated to philosophy. τῆς δὲ τοῦ βίου τῇ προαιρέσει (b24), "from the other (i.e., from sophistry) philosophy distinguishes itself in the way of choosing in advance the mode of existence," to translate literally. That is, the βίος of the philosopher is devoted purely to substance *[Sachlichkeit]* rather than semblance. The philosopher, as the representative of this radical research, has absolutely and purely decided in favor of substance over semblance. In the sophist, too, there is a προαίρεσις, but a different one. His concern is education, and his determinate mode of existence comes down to enabling others εὖ λέγειν, "to debate well," about everything the philosopher deals with. What is completely disregarded is whether this ability to speak about things says anything substantial about them. In sophistry, as a study of its history also shows, the only concern is to be able to speak in a splendid way about anything whatsoever under discussion. Sophistry's ideal is a spiritual existence oriented solely toward

3. *Sophistical Refutations* I, 11, 171b3f.: τὸ φάναι ἢ ἀποφάναι ἀξιοῦν . . . ἐστὶν . . . πεῖραν λαμβάνοντος.

the form of speech, which indeed meant much to the Greeks. Sophistry's ideal is the ability to speak and converse reasonably and beautifully about all things, regardless of whether what is said holds good or not. The sophist has made a decision in favor of the form, in favor of this aesthetic ideal of human existence, i.e., actually, in favor of an unconcern with substantive content, whereas the philosopher has a προαίρεσις in favor of the βίος of the pure θεωρεῖν of the ἀληθές, i.e., in favor of uncoveredness in itself. What thus for dialectics lies in the distance, in the direction of which the dialectician is moving, is something with regard to which the philosopher is not merely πειραστικός but γνωριστικός (b26); the philosopher is already at home in it. The philosopher has the possibility, the δύναμις, of exhibiting the whole in its Being and in the structure of its Being, provided this δύναμις is taken up seriously. Sophistry, on the other hand, is φαινομένη (ibid.), it merely seems like that, but in fact it has basically another ideal, οὖσα δ' οὔ (ibid.), it is not actually philosophy. So you see from this nexus, from the orientation dialectics and sophistry have toward the idea of philosophy, that Aristotle does not simply negate dialectics but instead characterizes it as πειραστική. Thus it has a determinate positive sense: in common with philosophy, the dialectician speaks, as Aristotle says in the *Topics*, κατὰ τὸ πρᾶγμα,[4] "with regard to the matters themselves," whereas the sophists are not concerned with saying anything of substance but are simply concerned with the εὖ, with arguing and discussing beautifully and brilliantly and in seeming to demonstrate things in a genuine way.[5]

In connection with dialectics we had the opportunity to determine something about sophistry and to characterize it at least formally. This first characterization must now be continued.

§31. First characterization of sophistry.[1] Continuation.

a) The idea of παιδεία in sophistry and in Aristotle. Εὖ λέγειν. Concern with substantive content and unconcern with substantive content. Predelineation of ἀληθεύειν as the ground of sophistry.

It must be noted that Plato makes only the single distinction, between dialectics and sophistry, whereas Aristotle, by reason of a more acute grasp of the meaning of the dialectical and of dialectics itself, proposes a threefold

4. *Sophistical Refutations* I, 11, 171b6.
5. See the appendix.
1. Title in Heidegger's manuscript.

articulation: philosophy, dialectics, sophistry. Aristotle distinguishes dialectics and philosophy with regard to their reach, and he distinguishes both over and against sophistry with regard to the way in which they comport themselves to the content of their speech: the sophist on one side and the philosopher and dialectician on the other. In opposition to the sophist, the dialectician and the philosopher are determined by the fact that they take that about which they speak seriously, they intend their speech to bring about an understanding of the content, whereas the sophist pays no attention to the substantive content of his speech but is simply concerned with the speech itself, its *apparent* reasonableness and its brilliance. Therefore the idea guiding the sophist is παιδεία, a certain education with regard to speaking about all things. This παιδεία characterizes the form, in the sense of being able to speak well, εὖ, about everything. Even Aristotle knows of this ideal of education in the sense of scientific training, and even with him, in a certain respect it refers to the form: i.e., παιδεία is not limited to a determinate realm of objects. Yet, with Aristotle, παιδεία means education with regard to the possibility of one's speech measuring up to the matter spoken about in each case, thus precisely the opposite of what the sophist means by παιδεία, namely education in the sense of an utter unconcern with substantive content, an unconcern that is, in fact, one of principle. For Aristotle, to be educated means that the person's speech measures up to precisely the content, to what is spoken about in each case. Since there are contents in many regions, παιδεία cannot be characterized simply in terms of content. It concerns, rather, a determinate kind of training, the methodical attainment of the scientific level in questioning and research. Through this delimitation, sophistry is at the same time brought into connection with ἀληθεύειν, the disclosure of beings, which is what defines philosophy itself.

I will not pursue the historical conditions and will not present a historical characterization of sophistry. For that, you should consult Diels, *Fragmente der Vorsokrater* II. The main genuine source is Plato himself. Therefore a discussion about the historical situation of sophistry, given the prejudices of Plato, presents certain difficulties. Our consideration will proceed in a different direction, not toward sophistry in its cultural significance but toward understanding, from the idea of sophistry itself, that with which the sophist as sophist is involved: semblance, the false, the not, and negation.

b) Critique of the traditional interpretation of sophistry.

The interpretation of sophistry, as it developed historiographically, and in the usual history of philosophy, took the sophists as exponents of definite philosophical positions as regards knowledge and life, so that the sophists were considered skeptics, relativists, and subjectivists, whatever these terms might mean. This view is untenable, since the sophists had, from the very outset, no interest in saying anything substantive about scientific questions. Therefore they lacked the concrete means to philosophize scientifically, so that one cannot attribute to them any definite scientific position, even if only the one of skepticism. What people have interpreted that way is thus for the sophists actually a mere object of speeches and argumentation and not something to be considered scientifically. For instance, the proposition of Protagoras, man is the measure of all things, is not the expression of a relativism or a skepticism, as if a theory of knowledge were to be found in that sophist. The traditional interpretation of sophistry was occasioned by the fact that the positive content of scientific research in philosophy was understood precisely in opposition to sophistry. But this way of understanding places that against which Plato, Aristotle, and Socrates worked their way forward on the same level as Plato and Aristotle themselves. It overlooks the fact that scientific philosophy did not arise as a counter-movement against certain doctrinal contents, schools, and the like, but arose instead from a radical reflection on existence, which in Greek public life was determined by the educational ideal of the sophists and not by a determinate philosophical movement. Only by passing through Plato could one think of making the sophists exponents of definite philosophical systems. And that is an inverted image of the spiritual development of the Greeks in general and, above all, of scientific philosophy itself.

c) Sophistry and rhetoric. Plato's position on rhetoric as distinct from Aristotle's. Their common judgment on sophistry (φαινομένη σοφία).

Since Plato identified sophistry with rhetoric (as even Aristotle still did in part), his battle against the sophists was at once a condemnation of the orators. That is, Plato did not succeed in attaining a positive understanding of rhetoric. Aristotle was the first to attain it, for he saw that this kind of speaking makes sense in everyday life, insofar as everyday discussions and deliberations are not so much a matter of disclosing the actual and strict truth but simply of forming a δόξα, a πίστις, a conviction. The positive reflections Aristotle carried out in his *Rhetoric* broke open Plato's identification of sophistry and rhetoric. Plato's identification of them is clear from the dialogues named after Greek sophists. The *Gorgias:* ταὐτόν ἐστιν σοφιστὴς καὶ ῥήτωρ, ἢ ἐγγύς τι καὶ παραπλήσιον (cf. 520a6ff.). "The sophist and the orator are the same, or in any case they come very close to one another and are similar." What is characteristic of the sophists, paid tutors of youth who claimed to have perfected this education, is also part and parcel of the orator, insofar as it is also the latter's goal to enact παιδεία in the sense of the δεινότης of the εὖ λέγειν, to enable one to speak well. The sophist who reached the highest spiritual level and who was esteemed accordingly even by Plato and Aristotle was Protagoras of Abdera. His work did not in fact stop with rhetoric, but in connection with reflections on speech he contributed to the development of certain basic grammatical concepts. Likewise Prodikos of Keos engaged in the question of significative nexuses.[2]

Aristotle's judgment on sophistry is basically the same as Plato's. The determination we encountered in Aristotle, namely that σοφιστική is φιλοσοφία φαινομένη, οὖσα δ' οὔ (cf. *Met.* IV, 2, 1004b26), we find almost verbatim in Plato's *Sophist:* πάντα ἄρα σοφοὶ τοῖς μαθηταῖς φαίνονται (233c8), "they seem to be and they pretend to be disciples in every respect, ones who know and understand." σοφοὶ φαίνονται, hence φιλοσοφία φαινομένη, οὖσα δ' οὔ. Plato says οὐκ ὄντες γε (233c8), "in fact they are not." The sophists do not have ἀλήθεια, i.e., their speaking does not disclose the things, but, instead, the sophists move in a δοξαστικὴ περὶ πάντων ἐπιστήμη (cf. 233c10), in a knowing which is only δοξαστική, which only looks like knowing and which claims to extend to everything. It only looks that way, it is only presumed knowledge, because it moves only in determinate opinions. Δοξαστική is to be taken in a double sense: on the one hand, it means the same as φαινομένη, "apparently," and at the same time there resides in it the reason this ἐπιστήμη is φαινομένη: because it does not provide ἀλήθεια but only δόξαι, opinions on matters, not the matters at issue themselves.

d) Ἀληθεύειν as ground of the question of μὴ ὄν (= ψεῦδος).

Our reflection on ἀληθεύειν has at the same time also provided the ground needed to understand why the sophist becomes thematic in the question about the Being of non-beings. That is, insofar as ἀληθεύειν has the sense of the uncovering of beings in their Being,[3] then its opposite, ψεύδεσθαι, distorting, deceiving, is the mode of comportment in which beings are covered over and distorted, the mode in which something shows itself—or "is"—as something it basically is not. The result is that non-being can be exhibited as being through the factual existence of error and deception. This is the inner connection between ἀληθές and ὄν, and between ψεῦδος and μὴ ὄν. The task is to draw closer to ψεύδεσθαι in order to gain the ground for presentifying μὴ ὄν itself.

2. See the appendix.
3. AH: ἀλήθεια—beingness.

§32. *Continuation: The idea of first philosophy in Aristotle.*

a) First philosophy as ontology (ὂν ᾗ ὄν) and as theology. Explication of this duality on the basis of the Greek understanding of Being (= presence).

Following Aristotle, we have gained some clarity concerning the question of ὄν, insofar as we can say it does not deal with a definite region of objects but with τὰ πάντα, with ὂν ᾗ ὄν, with the ὅλον. The question concerns the determinations which constitute beings in their Being. This idea of first philosophy, as Aristotle calls it, the original science of beings, is for him intersected by another fundamental science, which he designates as θεολογική, so that we have:

πρώτη φιλοσοφία
θεολογική
the science that considers ὂν ᾗ ὄν.

This latter came to be called "ontology." Aristotle himself does not ever use the term. For the science which considers ὂν ᾗ ὄν, Aristotle uses the expression πρώτη φιλοσοφία. Thus theology as well as ontology claim to be πρώτη φιλοσοφία.

This duality can be pursued further, into the Middle Ages up to the ontology of the modern period. People have sought to mediate between ontology and theology in Aristotle, in order to gain a "well-rounded picture" of Aristotle. This way is not fertile for an understanding of the matters at issue. Instead, the question should be raised why Greek science travelled such a path that it landed, as it were, with these two basic sciences, ontology and theology. Theology has the task of clarifying beings as a whole, the ὅλον, the beings of the world, nature, the heavens, and everything under them, to speak quite roughly, in their origins, in that by which they properly are.[1] It must be noted that the clarification of beings as a whole, nature, by means of an unmoved mover has nothing to do with proving God through a causal argument. Theology has the whole, the ὅλον, as its theme, and ontology too has the whole as its theme and considers its ἀρχαί. Both, theology and ontology, take their departure from beings as whole, as ὅλον; and it is their concern to understand the ὅλον, the whole in its entirety, as being. Why did Greek science and philosophy arrive at these two basic sciences? (In Plato they are still wholly intermingled; he leaves them even more unclarified than Aristotle does. But in fact

1. In the comments which follow, Heidegger takes his orientation from *Met.* XII, 1, 1069a18ff.

he already moves in both these dimensions.) It can be made understandable only on the basis of the meaning of Being for the Greeks.[2] Beings are what is present in the proper sense. Theology considers beings according to what they are already in advance, i.e., according to what constitutes, in the most proper and highest sense, the presence of the world. The most proper and highest presence of beings is the theme of theology. The theme of ontology is beings insofar as they are present in all their determinations, not tailored to a definite region, not only the unmoved mover and the heavens, but also what is under the heavens, everything there is, mathematical beings as well as physical. Thus the theme of theology is the highest and most proper presence, and the theme of ontology is that which constitutes presence as such in general.[3] The development of Greek science is pursued in these two original dimensions of reflection on Being. The real difficulty of understanding these matters and their proper productive formation and appropriation does not reside in θεολογική, whose approach is relatively clear to us, as it was to the Greeks as well, but in ontology and more precisely in the question: what is the sense of the characters of Being which pertain universally to all beings insofar as they are, in relation to the individual concrete being? Later, in scholaticism, this question was expressed as follows: do the universal determinations ontology provides concerning beings in their Being, i.e., concerning beings in general, have the character of genuses? Is ontology in some sense the science of the highest genuses of everything that is, or do these characters of Being have a different structural relation to beings?

A survey of the development of this entire question, thus of the basic questioning of ontology, from Aristotle and the Greeks up to the present, shows that we have in fact not advanced one step forward; indeed, quite to the contrary, the position the Greeks attained has for us been lost and we therefore do not even understand these questions any longer. Hegel's entire *Logic* moves within a complete lack of understanding and misunderstanding of all these questions. Husserl was the first, in connection with his idea of logic, to rediscover, as it were, the question of the meaning of the formal determinations of Being, though he did so, to be sure, only in a first—admittedly very important—beginning. It is no accident that this question emerged in connection with a clarification of the idea of logic, because—and here we arrive at a concluding characteristic of the fundamental science of the Greeks, πρώτη φιλοσοφία—this science is ultimately oriented toward λόγος, or, more precisely, because its theme is beings

2. See the appendix.
3. AH: Beings as a whole. Beings as such.

insofar as they are ὂν λεγόμενον, hence beings as addressed in speech, beings insofar as they are themes for λόγος.[4,5]

b) Λόγος as guideline for the research into Being carried out by σοφία. Explication of the guiding function of λόγος on the basis of the Greek understanding of Being.

As we have seen, Aristotle strives, precisely with his idea of σοφία, to go beyond λόγος to a νοεῖν that is free of λέγειν. But closer inspection shows that even his determination of the ultimate ἀρχή, the ἀδιαίρετον, is acquired only within an orientation toward λόγος. This is manifest in the fact that οὐσία, the basic determination of ὄν, has the character of ὑποκείμενον, of what is already there in advance, of utter and primary presence. That is the formal determination of anything at all. Now this ὑποκείμενον, what is already there in advance, is specifically seen in light of λέγειν: what, in speaking about something, in discussing some connection in beings, is there in advance, prior to all speech and on behalf of all speech. That is, what is spoken about is the ὑποκείμενον, ὄν, οὐσία, in a formal sense. The basic character of Being is drawn from the context of λόγος itself. Therefore—i.e., because λόγος is the guiding line—πρώτη φιλοσοφία, with regard to the question it raises (not with regard to theory), stands connected again to "logic," as we say today, i.e., connected to λέγεσθαι, dialectic. This is the meaning of the cliché heard every so often that for Aristotle metaphysics is logical and logic is metaphysical. The meaning is that even the ἀληθεύειν of σοφία, uncovering in the purest sense, still remains in a certain fashion μετὰ λόγου, that, consequently, for the explication of a given theme—even if only the sheer something in general—speech or discourse is the guiding line. This irruption of λόγος, of the logical in this rigorously Greek sense, in the questioning of ὄν, is motivated by the fact that ὄν, the Being of beings itself, is primarily interpreted as presence, and λόγος is the primary way in which one presentifies something, namely that which is under discussion. Let this suffice as a quite general preliminary orientation regarding questions we will subject to closer scrutiny in the context of Plato's *Sophist*.[6]

4. AH: Being and thinking.
5. See the appendix.
6. See the appendix.

MAIN PART

Plato's Research into Being
Interpretation of the *Sophist*[1]

Preliminary Remarks

§33. The meaning of the preceding preparation: the acquisition of the ground for an understanding of the issues in a specific Greek dialogue. The insufficiencies of the preparation.

If, now, armed with the preceding orientation, we go on to consider what is thematic in the dialogue, it will be clear at once that, although for many the preparation might already have been too lengthy and involved, it is still not enough and that it has by no means attained the ideal of a preparation for an interpretation. An ideal preparation would actually enable us to appropriate the dialogue, presupposing a rigorous and concentrated reading, at one stroke without entrammeling the understanding; i.e., it would render every pertinent horizon within which the dialogue moves completely perspicuous and available. Our introduction has admittedly not yet equipped us with all this, and under the present circumstances it never will.

Nevertheless, we have to retain the ideal of an interpretation which simply aims at allowing the dialogue to speak purely for itself. That goes without saying; today everyone claims to let the texts speak for themselves. It has become a watchword. In most cases, however, the obligation entailed by this claim is not understood. For it is not sufficient to lay out the largest possible text material and refrain from saying what is not in the text. That is no guarantee that even the slightest thing has been understood. On the contrary, this claim to let the text speak for itself involves the task not only of first pinning down, as it were, the issues discussed in the text but of letting these issues come forth in advance on the basis of a more penetrating understanding. The claim of allowing the texts to speak for themselves thus entails the obligation, as regards an understanding of the matters at issue, to be fundamentally more advanced than the object of the interpretation. Yet this claim, properly understood, is an occasion for modesty. For to be more advanced cannot mean (as I judge the situation) to be *superior* to Greek

1. Subtitle in Heidegger's manuscript.

scientific philosophy. It can only mean understanding that we have to enter into the service of this research in order to make a first attempt, following its guidance, to heed its immanent tendencies, to grasp and retain them in a more original elaboration, and in that way to fortify the ground upon which the discussion of the matters at issue must develop.

As regards ἀλήθεια, ἐπιστήμη, etc., it is not enough to find terminological equivalents and speak of the concepts of truth, science, semblance, deception, assertion, and the like. Nor is it enough, though this is often taken as a substantive interpretation, to leave everything in indeterminateness, to call on the end, itself not understood, to help explain the beginning, which has not been appropriated either, or in general to try to clarify any part, any passage, by means of another. Nor will it suffice to take passages from other dialogues dealing with the same theme and in this way attempt to understand Plato on the basis of Plato, Aristotle on the basis of Aristotle. All that is out of the question. What is decisive resides, as always, in a confrontation with the very matters at issue in the discussions. Unless we set out, in each case following the possibility of a development of an understanding, to exhibit and clarify that which is under discussion by basing ourselves on the matters at issue themselves, a comprehension of the philosophy of Plato and Aristotle, or of any philosophy at all, will be unthinkable.

To conceive of the task of interpretation in such a way is to know forthwith, even without being familiar with the history of philosophy, that there exists a continuity of radical questioning and research, a continuity not in the least manifest in the external aspect of what is commonly known about the trends, problems, systems, works, and personages in the history of philosophy. On the contrary, this continuity resides behind all that and cannot be the object of such a consideration. In this sense, the past comes alive only if we understand that we ourselves are that past. In the sense of our spiritual existence, we are the philosopher as well as, in general, the scientist we were, and we will be what we receive and appropriate from what we were, and here the most important factor will be *how* we do so. On the basis of these simple temporal relations, the temporal relations of human—and particularly spiritual—existence, we see the proper meaning of actual research to be a confrontation with history, a history which becomes existent *[existent wird]* only when the research is historical, i.e., when it understands that it is itself history. Only in this way does the possibility of the historiographical arise.[2] An appeal to supertemporal or eternal values and the like is not needed to justify historical research.

What I am saying is supposed to indicate that the interpretation, even

2. Thus in Heidegger's manuscript.

more than the preceding reflections, whose sense was to clarify what is peculiarly Greek, will require you to be prepared for an actual confrontation with the matters we are about to take up.

§34. Recapitulation: First characterization of sophistry. Delimitation of sophistry against dialectic and philosophy. The appreciation of the εὖ λέγειν*: unconcern with substantive content versus concern with substantive content.*

To comprehend the dialogue we need to adhere to the meaning of sophistry as delimited against dialectics and philosophy. Sophistry is characterized by an unconcern with substantive content, an unconcern in a quite determinate sense, not one that is haphazard, arbitrary, or occasional, but one that is a matter of principle. Yet this unconcern may not be understood as if there was alive in the sophists a basic intention to distort and conceal the matters at issue, as if they wanted to do nothing but deceive. We could determine their unconcern in a better way by calling it emptiness, a *lack* of substantive content; i.e., this unconcern is grounded in something positive, in a determinate appreciation of the domination of speech and the speaking person. The spoken word in its domination in single individuals as well as in the community is what is most decisive for the sophist. Now insofar as this obstinate adherence to the word and to the beautifully and strikingly spoken word always involves the obligation, as a mode of speaking, to speak about something, the interest in speaking is by itself already an unconcern with substantive content, simply by the fact that it emphasizes the form alone, i.e., the form of the speech and argumentation. In other words, insofar as all speech is about something and insofar as the sophist speaks, he has to speak about something, whether or not the content he speaks about is of interest to him. But precisely because it does not interest him, i.e., because he is not bound by the content of his speech, because for him the meaning of the speaking resides solely in its beauty, he is unconcerned with substantive content, i.e., he is unburdened by the substantive content of what he says. Now insofar as speech is the basic mode of access to the world and of commerce with it, insofar as it is the mode in which the world is primarily present—and not only the world but also other people and the respective individual himself—the emptiness of the speech is equivalent to an ungenuineness and uprootedness of human existence. That is the proper meaning of sophistry's unconcern with substantive content as a form of emptiness. Keep in mind that the Greeks see existence as existence in the πόλις. The opposite of this existence, of the one that is uprooted, and the opposite of the way it expresses itself in communal spiritual life, resides in genuine existence, i.e., in a concern with substantive content, in a concern with disclosing beings and in obtaining a basic understanding of them. In other words, genuine existence resides in the idea of scientific philosophy, as Socrates first brought it to life and as Plato and Aristotle then developed it concretely. We must now actually understand this simple matter of the opposition between unconcern with substantive content and genuine concern with it, i.e., genuine research. We must understand it in such a way that every one of us understands for his part and in his own place what it means to be concerned with substantive content. The difficulty of the dialogue lies neither in the specifically ontological treatise about non-being and negation and the like, nor in the complexity of the divisions with which the consideration begins. On the contrary, the real difficulty is to bring the connection of the whole into proper focus and thereby see the content that is genuinely and ultimately at issue, so that from it as from a unitary source the understanding of every single proposition will be nourished. To facilitate an insight into the whole of the dialogue, we will presentify its articulation and keep that on hand in order to be able to refer to it at any time.

§35. *Structure and articulation of the* Sophist.

a) General characterization of the structure of the *Sophist*. The traditional division: introduction, shell, kernel. Acceptance and critique.

The dialogue which is our primary theme, the *Sophist*, is relatively transparent in its structure and articulation. The lines marking the sections, in which the content is for the most part divided, are assigned by universal agreement, apart from a few minor deviations. I will follow the articulation Bonitz[1] offers, which is also the one most accepted. No special value is to be placed on this articulation; it has no significance for an understanding, it is only meant as an extrinsic orientation.

The dialogue, speaking very roughly, consists of an "introduction," and, it is said, an enclosing shell and a kernel. This image also characterizes the way such a dialogue is taken up. The introduction is the prelude to the dialogue; the enclosing shell, it is said, is the question of the essence of the sophist, which is the immediate issue, but which is then interrupted by the question of the Being of non-beings. Here we have the kernel. At the end of this, the dialogue leads again to the question taken up first, the question

1. H. Bonitz, *Platonische Studien*, 3. Auflage, Berlin 1886, p. 152ff.

of the essence of the sophist, so that the latter question, like a shell, encloses the question of the Being of non-beings.

Such a harmless division as that into "introduction," enclosing shell, and kernel already betrays the fact that it is confined to the extrinsic and the literary, to the material occurrences and themes of the dialogue, and is seeking an exemption from asking about the articulation of the matter at issue itself, i.e., from inquiring into *what* the dialogue is dealing with. This extrinsic articulation has given rise to equally extrinsic problems. In connection with the orientation expressed in this image, the difficulty has arisen that the title only touches what would constitute the shell and precisely not the inner core. For Plato's genuine aim, namely the question of the Being of non-beings, is not expressed in the title; what the title presents would thus be a mere playful imitation of sophistry. This division into shell and kernel is a classic example of how the image of a separation of matter from form, without an orientation toward the genuine questions, can breed pseudo-problems, e.g., the problem of why the dialogue is called the *Sophist*, whereas its main theme is the Being of non-beings.

From the very outset, i.e., already in our consideration of the prelude to the dialogue, we want to free ourselves from this extrinsic division. That means nothing else than that from the very outset we will take pains to expose the context in which the dialogue moves, i.e., the concrete connection of the phenomena which are thematic in the whole dialogue and are not merely treated within the inner core or as part of the shell. This connection between what the image characterizes as kernel and what it characterizes as shell must be worked out in terms of the very matters at issue.

The introduction of the dialogue comprises, according to the old division into chapters, chapters one and two, 216a–219a. This introduction is a prelude to the dialogue; its task is to pose the theme and to indicate the way the theme is to be dealt with. The shell, which in a certain sense encloses the kernel, is found, as it were, on both sides, initially (chapters 3–24) as ushering in the kernel.

b) The articulation of the *Sophist* (according to H. Bonitz).[2]

Introduction: Chapters 1–2, 216a–218b.

Ia) Search for the definition of the sophist, Chapters 3–24.

1.) An example of the method of definition. The definition of the ἀσπαλιευτής. Chapters 4–7, 219a4–221c4.

2. See the note on p. 160.

2.) The first six definitions of the sophist. Chapters 8–19, 221c5–231c9.

3.) The preparation for the indigenous or genuine definition. Chapters 20–24, 232b–236c.

The individual definitions of the sophist. Chapters 8–24.

a) Preparatory definitions. Chapters 8–19.

1st definition 221c–223b.

2nd definition 223b–224d.

3rd and 4th definitions 224d, e.

5th definition 224e–226a.

6th definition 226a–231c.

Summary 231d–232a.

b) Indigenous definition. Chapters 20–24.

7th definition 232b–236c.

(Cf. Continuation at 264c.)

The 7th definition of the sophist as ἀντιλογικός provides the point of departure for the consideration of the fundamental problem:

II The Being of non-beings. Chapters 25–47, 237b9–264b9.

1.) Difficulties in the concept of non-beings. Chapters 25–29. 237b9–242b5.

2.) Difficulties in the concept of beings. Chapters 30–36, 242b6–250e.

3.) The positive resolution of the problem through the κοινωνία τῶν γενῶν. Chapters 36–47, 250e–264c.

Ib. Conclusion of the definition of the sophist. Chapters 48–52, 264c–268c.

INTRODUCTION

The Prelude to the Dialogue[1]
(*Sophist* 216a–219a)

§36. First intimation of the theme and method of the dialogue. Introduction of the ξένος *from Elea. The fundamental theses of Parmenides.* Θεὸς ἐλεγκτικός*? The divinity of philosophy. Theme of the dialogue: the philosopher. Method:* διακρίνειν τὸ γένος*. The ground of* διακρίνειν*: immediate self-showing (*φάντασμα*) and popular opinion:* φιλόσοφοι = πολιτικοί-σοφισταί-μανικοί.

If we divide its content very schematically, the prelude of the dialogue has the task of determining, first, the theme, namely what a philosopher is, and, second, the method. The dialogue begins with Theodorus, together with Theaetetus, bringing a stranger to Socrates. Theodorus had already been a participant in a dialogue, namely the one immediately preceding, the *Theaetetus.* There (*Theaetetus,* 143b8) he was called γεωμέτρης. Theodorus was Plato's teacher of mathematics. He comes from Cyrene in North Africa. This Theodorus, along with Theaetetus, a younger philosopher, approaches Socrates κατὰ τὴν χθὲς ὁμολογίαν (216a1), "according to the appointment made yesterday." Thereby reference is made to the dialogue *Theaetetus.* Theodorus brings with him a ξένος, a foreigner. The dialogue begins with Theodorus' presentation of this foreigner to Socrates. We learn: 1.) τὸ μὲν γένος ἐξ' Ἐλέας (a2f.), that this ξένος comes from Elea, 2.) ἑταῖρον δὲ τῶν ἀμφὶ Παρμενίδην καὶ Ζήνωνα (a3f.), that he is a companion and associate of the disciples of Parmenides and Zeno, indicating his spiritual-scientific roots, and 3.) μάλα δὲ ἄνδρα φιλόσοφον (a4), that he is a very philosophical man, characterizing his very existence.

Thus a philosopher from the school of Parmenides is introduced. This indicates the entire spiritual atmosphere of the dialogue. For the genuine argumentation and the substantive discussion move within the horizon of the mode of questioning established by Eleatic philosophy, by Parmenides of Elea. Thereby at the very outset the substantive content of the dialogue is indicated in a provisional way, namely the question of whether there are also non-beings. That is only the counter-question to the fundamental proposition of the Eleatic school, the principle of Parmenides: beings are. That is the positive thesis, which now will be shaken in the course of this

1. Title in Heidegger's manuscript.

dialogue. For our knowledge of Parmenides, we do not have to rely on doxographic material, since we even have actual fragments of his didactic poem, entitled Περὶ φύσεως. We now want to take this didactic poem merely as a provisional indication of the fundamental conception of beings, from which the counter-position of the dialogue will be understandable.

Already the title, Περὶ φύσεως, points to the fact that beings, which are at issue there, are taken in the sense of the whole of nature and the world.[2] To characterize in a preliminary way the basic proposition of the Parmenidean school, we may quote a statement from fragment 6 (cited according to the order of Hermann Diels): χρὴ τὸ λέγειν τε νοεῖν τ' ἐὸν ἔμμεναι· ἔστι γὰρ εἶναι, μηδὲν δ' οὐκ ἔστιν· τά σ' ἐγὼ φράζεσθαι ἄνωγα. "It is necessary to assert and to apprehend about beings as such that they are"; it is necessary to say that beings are. Ἔστι γὰρ εἶναι, "for Being is." And now, in simple opposition to this formally universal proposition about Being: μηδὲν δ'οὐκ ἔστιν. That is how the proposition has been handed down. But according to a conjecture which first became known after Diels' edition, we should read, instead of μηδέν, μὴ δ' εἶν' οὐκ: "But non-being is not." *Positio:* Being is; *negatio:* Non-being is not. We see here already that this proposition has been obtained under the strong impress of speaking and asserting. It says, expressing, as it were, an archaic truth:[3] beings are, non-beings are not. Without looking at the phenomena any further, but merely on the basis of an obviously perceived content, the proposition says: beings are, and non-beings are not. The *Sophist* places the second assertion in question. Thereby the meaning of Being gets modified, and the first assertion is set on a more radical basis. The dialogue refers explicitly to the Eleatic school at 241aff. and at 258cff.

This presentation of the ξένος as a stranger from Elea, and as an adept of the school of Parmenides and Zeno, as a very philosophical man, indicates what is now properly to come. Socrates responds to this presentation of the stranger. We ask: how does Socrates react to the introduction of the stranger? We can at first say only: Socratically. Which must then be made more clear. Socrates turns the dialogue and the attention given to the foreigner as a important stranger away toward a wholly different connection. Ἀρ' οὖν οὐ ξένον ἀλλά τινα θεὸν ἄγων κατὰ τὸν Ὁμήρου λόγον λέληθας (cf. 216a5f.), perhaps it is a god you are bringing here—without knowing it, i.e., in such a way that you are concealed to yourself in what you bring and what you do—perhaps you bring along a god. We must understand that Socrates is here in his way altogether struck, as it were, by this meeting,

2. AH: The title came later! But then also φύσις: what in itself grows from itself; beings in themselves. Cf. Heraclitus: ἡ φύσις κρύπτεσθαι φιλεῖ (fragment 123).

3. AH: primordially and immediately.

insofar as we must presuppose that Socrates = Plato and accordingly must assume in Socrates the same enormous respect Plato himself had for Parmenides, since Plato (the dialogue *Parmenides* preceded the *Sophist*, if the chronology is correct)[4] had already properly understood and appropriated Parmenides' far-reaching discovery. Socrates hence is in the situation of encountering something out of the ordinary and of being offered an unusual opportunity. His reaction is not to burst forth into a wild discussion but to meditate quietly about what this occasion could bring to pass. In this connection, it must be taken into account that Socrates/Plato not only knew about the lofty meaning of the philosophy of Parmenides but also knew that Parmenides had founded a school and that, at the time of Socrates, precisely these Eleatics, the philosophers of this school, were making a particularly great sensation. They exhibited a special arrogance and fell into a blind negating of all other research. Yet they did so, as disciples very often do, without an awareness and appropriation of what the teacher himself once had to go through and what he thereby confronted and discovered. Socrates was aware of the esteem due the founder of the school but was also acquainted with the ill behavior of the disciples, who were causing a sensation to their own advantage. Socrates thus first refers positively, since basically he is positive, to this eminent possibility: οὐ ξένον ἀλλά τινα θεὸν ἄγων λέληθας. And he does not let it rest with a mere reference but clarifies what is properly at stake in this possibility, that here perhaps a god is coming in a concealed way. That is, by citing a passage from Homer's *Odyssey*, XVII, 485–487, he points out that often other gods, though predominantly the θεὸς ξένιος, accompany men and travel with them, συνοπαδὸν γιγνόμενον ὕβρεις τε καὶ εὐνομίας τῶν ἀνθρώπων καθορᾶν (b2f.), and "thereby look down on the transgressions and good deeds of men," and thus keep abreast of human affairs. Socrates again uses the expression καθορᾶν, at 216c6, to characterize philosophers and precisely the genuine ones. The gods who in this way are secret companions look upon the behavior[5] of man with a critical eye. And thus here, too, it could be that one of τῶν κρειττόνων (b4) is actually accompanying the philosophical stranger. The καθορᾶν, the looking down, of the θεός would then be ἐποψόμενος, "watching us"; the θεός would carry on an inspection of us, perhaps with the specific outcome φαύλους ἡμᾶς ὄντας ἐν τοῖς λόγοις (b4f.), "that we are deficient in our λόγοι," i.e., that we do not genuinely know what we are talking about, that in our λέγειν we fall short as regards the foundedness of our speech in the things themselves. Thus perhaps this god is at the same time ἐλέγξων (b5), the one who exposes us publicly,

4. AH: "contemporaneous" in production, not in publication.
5. AH: βίος.

makes us publicly visible and exhibits us for what we are and thereby confutes us. This is the possibility Socrates is referring to. Socrates thus is responding to the presentation of the foreigner in a peculiar fashion, by, as it were, looking away from this new acquaintance and envisioning a higher possibility, one which could be given along with the appearance of the foreigner: οὐ ξένον, ἀλλά τινα θεόν.

This reference to a higher possibility, as well as the more precise characterization of this possibility—that Socrates and those with him could be found wanting as regards their discussion of the matters they are about to take up—now have, however, the Socratic sense of forcing the stranger, or, rather, the one who has introduced him, Theodorus, to acknowledge this higher possibility held out to them. Thus Theodorus is compelled to reveal how things stand with the stranger. He is compelled to present the foreigner in the latter's true spirit. Hence the response of Theodorus: Οὐχ οὗτος ὁ τρόπος τοῦ ξένου, ἀλλὰ μετριώτερος τῶν περὶ τὰς ἔριδας ἐσπουδακότων. καί μοι δοκεῖ θεὸς μὲν ἀνὴρ οὐδαμῶς εἶναι, θεῖος μήν· πάντας γὰρ ἐγὼ τοὺς φιλοσόφους τοιούτους προσαγορεύω (cf. b7ff.), "That is not the character of the foreigner; on the contrary, he is of a more moderate temper than those who direct all their endeavors toward disputation." This answer shows Theodorus understood the reference Socrates made by speaking of the θεὸς ἐλεγκτικός (b5f.), i.e., the reference to the disputatiousness of the Eleatics, the disciples of Parmenides. In the face of the higher possibility of being a god, the ξένος now reveals himself more precisely, i.e., now there begins the proper presentation of what he is, over and against merely extrinsic characteristics. Now it is to be decided whether he has actually received his allotment from his school and wears, as we say, his school colors, i.e., whether he has his work from his school and understands his work to be this work, finding his limits in this work, or whether he is capable of being unprejudiced even with regard to the propositions and dogmas of his school. That is to say, it must now be shown whether he is ultimately capable of patricide, i.e., whether he can topple the standing of his teacher from the ground up. Only if he harbors this possibility could he perhaps be a person to be taken seriously in the matters at issue. Or is he just a shallow wrangler who derives prestige merely by belonging to the school and who plies his trade at the expense of the school and for the sake of a career?

The second intention of Socrates' response is to deflate any possible pretensions on the part of the newcomer to offer up a great philosophy. For the answer of Theodorus is very cautious; he draws back, as it were: καί μοι δοκεῖ θεὸς μὲν ἀνὴρ οὐδαμῶς εἶναι, θεῖος μήν (b8f.), the stranger I am bringing here is not a god, though in truth he is divine. And then the general characterization: πάντας γὰρ ἐγὼ τοὺς φιλοσόφους τοιούτους προσαγορεύω (b9f.), "I am accustomed to apprehend and address all philosophers as divine." This predicate of "divine," as applied to the philosophers, means that the object of their questioning is what is highest among beings. Moreover, already here in Plato, where the notion of the θεῖον has a more obscure and much more comprehensive sense than in Aristotle, "divine" does not have a religious meaning, as one might think, such that this person could then be characterized in a specific sense as religious. We must conceive the "divine" in a worldly sense, or—from the standpoint of Christianity—in a pagan sense, insofar as θεῖος, "divine," here simply means to relate, in one's knowledge, to those beings having the highest rank in the order of reality. Included here is nothing like a connection of the divine or of god to an individual man in the sense of a direct personal relationship. Thus Socrates forces Theodorus to present his companion in his proper spiritual provenance and to draw back to legitimate claims.

Socrates takes this answer literally, as it were, and thereby we are already given the theme of the dialogue. The last sentence of Theodorus' answer, πάντας γὰρ ἐγὼ τοὺς φιλοσόφους τοιούτους προσαγορεύω, becomes the point of departure for a reflection on Socrates' part, whose object is to distinguish, διακρίνειν (c3), these two realities, the philosopher and the divine, the god, and specifically to διακρίνειν with regard to the γένος. Socrates says: Alright, there is indeed a distinction, and the man you present to me might very well not be a god, but nevertheless it must be noted that both, the philosopher and the god, the divine, are equally difficult to disentangle, equal difficult to understand. We must notice that not just any arbitrary expression is used here for "understanding" or "close determination," but instead διακρίνειν τὸ γένος (cf. c2f.), κρίνειν, to distinguish, to set something off over and against something else, and specifically to delimit the γένος. We must take the expression γένος here as originally as possible: it means the origin of the philosopher, or of the god, the origin in the sense of ontological lineage. In the setting off of one against the other, in this differentiation of one against the other, the γένος from which each becomes what it is must therefore be extracted. This is the proper ontological meaning of γένος: that out of which something becomes what it is, the stem, ancestry, lineage, origination. Thus what is at stake here is not an arbitrary popular delimitation of the philosopher over and against the divine. Rather, the expression γένος already refers to this particular sort of questioning and differentiating.

Not only that; Socrates also indicates the ground more precisely, insofar as he points out at the same time how the question of what the philosopher is and what his γένος is presupposes a first orientation in terms of what we in an average and naive way, in everyday life, know about the object we are now interrogating. Socrates characterizes the popular knowledge about philosophers, and what philosophers are, by saying: πάνυ παντοῖοι (cf. c4f.), "with much variety, in many different ways," do they show themselves, φαντάζεσθαι. Φάντασμα does not here mean appearance as mere phantasy, over and against real perception, but instead has the original sense of φαίνεσθαι, self-showing, immediate apparition, in which the philosopher manifests himself to the people, to persons of average sophistication. If we ask the person of average culture what he thinks of philosophers, the first thing he will express is some kind of a judgment, either one of denigration or of esteem. To some, philosophers appear to be "of no value," τοῦ μεδενὸς τίμιοι (c7f.), a superfluous type of humanity; to others, however, they are "worthy of the highest veneration," ἄξιοι τοῦ παντός (c8). Hence we have here contrasting judgments which do not so much rest on an actual presentification of the matter at issue, but on an immediate common impression, on the predominating temper and opinion. And indeed the variety of the apparitions in which the philosopher figures results διὰ τὴν τῶν ἄλλων ἄγνοιαν (c4f.), "from the unfamiliarity of the others." Here οἱ ἄλλοι means the same as οἱ πολλοί, the multitude.

In connection with this characterization of the immediate popular view of the philosopher, Socrates provides at the same time a positive indication of the way the ὄντως φιλόσοφος (cf. c6), "the real philosopher," appears. Ὄντως φιλόσοφος stands in opposition to πλαστῶς (c6); πλάττω means to feign, to fabricate, to concoct a figure. In another context, ἀληθῶς replaces ὄντως. The feigned philosopher is thus opposed to the true one. Socrates now determines the true philosophers as καθορῶντες ὑψόθεν, "looking down from above on the βίος of those who are beneath them." οἱ μὴ πλαστῶς ἀλλ' ὄντως φιλόσοφοι, καθορῶντες ὑψόθεν τὸν τῶν κάτω βίον (c5f.). The occupation of the philosopher is therefore ὁρᾶν, to look upon the βίος. Notice that the word here is not ζωή, life in the sense of the presence of human beings in the nexus of animals and plants, of everything that crawls and flies, but βίος, life in the sense of existence, the leading of a life, which is characterized by a determinate τέλος, a τέλος functioning for the βίος itself as an object of πρᾶξις. The theme of philosophy is thus the βίος of man and possibly the various kinds of βίοι. "They look down from above." That implies that the philosopher himself, in order to be able to carry out such a possibility in earnest, must have attained a mode of existence guaranteeing him the possibility of such a look and thereby making accessible to him life and existence in general.[6]

If we ask more precisely what popular opinion, which is always affectively disposed to the philosophers in one way or another, finds to say about them, the result is threefold. For some, philosophers show themselves

6. AH: *outside the cave*. Οἱ κάτω. In the cave.

as πολιτικοί, for others as σοφισταί, and for still others as παντάπασι μανικῶς (cf. 216c8–d2), as "utterly deranged." These three determinations, politician, sophist, and madman, are not accidental; nor is the indeterminateness in which popular opinion about the philosopher moves an arbitrary one. On the contrary, we can see from the threefold characterization that it is a matter of men whose doctrine and teaching aim at human beings insofar as they live in the πόλις. For even the sophist, in his proper occupation, is a ῥήτωρ, an orator and teacher of rhetoric, a teacher of the speech that plays a substantial role in the public life of the πόλις: in the courts, in the senate, and in festivals. It is a matter then of people who are directed to the πολιτικά. And so despite all the indeterminateness surrounding the essence of the philosopher, a certain range of his possible activity is indeed already given: σοφιστής, πολιτικός, and παντάπασιν ἔχων μανικῶς. From this (217a3) and from what follows, people have drawn the conclusion that Plato intended to write a trilogy. We possess along with the *Sophist* a further dialogue under the title "Πολιτικός," and, as to content, in a certain sense they belong together. Plato left unfinished, it is said, the third dialogue, about the philosopher. Now this is a picture of Plato as a grade-school teacher, one who writes dramas and who is bent on composing a trilogy. Closer inspection will show that for Plato things were not so simple. On the contrary, it is precisely the dialogue on the sophist that accomplishes the task of clarifying what the philosopher is, and indeed it does so not in a primitive way, by our being told what the philosopher is, but precisely Socratically. In the last parts of the dialogue there occurs a passage (2253c8f.) where the protagonist says explicitly that in fact now, even before their discussion has arrived at the proper scientific definition of the sophist, they suddenly might have found the philosopher. That is noteworthy, not only as regards content, but purely methodologically, insofar as this makes it clear that Plato knew he could interpret the sophist as the antipode of the philosopher only if he was already acquainted with the philosopher and knew how matters stand with him. We shall thus dismiss this trilogy and attempt to derive from the *Sophist* the genuine answer to the question raised there: what is a philosopher?

§37. More precision on the theme. Explication of the thematic object of a question in general: the distinction between the matter at issue (τί), the determination of the matter (γένος), and the designation of the matter (ὄνομα). Λόγος as the unitary field of the threefold distinction. Task: application of this distinction to three objects: σοφιστής—πολιτικός—φιλόσοφος.

After Socrates provides Theodorus, or the ξένος, with a ground in this way—namely, first by indicating how that which is at issue, the philosopher, is manifest immediately, i.e., in natural opinion, and, further, by sharply fixing the question, insofar as what is to be sought is the γένος of the being at issue—he asks the ξένος to give him information on this point: τοῦ μέντοι ξένου ἡμῖν ἡδέως ἂν πυνθανοίμην, εἰ φίλον αὐτῷ, τί ταῦθ' οἱ περὶ τὸν ἐκεῖ τόπον ἡγοῦντο καὶ ὠνόμαζον (216d2ff.). He wants an answer from him about two things: 1.) τί ἡγοῦντο, what the Eleatic school, and hence ultimately Parmenides himself, maintained about the philosopher, how they conceived the philosopher or the man of science, and 2.) τί ὠνόμαζον, what they called him. Theodorus requires a more precise determination of the question. At that point it becomes evident that Socrates is not raising the question of the philosopher in isolation but is laying under it the whole ground: σοφιστής, πολιτικός, φιλόσοφος. And he provides a more precise explication of what exactly is now to be investigated in the dialogue. Quite roughly, there is given—using the expression "subject matter" in a completely formal sense—a subject matter to be interrogated: the philosopher. The question is how this subject matter is to be taken, and further, how it is to be denominated. The pregiven subject matter, the theme, is the "what," the τί. And this is to be determined as such and such, the philosopher as this or that, determined from his origination, according to his ontological provenance, thus out of his γένος. And the thematic object which in this way will be determined out of the γένος is to obtain its appropriate designation, its ὄνομα. The ὄνομα is hence not arbitrary but is given on the basis of the investigation into the subject matter itself. This question concerning what the subject matter is, and then concerning how it is to be taken and determined, and finally concerning the designation which nails it down, is now to be pursued with regard to the three given objects: σοφιστής, πολιτικός, φιλόσοφος. The question arises whether all this is one and the same subject matter, and only the names are different, or whether, along with the three names we have to do here with three different subject matters as well, whereby it becomes necessary to pursue a threefold genetic derivation of the Being of these three different matters and, accordingly, the three designations are justified. This is the more precise question which gradually emerges; hence it is the explication of what was called above, quite roughly, διακρίνειν τὸ γένος.

In order to do real justice to this questioning and to understand it, we must keep in mind the fact that for the science and philosophy of those times such a distinction within the subject matter, i.e., a distinction between the determination, or the provenance of the determination, of the subject matter and its denomination was anything but obvious and that Plato was the very first, precisely in these dialogues, to secure these quite primordial distinctions and make them bear fruit in a concrete investigation. We who think we know much more and take most things as obvious can no longer see in such questioning a great deal. We must therefore turn ourselves back in the right way, as it were, and presentify a kind of speaking about questions and subject matters which does not at all make these distinctions between denomination, determination of the subject matter, and subject matter itself. This is precisely what is characteristic of sophistry and idle talk, namely that it is caught up in words, indeed partly from an ingrained superficiality, but also partly from an incapacity to see these states of affairs themselves and to distinguish them. If we ask where this distinction itself belongs—the distinction between τί, γένος, and ὄνομα—hence where the unitary field is, within which these characters can be studied each for itself as well as connected together, it becomes evident that that is nothing else than λόγος. The way and the extent to which Plato, precisely in this dialogue, articulates his understanding of λόγος are also decisive for an elucidation of the structure of the τί, of the γένος, and of the ὄνομα, as well as for their connection. At the same time they are also concretely decisive for the response to the question posed, under the guiding line of this distinction, with regard to the sophist, the philosopher, and the politician. The κοινωνία τῶν γενῶν, which, in the consideration of the Being of nonbeings, is supposed to provide the genuine solution to the problem, can only be understood on the basis of a determinate conception of λόγος, i.e., from a definite interpretation of the structural moments of λόγος. For all speaking, as a speaking about something, has that which is spoken of, a τί, in the widest sense. Furthermore, all speaking is speaking about something *as something*, interpreting it on the basis of something, bringing it to intelligibility on the basis of something; hence all speaking possesses, formally, a γένος. Lastly, all speaking is, if concrete, something phonetic; the subject matter about which one speaks has its names, its denomination; it is called, as we say, so and so. And thus the concrete phenomenon of λόγος presents the "about which," the "as which," and the phonetic denomination.

The fact that the question about the philosopher remains oriented to these distinctions and is actually carried out in that way shows that for Plato it no longer sufficed to obtain a preliminary and popular clarity with regard to the distinctions within certain subject matters. A proof of this is the whole dialogue itself. At the end, one will say Plato knew all along that between the sophist and the philosopher there is a distinction to be made, and others perhaps knew it as well—just as we know of many things: they are distinct. But to clarify this distinctness properly, on the basis of a presentification of the subject matter, requires a scientific investigation. This shows that such scientific investigations for the most part come up against phenomena that are entirely unclarified and undetermined. And so, within the dialogue which intends to delimit the subject matters in question quite clearly and explicitly, we see that in connection with this task, which, within certain limits, does succeed, at the same time subject matters of new content become visible though they are not investigated. Yet this is sufficient for their philosophical significance.

The ξένος now has objections. He of course agrees to relate what his school thinks about these matters and their distinctions: it is not difficult to say that the three names apply to three things. καθ' ἕκαστον μὴν διορίσασθαι σαφῶς τί ποτ' ἔστιν, οὐ σμικρὸν οὐδὲ ῥᾴδιον ἔργον (217b2f.). "On the other hand, to clarify respectively each of the three, to delimit the one against the other, and to say what each for its part is—these are not slight matters and are not easy to bring about." In the meantime, however, Theodorus remarks to Socrates that he himself, Theodorus, on his way over, already discussed these questions with the foreigner and made the observation that the foreigner is very well informed about the subject matter, καὶ οὐκ ἀμνημονεῖν (b8), and above all, "he does not forget anything." That means he is able to survey the entire domain of the question at issue; he thus leaves nothing out, and everything important is present to him and at his disposal.

§38. More precision on the method.

a) Λόγος as the method of the investigation. The type of λόγος: mixed form between dialogue and monological treatise. Introduction of Theaetetus as collocutor. Agreement about the initial theme: the sophist. Ground rule of the method: τὸ πρᾶγμα αὐτο διὰ λόγων. The linking of substantive thinking and methodological thinking in Plato.

After establishing the question regarding the theme, Socrates makes his second and last move within this dialogue—for afterwards he withdraws completely from the discussion and acts merely as an auditor. He induces the foreigner to declare which method he prefers in the treatment of this question, whether he wants to deal with the question by way of a λόγος μακρός (cf. c3ff.), a lengthy treatise, which he αὐτὸς ἐπὶ σαυτοῦ, in a certain sense will "speak to himself" monologically, or δι' ἐρωτήσεων, "by way of question and answer," or, as it is called later, κατὰ σμικρὸν ἔπος πρὸς ἔπος (217d9), "in the form of brief speeches and counterspeeches." The foreigner will decide among these possibilities of method depending on the disposition of the one with whom he has to conduct the discussion. If the one with whom he will converse is ἀλύπως (d1), not overly sensitive, i.e., if within the argumentation and discussion he is not influenced by his moods, and if he is εὐηνίως (d1), easy to guide,[1] i.e., if he is not obdurate, not dogmatic, if he does not enter the discussion convinced he is right in every case, whether it is true or not—thus if he gets such a partner, who in perfect freedom is open to what is going to be discussed, then indeed in that case he prefers the way of λόγος πρὸς ἄλλον (cf. d2); if not, then he prefers to speak to himself alone and expose the subject matter to them in a long discourse. Socrates then proposes Theaetetus, who already in the preceding dialogue, which bears his name, was one of the discussants and who demonstrated his understanding of the subject matter. The ξένος consents, but in such a way that he once again excuses himself; he emphasizes he will speak πρὸς ἕτερον (e2), to an other and with him, thus not monologically, but that by reason of the difficulty of the subject matter the dialogue would likely turn out in such a way that he ἐκτείναντα ἀπομηκύνειν λόγον συχνὸν κατ' ἐμαυτόν (e1f.), "that he will have to conduct the discussion of connected subject matters by way of a λόγος which is συχνός, continuous"—συνεχές lurks in the background—so that many subject matters and determinations will be presented one after the other, as they are connected. In this way, a peculiar mixed form of the mode of treating the theme comes into being: indeed a dialogue, a discussion, which, however, in part already has the character of a monological treatise; and the reason for this resides in the difficulty of the subject matter. Finally the ξένος addresses himself to Theaetetus, with whom the discussion is now to be carried out, and they once more come to an agreement about what is properly in question. ἀρχομένῳ πρῶτον ἀπὸ τοῦ σοφιστοῦ, ζητοῦντι καὶ ἐμφανίζοντι λόγῳ τί ποτ' ἔστι (cf. 218b6ff.). "We are to begin first with the sophist, and in discussion we are to seek him and to bring what he is, i.e., what the subject matter is, to a self-showing." And now there follows once more the establishing of a common ground. νῦν γὰρ τοὔνομα μόνον ἔχομεν κοινῇ (cf. c1f.). "At first, in the question of what the sophist is, we have only the name in common"; τὸ δὲ ἔργον, "what is at issue here" is τάχ' ἂν ἰδίᾳ παρ' ἡμῖν αὐτοῖς ἔχοιμεν (c2ff.),

1. AH: not obstinate.

"for each of us, perhaps still conceived and intended differently." But now comes the rule under which they place themselves: δεῖ δὲ ἀεὶ παντὸς πέρι τὸ πρᾶγμα αὐτὸ μᾶλλον διὰ λόγων ἢ τοὔνομα μόνον συνωμολογῆσθαι χωρὶς λόγου (218c4f.). "It is always important in each case to find the subject matter itself and to agree upon it by way of discussion," i.e., by exhibiting, uncovering, "rather than simply agreeing on the word," the denomination, χωρὶς λόγου, "without a demonstration on the basis of the subject matter itself." In this way, therefore, the method and the specific interest of the question of the dialogue are elucidated. Because of this peculiar linkage of investigative thinking with methodological thinking in Plato, we can expect that, along with the determination of the essence of the sophist, or of the philosopher, we will also learn something important about the mode of treatment itself, i.e., about λόγος.

We have seen that Socrates gives precision to the question of the essence of the philosopher in two directions, first by asking the ξένος: τί ἡγοῦντο, what do your co-disciples and your teacher think about the person who is called a philosopher, and secondly by asking the ξένος: τί ὠνόμαζον, in what significative nexuses do they discuss and determine this subject matter? This double or, rather, threefold question—about the subject matter (τί), its determination (γένος), and its denomination (ὄνομα)—indicates at the same time that the methodological background (which we could sum up as λόγος) of this question is just as important as the resolution of the subject matter, i.e., the resolution of the question of the essence of the philosopher.

b) Elucidation of λόγος as a basic task of the Greeks. Domination of propositional logic over λόγος.

The elucidation of λόγος was for the Greeks a basic task and, moreover, one in which they made progress only with difficulty and very slowly and in which in a certain sense they got stuck at one point, if this point can be called Aristotelian logic in the traditional sense, the logic handed down to us. Insofar as the Greeks ultimately developed a doctrine of λόγος in a theoretical direction, they took the primary phenomenon of λόγος to be the proposition, the *theoretical* assertion of something about something. Insofar as λόγος was primarily determined on this basis, the entire subsequent logic, as it developed in the philosophy of the Occident, became propositional logic. Later attempts to reform logic, whatever they might have worked out, have always remained oriented to propositional logic and must be conceived as modifications of it. What we commonly know as logic is merely one particular, determinately worked out, logic, given direction by the research impetus within Greek philosophy, but by no means is it *the* logic; it does not dispose of all the basic questions connected to the phenomenon of λόγος. As oriented in this way, i.e., as taking the theoretical proposition for its exemplary foundation, propositional logic at the same time guided all reflections directed at the explication of *logos* in the broader sense, as language, and, insofar as it did so, the whole science of language as well as, in a broader sense, the entire philosophy of language, took their orientation from this propositional logic. All our grammatical categories and even all of contemporary scientific grammar—linguistic research into the Indo-Germanic languages, etc.—are essentially determined by this theoretical logic, so much so that it seems almost hopeless to try to understand the phenomenon of language freed from this traditional logic. Yet there does indeed exist the task of conceiving logic, once and for all, much more radically than the Greeks succeeded in doing and of working out thereby, in the same way, a more radical understanding of language itself and consequently also of the science of language. The understanding of this entire development, and of the usual, so-called systematic questions ordinarily found today in relation to logic, depends on a concrete investigation into the ground of the question of λόγος in Greek philosophy and hence here in Plato. We shall therefore focus our attention not only on the question of the essence of the sophist and of the philosopher, and on the substantive problems included therein, but also on the problem of λόγος and on the roots of the idea of logic as worked out by the Greeks.

§39. The question of philosophy in the present age. Increasing difficulty with regard to Plato. The influence of Christianity and the Renaissance. The stifling of the idea of substantive research. "Prophetic" and "scientific" philosophy (K. Jaspers). The freedom of substantiveness.

The question of the philosopher, posed by the *Sophist*, is for us at the same time a positive indication of the only way such an apparently cultural question can be solved and what sort of investigation it requires. We may not believe our present understanding of the question of the philosopher has advanced even one step. On the contrary, we must say that tendencies of another kind, which have thrust themselves forth in the meantime, and the influence of extra-philosophical questions have made the question itself, and *a fortiori* the answer, more difficult for us. What alone is telling is the fact that for the question of the essence of the philosopher and consequently of philosophy itself, the phenomenon of world-view, as it is called—how it is to be determined may remain in suspense—i.e., the practical, plays the major role. Even those philosophers who attempt to develop a so-called scientific philosophy, detached purely for itself, feel themselves constantly obliged in the end to emphasize the value for a world-view even of such detached scientific philosophy.[1] This is connected with the fact that the scientific philosophy of the West, insofar as it maintained itself as genuine on the basis of the Greeks, came under the authoritative influence of Christianity, and specifically of Christianity as a culture-religion, as a worldly-spiritual power. Thereby the classical Greek philosophy underwent a completely determinate transformation; philosophy was from then on subordinated to a quite definite world-view and its requirements. With the broader understanding of spiritual life in the Renaissance, philosophy was understood as a particular element of culture, as formative of the culture of the individual: philosophical work and philosophical literature found their place within culture in the same sense as did works of art, music, etc., with the result that philosophy got amalgamated with tendencies of that kind. In this way philosophy not only became a world-view, as another phenomenon over and against Christianity, but even became esteemed at the same time as a spiritual creation. And so it happened that more general spiritual tendencies completely stifled the idea of research, and quite definite cultural needs guided the idea of philosophy, with the consequence that one could in fact call a creation which, in an eminent sense, satisfies such needs "prophetic" philosophy, since it "foresees" intermittently, on behalf of the average spiritual situation, and in certain epochs is guiding. What otherwise still remained of the scientific tradition of the Greeks, such as logic and psychology, is usually designated as "scientific" philosophy, with a sign meant to express that it is properly only an academic matter. Jaspers, in his *Psychologie der Weltanschauungen,* drew this distinction between "prophetic" and "scientific" philosophy and thereby gave proper expression only to an unclear need regarding how matters stand today.[2] These distinctions are characteristic, however, of the fact that, measured by the classical philosophical research of the Greeks, the radical claim to be nothing but substantive research has disappeared from philosophy. Christianity is basically responsible for this phenomenon of the decline of philosophy (others interpret it as an advance), which should cause no wonder, insofar as philosophy was amalgamated with the need of deepening and elevating the soul. The need of universal spiritual entertainment is ultimately definitive with regard to the appreciation of philosophy in public life. It is to this feeble-mindedness that "metaphysics" owes its current resurrection. That indicates we are wholly uprooted, we suffer from a

1. AH: philosophy in its relationship to science and world-view, cf. W.S. 1928–29.
2. AH: The following is insufficient; concept of science 1.) not sufficiently elucidated 2.) exaggerated 3.) not acknowledged as subordinated to philosophy. The round circle = "scientific philosophy."

fatigue of questioning, and a real passion for knowledge has died in us. The reverse side of this fatigue and of the moribund state of the passion for knowledge is the tendency to require of philosophy or even of science something like a refuge, to look in them for a refuge for spiritual existence, in other words to abandon them should they fail. This tendency to look for a refuge is a fundamental misunderstanding of philosophical research. We must be able to abjure this claim to refuge with regard to science and *a fortiori* with regard to philosophical research. Conversely, the possibility of correct research and questioning, hence the possibility to exist scientifically, already presupposes a refuge, indeed not a refuge of a religious kind but a quite peculiar refuge, belonging only to this kind of existence, which I denominate the freedom of substantiveness.[3] Only where this freedom has developed is it at all existentielly possible to pursue science. And only from this position will it be possible to overcome historicism, which our age proclaims to be a special danger to spiritual life. Whoever understands the meaning of substantive research is in no danger at all from historicism, insofar as the latter is a theory of history which has not even ever bothered to ask what history is and what it means to be historical. Historicism is a characteristic modern theory which originated in such a way that its substantive subject matter itself, namely history, never properly became a problem for it. The freedom of substantiveness, I say, will first be able to make it possible for us to be historical in the genuine sense, i.e., not to protect ourselves from history with a sign of the cross, as if history were the devil, but to know that history, in general, is the residence of the possibilities of our existence. Only if we are historical will we understand history; and if we have understood it, we have *eo ipso* overcome it. Therein is included the task of substantive research, over and against which free-floating so-called systematic philosophy, with occasional stimulations from history, counts as an easy occupation.

Thus if we now orient ourselves, wholly in correspondence with the dialogue, concerning people's views of philosophy, we may not expect to be able to think out and present a cheap definition of the philosopher and thereby extricate ourselves from the difficulties. On the contrary, no other way is open to us than the one the Greeks traveled, namely to come to philosophy by philosophizing. This dialogue and the prelude to it thereby become, for each one of us, a test of whether he is a philosopher, or otherwise a person of science, a test as to what extent each of us disposes of the freedom of substantiveness, whether he has within himself a receptivity and openness for the impulse such a dialogue can release. He who has understood such a dialogue and the inner obligation it carries—i.e., a dia-

3. AH: Cf. *Essence of truth.*

logue which, quite freely, without any systematic background and without any aspiration, goes right to the substantive issues—does not need any cultural elevation of the significance of philosophy and the like. If you read the prelude to the dialogue at one stroke, you must sense the seriousness of this situation, which is still much higher and more decisive than the prelude to a duel, where only life and death are at stake.

§40. Transition to the substantive issue: the choice of the exemplary object. The twofold criterion: 1.) simplicity 2.) analogy and richness of the ontological structures. The ἀσπαλιευτής as exemplary object.

The prelude of the dialogue leads directly over to the substantive issue. First of all, both interlocutors, the ξένος and Theaetetus, again confirm what alone matters to them: συνομολογεῖσθαι (218c5), "to agree, to say the same as the other, to mean the same as the other," περὶ τὸ πρᾶγμα αὐτό (c4), "with regard to the substantive issue itself." What is decisive is thus to mean the same thing and to understand it in the same sense as the other, and to do so specifically διὰ λόγων, on the basis of having disclosed the matter at issue, having genuinely confronted it. That is what counts, not ὁμολογεῖσθαι <περὶ> τοὔνομα μόνον (cf. c5), "agreement merely with regard to the word," i.e., χωρὶς λόγου (c5), "freely, without any exhibition of the matter at issue." In this way they renounce all empty verbal knowledge. We have already seen, from Socrates' way of questioning, that he asks about the γένος. The task was τὸ γένος διακρίνειν (cf. 216c2f.) of the philosopher. There we translated γένος not as "genus" but as "ancestry." The justification of this translation will become clear from the following proposition: τὸ δὲ φῦλον ὃ νῦν ἐπινοοῦμεν ζητεῖν (218c5f.). Φῦλον, "lineage," means the same as γένος and makes it quite clear that γένος is not meant here in the sense formal logic later gave it, namely "genus." What we are to grasp is the lineage of the sophist, i.e., that out of which he became what he is. We are to disclose in λέγειν his entire pedigree, the ancestry of his Being. We are to interpret the Being of the sophist, or of the philosopher, in terms of its origination, its provenance. The disclosing of the ancestry, the unfolding of the origin of its coming to be, first makes the being itself understandable in its Being. The Being of a being becomes transparent in its provenance. The ξένος emphasizes once more the difficulty of the investigation, χαλεπὸν καὶ δυσθήρευτον ἡγησαμένοις εἶναι τὸ τοῦ σοφιστοῦ γένος (218d3f.), and suggests τὴν μέθοδον αὐτοῦ προμελετᾶν (d4f.), a first rehearsal of the way they are to carry out the disclosive research, i.e., the investigating. He says: ὅσα δ' αὖ τῶν μεγάλων δεῖ διαπονεῖσθαι καλῶς, περὶ τῶν τοιούτων δέδοκται πᾶσιν καὶ πάλαι τὸ πρότερον ἐν σμικροῖς καὶ ῥᾴοσιν αὐτὰ δεῖν μελετᾶν, πρὶν ἐν αὐτοῖς τοῖς μεγίστοις (218c7–d2). "Everyone has taught for ages," i.e., it is an old rule, an old universal doctrine, that "if, as regards important matters, something is to be διαπονεῖσθαι, worked out, καλῶς, in the most appropriate way, then that way should first be rehearsed ἐν σμικροῖς, in the ambit of what is insignificant and easy, before one tries it on the more important objects themselves." This is what the ξένος recommends, and Theaetetus acknowledges he does not know another way. Then the ξένος asks him: Would it then be agreeable to you if we worked through an insignificant object and tried παράδειγμα αὐτὸ θέσθαι τοῦ μείζονος (d9), "to pose it as an example of the more important one?" Theaetetus agrees.

Thus the question now arises as to how the exemplary object must be constituted in order to satisfy the task of a rehearsal of the mode of treatment. An object must be found on which to practice the mode of investigation that will be employed afterwards in regard to the sophist. The ξένος characterizes the qualities of the exemplary object of the method in a twofold way. It must:

1.) εὔγνωστον μὲν καὶ σμικρόν (218e2f.), be "well-known and insignificant." In a certain sense both these qualities belong together. Something which is well known in everyday experience, which poses no enigmas, within this experience, regarding what it is, how it is used, and what meaning it has, and whose ontological possibilities, as well as those of its factual variations, are familiar to everyone and well known—this is precisely something insignificant and commonplace. The more important matters of life are for the most part controversial; with regard to these, as, e.g., with regard to the philosopher, the sophist, and the politician, there indeed exists ἄγνοια (we heard this already in relation to the philosopher), no objective knowledge but instead an opinion based on feeling. In order to be able to rehearse the method effectively, an object must be present whose phenomenal content is accessible, within certain limits, to everyone and whose immediate self-showing is unmistakable. If such an object is to be present, what is at issue is obviously the task of taking up, as we say, the phenomenal content of the object, of the matter in question. "Phenomenal" here means nothing else than what shows itself in a first straightforward look at the thing. Now this first straightforward look may very well be confused. It does not yet have to be original at all, a genuine grasp of the thing; on the contrary, what is essential to the phenomenal content is simply that it is acquired out of a natural, precisely ordinary situation of considering and seeing. What purely shows itself in this situation is what is to be grasped first of all. It may turn out that quite ungenuine conceptions are determining this first aspect of the thing. Yet for the natural and immediate mode of approaching the thing and dealing with it, it is the obvious aspect. And the first task is to take it up, to establish it, in order to be able to pose a well-founded question to this thing. Thus it is not at all necessary for an investigation claiming to be philosophically significant that its matter be of special importance. Hence to pretend to be actually philosophizing it is not necessary to begin with the dialectic of the absolute, or to speculate about the essence of religion, or to lay the foundation for the meaning of world history; εὔγνωστον καὶ σμικρόν.

2.) What is also required is λόγον δὲ μηδενὸς ἐλάττονα ἔχον τῶν μειζόνων (218e3), that the exemplary object indeed be well known and insignificant, but not of less moment as regards what can be exhibited about it in the realm of speech. There, however, the being must be spoken of with regard to its γένος, its provenance. Thus what is required is an object whose factual significance might perhaps border on the ridiculously trivial but which, as regards the structures of provenance that can be exhibited in it, does not at all rank behind the μείζονα, the more important things. That is, despite the great difference in the factual role of the thing, it may be rich in the structures at issue. The ξένος suggests as object satisfying both these requirements, and known to all, the angler, the ἀσπαλιευτής; he says (219a1f.) that he hopes this indication of the way, μέθοδος, and this λόγος, this investigation, will not be without profit for the proper goal of their endeavors. And thus begins the consideration of the ἀσπαλιευτής in the sense of a paradigmatic object (219a–221c).

SECTION ONE

The Search for the λόγος of the Factual Existence of the Sophist (*Sophist* 219a–237b)

Chapter One

An Example of the Method of Defining. The Definition of the ἀσπαλιευτής.[1] (219a–221c)

§41. The scope of the exemplary object (ἀσπαλιευτής) and its method of treatment. The Sophist*: not a "purely methodological dialogue."*

It might appear that for a paradigmatic philosophical consideration the factual content of the exemplary object would, in principle, be completely arbitrary and that the determination of the exemplary object has merely the sense of obtaining an object which is suitable, in relation to the thematic object, for making the method visible. Thus it would be possible, ultimately, to exhibit the same structures and results in relation to entirely disparate things. Under this conception of the exemplary object, it would seem the method is completely independent of the matter to be dealt with, so that it would be identical with a formal technique or abstract routine of treatment, which runs its course as something enclosed in itself and which can be applied to any arbitrary object without the least knowledge of the particular thing in question. It seems so. Nevertheless, it would be premature to think that a complete arbitrariness obtains here, as if any random object could be employed within the determinate task the dialogue sets for itself. We will see that between the exemplary object, the angler, and the thematic object, the sophist, there also exists a connection in terms of content, and that consequently the structures brought out in the analysis of the angler are not proposed simply in the sense of examples. On the contrary, the structures, at least some of them, are taken up positively in the further determination of the sophist, so that even the basic thrust of the analysis of the angler ultimately provides the ground for the determination of the sophist. As far as I can see in the previous literature on Plato, no one has

1. Title based on Heidegger (see p. 161f. The articulation of the *Sophist*).

ever observed that the scope of the exemplary object and its treatment exceeds by far the determination I had expounded earlier, namely the sense of being a mere example, and that therefore some of these structures in fact enter into the definition of the sophist. And not only some structures, but the basic thrust, as well, are already sketched out for the idea of the sophist. We must therefore not fall prey to the opposite conception and believe the *Sophist* is a purely methodological dialogue, as is claimed especially by modern interpretations, as if Plato were merely interested here in demonstrating a newly discovered method of διαίρεσις. A closer consideration of the inner connection between the exemplary object and the thematic object also allows us to grasp the proper sense and the goal of the dialogue positively and more originally.

§42. Τέχνη *as the basic determination of the* ἀσπαλιευτής*; its two* εἴδη *(*ποιητική, κτητική*).*

a) Τέχνη as the basic determination of the ἀσπαλιευτής. The ζήτημα πρῶτον (the phenomenon serving as point of departure) as "pre-possession." Τέχνη: knowing-how to do something or other, δύναμις εἰς. Horizon: life, Dasein.

We now have to examine how the exemplary object looks, i.e., how the two, the ξένος and Theaetetus, arrive at a determination of the angler. The first question they raise is this: ὡς θήσομεν (cf. 219a5f.), more precisely: ὡς τί θήσομεν, "*as what* shall we posit in advance" the given object we now have to deal with? That is, how are we to determine it so that this determination will be the basis of the entire further examination? In other words, they are to determine the ζήτημα πρῶτον (221c8), "that which is first to be sought and found" and which will lay the foundation for all further determinations and all concrete elaborations of the phenomenon.[1] This ζήτημα πρῶτον is precisely what we ourselves have to grasp if we are going to interpret the dialogue, i.e., if we are to uncover what is unexpressed though already operative in it. But in order not to proceed here by way of pure fabrication, we are obliged to see for ourselves how that which is first sought and found unfolds itself, how it lies at the foundation, and in what way it is the πρῶτον.

Methodologically, we will interpret this ζήτημα πρῶτον, out of more original contexts, as a "pre-possession" *[Vor-habe]*, as that which the investigation at the very outset grasps of the phenomenon and what is held fast as something primarily grasped as such, held fast in all further looking

1. On the ζήτημα πρῶτον, cf. pp. 194f., 202f.

upon the object. Hence, as what is possessed at the very outset and held fast, it enters into every further determination of the phenomenon, though not arbitrarily, like, e.g., in a certain sense, the top of a pyramid, which is once made fast and then remains left to itself. Instead, it has the peculiar function of being operative in every concrete determination. This is the methodological sense of what we designate in a phenomenological characterization as the "pre-possession" of the phenomenon.

From the very beginning of the question it is clear that both interlocutors agree about the general field of phenomena in which the angler should be sought, namely τέχνη: i.e., is the angler a τεχνίτης or an ἄτεχνος (219a5)? From our introductory lectures, we know that τέχνη denotes a mode of ἀληθεύειν, of uncovering, and indeed one within a definite kind of dealing with things. Aristotle defines it as the ἕξις of ἀληθεύειν μετὰ λόγου ποιητική, as know-how in regard to something—to determine it for the moment quite formally. Thus is the angler one who has know-how in some regard, or is he an ἄτεχνος, "one who lacks something, namely know-how in some regard"? If he does lack this, does he have ἄλλην δὲ δύναμιν (219a5f.), i.e., does he have "another δύναμις" instead of this know-how? Thus we see already, on the basis of this quite concisely formulated question, that τέχνη, τεχνίτης, and ἄτεχνος are more originally determined in terms of δύναμις. Therefore τέχνη is determined as δύναμις, as an ability, a capacity, an aptitude for something, a δύναμις εἰς . . . (cf. 219b8f.), as it is later called explicitly. We can therefore represent the articulation of the consideration as follows:

δύναμις
τέχνη

The question is hence whether the angler is a τεχνίτης or an ἄτεχνος with another δύναμις. The ἄτεχνος is designated at 221c9 as an ἰδιώτης, someone who has not learned anything and does not understand anything. Theaetetus responds: ἥκιστά γε ἄτεχνον (219a7), "not in the least" can one say that the angler is an ἰδιώτης or an ἄτεχνος, that he is without know-how. For that is obvious to everyone; we all know in our natural understanding of life that the angler must have at his disposal a certain know-how, a certain ability to find his way about. It is something εὔγνωστον. This provides the answer to the question ὡς τί θήσομεν?—as τεχνίτης. His Being as an angler is determined by τέχνη. Accordingly, τέχνη is the basic determination of the exemplary object, the angler, but we must note that τέχνη is determined here in a wholly formal and general way without any further definition beyond immediate understanding. At the same time we see that τέχνη is determined here in such a way that it has the original character of δύναμις. Evidently (though unexpressed, this becomes factually transparent), because what is in question here is in a determinate sense a being that lives, it as such has a definite possibility for something, a δύναμις εἰς. . . . We now have to examine more closely how, on the basis of this fundamental determination, the disclosure, the δηλοῦν, of the ἀσπαλιευτής is carried out. For the consideration ends with Theaetetus saying: παντάπασι μὲν οὖν τοῦτό γε ἱκανῶς δεδήλωται (221c4). "Thus it (the exemplary object) has now been made quite sufficiently clear and disclosed."

b) The first εἶδος of τέχνη: ποιητική.

α) Adducing the phenomena. Exposition of the one identical basic phenomenon: ἄγειν εἰς οὐσίαν.

The question is how this τέχνη itself may be determined more precisely so that the determination is sufficient to allow us to see the angler as such. The ξένος answers: ἀλλὰ μὴν τῶν γε τεχνῶν πασῶν σχεδὸν εἴδη δύο (219a8), "but, in truth, of all modes of know-how," σχεδὸν εἴδη δύο, "there are" (and this is not asserted dogmatically, but σχεδόν) "more or less, perhaps, two." It becomes quite clear that Plato is not at all concerned with an absolute division but that he leaves the division open; it does not at all matter to him whether the system, as successive interpreters have often said, is correct or not, for he has entirely different interests, namely to work his way to the substantive issue itself. Know-how can thus appear outwardly in two ways. The question is in what regard a τέχνη is to be determined in order to uncover its εἶδος. About τέχνη itself nothing at all has been decided yet. Τέχνη, however, as know-how, is in itself know-how *in some regard*. Accordingly, that in regard to which one has know-how can perhaps provide the ground for the different classes, as they are usually called, of know-how—i.e., the "in regard to which" of the know-how in relation to the particular activity. About the connection between know-how in regard to a particular activity and this activity itself, nothing has yet been determined; the connection is simply announced by the "in regard to."

What are the distinctions in the various classes of the "in regard to"? The ξένος mentions, at 219a10ff., γεωργία μέν: in the first place then γεωργία, "the cultivation and care of the land, of the field"; and he expands this determination: καὶ ὅση περὶ τὸ θνητὸν πᾶν σῶμα θεραπεία, and all care directed to what is mortal, i.e., to everything that lives. Hence we have in the first place one class of that in regard to which one can have know-how: in regard to the cultivation of the field and the care of animals. Hence know-how in regard to cultivating and caring.

Cultivating,
Caring.

τό τε αὖ περὶ τὸ σύνθετον καὶ πλαστόν, ὃ δὴ σκεῦος ὠνομάκαμεν (219a11f.). This next determination is expressed very concisely. We might paraphrase it this way: know-how in regard to an activity, a concern, that extends to "what is composed, i.e., what *can* be composed, and to what can be formed." A summary characterization of this is σκεῦος, "implement." Hence know-how in regard to composing and forming, or, in summary, fabricating.

Fabricating,

and specifically a fabricating of household implements and tools; πλαστόν refers above all to what is decorative.

The final determination is ἥ τε μιμητική (219b1), know-how in regard to imitative formations, i.e., in regard to a producing which, in producing, imitates something. What is meant here is painting and the activity of the sculptor, i.e., the creation of a work of art:

imitating.

With this, the ξένος has now circumscribed a certain domain of various possibilities of know-how.

This multiplicity of possibilities of know-how in regard to something is to be fixed, as had been agreed upon earlier, ἑνὶ ὀνόματι (cf. b2), "with *one* name," in such a way that the one name can δικαιότατα, "quite rightly," be applied to the manifold of know-how in regard to these modes of activity. It is therefore not simply a question of an empty nominal designation but an ὄνομα διὰ λόγων, a giving of names that is thoroughly steeped in a disclosure of the matters at issue. A name is to be given to this multiplicity; i.e., in the manifold of these possibilities in which τέχνη can develop, we are to glimpse one identical phenomenon which would be the proper ground of the unitary designation. What then is the identical phenomenon we find in the cultivation of the field, in the caring for animals, in fabricating, and in imitating? This identical phenomenon is to be glimpsed, and in correspondence to it, a name will be given to these types of know-how. Thus what is decisive in name-giving is not the name as such, the fact that a name is available, but the identity of the matter in question. This appears clearly in several passages where the consideration stops at similar situations and the interlocutors are at a loss for the name: e.g., ἀμελῶμεν τοῦ ὀνόματος· ἀρκεῖ γὰρ καὶ τοῦτο (220d4), "let us not be overly concerned with the name; this name is already sufficient." The name has meaning and significance only as long as it has credentials; otherwise it is actually misleading.

What then is the identical phenomenon in cultivating, caring, fabricating, and imitating? The ξένος again provides the answer: ὅπερ ἂν μὴ πρότερόν τις ὂν ὕστερον εἰς οὐσίαν ἄγῃ (219b4f.), "conducting into being what at first is not there." This phenomenon is peculiar to all these various types of know-how, as the one identically the same moment that can be found in all of them: ἄγειν εἰς οὐσίαν. Accordingly, this τέχνη, as know-how, is related to an ἄγειν, "conducting, bringing," in the broadest sense, an action we can also call πρᾶξις.

β) Outlook: the meaning of Being for the Greeks. Being (οὐσία) = presence, to be available, to be pro-duced. Ἄγειν εἰς οὐσίαν = to pro-duce, ποιεῖν. Reading off the meaning of Being from the surrounding world. The natural ontology of Dasein. Ποίησις and οὐσία.

We must attend to the expression ἄγειν εἰς οὐσίαν. Within certain limits, οὐσία is already a significant term for Plato. Especially in Aristotle, οὐσία means ὑποκείμενον and designates the basic character of Being. Here, however, οὐσία has a much more natural and original sense. We can read off the meaning of οὐσία immediately from the context. The crux of the matter is that in these kinds of doing and acting, in the broadest sense, something is brought into being. At issue is the Being of growing plants, of fruits of the field, the Being of animals taken care of, and the Being of implements and works of art set up as decorations to be contemplated. Here, therefore, Being signifies, in a wholly determinate sense, the presence of definite things in the circuit of everyday use and everyday sight. Οὐσία means availability for this use. Εἰς οὐσίαν ἄγειν, to conduct into being, means therefore: to con-duce into availability for everyday life, in short: to produce. The ξένος expands on this: τὸν μὲν ἄγοντα ποιεῖν, τὸ δὲ ἀγόμενον ποιεῖσθαί πού φαμεν (b5f.), we call the behavior of someone who brings or conducts something into being ποιεῖν; the ἀγόμενον, that which is brought into being and which stands there as produced, is the ποιούμενον, ποιεῖσθαι. Being thus means to be produced. That corresponds to the original sense of οὐσία. Οὐσία meant possessions, wealth, household chattels, that which is at one's disposal in everyday existence, that which stands in availability. Being means to stand there as available.

We see that the objects in question here are those of a quite definite domain, that of everyday use and everyday concern. The term for this entire world of immediate beings is "surrounding world." We see at the same time that here for the Greeks an entirely natural interpretation of the meaning of Being was alive, that they read off the meaning of Being from the world as surrounding world. It is a natural and naive interpretation, since this meaning of Being is taken at once (precisely this characterizes naiveté) as the absolute meaning of Being, as Being pure and simple. This shows the Greeks had no explicit consciousness of the natural origin of their concept of Being, hence no insight into the determinate field from which they actually drew the meaning of Being, such that οὐσία could precisely at the same time take on the further terminological significance of Being in general. Furthermore this makes it visible that natural human Dasein, insofar as it sees and uncovers, and discusses what is uncovered, i.e., what is there, even if it does not pursue science, already possesses an original and natural ontology and operates with a quite definite sort of interpretation of the world and of its Being. This natural ontology is not accidental and must be understood in its own character if we are to have any grasp at all of the problematic delimited under the title "ontology." The Greeks have a characteristic expression for the field of beings in question here, ones delimited by these sorts of ποιεῖσθαι: they are πράγματα, that with which one has to deal, that which is there for πρᾶξις. Therefore the terms ὄν, εἶναι, οὐσία, and πράγματα are synonyms.

The ξένος again recapitulates: τὰ δέ γε νυνδὴ ἃ διήλθομεν ἅπαντα εἶχεν εἰς τοῦτο τὴν αὐτῶν δύναμιν (219b8f.), "all the things we have traversed (these various classes, in regard to which there is know-how) have in themselves a potentiality εἰς, for something or other," εἰς τοῦτο, namely for ποιεῖν. In all of them, the identical phenomenon of a capacity for something or other is manifest, a capacity, namely, for bringing something into being which previously was not there, i.e., a potentiality for ποιεῖν. The Greek language expresses the potentiality for something or other, the capacity for something or other, by the ending -ικος: τέχνη ποιητική. ποιητικὴν τοίνυν αὐτὰ συγκεφαλαιωσάμενοι προσείπωμεν (219b11f.). To summarize (and that always means to go to the heart of the matter, the crux), we can call these phenomena τέχνη ποιητική. That is *one* way τέχνη looks: know-how in regard to the production of something.

I am deliberately lingering over this passage and heeding it carefully, because it betrays a fundamental connection between the meaning of οὐσία and that of ποίησις. This connection is not accidental, and, as we will see later, our interpretation of the passage is by no means forced. On the contrary, this precise passage is the basis upon which the forthcoming proper determination of the sophist will rest and upon which the question of the Being of non-beings will play out. Indeed, Plato refers explicitly to this connection through a definite way of questioning, insofar as the phenomenon of ποιεῖν is taken up again in a later passage: 233d9ff. There ποιεῖν is not only brought into connection with Being but also with εἰδέναι, knowing, the disclosure of beings. Hence precisely this first characteristic of the comportment to which τέχνη is related—ποίησις—is of particular importance for the further work of the dialogue, insofar as ποιεῖν, on the basis of its intrinsic relation to Being (being there on hand or coming to be there on hand) is introduced again later into the proper discussion of Being and non-being. We need to keep in mind that the determination of ποιεῖν is not involved in the definition of the ἀσπαλιευτής or of the sophist—i.e., in the first six definitions of the sophist—and seems at first to be forgotten; only later does it receive a central significance.

Thus far we have pursued *one* direction of the structure of τέχνη and have gained *one* εἶδος. The task is now to see the other εἶδος. Only if we have both in view will we be capable of understanding more precisely the δύναμις of τέχνη in relation to the various basic possibilities of know-how.

c) The second εἶδος of τέχνη: κτητική.

α) Adducing the phenomena. Exposition of the one identical basic phenomenon: κτῆσθαι (appropriating). The basic possibilities of appropriating: 1.) λόγος, 2.) πρᾶξις.

Plato, of course, did not place the first εἶδος first by accident. We will see that the second εἶδος of τέχνη is acquired in regard to the first and in contrast to it. Purely schematically, the explication of τέχνη unfolds as follows:

τέχνη

ποιητική (1st εἶδος) | κτητική (2nd εἶδος)

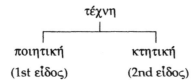

Notice how Plato is proceeding in each case: first of all he lays out the matter at issue, i.e., he adduces the actual phenomena, and then he determines the εἶδος on that basis. Τὸ δὴ μαθηματικὸν αὖ μετὰ τοῦτο εἶδος ὅλον καὶ τὸ τῆς γνωρίσεως τό τε χρηματιστικὸν καὶ ἀγωνιστικὸν καὶ θηρευτικόν (219c2ff.). Our task is now to see how, in the further course of the determination of the phenomena, the εἶδος acquired earlier comes into play. We have already discerned the τέχνη ποιητική, know-how in regard to the pro-duction of what did not previously exist, i.e., in regard to bringing something into being. In the present case, we are given a series of phenomena in relation to which there can be know-how of another kind: μαθηματικόν, μάθημα, learning in the broadest sense, γνώρισις, γνῶσις, "taking cognizance of something," χρηματίζειν, ἀγωνίζειν, θηρεύειν. Learning is understood in the sense of "bringing something close to oneself"; γνωρίζειν is "making oneself familiar with something," "getting to know something," or, as we say, "taking something into cognizance." As above, the question is of course to discover one identical basic content in these phenomena. Thus far we have: bringing something close to oneself, taking something up to oneself. As for χρηματίζειν, χρῆμα means the same as πρᾶγμα (or οὐσία): something there that one can do things with, something one can use, something one can appropriate. Χρηματίζειν means "to pursue what is there, what is available," "to procure it," in the broadest sense "to busy oneself with something," "to be out to acquire something" by taking pains. The final phenomena are ἀγωνίζειν, "to struggle to get something," "to obtain something by means of a struggle," and θηρεύειν, "to hunt something down." The text itself contains a clear indication of the basic structure, first of all negatively: δημιουργεῖ οὐδὲν τούτων (cf. 219c4), none of these phenomena have the character of δημιουργεῖν. Δήμιον means "publicly"; δημιουργεῖν is "to produce something used in everyday public life." The δημιουργός is the craftsman, he who produces the things of everyday use. Here δημιουργεῖν has the broad sense of ποιεῖν. None of the phenomena now in question have the character of ποιεῖν; that to which they relate, their object, does not have a structure like that of the object of ποίησις. Their object is not one that πρότερον μὴ ὄν, previously was not and is brought into being only by someone's efforts. On the contrary, τὰ δὲ ὄντα καὶ γεγονότα (c4f.) the present case is a relation to beings already at hand, no matter whether they have always already been there or whether they only come into being through ποίησις. A constitutive moment of all appropriating, all bringing something close to oneself, acquiring something, getting something by struggle, and hunting something down is that the "something" be already there. The objects to which these comportments relate have an entirely different ontological structure than the ones to which ποίησις relates. And the one identical phenomenon in these comportments is not a ποιεῖν, an ἄγειν εἰς οὐσίαν, but a χειροῦσθαι, a "grasping something with the hand," bringing something close to oneself, appropriating it. And, specifically, there are various possibilities here: τὰ μὲν χειροῦται λόγοις καὶ πράξεσι (c5), something can be appropriated in λόγος or else in πρᾶξις. Thus it is a matter here of beings which can become objects of an appropriation, or rather τὰ δὲ τοῖς χειρουμένοις οὐκ ἐπιτρέπει (c5f.), beings which resist being grasped and appropriated and which therefore must be appropriated by cunning or perhaps by violence, struggle, or hunting. All these modes of dealing with beings are characterized by χειροῦσθαι, "bringing something to oneself." And this appropriation is, as we said, determined negatively by the fact of οὐδὲν δημιουργεῖ, i.e., these modes of comportment having the character of appropriation "produce nothing." Χειροῦσθαι, "to take something in hand," "to bring something to oneself," understood here in the broadest sense, though employed later in a stricter sense, is meant to indicate, in contrast to producing, a simple bringing to oneself of something that is already there, i.e., taking possession of it, making it one's possession, in Greek κτῆσθαι. Therefore the know-how related to this is called τέχνη κτητική (cf. c7).

We see here to what degree the first εἶδος of τέχνη, namely τέχνη ποιητική or ποίησις, in a certain way provides the ground for the delimitation of the second mode, insofar as the appropriation of something relates, according to its very sense, to a being which is already there. This being which must already be there on hand in order to become a possible object of an appropriation can for its part be there precisely in virtue of having once been fabricated, and so would be an ὄν which is in fact a ποιούμενον. Thus one can say that appropriation is related to ποίησις, insofar as definite objects, utensils, and tools can be produced by one person and then appropriated by another. Taken strictly, however, the appropriation of something is not necessarily founded in ποίησις. For there are many beings which, according to their sense, are not produced, beings which always are, such as the beings of nature, which hence are always already there but which nevertheless can as such be appropriated, specifically in the determinate modes of learning, taking cognizance, or taking possession—of, e.g., a parcel of land. Structurally conceived and strictly understood, therefore, appropriation, χειροῦσθαι, is not founded in ποίησις.

β) Outlook: the Greek understanding of λόγος. Λόγος as appropriation of the truth of beings.

Just as the first εἶδος of τέχνη, τέχνη ποιητική or ποίησις, provided us with an outlook on the Greek understanding of οὐσία and gave us an opportunity to set in relief the natural (uncontrived) meaning of Being for the Greeks, so the characterization of the second εἶδος of τέχνη, i.e., χειροῦσθαι, provides access to the Greek understanding of λόγος. Beyond the determination of the new εἶδος of τέχνη, it is also of essential significance that λόγος receive here a quite fundamental interpretation. Μάθησις, to learn, and λέγειν, to discourse on something, are characterized as χειροῦσθαι, "bringing to oneself"; this χειροῦσθαι is for its part characterized as οὐδὲν δημιουργεῖ. The Greeks, and Plato above all, understood knowing, γνώρισις, and λέγειν as appropriation, as a mode of appropriating something already there on hand. More precisely, this *taking* (which characterizes knowledge and discourse here) is a disclosive taking. Then what of beings is appropriated in knowledge and discourse, and how is this appropriated? Knowledge is precisely a mere taking cognizance of something; this, or mere onlooking, or mere speaking about something, is characterized by the fact that it does not "do anything," as we say, with the object. It simply lets it stand there just as it is; it does not manipulate the object.[2] Nor is the object removed in any sense from its place and transposed "into" the subject, placed into consciousness;

2. AH: Letting-be.

on the contrary, it remains, in accord with the very meaning of knowledge, precisely where it is. Knowledge is a peculiar taking to oneself of something already there on hand, such that the thing, in being taken up, remains precisely what and where it is. We can understand this only if we are clear about what of beings is properly taken up in the act of appropriating them. And that is nothing other than their being-there-in-themselves, their presence, and specifically their full presence, as this offers itself without distortion. What is appropriated in knowledge and speech is the truth of beings, their unconcealedness. Λέγειν, speaking about something, is a mode of appropriating beings with regard to their outward look.[3] This is the basic thrust of the Greek interpretation of λέγειν and of knowledge; it was established among the Greeks quite originally, i.e., phenomenally, without dependence on a theory or an epistemology. It is all the more astonishing in view of the fact that it was preceded by Parmenides' theory of Being, which asserts baldly that perceiving, knowing, and Being are the same. This proposition obviously did not for the Greeks smack of idealism, if indeed the Greeks understood knowledge and discourse as taking beings and allowing them to give themselves.

γ) Ποίησις and κτῆσις as modes of commerce with the world. The structures of the commerce of Dasein with the world as the horizon for an interpretation.

We have thus exhibited two basic modes of comportment, two possibilities of commerce with the world, related to τέχνη: production and appropriation. Both these modes of commerce with the world are ones of everyday Dasein; they are comportments that originate in life. Later the substantive questions of the dialogue will force us to return to these phenomena with greater attention and to see them more originally. Within appropriation and production, identical phenomena manifest themselves, ones unrelated to τέχνη, know-how, as such. The term "commerce," i.e., the commerce of a living being, namely man, with his world, indicates such a basic state of affairs, identical to both appropriation and production.[4] From this character, τέχνη, for its part, receives an interpretation. Accordingly, even know-how in regard to something, insofar as it is a kind of knowledge, is a determinate appropriation, with the remarkable result that τέχνη ποιητική, the productive commerce with beings, is guided and directed by a prior *appropriation* of what is there, i.e., of what is to be made into something. That which τέχνη primordially appropriates and anticipates was subsequently deter-

3. AH: Taking to oneself *[An-sich-nehmen]*. Perception *[Wahr-nehmen]:* to take the truth *[Wahre-nehmen]*.

4. See the appendix.

mined by Aristotle as the εἶδος, as we explained with the example of the shoe.[5] The traditional interpretation of Plato left these matters out of account because they were obviously too primitive and too self-evident for such a lofty science as contemporary philosophy, and because our epistemology is much more advanced and takes Plato to be beating his brains over trivialities. The proper meaning of these connections, of course, can be seen only if the phenomena are appropriated positively in advance, i.e., only if the original phenomena, such as the act of procuring, the Being of the immediate world, etc., are investigated on the basis of the matters themselves, for in this way alone do the horizons become available for measuring the meaning of those things. This is the proper sense of so-called systematic work in philosophy. We do not pursue systematics in order to construct a system but in order to understand ourselves in the foundations of our Dasein. And if, for the sake of a more thorough interpretation, we examine these phenomena phenomenologically, our intention is not to construct a system of phenomenology, or to inaugurate a new movement, but simply to make available the horizons that will enable us to understand what Plato already knew in a much better way.

For the further determination of τέχνη, the question now arises: which direction of its provenance must we pursue in order to gain an actual grasp of the phenomenon which set the consideration on its way? Do not let yourselves be led astray by the literary form of the presentation and see here a deduction. Keep in mind that for the first beginning what is directive is the view of the initial phenomenon, namely angling or catching fish. The step from ποίησις to κτῆσις already points to the form: catching. Catching fish is a mode of appropriation, so that, starting from the initial phenomenon, the further explication does not proceed in the direction of ποίησις but in the direction of κτῆσις. For catching fish is a mode of commerce with things which has the character of appropriation. And so arises the task of grasping more precisely the δύναμις of appropriation for its own part.

§43. *The determination of* τέχνη κτητική.

a) The determination of κτῆσις in terms of its "how." The possible modes of appropriation. Seizing (χειροῦσθαι). Hunting (θηρευτική).

Plato makes a distinction, at 219d5ff., into two forms:

5. Cf. p. 28ff.

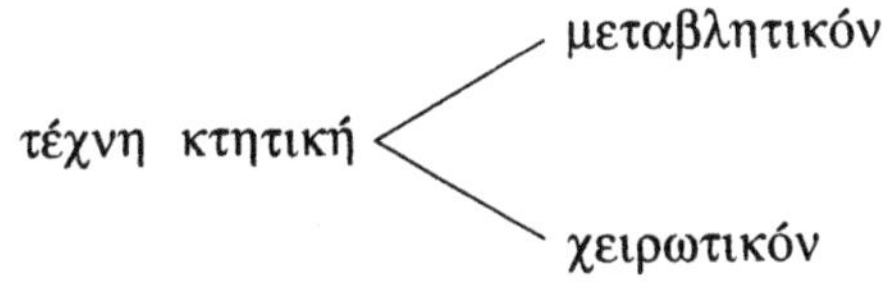

Both of these, insofar as they possess the character of κτῆσις, have the peculiarity of relating to something already there on hand. They both deal, in the mode of appropriation, with something that already is.

I.) Μεταβλητικόν. Μεταβάλλω means "to change"; here it signifies "to exchange something for something else," and specifically ἑκόντων πρὸς ἑκόντας μεταβλητικόν (219d4f.); i.e., this exchange is carried out "freehandedly." That which someone possesses is appropriated by another in a μεταβάλλειν; they allow the exchange to take place. It is a matter here of an appropriating in which someone does not properly seize and take something by himself. Instead, it is an appropriating in the mode of both parties' allowing the exchange to take place, specifically such that the other gives me a thing, which I appropriate, and I for my part give something in exchange for what I have thus appropriated. Plato calls this type of freehanded exchange ἀλλακτικόν (223c7); ἀλλάσσω means "altering." The determinate modes of μεταβάλλειν are the following: 1.) For a gift I have received, I exchange a gift in return. 2.) For some service, I give wages. 3.) For goods, money. It is characteristic of this mode of appropriation in the sense of exchanging that the appropriating is not unilateral.

II.) Χειρωτικόν. This is the determination: τὸ δὲ λοιπόν, ἢ κατ' ἔργα ἢ κατὰ λόγους χειρούμενον σύμπαν (219d6f.), "sheer seizing." The other does not voluntarily let go of the thing, and, above all, I do not give something in return; it is nothing but taking. Versus κτῆσις, appropriating in general, the χειρωτικόν is in the stricter sense a seizing, where I on my own snatch something, as it were. Obviously this is where catching belongs, so that its further explication remains tied to this phenomenon.

The articulation, in this sense of splitting into two, dichotomizing, has, besides other connections, above all the meaning of repulsion—to repel from the phenomenon in question whatever is irrelevant and in that way to arrive at the characteristic determinations which make it finally possible to determine catching fish as a mode of catching.

The χειρωτικόν is apprehended more precisely as a bringing to oneself in the mode of seizing, in exchange for which the one who seizes does not give anything. Furthermore, it is characteristic of the χειρωτικόν that what is appropriated in the seizing does not willingly give itself. Therefore the χειρωτικόν is subdivided into:

1.) the ἀγωνιστικόν, seizing in battle. This is determined by the fact that it is ἀναφανδόν (219e1), "open." That means the one who seizes relates to what he acquires by seizing and to the one he is attacking in such a way that the latter knows in a certain sense about the attack and can stage a defense. Hence this is openly going after what is to be appropriated, battling for it. Versus this ἀναφανδὸν χειροῦσθαι, there is

2.) a κρυφαῖον, hidden, χειροῦσθαι, such that the one under attack does not notice anything: to slay under cover, to shoot down, ambush, set a trap, take by surprise, to appropriate something by letting it fall into a trap. Here what is appropriated, captured, caught, has no possibility of initiative. It does not have the possibility of an open defense but instead is captured with one stroke. It has no chance to offer resistance, οὐκ ἐπιτρέπει (219c6), as it was called.

With this last determination of χειροῦσθαι as θηρεύειν, we come quite close to the kind of appropriation in question, namely catching, catching fish. The phenomenon of catching is indeed the ζήτημα πρῶτον, which, as the starting phenomenon, provides the first direction for the inquiry into the provenance of the ἀσπαλιευτής.

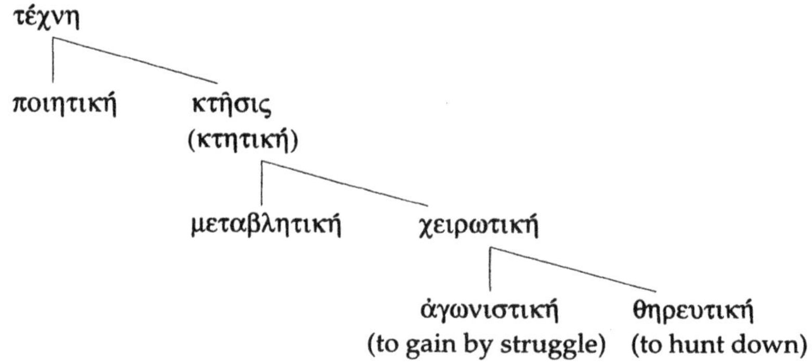

This analysis of κτῆσις brings the consideration to a provisional limit.

b) The determination of κτῆσις in terms of its "what." Living things.

The delineation of the phenomenon of appropriation has thus far turned merely on the character of the type and mode of comportment toward something which is there (or is not yet there): the "how" of the comportment to something, the "how" of the having of something, and this entirely in general in the sense of a seizing appropriation of something. The comportment, however, as commerce with something or other, is always related to a determinate stock of beings. The relatedness to things is not accidental to this phenomenon of possessing and seizing but pertains to it intrinsically.

We have here a structural appurtenance; the seizing or appropriating, as an appropriating, appropriates *something*. Even if there is nothing there, and if what is appropriated is not appropriated as it should be, still, by its very sense, the appropriation has a direction to something or other, with the result that the full characterization of the phenomenon of appropriation can obviously not be carried out in disregard of this second structural moment, namely that which is appropriated. The deflection to the second structural moment of κτῆσις can be seen clearly, starting at 219e4; in general the focus deflects from the *mode* of commerce with things to the *things* dealt with in the commerce. Only on this basis does the consideration advance. The "what," to which the κτῆσις is related, must be understood constitutively. Only in later contexts will we have an opportunity to understand this peculiar appurtenance of the phenomenal parts, the being related to something and the "to which" of the relation, provided we succeed in exhibiting more original phenomena, on the basis of which the appurtenance becomes visible. Hence it is not the case that there is something in the subject and also something on the outside, namely an object, and then occasionally a relation between the two. The question is which basic stock of phenomena has to be exhibited in order to see that the analysis of the act of relating must necessarily also take into account that to which the relation is directed.[1]

Even the further steps of the analysis of the "to which"—from 219e4 on—are already predelineated in the initial phenomenon of catching fish, so that again there is not a simple blind deduction. Just as "catching" was prescriptive for the previous consideration, so "fish" is for the further one. Thus it is a matter of catching something that is alive. Accordingly, the basic distinction is the first one made within the many possible objects of hunting: the living and the non-living, ἔμψυχον and ἄψυχον (219e7). The ξένος says of the ἄψυχον: χαίρειν ἐᾶσαι (220a3f.), we can immediately dismiss hunting for non-living things, since what is at stake is the catching of fish. Nor is a definite designation necessary for it; we can leave it without a name, ἀνώμυνον (220a2). On the other hand, it becomes necessary, in view of the initial phenomenon, to determine more precisely hunting for ἔμψυχα, ζῷα. Now the further articulation does not proceed according to the mode of appropriation but according to the thing hunted. Therefore the next step leads from the θηρευτικόν to the ζῳοθηρική, the hunt for living things. This phenomenon is taken up again later, insofar as man too is a ζῷον and the sophist in a certain sense hunts man. The ζῷα, the many things alive in the world, are interrogated in terms of the way they comport themselves,

1. See the appendix.

as living beings, to the world. When we look further into the development of the determination of ζωή, we will see that Aristotle determines ζωή by κινεῖν κατὰ τόπον, local movement, and by κρίνειν.[2] Κρίνειν corresponds to what we are now calling τέχνη: to make prominent and to distinguish, to orient oneself in the broadest and most primitive sense: perception, instinct. The κινεῖν κατὰ τόπον, the bestirring oneself in one's surrounding world, is the characteristic comportment. And this can be carried out in two ways: the movement can be 1.) that of a πεζόν, or 2.) that of a νευστικόν (cf. 220a6f.), the movement of a living being that "walks" or of a living being that "can swim." The class of land animals we call πτηνὸν φῦλον (220b1), "poultry," can also swim, and so can certain birds, but they do not move by swimming alone. Only the things that live entirely in water, the ἔνυδρα (cf. b2), move by swimming alone. Thus there results, as regards the continuous orientation toward catching fish:

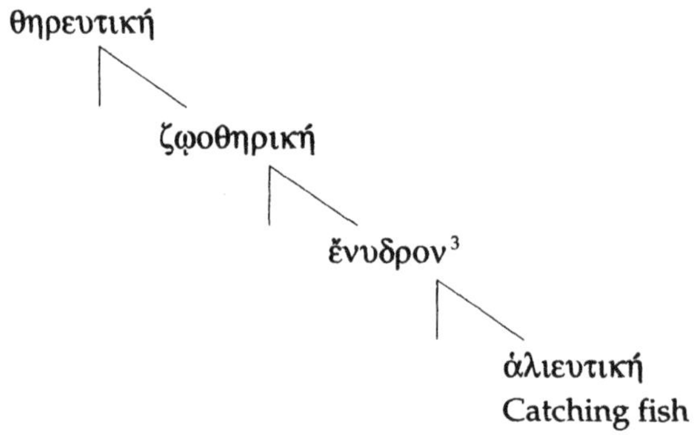

Thus the phenomenon from which we set out has been determined, on the one hand, in terms of the appropriating, the catching, and, on the other hand, in terms of that which is appropriated. Thereby the phenomenon is made concrete from both sides, from the "how" and the "what" of the appropriation. Only now are we given the basis for a more precise determination of catching fish as a mode of hunting. The consideration now therefore turns back to the mode, to the "how" of the hunting.

c) Further determination of θηρευτική in terms of its "how." Summary: history of the provenance of the ἀσπαλιευτής.

How then is the κρυφαῖον χειροῦσθαι carried out, the clandestine bringing to one's hand in the case of catching fish? According to what are we to

2. *De An.* III, 9, 432a15ff.
3. Cf. 220a11: ἐνυγροθηρική.

distinguish ἁλιευτική? The two modes of catching are characterized by ἕρκος, nets, and πληγή, beating, striking, wounding: καθ' ἃ τὸ μὲν ἕρκεσιν αὐτόθεν ποιεῖται τὴν θήραν, τὸ δὲ πληγῇ (220b12f.). Most texts have αὐτόθι, as if catching with nets were determined by the "immediately," but the reading αὐτόθεν is preferable. For it is a matter ἕνεκα κωλύσεως εἴργῃ τι περιέχον (220c1f.), of not allowing what is to be appropriated to have any room, εἴργειν, enclosing it, περιέχειν, encompassing it, hemming it in. What is characteristic of this catching is the αὐτόθεν, "by itself." Nets and traps bring about hunting by themselves, and specifically in such a way that what is hunted down is captured just as it is; i.e., it is still alive, it is spared, it is merely hemmed in but is untouched, whereas in hunting by means of πληγή, in πληκτική, what is hunted can be taken only by means of wounding and maiming.

This last moment, namely the ἁλιευτικὴ πληκτική, ushers in the final step in the determination of the ἀσπαλιευτής. The angler catches in the mode of πληκτική, striking and wounding, but not from above downward, as in the case of fishing with harpoons, but in the reverse direction. Angling is a catching in the sense of ἀνασπᾶσθαι κάτωθεν εἰς τοὐναντίον ἄνω ῥάβδοις καὶ καλάμοις (cf. 221a2f.), from below upward, a drawing up with rods or canes. Furthermore it is characteristic of the πληγή of the angler that, unlike the harpoonist, he is not simply out to strike the hunted object and wound it in any which way. Instead, he must see to it that it bites: περὶ τὴν κεφαλὴν καὶ τὸ στόμα (221α1), the booty is to be grasped only in a quite determinate place. On the basis of this determination, the whole explication is once more run through at 221b, and in a certain sense the lineage, the provenance, of the ἀσπαλιευτής is made visible. The consideration concludes: "And in this way we have disclosed, in a thoroughly sufficient fashion, what we desired," ἱκανῶς δεδήλωται (221c4), and precisely through λόγος.

§44. General characterization of the method. Dichotomy and diairesis as modes of δηλοῦν. *The echo of the Platonic dichotomy in the* ἄτομον εἶδος *of Aristotle. Dichotomy and diairesis as Plato's way of treating beings and Being.*

Our discussion of the example has given us a preliminary insight into the method for presentifying some matter at issue in its essential content. If we were to determine this method according to its immediate aspect, while retaining Plato's own terms, then we would have to call it "dichotomizing." It is a matter of a cutting, τέμνειν, a "dissecting," of something previously undissected. The proper term for this τέμνειν is διαιρεῖν; Plato often also uses σχίζειν, "splitting." The use of these designations shows that Plato and the Greeks also viewed this procedure in such a way that for them τέμνειν had a concrete sense. Yet we must not forget that this διαιρεῖν is designated as λέγειν and that λόγος for its part has the character of δηλοῦν, "revealing," so that τέμνειν is not an arbitrary operation to be taken as identical with physical cutting and breaking. On the contrary, we have to recognize that this τέμνειν itself, and διαιρεῖν, have the function of showing, of revealing. The being is dissected until its substantive contents, the εἴδη, are revealed. This methodological state of affairs, namely that λέγειν is apprehended as τέμνειν, and specifically as τέμνειν of the εἶδος, results in an expression which later plays a certain role even in Aristotle: ἄτομον εἶδος, that outward look (of some matter at issue) that can be dissected no further, i.e., the substantive content at which the λέγειν rests, and in relation to which the λέγειν cannot further exhibit anything substantive. Closer examination shows that the ἄτομον εἶδος, the substantive or ontological content of the thing, is to be considered simply as it is in itself and not as delimited against something else. The latter is precisely what is characteristic of dichotomization and τέμνειν, namely that something is determined with respect to something else, or, more precisely, that the determination of the γένος as such keeps going on. Aristotle's use of the expression ἄτομον εἶδος recalls the Platonic way of seeing and explicating. To be sure, the expression ἄτομον εἶδος no longer made sense for Aristotle, in view of the methodological ground he later attained, and to that extent τέμνειν and διαιρεῖν lost their methodological significance. The expression ἄτομον εἶδος is a remnant in Aristotle of a methodological position he no longer shares. We first experience all this about the εἶδος, and about the procedure that determines the εἶδος, by going through the delimitation of the ἀσπαλιευτής. We must not allow ourselves to be led astray by this kind of dichotomizing and see the systematization of concepts as what is essential in it. On the contrary, the δηλοῦν remains what is essential, i.e., the showing and revealing of the matter at issue itself.

On this basis we can measure the extent to which the presentation of this example is important for the substantive disclosure of the sophist. The example is not at all an "overview of the factual relations prevailing in the world of concepts," as has been said.[1] It is neither formal logic nor "empirics." On the contrary, it is meant to disclose the horizon of the phenomena we have come to know under the title τέχνη, in accord with its fundamental differentiation into ποίησις and κτῆσις.

The method of τέμνειν and διαιρεῖν has been carried out here quite *naively*, i.e., in relation to objects taken as occurring in the world, whereas

1. Constantin Ritter, *Neue Untersuchungen über Platon*. München, 1910, p. 3.

we will see later that this τέμνειν and διαιρεῖν are not only applied to beings but are also carried over to Being and its structures. Consequently, for Plato there is no distinction between the way of dealing with beings versus the way of dealing with Being. This state of affairs is important for an understanding of the Being of the so-called Ideas, as Plato conceived it.

Chapter Two

The Definitions of the Sophist. Definitions 1–5. (221c–226a)

§45. Preliminary remarks. The difficulty of defining the sophist. The indeterminateness of the ζήτημα πρῶτον. The meaning of the definitions: the securing of the immediate aspects (φαντάσματα) of the sophist in the usual horizons. Actually not definitions but descriptions. Articulation of the definitions.

The explication of τέχνη provides a concrete horizon for the determination of the sophist. The determination of the ἀσπαλιευτής is relatively easy in comparison with that of the sophist, because there is no controversy regarding what the ἀσπαλιευτής genuinely is, i.e., regarding the τέχνη of catching fish. This activity is unproblematic to anyone with an elementary understanding of Dasein in general. Therefore the preliminary determination of the γένος out of which the ἀσπαλιευτής takes his origin can be acquired in relatively univocal terms. But matters are quite different as regards the thematic object, the sophist. As the ξένος says: οὐ γάρ τι φαύλης μέτοχόν ἐστι τέχνης τὸ νῦν ζητούμενον, ἀλλ' εὖ μάλα ποικίλης (223c1f.). "The sophist participates in a know-how that is quite variegated and manifold." The phenomenal content of what is designated by the term "sophist" is from the very outset not given as univocally as is the content in the case of the angler. Accordingly, it is not clear without further ado which γένος is to be put forth as the ζήτημα πρῶτον. What is lacking is a secure ground for the disclosure of the ontological provenance, the proper γένος, of the sophist, because the phenomenon from which to depart is indeterminate. Therefore the very first task of an inquiry into what the sophist genuinely is is not to formulate an arbitrarily conceived definition but to ascertain the most immediate aspects presented by this new thematic object, the sophist. Furthermore, these immediate aspects are to be discussed at first in the familiar horizons, and according to the directions, known in the relations of everyday life, if indeed it is a matter of determining a relation in life. For that, τέχνη, ποίησις, and κτῆσις provide a very general predelineation. Thus the immediate definitions, above all the first six, are not arbitrary amusements or jests, as the philologists maintain; nor are these dichotomies examples of formal logic. On the contrary, these definitions have the quite specific task of securing the domain of the immediate φαντάσματα in which the sophist shows himself, in order to acquire a ground for the determination of the concrete content of the object in question. The orientation toward the concrete horizons, those given in the discussion of the παράδειγμα, is not a rigid and schematic repetition, which is shown above all by the sixth definition. For this definition approaches the phenomenon in an entirely new way, with a determination, the διακρίνειν or τέχνη διακριτική, not previously given in the explication of τέχνη under the παράδειγμα of the ἀσπαλιευτής. From this it is clear that what is at stake in the carrying out of these *descriptions*, as we should really call these definitions, is not a mere ordering or classification. In the process, Plato acquires something new: in virtue of this provisional sort of description of the sophist, Plato can then for the first time actually contrast philosophical explication, as it follows later, against naive description.

We need to presentify briefly the textual articulation of the definitions. The descriptions extend from chapter 8 to chapter 24. At 231 c–e, the ξένος himself presents a summary of the previous definitions: "We want to stop and, as it were, catch our breath and discuss once again, ὁπόσα ἡμῖν ὁ σοφιστὴς πέφανται, how manifoldly the sophist has shown himself to us. . . . " Thus there is nothing here of a conceptual system, a systematic articulation, ordering, or derivation of the definitions. Instead, what is at issue is ὁπόσα φαίνεται, "how manifoldly and in what guises did the sophist show himself." At 231 d–e, the six descriptions of the sophist are enumerated. We will adhere to this articulation, although the numbering concurrent with the exposition counts only five, since the third and forth are amalgamated.

First description: 221c–223b.

Second description: 223b–224d.

Third and fourth description: 224d and e (the third in d and the fourth in e).

Fifth description: end of 224e–226a.

Sixth description: 226a–231c.

At 232b, we find the beginning of the proper explication and the transition to the question of the Being of non-beings. The connection between the first six descriptions and the seventh is this: the first six are the springboard for the seventh and facilitate it.

§46. The first definition of the sophist: hunter (221c–223b). Ζήτημα πρῶτον: τέχνη. *The common course of the history of the origination of the sophist and of the* ἀσπαλιευτής*:* τέχνη—κτῆσις—χειρωτική—θηρευτική. *Distinction with respect to the "what" of the* θηρευτική*: man. Factual comportment as the standard.* Λόγος *as the tool of the sophist. Rhetoric as horizon.* Ἀρετή. Δοξοπαιδευτική.

The consideration of the sophist begins with a recollection of the ζήτημα πρῶτον. What was first sought and investigated was whether the ἀσπαλιευτής is an ἰδιώτης, ἄτεχνος, or whether he has a τέχνη. Thereby the first description of the sophist is drawn into the horizon worked out in the consideration of the example. In the discussion, Theaetetus finally decides that in fact a τέχνη must be attributed to the sophist. That is clear to everyday understanding as well, insofar as we obviously recognize in the sophist, if presentified concretely, someone who understands his own business, whatever that may be. Before the more precise determination begins, the interlocutors recall that they have previously overlooked the fact that both, the ἀσπαλιευτής and the sophist, are ὄντα συγγενῆ (221d9), have the same γένος in common, the same provenance. That means each of them is not only to be addressed quite generally and formally as τεχνίτης, but they go together for a quite determinate extent ἅμα πορεύεσθαι (cf. 222a3), and specifically in their ontological provenance, not only in their formal determination. Both turn out to be, show themselves to be, in a certain sense hunters: θηρευτά τινε καταφαίνεσθον ἄμφω μοι (221d13). This now also indicates which course in the history of their provenance the two have in common: from τέχνη to κτῆσις and the χειρωτικόν up to θηρευτικόν, acquisition in the sense of a hunting that seizes. The sophist has this entire ontological history in common with the ἀσπαλιευτής.

We saw in the previous consideration that precisely at the place the explication of the modes of comportment arrived at the phenomenon of hunting the investigation took a turn. It diverted its gaze from the mode of appropriation to the possible object of the appropriation. This place now also marks the divergence of the previously common provenance of the sophist and the angler. Hunting was determined earlier as the hunting of ἔμψυχα and of ἄψυχα, and the former divided into hunting of the πεζὸν γένος and hunting of the ζῷα νευστικά (cf. 220a8f.). Now the ξένος says: τὸ δὲ πεζὸν εἰάσαμεν ἄσχιστον, εἰπόντες ὅτι πολυειδὲς εἴη (21e6f.), "we have left ἄσχιστον the outward look of those possible objects of hunting we spoke of as beings that move on feet." Specifically, they said this εἶδος itself has a manifold form, but its exhibition was not important then. This is the point of divergence of the paths of the ἀσπαλιευτής and the sophist.

The expression the ξένος uses for the determination of this divergence is telling: ἐκτρέπεσθαι. Μέχρι μὲν τοίνυν ἐνταῦθα ὁ σοφιστής καὶ <ὁ> ἀσπαλιευτὴς ἅμα ἀπὸ τῆς κτητικῆς τέχνης πορεύεσθον (222a2f.). "From the point of departure, τέχνη κτητική, up to now, both went together." ἐκτρέπεσθον δέ γε ἀπὸ τῆς ζῳοθηρικῆς (a5), "starting with ζῳοθηρική, they diverge" and specifically in separate directions. It is significant that the conversation is not now about ontological relations but about the comportment of the beings themselves; at issue here are not the ontological relations of the εἴδη, but instead the investigation turns concretely to the factual comportment of the beings which correspond to the εἴδη. Plato thereby gives a very apt reference to the perceptual field in which we now find the sophist, and indeed according to his factual behavior. The angler turns in one direction, to the sea, to rivers and brooks; the other, the sophist, turns to the land, to other rivers, οἷον λειμῶνας ἀφθόνους (222a10), to "fields which begrudge nothing," which give generously of themselves, which yield up richness and youth. And the sophist turns there "in order to seize and to get in hand," χειρωσόμενος τὰν τούτοις θρέμματα (cf. a10f.), "that which is nurtured and grows there." This χειρωσόμενος again indicates and calls to memory that this hunt is a matter of appropriation and indeed an appropriation of definite men. And now the dialogue considers how hunting, i.e., that which is hunted, that which lives on land, should be divided. The ξένος refers to the distinction between tame and wild. And then the question arises as to whether man is to be counted among the tame or the wild living beings. It is characteristic that the ξένος challenges Theaetetus to decide one way or another. He decides: ζῷον ἥμερον ἀνθρώπους εἶναι (cf. 222c1f.), "man is a tame living being." But he decides without actually deliberating on the matter. Ἡγοῦμαι (c1), "I deem it" on the basis of the natural knowledge of man available to me. Ἡγεῖσθαι is the common expression for such convictions. (This is further testimony that the explication of the sophist is carried out on the basis of the intuitive field of natural cognition.) What results is the possibility of ἡμεροθηρική (cf. c3), the hunting of tame living beings, specifically man.

This hunting of man, in the sense of the intention to dominate people and to have such a hold on them that they are at one's disposal, has two possibilities. These were already predelineated in our earlier considerations, if we recall that the χειροῦσθαι, where it occurred for the first time, divided into an appropriating κατ' ἔργα and an appropriating κατὰ λόγους (219d6f.), i.e., an appropriation by way of actually laying one's hands on the object and an appropriation by way of speaking and persuading. Here, at 222c3, we have, on the one side, βίαιος θήρα, hunting by force. To this belongs πολεμικὴ τέχνη, everything related to war. For the Greeks, war is characterized basically by an intention to acquire something precisely through force, through violent means. On the other side, there is also a way of getting a hold on people, such that they come to be at one's disposal, through λόγος, through a λέγειν whose specific possibilities are: δικανική (cf. c9), speaking before the courts; δημηγορική (cf. c9), speaking in parliament; and προσομιλητική (cf. c9f.), speaking with one another in daily commerce, on everyday occasions and for everyday reasons. This appropriation of others through λόγος is characterized on the whole as πιθανουργική (cf. c10): i.e., πιθανόν and ἔργον. Ἔργον means effectuate, carry out; πιθανόν means that which speaks in favor of some issue. Πιθανουργική thus means to bring the other to a definite conviction, to talk someone into something, to occasion in the other the same conviction one has oneself, thereby bringing him over to one's own side. It means to speak so as to procure a following, i.e., to make disciples, and, further, to persuade ἰδίᾳ (d5), "all the individuals," and μισθαρνητικόν (d7), "even get paid by them for doing so," i.e., take money from them. This reference to the preeminent possibilities of winning people over by means of λόγος places the characterization of the sophist within the general horizon of speaking, of rhetoric. This passage is important for the development of the understanding of λόγος and for the elaboration of rhetoric because here Plato gives a complete enumeration of the possible types of pretheoretical discourse: speech in court, in parliament, and in ordinary conversation. We will have to orient ourselves still more precisely concerning Plato's position toward what we call rhetoric, in order to understand on that foundation his basic judgment about the sophists.

At issue is a χειροῦσθαι, a seizing directed at other people or, more precisely, a hunting for them. The means, the net or trap, as it were, with which the sophist catches people, his tool, is specifically λόγος, a persuading of people, a persuading that has the sense of ὁμιλίας ποιεῖσθαι (cf. 223a4), "nurturing commerce," προσομιλεῖν (cf. 222e5), "bringing another into commerce with oneself," drawing the other to oneself. That is the phenomenon focused on in this first description: the comportment of a man who by a certain way of speaking draws people to himself—by talking them (223a3f) into something, i.e., by convincing them that he is out to give them ἀρετή. Here ἀρετή is identical in meaning with παιδεία, correct formation as the possibility of bringing oneself into a proper existence within the πόλις. The sophist does not want to give others something to take pleasure in; his τέχνη is not ἡδυντική (cf. 223a1), but instead he places the others under definite demands while he claims their interest for a positive task, ἀρετή, and does so by persuading them that they can learn something from him, from commerce with him, and only from him. The summary of this description at 223b contains the characteristic expression for this proclamation and this pretension: δοξοπαιδευτική; δοκεῖ, "it looks" as if he could provide the correct παιδεία.

It is important to keep in mind that this description does not evaluate *what* the sophist has to say but concerns only his peculiar comportment to others insofar as he hunts them and wins them over to himself by means of a certain kind of persuasion and influence. Thus this first description of the τέχνη of the sophist remains entirely restricted to the characters of κτῆσις and χειροῦσθαι. We can now understand better the previous reference to the factual comportment of the sophist. This first description grasps the sophist in his factual comportment to others, in the aspect he displays as he walks about on the streets trying to procure for himself a following and thereby pursuing his occupation. To be sure, this aspect is objectively founded, but the question is whether this determination provides a genuine understanding of what the sophist properly is.

It is clear that the first description of the sophist is in this sense linked up with the example of the ἀσπαλιευτής and that his manners and habits are therefore immediately understandable out of well-known horizons of human commerce and existence. There are immediate aspects of this existence, like those of any other. The framing of the first description and the following one within the horizons obtained from the determination of the angler makes it clear that the sophist will be described here quite naively, the way people in general know him and talk about him. Yet this initial description is not without importance for the inception of the proper understanding, since it is precisely something factual, and must be comprehended, and is not a mere fantastic idea of the sophist. This procedure already results in a series of determinate structures, ones which are not somehow illusory but which, on the contrary, expose a fixed content in the behavior and existence of the sophist. The more manifold precisely these aspects become, i.e., the ones the sophist shows to anyone who has anything to do with him, the more puzzling and difficult becomes the task of grasping him unambiguously, i.e., obtaining the determination of him appropriate for comprehending this manifold of immediate aspects and for providing them with a first proper foundation. It is in these terms that we must understand the connection between the individual descriptions of the sophist and the horizons that pertain to the ἀσπαλιευτής.

§47. The second, third, and fourth definitions of the sophist: merchant (223b–224e).

a) The second definition. Retailer (223b–224d). Link to the first definition: ἀρετή, παιδεία. Κτητική—μεταβλητική—ἀγοραστική. Trading in λόγοι καὶ μαθήματα ἀρετῆς. Λόγος as the sophist's merchandise.

The transitions between the individual descriptions of the sophist are revelatory of this connection. It seems the transitions are carried out quite extrinsically, in the form of mere adjuncts. At the end of the first definition, for example, the second is taken up by a simple ἔτι. Ἔτι δὲ καὶ τῇδε ὁδῷ ἴδωμεν (223c1): "Furthermore, we also want to examine how he appears in this regard." This is the passage which emphasizes expressly that the sophist is μέτοχος τέχνης μάλα ποικίλης: οὐ γάρ τι φαύλης μέτοχόν ἐστι τέχνης, ἀλλ' εὖ μάλα ποικίλης (cf. 223c1f.). But the link is not as extrinsic as the ἔτι might suggest and as seems to be the case according to the summary at 224c. We will see that there is a connection only insofar as we correctly grasp the method of this description. The sentence immediately following, for example, explicitly takes into account what was previously brought out about the sophist and at the same time allows for the horizons in which he is located in immediate self-evidence. καὶ γὰρ οὖν ἐν τοῖς πρόσθεν εἰρημένοις φάντασμα παρέχεται μὴ τοῦτο ὃ νῦν αὐτὸ ἡμεῖς φαμεν ἀλλ' ἕτερον εἶναί τι γένος (223c2ff.). "For even in what we have discussed above, παρέχεται φάντασμα, he—the sophist—gives and imparts an appearance, a self-showing." That is, even on the basis of what we have discussed above, something becomes visible about the sophist (to be understood in the sense of how he can be recognized and how he shows himself) namely "that the provenance we have just now attributed to him," namely θήρα, "does not fit him but that some other provenance must be accorded him." This shows that the taking up of the next description is grounded in a regard back upon the previous appearance of the sophist. That is to say, insofar as he was characterized as θηρευτής he was placed in the γένος of κτητική; he was understood in this respect, namely that he brings something to himself, appropriates something, specifically in the unilateral way of hunting, which gives nothing in exchange for what it appropriates. But at the same time it was already clear in the first description that the sophist does not merely hunt unilaterally; he also gives something in return. Indeed he draws attention to himself and he broadcasts his claims to teach ἀρετή. At 223b5, his τέχνη is characterized as δοξοπαιδευτική, as conveying and awakening παιδεία. Accordingly, in view of the state of affairs already brought out in the first definition, we must say that the γένος of unilateral seizing and hunting is incommensurate with the facts and that the determination of χειροῦσθαι is in any case insufficient. The φάντασμα is ποικίλον, manifold, variegated; the matter itself requires that we determine it in terms of still another line of provenance. That is therefore the sense of the connection, and the sentence at 223c2ff. does not at all mean (despite being understood this way very often): we intend to place the sophist in still another one of the γένη made explicit in the example, as if the articulation is given schematically with the ἀσπαλιευτής and now it simply remains to examine which γένος fits the sophist. On the contrary, the standard here is the way the sophist shows himself. Accordingly, the comportment of the sophist is an appropriation, a drawing of people to himself, but one that at the same time gives something in return, so that the sophist does not merely draw people to himself and let himself be paid by them, but he also gives something in exchange for this wage. We are already familiar with this sort of appropriation from the first division of κτητική into μεταβλητική and χειρωτική. Μεταβλητική, letting oneself be given something and then giving something in return, is the phenomenon which now characterizes the comportment of the sophist in a more fitting way. At 219d5ff., a series of possibilities of μεταβλητική was introduced: exchanging gifts, receiving a wage, selling. This last type of μεταβλητική—called here (at 223c9) ἀλλακτική—is now enlisted to determine more precisely the comportment of the sophist. The sophist is exposed as an ἀγοραστικός, and his τέχνη is ἀγοραστικὴ τέχνη.

This τέχνη is itself now articulated with respect to whether the seller sells products he himself has made, τῶν αὐτουργῶν (d2), or whether he sells τὰ ἀλλότρια ἔργα (d3) what others have produced, i.e., whether he turns over, μεταβάλλεται, foreign products, i.e., trades in them. The consideration proceeds to this last determination, which amounts in Plato's eyes to a sharp negative criticism of the sophist, insofar as that which he retails is not something he himself has produced.[1] (Later, this determination is retracted to a certain extent.) This trading in or retailing of foreign products has two possibilities: on the one hand κατὰ πόλιν (223d5), such that the merchant remains in town, has a permanent residence there. We call such a one κάπηλος, "shopkeeper." He has his established stand or stall and sells things there. Others, in contrast, do not trade κατὰ πόλιν, but instead ἐξ ἄλλης εἰς ἄλλην πόλιν διαλλατομένων (cf. d9), "they travel from one town to another" and carry on a peripatetic trade.

This latter determination of trading in and retailing foreign goods, things produced by others, is now again in need of a characterization as regards content, insofar as, within the orientation toward what was already ex-

1. Reading *hergestellt* ["produced"] for *zugeeignet* ["appropriated"]—Trans.

posed, namely ἀρετή, it is a matter of determining what it actually is that the sophist offers for sale and does sell. Accordingly, there follows, at 223e1, a preliminary and quite rough distinction between what is beneficial and necessary for the τρέφεσθαι of the body and what is such for the soul. Concerning the latter goods and wares, ἀγνοοῦμεν (e5), "we are unclear"; we do not properly know what they might include. Here again there arises the same distinction we encountered already in the characterization of ὁμιλεῖν, where it was claimed that the τέχνη of the sophist does not aim at pleasure but instead claims a certain seriousness since it concerns one's proper formation. The same point is made again here at 224a1ff.: the sophist does not trade in music, pictures, or other illusions; on the contrary, what he imports and sells is σπουδῆς χάριν (a5), "for the sake of seriousness," since it is a matter of education leading to the proper mode of Dasein, the proper mode of existence in the πόλις. It has nothing to do with ἡδονή but instead concerns the higher possibilities of the life of the soul and of the spirit, namely μαθήματα (b1), cognitions in the broadest sense. The sophist buys them in bulk, stocks them, and then retails them, going from town to town. Thus what he buys wholesale and then sells are things which are important for the soul and for life, for the proper life of the soul. The sophist does not display these wares, and they are not things which can simply be displayed. On the contrary, they relate to the πρᾶξις of the ones to whom he sells these χρήματα. Hence the objects the sophist trades in have a quite general relation to the ψυχή, and they are further determined as μαθήματα (224c1), cognitions, and then, in the summary at 224c9ff., they are still more precisely determined as περὶ λόγους καὶ μαθήματα. The sophist does not trade in definite speeches, or in the results of definite discussions, which the trader in question would impart to others by means of discourse. Nor is he a τεχνοπωλικόν (c4); "he does not sell cognitions belonging to τέχναι," belonging to the various practical professions. Instead, he is a μαθηματοπωλικόν (cf. 224b9), "he sells the μάθημα, the knowledge," related to ἀρετή and παιδεία. This determination concludes again in a summary: ἴθι δὴ νῦν συναγάγωμεν αὐτὸ λέγοντες ὡς τὸ τῆς κτητικῆς, μεταβλητικῆς, ἀγοραστικῆς, ἐμπορικῆς, ψυχεμπορικῆς περὶ λόγους καὶ μαθήματα ἀρετῆς πωλητικὸν δεύτερον ἀνεφάνη σοφιστική (224c9ff.). That is how σοφιστική shows itself.

b) The third and fourth definitions. Shopkeeper (224d–e). The differentiation of the third definition (shopkeeper) according to the summary of the definitions (225e). Trading in: 1.) foreign or 2.) self-produced λόγοι. Increasing concentration of the definitions of the sophist on λόγος.

The third and fourth definitions are now in fact extrinsically thrust together with one another and with the second definition as well. For the introduction of the third definition, τρίτον δέ γ' οἶμαί σε (d4), is simply linked to the preceding δεύτερον in the sense of a mere further enumeration. This has a certain justification, since the third and fourth definitions remain within the same γένος. The ξένος here merely provides a restriction on the preceding description, yet at the same time, insofar as this restriction is taken up into the definition, he enriches our understanding of the substantive content of the sophist, to the extent that the sophist is looked upon as one who trades in μαθήματα. The third and fourth determinations consider it of value to distinguish something already mentioned earlier: whether the retailing merchant is a strictly local one and whether he has himself produced the things he sells. These two determinations, 1.) that he αὐτοῦ καθιδρυμένος ἐν πόλει (d4f.) and resells what he has purchased in bulk, and 2.) that he sells things he has made himself, can now be taken together as one or can be separated. We can thus conceive the sophist either as κάπηλος, as a "shopkeeper," who remains in the same town, or as someone who travels about. Furthermore, we can take him as a merchant who retails things others have made or as one who trades in things he himself has produced. The latter distinction makes it possible to increase the number of definitions by one, depending on whether or not the two moments are taken together or distinguished. Here they are taken together: μαθηματοπωλικόν (224e3). On the other hand, in the enumeration at 231d a distinction is made: the second description portrays the sophist as ἔμπορός τις, the third as a shopkeeper who retails locally things made by others, and the fourth as a merchant who sells what he himself has made. In the recapitulation, both these moments are distinguished, and accordingly we find there one extra definition. On the other hand, the summary at 225e concludes with: τέταρτον, as fourth. I have already said we will take up the enumeration according to the recapitulation at 231d.

What is substantively important in this second description (and consequently also in the third and fourth descriptions, which depend on the second) is the emergence of the fact that the sophist is not only engrossed in speaking in the sense of persuading others but that he trades in λόγοι, in things said, either what others have expounded or what he has discovered himself. Thus he has to do with λόγος also by way of retailing λόγοι, things said, whether produced by others or created by himself. Hence for the sophist λόγος is not only the way to win others but is also his stock in trade. And so it is already becoming clear how the whole comportment of the sophist is increasingly concentrated on λόγος and how his whole existence is engrossed in λέγειν.

§48. The fifth definition of the sophist. Disputer (224e–226a). Orientation toward the horizons of the definition of the ἀσπαλιευτής: κτητική—χειρωτική—ἀγωνιστική. Battle by means of λόγοι. Λόγος as the basic phenomenon of the definitions of the sophist; recapitulation. Ἀντιλογική, ἐριστική. The babbler (Theophrastus, Characters, *3).*

The fifth description also begins with an ἔτι, here, to be sure, in another form. Ἔτι δὴ σκοπῶμεν εἴ τινι τοιῷδε προσέοικεν ἄρα τὸ νῦν μεταδιωκόμενον γένος (224e6f.). Now the question is turned around, but in such a way that the orientation remains directed toward the content exposed up to now: the one we have hitherto presentified in the descriptions and characterized by so many different τέχναι—"whether there also applies," προσέοικεν, i.e., must be attributed to him, "this other lineage that we now have to pursue." Which one? The answer is a reference back to a kind of χειροῦσθαι that was already brought out; and we see thereby that the description of the sophist keeps taking its orientation, quite clearly and certainly, from the horizons of the ἀσπαλιευτής. This is evident if we schematically present the articulation of the investigation and the course it has taken:

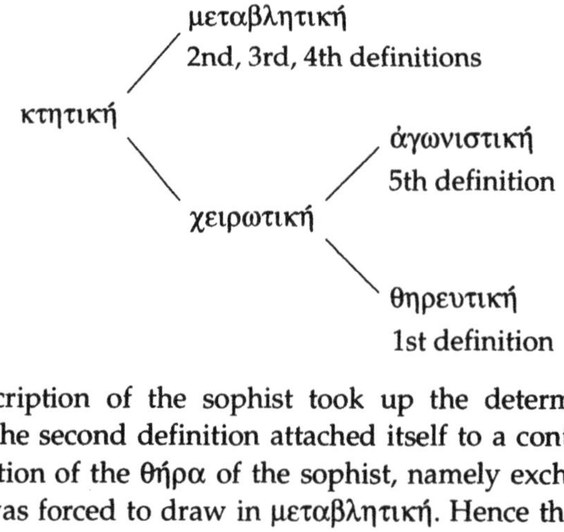

The first description of the sophist took up the determination of the θηρευτικόν. The second definition attached itself to a content introduced in the description of the θήρα of the sophist, namely exchanging, and so this content was forced to draw in μεταβλητική. Hence the only moment in the pregiven horizon to remain untouched is ἀγωνιστική. The fifth definition now claims it. We then see clearly that the sophist is being described quite primitively, solely in terms of his behavior.

Ἀγωνιστική, appropriation by means of battle, now allows further determinations. For ἀγών properly means for the Greeks "contest," "competition." And so the original determination of this battling is ἀμιλλᾶσθαι, in Latin *contendere,* contesting, competing with an other over first place in something. It does not mean fighting against the other in the sense of attacking him violently, in order to bring him down, but competing with him over something held out to both. Juxtaposed to battling as ἀμιλλᾶσθαι is μάχεσθαι, in Latin *pugnare,* confrontation not *with* the other but *against* him. This μάχεσθαι again has two possibilities: battling against another σώματι πρὸς σώματα (225a8), using violence, with arms and implements, thus βίᾳ, βιαστικόν (a10), or, on the other hand, battling, confronting, striving against the other, λόγοις πρὸς λόγους (a12), i.e., by means of λόγοι. The latter confrontation is carried out in speech. And so you see how, in the fifth description as well, the basic phenomenon of λέγειν is decisive. In all these descriptions, the focus is on λέγειν in its various possibilities. The goal is not only to win people through λόγοι, nor only to sell λόγοι, but the very way of winning over and selling is a λέγειν. Moreover, what the sophist sells, λόγοι, ultimately become in turn a δύναμις of λέγειν for the others, for those who are brought into this παιδεία.

The battling by means of speech is again articulated according to familiar distinctions, ones that simply arose in the public life of that time. The first distinction is made with respect to whether the speeches are "long," μήκεσι (225b5f.), and "public," δημοσίᾳ, i.e., whether it is a matter of confrontations in long speeches and counter-speeches as happens "in court," δικανικόν (b6), or whether the confrontation the sophist pursues is of another character: ἐν ἰδίοις (b8), "related to individuals." This latter mode does not play out in public life and is carried out κατακεκερματισμένον ἐρωτήσεσι πρὸς ἀποκρίσεις (b8f.) (κερματίζειν means to fragment, to transform into small change, as it were) in speeches which are not continuous like a long oration in court or a formal accusation but instead "break down into question and answer." This type is battling in the sense of ἀντιλέγεσθαι, ἀντιλογικόν (b10). This ἀντιλέγεσθαι, this verbal confrontation in the form of speech and counter-speech, can be carried out ἀτέχνως (c1), without any special education or preparation that could make one versed in the particular object. And indeed this is the usual type of discussion on everyday occasions, in commercial transactions, and the like, for which there is no name and which here (225c) will not be dealt with further. In addition, there is the ἔντεχνον (c7), the confrontation carried out according to certain rules and on the basis of a definite τέχνη. This is called ἐριστικόν (ς9), genuine disputation, which, as essentially theoretical, has a function in theoretical questions and cognitions. Within this class of discourse in question and answer, i.e., argumentation, theoretical-scientific discussion in the broadest sense, there is a type Plato calls ἀδολεσχικόν (cf. d10), mere pedantic babble. From that he distinguishes a kind of speech whose only possible name is σοφιστικόν. It is thereby evident that the sophist's sort of ἀντιλέγεσθαι has indeed a serious character; his speeches are concerned with some matter or other. The ἀδολέσχης is the babbler, used in the special sense of one who babbles pedantically about trifles. Meant here are those who do not pass a minute of their lives without philosophizing about trifles or speaking about them, who cannot even climb a mountain without pouring forth all their knowledge to their companion, indeed with the intention of provoking the other to a response and leading him into a debate. What is characteristic is that this sort of man speaks constantly and seeks ever new opportunities to set a dialogue in motion. Theophrastus has handed down to us, in his *Characters*, a classic description of this type of person. According to Theophrastus, babbling is a matter of λόγοι μακροί, whereas here for Plato it is a question of λόγοι μικροί. That is not a contradiction. Theophrastus does not mean by μακροί extended speaking in the sense of *one* discourse but rather constantly bringing up new topics in order to draw the other into a dialogue. This is Theophrastus' account in *Characters*, 3:

> Ἀδολεσχία is a mode of circumlocution in rambling and rashly chosen words, and the ἀδολέσχης is, e.g., a man who approaches someone he does not at all know (in a train or wherever) and gives him a long speech in praise of his own wife, or relates to him what he dreamt that night, or treats in detail what happened during the afternoon. After that, if the other is still listening, he goes on to say that people today are much worse than formerly, that the price of wheat on the market has risen, that there are many foreigners in town, that since the Dionysian festivals the sea has become navigable again (these are all obvious things), that if Zeus would send more rain it would be better, that the harvest will be such and such this year, and that in general life is difficult.[1]

§49. Transition to the further task: orientation with regard to Plato's position on λόγος by means of a clarification of his position on rhetoric.

The consideration of the last definitions has demonstrated, above all, the significance of λόγος, in various regards, for the comportment of the sophist. The sophist moves in λόγος:

1. Theophrastus, *Characters*, 3. Heidegger's translation.

1.) insofar as λόγος is the means he employs to procure his objects, namely other people,

2.) insofar as correct speaking, εὖ λέγειν, παιδεία, is what he himself has to give, and

3.) insofar as λέγειν, in the form of ἐριστική, disputatiousness, is what his παιδεία brings about in individuals.

This predominance of the phenomenon of λόγος may not be passed over, provided one sees it at all. The interpretation of the dialogue must take it into account. Our introduction has already pointed to the fundamental significance of λόγος, though indeed only in its quite general and basic determinations. Thus we indicated, above all, that the Greeks understood λόγος as the very phenomenon on which their interpretation of human existence was based.

Furthermore, we pointed out that λόγος as idle talk, its natural mode, predominantly determines everyday Dasein. Rhetoric and sophistry orient the Greek idea of education, παιδεία, toward λόγος. Moreover, we saw in Aristotle's positive consideration that every single ἀληθεύειν, every single disclosive comportment—other than νοῦς—all the way up to theoretical research, is determined μετὰ λόγου, by the way it carries out λέγειν. And so we have anticipated the fundamental significance of λόγος for human Dasein. Now, however, we face the task of understanding the phenomenon of λόγος in Plato's sense, since this phenomenon itself presses forward more intensely in the dialogue. That is, we have to ascertain Plato's own position on λόγος and on the cluster of phenomena grouped around it. Does Plato himself express this predominance of λόγος within Dasein, or will the foregoing characterization ultimately prove to be nothing but a groundless invention?

To procure this orientation we cannot possibly discuss all the passages where Plato considers λόγος; instead, it can only be a matter of certain references, ones which make it clear that the question of λόγος resides in the central questions of Plato's thinking, indeed is even identical with them. We will begin with a quite specific question, in order to gain our orientation regarding Plato's position on λόγος. We will ask: what is Plato's position on rhetoric? For rhetoric is the τέχνη that develops and teaches correct speech and even claims to be it itself. Plato's position on rhetoric must make visible, at least indirectly, his position on λόγος.

Chapter Three

Excursus
Orientation regarding Plato's Position on λόγος. Plato's Position on Rhetoric.[1] Interpretation of the *Phaedrus*

§50. Introductory remarks.

a) Plato's ambiguous attitude toward rhetoric. General characterization. Rhetoric before Plato: πειθοῦς δημιουργός. Plato's attitude: negative in the *Gorgias*, positive in the *Phaedrus*.

The orators of earlier times, i.e., before Plato and Socrates, made it their occupation to speak not—as Cicero says—*de arte,* "about τέχνη," but *ex arte,* "out of τέχνη";[2] i.e., their work consisted in composing speeches, writing and delivering exemplary speeches. A certain theory, which they themselves called θεωρία, accompanied it, but this was not such that it could become θεωρία in the proper Greek sense. What we possess as the tradition of ancient rhetoric indicates that the meaning of ῥητορικὴ τέχνη, and consequently also the meaning of public speaking, was understood to be the forming, by means of speech, of a definite conviction in the ones addressed, the listeners. Rhetoric is πειθοῦς δημιουργός,[3] "it inculcates an opinion" about something. That is the proper meaning of this λέγειν. A predominant view is taken up, taken into account, and a particular case is discussed, in court or in parliament, in such a way that the case is seen to agree with public opinion and thereby receives the approval of public opinion. The primary orientation derives from public opinion, from εἰκός, and the aim is to prevail in public opinion and to procure power and reputation. The intention in speaking is not at all to comprehend the affairs about which the speech is made; on the contrary, the intention is simply and precisely to remain oriented toward the views of public opinion.

And that is the way, in the *Gorgias,* even Plato understands rhetoric.

1. Heidegger's manuscript alludes to the following literature:

L. Spengel, "Die Definition und Eintheilung der Rhetorik bei den Alten," in *Rheinisches Museum für Philologie,* XVIII, 1863, pp. 481–526.

L. Spengel, "Ueber der Rhetorik des Aristoteles," in *Abhandlungen der philosoph.-philologischen Classe der Königlich Bayerischen Akademie der Wissenschaften,* Sechster Band, München, 1852, II. Abteilung, pp. 455–513.

2. *De Inventione* I, 8.

3. *Gorgias* 453a2.

Socrates observes, after having asked Gorgias about the essence of rhetoric, that the latter's opinion about rhetoric would amount to this: Νῦν μοι δοκεῖς δηλῶσαι, ὦ Γοργία, ἐγγύτατα τὴν ῥητορικὴν ἥντινα τέχνην ἡγῇ εἶναι, καὶ εἴ τι ἐγὼ συνίημι, λέγεις ὅτι πειθοῦς δημιουργός ἐστιν ἡ ῥητορική, καὶ ἡ πραγματεία αὐτῆς ἅπασα καὶ τὸ κεφάλαιον εἰς τοῦτο τελευτᾷ· ἢ ἔχεις τι λέγειν ἐπὶ πλέον τὴν ῥητορικὴν δύνασθαι ἢ πειθὼ τοῖς ἀκούουσιν ἐν τῇ ψυχῇ ποιεῖν; (452e9ff.). "Now it seems to me, Gorgias, that you have revealed to me precisely what sort of τέχνη you attribute to rhetoric, and, if I have understood correctly, you are saying" πειθοῦς δημιουργός ἐστιν ἡ ῥητορική, "the main concern of the entire occupation is to achieve this end. Or are you saying that rhetoric might possibly be capable of something else than the inculcation of a definite opinion in the audience?" This is Plato's conception of rhetoric in the *Gorgias,* hence a negative one. That is, as the subsequent considerations make clear, such a τέχνη—this is what Socrates demonstrates—cannot be a τέχνη at all. For it does not have any content. It precisely refuses to deal substantively with that regarding which it is supposed to teach others how to speak. It is a know-how that is not oriented toward any substantive content but instead aims at a purely extrinsic, or, as we say, "technical," procedure. This negative attitude of Plato toward rhetoric—that he does not even recognize in it a proper τέχνη—obviously has its motives in the excesses committed by the orators of that time. What is remarkable, however, is that already in this dialogue Plato holds in his hand positive possibilities for a real understanding, without letting them become effective.

In the *Phaedrus,* Plato's attitude toward rhetoric is quite different. There it is positive, but not such that Plato recognized in rhetoric a proper τέχνη, as Aristotle later did. It is the *Phaedrus* that can provide us with central information about the whole question now occupying us. To be sure, this dialogue is precisely the most controversial both with regard to its proper content and its main intention, as well as with regard to its chronological place.

b) The controversial character of the *Phaedrus.* Schleiermacher's theses about the *Phaedrus* and about Plato in general. The beginnings of historiographical-critical research into Plato. Dilthey and Schleiermacher.

Schleiermacher places the dialogue at the beginning of Plato's literary activity.[4] He sees the soul of this work,[5] as he says, in the dialectic. It is the idea of the dialectic which Plato shows to the Greeks for the first time in a

4. F. Schleiermacher, *Platons Werke.* Ersten Theiles erster Band, zweite verbesserte Auflage, Berlin, 1817. Cf. p. 67.

5. Cf. ibid., p. 65.

positive way. Schleiermacher determines dialectic as "the art of free thinking and of formative communication."[6] The thesis of Schleiermacher—that the *Phaedrus* is the earliest work of Plato—opened up the question of the historical development of Plato's thinking, just as in general Schleiermacher's work on Plato (his translation is unsurpassed even today, and the same holds for his introduction to the dialogues) brought the Platonic research of modern times to the level of historiographico-philological criticism. This occurred in initial collaboration with Friedrich Schlegel, who, however, because of his literary preoccupations, did not find it possible to accomplish real work but left it at pronunciations and programs. The classical philologist Heindorf[7] was also a collaborator of Schleiermacher's, and even today, as far as the establishment of the text is concerned, he is still important for research on Plato. In 1896, Dilthey delivered a lecture in the Berlin Academy about the work of Schleiermacher on Plato, "Schleiermacher's Plato," which until recently was unpublished. Today the lecture is available; it is inserted in the second edition (1922) of Dilthey's book on the life of Schleiermacher, which augmented the first edition with posthumous fragments.[8] His appreciation of Schleiermacher's work on Plato is characteristic of Dilthey. He emphasizes above all the historical significance of philological-historiographical criticism for the formation of the modern scientific consciousness and refers back to the first predecessor of this critical consciousness, Semler, and his "Biblical criticism."[9] Actual philological-historiographical research was introduced by Friedrich August Wolf in his *Prolegomena zu Homer* of 1795.[10] Niebuhr's *Römische Geschichte* followed in 1811.[11] In this context belongs Schleiermacher's translation of Plato, 1804–28.[12] Dilthey points out that the aids created by these three great critics came together and were elaborated by Ferdinand Christian Baur. He applied this critical consciousness to research on Christianity and tried to offer a historiographical-critical presentation of ancient Christianity.[13]

6. Ibid., p. 65f.

7. Ludwig Friedrich Heindorf (1774–1816). Philologist. Teacher at the classical high school, then professor, in Berlin.

8. W. Dilthey, *Leben Schleiermachers*. 2. Aufl., vermehrt um Stücke der Fortsetzung aus dem Nachlaß des Verfassers. Hg. von H. Mulert. Berlin and Leipzig, 1922. Bd. 1, pp. 645–663.

9. Johann Salomo Semler, e.g., *Abhandlung von freier Untersuchung des Canon*, 4 Teile. Halle, 1771–1775.

J. S. Semler, *Vorbereitung zur theologischen Hermeneutik, zu weiterer Beförderung des Fleißes angehender Gottesgelehrten*, 1.–4. Stück. Halle, 1760–1769.

10. Friedrich August Wolf, *Prolegomena ad Homerum, sive de operum Homericorum prisca et genuina forma variisque mutationibus et probabili ratione emendandi*. Halle, 1795.

11. Bartholt Georg Niebuhr (1776–1831), *Römische Geschichte*, 2 Bde., Berlin, 1811–1812.

12. *Platons Werke*, übersetzt von F. Schleiermacher, 2 Teile in 5 Bänden. Berlin, 1804–1810.

13. Ferdinand Christian Baur (1792–1860), e.g., *Kritische Untersuchungen über die kanonischen Evangelien*. Tübingen, 1847.

F. C. Baur, *Lehrbuch der christlichen Dogmengeschichte*. Stuttgart, 1846.

It is on this basis that we are to understand and evaluate Schleiermacher's work on Plato, and it is on the same basis that we are to see the origin of his remarkable thesis of the chronological position of the *Phaedrus*. This determination is all the more remarkable in view of the fact that that dialogue presents an extraordinary level of questioning throughout its entire extent. There is a whole series of Platonic dialogues which remain essentially beneath that level. Schleiermacher's work on Plato took its philosophical orientation from its own epoch. The way Schleiermacher interpreted the past in terms of his own present is characteristic of the construct in which he locates Platonic philosophy. Schleiermacher identified Plato's predecessor Socrates with the Enlightenment; he saw in Socrates the genuine enlightener, who battled against superstition and popular opinion. He then saw in Plato the position of Kant and Fichte, the return to consciousness, subjective idealism. In these terms, he interpreted the work of Schelling and Hegel back into Aristotle's own research. This is an interesting construct which later became fashionable and today still thoroughly determines the usual conception. Yet it is by no means defensible. In his presentation of this interpretation, Dilthey is unsure, because he himself knew little about the Greeks (which is made clear in his *Einleitung in die Geisteswissenschaften*)[14] and because he did not possess a grounding in systematic philosophy radical enough to allow him to press on to a real interpretation of Kant and of idealism. And so Schleiermacher's work on Plato, though indeed important for the history of the development of the human sciences and even unsurpassed as a translation, remains, in terms of a philosophical appropriation of Plato, beneath the demands we have to make on a philosophical interpretation. Schleiermacher's assessment of the *Phaedrus* as early was subsequently taken up by no less a figure than Hermann Usener,[15] who sought to support it with external, philological criteria. He based himself on an ancient tradition: Alexandrian philosophy seemed to suggest the *Phaedrus* had to be taken as Plato's earliest work. The question has not yet been sufficiently decided. The general opinion inclines today rather in the direction of placing the *Phaedrus* in the time of the *Theaetetus*, the *Sophist*, and the *Statesman*, i.e., in the time of the properly scientific dialogues. There might be a certain justification in saying that the *Phaedrus* is a programmatic writing for the opening of the Academy, if such a characterization were not so cheap. Another conception, still defended tenaciously today, places the *Phaedrus* at the beginning but sees interspersed in it fragments from a later time, so-called revisions. This conception is

14. Wilhelm Dilthey, *Einleitung in die Geisteswissenschaften*. Leipzig and Berlin, 1883.
15. Hermann Usener (1834–1905). Classical philologist. Professor in Bern, Greifswald, and Bonn; foundational work in the area of the history of Greek philosophy and religion.

characteristic of contemporary philology. This tack will certainly not get us over the difficulties. The only way over them is a substantive interpretation of the dialogue.

§51. *General characterization of the* Phaedrus.

a) The putative disparity and the central theme of the *Phaedrus:* human Dasein itself in its relation to Being (love, beauty, the soul, speech).

The basic difficulty in the interpretation of the *Phaedrus* has to do with the content of the dialogue, which initially seems to involve a great disparity: the first part contains three speeches about love, the second part concerns rhetoric. The content of the speeches and, above all, that of the second and the third, which are delivered by Socrates, is certainly such that these speeches cannot be taken simply as rhetorical παράδειγματα. These speeches are also significant in terms of content. Thus the articulation of the dialogue cannot simply be that the first part presents the examples, and the second part the theory. In fact, even the ordinary, traditional view of the *Phaedrus,* a dialogue which must actually be considered central for an understanding of Plato, placed little value on the second part and instead saw in the two speeches of Socrates the proper kernel of the work. This occurred primarily on account of a conception of Plato as an idealist, a view adopted merely as a matter of custom or, for some, on more theoretical grounds. Basing themselves on an aesthetic-literary appreciation of Plato, which was current at the same time, and finding support in the tradition, people took the proper content of the dialogue to be Plato's doctrine of the soul. In fact such claims originated very early. Some of them said the dialogue deals with love, others with the beautiful, and others with the soul. What is decisive, in my judgment, for an understanding of this remarkable dialogue, whose purely substantive parts pose grave difficulties to an interpretation, difficulties which have by no means been overcome as of yet—or, in other words, what is decisive for a proper access to this dialogue—resides precisely in not taking the second part as a doctrine of rhetoric or of dialectic even in the broadest sense. That is, we must see that what is at stake there is not speaking in the sense of orating, such as public speakers carry out and of which rhetoric is the theory. On the contrary, the theme is speaking in the sense of self-expression and communication, speaking as the mode of existence in which one person expresses himself to an other and both together seek the matter at issue. The best evidence in favor of taking λόγος here in this broad sense is the fact that the *Phaedrus* does not deal merely with the spoken λόγος but also with the written, the γράμματα: not only with what is said in the stricter sense, but also with outward expression in the sense of writing, the written work, the treatise. Likewise, in the first part, Socrates' second speech deals with the soul, but his aim is not to present a psychology, not even a metaphysical one. On the contrary, his concern is to expose the basic determination of the existence of man, precisely the concern of the second part of the dialogue, and human Dasein is seen specifically in its basic comportment to beings pure and simple. And the love Socrates speaks of, both the natural and the purified, is nothing else than the urge toward Being itself. Thus the three main topics of the dialogue, love, speech, and the soul, all center around one phenomenon, namely human Dasein, or around Socrates himself, to refer to a single individual.

b) General characterization of the first part of the *Phaedrus*. The preeminent significance of λόγος for the central theme of the *Phaedrus*. Socrates' love for λόγος (or for speaking) as a passion for self-knowledge.

The strength of the phenomenon of λόγος in this context of human existence is already evident in the first part (it is not at all necessary here to appeal to the second part) where Socrates characterizes himself, somewhat ironically, in opposition to Phaedrus, who is enraptured with the rhetoric of the time and always carries in his pocket the speeches of Lysias. Just as Phaedrus is coming from Lysias' school, he encounters Socrates, who stops him and says, ἀπαντήσας δέ τῳ[1] νοσοῦντι περὶ λόγων ἀκοήν[2] (228b6f.). "You have met someone who is love-sick over hearing speeches." Thereby it is already clear (and we will see it again in another passage) how much, i.e., how completely, Socrates was concerned with λόγος, correct self-expression, insofar as he understood self-expression to involve nothing other than self-disclosure, i.e., the disclosure of the self to itself. Therefore he speaks of being love-sick for speech, for hearing speeches, and, as one with that, he speaks of his passion for self-knowledge. A telling passage, which seems to me to be characteristic of Socrates in general occurs at 229e5ff., where Socrates admits: οὐ δύναμαί πω κατὰ τὸ Δελφικὸν γράμμα γνῶναι ἐμαυτόν· γελοῖον δή μοι φαίνεται τοῦτο ἔτι ἀγνοοῦντα τὰ ἀλλότρια σκοπεῖν. ὅθεν

1. Stephanus' reading.
2. Cf. 228c1f., where Socrates calls himself a λόγων ἐραστής.

δὴ χαίρειν ἐάσας ταῦτα, πειθόμενος δὲ τῷ νομιζομένῳ περὶ αὐτῶν, ὃ νυνδὴ ἔλεγον, σκοπῶ οὐ ταῦτα ἀλλ' ἐμαυτόν, εἴτε τι θηρίον ὂν τυγχάνω Τυφῶνος πολυπλοκώτερον καὶ μᾶλλον ἐπιτεθυμμένον, εἴτε ἡμερώτερόν τε καὶ ἁπλούστερον ζῷον, θείας τινὸς καὶ ἀτύφου μοίρας φύσει μετέχον. "I have not been able to achieve self-knowledge, in accord with the Delphic injunction; I have not yet got so far. Therefore it seems to me to be ridiculous, as long as I am not yet advanced far enough there, hence am in ignorance about myself, to try to grasp what is alien to me and does not pertain to me. Therefore I leave that alone, and in all these things—nature and the like—I adhere to what people generally believe. In these matters I can indeed be satisfied with opinions; but as regards myself I want knowledge. I do not look into anything but myself, and in particular I investigate whether I am perhaps an animal like Typhon with a much confused form, and am just as monstrous or even more so, or whether I am tamer (recall the same question arose in the *Sophist*), a tamer and simpler animal, whose existence partakes somewhat of the divine."[3] In this connection he says φιλομαθὴς γάρ εἰμι (230d3), "I am possessed by the love of learning," and this is to be understood in the sense already mentioned: the love of hearing what people say, λόγων ἀκοή (cf. 228b6f.). Socrates is obviously not referring here to the degenerate speaking of the orators but to genuine, substantive speaking. τὰ μὲν οὖν χωρία καὶ τὰ δένδρα οὐδέν μ' ἐθέλει διδάσκειν, οἱ δ' ἐν τῷ ἄστει ἄνθρωποι (230d4f.). "The fields and the meadows and the trees cannot teach me anything; on the other hand, I can learn from the people in the city." That is why, he says, he rarely leaves the city. But this afternoon Phaedrus and Socrates walk together outside the city and then recline beside a brook. In this setting, Socrates brings up the fact that Phaedrus is carrying the transcription of the speech of Lysias in his pocket and that at the beginning of the dialogue he enticed Socrates out of the city with it. σὺ μέντοι δοκεῖς μοι τῆς ἐμῆς ἐξόδου τὸ φάρμακον ηὑρηκέναι. ὥσπερ γὰρ οἱ τὰ πεινῶντα θρέμματα θαλλὸν ἤ τινα καρπὸν προσείοντες ἄγουσιν, σὺ ἐμοὶ λόγους οὕτω προτείνων ἐν βιβλίοις τήν τε Ἀττικὴν φαίνῃ περιάξειν ἅπασαν καὶ ὅποι ἂν ἄλλοσε βούλῃ (230d6ff.). "It seems to me you have indeed found the proper means of enticing me out here. Just like ones who lead hungry animals by dangling before them greens or some other fruit, so you could, λόγους οὕτω προτείνων, by enticing me with speeches, lead me around the whole of Attica or wherever you want." This expresses quite clearly enough the strength of Socrates' genuine love for λόγος and how important it is for him to gain clarity about λέγειν itself. We cannot here go into the content of the speeches of Socrates. We will limit

3. Heidegger's paraphrasing translation.

ourselves to some of the main points of the second part of the dialogue and try to see thereby, with more precision, Plato's attitude toward λόγος.

c) General characterization of the second part of the *Phaedrus*. Its articulation into three moments (Rhetoric and truth. Truth and dialectic. Rhetoric as ψυχαγωγία). Plato's positive evaluation of λόγος. Outlook: his skepticism with regard to λόγος as "writing."

We can articulate the second part into three moments:

1.) Plato shows that even rhetoric, rhetorical technique, insofar as it aims at λόγος as πειθοῦς δημιουργός, hence insofar as it deals with what is probable or with opinions, is actually possible only if it has an insight into ἀλήθεια itself, i.e., into truthful speech (273d3ff.). Thus Plato shows in the first place that the orators are altogether misinformed about the conditions of the possibility of their own τέχνη. That is, an orator must consider something much more fundamental than technique proper, something prior to technical artifices and tricks, prior to composition, harmony etc., if he is to be able to fulfill his task, even if he merely intends to speak in accord with popular opinion. For even εἰκός, ἀπάτη, deception, is possible, and can be genuinely carried out, only if one sees the truth. This position actually amounts to an acknowledgment of something positive in rhetorical technique. Thus it justifies our saying that Plato's attitude toward rhetoric has here become more positive.

2.) This seeing of the truth is carried out in dialectic. Plato characterizes dialectic with regard to two aspects: on the one hand, insofar as it grasps in general that which is spoken of, namely the ζήτημα πρῶτον, and on that basis, constantly oriented toward it, articulates its content. For Plato, then, what could make rhetoric genuine, if it were a τέχνη, belongs—and this is the other aspect—to the realm of dialectic. Dialectic shows what properly is and how undisclosed beings can be made visible.

3.) Only if we give rhetoric this foundation, i.e., understand it on the basis of true speech, and only if the latter is not limited to speeches in court or in parliament but instead relates to the speech of every moment, hence also to speech ἐν ἰδίοις (261a9)—only then can we also attribute to ῥητορικὴ τέχνη a certain justification. Then we can say rhetoric is perhaps something like a τέχνη ψυχαγωγία τις διὰ λόγων (261a7f.), "know-how in guiding the existence of others by means of speaking with them."

This threefold reflection with regard to λόγος shows quite clearly now that Plato's interest in λέγειν in fact is not oriented toward rhetoric and its possibility, but that for him λέγειν—in the sense of Socrates' self-characterization—concerns human existence itself.

This positive appreciation of the sense of λόγος shall be our basis for understanding Plato's positive skepticism regarding λόγος as well. He expresses this skepticism, precisely in this second part of the *Phaedrus*, and in particular when he speaks about the written word and then about the word as communicated in general (274bff.). In the following session,[4] we will examine this more closely. And we will also employ concrete examples to expose the three points just mentioned. At the same time, we will have occasion to see the connection with an important passage from the "Seventh Letter," where Plato deals with knowledge,[5] a passage that can be understood only on the basis of this connection. That is all the more so precisely because there an even more acute skepticism with regard to λόγος comes to light. This skepticism is not a matter of feebleness or exhaustion and is not the kind philosophers of today's caliber could bear. On the contrary, it requires a philosophy of quite a different level and orientation, precisely what Plato acquired in seeing the fundamental significance of λόγος for existence.

§52. Recollection of the sense of the interpretation of the Phaedrus *in connection with that of the* Sophist. *Gaining a fundamental grasp of the meaning of λόγος as the field of scientific philosophy for the Greeks. Transition to the interpretation of the second part of the* Phaedrus.

Let us first recall the task. We want to ascertain the fact, and the sense, of the priority of λόγος in the questioning characteristic of scientific philosophy. Our previous consideration of the definitions of the sophist has led us to see that the phenomenon of λόγος comes to the fore everywhere. A fundamental grasp of the meaning of λόγος as the field of the investigations of the Greeks, and as the horizon and the way of the other basic questions of their science, requires more than a general orientation, more than the observation that λόγος played a special role, and more than an appeal to Aristotle. Instead, insofar as what is at stake here is an interpretation of Plato's *Sophist*, we are obliged to examine the role played by the phenomenon of λόγος in Plato himself. Within the framework of our lectures, we can most easily carry out this task by limiting ourselves to the dialogue which in a certain manner forms the central point for all the questions raised in Plato's philosophy, not in the sense that all these

4. The "following session" was the thirtieth, held on Friday, January 23, 1925. The current one was the twenty-ninth, held on Thursday, January 22. The comments on Plato's skepticism in relation to λόγος occur on p. 235ff.

5. *Epistula* VII, 344c.

questions are treated there equally, but because it is the framework in which the basic questions, as they were present in Plato, are coiled up. The peculiarity of the *Phaedrus* is that it does not contain a genuine investigation, or even only the beginning of one, in any domain of the questions coiled up there. Hence our strong emphasis on the phenomenon of λόγος in Plato is not a matter of offering a new interpretation of his philosophy (although we could hardly attempt anything else, given the usual boring concentration on the theory of Ideas). This point became clear to me from a question I was once asked: is it possible to defend the view that what is new is altogether without interest? What is at issue here, rather, is to make you familiar with the field of investigation out of which the basic concepts of Greek philosophy grew and thus to enable you to go to the root of contemporary philosophy and from there to evaluate what is right and what is wrong in its handling of philosophical terms and questions—so-called "problems." If comparisons have any use, then we might compare the current situation of philosophy with that of the Presocratics at most. And even then, the comparison would have a privative sense, insofar as we still have not come into possession of the fundamental prerequisite of every philosophy, what I call the concrete realization of rigor, i.e., the elaboration of the elementary conditions of evidence and of proof regarding its propositions and concepts, conditions which are necessary for such a science. It is a matter of elaborating, not contriving or dreaming up. And to elaborate means to run through the basic directions within the sphere of the substantive research. Our entire interpretation of Plato is carried out precisely from such a purely substantive interest, and so is our explicit orientation toward λόγος.

The *Phaedrus* poses a series of difficulties for the interpretation as a whole, difficulties we will not merely leave unsolved here but cannot even take up in the sense of a simple presentation of all the items in the series. We will limit ourselves to the questions which make it clear how for Socrates/Plato the basic concern of their research in fact hovered around λόγος, insofar as they asked about the condition of the possibility of genuine self-expression about something to an other or with an other. The formula "condition of possibility" echoes Kant. Nevertheless this formula is to be taken here merely in a wholly formal sense, without reference to the actual questions raised by Kant. What is meant are not conditions in consciousness; on the contrary, the character of these conditions remains at first undetermined. Through this formula, the Greek term λέγειν is already taken in a phenomenologically more precise way: to express oneself about something to an other or with an other. Thus definite moments of the structure are intimated; the phenomenological horizon becomes richer and more determinate. Insofar as we adhere to this horizon we will later be able to understand the characteristically restricted way in which the Greeks placed the theme of λόγος at the foundation of their considerations.

§53. The foundation of rhetoric as a positive possibility of human Dasein (Phaedrus, *second part, 259e–274a).*

a) The seeing of the truth as a condition of the possibility of rhetoric.

α) The question of the condition of the possibility of rhetoric. Εἰδέναι τὸ ἀληθές. Δόξαντα πλήθει. Ὀρθότης.

The questioning at work in the second part of the *Phaedrus* becomes clear at 259e1f.: σκεπτέον, "what is to be examined and grasped" is λόγος, and specifically ὅπῃ καλῶς ἔχει λέγειν τε καὶ γράφειν καὶ ὅπῃ μή. Λόγος as self-expression in the widest sense, publicizing oneself, as it were, is to be examined in terms of "how one speaks and writes in the correct way and how not." We need to note the broad concept of λόγος here, on account of which I would characterize the phenomenon as "publicizing" oneself, communicating oneself to others. At issue is the condition of the possibility of καλῶς λέγειν τε καὶ γράφειν or μὴ καλῶς. Thus the intention is to expose the condition of the possibility even of deceptive communication, the ungenuine, the ἀπάτη. The basic answer to the question of the condition of correct self-expression is given at 259e4ff.: ὑπάρχειν δεῖ τοῖς εὖ γε καὶ καλῶς ῥηθησομένοις τὴν τοῦ λέγοντος διάνοιαν εἰδυῖαν τὸ ἀληθὲς ὧν ἂν ἐρεῖν πέρι μέλλῃ. Διάνοια, the grasping, in the widest sense, and determining of beings, as carried out by the λέγων, the one who is expressing himself, δεῖ ὑπάρχειν, "must be present in such a way" that it is εἰδυῖα τὸ ἀληθὲς ὧν ἂν ἐρεῖν πέρι μέλλῃ. Εἰδώς, εἰδέναι, usually translated as "to know," is connected to the Latin *videre*, "to see." Διάνοια "must be present in such a way that from the very outset it has already seen" τὸ ἀληθὲς ὧν ἂν ἐρεῖν πέρι μέλλῃ, "the beings, about which it wants to speak, in their unconcealedness." I must ask you not to take this as obvious, for it is a proposition Socrates, i.e., Plato, had to struggle with.

Phaedrus now characteristically appeals to the opposite, i.e., not to what he knows but to something ἀκήκοα (e7), something "he has heard." Thus, on the basis of hearsay, he raises a determinate objection to Socrates: οὐκ εἶναι ἀνάγκην τῷ μέλλοντι ῥήτορι ἔσεσθαι τὰ τῷ ὄντι δίκαια μανθάνειν ἀλλὰ τὰ δόξαντ' ἂν πλήθει οἵπερ δικάσουσιν, οὐδὲ τὰ ὄντως ἀγαθὰ ἢ καλὰ ἀλλ' ὅσα δόξει· ἐκ γὰρ τούτων εἶναι τὸ πείθειν, ἀλλ' οὐκ ἐκ τῆς ἀληθείας (259e7ff.). He appeals to the fact that for those who want to be orators (e.g., in court) it is of no matter to learn and to know τὰ τῷ ὄντι δίκαια, "what is true and correct in actuality, according to its Being." On the contrary, ἀλλὰ τὰ δόξαντ' ἂν πλήθει, it suffices for them to know "the opinions of the many." With the result that πείθειν, "persuasion," is not carried out ἐκ τῆς ἀληθείας, "in terms of beings, insofar as they are unconcealed," but ἐκ τούτων (a3), i.e., on the basis of δόξαντ' ἂν πλήθει. The needs, demands, dispositions, inclinations, and cognitive horizons of the multitude are decisive, and they serve as the guidelines for the discourse.

Yet Socrates goes still further in his demand, insofar as he applies the condition of the possibility of genuine discourse not only to public speech, in court and in parliament, but in fact says explicitly: every self-expression comes under this condition, if it is to be genuine: ἀλλὰ καὶ ἐν ἰδίοις, ἡ αὐτὴ (261a9), "even in everyday conversation the same idea of τέχνη ῥητορική is to be found," σμικρῶν τε καὶ μεγάλων πέρι (a9), whether this speaking in everyday life is a matter of "something trivial or something important." καὶ οὐδὲν ἐντιμότερον τό γε ὀρθὸν περὶ σπουδαῖα ἢ περὶ φαῦλα γιγνόμενον (b1f.): "taking direction, i.e., speech taking direction from the matter at issue, has no prerogative in discourse about serious and important things over speech concerned with trivialities and things without interest." According to Socrates, no fundamental distinction may be drawn between these types of discourse; on the contrary, all speech is subject to the idea of the ὀρθότης, the taking direction from the matter at issue. ἢ πῶς σὺ ταῦτ' ἀκήκοας; (b2). Socrates returns the question by referring to the appeal to hearsay. With this counter-question, Plato makes it explicit that Socrates is fully conscious of the opposition between his conception and the ordinary opinion about the meaning of discourse. Yet the significance of Socrates' requirement and of what it can accomplish, if carried out, goes still further. Socrates stresses that the one who is competent in this τέχνη is also enabled by it to deceive in a perfect way (261e). What Socrates here demands as a condition of the possibility of genuine self-expression is also a condition of the possibility of perfect deception and misrepresentation. Hence this demand still accommodates our ungenuine conception of the intention of discourse, insofar as it places in our hands the weapons we need to carry out the business of deception, now based for the first time on, as it were, a scientific foundation. With this last, extreme interpretation of the significance of the demand, Socrates/Plato finally places the rhetoric of the time back on its most proper foundations.

β) The essence of the ἀπάτη. General characterization. Its structure: ὁμοιοῦν. Its object: the "essential" things.

The question is: What must ῥητορική accomplish as τέχνη, in order for it to make possible a convincing deception? It must be such ᾗ τις οἷός τ' ἔσται πᾶν παντὶ ὁμοιοῦν τῶν δυνατῶν καὶ οἷς δυνατόν, καὶ ἄλλου ὁμοιοῦντος καὶ ἀποκρυπτομένου εἰς φῶς ἄγειν (261e2ff.), on the basis of which a person is capable: 1.) πᾶν παντὶ ὁμοιοῦν, 2.) εἰς φῶς ἄγειν. The proper laying of the foundations of rhetoric thus accomplishes two things: 1.) It transposes the speaker into the possibility of ὁμοιοῦν, and 2.) it gives him the possibility εἰς φῶς ἄγειν.

1.) Ὁμοιοῦν means in the first place "to assimilate" something to something. The orator is capable, if he has substantive knowledge about the things of which he speaks, to assimilate anything to anything else admitting of such assimilation. His λόγος thereby has the possibility of ὁμοιοῦν. Ὁμοιοῦν must be understood here as a mode of carrying out λέγειν in the sense of δηλοῦν, revealing. Ὁμοιοῦν thus means to speak about something in such a way that it looks like something else which it precisely is not but which it is to be seen as. This being seen as, this sight, is to be formed precisely by λόγος. Let us take an example from oratory in court: the counsel for the defense can present an assassination as a heroic deed, despite knowing very well it was a case of paid murder. This defense will have the best chance of success if counsel genuinely understands something of the hero and a heroic act and does not merely have a representation of them from the movies. If a defender does speak of the hero and heroism, we usually say he is becoming "moralistic." That means, though expressed improperly, that he is taking his orientation from an idea. If the defender possesses a substantive idea of the hero, then it is possible for him to extract from the actual deed the moments which correspond to this idea and then exaggerate them as he wishes. If he does not have this idea, then he feels at a loss, assuming he wants to do more than merely babble. And thus, precisely for an ungenuine objective, what is guiding is a disclosure of the true state of affairs and its meaning. This makes it possible to put a certain face on the actual deed, so that the thing then shows itself under such a guise. This is the phenomenal character of the face of something, the outward look as such and such. The actual "what" is thereby precisely hidden and unknown to the one who is presented with this face of the thing; he depends and remains dependent on the face it wears. For the one who is perpetrating the deception, however, this "what," to which the face is oriented, must precisely be revealed. Thus the one who knows the ἀληθές is at any time capable of this ὁμοιοῦσθαι, this assimilation, this putting of a certain face on things.

2.) If, now, one's opponent has the same genuinely substantive knowledge, then he is himself capable of accomplishing the second point (which the other person could accomplish as well), namely, εἰς φῶς ἄγειν, "bringing to light." That is, if someone is proceeding with the ὁμοιοῦν in this way, putting a face on things that does not correspond to the true state of affairs, such an opponent can detect the deception and bring to light the fact that he is not speaking about the things themselves but is precisely concealing them and covering them over.

This indicates quite generally the structure of the ἀπάτη, the deception, in the conditions of its possibility. In the case of the sophist, we will encounter these phenomenal structures in still more detail. What now is important is only that you see the general horizon to which these phenomena belong.

The ἀπάτη, the deception, the ὁμοιοῦν, will thus "be most successful" ἐν τούτῳ μᾶλλον γίγνεται (cf. 261e6f.), where the matters spoken of are poorly distinguished, ἐν τοῖς ὀλίγον διαφέρουσι (cf. e6–262a1). κατὰ σμικρὸν μεταβαίνων, μᾶλλον λήσεις ἐλθὼν ἐπὶ τὸ ἐναντίον ἢ κατὰ μέγα (a2f.). The deception is easier when speaking of matters with regard to which the intuitions and available concepts run into one another, for then μᾶλλον λήσεις ἐλθὼν ἐπὶ τὸ ἐναντίον, "you are then more likely to remain in concealment if in the course of the speech you suddenly cross over to the opposite." Therefore, where the states of affairs are distinguished only in very small part, such that the transition is a μεταβαίνειν "over something trivial," κατὰ σμικρόν, then it is much more possible ἐπὶ τὸ ἐναντίον ἐλθεῖν, "to switch to the opposite," much more likely than when the matters are far apart and their distinctions catch the eyes of everyone. Consequently, it is important τὴν ὁμοιότητα τῶν ὄντων καὶ ἀνομοιότητα ἀκριβῶς διειδέναι (a6f.), "to see through," διειδέναι, "in a rigorous way," ἀκριβῶς, "the peculiar substantive affinity, and divergence, of the matters at issue, the concepts, and the assertions." But it is possible to see the ὁμοιότης and the ἀνομοιότης of the matters only if I possess the matters themselves on the basis of their ἀλήθεια (cf. a9), hence only if the διάνοια is εἰδυῖα τὸ ἀληθές (cf. 259e5). And so it has become clear that genuinely convincing deception depends precisely on an antecedent knowledge of the truth.

Socrates now asks where we are most deceived (263aff.): obviously in regard to matters whose limits most run into one another, where ἄλλος ἄλλῃ φέρεται (a9f.), "everyone is carried in a different direction," and where we ἀμφισβητοῦμεν (b3), "are in conflict" with one another and also with ourselves. We can be deceived much easier, εὐαπατητότεροι (b3), where we πλανώμεθα (b5), "drift about," where our assertions and concepts have no stable foothold in the matters themselves. We do not drift about in regard to everyday things, in saying, e.g., what iron or silver (263a6) is, or, recalling the *Sophist,* what fishing is, or what a fish is as an object of hunting, etc. We can sufficiently determine these without further ado. Here we have fixed limits within the sphere of evidence required in everyday life; here we are not readily deceived. But it is quite different when it is a matter of the δίκαιον or the ἀγαθόν (cf. 263a9). In all these issues, people's opinions diverge. Accordingly, whoever does not have the correct attitude with regard to these states of affairs, i.e., a διάνοια that is εἰδυῖα τὸ ἀληθές (cf. 259e5), but is instead ὁ τὴν ἀλήθειαν μὴ εἰδώς (262c1f.), i.e., "one who has never seen the matters at issue in their unconcealedness," who rather pursues mere opinions, hearsay, and common beliefs, will not be able to develop a genuine τέχνη of λόγοι but only γελοία (cf. c2), "a ridiculous one," one that is ἄτεχνος (cf. c3), without orientation. Thereby, from a negative side, in relation to deception and delusion, the necessity of substantive knowledge, i.e., a knowledge of the matters at issue themselves, and thus the necessity of research into truth have been demonstrated.

But this still says nothing as to how the disclosure of the truth, the disclosure of beings in the proper sense, looks. That is the second thing Plato will show in this latter part of the *Phaedrus*. What then does this εἰδέναι ἀλήθειαν properly accomplish? Which are the ways we can properly appropriate beings? The answer is διαλέγεσθαι, dialectic.

b) The seeing of the truth by means of dialectic. General characterization of dialectic. The two component parts of dialectic: συναγωγή and διαίρεσις. Συναγωγή as ἀνάμνησις. Dialectic as a condition of the possibility of rhetoric.

Plato deals with the modes of the proper appropriation of beings at 265dff., and he does so, specifically, as I have already stressed, not by carrying out a dialectical investigation but by describing dialectic in general, in its methodological character. We will see dialectic actually carried out in the *Sophist*, with regard to a determinate phenomenon, one connected precisely to the accomplishment of deception. Thus it has become clear negatively that there must be a way to see the truth of things first, just in order to be able to deceive, quite apart from the positive possibility of being able to speak correctly at any time. Socrates skillfully leads the conversation to the question of dialectic by recalling the discourse of Lysias which Phaedrus read to him earlier. They discuss this discourse, and Socrates brings Phaedrus to the insight that it has been composed in quite a confused manner: i.e., Lysias places at the beginning what he actually wants to say at the end. Phaedrus concedes this, and, at 264c2ff., Socrates formulates his concession more clearly: "But I believe what you actually mean by this concession, is δεῖν πάντα λόγον ὥσπερ ζῷον συνεστάναι, σῶμά τι ἔχοντα αὐτὸν αὑτοῦ, ὥστε μήτε ἀκέφαλον εἶναι μήτε ἄπουν, ἀλλὰ μέσα τε ἔχειν καὶ ἄκρα, πρέποντα ἀλλήλοις καὶ τῷ ὅλῳ γεγραμμένα, "every λόγος must συνεστάναι, hold together in itself, ὥσπερ ζῷον, like a living thing, which σῶμά τι ἔχοντα, has a body, αὐτὸν αὑτοῦ, with its own coherence, so that this ζῷον is neither ἀκέφαλον, without head, nor without feet, and also has a middle and ends, ἄκρα, and everything is πρέποντα ἀλλήλοις: all the parts are articulated, γεγραμμένα, in a suitable way, among themselves and also in the context of the whole." Here Socrates is comparing λόγος, the completed discourse, whether written or spoken, to a ζῷον and its organic structure. He does so first of all with reference to the present theme of the dialogue, the actual composition of the discourse, of the λόγος. Socrates turns this rather extrinsic question of the structure of the λόγος with respect to its composition toward something quite different, namely toward the matters the λόγος is supposed to address and toward the exposition of these matters. He says two conditions are necessary for λόγος to be able to accomplish its task of letting the matters at issue be seen:

1.) the λόγος, and thereby the orator, must be capable εἰς μίαν τε ἰδέαν συνορῶντα ἄγειν τὰ πολλαχῇ διεσπαρμένα (265d3f.), of "taking τὰ πολλαχῇ διεσπαρμένα, that which is in a manifold way dispersed, and leading it, orienting it, to one view, to one single thing seen." And the orator must perform this ἄγειν in the specific mode of συνορᾶσθαι, "such that he sees together" (note the emphasis on seeing, which is the proper grasping of a matter at issue) and indeed ἵνα ἕκαστον ὁριζόμενος (d4), "such that he delimits every one of the dispersed manifolds against the others," and thereby, in this ἄγειν εἰς μίαν ἰδέαν (cf. ibid.), "reveals" δῆλον ποιεῖ, περὶ οὗ ἂν ἀεὶ διδάσκειν ἐθέλῃ, "that which he wants to teach, in his entire discourse or treatise, ἀεί, for the future and always." This first determination is therefore a constitutive moment of dialectic, but the statement is not immediately clear. Its interpretations have been as divergent as possible. As far as I know, none of the previous works on this topic have really understood what is involved here, because they have been oriented toward some sort of historiographical dialectic or else toward formal logic. What Plato is saying is that that which is spoken of, the matter of fact, e.g., love, gathers up its various phenomenal aspects and lets them be seen together in one basic content, so that with this συνορῶντα ἄγειν εἰς μίαν ἰδέαν the total phenomenal content of whatever is at issue is taken up, specifically in such a way that it can be understood from *one* view. Thus the first accomplishment of this διαλέγεσθαι is the taking up of the totality of the state of affairs in an orientation toward a μία ἰδέα, such that in this connection the matter of fact in its concrete totality, that which is at issue, becomes visible. It is not a question of exposing one idea in isolation and then ordering the other εἴδη to it, thereby forgetting the thing itself, as it were. On the contrary, it is a question of comprehensively taking up the state of affairs into a first horizon of an orientation toward the phenomenon in its totality. Thus it is a matter of nothing else than what the *Sophist*, e.g., accomplishes in its first considerations and preliminary descriptions, all of which already have their quite definite capacity to be seen together εἰς μίαν ἰδέαν. The aim is not to produce a system but to make clearly visible for the first time this ἰδέα itself, in all its content, and to gain a foundation for the explication of this idea itself. The latter then becomes the second task of dialectic, διατέμνειν or διαιρεῖν, which cannot be separated from the first. Thus the initial component of dialectic, συναγωγή (cf. 266b4), has the task of first "bringing together in one view," εἰς μίαν ἰδέαν ἄγειν, the entire realm of the state of affairs, as that realm was initially intimated. This συναγωγή does not accomplish anything else than making what is spoken of 1.) σαφές, "clear," and 2.) ὁμολογούμενον, "harmonious." τὸ σαφὲς καὶ τὸ αὐτὸ αὑτῷ ὁμολογούμενον διὰ ταῦτα ἔσχεν εἰπεῖν ὁ λόγος (cf. 265d6f.). The clarity and harmony of whatever is said are accomplishments of the first structural moment of the dialectical process, συναγωγή. At another place in the dialogue (cf. 273e2f.), Plato calls this moment μιᾷ ἰδέᾳ περιλαμβάνειν, "encompassing in *one* view." That means the ἰδέα provides for what is encompassed an illuminating view. If I see the idea, if I see what love is, then, and only then, can I clearly distinguish its various phenomena and their structures. And, on the basis of this idea, I can proceed harmoniously in the whole consideration. I will not speak in the first part of my speech about something with which the third part has nothing in common except for the name. This accomplishment is the work of a συναγωγή directed toward something primarily seen, seen in the sphere of objects of a certain content.

2.) The second component of dialectic is διαίρεσις. This is a matter of διατέμνειν, "cutting through," guided by a constant regard toward the idea, τὸ πάλιν κατ' εἴδη δύνασθαι διατέμνειν (265e1), what is seen together in one view, the πρῶτον ζήτημα. That which is initially an undiscriminated manifold of objects in an imprecise knowledge of the meaning and the possibilities—of love, e.g.—is now to be split apart on the basis of the μία ἰδέα. Plato compares this διατέμνειν with the process of dissecting an animal in such a way that the whole organism remains preserved, and nothing, "no part, is broken or broken off," καταγνύναι μέρος μηδέν (265e2), as is done, for instance, by a bad cook working on some game or other. Thus it is a matter of διατέμνειν κατ' ἄρθρα (e1), cutting through, i.e., exposing the connections in the object, in such a way that the joints become visible, namely the connections among the respective origins of the determinations of the things, so that in this dissection of the whole organism, cutting through the connections of its joints, the entire ontological lineage of the being becomes visible.

These are the two accomplishments required of those Plato calls διαλεκτικοί. τοὺς δυναμένους αὐτὸ δρᾶν . . . καλῶ . . . διαλεκτικούς (266b8ff.). Socrates himself now says: τούτων δὴ ἔγωγε αὐτός τε ἐραστής, τῶν διαιρέσεων καὶ συναγωγῶν (cf. 266b3f.). "I am a friend of these two procedures, namely διαίρεσις and συναγωγή." And a person who can carry out these two procedures of διαλέγεσθαι is δυνατὸς εἰς ἓν καὶ ἐπὶ πολλὰ πεφυκόθ' ὁρᾶν (cf. b5f.) capable of seeing a) the *one* in διαγωγή, where he takes direction for the διατέμνειν, and b) in the διατέμνειν, ὁρᾶν ἐπὶ πολλά. What is at stake in both cases is primarily and essentially the seeing of the matters at issue.

In the first part of the dialogue, at 249b, Plato had already begun to speak allusively of this dialectical procedure, and there he touched upon a moment which clarifies the first step of dialectic, the συναγωγή. δεῖ γὰρ ἄνθρωπον συνιέναι κατ' εἶδος λεγόμενον, ἐκ πολλῶν ἰὸν αἰσθήσεων εἰς ἓν λογισμῷ συναιρούμενον· τοῦτο δ' ἐστιν ἀνάμνησις ἐκείνων ἅ ποτ' εἶδεν ἡμῶν ἡ ψυχὴ συμπορευθεῖσα θεῷ καὶ ὑπεριδοῦσα ἃ νῦν εἶναί φαμεν, καὶ ἀνακύψασα εἰς τὸ ὂν ὄντως. . . . πρὸς γὰρ ἐκείνοις ἀεί ἐστιν μνήμῃ κατὰ δύναμιν, πρὸς οἷσπερ θεὸς ὢν θεῖός ἐστιν (249b8ff.). The συναγωγή, the seeing of the idea, is an ἀνάμνησις, a re-seeing of something already seen once before. It is hence not a concocting or fabricating of a determinate nexus in the matter at issue, out of separate individual elements; on the contrary, the μία ἰδέα is as such already present in its substantive content, although it is not immediately accessible. It is accessible only to one who has the possibility of ἀνάμνησις, i.e., to one who possesses genuine μνήμη and genuinely retains what he once already saw. That means συναγωγή is possible only to one who has formed an original relation to the matters at issue. A knowledge, no matter how great, of the πολλαχῇ διεσπαρμένα (265d3f.), the dispersed multiplicities and of a thousand other things does not result in any understanding if the primary relation, the ἀνάμνησις, is not present. Plato interprets this ἀνάμνησις as a re-seeing of what our soul previously saw while traveling with a god. If one liberates this interpretation from everything mythical and presentifies the genuine meaning, then it can only signify that the basic accomplishment of συναγωγή is not at all obvious, not given immediately to man, but instead that it requires an overcoming of definite resistances residing in the very Being of man himself, precisely insofar as a man is a man. Later we will still more closely see in what the basic resistance resides and precisely what makes the συναγωγή and hence the διαλέγεσθαι factually impossible most of the time.

In συναγωγή, the μία ἰδέα is not something fabricated but is itself a finding, something found, yet not something extracted from things in the sense that it did not reside there already, as if it were simply a product of individual determinations, a summation. On the contrary, the ἰδέα is already there. That is the reason for the remarkable designation for the Being of the ideas: παρουσία, presence. On the basis of their presence for correct seeing, Plato can say of συναγωγή, e.g. in the *Philebus,* with respect to the same function of διαλέγεσθαι: δεῖν οὖν ἡμᾶς τούτων οὕτω διακεκοσμημένων ἀεὶ μίαν ἰδέαν περὶ παντὸς ἑκάστοτε θεμένους ζητεῖν (16c10ff.). In every case to be treated in λόγος, an idea, a view, which provides the proper substantive content, must be sought, and εὑρήσειν γὰρ ἐνοῦσαν (d2) "one can find it as something lying in the matters themselves," arising out of the matters themselves; but it is not the product of a determinate elaboration of those matters. In this way, the λέγειν κατ' εἴδη (cf. 249b7), the διαίρεσις, is first possible on the basis of this μία ἰδέα, which is the proper foundation of all διαλέγεσθαι; i.e., it is the primary disclosure of the matters, of the γένος.

After the exposition of this idea of διαλέγεσθαι as a cognition which first properly gives us the matters to be taken up in speech, Socrates/Plato asks what then actually remains as genuinely scientific in rhetoric, if the dialectic is removed. λεκτέον δὲ τί μέντοι καὶ ἔστι τὸ λειπόμενον τῆς ῥητορικῆς (266d3f.). The answer is: it is then nothing but the manipulation of technical devices regarding the external composition of a discourse. Put positively: dialectic makes people δυνατοί (cf. 273e2); it develops their ability to speak in the correct way. οὔ ποτ' ἔσται τεχνικὸς λόγων πέρι (273e3); there is no one who has the ἕξις of knowing how to speak correctly, ἐὰν μή τις τῶν τε ἀκουσομένων τὰς φύσεις διαριθμήσηται, καὶ κατ' εἴδη τε διαιρεῖσθαι τὰ ὄντα καὶ μιᾷ ἰδέᾳ δυνατὸς ᾖ καθ' ἓν ἕκαστον περιλαμβάνειν (273d8ff.). That expresses it quite clearly: there is no τεχνικὸς λόγων who is not first of all διαλεκτικός. And insofar as he is that, it is also possible for him διαριθμεῖσθαι the present Being and comportment of his hearers. Thereby we arrive at rhetoric in its concrete relation to the hearers.

c) Rhetoric as ψυχαγωγία. The conditions of its possibility and its justification. Summary: dialectic as the ground of rhetoric.

It is clear that the τεχνικὸς λόγων must be capable διαριθμεῖσθαι τὰς φύσεις τῶν ἀκουσομένων (273d8ff.), "of taking full account of the present Being and comportment of the hearers." Thereby we touch a further phenomenon, pertaining to the concretion of speaking and, above all, public speaking. Those who are addressed in the speech can be understood in the multiplicity of their comportments (later conceived by Aristotle as πάθη) and taken into consideration in the correct way, only if the τεχνικὸς λόγων has acquired in advance a substantive knowledge of the ψυχή, i.e., only if he has gained clarity about this ὄν, life itself. And he can do so only if he understands in general the procedure of the dialectician. For the ψυχή is only one φύσις, one determinate being, among others. Ψυχῆς οὖν φύσιν ἀξίως λόγου κατνοῆσαι οἴει δυνατὸν εἶναι ἄνευ τῆς τοῦ ὅλου φύσεως; (270c1f.). "Do you really believe someone could grasp the Being of a living thing, the ψυχῆς φύσιν, as it requires the correct mode of treatment, without having first seen the whole?" That means: without having understood the question of a being or of beings in general. Thereby it is clear that anyone who σπουδῇ τέχνην ῥητορικὴν διδῷ (271a5), "who intends to elaborate an actual rhetoric," πρῶτον . . . ψυχὴν ἰδεῖν (a5f.), "must in the first place grasp the soul," i.e., the various possible types of Being of man (you see here a clear preparation for Aristotle's entire research) and specifically must look upon the soul with regard to πότερον ἓν καὶ ὅμοιον πέφυκεν ἢ κατὰ σώματος μορφὴν πολυειδές (a6f.), "whether there is only one possible mode of Being of psychic comportment or as many as there are in the case of the body." τοῦτο γάρ φαμεν φύσιν εἶναι δεικνύναι (a7f.): "we call such a demonstration φύσιν δεικνύναι, exhibiting nature—i.e., taking something which is and exhibiting that from which it has its Being." This, then, is first: to analyze the ψυχή.

Δεύτερον δέ γε, ὅτῳ τί ποιεῖν ἢ παθεῖν ὑπὸ τοῦ πέφυκεν (a10f.). Secondly, he must exhibit ὅτῳ, that to which the ψυχή relates in its comportment, and τί, what it thereby accomplishes or what it itself undergoes from another, how it itself can be touched—i.e., through speech. Hence he must know the various possible modes of leading and guiding the comportment of the soul of others.

In the third place, finally, he must examine <τὰς> αἰτίας (271b2), all "the causes" (which is here simply another way of saying "the means") necessary for the development of any correct speaking, so that the τεχνικὸς λόγων must see οἵα οὖσα ὑφ' οἵων λόγων δι' ἣν αἰτίαν ἐξ ἀνάγκης ἡ μὲν πείθεται, ἡ δὲ ἀπειθεῖ (b3ff.), which constitution of the soul may be, and which may not be, brought to a conviction through which speeches and through which means. If rhetoric develops in this manner then we must in fact say that it can be a directing of the soul, a ψυχαγωγία (271c10), a directing of the life of others by means of speaking with them and to them. Thereby the positive foundations of rhetoric are elaborated with explicit reference to its possible idea.

At 277b, Plato offers a brief summary of the idea of such a rhetoric. He gives us to understand—and this is essential—that λόγος as self-expression, as speaking out, communication, making public, has its ground in διαλέγεσθαι. This λόγος is hence in need of a definite direction, which is given to it by the way the matters at issue are disclosed, and Plato calls this way dialectic. Hence if we want to understand the term "dialectic" in the Platonic sense, we must accordingly keep it completely free of all the determinations heaped on it in the course of history even to this very day. Διαλέγεσθαι is the primary mode of the disclosure of beings themselves, such that thereby λέγειν maintains, in the broadest sense, its ground.

d) Plato and Aristotle on rhetoric.

We have presentified the positive grounding of the possibility of a rhetoric according to Plato. This ground lies in the Platonic idea of dialectic. In the *Phaedrus,* Plato does not retain the negative attitude toward rhetoric expressed in the *Gorgias.* We must keep in mind that Plato does not intend to develop a rhetoric, as Aristotle later did. And indeed it is not simply that Plato does not in fact care to do so, but he even considers it unnecessary, since dialectic occupies a different position within his concept of science than it will later for Aristotle. Plato sees his dialectic as the only fundamental science, such that in his opinion all other tasks, even those of rhetoric, are discharged in it. The reason Plato does not take up the task of developing a rhetoric, as Aristotle will later, lies in his exaggeration of dialectic or, more precisely, in this peculiarity, that although he in a certain sense understands the secondary significance of λόγος, yet he does not proceed to make λόγος itself thematic in its secondary position and to penetrate positively into its proper structure. Nevertheless, what Plato presents here in the latter part of the *Phaedrus* is the foundation for the concrete work Aristotle carried out. It is undeniably puzzling that Aristotle's *Rhetoric,* which without doubt is nothing other than the realization of the idea of such a τέχνη, does not mention the important preparatory work of Plato and refers to Plato only in the first part, and even then critically, with a caustic remark against the *Gorgias,* where Plato in fact still conceives of rhetoric in a very primitive way. This puzzle remains, and we have no prospect of clearing it up. On the other hand, we must be very cautious in our judgment on Aristotle's silence, because precisely the first part of the *Rhetoric* gives the impression this is not a fully elaborated treatise but two preparatory works clearly folded into one another, and in such a context, namely private expositions and remarks, it would not at all be necessary to quote Plato. The fact remains that Aristotle brought to realization the idea of rhetoric, the idea Plato himself positively elaborated with the help of his dialectic. Aristotle's success in penetrating through to the proper structure of λόγος makes it possible to institute a genuine investigation into λόγος itself. It likewise makes it possible for the λόγος that is not theoretical, i.e., for speech that is not in service to διαλέγεσθαι, to receive a certain justification within the context of everyday Dasein. The result is that the insight into the justification of everyday interlocution can provide the motive to create a rhetoric. For this everyday speaking (here we have Aristotle's genuine discovery) does not aim at ἀλήθεια yet still has a certain justification, since it pertains to the sense of everyday Dasein to move within the circuit of appearances. On this basis, then, even the speaking that is not explicitly an ἀληθεύειν receives its independent justification. Thereby rhetoric comes by a more positive justification than it does in Plato, who to be sure provided the guiding lines for the elaboration of the phenomenon. What is important, above all, in Plato's predelineation of the idea of rhetoric is that he does not stop at anchoring λέγειν in ὁρᾶν but goes on to maintain that the ψυχή of the auditor also belongs to the field of such dialectic, i.e., to rhetoric.

In the second part of the *Phaedrus*, Plato first shows rhetoric as a positive possibility, and then he proceeds to manifest his skepticism with regard to λόγος and specifically with regard to it as free-floating and as communicated.

§54. Plato's skepticism with regard to λόγος[1] *(*Phaedrus*, second part, 274b–279c).*

a) The ontological possibility of free-floating λόγος.

It has become clear that λόγος is dependent on ὁρᾶν and therefore has a derived character. On the other hand, insofar as it is carried out *in isolation*, insofar as it is a *mere* speaking about things, i.e., babbling, it is precisely what in the Being of man makes it possible for one's view of things to be distorted. Thus in itself, insofar as it is free-floating, λόγος has precisely the property of disseminating presumed knowledge in a repetition that has no relation to the things spoken of. It is not accidental that precisely in this dialogue, where Plato exposes the positive conditions of correct self-communication and self-publicizing, he focuses at the same time, with great acumen, on this other role of λόγος in factual existence, i.e., on that which λέγειν, insofar as it is left to its own devices, presents as an ontological possibility of life itself. This is just what λόγος means in the term ζῷον λόγον ἔχον (the determination of man) insofar as λόγος comes to dominate. Therefore the insight into the foundation of correct speaking in διαλέγεσθαι at the same time offers Plato a horizon for understanding λόγος in its opposite power, as it were, i.e., as that possibility in Dasein which precisely keeps man far from the access to beings.

b) The critique of writing. The legend of Theuth. Writing as debilitation of μνήμη. Λήθη. Σοφίας δόξα. Writing as mere impetus (ὑπόμνησις). The silence and defenselessness of the written λόγος. Genuine and written λόγος. The written λόγος as εἴδωλον.

Socrates, i.e., Plato, clarifies the ontological function of the free-floating λόγος in Dasein by means of a so-called ἀκοή (cf. 274c1), something he has heard, a legend. It tells of an Egyptian god, Theuth, who invented, among

1. Title in Heidegger's manuscript.

other things, number, board games, dice, geometry, astronomy, and even writing. This god Theuth came to see king Thamos, brought him all these treasures, and urged him to share them with all the Egyptians. Thamos allowed Theuth to relate the advantages of each of his inventions and then he himself passed judgment on them. When Theuth came to writing, the god said: Τοῦτο δέ, ὦ βασιλεῦ, τὸ μάθημα σοφωτέρους Αἰγυπτίους καὶ μνημονικωτέρους παρέξει· μνήμης τε γὰρ καὶ σοφίας φάρμακον ηὑρέθη (cf. 274e4ff.). "This knowledge, this μάθημα, namely writing, the ability to write down and, in the broadest sense, communicate what is said, will render the Egyptians σοφωτέρους, wiser, by making it easier for them to retain." Hence he had discovered a means for μνήμη. Recall what we said earlier about μνήμη: it is the soul's retention of what was seen once before, the retention of what is prepared for the soul from the very outset, provided the soul has the correct access. A φάρμακον has now been found for this μνήμη. Thamos, however, responded: ἄλλος μὲν τεκεῖν δυνατὸς τὰ τέχνης, ἄλλος δὲ κρῖναι τίν' ἔχει μοῖραν βλάβης τε καὶ ὠφελίας τοῖς μέλλουσι χρῆσθαι (274e7ff.). "It is one thing to be capable τὰ τέχνης τεκεῖν, of inventing and developing for the first time what belongs to a determinate knowledge and a definite know-how; it is another thing, however, κρῖναι, to judge how the invention contributes to the advantage or disadvantage of the ones who are going to use it." And he said to the god: δι' εὔνοιαν τοὐναντίον εἶπες ἢ δύναται (275a1), your praise asserts "the opposite of what the γράμματα are really capable of." Now comes the decisive statement, which stands in close connection to συναγωγή, i.e., to the proper seeing of the things, one founded in genuine ἀνάμνησις: τοῦτο γὰρ τῶν μαθόντων λήθην μὲν ἐν ψυχαῖς παρέξει μνήμης ἀμελετησίᾳ (275a2f.). This knowledge, this μάθημα, this making public in writing of what has been said, ἐν ψυχαῖς παρέξει, "will create in people λήθην, forgetting," or, more properly, λανθάνω, a concealing, a covering, "of themselves, in relation to what they have learned," τῶν μαθόντων. Hence what the god is offering will cover over in people precisely that to which they relate in their comportment toward the world and themselves, because the knowledge of writing entails ἀμελετησία μνήμης, "unconcern with retention," i.e., with retaining the things themselves. Λόγος as communicated in writing is capable of promoting an unconcern with retaining the matters spoken of, i.e., with retaining them in their proper substantive content. And then comes the more precise reason: ἅτε διὰ πίστιν γραφῆς ἔξωθεν ὑπ' ἀλλοτρίων τύπων, οὐκ ἔνδοθεν αὐτοὺς ὑφ' αὑτῶν ἀναμιμνησκομένους (a3ff.). They will retain what they learn διὰ πίστιν γραφῆς, "by relying on what is written," ἔξωθεν, "from the outside," i.e., on the basis of the written word, "by means of foreign signs," ones which have, in their own character, nothing at all to do with the matter they refer to. The written form of the word "chair" does not have the least kinship with the thing itself; it is something completely foreign to the thing itself. And this reliance on writing promotes an unconcern with regard to retaining: people will retain their knowledge from the outside and will not remember from their own resources, from the inside, i.e., from a possibility they themselves possess, namely ὁρᾶν. The πίστις γραφῆς, reliance on what is said, in the broadest sense of what is talked about publicly, considers itself absolved from having to look into what is talked about. οὔκουν μνήμης ἀλλὰ ὑπομνήσεως φάρμακον ηὗρες (a5): "Thus you have not found a means to a proper repetition and re-possession of matters but only a means of being reminded of them." Therefore μνήμη and ὑπόμνησις are essentially different: μνήμη is a going back, a repetition and appropriation of the matters themselves; ὑπόμνησις is a mere reminder, one that adheres to the spoken word. σοφίας δὲ τοῖς μαθηταῖς δόξαν, οὐκ ἀλήθειαν πορίζεις (a6f.). "That is the reason you are not inculcating in your pupils σοφίας ἀλήθεια, true and correct research, but only δόξα, semblance." πολυήκοοι γάρ σοι γενόμενοι ἄνευ διδαχῆς πολυγνώμονες εἶναι δόξουσιν, ἀγνώμονες ὡς ἐπὶ τὸ πλῆθος ὄντες, καὶ χαλεποὶ συνεῖναι, δοξόσοφοι γεγονότες ἀντὶ σοφῶν (a7–b2). On account of their adherence to the γραφή, to what is for public consumption, to what is bruited about, to what is fashionable, "they hear much, but without the proper training, and so they fancy themselves to be familiar with many matters, whereas in fact they are quite unfamiliar with them; and it is difficult to be together with such persons," συνεῖναι, because they cannot speak about anything. They have become δοξόσοφοι ἀντὶ σοφῶν, "ones who merely look like those who are really striving for correct knowledge." And so you see here quite clearly the function of the γράμματα and γραφή within the existence of man, and indeed precisely in relation to the possibility of disclosing what is there to be uncovered. You see the relation of the free-floating λόγος to the genuinely substantive task of dialectic.

Plato now supplies a still more precise foundation for this peculiar function of λόγος, namely that it leads to ἀμελετησία μνήμης: λόγος as made public, as communicated and written, has nothing in common with the σαφές and the βέβαιον (275c6), the clear and the certain. All that can be attributed to the public, communicated, λόγος, i.e., to the written one, is that it does nothing more than τὸν εἰδότα ὑπομνῆσαι περὶ ὧν ἂν ᾖ τὰ γεγραμμένα (275d1f.), nothing more than ὑπομνῆσαι, "allow τὸν εἰδότα, the one who has already seen something, to encounter it again, i.e., to encounter again the matter at issue in the γεγραμμένα." What is written, what is said and made public, can only be an impetus and a basis for going back to the matters themselves. Consequently, to take up and understand something written or said, an individual must have previously already seen that which is spoken of. He must set out to see the matters on his own.

What is said and written—this is essential—can by itself deliver nothing. Therefore Plato says: Δεινὸν γάρ που τοῦτ' ἔχει γραφή, καὶ ὡς ἀληθῶς ὅμοιον ζωγραφίᾳ (cf. d4f.): "What is written is as uncanny as a painting." καὶ γὰρ τὰ ἐκείνης ἔκγονα ἕστηκε μὲν ὡς ζῶντα (d5f.), what is presented in it looks as if it were alive, ἐὰν δ' ἀνέρῃ τι, σεμνῶς πάνυ σιγᾷ (d6), yet "if you interrogate it, it maintains a solemn silence." Thus what is spoken and written is silent and delivers nothing. Plato then asks: δόξαις μὲν ἂν ὥς τι φρονοῦντας αὐτοὺς λέγειν (d7f.); "do you really believe that what is written down could speak ὥς τι φρονοῦν, as if it had understanding?" No, on the contrary, to anyone who wants to learn something on the basis of what is said there, "it always shows one and the same thing and no more"; ἕν τι σημαίνει μόνον ταὐτὸν ἀεί (d9). This ἕν τι μόνον is nothing else than the word sound itself. What is said, and is fixed once and for all, is in fact always one and the same. And if it is taken up, without preconditions, for a substantive understanding, it says always the same thing, i.e., basically nothing; it keeps silent. Therefore Plato can say: ὅταν δὲ ἅπαξ γραφῇ, κυλινδεῖται μὲν πανταχοῦ πᾶς λόγος ὁμοίως παρὰ τοῖς ἐπαΐουσιν, ὡς δ' αὔτως παρ' οἷς οὐδὲν προσήκει, καὶ οὐκ ἐπίσταται λέγειν οἷς δεῖ γε καὶ μή (275d9–e3). "If a λόγος is once written down, it roams around everywhere and equally approaches those who understand the matter and those who do not, and it has no way of distinguishing between the one to whom it should speak and the one to whom it should not." Such a written λόγος or communicated word, the end result of some research, can then be mistreated and improperly abused; it cannot defend itself. It can be watered down, and everything possible can be made out of it; the *logos* cannot defend itself. τοῦ πατρὸς ἀεὶ δεῖται βοηθοῦ (e4): "It is always in need of the father's help," i.e., help from the one who expressed it on the basis of a knowledge of the matters themselves, help from the one to whom it owes its Being. αὐτὸς γὰρ οὔτ' ἀμύνασθαι οὔτε βοηθῆσαι δυνατὸς αὑτῷ (e5): "It itself cannot defend itself and cannot help itself." Thus the peculiar ontological character of what is spoken and said publicly, what is bruited about, makes it clear that it is by itself unable to be anything but a mere impetus, and can be this only for persons who have already seen; otherwise it simply shows how superfluous it is.

Consequently, genuine λόγος and genuine communication are obviously something else; only that λόγος is genuine ὃς μετ' ἐπιστήμης γράφεται ἐν τῇ τοῦ μανθάνοντος ψυχῇ (276a5f.), "which is written on the basis of a knowledge of the matters themselves," on the basis of a relation to the matters themselves, written not, as it were, in the public realm but rather "in the soul of the one who learns" such that he does not adhere to the said and spoken but instead—i.e., precisely in the soul—the one who learns νοεῖ, "sees" for himself. This λόγος, the one written in this way, is δυνατὸς ἀμῦναι ἑαυτῷ (cf. a6), "able to defend itself," and ἐπιστήμων λέγειν τε καὶ σιγᾶν πρὸς οὓς δεῖ (a6f.), "it understands, i.e., is clear about, to whom it may speak and should speak and to whom, on the other hand, it ought to keep silent." It is silent to that ψυχή which does not in itself have the possibility of hearing it, i.e., is not prepared for it and does not possess genuine παιδεία. It is thus clear that this writing μετ' ἐπιστήμης presupposes that the ψυχή upon which it is written has put aside prejudices and has liberated for itself the horizon to the matters themselves. Only then is the written λόγος a living one.

Phaedrus now draws the consequence. Τὸν τοῦ εἰδότος λόγον λέγεις ζῶντα καὶ ἔμψυχον, οὗ ὁ γεγραμμένος εἴδωλον ἄν τι λέγοιτο δικαίως (a8f.). There is a double λόγος, the living, i.e., the one that takes its life from a relation to the matters themselves, from διαλέγεσθαι, and the written one, in the broadest sense the communicated one, which is a mere εἴδωλον of the other, the living λόγος. Εἴδωλον is usually translated as image, imitation, or the like. Recall that εἶδος means the outward look of something, i.e., that ontological determination which presents something as what it is. Εἴδωλον, on the other hand, refers to *mere* outward look; it is not nothing, but it is such that it merely appears to be so and so. The written λόγος is in fact a λόγος, but it merely looks like the living one.

This position on the function of λόγος recurs in Plato's "Seventh Letter."

c) Plato's position on λόγος in the "Seventh Letter."

Here Plato is defending himself against the abuse of his philosophical work carried out by disciples who did not understand it. His indignation over this abuse leads him to a very harsh appraisal, almost purely negative, of the role of λόγος. In this "Seventh Letter," he takes up the question of how it was possible for him to be so misunderstood, and he does so by engaging in a lengthy treatise on knowledge. He does not offer anything new but simply summarizes what determined all his work: that all knowledge, if taken in its total structure, is constructed out of the phenomena of ὄνομα, λόγος, εἴδωλον, ἐπιστήμη, and ἀληθές (342a7ff.). But we may not conceive of the connection of these five moments as if it were a matter of an epistemological system; on the contrary, it is a matter of one and the same phenomenon of knowledge, one and the same disclosure of beings, according to the various directions of its structure. Ὄνομα: the word, the word sound. Λόγος: what is said as such. Εἴδωλον: mere outward look, mere appearance, from which I depart in speaking about something. Ἐπιστήμη: the pressing on from the εἴδωλον to the matter itself. The most proper element is the ἀληθές; it is that toward which ὄνομα, λόγος, εἴδωλον, and ἐπιστήμη are already oriented in their very sense. These have in themselves a directedness toward the ἀληθές; they cannot be understood otherwise than as determined by the functional character of disclosing beings. Plato here recalls these structures of genuine knowledge. He concludes the consideration with the following statements: διὸ δὴ πᾶς ἀνὴρ σπουδαῖος τῶν ὄντων σπουδαίων πέρι πολλοῦ δεῖ μὴ γράψας ποτὲ ἐν ἀνθρώποις εἰς φθόνον καὶ ἀπορίαν καταβαλεῖ (344c1ff.). "Certainly, therefore, no serious man would ever write about serious things and thereby deliver his discoveries to the envy and misunderstanding of men." Then he adds: ἑνὶ δὴ ἐκ τούτων δεῖ γιγνώσκειν λόγῳ, ὅταν ἴδῃ τίς του συγγράμματα γεγραμμένα εἴτε ἐν νόμοις νομοθέτου εἴτε ἐν ἄλλοις τισὶν ἄττ' οὖν, ὡς οὐκ ἦν τούτῳ ταῦτα σπουδαιότατα, εἴπερ ἔστ' αὐτὸς σπουδαῖος, κεῖται δέ που ἐν χώρᾳ τῇ καλλίστῃ τῶν τούτου (c3ff.). "In a word, this means that if someone sees συγγράμματα γεγραμμένα τινός, something made public by a person, be it laws or other matters" (here these "other matters" are obviously philosophical, scientific writings) "it can be taken for granted that what the person in question made public was not for him anything serious," εἴπερ αὐτὸς σπουδαῖος, "if indeed he himself is a serious man." For, "on the contrary, what most properly concerns him, what is most proper to him, resides in the most beautiful place, i.e., in the soul itself." εἰ δὲ ὄντως αὐτῷ ταῦτ' ἐσπουδασμένα ἐν γράμμασιν ἐτέθη (c8f.): "And if in fact a person exposes in writing what is for him ἐσπουδασμένα, the most decisive," i.e., if he in fact makes it public, "ἐξ ἄρα δή τοι ἔπειτα," θεοὶ μὲν οὔ, βροτοὶ δὲ "φρένας ὤλεσαν αὐτοί" (d1f.), "then it was not the gods, but men, who have deprived him of his understanding." This is Plato's haughty denunciation of all the epigones of his work. It is perhaps an irony of history that this letter has been considered to be spurious.

d) The correct condition of the ψυχή as presupposition for genuine λόγος (διαλέγεσθαι).

To summarize, λόγος, in its genuine function, is founded on dialectic. But, at the same time, we see that λέγειν, if it is living speech—living in the sense that it lets others see—necessarily presupposes a readiness to see on the part of the ψυχή of those others. Yet, on the other hand, in fact most men do not possess this readiness, and διαλέγεσθαι, as Plato says explicitly in the *Phaedrus*, is a πραγματεία (cf. 273e5), a real labor and not something befalling a person by chance. To that extent, a special task and a special kind of speaking are necessary in the first place, in order to develop this readiness to see on the part of the very one who is investigating and also on the part of the other, the one to whom something is to be communicated. Therefore everything depends on this, that the ψυχή, the inner comportment, the Being of the existence of man, lies in the correct condition with regard to the world and to itself, i.e., in the correct συμμετρία, in an adequacy to the things themselves which are to be grasped in their uncoveredness. Socrates summarizes this once more at the end of the *Phaedrus*, now specifically not in a theoretical explication but in an invocation of the gods. Ὦ φίλε Πάν τε καὶ ἄλλοι ὅσοι τῇδε θεοί, δοίητέ μοι καλῷ γενέσθαι τἄνδοθεν· ἔξωθεν δὲ ὅσα ἔχω, τοῖς ἐντὸς εἶναί μοι φίλια. πλούσιον δὲ νομίζοιμι τὸν σοφόν· τὸ δὲ χρυσοῦ πλῆθος εἴη μοι ὅσον μήτε φέρειν μήτε ἄγειν δύναιτο ἄλλος ἢ ὁ σώφρων (279b8–c3). "O dear Pan and all ye gods here"—Socrates is outdoors with Phaedrus, beyond the city—"grant it to me to become beautiful" (καλός is nothing else than the opposite of αἰσχρός, ugliness, and signifies συμμετρία versus ἀμετρία, the proper adequacy versus inadequacy) "grant it to me to become beautiful, to come into the correct condition in relation to what is in myself, what comes from the inside, and grant that whatever I possess extrinsically may be a friend to what is inner, and grant that I repute as rich the one who is wise, i.e., the one who is concerned with the disclosure of things, the disclosure of beings, and grant that to me the amount of gold, the quantity of treasure, I possess in this world[2] will have for me as much value, and that I will claim for it only as much value, as a man of understanding should claim." That is, he beseeches here specifically for this correct condition with regard to the things themselves, and at the same time also for the correct bounds. Thus nothing in excess, for that could again turn into ignorance and barbarism. This καλὸν γενέσθαι, this becoming beautiful from the inside, is nothing other than what Plato fixes conceptually in the *Sophist* while attempting the sixth definition.

§55. *Transition: Dialectic in the* Phaedrus *and in the* Sophist.

a) Result and limits of the characterization of dialectic in the *Phaedrus*. Plato and Aristotle on dialectic and rhetoric.

The meaning of Plato's dialectic is the genuine root for our understanding of Greek logic and consequently for the ways of posing questions in logic as these became traditional in subsequent philosophy up to the present day. What we have thus far acquired from indications in the dialogue *Sophist*, as well as from our consideration of the *Phaedrus*, is actually a mere extrinsic characterization of dialectic and requires further work. The question of the Being of non-beings will lead us to ask what it really is that transforms the idea of dialectic as we have known it up to now and thus to ask where the

2. Reading *Reich* ["realm"] for *Reichtum* ["riches"].—Trans.

motives for the further development of Plato's dialectic reside. In order to understand this step, which Plato takes in the *Sophist* and which then determines the lawfulness of the stages of the further development of logic, we must constantly keep in mind the idea of dialectic exposed up to now. In the *Sophist*, Plato also calls διαλέγεσθαι διαπορεύεσθαι διὰ τῶν λόγων (cf. 253b10) or ἡ τῶν λόγων μέθοδος (cf. 227a8), "the direction taken with the λόγοι." Above all we must exclude—this should be clear on the basis of the foregoing—every extrinsic technical interpretation of dialectic. The essential element in it is the ὁρᾶν. Συναγωγή is a mode of seeing, i.e., seeing the ἕν; and even διαίρεσις, as an uncovering, is carried out on the basis of the constant looking upon the ἕν. The διαίρεσις of the εἴδη is a setting off of an outward look in opposition to an outward look, something which can itself be accomplished only in seeing. In this constant looking upon the ἕν, i.e., upon the γένος, an outward look is constantly there, and specifically in such a way that it remains present in every further setting off or in that which is set off against the other. And thus λέγειν in the sense of διαλέγεσθαι is a speaking about things which looks upon them. Where now nothing is capable any longer of being set off, where, on the basis of the thematic matter, there no longer exists the possibility of casting a regard from one pregiven εἶδος to another and thereby delimiting the pregiven against this other, thus where the content of an εἶδος compels us simply to dwell with it, there διαλέγεσθαι in the sense of διαίρεσις returns to the original attitude of sheer seeing, ὁρᾶν, as it is constantly carried out in relation to the ἕν. This "nothing but looking on" is the simple having of the ἄτομον εἶδος, specifically such that the entire connection of the διαλέγεσθαι, starting with the ὁρᾶν of the ἕν up to the seeing of the εἶδος, is a seeing enclosed in itself, a seeing of the history of the provenance of the being in question. Here we must note that, with regard to this idea of dialectic and of διαλέγεσθαι, it is still not decided whether the theme of διαλέγεσθαι is a being chosen entirely arbitrarily—e.g., the angler, the sophist—or Being. The ontological character of what is thematic in διαλέγεσθαι has not yet been discussed here. But it is exactly here that the determination of διαλέγεσθαι becomes more precise. In other words, the transformation of the idea of dialectic, in the later sense of logic, is motivated by the transformation of the concept of Being and of the idea of ontological constitution in general.

I indicated in the last session[1] that Aristotle brings this dialectic into a quite different scientific-theoretical position. Aristotle emphasizes that dialectic is the ἀντίστροφος[2] of rhetoric, or vice versa; they are opposites. That

1. The thirty-second session, on Tuesday, January 27, 1925. P. 233f.
2. *Rhetoric* A, chapter 1, 1354a1: Ἡ ῥητορική ἐστιν ἀντίστροφος τῇ διαλεκτικῇ.

means they are both on the same footing. For Plato, on the contrary, we have seen that διαλέγεσθαι and dialectic are in principle preordained to rhetoric, they are what first makes it possible, whereas for Aristotle rhetoric is ἀντίστροφος, it resides on the same level, as regards its epistemic character, as dialectic itself. Indeed Aristotle also says rhetoric is in a certain sense a παραφυές of dialectic.[3] This cannot have the sense it has in Plato, namely that rhetoric has "grown up next to" dialectic. It means rather, according to Aristotle's transformed concept of dialectic, that rhetoric belongs in the same field of the theory of λόγος in the largest sense. Hence here dialectic is limited to λόγος itself and its possible structures. We need to note now that Aristotle does not at all abandon what Plato calls dialectic but for the first time takes up precisely Plato's dialectic in an actually radical way in his idea of πρώτη φιλοσοφία. Of course, I cannot here pursue the concrete idea of dialectic in Aristotle; it is enough that you are aware of this connection.

b) The motive for the further development of dialectic in the *Sophist:* the differentiation of the "object" of dialectic (beings—Being and ontological structure).

For the following consideration we must keep in mind this question: What is it about the thematic content dealt with in the *Sophist* that transforms dialectic? More precisely, how can the κοινωνία τῶν γενῶν, toward which the discussion of the meaning of Being and non-being leads, be the substantive ground for a new determination of διαλέγεσθαι? You can see already in the term κοινωνία τῶν γενῶν that at issue here is the connection of the γένη, whereas up to now we have seen only *one* γένος and, oriented toward that one, a taking apart of the εἴδη. This is an indication that now the whole dimension of questioning and determining in the sense of διαλέγεσθαι is set differently, that here it will no longer be a matter of concrete beings but of the γένη and of the connection of the ontological structures as such.

Before we can see these substantive connections themselves, ones which compel a transformation of dialectic, we must provide ourselves with the access to them. That is to say, on the basis of a concrete presentification of what the sophist is, we must come to understand that this phenomenon of the sophist in fact itself already exemplifies the Being of non-beings. Because of the fact that the sophists, in a manifold way yet according to the structure we shall now gradually extract, make present the Being of non-

3. *Rhetoric* A, chapter 2, 1356a25: συμβαίνει τὴν ῥητορικὴν οἷον παραφυές τι τῆς διαλεκτικῆς εἶναι.

beings, our endeavor will amount to getting the sophist in view in his factual existence and, as it were, from all sides. For if it is clear and evident that the sophist in fact is and in himself constitutes a properly possible mode of Dasein, then the Being of non-beings, i.e., the existence of deception and error, is given *ipso facto*. Insofar as the demonstration of the existence of deception and error is at the same time a matter of a demonstration of something negative, it is necessary that Plato's consideration of the sophist in a certain sense leap over this negative phenomenon—in order to arrive at something positive, on the basis of which he sees the negative. This is the proper sense of the description in the sixth definition, which indeed then quite significantly ends in both collocutors agreeing they have now basically found the philosopher.

Chapter Four

The Definitions of the Sophist. Sixth and Seventh Definitions. (226a–236c)

§56. The sixth definition of the sophist. Refuter (226a–231c).

a) The question of the classification of the sixth definition. The concrete structure of the definitions. The sixth definition as a union of the fifth and the seventh definitions (ἀντίλογος).

The sixth definition of the sophist always struck commentators as a consideration lying outside the framework of the previous definitions. Above all, they were at a loss to see how this definition could be brought into the framework of the dichotomies. If one understands the preparatory definitions to be connected through Plato's supposed concern with building a conceptual pyramid, then indeed it will be difficult to fit this sixth definition among the others. For our consideration of the fifth definition has already shown that in going back to the χειροῦσθαι, this definition claims the last remaining structural moment out of the framework which determines the angler and so exhausts this pregiven frame, if one's gaze does not go beyond it. But we have emphasized repeatedly that our aim is not to provide an articulation of an extrinsic sort but to bring the phenomenon of the sophist closer and closer through the individual definitions. Thus we said the inner concatenation of the individual definitions is grounded in the matter itself, i.e., in definite objective characters graspable in the sophist as he ultimately shows himself. If we orient the definitions around the earlier framework, then the sixth definition will clearly and immediately conflict with that mode of consideration. To the extent that the sixth definition cannot be inserted into that schema, it precisely proves that the latter is not genuinely the issue.

Versus the earlier definitions, the sixth already has a more positive descriptive character, since it immediately prepares the way for the seventh, where the positive consideration begins. To understand the sixth definition we need to be clear about the onset of this new description within the previously articulated phenomena of the sophist. The sixth definition is, of course, not an arbitrary introduction of a new point of view but precisely takes up the decisive phenomena of the sophist as already described and propels them in a direction that would make possible a genuine elaboration.

Specifically, what is taken up is the phenomenon of ἀντιλέγειν, dealt with in the fifth definition and itself already encompassing the earlier ones. That may not be visible immediately, if the sixth definition is taken extrinsically, in terms of surface content, but a more precise interpretation will make it clear. We will then see that the sixth definition, insofar as it takes up ἀντιλέγειν and makes it more acutely explicit, links precisely the fifth definition with the seventh, inasmuch as the seventh again makes the ἀντίλογος thematic.

Thus you need to note well that the great emphasis I place on the structure does not have anything to do with an intention to determine the literary form of the dialogue, in order, thereby, to fix the chronological order of the dialogues, based on stylistic criticism. Our aim is simply to understand the substantive content, if indeed we have a right to presuppose that Plato designed his *logos* in accord with the outward look of the matters themselves, i.e., that he, in correspondence with the multiform aspect of the sophist, begins with that and drives this multiformity on toward a ἕν, toward that which allows it to be seen together—in the mode of συναγωγή—and thereby to be properly determined. Thus it is also impossible to partition this dialogue, based on pre-determined philosophical theorems and disciplines, into inferior parts, written merely for the purpose of training, and the kernel for the more advanced.

At the place of transition from the fifth to the sixth definition, the text makes superabundantly clear what is at issue. Ὁρᾷς οὖν ὡς ἀληθῆ λέγεται τὸ ποικίλον εἶναι τοῦτο τὸ θηρίον καὶ τὸ λεγόμενον οὐ τῇ ἑτέρᾳ ληπτόν (226a6f.). We are once more reminded that this θηρίον, namely the sophist, was correctly addressed as ποικίλον, something "multiform and variegated," and therefore as something which οὐ τῇ ἑτέρᾳ ληπτόν, cannot be grasped "with one hand" on the first attempt. ἀμφοῖν χρή (a8): "Both hands are needed." καὶ κατὰ δύναμίν γε οὕτω ποιητέον, τοιόνδε τι μεταθέοντας ἴχνος αὐτοῦ (b1f.). "And in accord with possibility, the grasping and conceiving of the sophist must be carried out by following the trace." This mention of a "trace" indicates precisely that the sophist himself, the substantive content thus far, the object, himself provides us with something that makes it possible for us to track him down, as we say, i.e., to follow him and actually get him in sight.

b) Formal depiction of the way of the sixth definition. Diairesis. To take apart (διαίρεσις)—to set in relief (διάκρισις)—to extract—to render free, to purify (κάθαρσις). Preview of the genuine object of κάθαρσις: ἄγνοια. Κάθαρσις as ἔλεγχος.

Someone merely following the text extrinsically is in for a surprise from the question now posed by the ξένος, i.e., after the just-mentioned methodological requirement: τῶν οἰκετικῶν ὀνομάτων καλοῦμεν ἄττα που; (226b2f.). "Does our language have designations τῶν οἰκετικῶν (τεχνῶν is left understood), for the modes of comportment, for the know-how, related to domestic servants?" This is indeed immediately very striking, if approached directly from the earlier definitions; it is an entirely strange question, but one we will later understand better. We will see that the reference to those who have duties around the house is not accidental, quite apart from the fact that there is a definite purpose behind the choice of the modes of behavior attributed to them. The ξένος now lists a quite definite number of activities; they are not arbitrarily chosen but, on the contrary, are already determined by his general aim (226b4ff.). He mentions διηθεῖν (b4): "to strain, to pass through a filter"; διαττᾶν (b4): likewise "to strain"; βράττειν (b6) (a characteristic expression for something we will want to understand later): "to shake back and forth and by this very shaking to cast something out," e.g., the chaff from the wheat, "to winnow"; and instead of διακρίνειν another reading has διασήθειν, which again means "to sift." And then the list continues with ξαίνειν (b8): "to comb"; κατάγειν (b8): "to spin"; and κερκίζειν (b8): "to weave." At 226c1f., Theaetetus quite justifiably asks what the ξένος is actually trying to accomplish with these remarkable things which at first have as little to do with the angler as with the sophist. The ξένος answers: διαιρετικὰ τὰ λεχθέντα σύμπαντα (cf. c3); "these are all activities which take apart," διαιρεῖσθαι, or, as it is characterized immediately afterwards, μίαν οὖσαν ἐν ἅπασι τέχνην (c5f.), and this τέχνη is διακριτική (c8). Διακρίνειν, "to set in relief," expresses it more precisely than does διαιρεῖσθαι, for διακρίνειν means not only to take apart in general but to set off against one another and to distinguish from one another the things taken apart in the taking apart. Thus there is a phenomenal distinction between a simple taking apart of something given and leaving it at that and taking apart in the sense of setting in relief, i.e., distinguishing some one thing against an other.

This διάκρισις can now again be carried out in such a way that it is a διακρίνειν τὸ δ' ὅμοιον ἀφ' ὁμοίου (cf. d2f.), i.e., such that "things that are the same are set off against each other," or, on the other hand, such that the διακρίνειν is an ἀποχωρίζειν, a "segregating" and specifically τὸ χεῖρον ἀπὸ βελτίονος (cf. d1f.), "of the worse from the better." Thus there is one taking apart, and there is another in the sense of setting in relief, and this latter can be such that both the things set off against each other are equal in their ontological character or such that they are different. In that case, the setting off is a separating of the worse from the better. This setting off is an extracting, namely of the worse from the better, such that that from which the extraction takes place, the better, remains left over; it is a ἀποβάλλειν τὸ χεῖρον and a καταλείπειν τὸ βέλτιον (cf. d5ff.). Thus we see that the structure of διαιρεῖσθαι is organized in an entirely determinate way. Purely terminologically, we can make the distinction still sharper by grasping the sense of the setting off of the worse against the better as a simple remaining left over of the better, which we can designate as "sifting." A second sense of setting off, however, derives from the extraction of the worse from the better, such that the latter is made free of the former, and we call this sort of sifting "purifying." Such a taking apart that also sets in relief is therefore καθαρμός (d10), "purification." The distinction between purification and sifting indicates that the sense of the καταλείπειν (cf. d6), the "leaving behind," is different in the two cases. Purification does not simply have the sense of removing something from something else and leaving at rest in itself that from which the removal takes place. On the contrary, the sense resides precisely in the making free and the consequent bringing of the thing to its proper possibilities. Hence the sense is a clearing away of obstacles, ἐμποδίζοντα, as the ξένος later says (230c6), "that which lies in the way," so that what is purified can now come into its own.

The establishment of the structures of διαίρεσις is important because the theme of the specifically ontological parts of the dialogue will be worked out precisely as the proper object of a definite διαίρεσις or κάθαρσις. Specifically, it is something that unifies in itself a βέλτιον and a χεῖρον, indeed in such a way that the one suppresses the other. This χεῖρον, the proper object of the κάθαρσις, is nothing other than something which, insofar as it is, at the same time is not. And so this peculiar object entails a συμπλοκή of ὄν and μὴ ὄν. The task was to see this συμπλοκή as something original. This means, however, that the fundamental dogmas then dominating philosophy had to be abandoned. For a συμπλοκή of μὴ ὄν with ὄν was at that time unheard of, i.e., insofar as it was held that only beings are, non-beings are not, and there is no other possibility. We will encounter this peculiar object as we come to understand better the proper theme of κάθαρσις, as carried out respectively by the sophist or by the genuine philosopher. Therefore the sixth definition is a *positive* description of the sophist, positive in the sense that it goes back to the foundations of his existence in general.

Thus διαίρεσις is 1.) a taking apart, and as διάκρισις this taking apart is

2.) a setting off and distinguishing of something from something else. In this context, I cannot yet pursue the fact that this taking apart in the second sense already entails an entirely new structural moment, insofar as the setting in relief which distinguishes something versus something else presupposes a determinate view of that according to which the two are distinguished. That moment is not yet present in the mere taking apart. This setting in relief which distinguishes one against another can now be 3.) a distinguishing that extracts, such that the distinguishing is an extracting in the sense of sifting. This taking apart that sifts, in the sense of extracting, can be 4.) a sifting that sets free in such a way that what is liberated itself remains and is preserved, a λειπόμενον. Hence such a sifting at the same time properly aims at what remains behind and grasps it. This διαίρεσις has the character of κάθαρσις.

If we look toward what the object of such a διαίρεσις in the sense of κάθαρσις can be, we see it is a matter of something having the character of a χεῖρον and a βέλτιον, and specifically such that both of these are initially given together and are unitarily determinative of a being. The more concrete grasp of διαίρεσις as performed in the sophistical teaching activity shows then that the proper object of the κάθαρσις is ἄγνοια and that thereby, to characterize it in an anticipatory way, the κάθαρσις ultimately proves to be ἔλεγχος. Ἔλεγχος means "to pillory, to expose publicly." It applies to something which, in accord with its possibility, possesses a βέλτιον but which is suppressed by a χεῖρον. The κάθαρσις as ἔλεγχος exposes the thing publicly, and this making public is in itself an ἐκβολή, a casting out of the χεῖρον, and consequently is a liberation of the βέλτιον. In a wholly formal and preliminary sense, this is the path taken by the description constituting the sixth definition of the sophist.

We intend to follow this path in detail.

c) Detailed depiction of the path of the sixth diairesis.

α) The differentiation of the καθάρσεις with respect to the sophist's object (ψυχή). Κάθαρσις of the body and κάθαρσις of the ψυχή. Remark on dialectic. Κάθαρσις as ἐκβολὴ τῆς κακίας.

It was quite advisedly that the modes of διακρίνειν were made visible in terms of activities related to everyday existence at home, i.e., related to the maintenance and fitting out of everyday life. Recalling what we made clear earlier about the sophist, we can say his τέχνη is characterized as δοξοπαιδευτική: his comportment thus includes a claim to παιδεύδειν. More precisely formulated, his τέχνη is μαθηματοπωλική; his comportment is a "provision, a selling, of μαθήματα," i.e., of λόγοι. And his way of dealing with those to whom he sells his treasures is ἀντιλογική, i.e., ἐριστική. All these modes of comportment, in their very sense, are clearly directed toward other people, toward their possible modes of existence, toward their ψυχή. More precisely, insofar as it is a matter here of the formation of παιδεία, a matter of the selling of μαθήματα, a matter of ἀντιλέγειν, this comportment aims at the ψυχή to the extent that νοεῖν, knowing in the largest sense, resides in it. Thus we must maintain 1.) that the determination of λόγος permeates the entire comportment of the sophist, and 2.) that the object he hunts is the ψυχή of another person.

It is in these terms that we need to understand the turn now taken by the consideration of διαιρεῖσθαι. For this διαιρεῖσθαι is meant to express nothing other than the anticipation of a phenomenon which will subsequently be claimed for the behavior of the sophist. Accordingly, insofar as the soul is concerned, even this διαίρεσις, i.e., the καθαρμός, will be directed toward the soul, toward the existence of other people, and specifically with regard to διάνοια. Thus the differentiation now made with respect to the object of καθαρμός is not an extrinsic, scholastic one, but is already predelineated in the very idea of the sophist, i.e., in the object of his comportment. Therefore the καθάρσεις are now again differentiated into ones περὶ τὸ σῶμα and ones περὶ τὴν ψυχήν (227c8f.). This differentiation at the same time serves to clarify in a preliminary way the sense of the κάθαρσις related to the ψυχή. It is not accidental here that the possible modes of the κάθαρσις related to σώματα function in a certain sense as examples for the modes of purification relative to the soul, insofar as it is manifest that even the existence, the soul, i.e., the full Being of the living man, is grasped here in the sense of form, καλῶς, εἶδος.

Thus there is first of all (as the most well known) a καθαρμὸς περὶ τὰ σώματα (cf. 226e5). And a distinction must be made between, on the one hand, the σῶμα τῶν ἀψήχων (cf. 227a3), "the body of what is without a soul," what does not live, the non-living, what is merely material, and, on the other hand, the σῶμα τῶν ἐμψύχων (227b7), "the body of what is alive." Such a body, one partaking of life, we call "flesh." It is characteristic of such a body to be given not only from the outside, for αἴσθησις, for ἁφή and ὁρᾶν, but to be given from the inside, as we say, i.e., given as a body for the living being whose body it is. My relation to my body is therefore one that is specifically psychic, i.e., this relation includes the possibility of my being "disposed" in relation to my body. This is why we speak of a bodily disposition. Only a body having the character of flesh contains in its objective content this structure of one's being disposed toward it in some way or another. A chair and a stone, although they are bodies, have no bodily disposition. Therefore the possible ways of influencing a body are different, depending on whether the body is flesh or a mere physical thing. The latter can be purified only in the sense of "washing" or "decoration," γναφευτική or κοσμητική (227a3f.). But one can exercise an influence, in the sense of καθαρμός, on the flesh by γυμναστική and ἰατρική (226e8f.), "gymnastics" and "healing." Both these latter kinds of purification, ἰατρική and γυμναστική, will be taken up again later when it is a matter of determining the purifications pertaining to the psychic as such.

This consideration of apparently quite primitive everyday activities provides Plato an opportunity to make a parenthetical remark about dialectics; at 227a7ff., he calls it ἡ μέθοδος τῶν λόγων (cf. a7f.). He explicitly emphasizes what is at issue in this dialectical analysis of τέχναι: it is not a matter of which accomplishes more within life and which less, which has the higher function of purification and which the lower; i.e., it is not a matter of ranking the factual modes of purification. For τοῦ κτήσασθαι . . . ἕνεκα νοῦν . . . πειρωμένη (227a10f.): "Our aim here is simply to take possession of νοῦς, to discern, to see." This is an abbreviated way of speaking: νοῦς stands for νοούμενον, as λόγος does for λεγόμενον. Hence the aim is merely to take possession of what is discerned, what is seen. That is to say, at issue here is merely the discernment of the ontological connections: τὸ συγγενὲς καὶ τὸ μὴ συγγενὲς κατανοεῖν (b1f.), "to get in sight what belongs in one γένος, in one ἕν, i.e., what belongs together in the same provenance and what does not." Since only this structure of provenance, and nothing else, is the theme, therefore τιμᾷ πρὸς τοῦτο ἐξ ἴσου πάσας (b2), "all these different τέχναι are equal in value." The consideration is indifferent with regard to their factual significance, and therefore σεμνότερον δέ τι τὸν διὰ στρατηγικῆς ἢ φθειριστικῆς δηλοῦντα θηρευτικὴν οὐδὲν νενόμικεν (b4f.), "it does not at all take it to be more worthy, more important, or more excellent to explain the structure of θηρεύειν with regard to the comportment of a field-marshal than to show the same thing with regard to the hunting of lice." In a similar fashion, someone who believes in logic might think (as happens frequently) that in order to be able to explicitate the structure of a proposition or of a concept he has to employ an example from theoretical physics at the very least. But that precisely proves that the person in question does not know what is at stake, that the objective content is at first indifferent, and that διαλέγεσθαι is rather a matter of *structures*, ones occurring prior to everything that constitutes the practical applicability in each case, i.e., the factual rank of the beings themselves. This is a clear indication of the direction followed by the transformation of διαλέγεσθαι. The ξένος concludes this methodological interlude by going back over what preceded and emphasizing (227b6ff.) that here the issue is simply—no matter whether inconsequential or very valuable activities are under discussion—to keep separated the κάθαρσις related to σώματα and the one περὶ τὴν διάνοιαν;

and it is precisely this latter κάθαρσις which we had in a certain sense "taken in hand" at the very outset, ἐπικεχείρηκεν ἀφορίσασθαι (227c4f.), "in order to delimit it."

Thus now the analysis gets a foothold in the διαίρεσις περὶ τὴν ψυχήν, and the question is to what extent we can speak of a κάθαρσις περὶ τὴν διάνοιαν. Let us recall the structure of κάθαρσις: 1.) ἐκβάλλειν, "to cast out," and specifically in the sense of καταλείπειν, "leaving behind," namely of the βέλτιον; 2.) διακρίνειν ὅμοιον ἀφ' ὁμοίου (cf. 226d1–7). The immediate question is: is there in the soul something which renders possible such comportment to it, the casting out of a χεῖρον and the retaining of a βέλτιον? Our everyday knowledge of factual Dasein, of life, shows us that there is ἐν ψυχῇ πονηρία and ἀρετή (cf. 227d4). These terms are to be taken here provisionally in a very general sense: "badness" and "excellence." In relation to this constitution of the soul, the καθαρμός would then be nothing other than ἐκβολὴ πονηρίας or κακίας ἀφαίρεσις (cf. d9f.).

The more precise determination of κάθαρσις has to take into account what this κακία itself is; it has to see to what extent there is a κακία in the soul. This is the place where the significance of the σῶμα as an example penetrates the conception of the ontological structure of the soul. In order to determine the κακία of the soul, we will go back to the κακία in the σῶμα, in flesh. The guiding line for the more precise determination of the object toward which the endeavors of the sophist are directed derives from the purification that relates to the flesh, σῶμα.

β) The determination of the κακία in the ψυχή, with the flesh as guiding line.

αα) The κακία of the flesh. Sickness and ugliness. Sickness: στάσις (insurrection). Ugliness: ἀμετρία, δυσειδές (deformity). Directedness-toward as condition of the possibility of the ἀμετρία of a comportment: general structural analysis.

The human body can manifest a χεῖρον in two ways: in the first place, as νόσος, "sickness," and secondly as αἶσχος, "ugliness" (cf. 228a1), the opposite of καλῶς. The structures of these two forms of badness are essentially different.

Νόσος, "sickness," is determined as στάσις (cf. a4), "insurrection," and this στάσις is determined as διαφορὰ τοῦ φύσει συγγενοῦς ἔκ τινος διαφθορᾶς (cf. a7f.), "a diremption of what is συγγενές, what in its very Being belongs properly together, due to a disturbance," i.e., due to destruction in the largest sense. What is characteristic of νόσος is thus στάσις, the stepping apart, the opposition against, the insurrection, of determinations which properly belong together in the being itself and which are thus likewise constitutive of the φύσις of the being. Δόξα, ἐπιθυμία, θυμός, ἡδονή, λόγος, λύπη (cf. b2f.): all these determinations are constitutive of the Being of man. But for someone who finds himself in an unfortunate situation with regard to his soul, these structural moments do not simply step apart but they oppose themselves against one another, such that an insurrection arises. This character of insurrection determines νόσος. What is essential here is hence that a mode of comportment comes into conflict with another and against another.

Αἶσχος, on the other hand, is τὸ τῆς ἀμετρίας . . . γένος (cf. a10f.); it is a γένος of ἀμετρία, "inadequacy." This is not a matter of the relation of one comportment to another but is something residing purely and simply in the comportment itself. It is not a matter of a relation, e.g., between the way I speak about something and my disposition: that I speak in this or that way depending on my disposition at the time, my passions and prejudices, i.e., that my disposition encroaches on my speaking about the thing. Hence αἶσχος is not a matter of the relation between λόγος and λύπη but on the contrary concerns merely one comportment, i.e., νοεῖν by itself, to take the example set in relief here. Νοεῖν has in itself the character of αἶσχος insofar as it manifests an inadequacy residing in its very Being. Αἶσχος is therefore a matter of the ἀμετρία, the inadequacy, of a comportment not with regard to another but with regard to itself. Where this γένος of ἀμετρία occurs, there πανταχοῦ δυσειδές (cf. a10f.), "there beings do not at all have the εἶδος, the outward look," which properly fits them. Instead, we find there *de-formatio,* disfiguration; the εἶδος is not what it should be. Αἶσχος is distinct from νόσος by virtue of the fact that there the inadequacy resides within the comportment itself and concerns its own specific constitution.

We must then ask what sort of structure has to be presupposed in a comportment for it to be able to display something like αἶσχος and ἀμετρία. Not every comportment of the soul possesses the possibility of this δυσειδές. We must ask, accordingly, what εἶδος, what ontological structure, of a mode of comportment renders possible such δυσειδές, such deformation? The analysis makes this plain at 228c1ff.: ὅσ' <ἂν> κινήσεως μετασχόντα καὶ σκοπόν τινα θέμενα πειρώμενα τούτου τυγχάνειν καθ' ἑκάστην ὁρμὴν παράφορα αὐτοῦ γίγνηται καὶ ἀποτυγχάνῃ, πότερον αὐτὰ φήσομεν ὑπὸ συμμετρίας τῆς πρὸς ἄλληλα ἢ τοὐναντίον ὑπὸ ἀμετρίας αὐτὰ πάσχειν; We want to extract the individual moments packed in this very condensed analysis. It is a matter of the ψυχή, of a comportment of the soul, which:

1.) is characterized as κινήσεως μετασχόντα, therefore as something "that bears in itself κίνησις." That means it is a psychic comportment having in itself the character of the "from-to," a comportment which in its Being as such is underway to something else. That is the sense of this κινήσεως μετασχόν.

2.) σκοπόν τινα θέμενα, in this being underway to, it has posited that to which it is underway, as σκοπός. Σκοπός is usually translated "aim." Provided the term is interpreted correctly, it does capture the meaning. The toward-which of a κίνησις is that in which it comes, in accord with its own proper sense, to its end, its τέλος. Σκοπός is such a τέλος which is "sighted," σκοπεῖν, as τέλος, and hence is uncovered. In this movement, its own proper end is by itself seen in advance. That is the genuine meaning of "aim."

3.) πειρώμενα τούτου τυγχάνειν: this κίνησις is not merely underway toward but possesses ὁρμή, "a striving to reach the goal," thus a positive tendency, an "urge," which is a new moment in opposition to a merely factual movement toward the goal. Where this is given, there can occur:

4.) a παραφορά, a "going awry." For only where there is a φορά, i.e., a κίνησις, in the sense of a striving to arrive at a τέλος which is σκοπός, is there, properly speaking, a going awry. Only in relation to a φορά oriented by a definite striving can there be a παραφορά.

Αἶσχος in the sense of this de-formation is thus possible only in the case of a formation which has in itself a direction toward something but which can also fail, by being deflected from its σκοπός. Such a comportment is a διαφέρειν not from another but from itself, from the meaning of Being residing in this being itself. The being is in itself, in its factual formation, inadequate to that toward which it itself as such is underway. Αἶσχος as ἀμετρία is thus an inadequacy which, out of the being itself, recoils back on itself.

Now arises the substantive question: where is such a phenomenon given in the ψυχή and what is it?

ββ) The ἀμετρία in the ψυχή: ἄγνοια. Structural analysis of νοεῖν. The orientation (ὁρμή) of νοεῖν toward the ἀληθές. Ἄγνοια as ugliness in the ψυχή. Ἀληθεύειν as καλόν.

The substantive question is hence: where and what in the ψυχή is this phenomenon of κίνησις which bears in itself a ὁρμή and the possibility of παραφορά? This phenomenon in the ψυχή is νοεῖν, or, more concretely, φρονεῖν, φρόνησις, which in Plato is still undifferentiated from σοφία and ἐπιστήμη. The most general term is νοεῖν. The τέλος of this κίνησις as νοεῖν is the ἀληθές: that in which the seeing comes to an end, the perceived, i.e., beings present as they are uncovered in themselves. Therefore what constitutes the inadequacy of this νοεῖν itself with regard to itself is παραφροσύνη: ἐπ' ἀλήθειαν ὁρμωμένης ψυχῆς, παραφόρου συνέσεως γιγνομένης, οὐδὲν ἄλλο πλὴν παραφροσύνη (228c10ff.). Παραφροσύνη is a very difficult term to translate, and in particular the usual translation is not a very happy one. The proper sense is "perception gone awry" or "misperception," i.e., it is not blindness, not mere non-seeing, but a much more radical deformation, precisely a "misperception," hence indeed a perception, a seeing. An extreme phenomenon of παραφροσύνη is infatuation. The idea that the νοεῖν in the soul is a phenomenon which makes possible a παραφροσύνη, that there is hence an ἀγνοεῖν, and that this ἀγνοεῖν is itself a deformation, quite apart from whatever sort of practical comportment results from this ἀγνοεῖν—that idea is founded in a more original one, expressed in the preceding statement: Ἀλλὰ μὴν ψυχήν γε ἴσμεν ἄκουσαν πᾶσαν πᾶν ἀγνοοῦσαν (228c7f.). "We know that every soul (that means all human knowing, for here it is a matter of νοεῖν) is in ignorance, ἄκουσα, without a positive impetus in that direction arising from itself." There is in the soul no positive ὁρμή toward this failing, this misperceiving. On the contrary, precisely even in misperception, the ὁρμή aims at the ἀληθές. This expresses the claim and the opinion that even the νοεῖν which is factually an ἄγνοια is oriented toward the ἀληθές. Thus we see that in fact there resides in the soul such an ἄγνοια, that (this is Plato's main concern) this ἄγνοια κακία αὐτὸ ἐν ψυχῇ μόνον γιγνόμενόν ἐστιν (cf. 228d10f.), this ἄγνοια "purely as such," αὐτὸ μόνον, insofar as it is present at all, already constitutes a deformation, and that therefore the δυσειδές within this basic comportment determines the κακία. Positively expressed, this means that the proper and genuine νοεῖν, i.e., ἀληθεύειν, is the καλῶς and is hence that which is properly to remain in the soul and is to be set free. In this connection, we must keep in mind that καλῶς, or τὸ καλόν and αἶσχος, are for the Greeks decisive predicates for a thing and concern its proper ontological character. Our expression "beautiful" or the like is much too pale and worn out to render the sense of καλῶς in any significant fashion. What is essential is that νοεῖν, this ὁρμή of soul toward the ἀληθές, be seen as what is most original in the constitution of man.

We encounter here a wholly original structure, one visible to the Greek philosophy of the time, a structure of Dasein, which to be sure would not be pursued in an explicit anthropological reflection.

γγ) Directedness-toward as an original structure of Dasein as Being-in (Being-in-a-world). The Greek discovery of Being-in. The Greek interpretation of existence as illuminated from the "world." The darkness of the history of anthropological questioning (Dilthey). The ontology of Dasein as presupposition for an insight into this questioning.

The structure of Dasein's being-underway toward what is to be uncovered touches that ontological structure of Dasein we designate phenomenally as

Being-in. Dasein, always used here as a title for the Being of man, is characterized by the basic phenomenon of Being-in or, more fully expressed, Being-in-a-world. Being-in-a-world is a basic phenomenon and is not resolvable further; on the contrary, it is a primary and perhaps *the* primary ontological fact of Dasein itself. This Being-in is initially permeated by ἄγνοια, by a knowledge of the immediately given world which is at the same time a lack of knowledge. It is a certain infatuation with immediately given appearances, on the basis of which all further experiences of the world are interpreted, interrogated, and explained. The knowledge arising in this way can become science and as such can be nurtured and cherished. At the same time, it is clear that this ἀγνοεῖν harbors a positive ὁρμή toward an ἀληθεύειν which has the potential to break through the actual ignorance. I emphasized that the Greeks, in all their scientific questioning, did not primarily focus on anthropological contexts but instead were concerned with elucidating the Being of the *world* in which man lives. Quite naively and naturally, they then likewise interpreted existence, the Being of the soul, with the same means they employed to elucidate the beings of the world in their Being. This is a tendency already pregiven in natural Dasein, insofar as natural Dasein takes the means even for its self-interpretation from the immediately experienced world. Greek research merely follows this quite primitive and in itself justifiable tendency toward self-interpretation on the basis of what is given immediately. But in order to see anything of the anthropological structure in which man stood within Greek research, we need to return to the phenomena of ἀληθεύειν, the uncovering and disclosure of the world. To be sure, this is only one direction in which we find access to these still wholly obscure contexts of the ontological structures of human existence, quite apart from the fact that we today still have very little clarity concerning the concrete history of the development of anthropological questioning. Dilthey was one who dedicated his entire long life to gaining insight into this matter, and, as he himself conceded in his discourse on the occasion of his seventieth birthday, he always remained underway.[1] We lack not only the factual concrete contexts of Greek anthropology but also the connection between Greek and Christian anthropology and, even more, the connection between Luther's anthropology and the preceding ones. In view of this state of research, we may not nurture the thought of being able to say anything definite about these phenomena, especially since the proper substantive preparation for an investigation into them is still in its infancy. For one can see these structures only if the ontology of Dasein itself is made the theme of its own proper research.

1. W. Dilthey, "Rede zum 70. Geburtstag," in *Die geistige Welt: Einleitung in die Philosophie des Lebens*. Wilhelm Diltheys Gesammelte Schriften, Band V, Erste Hälfte. Leipzig and Berlin, 1924, cf. p. 9.

It is in this context that the structures now becoming visible through the elucidation of ἄγνοια belong. To this ἄγνοια there corresponds, in terms of κάθαρσις, a definite mode of purification. What is that mode?

γ) The determination of the κάθαρσις of ἄγνοια.

αα) The κάθαρσις of ἄγνοια as διδασκαλική.

If ἄγνοια is an αἶσχος, a deformation, then its structure contains a δυσ-, a χεῖρον. So the question arises: is there a τέχνη that can cast out this δυσ- and set free the βέλτιον, the ἀληθεύειν, the νοεῖν? Insofar as this would be a τέχνη concerned with knowing and not-knowing, it will have the general character of διδασκαλική (cf. 229a9), "instruction." Instruction brings about the disappearance of ignorance by communicating knowledge. The question, however, is whether such διδασκαλική which communicates knowledge (and this is comparable to the sophist's selling of λόγοι) is capable of removing the deformation in the soul. And in this way a question arises concerning the διδασκαλική directed to ἄγνοια. The deliberations aim at elaborating, versus the διδασκαλική immediately given, a quite peculiar one, one whose single unique goal is the removal of this ἄγνοια.

ββ) Further determination of ἄγνοια. Ἄγνοια as ἀμαθία, as presumptive knowledge and infatuation, as the actual κακία in the ψυχή.

The ξένος says of ἄγνοια: Ἀγνοίας γοῦν μέγα τί μοι δοκῶ καὶ χαλεπὸν ἀφωρισμένον ὁρᾶν εἶδος, πᾶσι τοῖς ἄλλοις αὐτῆς ἀντίσταθμον μέρεσιν (229c1ff.). "I believe I see an ignorance, namely the one just characterized, which is μέγα, great, a great and difficult field delimited in itself, an ignorance which is ἀντίσταθμον, which has the same weight as all other kinds of ignorance together," which includes all ignorance in the sense of mere unfamiliarity. The ξένος now characterizes this ἄγνοια more precisely: it is τὸ μὴ κατειδότα τι δοκεῖν εἰδέναι (c5), that state and constitution of man which consists in "not yet having seen something or other, μὴ κατειδότα τι, yet appearing to oneself and in the eyes of others as if one had knowledge of it." "Not yet having seen the thing," μὴ κατειδότα τι (this κατά signifies precisely a looking upon something in the correct way) is not yet having seen the thing and yet appearing to oneself and to others (the word δοκεῖν requires this to be supplemented) as if one did know it. At 230b, the same state of affairs is once more formulated, so briefly that we cannot express it that way in our language at all, and specifically with regard to the phenomenon which will be discussed later, namely λόγος. οἴηταί τίς τι πέρι λέγειν λέγων μηδέν (b4f.): such a one "believes he is saying something about a thing," letting it be seen, ἀποφαίνεσθαι, "yet is not saying anything about it," and, on the contrary, is distorting it. This μὴ κατειδότα τι δοκεῖν εἰδέναι or οἴεσθαί τι πέρι λέγειν λέγων μηδέν is what δι' οὗ κινδυνεύει πάντα ὅσα διανοίᾳ σφαλλόμεθα γίγνεσθαι πᾶσιν (229c5f.): "this peculiar phenomenon of ἄγνοια is what makes all of us be deceived in our discernment, our διάνοια." This μὴ κατειδότα τι δοκεῖν εἰδέναι, the presumed familiarity with something, is the proper origin of deception and error. What is essential is not mere ignorance, mere unfamiliarity, but a positive presumption of knowledge.

This ἄγνοια is designated at 229c9 as ἀμαθία, unproficiency, inexperience. The positive phenomenon opposed to ἀμαθία is παιδεία, proper "upbringing." Παιδεία is usually translated as "education," and ἀμαθία as "lack of education." But the term "education" in our language does not at all capture the sense. For we understand an educated, or cultured, man to be precisely one who knows a great deal and indeed knows everything possible to know in all realms of science, art, and the like, and not only has a general acquaintance but knows the most valuable details, and judges with taste, and to all questions put to him from any of these realms always has a ready answer, and acquires each day what is newest and most valuable. Now such an education does not at all require what the Greeks understand by παιδεία. For that education does not make one capable of posing a proper substantive question. One will not thereby have the proper disposition to be a researcher, though this does not mean every researcher has to be uneducated. Yet our contemporary philosophy is to a large extent made up of such education. It does not have to be a historiographical education, but there is also an education in systematics. By the same token, there are also such educative sciences in other disciplines, e.g., in theology. And therefore it can happen that a theologian or a theological faculty, with simultaneous appeal to the general disposition, will endorse another theologian's paper by saying that special merit must be attributed to it for emphasizing that sin is the opposite of faith. It would be precisely the same if a mathematician were to say to his colleague, after hearing him lecture, that his paper was indeed methodologically insufficient, perhaps even completely beside the point, but we mathematicians all agree we owe the author thanks for having proclaimed with emphasis that a + b = b + a. Thereby wailing misery is transformed into ludicrousness. I do not know whether the state of our contemporary spiritual make-up has struck the soul of the present public or not. But παιδεία is not education in this sense; on the contrary, it is a πραγματεία, a task, and hence not a self-evident possession. It is not a task any person can take up according to whim but is one which precisely encounters in each person its own proper resistances. And this is the way it stands with the διδασκαλική that is to have the function of ἐκβάλλειν.

In order to grasp the genuine aim of the whole dialogue at the end, it is important to see here that ἄγνοια is a κακία. That means that purely in itself, as a determinate formation, or, rather, de-formation, of the soul, it denigrates the Being of man with regard to his ontological possibilities. Therefore this ἄγνοια does not require a relation to determinate objects, ones it precisely does not know. A definite realm of objects is not constitutive of ἄγνοια. Its very existence as such is already sufficient to characterize it as κακία. By reason of the peculiar sort of Being of this κακόν, a corresponding τέχνη proves necessary, one which is to have the sense of a κάθαρσις, a purification.

γγ) Further determination of διδασκαλική as κάθαρσις of ἄγνοια. Not a communication of knowledge but a liberation toward ἀληθεύειν: παιδεία. Λόγος as essential element of παιδεία. Its types: νουθετητική (admonition) and elenchtics. Rejection of νουθετητική.

This ἄγνοια is not such that it can be eliminated through the infusion of definite bits of knowledge. Therefore the διδασκαλική cannot have the character of δημιουργική (cf. 229d1f.); i.e., it cannot be something that provides or produces a definite stock of objective knowledge and that imparts definite objective cognitions. And so the question arises concerning a τέχνη which alone would bring about the elimination of the ἄγνοια. In positive terms, it would allow the ἀληθεύειν itself to become free. This τέχνη is hence a μέρος διδασκαλικῆς ἀπαλλάττον τοῦτο (cf. 229c11f.), "a mode of διδασκαλική which removes τοῦτο," namely the ἄγνοια or the ἀμαθία. And this διδασκαλική is precisely παιδεία (cf. d2). Specifically, it is a matter of a διδασκαλικὴ ἐν τοῖς λόγοις (cf. e1), a διδασκαλική carried out in the mode of speaking with one another and to one another. You see here again how the phenomenon of κάθαρσις is incorporated into that which has already been of constant interest in the determination of the sophist: λόγος. The κάθαρσις is something carried out in λέγειν and is related to λόγοι.

This is the occasion to distinguish two modes of διδασκαλική: first, the νουθετητική (cf. 230a3), which works with mere admonitions, mere remonstrance. It is not a matter of imparting knowledge but has merely the sense of bringing the other to a definite decision and comportment. Such a διδασκαλική, however, obviously cannot accomplish the desired purification of the soul with regard to ἄγνοια. So Plato says: εἴξασί τινες . . . ἡγήσασθαι (230a5f.), "some seem to be of the opinion," and specifically not on the basis of arbitrary whim but λόγον ἑαυτοῖς δόντες (a5), after they have presentified the matter itself under discussion. They seem to be of the opinion:

1.) πᾶσαν ἀκούσιον ἀμαθίαν εἶναι (a6). This is a repetition of the proposition we have seen above: "All unproficiency comes to be without a positive decision in favor of it."

2.) μαθεῖν οὐδέν ποτ' ἂν ἐθέλειν τὸν οἰόμενον εἶναι σοφὸν τούτων ὧν οἴοιτο πέρι δεινὸς εἶναι (a6ff.): "No one will learn anything about a subject he considers himself an expert in and thinks he is already thoroughly familiar with."

3.) μετὰ δὲ πολλοῦ πόνου τὸ νουθετητικὸν εἶδος τῆς παιδείας σμικρὸν ἀνύτειν (a8f.): against such ignorance as this ἄγνοια in the strict sense, the mode of education in question, the νουθετητική, admonition and remonstrance, would be able μετὰ δὲ πολλοῦ πόνου σμικρὸν ἀνύτειν, "even with great pains and at great cost, to accomplish but the slightest thing."

The νουθετητική must fail, because the comportment which needs to undergo the purification, by its very sense, shuts itself off from such instruction by considering itself dispensed with the necessity of purification in the first place. Indeed it is part of the very sense of ἄγνοια to believe that it already knows. It is precisely this pretence to knowledge that the διδασκαλική must attack. This pretence must, as it were, be emptied, undermined, and thereby brought to the point that it collapses upon itself.

δδ) The κάθαρσις of the ἄγνοια by ἔλεγχος. The procedure of ἔλεγχος. Setting the δόξαι against each other through the συνάγειν εἰς ἕν. Rejection of the purported discovery of the principle of contradiction. Its discovery in Aristotle. The ἐκβολή of δόξα as μεγίστη τῶν καθάρσεων. The liberation of Dasein toward ἀληθεύειν.

Plato now says that those who know how things stand with this ἄγνοια—that it is precisely grounded in the fact that πᾶσαν ἀκούσιον ἀμαθίαν εἶναι, "all unproficiency comes to be without a resolution toward it"—already possess the path to the ἐκβολή (cf. 230b1). Διερωτῶσιν, they "question" anyone who οἰόμενος λέγειν τι λέγων μηδέν (cf. b4f.); "they question him thoroughly." Διερωτᾶν means to question so as to shake someone thoroughly, as it were, i.e., to overwhelm him with questions so that he is altogether shaken in his εἰδέναι and is thereby disabused of his purported familiarity with things. Here we see the concrete connection with the modes of everyday activity mentioned at the beginning, e.g., the winnowing of grain. The thorough questioning has determinate stages. What is essential is that the ones who carry it out, take τὰς δόξας, "the opinions" of the person concerned, the one who is undergoing the questioning, and συνάγοντες τοῖς λόγοις εἰς ταὐτὸν τιθέασι (cf. b6), "in discussion they bring together, συνάγειν, the person's opinions about some matter and relate them to one and the same thing." That is to say, they accomplish something we have already become familiar with, the συνορᾶν: they "see together" the very different things someone has said about one single matter. Τιθέντες (b7), when that happens, "they let be seen," ἐπιδεικνύουσιν (b7), what? Αὐτὰς αὐταῖς . . . ἐναντίας (b7f.), that the opinions "as it were, slap each other in the face," that one opinion, which has always claimed to show the matter about which it speaks, covers over what the other opinion shows, and vice versa. They let be seen this peculiar ἐναντίον among the δόξαι and specifically αὐτὰς αὐταῖς ἅμα . . . ἐναντίας (b7f.). The sense of this ἅμα cannot be grasped here in a wholly univocal way. We are tempted to take it without further ado as a temporal determination: "at once"—insofar as the δόξαι are understood as grasping one and the same matter in the very same sense of making present. That means the object of the opinions and the opinions themselves dwell in the character of the now: now the matter is so and so, or now the one opinion says this and the other says the opposite. But we must indeed leave the meaning of the ἅμα open here, and the same applies in general to the entire explication of what is really at issue, as I will show later. First of all it is a question of simply making visible the structures that are supposed to be uncovered in the διερωτᾶν, ἅμα περὶ τῶν αὐτῶν πρὸς τὰ αὐτὰ κατὰ ταὐτὰ ἐναντίας (b7f.). Ἅμα: the δόξαι speak "at the same time," "at once," against each other; περὶ τῶν αὐτῶν: as opinions "about the same matters"; πρὸς τὰ αὐτά, considering the same matters "in relation to the same other ones"; κατὰ ταὐτά, taking this relation itself for its part "in the same regard." This is a very rich formulation of what ταὐτόν properly means, in regard to which those who question thoroughly in this way see the δόξαι together and bring them together. All these terms, ἅμα περὶ τῶν αὐτῶν πρὸς τὰ αὐτὰ κατὰ ταὐτά, are meant to extract clearly the ἕν which must already be seen at the very outset and in relation to which the questions are oriented. What is essential to this διερωτᾶν is to lead the οἰόμενος λέγειν τι λέγων μηδέν in such a way that he sees the inconsistency with himself, the inconsistency within his own comportment. That means it has to be shown to him that he presents the matter at issue sometimes in one way and then again in another way: i.e., he does not have any relation at all to the matters themselves. Here it is always a question of the ἐναντίον of δόξαι, opinions. We must still take the term δόξα in an indeterminate sense, although, if the usual chronology is correct, Plato had already given in the *Theaetetus* a more precise characterization of δόξα, one which, to be sure, did not yet grasp the genuine phenomenon. What we have here then is a playing off of the δόξαι against each other, in order to make the one who has them confused about himself. But this is in no sense a discovery of the principle of contradiction. That is out of the question.

The principle of contradiction can be discovered only if the principle is grasped as a principle. Plato never presses on to that, as we will see in the second part of the *Sophist*. It is thus fundamentally impossible to say that Plato has discovered the *principle* of contradiction. But he has certainly exposed very definite structural connections in the act of contradicting, which Aristotle undoubtedly elaborated in his discussion of contradiction in *Metaphysics* IV, chapter 3ff. We can at most say that in a certain sense the principle of contradiction is *potentially* there in Plato. I cannot now enter into the substantive questions connected to this principle of contradiction. I merely emphasize that the principle of contradiction even still today, and actually throughout history, is a matter of controversy, with regard to its formulation as well as with regard to its origination, i.e., whether it is deducible from the principle of identity and is founded therein, or whether it is an independent principle. Likewise, its character as law and norm is controversial: i.e., whether it is a rule for the formulation of propositions, a law of propositions, or whether it is a law of Being, expressing an ontological state of affairs. People have even taken both these together. It is impossible to decide anything correctly here as long as the proposition itself, this definite mode of λόγος, remains unclarified.

What is now important to us is simply the central point of this part of the dialogue: that such thorough questioning, and consequently the shaking and ultimate casting out of the ungenuine δόξαι, are possible only on the basis of a previous συνάγειν εἰς ἕν. This ἀπαλλαγή (cf. 230c2), this "clearing away" of δόξαι, is at the same time an ἐξελεῖν (cf. ibid.), a removal of what stands in the way of the μαθήματα (cf. ibid.), the proper positive learning. Once this ἐκβολή, this κάθαρσις, succeeds, then the one who is purified is one who ἡγούμενος ἅπερ οἶδεν εἰδέναι μόνα, πλείω δὲ μή (cf. d3), "is of the opinion he knows only and exclusively what he has seen," what he has appropriated insightfully, "but no more than that." This κάθαρσις is called the μεγίστη *and* κυριωτάτη (d7), "the highest and properly decisive," precisely because it first opens up Dasein for a possible encounter with the world and with itself. On this basis, the ξένος could already say earlier that this διδασκαλική or this κάθαρσις is ἀντίσταθμος in relation to the whole multiplicity of other possible modes of communicating, of communicating knowledge. Thereby it is clear that Plato is not at all speaking about the material content of knowledge; here it is a matter simply of the Being of Dasein itself: to what extent does it dwell in ἀληθεύειν or in ἄγνοια. This is in accord with ἄγνοια itself, which is merely an ontological character, free from all material content, from the known as such. Consequently, even the foregoing consideration of the sophist has carried out its teaching completely formally. We have actually learned nothing at all about the content of the sophists' philosophies and doctrines, because at the very outset the orientation was to expose their knowledge, i.e., their ignorance, their ἀμαθία, in its proper ontological structure, which naturally is formal in opposition to all concrete, material knowledge.

And so now we ask: the ones "who employ this τέχνη," χρώμενοι ταύτῃ τῇ τέχνῃ (cf. 230e5), are they the sophists we are seeking?

d) The result of the sixth diairesis: philosophy as "legitimate sophistry." The similarity between philosophy and sophistry. The aporia in relation to the sophist.

We can say that what has now been found προσέοικέ γε τοιούτῳ τινί (231a4), "is in a certain sense similar to such a one," i.e., it comes close to the sophist. But at the same time the ξένος has misgivings: δεῖ πάντων μάλιστα περὶ τὰς ὁμοιότητας ἀεὶ ποιεῖσθαι τὴν φυλακήν (a7f.), "when it comes to similarities, we have to be on our guard." Recall what the *Phaedrus* said about the ὁμοιοῦν and ὁμοιοῦσθαι. This sort of presentation and interpretation of the διδασκαλικὴ τέχνη naturally aims at bringing the sophist and the philosopher very close together. But initially this accomplishes nothing else than what the natural public conception already has at its disposal: the sophists, the philosophers, and the πολιτικοί are all muddled together, the one is taken for the other, and no one is capable of distinguishing them. Now this appearance is made still more explicit and sharper, such that when the sophist and the philosopher are brought so close to each other, whatever might be there to distinguish them will distinguish them in a *fundamental* way. But in order to hold this back and perhaps even in order to characterize philosophy intentionally in a non-positive fashion as regards content, Plato calls what has been discovered σοφιστική, though to be sure a quite peculiar σοφιστική—γένει γενναία (231b8), the "legitimate" one, the one that comes forth out of the genuine stem of its proper Being, the one that actually is what the factual sophist simply pretends to be. Versus this designation of φιλοσοφία as σοφιστικὴ γένει γενναία, Aristotle calls σοφιστική φαινομένη φιλοσοφία.

So we now have apparently less clarity than ever as regards the question of what the sophist properly is. We are in a certain sense thrown back to the beginning; it is just that now our ignorance or confusion has become explicit and, as it were, clarified. Therefore Theaetetus says: ἀπορῶ δὲ ἔγωγε ἤδη διὰ τὸ πολλὰ πεφάνθαι, τί χρή ποτε ὡς ἀληθῆ λέγοντα καὶ διισχυριζόμενον εἰπεῖν ὄντως εἶναι τὸν σοφιστήν (231b9ff.). διὰ τὸ πολλὰ πεφάνθαι, "because so many things have now been shown" in relation to the sophist, "I can no longer find a way out," ἀπορῶ, I do not know, τί ὄντως εἶναι, "what then the sophist actually is" and how he is to be determined in reality. I do not know what I am supposed to say, if I ὡς ἀληθῆ λέγω (cf. c1), "if I am to speak in such a way that I present the matter at issue," and specifically διισχυριζόμενον (c1), "on firm ground."

§57. Summary of the previous six definitions. The unitary basic structure: the sophist as ἀντιλογικός *(231d–232e).*

Before the new approach to a positive determination of the sophist, there occurs, as I have already emphasized, one more summary of the previous discussions: ὁπόσα . . . πέφανται (231d1f.), "everything which has shown itself up to now." It is telling that this summary is a mere recounting of what was gained in successive steps; it is not a summary in the sense of a συναγωγή. It cannot be a συναγωγή, since precisely what is still lacking is the ἕν with regard to which the συναγωγή would be carried out. But, at the same time, the summary is also oriented positively, precisely with a view toward preparing for the task of making the ἕν visible. Thus we have here again the distinction between a mere gathering together of what was dispersed, διεσπαρμένα, and a proper συναγωγή. The συναγωγή should take the ἕν as guideline, and this ἕν should be gained from the matter at issue, whose phenomena are here taken together.

The basic character of the matter at issue, for which we are seeking the ἕν, is τέχνη. Under this peculiar aspect of τέχνη, the sophist was indeed seen from the very outset. And now it has been shown that the sophist is an ἐπιστήμων τις πολλῶν (232a1). We have before us a τέχνη related to a manifold, related to what was exposed in the various definitions. μιᾶς δὲ τέχνης ὀνόματι προσαγορεύηται (a2). And for this τέχνη, in these manifold aspects, we have *one* ὄνομα, *one* designation. With such a state of affairs, however, i.e., a phenomenon showing itself in so manifold a way and yet always being designated with the same name, "something must not be right," τὸ φάντασμα τοῦτο ὡς οὐκ ἔσθ' ὑγιές (232a2f.). He who finds himself in such a situation, being given a phenomenon in a manifold of aspects without an orientation toward the ἕν, with the result that he cannot attribute the uniqueness of the name to a unitary matter in a founded way, such a one οὐ δύναται κατιδεῖν ἐκεῖνο αὐτῆς <έχνης> (a4), "cannot in that case properly see that in the τέχνη" εἰς ὃ πάντα τὰ μαθήματα ταῦτα βλέπει (a4f.), "to which all these capacities refer," this ἕν toward which they are oriented. Thereby the path is predelineated for us to acquire the ἕν for the manifold aspects of τέχνη: not from τέχνη itself insofar as it is a multiform comportment to something, but from that toward which it comports itself. And so the question must now be raised: in regard to what, properly speaking, is this τέχνη a know-how in the genuine sense, notwithstanding its multiform capacities? Hence we are seeking the object of this know-how as a ἕν. The ξένος says: ἓν γάρ τί μοι μάλιστα κατεφάνη αὐτὸν μηνῦον (232b3f.). "One thing appeared to me most able to make him visible, αὐτὸν μηνῦον." Μηνύειν means "to indicate something concealed." This, this structure, which is appropriate for making visible the proper ἕν, the ἕν toward which the entire sophistical τέχνη is oriented, is called ἀντιλογική; i.e., the sophist is understood as ἀντιλογικός (cf. b6). This is the mode of comportment elaborated in the fifth definition, at 225b. This ἀντιλέγειν is not only an ἀντιλέγειν, a speaking against and a contradicting as a comportment toward others, but also what the sophist provides and what he sells is itself nothing other than the ἀντιλογική, καὶ τῶν ἄλλων αὐτοῦ τούτου διδάσκαλον γίγνεσθαι (232b8f.), and the sophist is at the same time the teacher of the very same thing that constitutes his proper comportment.

Thereby the six definitions are joined together in unity. The ἀντιλέγειν comprises:

1.) the way of dealing with other people in the sense of hunting them. The sophist seizes others when he can, and by his way of speaking he makes them objects of his hunt. While he speaks with them as ἀντιλογικός, he presents his τέχνη. That is the first definition.

2.) What he claims to provide them, what he sells (definitions 2–4) is again this ἀντιλέγειν. And finally

3.) the mode of carrying out the ἔλεγχος, by exposing publicly, by shaking (also in the negative sophistical sense), as characterized in the sixth definition, is again a διερωτᾶν in the sense of ἀντιλέγεσθαι.

Thus we see that the ἀντιλογικός gathers together in a basic structure the phenomenal content acquired up to now with regard to the sophist. Yet the ἕν itself, insofar as we understand it as the εἰς ὅ, that toward which this τέχνη ἀντιλογική is directed, still remains undetermined. The comportments are centered in the ἀντιλέγειν or, put briefly, in λέγειν, in λόγος. The question to be asked is: what then does this ἀντιλέγειν deal with?

§58. The seventh definition of the sophist. Semblant artist (232b–236c).

a) The "object" of sophistical λόγος: τὰ πάντα.

α) Enumeration of the individual "objects" of sophistical λόγος. The orientation of Greek-Platonic philosophy.

The consideration continues, properly speaking, at 232b: σκοπῶμεν δή, περὶ τίνος ἄρα καί φασιν οἱ τοιοῦτοι ποιεῖν ἀντιλογικούς (b11f.). What is the actual field of ἀντιλέγειν? That must now be subjected to a σκέψις, a searching inquiry; we must determine what this τέχνη ἀντιλογική encompasses.

This σκέψις must be carried out ἐξ ἀρχῆς (b12), from the very beginning, since, ultimately, everything belongs in this field. The consideration extends from 232c to 232e.

The speeches of the sophists deal with:

1.) τὰ θεῖα, ὅσ' ἀφανῆ τοῖς πολλοῖς (cf. c1), "the divine, that which for most people, for the multitude, is not visible," and here the sophists are simply trying to make an impression. It is essential to see that τὰ θεῖα, the divinities, are beings, indeed are most properly beings, in the sense of the most excellent of everything that is.

2.) ὅσα φανερὰ γῆς τε καὶ οὐρανοῦ καὶ τῶν περὶ τὰ τοιαῦτα (c4f.), "everything lying there open to view on earth and in heaven": hence, in addition to the most excellent beings, those that are given first and what everyone can see, σώματα.

3.) The sophists speak about γένεσις and οὐσία κατὰ πάντων (cf. c8), about Being and about coming into being with regard to all the beings just mentioned. That is, the sophists speak not only about the most excellent beings, and the first given beings, but also about the Being of these beings.

4.) They deal with the νόμοι and σύμπαντα τὰ πολιτικά (cf. d1), everything whatsoever connected to the πόλις and to the Being of the πόλις: above all, whatsoever touches the ζῷον πολιτικόν, i.e., the Being of man. Hence the sophists treat human life itself as a being.

5.) The sophists deal with τέχναι and, specifically, περὶ πασῶν τε καὶ κατὰ μίαν ἑκάστην τέχνην (d5f.), with all possible modes of know-how in regard to something or other, both as a whole and in every single particular, and this includes all knowledge, all sciences, and every discipline.

This completes the circuit of that in which the ἀντιλογική moves. It deals with all beings, Being, and all know-how, i.e., the comprehension of all beings and of Being. Φαίνεται γοῦν δὴ σχεδὸν οὐδὲν ὑπολιπεῖν (232e5), "outside of this, there is obviously nothing more," such that the sophists in fact ἐν κεφαλαίῳ περὶ πάντων (e3), speak "in summary, about everything" and claim to impart the correct δύναμις of ἀντιλέγειν about everything. This summary is naturally also important for the positive characterization of the horizon surrounding Plato, surrounding his philosophy: beings as god and world, beings in the sense of man, whatever relates to the Being of these beings, and, at the same time, the modes of know-how in regard to all these modes of beings and of Being. We now have to ask how this determination which relates the ἀντιλογικὴ τέχνη to τὰ πάντα provides an essential, and indeed *the* essential, characteristic of this τέχνη itself. That is, we need to see how its peculiar object characterizes this τέχνη itself in its Being.

The sophist has shown himself in a manifold of aspects and specifically in such a way that this manifold was given in everyday perception. If one clings to the surface of the text, then this manifoldness is based in τέχνη and its possible articulation. And indeed this path would certainly lead to a manifold and would also make it possible to articulate schematically the connection of the various determinations. For us, however, the task is to go back behind this external structure to that in which the manifoldness is founded. This plurality of the aspects does not reside in the arbitrariness of the everyday way of perceiving and considering; on the contrary, it is grounded in the structure of the very beings at issue here. The manifoldness derives not from the imprecision and preliminary character of the everyday mode of consideration but from the very structure of what is standing under consideration.

β) Explication of the τέχνη σοφιστική as a mode of commerce with things. The structural moments of this commerce (the objects—the mode—the end, εἰς ὅ). The primacy of the εἰς ὅ in Plato.

Τέχνη, which we have indeed determined as know-how, is, precisely as know-how, a structural moment of our commerce with things in the broadest sense. Human Dasein enters into commerce with things, has something to do with things. This commerce includes: 1.) the objects, 2.) a definite mode of commerce, of concern, and 3.) the precise end of the commerce or concern. Limiting ourselves initially to these three structural moments, it is clear that they are included in every commerce as commerce and hence in every τέχνη as τέχνη. Thus every τέχνη can be seen from these three sides. In terms of the sophist, the objects of his commerce, that with which he properly has to do, are men, beings of his own kind, beings that occur in the world and are in it with him. Such beings, which share our own Being, comprise the "shared world" *[Mitwelt]*. On the other hand, the beings we have commerce with, but which do not share our own mode of Being, comprise the "surrounding world" *[Umwelt]*: trees, stones, land, sea. The beings with which the sophist has to do are the former, other men. Now the Being of man is determined as ζῷον λόγον ἔχον, and thus the beings with which the sophist has to do are λόγον ἔχοντες. As to the mode of commerce, the manner of the concern, it is ἀντιλέγεσθαι, i.e., λέγειν. And the end, that which the commerce aims at, is παιδεία, i.e., a determinate δύναμις of ἀντιλέγεσθαι. And in this way the ontological structure of the sophist, which at first was characterized quite formally as τέχνη, now becomes concrete. The objects of the commerce are beings characterized by λέγειν; the mode of the commerce is λέγειν; and what the commerce aims at is again λέγειν. Thus precisely here, in the τέχνη σοφιστική, we see at the same time the multiformity of the structure of λόγος.

These various structures—the objects of the commerce, its mode, its aim—which pertain to the very Being of the beings under consideration can for their part be considered either provisionally or properly. These basic structures themselves offer sundry aspects. Thus it is clear that as long as the beings at issue here, ones designated by the title τέχνη—as long as these beings themselves (and that means nothing else than the Being of man)—are not exposed according to all their basic structures, there will persist an incertitude in the interpretation of these structures, which are always visible in some way or another. And thus it happened, as the history of philosophy shows, that some structures of Dasein were indeed always seen, but that one or the other structure always had priority and the rest were interpreted on the basis of the former.[1]

This deficiency, which naturally is present even in Plato, shows itself in the fact that the question of the ἕν, within the multiform moments taken up in the sophist, initially follows a quite determinate direction. On what do all these structures center, the ones we have seen thus far in the sophist? That is the question Plato asks, and he determines this direction toward the ἕν, this possible unification (insofar as it must precisely be a concrete one) from the concrete matter at issue itself, from the τέχνη. He determines it specifically in terms of that to which the commerce as commerce is related, in the sense of the end or aim of the commerce. To speak quite roughly, the unity derives from what the sophist is properly trying to accomplish, the aim of his comportment. That is the sense of the εἰς ὅ of τέχνη. If a consideration of τέχνη takes this direction, toward the aim, then it faces the task of provisionally characterizing its domain, i.e., the objects encompassed by this aim. And this characterization of content leads necessarily to a determination of the mode of comportment related to the objects. That is to say, the characterization of the εἰς ὅ (ἀντιλέγεσθαι and ἀντιλέγειν) provides at the same time the possibility of determining the Being of this λέγειν itself.

The εἰς ὅ encompasses, in terms of the objects in its domain, as Plato's enumeration shows, everything that can at all be a possible object of discussion. In his enumeration, Plato proceeds from the most excellent beings to the most common, and he then determines the possibility of a consideration of these beings with regard to their Being. Then he turns to the beings connected to Dasein itself, and he finally moves to the comportment which can make accessible all these beings and the Being of these beings, namely τέχνη. This sketch of the range of ἀντιλέγεσθαι shows that, in the case of the sophist, it encompasses everything. The domain of the ἀντιλέγεσθαι of the sophist includes all beings, in regard to their Being, and also includes the mode of know-how relative to them.

1. See the appendix.

γ) First intimation of the ontological problematic of the τέχνη σοφιστική: the Being of non-beings.

The peculiar thing is that this ἀντιλέγεσθαι, i.e., the τέχνη of the sophist, is impossible in terms of that to which it relates. Thus the τέχνη of the sophist shows itself as an impossibility, i.e., something which cannot be. For πάντα ἐπίστασθαι (233a3) could pertain only to the gods. This is indeed a negative determination, but we have already seen in the earlier consideration, in the sixth definition, that there parenthetically, though of course intentionally, the comportment of disclosing beings, ἀληθεύειν, was characterized as κίνησις, ὁρμή.[2] In other words: the Being of man, insofar as it is oriented toward knowledge, is as such *underway*. Its uncovering of beings, ἐπίστασθαι, is never finished. Hence the claim πάντα ἐπίστασθαι is in itself an ontological impossibility. Thus, on the basis of the εἰς ὅ, the τέχνη of the sophist reveals itself as impossible in its Being. At the same time, however, the foregoing interpretation has demonstrated that this τέχνη is in fact given along with the existence of the sophist, so that in the case of the sophist, in the case of the sophistical τέχνη, we are presented with a being which is factually there and yet is, according to its Being, impossible. Hence, anticipating what is to come, we have here the Being of a non-being.

At this point, to be sure, Plato does not immediately proceed to the question we have indicated. But what follows shows precisely how much he is concerned with demonstrating the factual existence of such a τέχνη and consequently precisely with demonstrating the existence of a non-being. Initially, therefore, he does not interrogate the ultimate possibility and the ultimate grounds which found something like the Being of non-beings. Instead he asks: how can such a peculiar τέχνη be made understandable on the basis of what we hitherto came to know in general about the various possibilities of τέχνη? Thus Plato does not now proceed as far as he will later, but already here, as regards this peculiar phenomenon, the Being of non-beings, he allows the previous theory of Being to run on and, as it were, dash itself to bits. And, once again, the first move is into the concrete.

b) Concrete demonstration of the factual Being of the τέχνη σοφιστική from the example of τέχνη μιμητική.

α) The factual Being of the τέχνη σοφιστική as ἐπιστήμη δοξαστική.

The question is: how can such a τέχνη, the τέχνη σοφιστική (which is precisely a non-being) be made understandable? Can there be something

2. Cf. p. 254ff.; *Sophist* 228c1–d2, 228c10–d1: ἐπ' ἀλήθειαν ὁρμωμένης ψυχῆς.

like that at all? Can it be made intelligible by means of the natural self-interpretation of τέχνη? For if there is such a τέχνη, then, within its connection to other people, it must have a certain intelligibility, and all the more so because its very sense relates it to others. And so once again explicit reference is made to the fact that the sophists actually have a following, that they are paid for their ἀντιλέγειν, and that this shows they actually πάντα ἄρα σοφοὶ τοῖς μαθηταῖς φαίνονται (233c6). "In the eyes of their disciples they do look like that and are in fact accepted as πάντα σοφοί, as possessing know-how in regard to everything," οὐκ ὄντες γε (c8), "although this is not so." Hence this ἐπιστήμη is δοξαστική (cf. c10), "one which in itself has the possibility of posing as something it is not."

Thus arises the task of inquiring into this peculiar phenomenon—something posing as what it is not—and of attempting to track down once and for all the place within this τέχνη where the phenomenon of semblance and mere appearance resides. Plato does not clarify this character of semblance and mere appearance, δοξαστικόν, directly in terms of the τέχνη σοφιστική and the ἀντιλέγειν. Instead, he says: λάβωμεν τοίνυν σαφέστερόν τι παράδειγμα περὶ τούτων (233d3f.). "Let us therefore take an example" and by its means clarify where something like the δοξαστικόν can reside within a τέχνη and what that means. It is no accident that Plato here resorts to a παράδειγμα, does not make the ἀντιλογική the direct theme of the analysis, and hence shows the character of semblance in terms of this παράδειγμα and not in λέγειν itself. Indeed later, on the basis of an elucidated concept of non-being, he comes to speak once more of λόγος and of the phenomenon of ψεῦδος, which here lies at the foundation. But nowhere, even in other dialogues, does Plato successfully disclose, within the structure of λόγος itself, the peculiar constitution of ψεῦδος and its possibility in λέγειν. This derives from the fact that he did not yet see λόγος in its main structures, and consequently his concepts of φαντασία and of δόξα remain uncertain. And yet we have here already a remarkable indication for the interpretation of the τέχνη ἀντιλογική. Earlier, λέγειν was indeed determined as χειροῦσθαι, as an appropriation of beings in their ἀληθές. If we understand λέγειν in this way, as appropriation, as taking possession of beings as uncovered, and if we clarify the claim residing in the ἀντιλογική, then the result is that the ἀντιλογική is impossible in its pretense to be able to possess all beings in their uncoveredness.

β) Τέχνη μιμητική as ποιεῖν δοκεῖν. Τέχνη σοφιστική as ποιεῖν δοκεῖν λέγεσθαι.

To what extent can the δοξαστικόν and consequently this ontological impossibility of the τέχνη ἀντιλογική be understood in themselves? Plato's method here is peculiar: he shows that the existence of this impossibility, i.e., of the τέχνη σοφιστική, is possible on the basis of the existence of a still higher impossibility. He steers the consideration toward a context which to us is not entirely strange. Εἴ τις φαίη μὴ λέγειν μηδ' ἀντιλέγειν, ἀλλὰ ποιεῖν καὶ δρᾶν μιᾷ τέχνῃ συνάπαντα ἐπίστασθαι πράγματα (233d9f.): "If someone were to say ἐπίστασθαι, he knows, not only how to discuss and argue with others in regard to everything there is, but that he even knows how to make everything in *one* τέχνη," i.e., if he goes beyond what we have previously seen as an impossibility, namely λέγειν, speaking about everything that already exists, and then even claims to be able to bring into existence something—indeed everything—that does not yet exist, what could we say against him? At first, Theaetetus does not understand precisely what is meant here; i.e., Plato wants to make still more clear that in fact we would be introducing the idea of a ποίησις through which everything—i.e., everything previously enumerated as possibly in the realm of ἀντιλέγειν—would be produced, ἄγειν εἰς οὐσίαν (cf. 219b4f.). Regarding such a possibility, i.e., the possibility of bringing everything whatever into being, not only discussing what already exists, Theaetetus says: that could only be said in jest, παιδιὰν λέγεις τινά (234a6). Such a comportment could only be a jest; as for making and producing, it could only look as if it actually made that to which it relates. If it is possible only as a jest, then this ποιεῖν is not a genuine ποιεῖν. But then what kind of ποιεῖν is it? Where shall we find the ungenuineness of this ποιεῖν, a ποιεῖν which is indeed conceded within certain limits? This ποιεῖν is not a ἄγειν εἰς οὐσίαν but a ποιεῖν πάντα δοκεῖν, "a making everything appear as such and such"; hence it is not a ποιεῖν in the sense of producing but—in a certain sense akin to that—a making which lets be seen. For you must recall here what we emphasized earlier: that there is a peculiar connection between the existence of a ready-made being, in the sense of something present, something visible as such, and ποιεῖν as ποιεῖν δοκεῖν in the sense of letting be seen. According to the Greek conception, even one who most genuinely produces something lets that something be seen; i.e., an εἶδος is thereby given concreteness. Even in genuine ποιεῖν, as ἄγειν εἰς οὐσίαν, the sense oscillates between bringing into presence and letting be seen in such a way, in such a way, to be sure, that the thing is present in itself. But in the case of this ποιεῖν, the ποιεῖν does not extend to the thing but to the δοκεῖν: it appears in such a way. What is thus produced is not the thing itself but its μίμημα, its "imitation." Yet this imitation is now designated with the same word as is the existing thing: μιμήματα καὶ ὁμώνυμα τῶν ὄντων (234b6f.); the painted tree is addressed as a tree the same way the real tree is. And insofar as the consideration of the world, as well as the judgment about the world in natural speech, dwell in words, in speaking, there also exists the possibility of taking one's orientation from what is said in everyday average speaking, with the result that it cannot be decided without further ado from the ὄνομα itself whether it is a matter of a μίμημα or an ὄν in the proper sense. This applies to those who explicitly intend ποιεῖν πάντα δοκεῖν, to let be seen πόρρωθεν (b8), "from afar," what they show: thereby they do not allow us any possibility of investigating the thing itself. This sort of letting be seen from afar, πόρρωθεν, and not ἐγγύθεν, as it is called later (d4), makes them capable λανθάνειν (b9), of "remaining concealed" in what they are actually doing. δυνατὸς ἔσται τοὺς ἀνοήτους τῶν νέων παίδων, πόρρωθεν τὰ γεγραμμένα ἐπιδεικνύς, λανθάνειν ὡς ὅτιπερ ἂν βουληθῇ δρᾶν, τοῦτο ἱκανώτατος ὢν ἀποτελεῖν ἔργῳ (b8ff.). It is hence a matter here of someone who paints pictures and shows them to inexperienced young people from afar, such that they then believe that these are the things themselves and that he is capable of actually making them.

This procedure is that of a τέχνη which lets something be seen from afar and allows someone to pose as actually capable of making things. And Plato now says there is such a τέχνη, in the end, περὶ τοὺς λόγους (c2), in the field of λέγειν. Thus even here there would be a πάντα λέγειν, one which would not be a genuine λέγειν but a ποιεῖν πάντα δοκεῖν, a speaking about things which "shows and lets be seen," δεικνύναι εἴδωλα (c5f.), "things which only look" like the things spoken about, and indeed it would speak that way about everything. Hence it is not the εἶδος and the οὐσία which are shown but the εἴδωλον, not the thing itself as it is in itself but merely as it looks in its immediate aspect. This ποιεῖν λέγεσθαι is characterized pointedly at the end of 234c as ποιεῖν ἀληθῆ δοκεῖν λέγεσθαι (c6f.), "making it appear that the truth was spoken." The peculiar phenomenon in the τέχνη μιμητική is the ποιεῖν δοκεῖν and, in reference to λόγος, the ποιεῖν δοκεῖν λέγεσθαι.

γ) The classification of the sophistical λόγος within ποίησις. Τέχνη σοφιστική as εἰδωλοποιική. The sophist as μιμητής. Τέχνη σοφιστική as τέχνη μιμητική. The one identical basic meaning of ποιεῖν, μιμεῖσθαι, λέγειν: to let be seen. The sense of Being for the Greeks: presence.

This places us in a wholly new context: a completely different mode of execution is serving to interpret the τέχνη of the ἀντιλογικός as a τέχνη of λέγειν. Earlier, λέγειν in the proper sense was acquisition, κτῆσις, χειροῦσθαι; here, however, the τέχνη ἀντιλογική is a ποιεῖν. Thus structurally it is an entirely different comportment than λέγειν proper in the sense of acquisition, receiving the things in their self-presentation. But this ποιεῖν, although opposed to the χειροῦσθαι of something already extant, is not an ἄγειν εἰς οὐσίαν;[3] instead, it is related to δοκεῖν. That is to say,

3. *Sophist* 219b4f.; cf. p. 186ff.

what are produced in the τέχνη of the sophist are not the things themselves but only a determinate mode of presentation of the things.[4] The determinate mode of presentation is, however, a presentation in mere appearance, in εἴδωλον. Here, thus, λέγειν is, as we said, not χειροῦσθαι, not κτῆσις, but ποιεῖν, and as such it is a ποιεῖν of mere appearances, ποιεῖν τὰ εἴδωλα. Therefore the τέχνη σοφιστική is εἰδωλοποιική (cf. 2235b8f.); and accordingly the sophist is called μιμητής: μιμητὴν θετέον αὐτόν τινα (cf. 235a8), "he is in a certain way an imitator of what is."

In this roundabout fashion, Plato grasps the εἰς ὅ, that to which this τέχνη is directed, more precisely: the εἰς ὅ are the εἴδωλα. And the sophist's comportment to that with which he ultimately is occupied is a ποιεῖν and not what it properly should be, insofar as it is a λέγειν, namely a χειροῦσθαι, a receiving of the things themselves. Yet, in a certain sense, the sophist has at his disposal the modes in which the beings under discussion can be encountered. The ἀντιλέγειν in the sense of the δυνατὸς λέγειν περὶ πάντα is thus actually there in the mode of τέχνη μιμητική. But this means therefore that the ποιεῖν is not a genuine one but is only in jest. And so the sophist's craft is possible only by aiming at people who πόρρω τῶν πραγμάτων τῆς ἀληθείας ἀφεστῶτας (234c4f.), "who are very far removed from the uncoveredness of things," who thus are not capable of testing, on the basis of the things themselves, what the sophist palms off on them in his speeches. The ξένος, to be sure, points this out: in the course of time and by means of the παθήματα (cf. d5), "what they experience," even those who have been taught in the school of the sophists will be brought ἐγγύθεν (d4), "closer," to the things themselves. They will be forced ἐναργῶς ἐφάπτεσθαι τῶν ὄντων (d5f.), "to grasp things clearly and unambiguously," so that a distinction will be obvious to them between τὰ φαντάσματα ἐν τοῖς λόγοις (cf. 234e1), "what merely appears first of all in speaking about the things," and τὰ ἔργα (cf. e2f.), that which is actually there in genuine dealings with the things, in genuine commerce with them. But even now, although the σοφιστικὴ τέχνη in this way becomes intelligible as μιμητική, Plato is still not satisfied. The peculiar existence of semblance must be exposed still more sharply, in particular so that not every arbitrary non-being, i.e., non-genuine being, could become the thematic foundation for the discussion he is pursuing. A further clarification of the peculiar Being of non-beings and of the possibility of the existence of this impossibility results from a more precise consideration of what the εἰδωλοποιική properly means, i.e., of what the εἴδωλον signifies in itself: which possibilities of mere appearing and of posing as something reside in the εἴδωλον as εἴδωλον.

4. AH: δόξα.

The very difficult connection we have pursued today[5] in a certain sense is the last preparation for the leap into the discussion of the Being of non-beings. To master this connection is to gain clarity about the basic intention already contained in the preceding definitions: to demonstrate the factual existence of something impossible, namely the Being of non-beings. This impossible existence is for Plato always an impossibility, precisely insofar as the proposition still holds: beings are, non-beings are not. It is precisely this obviousness, predominant all the way up to Plato, that makes necessary this complication and this endeavor to demonstrate, once and for all, the factual existence of this impossibility and to pursue it into the most inner structure of the τέχνη of the sophist. We will see that as soon as this goal is attained the consideration will apparently completely lose its previous ground, to return to it only later, at the end of the dialogue. Plato's first demonstration of the factual existence of the Being of non-beings has to be carried out in accord with the structure of the dialogue; i.e., he cannot yet make use of the knowledge he will acquire later on but instead has to show the Being of non-beings while, in a certain sense, constantly keeping the proposition of Parmenides in the background, and this proposition prohibits the idea of the Being of non-beings as an absurdity. Here reside the peculiar difficulty as well as the peculiar character of the path Plato has chosen: he does not show directly in relation to λέγειν, which is his central interest, nor in relation to the τέχνη of the sophist himself, that there factually is a non-being. Instead, he attempts to place the τέχνη of the sophist within the horizon of another τέχνη, in which there is in fact something like non-being and which is closer to natural understanding: the horizon of τέχνη μιμητική.

Now Plato is not proceeding arbitrarily by elucidating the σοφιστικὴ τέχνη out of the horizon of the τέχνη μιμητική. That is evident from the fact that the comportment of both these τέχναι, on the one hand ποιεῖν in the sense of μιμεῖσθαι, and on the other hand λέγειν, have something in common in a structural sense. Already earlier, in considering the pre-possessed horizon for the determination of the angler, Plato spoke of ποιητική, and it was for him the opportunity to point out that the concept of οὐσία is connected with ποιεῖν and that ποιεῖν is nothing other than ἄγειν εἰς οὐσίαν.[6] Ποιεῖν means "to produce"; μίμησις, μιμεῖσθαι, means "to present"; and λέγειν means "to reveal," δηλοῦν. All three modes of comportment have the same basic relation to their object: they let be seen. Producing in the sense of fabricating is a making available and thereby is a placing into availability, a placing into presence, and thus is a letting be seen.

5. Session 36, Monday, February 2, 1925.
6. Cf. p. 186ff.

Similarly, presenting in the sense of presenting in images, μιμεῖσθαι, is a letting be seen, and λέγειν has the same function as well. The basic sense of the accomplishment is important here. It is the identity of this basic sense which suggests elucidating the modes of letting be seen that reside in λέγειν from μίμησις as letting be seen in the mode of presenting or from ποίησις as letting be seen in the mode of producing. In ποίησις resides the ποιούμενον = οὐσία = εἶδος, what is seen, what is there. Correspondingly, the δηλούμενον, the ὄν in the sense of the ἀληθές, resides in λέγειν. In μιμεῖσθαι, the μιμούμενον is the εἴδωλον. Correspondingly also in λέγειν, insofar as it is a kind of μίμησις, the λεγόμενον will be a kind of εἴδωλον. Ἀληθές, εἶδος, and εἴδωλον are, taken together, modes of uncoveredness and as such are related to seeing. Hence when Plato places the τέχνη σοφιστική in the horizon of the μιμητική his choice of this horizon is not accidental but, quite to the contrary, is grounded in the matter itself, i.e., in the mode of the connection between ποιεῖν and λέγειν, or between οὐσία and λεγόμενον, insofar as, for the Greeks, Being means precisely to be present, to be in the present.

The consideration initially began with the sophist: the establishing of the object of his ἀντιλέγειν—establishing that it is πάντα—showed that this ἀντιλέγειν is in itself an impossibility. Nevertheless it is indisputable that it exists. Accordingly, that which cannot be but which nevertheless is can only be in virtue of a modification toward ungenuineness. This modification is expressed by the term παιδιά: it is properly a mere jest. This modification toward ungenuineness is in fact present in every art, which is not to say that art as such is ungenuine but that the modification is in fact there and has its justification. Yet precisely this factual existence of art demonstrates the Being of non-beings. The question is now: how, out of the horizon of μιμητική, can the Being of non-beings show itself more sharply? More precisely: where actually are these non-beings in their Being? What is it about the μιμητικὴ τέχνη that requires us to acknowledge the existence of non-beings?

c) Sharpened demonstration of the factual Being of the τέχνη σοφιστική out of the horizon of τέχνη μιμητική.

α) The two types of τέχνη μιμητική: εἰκαστική and φανταστική. The two types of εἴδωλον: εἰκών and φάντασμα. The impossibility of clarifying the phenomenon of knowledge through the phenomenon of the image. Husserl's elucidation of the image.

The ποίησις alive in μιμητική has the task of ποιεῖν εἴδωλα, which means nothing else than ἀπεργάζεσθαι τὴν τοῦ μιμήματος γένεσιν (cf. 235e1f.), "to accomplish, to fabricate, the becoming, the coming into being, of the μίμημα, the imitation." Put more sharply, it is ποιεῖν δοκεῖν, to bring into being, εἰς οὐσίαν ἄγειν, that which only looks like something but properly is not. In order to make thoroughly clear this Being of non-beings in the case of μίμησις, Plato investigates this ποιεῖν εἴδωλα of the εἰδωλοποιική more closely and distinguishes two εἴδη: 1.) the εἰκαστική (cf. d6), a determinate type of making εἴδωλα, where the εἴδωλον has the character of εἰκών (cf. 236a8); and 2.) the φανταστική (cf. c4), in which the εἴδωλον, in comparison to the εἰκών, has a modified character. As we will see, this latter εἴδωλον is a φάντασμα (b7). Thus a distinction resides within the εἰδωλοποιική insofar as it produces εἰκόνα on the one hand and, on the other hand, φαντάσματα. Both, however, are εἴδωλα. Therefore the distinction must apply to the very character of the εἴδωλον. The task is to work out this distinction in the εἴδωλον in terms of the character of the "appearance-as" or, more precisely, in terms of the relation of the appearance to genuine presentation. Thus the more precise explication of the sense of εἴδωλον and its various possibilities is a matter of the connection between what presents and what is presented, or between the image and the imaged. I do not say the "pictured," because picturing is only one determinate form of an imaging.

The phenomenon of the image, which plays a great role here, ushers in a very important context. Image-ness *[Bildlichkeit]*, in the sense of something being an image of something else, has played an immense role in philosophy (in part precisely in connection with Greek philosophy) with regard to the question of the elucidation of knowledge. For philosophers have said that in a certain way the objects outside of us, outside of consciousness, i.e., in other terms, "transcendent" objects, are pictured by immanent objects, or conversely, that we attain transcendent objects only through immanent objects. The structural connection of image-ness, of something being an image of something else, even when not explicitly recognized as such, is often made foundational for the interpretation of knowledge, though to be sure always without any attempt to see more precisely what properly is involved in the phenomenon of image-ness, i.e., in being an image of something. To attempt it would mean seeing immediately that this context of images will never help elucidate knowledge. Husserl's *Logical Investigations* demonstrated this twenty-five years ago in an absolutely convincing and irrefutable way, but today people act as if nothing had happened. According to the Fifth Investigation, chapter two, supplement,[7] a primary distinction must be drawn in the phenomenon of the image between:

7. The title of the supplement is "Toward a critique of the 'image-theory' and of the doctrine of the 'immanent' objects of acts."

1.) the image-object, which means the image itself, i.e., the object which, e.g., is hanging on the wall, or the sculpture standing on some pedestal or other, and 2.) the image-subject, that which is presented, as we say, in the image itself. Husserl points out that the similarity of two things—even if it were so great that the content of these two things coincided—does not suffice to make the one the image of the other. On the contrary, essentially new structural moments are required for something to be the image of something else.

Now Plato is interested here in the Being of the image as such, but he is not interested in the phenomenon of image-ness as such; he does not even have the means of uncovering these structural connections. Within the structural connection of image-ness he is concerned rather with showing that the image-object, as we say, hence that which presents, indeed exists but that, as this extant object, it is precisely not what it, as image, shows. Plato is concerned with this distinction: the fact that in the image and with the existing image, there is something there which itself is not that which it shows; i.e., what it properly poses as is not itself. What interests Plato in the image is the relation of the mode of Being of the image-object to what is presented as such.

β) The relation between the image (εἴδωλον) and the imaged (ὄν) in εἰκαστική and φανταστική. The determination of both types of εἴδωλον: εἰκών and φάντασμα. The enhancement of non-being in φανταστική. The indisputability of the Being of non-beings.

Now within the production of images, within εἰδωλοποιική, there is one type which μάλιστα (235d7), "most of all," is what it can be, namely the one which produces the μίμημα, forms the image, in such a way that this image has the character of ἀποδιδόναι τὴν ἀληθινὴν συμμετρίαν (cf. e6f.) or ἀπεργάζεσθαι τὰς οὔσας συμμετρίας (cf. 236a5f.). Thus such a μιμεῖσθαι as it were extracts, ἀποδιδόναι, from what is to be presented its exact proportions and reproduces them in the presentation itself. This is the character of the ἀποδιδόναι: to extract from what is to be presented, and then reproduce in the presentation τὰς οὔσας συμμετρίας, the proportions precisely as they are in what is to be presented, in the model, τὰς τοῦ παραδείγματος ἐν μήκει καὶ πλάτει καὶ βάθει (cf. 235d7f.), "according to length, breadth, and depth." And it reproduces not only these proportions but also whatever else is visible, e.g., the colors, χρώματα (335e1), precisely as they are in the actual being, in the ἀληθινόν. What is produced and is present in such reproduction is an εἴδωλον having the character of εἰκὸς ὄν (cf. 236a8)—εἰκός means "same." This εἴδωλον, in its proportions and color, is the same as the model; it looks exactly like it. It is a picture in the quite strict sense of an exact copy, e.g., a life-size, slavishly produced sculpture. But although this εἴδωλον is εἰκός, and therefore is an εἰκών, an image in the proper sense, yet as εἰκών, i.e., as εἴδωλον, it still possesses the character of mere appearance in the sense of not genuinely being what it presents. This is one possible type of presentation, one way of producing an εἴδωλον.

The second is the φανταστική. What distinguishes it from the first-mentioned, the εἰκαστική, is that what this production of images properly produces is no longer the same as the model, the way a picture is. The contents, and the proportions given in them, are other than those of the actual being. Theaetetus asks, concerning the characterization of the εἰκαστική (235d7ff.): Τί δ'; οὐ πάντες οἱ μιμούμενοί τι τοῦτ' ἐπιχειροῦσι δρᾶν; (e3f.). Do not all who take up the τέχνη of μιμεῖσθαι proceed in this way; do they not all create εἴδωλα in the sense of εἰκών, and thus does the εἴδωλον not have to be εἰκός? The ξένος (235e5ff.) says no; when it is a matter of creating a huge presentation, e.g., a frieze, or the presentation of a battle or of a parade in an entire facade of a building, then the figures of the people and soldiers that will be placed up above must be bigger in order for them, since they are so far removed, to appear exactly as large as the ones beneath—insofar as these figures are seen in natural vision. If the ones up above were also presented in life size, they would seem too small, and a mis-proportion would enter into the image as a whole. Such a presentation is hence oriented so that what is presented has a unitary effect, as *one* parade, and so that the actual connections presented in the image have the effect of something integrated. The fact that some things we see are farther from us than other things requires the sculptor to enlarge whatever is more distant. If seen from a height, from a ladder, these figures are too big. Thus here it is not a matter of shaping the εἴδωλον in the sense of εἰκός; instead, the production of the εἴδωλον is oriented toward the image as a whole, with the intention of merely making it appear as an integrated real thing. This mere appearance goes by the name of φάντασμα. τί καλοῦμεν; ἆρ' οὐκ, ἐπείπερ φαίνεται μέν, ἔοικε δὲ οὔ, φάντασμα; (236b6f.). This εἴδωλον is μηδ' εἰκὸς ᾧ φησιν ἐοικέναι (b6), not at all the same as what it claims to be like and to present; it is no longer a picture or exact copy. We have already seen that a picture is not the actual thing itself, and the φάντασμα is even less that which it presents. This is what the distinction between εἰκαστική and φανταστική is meant to indicate. The mode of Being of the image in φανταστική possesses still less of that which it is designed to present and render, not even its proportions in the sense of the same size, length, breadth, and depth. That is to say, the φάντασμα, in its existence as an image, is even more *not* that which it poses as; in it, non-being is all the more genuine. And now the ξένος makes the remarkable observation that the μιμητικὴ τέχνη proceeds πάμπολυ (cf. b9f.), "on the whole," almost always, in the sense of τέχνη φανταστική. Almost all art is art not in the sense of εἰκαστική but in the sense of φανταστική. Now if, in this τέχνη φανταστική, something exists which is still more *not* what it presents and if it is actually the most widespread type of μιμητική, then the factual existence of non-beings can by no means be disputed any longer. Thus we have exposed in μιμητική a ποιούμενον, something fabricated, something produced, which is altogether *not* what it poses to be.

Plato thus emphasizes the distinction within the εἰδωλοποιική in order to show how extensively a non-being is contained in the output of τέχνη μιμητική and, analogously, in the productions of the sophist. The εἴδωλον in the sense of the εἰκών is already not the same as what it presents. The φάντασμα, however, is not only in general, simply as an image, not actually what it presents, but it is also in its very content altogether dissimilar to that which it presents yet is not. Thus the character of the φάντασμα as an image contains still more of μὴ ὄν. In this context, Plato is concerned with demonstrating precisely the existence of non-beings, μὴ ὄν. That is clear from the fact that the later discussion, where Plato again speaks of the εἴδωλον and the φάντασμα, does not again take up the distinction between εἰκαστική and φανταστική. And that is because it matters there only that Plato have at his disposal in the εἴδωλον in general this phenomenon of μὴ ὄν. This non-being corresponds to what the sophist himself produces in his own activity. But what he properly produces, and what there possesses the character of μὴ ὄν, is not yet directly clear. This whole consideration has not spoken of λέγειν; instead, the entire demonstration of the actual existence of non-beings in the φάντασμα has revolved around μιμητική.

Thereby, indeed, the factual existence of non-beings is laid before our eyes; but at the same time the ξένος says: εἰς ἄπορον εἶδος καταπέφευγεν (cf. 236d2f.), "the sophist has escaped us." He has again slipped out of our hands into an εἶδος, an outward look, in which we do not at all know our way about, "where we have no exit."

γ) The complete aporia of grasping the sophist. The sophist's hiding in the darkness of μὴ ὄν. The further task: the discovery of the εἶδος of μὴ ὄν.

The situation now is properly this: the actual existence of non-being has been established and the sophist is thereby, if we may speak this way, the walking incarnation of μὴ ὄν. But precisely here complete perplexity faces us, insofar as the principle indeed remains correct: beings are, non-beings are not. It is telling that Plato emphasizes several times in this context that the sophist has in a certain sense disappeared through a trap door. εἰς ἄπορον τόπον καταδέδυκεν (cf. 239c6f.): "He has dived down to a place with no access and no exit." ἀποδιδράσκων εἰς τὴν τοῦ μὴ ὄντος σκοτεινότητα (254a4f.): "He has escaped and hidden himself in the obscurity of non-being." διὰ τὸ σκοτεινὸν τοῦ τόπου κατανοῆσαι χαλεπός (254a5f.): "Because the place he has flown to, namely non-being, is dark, he himself is difficult to see." Corresponding to this σκοτεινόν, Plato says at 260d: up to now we have had no εἶδος for the sophist, i.e., no vision. Thus "having no εἶδος" of something corresponds to the σκοτεινόν, to hiding in darkness. Obviously the sophist can be drawn out of his hiding place, out of the darkness, only if the εἶδος is found for what he is, namely for μὴ ὄν, i.e., only if the meaning of Being is discussed anew. The ἰδέα, the ἕν, toward which the whole consideration of the σοφιστικὴ τέχνη aims, has not yet been discovered. On the contrary, Ὄντως ἐν παντάπασι χαλεπῇ σκέψει (cf. 236d9f.): "We find ourselves now altogether left with a difficult consideration." The difficulty is only now beginning. It is not accidental that at the start of the new investigations, where we will search for the εἶδος of μὴ ὄν, where light is supposed to be brought into the darkness of the Being of non-beings, i.e., into the existence of the sophist, the ξένος reminds Theaetetus once more of the correct comportment required for such a consideration. He asks Theaetetus: Ἆρ' οὖν αὐτὸ γιγνώσκων σύμφης, ἤ σε οἷον ῥύμη τις ὑπὸ τοῦ λόγου συνειθισμένον συνεπεσπάσατο πρὸς τὸ ταχὺ συμφῆσαι; (236d5ff.), whether in the previous course of the consideration he has said "yes" and "Amen" to the ξένος merely out of habit, or whether he has always had the matter itself in view, and has presentified it to himself, before he voiced his agreement. He once more appeals to Theaetetus' conscience to see for himself whatever is under discussion. For now non-being is indeed under discussion, and the question is whether something like that can be seen at all. The question is: what is addressed in the ὄνομα "μὴ ὄν"?

SECTION TWO

Ontological Discussion[1]
The Being of Non-beings[2] (*Sophist* 236e–264b)

Introduction

(236e–237a)

§59. Exposition of the ontological problematic.

a) Summary of the result of the seventh definition of the sophist. The contradictoriness of ψευδὴς λόγος.

The consideration begins at 236e with a certain quite formal summary of the result obtained thus far. The factual existence of images—or the factual existence of the sophist—presents us with something we can characterize as follows: τὸ . . . φαίνεσθαι τοῦτο καὶ τὸ δοκεῖν, εἶναι δὲ μή (e1f.), or, in relation to the sophist, who moves in λέγειν: τὸ λέγειν μὲν ἄττα, ἀληθῆ δὲ μή (e2). That is, we possess the state of affairs of φαίνεσθαι, "self-showing as something," or of δοκεῖν, "appearing as something," εἶναι δὲ μή, "without actually being that something." Similarly, we have encountered the λέγειν μὲν ἄττα, "addressing something," or, more precisely, letting something be seen by addressing it, ἀληθῆ δὲ μή, "yet not letting it be seen in its uncoveredness." "This whole state of affairs," τὸ φαίνεσθαι τοῦτο καὶ τὸ δοκεῖν, εἶναι δὲ μή, καὶ τὸ λέγειν μὲν ἄττα, ἀληθῆ δὲ μή, says the ξένος, "is full of difficulties," πάντα ταῦτά ἐστι μεστὰ ἀπορίας (e2f.), not only now but ever, ἀεὶ ἐν τῷ πρόσθεν χρόνῳ καὶ νῦν (e3), now and before. ὅπως γὰρ εἰπόντα χρὴ ψευδῆ λέγειν ἢ δοξάζειν ὄντως εἶναι, καὶ τοῦτο φθεγξάμενον ἐναντιολογίᾳ μὴ συνέχεσθαι, παντάπασιν χαλεπόν (cf. e3ff.). "And it is altogether difficult to see how someone who says there really is a ψευδῆ λέγειν or ψευδῆ δοξάζειν does not necessarily contradict himself," ἐναντιολογίᾳ συνέχεσθαι. That is, whoever contends there is a ψευδὴς λόγος is forced to speak against himself. For he is in effect saying that there is a λόγος, a δηλοῦν, a revealing, and that this λέγειν is ψευδῆ, it distorts.

1. Title in Heidegger's manuscript.
2. Title based on Heidegger (see p. 161f., the articulation of the *Sophist*).

Thus whoever says there exists a ψευδής λόγος is saying there is a letting be seen that conceals—or an opening up that occludes.

Plato now formulates μὴ ὄν in a double way (as just happened regarding μιμητική and as happened earlier regarding the sophist, i.e., in terms of the ἀντιλέγεσθαι περὶ πάντα), namely: 1.) as φαίνεσθαι καὶ δοκεῖν, εἶναι δὲ μή, and 2.) as λέγειν μὲν ἄττα, ἀληθῆ δὲ μή. This shows he is orienting the further consideration of μὴ ὄν toward the phenomena of δόξα and λόγος. Upon closer inspection, these two phenomena are not as different as might appear at first. It is precisely the intrinsic connection between δόξα and λόγος which justifies their alliance in this questioning. For, in Plato's eyes, δόξα, or δοξάζειν, is a determinate type of λόγος.

b) Excursus: δόξα and λόγος.[3] Δόξα as a mode of λόγος, i.e., of διάνοια.

Δοξάζειν means "to be of the opinion." What that denotes varies according to the specific level of philosophical insight Plato attains with regard to the genuine meaning of ἐπιστήμη. Where he is still essentially more uncertain than in our dialogue, e.g. in the *Theaetetus*, δοξάζειν means indeed to have an opinion about something, but in the sense of having a conviction about it, knowing it is so. Consequently, in the *Theaetetus* Plato can characterize genuine ἐπιστήμη, knowledge proper, and indeed at first negatively: ὅμως δὲ τοσοῦτόν γε προβεβήκαμεν, ὥστε μὴ ζητεῖν αὐτὴν ἐν αἰσθήσει τὸ παράπαν ἀλλ' ἐν ἐκείνῳ τῷ ὀνόματι, ὅτι ποτ' ἔχει ἡ ψυχή, ὅταν αὐτὴ καθ' αὑτὴν πραγματεύηται περὶ τὰ ὄντα.—Ἀλλὰ μὴν τοῦτό γε καλεῖται, ὡς ἐγῷμαι, δοξάζειν (cf. 187a3ff.). In sense perception, ἐν αἰσθήσει, οὐ, there is no genuine knowledge, but in δοξάζειν there is. And he determines δοξάζειν as a πραγματεύεσθαι περὶ τὰ ὄντα, the soul's "having to do with beings,"[4] and specifically τῆς ψυχῆς αὐτῆς καθ' αὑτήν, insofar as the soul is purely posited on itself and purely relates to itself. The αὐτὴ καθ' αὑτήν means that this comportment of the soul toward beings does not involve αἴσθησις; on the contrary, the soul is relating to beings purely out of its own possibilities. At 189e of the *Theaetetus*, Plato then determines the meaning of δόξα positively. Ἐπιστήμη is, as was said, in opposition to sense perception, αἴσθησις, a conceiving of something. To take an example: genuine knowledge is not the perception of a table—of this table here, as a determinate table here and now—but is conceiving in the sense of perceiving that there is here something like tableness in general. So knowledge in the proper sense is not related to the this-here-now but to the essence of

3. Title in Heidegger's manuscript.
4. AH: cf. W.S. 31–32.

what is here: table as such. I cannot see table as such with my eyes; I can only conceive it, i.e., see it in the sense of pure seeing—with the soul, with νοῦς. Thus the *Theaetetus* already orients genuine knowledge toward this, although Plato himself does not reach clarity about the proper character of this seeing and conceiving. Yet he does determine δόξα as λόγος. τὸ δὲ διανοεῖσθαι ἆρ' ὅπερ ἐγὼ καλεῖς; —Λόγον ὃν αὐτὴ πρὸς αὑτὴν ἡ ψυχὴ διεξέρχεται (*Theaetetus,* 189e4ff.). Δόξα, i.e., seeing and conceiving, διανοεῖσθαι, is a λόγος, "a speaking, which the soul traverses in itself and which is directed to itself," διεξέρχεσθαι (this is consistent with the description of dialectic as διαπορεύεσθαι διὰ τῶν λόγων[5]—notice the διά!), an addressing, a discussing, a traversing περὶ ὧν ἂν σκοπῇ (e6f.), of that which the soul itself has in its field of view, the soul taken purely for itself, without sense perception. Plato characterizes this λόγος as εἰρημένος οὐ μέντοι πρὸς ἄλλον οὐδὲ φωνῇ, ἀλλὰ σιγῇ πρὸς αὑτόν (cf. 190a5f.), speech "which is not spoken to someone else" but, as was said above, πρὸς αὑτήν, "to itself," i.e., not out loud, οὐδὲ φωνῇ, but σιγῇ πρὸς αὑτόν, "silently to itself." This delimitation clarifies at the same time the usual structure of λόγος: λέγειν πρὸς ἄλλον and φωνῇ, "speaking with and to an other," "out loud." But in this case the λόγος is οὐ μέντοι πρὸς ἄλλον, ἀλλὰ σιγῇ πρὸς αὑτόν, "not a speaking to another but silently to oneself." That is, this speaking is a matter of an *appropriation* and not a matter of communication with an other. Everything in this λόγος is oriented toward the appropriation of what is seen in its unconcealedness, the appropriation of what is in sight. Just as δόξα is interpreted here as λόγος, so the *Sophist* expressly characterizes διάνοια, i.e., thinking proper, genuine discernment, as διάλογος. Οὐκοῦν διάνοια μὲν καὶ λόγος ταὐτόν· πλὴν ὁ μὲν ἐντὸς τῆς ψυχῆς πρὸς αὑτὴν διάλογος ἄνευ φωνῆς γιγνόμενος τοῦτ' αὐτὸ ἡμῖν ἐπωνομάσθη, διάνοια; (*Sophist,* 263e3ff.). διάνοια μὲν αὐτῆς πρὸς ἑαυτὴν ψυχῆς διάλογος (264a9). The διανοεῖν is a διάλογος, a dialogue. You see here everywhere διεξέρχεσθαι, διαλέγειν, and in the *Philebus* the expression is διαδοξάζειν (38b13). Everything is oriented toward the διά: taking apart in the sense of διαίρεσις. If the discernment proper, διανοεῖν, is characterized as διάλογος, and specifically as a speaking of the soul with and to itself, then this indicates that λέγειν, as it is determined in διαλεκτική, is actually nothing else than a νοεῖν. Thus the διαλέγεσθαι is a νοεῖν in an emphatic sense. Plato touches upon the same connection in the *Philebus* as well. Seen in this perspective, namely insofar as δόξα is interpreted as λόγος, the peculiar parallels in the *Sophist* between φαίνεσθαι, δοκεῖν, and λέγειν are no longer surprising.

5. *Sophist* 253b10: διὰ τῶν λόγων πορεύεσθαι.

c) The ontological possibility of ψευδὴς λόγος: the Being of non-beings.

What corresponds to μιμητική in the τέχνη of the sophist is the existence there of a λόγος which λέγει μὲν ἄττα, "says something," ἀληθῆ δὲ μή, but does not uncover the being as it is; this λόγος is ψευδής, it distorts. The question is how something like that can be. A ψευδὴς λόγος, i.e., an opening up that occludes, is something actual only if non-beings can be. There is a ψευδὴς λόγος only under the presupposition that non-beings can be. With the interpretation of the sophist as ἀντιλέγειν περὶ πάντα, i.e., basically, as ψευδῆ λέγειν, we have dared τετόλμηκεν ὑποθέσθαι τὸ μὴ ὂν εἶναι (cf. 237a2ff.), "to posit in advance that non-beings are." Only under this presupposition, τὸ μὴ ὂν εἶναι, is there something like a sophist at all. If this presupposition is incorrect, i.e., if we adhere to the principle of Parmenides, unshaken up to now, that non-beings are not, then there can be no sophist. But then there is also no distinction between scientific investigation and the activity of the sophists, namely idle talk. Then all speaking is, as speaking, equally correct. Here we see for the first time the genuine meaning of all the previous, apparently merely scholastic, definitions: they compel us to take up, in opposition to the dogmas of the tradition of a Parmenides, research into the matters themselves.[6]

§60. The relation of philosophy to the tradition.

a) Conclusive establishment of the meaning of the "definitions" of the sophist: compulsion toward research into the matters themselves. The repudiation of the dogmatic tradition (Parmenides).

Thus we now see for the first time the meaning of the apparently merely scholastic definitions of the sophist. They force Plato to choose either: 1.) further complicity with the well-established dogma of the school of Parmenides that non-beings are not. Accordingly, there is no ψευδὴς λόγος, and the ἀντιλέγειν περὶ πάντα is also impossible. It must be conceded then that there is no sophist, because there cannot be one. Complicity with the dogma of the school of Parmenides would thus amount to Plato's acknowledging the sophists as philosophers and renouncing himself. For there would then be no distinction between what the sophists do and what he

6. See the appendix.

is attempting in opposition to them. Or, 2.) Plato can acknowledge the factual existence of the sophist and accordingly of μὴ ὄν, of the ψεῦδος, and take the factual existence of deception, distortion, and misrepresentation as it is and so transform the theory of Being. Thus the alternatives are now given: either to allow the matters themselves their right and bind oneself on the basis of them to a ruthless opposition against all pre-established theory, or to adhere to the tradition simply because it is venerable and thereby renounce oneself and give up research, which is always research into the matters themselves.

Plato decides in favor of the first possibility, or, more precisely, he has already decided in favor of it. For the entire consideration has indeed a positive, independent sense only if it is possible to make μὴ ὄν intelligible as a being. Precisely then does the consideration of the sophist have the positive meaning of first making visible the phenomena which the further investigation can latch on to. In terms of the image introduced earlier, i.e., the usual characterization of the content of the dialogue as a matter of a shell enclosing a kernel, the shell being what we have dealt with up to now, and the kernel the ontological discussion, we can say that for us it is precisely the reverse: what we have been dealing with up to now is the kernel of the dialogue and what follows is nothing else than the liberation of this kernel in its structure. There is no shell here but only one continuous train of investigation.

The alternatives facing Plato recur in every philosophical investigation which understands itself; yet, to be sure, nothing is gained by the mere formulation of the alternatives themselves. Even an understanding of them in their concrete demands and a decision comparable to Plato's are no guarantee that one's investigation will be able to set the first possibility in motion. For it is precisely Plato who shows, not only in this dialogue but in his entire work, how difficult it is, even with an interest directed purely at the matters themselves, to make any forward progress here, and how everything can remain in a preliminary state. This applies to Aristotle just as much as to Plato. The Romantic appreciation of Plato within the history of philosophy precisely does not see what is properly positive in him, i.e., what is not well-rounded, what is fragmentary, what remains underway. That is the genuinely positive element in all research. To be sure, this does not mean that every imperfection would as such already be positive, but only that it harbors the possibility of growth.

The situation Plato now faces (and we could hardly represent better the tremendous significance of Parmenides in the thinking of Plato) is also one we face, admittedly with this difference, that we are chained to the tradition in an entirely other measure, and even in an entirely other sense, than were Plato and Aristotle.

b) The relation of contemporary philosophy to the tradition. The "destruction" of the dogmatic tradition. The appropriation of the past research into the matters themselves.

Even here, and even today still, and not for the last time, in phenomenology, there is a romanticism which believes that it can step directly into the open space, that one can, so to speak, make oneself free of history by a leap. Philosophical questioning—precisely the one intending to press on to the matters themselves—is not concerned with freeing us from the past but, on the contrary, with making the past free for us, free to liberate us from the tradition, and especially from the ungenuine tradition. For the latter has the peculiar characteristic that in giving, in *tradere,* in transmitting, it distorts the gifts themselves. Only if we do justice to our own past, in the sense of past research, will we be able to grow in it, i.e., only then will we be capable of raising our liberated research to its level of questioning. This kind of historical consideration lets us understand that what remains in history—not in the sense of an eternal present but as a proper temporal historicality—are not systems but the often difficult to recognize pieces of actual research and work, that which we will grasp as pieces of actually accomplished labor. Genuine communication with the past is to be gained only on this basis. And only if we have attained this communication does there exist a prospect to be historical. Ruthlessness toward the tradition is reverence toward the past, and it is genuine only in an appropriation of the latter (the past) out of a destruction of the former (the tradition). On this basis, all actual historiographical work, something quite different from historiography in the usual sense, must dovetail with philosophy's research into the matters themselves.

Chapter One

Difficulties in the Concept of Non-beings[1] (237a–242b)

§61. Examination of the principle of Parmenides. The unutterability of μὴ ὄν.

a) First exhibition of the difficulties of the λέγειν of μὴ ὄν. The fundamental contradiction between μὴ ὄν and λέγειν as λέγειν τί.

Plato does not simply overthrow the principle of Parmenides with a violent stroke but instead emphasizes, after citing the principle, "we want to examine it," θεασώμεθα (237b3), "we want to investigate the character of this principle," namely the principle:

Οὐ γὰρ μή ποτε τοῦτο δαμῇ, εἶναι μὴ ἐόντα, ἀλλὰ σὺ τῆσδ' ἀφ' ὁδοῦ διζήσιος[2] εἶργε νόημα (cf. 237a8f.)

"You will never conquer this," in the sense of being able to maintain it; i.e., you will never be able to contend, "that non-beings are. Instead, keep away from it, keep your νοεῖν, your reflection, your seeing, far from this path of investigation." In other words, if you do direct your mind to that, you will never acquire a theme of real discernment, a theme of νοεῖν.

Against this prohibition, εἶργε νόημα, the ξένος says, in the form of a question: τολμῶμεν, "shall we dare" τὸ μηδαμῶς ὄν που φθέγγεσθαι; (cf. 237b7f.), "to somehow utter what is altogether non-being?" Note that it is a matter of φθέγγεσθαι, "uttering," λέγειν in a quite determinate sense. Theaetetus responds: Πῶς γὰρ οὔ; (237b9), "Why not?" He does not hesitate to accept it as obvious; he sees no difficulty, i.e., he appeals quite spontaneously to idle talk, which is what we have indeed been making thus far. He finds no difficulty because he is not at all attempting to investigate what the expression μὴ ὄν, understood by everyone, really means. He just says μὴ ὄν, without rigorously seeing what it properly means. He has already forgotten again the admonition the ξένος gave him at the outset of this new examination, namely to answer only on the basis of seeing.

The ξένος challenges him. It is not a matter of speaking ἔριδος ἕνεκα μηδὲ παιδιᾶς (b10), "in jest and for the sake of an arbitrary discussion," but

1. Title based on Heidegger (see p. 161f, the articulation of the *Sophist*).
2. According to 258d3.

σπουδῇ (ibid.), now it is "serious": I desire from you an answer, after you have, along with me, seen the thing with your own eyes. That is how you have to answer me this: ποῖ χρὴ τοὔνομ' ἐπιφέρειν τοῦτο, τὸ μὴ ὄν (c2), "to what should the expression μὴ ὄν properly be applied?" That means: what does it properly mean? What is given to us when we utter the expression μὴ ὄν meaningfully? For an ὄνομα, a word, is indeed not a mere sound in the sense of noise. It is not that a sound becomes audible and that next to it, or with it, a so-called representation emerges incidentally. On the contrary, the word itself—and this is its primary sense—means something. Already in natural speaking with one another, in discussion, we are not at all focused on the sounds themselves but primarily and quite naturally on what is said. We certainly hear the sounds, but they are not in the least thematically given to us as sounds and grasped as such. Even when we do not understand someone speaking, and are thus incapable of investigating the meaning of the words and sentences, even then we do not hear noises but un-understood words and sentences. Hence even then the primary mode of grasping is the understanding of what is said itself. The ὄνομα as such—I am anticipating some determinations in order to elucidate these connections—already contains the ἐπί, the "unto the matter itself." A word is a sign of something in the quite peculiar sense of signifying; it shows something, σημαίνει. The question is hence εἰς τί καὶ ἐπὶ ποῖον αὐτόν τε καταχρήσασθαι; (c2f.): "In regard to what, to what sort of thing, do we apply the expression μὴ ὄν?" Τί . . . τῷ πυνθανομένῳ δεικνύναι; (c2ff.): "What will we show someone who asks what it means?" After this more precise explication of the sense of φθέγγεσθαι τὸ μηδαμῶς ὄν, Theaetetus' answer changes essentially: παντάπασιν ἄπορον (c6), I am now "completely unable" to answer you. The ξένος comes to his rescue. But at first he says: δῆλον, ὅτι τῶν ὄντων ἐπί <τι> τὸ μὴ ὄν οὐκ οἰστέον (c7f.), "it is obvious, it is clear, that the expression μὴ ὄν, in its signification, cannot be oriented toward something having the character of ὄν." Theaetetus declares himself to be in agreement.

The ξένος then carries the thought further, in the direction of clarifying what in general it means τὶ λέγειν, to speak about something, to "say something." Obviously, he says, in connection with what preceded, οὐδ' ἐπὶ τὸ τί (c10), if we were indeed to relate the expression μὴ ὄν, in its signification, "to something," we would not ὀρθῶς φέρειν (c11), be "carrying the expression in the right direction." Hence μὴ ὄν cannot mean an ὄν; nor can it mean a τί, "something." Καὶ τοῦτο φανερόν, ὡς καὶ τὸ "τὶ" τοῦτο τὸ ῥῆμα ἐπ' ὄντι λέγομεν ἑκάστοτε (cf. d1f.), for "it is certainly clear that when we say 'τί,' we in each case ἐπ' ὄν τι λέγομεν, employ it in the direction of some being." The text here has ἐπ' ὄντι, i.e., the dative. Corresponding to the sense of the whole discussion, I suggest changing it to ἐπ' ὄν τι: "it is also clear that when we say τί, we carry it over to some being." I believe this is justified linguistically since the entire previous discussion, which employed the term ἐπί throughout, invariably construed it with the accusative, although, purely grammatically, ἐπί may also take the dative. But this kind of formulation first provides the thought its genuine edge. μόνον γὰρ αὐτὸ λέγειν, ὥσπερ γυμνὸν καὶ ἀπηρημωμένον ἀπὸ τῶν ὄντων ἁπάντων, ἀδύνατον (d2ff.): "To say it, namely τί, in its nakedness, as it were, isolated in a certain sense from every determination of Being, that is ἀδύνατον." I cannot say τί, "something," denuded of Being in general. Every something *is* as something, though the meaning of "is" and "Being" remains wholly indeterminate. But insofar as I speak at all about *something,* it *is,* with the result that "τὶ" λέγειν is to co-say ὄν and also, as we will see, ἕν. Every something *is,* and every something is *one* something. "Τὶ" λέγειν is therefore not at all possible without co-intending, in the very sense of the λέγειν, in the very saying of something at all, Being and one. Accordingly, he who would utter μὴ ὄν, i.e., μή τι, "not-something," must necessarily μηδὲν λέγειν (e2), be "saying nothing." Such a person, who utters μὴ ὄν, would, if he understood himself correctly, altogether keep silent. For every λέγειν is, in its very sense, a λέγειν τί, and every λέγειν τί is a co-saying of ὄν and ἕν. Thus in saying μὴ ὄν, insofar as λέγω, "I say" at all, I already co-say ὄν and ἕν. An entirely original structure of λέγειν is becoming visible here, a structure still completely detached from the sphere of the content to which λέγειν, addressing and discussing, could potentially relate. Insofar as λέγειν is λέγειν τί, an "addressing of something," it thereby co-says, in what is addressed itself, definite characters of its Being and Being itself. This means, however, that λέγειν in itself, insofar as it is λέγειν τί, harbors fundamental difficulties for uttering μὴ ὄν.

This difficulty must now be thought through to its end; i.e., we must ask what the difficulty residing in λέγειν itself means for διαλέγεσθαι as λέγειν of μὴ ὄν. If we dare to utter μὴ ὄν, then it is evident we are *ipso facto* speaking about *something* and are co-saying, in the very sense of any saying, along with the "something," ὄν and ἕν. If, therefore, we are to be able at all to make μὴ ὄν understandable as a potential object of λέγειν, the question arises as to how this λέγειν itself must be constituted in order to make possible a μὴ ὄν λέγειν, i.e., a μὴ ὄν δοξάζειν. Formulated differently, what we are seeking is the ὀρθολογία τοῦ μὴ ὄντος (cf. 239b4), "the correct way to address non-beings." This form of posing the question already implies that the first difficulty resides less in the μὴ ὄν than in λέγειν itself, and that every addressing of non-beings as being harbors, structurally, a συμπλοκή (cf. 240c1), an entwining of non-being and Being. Thus non-beings *are,* in some sense or other, if this entwining rightfully exists. If, however, non-beings are supposed to be, whatever that may mean, then obviously the "non" is used here in a quite specific sense, one which, prior to Plato himself, still lay in the realm of the unknown. Hence what are required here are a revision of λόγος and of its sense as well as a revision of the meaning of the "non." But insofar as the "non" is correlative to "saying no" and negation, the question of μὴ ὄν is concentrated again on the λέγειν of μὴ ὄν. This is the path the following considerations take; but their individual progressions are not clear without further ado.

b) Continuation of the difficulties in the λέγειν of μὴ ὄν. Further determination of the structure of what is meant in λέγειν. Ἀριθμός and ὄν. Further determination of the conflict between μὴ ὄν and λέγειν. Intentionality as basic structure of λέγειν.

We dare φθέγγεσθαι τὸ μὴ ὄν. We have already acquired an insight insofar as we have seen that the τί, the object of every λέγειν, is not γυμνόν, "naked," denuded of Being; and, furthermore, we know that every τὶ λέγειν is a ἓν λέγειν. τόν τι λέγοντα ἕν τι λέγειν (cf. 237d6f.). Every something, that which is said in saying anything, is *one* something. Or, as Plato expresses it, the τί is σημεῖον of the ἕν (d9). The τί, the "something" as such, signifies the ἕν. That means that in the meaning of the "something" there resides the *one*. This expression σημεῖον is not arbitrary here. It later became a special term in Aristotle. For him, σημαίνειν is a particular kind of thinking, namely one that pertains to the word as word, namely signifying. Thus every τί co-signifies a ἕν, i.e., in the broadest sense, a number. The "co" in "co-signify" means "in advance." Furthermore, the expression τινέ, the double of τί, hence "both," the one and the other, co-signifies "two." And τινές, "some," "more," co-signifies plurality. Τί, τινέ, and τινές co-signify ἕν, δύο, πολλά, as numbers. Hence a quite broad concept of number is operative here, whereby number becomes identical with a constitutive determination of every something as something. A manifold of somethings is a plurality or multitude, as some or more. One, some, and more are numbers in an entirely original ontological sense. We need to keep in mind this broad concept of ἀριθμός, both for an understanding of the role number plays in Plato himself, in his ontology, as well as for an understanding of the historical fact that there was among the Greeks a philosophical school, the Pythagorean, which conceived numbers as the proper basic determinations of beings. This has nothing to do with a mathematical interpretation of the world or anything like that; on the contrary, it stems from this wholly original meaning of number, whereby to count means nothing else than to say "something," "several," "some," "more," and in so doing to articulate the manifold. Recently people have attempted to reduce the role of number in Greek philosophy essentially to Greek mathematics, and Stenzel specifically tries to do this in his study "Number and figure in Plato and Aristotle."[3] This investigation has a certain significance, since it goes back at any rate to the sources of Greek mathematics. But it suffers by fundamentally misperceiving these sources. Number means something quite different than what mathematics could contribute to its understanding.

Therefore, insofar as the τί as λεγόμενον necessarily co-signifies ὄν and ἕν, μή τι λέγειν, "not saying something," means the same as μηδὲν λέγειν (e1f.), "saying nothing." And this of course comes down to not speaking at all (e5). It appears as if the consideration has now arrived at the most extreme difficulty, as if there were no way out with regard to the clarification of the λόγος of μὴ ὄν, since we have been led to see that one cannot at all even speak about μὴ ὄν. But the ξένος submits to Theaetetus a still greater difficulty and indeed ἡ μεγίστη καὶ πρώτη (238a2), "the highest and first," on the basis of which everything we have seen thus far regarding the difficulties in μὴ ὄν is really to be grasped. It is this, by way of anticipation: if we cannot speak about μὴ ὄν, insofar as every λέγειν is a λέγειν τί, then we cannot at all speak against the sophist, because we can not speak about him at all, if indeed the sophist represents the factual existence of μὴ ὄν itself. That means the sophist has completely barricaded himself behind his redoubt and is completely inaccessible to διαλέγεσθαι as λέγειν. This difficulty, which in a certain sense reverts back onto the one who intends to refute the sophist, is now to be analyzed more precisely. Naturally, the aim is not simply to debate but to expose new structures in this μὴ ὄν and in the λέγειν of μὴ ὄν, structures which are only emphasized provisionally here but which later, in the last section of the dialogue, will receive their justification.

The ξένος points out that in the λέγειν of μὴ ὄν obviously this takes place: Τῷ μὲν ὄντι που προσγένοιτ' ἄν τι τῶν ὄντων ἕτερον (238a5), "in speaking, a ἕτερον τῶν ὄντων may be προσγίγνεσθαι, added on, appended, to a being." Here, for the first time in such a context, there emerges the concept of ἕτερον, "other." This concept of ἕτερον is the one on which Plato will base his revision of the concept of the μή of ὄν, i.e., negation. Such a προσγένεσις, adding on, co-saying, of one being with an other, obviously presents no difficulty; if I address the τί as ὄν and at the same time as ἕν, that is altogether intelligible. But what about this case: Μὴ ὄντι δέ τι τῶν ὄντων ἀρά ποτε προσγίγνεσθαι φήσομεν δυνατὸν εἶναι; (a7f.): "Will we say it is possible to attribute ὄν to μὴ ὄν," i.e., to co-say ὄν along with μὴ ὄν? (Keep in mind the expression προσγίγνεσθαί τι τῶν ὄντων μὴ ὄντι.) How

3. J. Stenzel, *Zahl und Gestalt bei Plato und Aristoteles*, Berlin/Leipzig, 1924.

could that happen, Theaetetus asks. The ξένος refers him to a phenomenon they have already discussed, number. Ἀριθμὸν δὴ τὸν σύμπαντα τῶν ὄντων τίθεμεν (a10). "Everything in numbers we indeed count among beings." If anything is a being, it is number. Μὴ τοίνυν μηδ' ἐπιχειρῶμεν ἀριθμοῦ μήτε πλῆθος μήτε ἓν πρὸς τὸ μὴ ὂν προσφέρειν (b2f.). Accordingly, if every number is an ὄν, then "we will never try πρὸς τὸ μὴ ὂν προσφέρειν, to carry over to μὴ ὄν, anything pertaining to number, neither πλῆθος, many, manifoldness, nor ἕν, one." It will obviously not be possible προσφέρειν a number, as ὄν, to μὴ ὄν. On the other hand, however, Πῶς οὖν ἂν ἢ διὰ τοῦ στόματος φθέγξαιτο ἄν τις ἢ καὶ τῇ διανοίᾳ τὸ παράπαν λάβοι τὰ μὴ ὄντα ἢ τὸ μὴ ὂν χωρὶς ἀριθμοῦ; (b6ff.), how is it supposed to be possible to speak of a μὴ ὄν or τῇ διανοίᾳ λαβεῖν, to grasp it in discernment, χωρὶς ἀριθμοῦ, without intending it as *one* μὴ ὄν or as *many* μὴ ὄντα? The intending of a μὴ ὄν or of μὴ ὄντα thus necessarily co-intends an ἀριθμός. We have established, however, that an ἀριθμός is an ὄν. Accordingly, seen also from this perspective, μὴ ὄν cannot be grasped χωρὶς ἀριθμοῦ, i.e., χωρὶς ὄντος. Yet we know: οὔτε δίκαιόν γε οὔτε ὀρθὸν ὂν ἐπιχειρεῖν μὴ ὄντι προσαρμόττειν (cf. c5f.), "we have no right, nor does it make sense, to attempt ὂν μὴ ὄντι προσαρμόττειν, to bring beings into harmony with non-beings." (Pay attention here to the various expressions for the peculiar συμπλοκή of ὄν and μὴ ὄν: προσφέρειν at 238b3, προστιθέναι at c1, προσαρμόττειν at c6.) And so we will have to say: τὸ μὴ ὂν αὐτὸ καθ' αὐτό, non-beings, seen purely in themselves, ἔστιν ἀδιανόητόν τε καὶ ἄρρητον καὶ ἄφθεγκτον καὶ ἄλογον (c9f.), are altogether ἀδιανόητον, "indiscernible," they cannot at all be conceived or intended as something. They are ἄρρητον, "unsayable," ἄφθεγκτον, "unutterable," and altogether (this sums it up) ἄλογον: they are not possible objects of any λέγειν; there is no λόγος about μὴ ὄν. And this implies καὶ τὸν ἐλέγχοντα εἰς ἀπορίαν καθίστησι τὸ μὴ ὂν οὕτως (d5): even someone (like Parmenides) who formulates this negation, i.e., who says non-beings are not, incurs the same difficulty. If he says non-beings are not, he is speaking against himself. Moreover, to aggravate matters, ἄλογον ἔφην εἶναι (e6), *we* have said non-being *is* ἄλογον, and αὐτό (239a9), *it* is ἄλογον. Basically, we cannot even say that, if the principle of Parmenides is valid. In this way the ξένος carries the difficulty to an extreme, and does so simply with the intention of showing once again that λέγειν is λέγειν τί. Speaking about μὴ ὄν deprives the speaker of the possibility of his own undertaking. Insofar as speaking-about is always speaking about something, and insofar as speaking is in general the primary mode of uncovering and gaining access to what is, μὴ ὄν is always closed off from λόγος.

This sharp emphasis on λέγειν as λέγειν τί is nothing else than the disclosure and clear appropriation of a basic structure in λέγειν as well as in νοεῖν and in δοξάζειν: speaking is speaking about something. That is by no means trivial. It is precisely Plato's exertions that show what it cost to see this basic fact of λέγειν as λέγειν τί and then not to leave it at this constatation but to proceed to a modification of λέγειν and ὄν. This basic structure of λέγειν and νοεῖν, and, more broadly taken, of every human comportment and in general of the comportment of every living thing,[4] has the sense of directedness toward something. Phenomenology, appropriating the scholastic term *intentio,* calls this basic structure "intentionality." This word is perhaps inappropriate to the matter, since it harbors a whole series of difficulties. Even today it still suggests that this phenomenon of intentionality involves a special attitude, a peculiar observing, attending to, or aiming at something. But all that is what is not meant. On the contrary, intentionality is a structure pertaining to the living being with regard to its very Being.[5] This structure obtains even when, in a mere passive having of something present to me, I, in a certain sense, do not at all carry out an explicit act of attention, an intending properly spoken. Precisely because *intentio,* both linguistically as well as historically, has a close connection with "attention," it is easily misunderstood, especially when it is applied to so-called lived experiences and acts of consciousness and is then seen exclusively from that standpoint.

For us it is important to see how this basic structure of λέγειν as λέγειν τί sustains the whole discussion. As long as we actually adhere to this structure, we cannot touch the sophist with any argument, and indeed not only because no arguments can be proffered against him but because it is not even possible to begin to speak about him. What was said earlier about the sophist is justified and makes sense only if it is possible to speak about non-beings, i.e., about the sophist himself. Hence the demonstration of the phenomena of μὴ ὄν as regards the sophist, i.e., the various definitions, as a pre-possessing of the ground of the ontological research, receives precisely on the basis of this research its first justification. Thus it becomes clear that an intrinsic substantive connection permeates the entire discussion, the entire dialogue.

4. In the Moser transcript, Heidegger places in brackets the words "and in general of the comportment of every living thing."

5. In the Moser transcript, Heidegger places a question mark in the margin beside this sentence. In addition, he places the word "living being" in quotation marks.

§62. *Difficulties in the concept of* εἴδωλον.

a) The essential determination of the εἴδωλον. The shaking of the rigid sense of Being in Parmenides by means of the phenomena of the εἴδωλον and ψεῦδος: the συμπλοκή of μὴ ὄν and ὄν in the sense of the εἶναί πως. Outlook: the κοινωνία τῶν γενῶν as the possibility of this συμπλοκή.

Thus the sophist has up to now remained completely protected against every assault. On the other hand, he himself has the possibility of mounting an assault, insofar as he is indeed the factually existing μὴ ὄν which speaks. We say of him that his τέχνη is τέχνη φανταστική (cf. 239c9f.), he is εἰδωλοποιός (cf. d3). Ἀντιλαμβανόμενος (d1f.), "he himself in a certain sense now takes us at our word": we are now supposed to give him an account of that which, according to our own consideration, cannot properly be spoken at all. If we call him εἰδωλοποιός, he will ask what we mean by εἴδωλον. And so the consideration comes back to the explication of the εἴδωλον; but it no longer stands on the same level as it did earlier. It is no longer a matter of merely demonstrating the factual existence of the εἴδωλον, i.e., of non-being. Now the task is to understand the εἴδωλον itself as such, i.e., to prepare an understanding of it. And indeed this is to be accomplished not in connection with a τέχνη μιμητική, drawing or painting, but specifically in regard to the ποιεῖν of the εἴδωλον within the actual τέχνη of the sophist. Hence the discussion of what the εἴδωλον is must now be conducted not in terms of the παράδειγμα but in relation to the sophist himself, whose τέχνη is λέγειν. That is, we must now make intelligible the meaning of εἴδωλα λέγειν or ψευδῆ λέγειν. Thus we have here no simple repetition of what came before, but instead the consideration now stands on an entirely different level.

This becomes clear from the fact that a methodological reflection is again inserted at 239dff., corresponding to the one at 227a. The ξένος lets Theaetetus be tripped up, as it were. He asks him: what would you answer if the sophist raises the question: τί ποτε τὸ παράπαν εἴδωλον; (239d3f.), "What then, in general, is an εἴδωλον?" Theaetetus says: It is quite clear, I would say an εἴδωλον is τὰ ἐν τοῖς ὕδασι or τὰ ἐν τοῖς κατόπτροις εἴδωλα, ἔτι καὶ τὰ γεγραμμένα καὶ τὰ τετυπωμένα καὶ τἆλλα ὅσα που τοιαῦτ' ἔσθ' ἕτερα (cf. d6ff.), "it is, e.g., reflections in the water, images in a mirror, what is drawn or painted, what is chiseled, what is printed, and other things like that." Theaetetus answers in this sense,[1] that he refers to concretely existing

1. AH: the "educated" one.

εἴδωλα. The ξένος responds: φανερὸς εἶ σοφιστὴν οὐχ ἑωρακώς (cf. e1); "Now you reveal yourself as one who obviously never saw a sophist." He means to say that Theaetetus does not at all understand what a sophist is really about. If you answer him in such a way, the sophist δόξει σοι μύειν ἢ παντάπασιν οὐκ ἔχειν ὄμματα (e3), "will present himself as someone whose eyes are closed, or indeed as someone who has no eyes at all." He will laugh at you, if you speak to him as someone who sees with eyes and if you refer him to such factually existent images. You mistake his question completely if you answer by offering him various sorts of images. Προσποιούμενος (e7), he will pose as someone who knows nothing at all about such things; he will say to you: I know nothing about mirror images, drawings, and the like. Instead, he will ask τὸ ἐκ τῶν λόγων μόνον (cf. 240a1f.), "exclusively about that which becomes visible through λόγοι." What does this mean: that which becomes visible through the λόγοι themselves and hence is seen even if one closes his eyes? What is visible in λέγειν is the λεγόμενον, that which something is addressed as. This is what is properly sought, what is properly at issue in speaking of images here. But this is not one particular thing or another; it is not what I see with sensible eyes. On the contrary, it is precisely that which provides to whatever is seen with those eyes its intelligibility, i.e., its utterability, so that I can address a mirror image or an image in water as an εἴδωλον. What is properly sought is hence not what Theaetetus is offering but τὸ διὰ πάντων τούτων (240a4), "that which in a certain sense permeates all these particulars," i.e., what is already present as Being in all these things. Or, as it is expressed at 253d5–6: μίαν ἰδέαν διὰ πολλῶν πάντῃ διατεταμένην, what is sought is "*one* aspect, which resides, is present, everywhere throughout the many." And the ξένος indicates clearly that Theaetetus has basically, without knowing it, something like that already in sight, ἠξίωσας ἑνὶ προσειπεῖν ὀνόματι φθεγξάμενος εἴδωλον ἐπὶ πᾶσιν ὡς ἓν ὄν (240a4ff.), "if you indeed believe you can προσειπεῖν, address, all these εἴδωλα ἑνὶ ὀνόματι, with one name." φθεγξάμενος εἴδωλον, "when you attribute εἴδωλον ἐπὶ πᾶσιν, to all these, you utter this word εἴδωλον ὡς ἓν ὄν, as if they were one." Thus in his way of addressing, one which is quite natural and obvious, in his spontaneous use of words, he has already, in a certain sense, meant a ἕν. And this is what the sophist means when he asks about the εἴδωλον. The question is hence about a self-sameness, about the self-same εἴδωλον versus the arbitrary succession of εἴδωλα in various concrete forms. In this way the ξένος first elevates Theaetetus to the genuinely correct methodological level. Thus it has become clear that the discussion of the εἴδωλον is not a matter of seeing with the sensible eyes but with the eyes of νοῦς. Perhaps—I do not know whether it is an artifice—this characterization of the sophist is at the same time meant ironically: e.g., when the ξένος says the sophist will laugh at Theaetetus if he takes him ὡς βλέποντι, as one who sees. For Plato is convinced that the sophist, with regard to genuine seeing in λόγος, is the truly blind one.

After the question of the τί of the εἴδωλον has been clarified, Theaetetus attempts to give an answer. εἴδωλον ἂν φαῖμεν εἶναι τὸ πρὸς τἀληθινὸν ἀφωμοιωμένον ἕτερον τοιοῦτον (cf. 240a8f.). Note well that this formulation of the determination of the εἴδωλον is marked by the occurrence in it of the expression ἕτερον, which later will go to form the actual solution to the basic difficulty in the question of the Being of non-beings. Theaetetus' formulation of the determination of the εἴδωλον is difficult to render in translation. I will take the statement apart. The εἴδωλον, image, is τὸ ἕτερον τοιοῦτον, "that which is another such thing," other, namely, than what is presented, yet thereby ἀφωμοιωμένον πρὸς τἀληθινόν, "like the actual being," like it in the sense of ἀφ-, ἀπό: as if it were, so to speak, "drawn from" it. This determination is not immediately intelligible, as is shown by the question the ξένος raises: Ἕτερον δὲ λέγεις τοιοῦτον ἀληθινόν, ἢ ἐπὶ τίνι τὸ τοιοῦτον εἶπες; (240a9f.). To what does this ἕτερον τοιοῦτον, this "another such thing," refer? To an ἀληθινόν, i.e., to another such actual being, or, if not, then to what? Theaetetus answers: Οὐδαμῶς ἀληθινόν γε, ἀλλ' ἐοικὸς μέν (b2), "By no means to an ἀληθινόν," yet it is not that this ἕτερον τοιοῦτον would altogether be unreal; on the contrary, in its very structure it is ἐοικός, "it looks like the true thing," it is similar to the ἀληθινόν. But the ξένος does not let up. Ἆρα τὸ ἀληθινὸν ὄντως ὂν λέγων; (b3): ἀληθινόν certainly means, does it not, ὄντως ὄν, being in the only way something can be, genuine Being? If, therefore, the εἴδωλον, i.e., the ἐοικός, is οὐδαμῶς ἀληθινόν, then it is μὴ ἀληθινόν (b5); that, however, is indeed ἐναντίον (ibid.), against, the opposite of, the ἀληθινόν. The opposite of true being, of the ὄντως ὄν, however, is obviously μὴ ὄν. Οὐκ ὄντως <οὐκ> ὂν ἄρα λέγεις τὸ ἐοικός, εἴπερ αὐτό γε μὴ ἀληθινὸν ἐρεῖς (240b7f.). "You thus address the ἐοικός, the image, as utter non-being, if indeed you name it the μὴ ἀληθινόν." The ξένος hence wants to elicit from Theaetetus the concession that the εἴδωλον, if indeed it is a ἕτερον to the ἀληθινόν, is the ἐναντίον of the ἀληθινόν and hence is οὐκ ὄν. Here lies the sophistry, namely in that the ξένος simply interprets the ἕτερον of the ἀληθινόν, or of ὄν, in the sense of an ἐναντίον to the ὄν, as μὴ ὄν.

Theaetetus, however, defends himself against this attempt to interpret the Being of the εἴδωλον as non-being; he emphasizes: Ἀλλ' ἔστι γε μήν πως (b9), "yet in some way it is indeed there!" The image in the water does exist! Theaetetus does not have a positive concept of the Being of the image, but he sees that the image is, specifically πώς, "in some way," in some sense. Thus he will not allow arguments to lead him away from what he sees. Οὔκουν ἀληθῶς (b10), the ξένος again objects: it is certainly not the presented being itself. Theaetetus, taking his orientation from what he sees, specifies: Οὐ γὰρ οὖν, "to be sure, it is not"; πλήν γ' εἰκὼν ὄντως (b11), "I am only saying that *as an image* it is real." It really is—as an image. The image is something, precisely as an image. And the image must be something, just in order for it to show itself and pose as that which it is not. Therefore, in fact, in some way or other it is: ἔστι πως. This εἶναί πως, however, as the further consideration will show, shakes the previous traditional sense of ὄν, the rigid sense of Parmenides. The first result of the fact that the image ἔστι πως is that we must grasp the image conceptually in this way: it is non-being and yet it is. Οὐκ ὂν ἄρα ὄντως ἐστὶν ὄντως (b12),[2] properly non-being, it is properly a being. This λόγος of the εἰκών, however, implies, it seems, a συμπλοκή of μὴ ὄν with ὄν. Κινδυνεύει τοιαύτην τινὰ πεπλέχθαι συμπλοκὴν τὸ μὴ ὂν τῷ ὄντι (c1f.). Here we have the proper phenomenon toward which the consideration now is headed: the συμπλοκή. If the image has a Being, we will maintain that non-beings can enter into a συμπλοκή with beings. This is something quite different from the mere contention that non-beings are.

This συμπλοκή becomes the guiding line for the further course of the consideration and at the same time is the phenomenon which will find its solution in the κοινωνία τῶν γενῶν. The κοινωνία τῶν γενῶν demonstrates the possibility of the συμπλοκή and, consequently, the possibility that there is something which is and yet is not.[3] In order to see the real questioning clearly, we must not take our orientation from the naked question of the Being of non-beings but from the συμπλοκή. Therefore I have also called attention to the fact that the expressions προσφέφειν, προσαρμόττειν, and προσαγορεύειν indicate that λέγειν has a determinate structure:[4] πρός, something to something, or, as we can say more precisely, to address something as something. Συμπλοκή is the expression for this peculiar character of λόγος as addressing: something as something. Is it at all possible that something can be addressed as something it itself is not? The question of the possibility of such a λόγος and of λόγος in general, the question of the possibility of addressing something as something, is grounded in the question of whether, in general, with regard to beings, there is something which can be other than what it itself is. Only if there is such a being, which can be something it is not, can there be a λόγος able to disclose this being. Thus the συμπλοκή at the same time orients us toward λόγος, a phenomenon we already brought to the forefront in our discussions of the sophist.

2. This reading occurs in Heidegger's manuscript. Burnet's reading: Οὐκ ὂν ἄρα <οὐκ> ὄντως ἐστὶν ὄντως.

3. AH: thereby proven: non-beings *are*.

4. Cf. p. 291f.

We are forced, says the ξένος, ὁμολογεῖν τὸ μὴ ὂν εἶναί πως (cf. 240c5), "to concede that non-beings are in some sense or other."[5] But if they are possible, then it may also be possible for something like an εἴδωλον, a ψεῦδος, to exist. In that case, however, there may also possibly be something like an ἀπατᾶν (240d1), a deceiving, a working with εἴδωλα, i.e., with an ὂν which is μὴ ὄν. Then there can also be a ψευδὴς δόξα (cf. d6). At first, this possibility is quite problematic (240d–e). The discussion is still on such a level that the ξένος can ask: ψευδὴς δόξα indeed means to have an opinion, to be of an opinion, about something which is in itself deceptive, a τὰ ψευδῆ δοξάζειν; and this τὰ ψευδῆ δοξάζειν is indeed the same as τὰ ἐναντία τοῖς οὖσι δοξάζειν (cf. d6f.), such that the ψευδὴς δόξα is the same as τὰ μὴ ὄντα δοξάζειν (d9), is it not?

The theme of δόξα, as ψευδὴς δόξα, is, accordingly, the nothing. But Theaetetus resists this conclusion: Εἶναί πως τὰ μὴ ὄντα δεῖ γε, εἴπερ ψεύσεταί ποτέ τίς τι καὶ κατὰ βραχύ (e3f.). Μὴ ὄν, which, as ψεῦδος, is the theme of a ψευδὴς δόξα, is not the nothing, but is μὴ ὂν which in some sense is. Λόγος as ψευδὴς λόγος, or δόξα as ψευδὴς δόξα, involves the saying, or the addressing, of a non-being as a being, or of a being as not being. λόγος ψευδὴς νομισθήσεται τά τε ὄντα λέγων μὴ εἶναι καὶ τὰ μὴ ὄντα εἶναι (cf. 240e10f.). For this is the character of what we call a false assertion: to proffer a being as not being or a non-being as being. Notice that Plato is still using the expression λόγος in a quite preliminary way and in an undifferentiated sense, such that λόγος here simply means to address something as something. We had better leave out completely the term "judgment," which even in logic is ambiguous enough. Toward the end of the dialogue, Plato offers a determination of λόγος which comes close to Aristotle's.[6] I have already emphasized that the συμπλοκή is the phenomenon on which the ontological consideration, in the strict sense, focuses, that the problem of the συμπλοκή is solved by the κοινωνία, and that only on the basis of the κοινωνία is it possible for a λόγος to be a ψευδὴς λόγος. In a certain sense, Plato grasps this state of affairs of ψευδὴς λόγος from the outside, namely in such a way that he sees therein a συμπλοκή of λόγος with ψεῦδος, where the ψεῦδος is a μὴ ὂν and the λόγος an ὄν. Thus he sees in the ψευδὴς λόγος a συμπλοκή of ψεῦδος as μὴ ὂν with λόγος as ὄν.[7] Therefore it is too early for an interpretation that would already attempt to elucidate the phenomenon of imposture or deception phenomenally. We will see later that Plato does not at all enter into the dimension of a so-called intrinsic philosophical consideration of λόγος and of ψεῦδος but proceeds

5. See the appendix.
6. 261c–262e. Λόγος is determined as a συμπλοκή of ὄνομα and ῥῆμα (especially 262d4).
7. See especially 260a.

in such a way that he resolves the possibility of the Being of a λόγος ψευδής by means of a formal-ontological consideration, as is shown toward the end of the dialogue. On the other hand, in order to show the difference in kind between this and the contemporary way of questioning, we will now submit the phenomenon of deception to a closer investigation.[8]

b) Determination of the proper task: the revision of the principle of Parmenides. The modification of the meaning of Being.

His counter-question has placed the sophist in a safe position. For the ξένος and Theaetetus cannot take hold of him in their discussions so long as they have not surmounted the barrier which they constantly come up against, namely the principle of Parmenides, which is designated at 241c as ἰσχυρὸς λόγος (cf. c9), a principle that is strong, i.e., difficult to get the better of. Before taking up the proper solution of the ontological problem, the ξένος makes three requests of Theaetetus:

1.) He asks him to be satisfied if they succeed only "to a very small extent," κατὰ βραχύ (241c8), in freeing themselves from this forceful principle of Parmenides. He requests Theaetetus thus not to expect too much.

2.) A still more urgent request is not to believe that his attack on the principle of Parmenides will make him a πατραλοίας (cf. 241d3), a parricide. For the ξένος is indeed from Elea and so is directing his attack against his own spiritual father. He emphasizes: we *must* ἀναγκαῖον ἡμῖν . . . βιάζεσθαι (d5f.), penetrate with knowledge: τό τε μὴ ὂν ὡς ἔστι κατά τι καὶ τὸ ὂν αὖ πάλιν ὡς οὐκ ἔστι πῃ (241d6f.). It is significant that this formulation does not simply say τὸ μὴ ὂν ὡς ἔστι but τό μὴ ὂν ὡς ἔστι κατά τι, in a certain respect non-beings are, and not simply: τὸ ὂν ὡς οὐκ ἔστι, but ὡς οὐκ ἔστι πῃ, beings are πῃ, in a certain respect, not. Thus we do not have here a radical opposing of non-being and Being or a συμπλοκή of both, as was the case up to now, but instead: τὸ ὂν ὡς οὐκ ἔστι πῃ, i.e., ὄν is *not*, yet not in the sense of the μὴ ὄν, but differently; and μὴ ὂν *is*, yet not in the sense of ὄν, but differently, ὡς ἔστι κατά τι. This implies, however, a modification of the meaning of Being in general. That is the genuine theme. The question of μὴ ὄν is ultimately reduced to the question of Being, and that is why the tradition has a certain justification in giving the dialogue the subtitle: "Περὶ τοῦ ὄντος," "About Being." The ξένος repeats: as long as we have not overcome this principle we are not capable λέγειν περὶ λόγων ψευδῶν ἢ δόξης, εἴτε εἰδώλων εἴτε εἰκόνων εἴτε μιμημάτων εἴτε

8. See the appendix, p. 455: "From the notes of Simon Moser."

φαντασμάτων αὐτῶν, ἢ καὶ περὶ τεχνῶν τῶν ὅσαι περὶ ταῦτά εἰσι (cf. 241e2ff.). The ξένος says we must press on: τὸ μὴ ὂν ὡς ἔστι κατά τι. Only if we succeed can we assert something about δόξα, i.e., about the δοξαστικὴ τέχνη, about εἴδωλον or εἰδωλοποιική, about εἰκών, μίμημα, φάντασμα. All these phenomena will remain obscure as long as the principle of Parmenides remains unshaken. Only if we are actually able to deal with δόξα, εἴδωλον, and εἰκών in a way that accords with the matters themselves will we be able to discuss the τέχνη related to them, i.e., to genuinely grasp the sophist.

3.) He asks Theaetetus not to think he is deranged, μανικός (242a11), if he now sets out to solve this difficult question, whereas previously (239b1–3) he had said he always considered himself inadequate to take up this principle of Parmenides.

Chapter Two

Difficulties in the Concept of Beings.[1] The Discussion of the Ancient and Contemporary Doctrines of ὄν[2] (242b–250e)

Introduction

§63. The point of departure for the solution of the task: the discussion of the ancient and contemporary doctrines of ὄν.

a) General characterization of Plato's and Aristotle's confrontation with the "ancients." Aristotle's solidification of the concept of ἀρχή. The elaboration of the "milieu" (λόγος) as the center of the development of Greek ontology.

The question now is how the discussion of the principle of Parmenides is supposed to mount its attack. We have seen in the formulation at 241d that non-beings, in a certain sense, *are* and that beings, in a certain sense, *are not*. Thus the proper theme is Being. It is therefore that the substantive discussion begins with an account of what has previously been thought and said about this question, and indeed τὰ δοκοῦντα νῦν ἐναργῶς ἔχειν ἐπισκέψασθαι πρῶτον (242b10f.), "what we want to examine first is precisely what seems to be wholly transparent." It is precisely the obvious, the seemingly transparent, which is to be the theme. The ξένος recalls that Parmenides, as well as everyone else who set out to deal with beings, did so without great claims to rigor, εὐκόλως (242c4). What was it these ancients were seeking methodologically in their treatment of beings? διορίσασθαι <τὰ ὄντα> πόσα τε καὶ ποῖά ἐστιν (cf. c5f.); they sought "to delimit beings: how many beings are there and how are they constituted?" That was the question of the ancients: what is the number of beings and what is their constitution? The question is formulated here in a very careful way. It genuinely touches the question of the ancients and so is superior to the formulation of Aristotle, who indeed carries out a similar consideration in the first Book of the *Physics* as well as in other writings.[3] But Aristotle posits

1. Title in Heidegger's manuscript (see p. 161f., the articulation of the *Sophist*).
2. Title based on Heidegger (see p. 304).
3. See p. 302.

the central question of the ancients to be the question of the ἀρχή—ἀρχή as conceptually formulated in terms of his own position—which, however, does not so faithfully render the mode of questioning of the ancient φυσιολόγοι. Aristotle's investigation of the questioning of the ancients is thus sharper and more violent, insofar as the ancients did not possess Aristotle's precise concept of ἀρχή but instead used ἀρχή ontically, in the sense of mere beginning, and not ontologically. The ancients tried to clarify and to make intelligible beings, i.e., φύσις in a broad sense—what is already there—by deducing them from particular beings. Parmenides, to be sure, already made a first advance: he considers beings as such, i.e., he sets apart the whole of beings in an ontic sense and says that "they are." There is as yet no guiding line for the question of Being. Still, even in the naive endeavors of the ancients there is already a tendency toward definite ontological structures. In his rendering of the ancients' question of ὄν, Plato does not employ the term ἀρχή. The word has no terminological significance for him. Plato's mode of questioning is much more appropriate to the undeveloped questioning of the ancients.

Plato thus prepares his discussion of ὄν by confronting the previous age. Such confrontations can be found in Aristotle in manifold forms: *Physics,* Book I; *Metaphysics,* Book I; *De generatione et corruptione,* Book I. These three confrontations with history are all different, according to the respective thematic question. In the *Physics,* this is the intention to show κίνησις as determinative of the φύσει ὄντα. They are the ground on which the question of the ἀρχαί is posed. They are the phenomena from which the ἀρχαί are to be read off. The question of the ἀρχαί of the φύσει ὄντα thereby rules this discussion of the ancients. Moreover, Aristotle already takes the concept of φύσις in a completely determinate sense, one elaborated by him himself, whereas, for the ancients, φύσις has a broader meaning, namely the one which gets conceptually fixed later, precisely by Aristotle, in the term οὐσία. For the ancients, φύσις is that which is always already there.[4] Even Aristotle, in the *Metaphysics,* still at times uses φύσις in the sense of οὐσία, e.g., in *Metaphysics,* Γ, chapter 1. Alongside it, there can also be found in Aristotle the specific concept of φύσις as ἀρχὴ κινήσεως, elaborated in the second Book of the *Physics.* In the *Metaphysics,* Aristotle is not asking about the φύσει ὄντα but about the ὂν ᾗ ὄν. He is asking about the ἀρχαί in general, with the intention of acquiring the structure of ὄν itself, which is not only φύσει ὄν. Therefore, in the *Metaphysics,* the discussion of the ancients aims at the fundamental question of how many ἀρχαί or αἰτίαι in general can be exposed in the course of research. Aristotle distinguishes four kinds of

4. AH: Cf. SS 1930, WS 1929–30, *Einleitung über Seinsfrage.*

causes; three of them are supposed to have been discovered by the ancients, and the fourth, the proper one, is then established by him. Finally, in *De generatione et corruptione*, Aristotle inquires into the στοιχεῖα, which are themselves quite particular ἀρχαί within the φύσει ὄντα. And that is the reason ἀρχή, αἴτιον, and στοιχεῖον are occasionally identical in meaning for Aristotle, but only in a formal sense; taken strictly, they are tailored for particular realms of Being. This confrontation with the ancients is, in all three ways Aristotle carries it out, different from the Platonic one, since Aristotle already had a univocal, even if not radically conceived, basis for the ontological mode of questioning, acquired not without the preliminary work of Plato himself.

The development of Greek ontology does not proceed to a collection of ontological results in the sense of a heaping up of newfound categories. On the contrary, its proper work is concentrated upon the elaboration of the milieu in which ontological research can move in general. Here is the proper center of Greek research. Only if we learn to understand this, will there exist the prospect of making our past productive again. Parmenides begins the elaboration of the milieu from which the question of the Being of beings can be raised. This peculiar foundational research was not, for the Greeks, explicit as such, but in fact their work moved just as much in the field of λόγος as in that of ὄν. Specifically, λόγος is, for Greek ontological research, the way of access to the Being of beings. This does not mean, however, that Greek ontology is dependent on "logic";[5] we would first have to ask what logic was for the Greeks, and we may not impute to them the modern concept of logic. Plato's critique of the previous age has the intention of carrying out the ontological over and against the ontic, the categorial explication of Being over and against an ontic description of beings, i.e., of making this ontological research visible for the first time in its basic parts. For it was indeed an unheard of discovery to see Being over and against beings, though, to be sure, Parmenides, who himself was not clear about it, took the first step in this direction with the seemingly trivial principle: beings are. This principle places him fundamentally beyond beings in the sense of a description.[6]

The historical consideration Plato prefixes to his proper dialectical discussion is meant to confront not only all the previous philosophies but the one of his contemporaries as well. The consideration thereby acquires a clear articulation.

5. AH: But "logic" precisely from onto-logy; the "logy" more original than logic.
6. AH: of beings through beings.

b) The articulation of the discussion of the ancient and contemporary doctrines of ὄν.

The discussion of the ancient and contemporary doctrines of ὄν extends from 242c to 250e.

1.) The discussion begins, at 242c–243d, with a general characterization of the first ontological attempts.

2.) There follows at 243d–244b a proper critical consideration of those ὅσοι πλεῖον ἑνὸς λέγουσι τὸ πᾶν εἶναι (244b2f.), who address beings as something manifold rather than one, who therefore say beings are manifold.

3.) The passage at 244b–245c discusses those οἱ ἓν λέγοντες (cf. b6), who say beings are only one, i.e., the Eleatics.

4.) The passage at 246a–250e deals with the contemporary doctrines of Being; Plato speaks of a γιγαντομαχία περὶ τῆς οὐσίας (cf. 246a4f.), a battle of the giants over Being. There are two factions. First, those who say οὐσία = σῶμα or γένεσις, Being is body, becoming (246e–248a). The other faction (Euclid and the Megarians) says: οὐσία = εἴδη (248a–250e). This is a position to which Plato was once close but which he now no longer holds. That is already manifest, entirely apart from what follows substantively, by the peculiar characterization at 246c, where Plato says: between these two, the ones who say οὐσία = σῶμα and those who say οὐσία = εἶδος, ἐν μέσῳ δὲ περὶ ταῦτα ἄπλετος ἀμφοτέρων μάχη τις (246c2f.), "between them, in their midst, there rages an endless battle." This μέσον between them is a battle place, but it is also the place of a decision. For the solution of the question resides for Plato precisely in resolving the unilaterality of each position and acquiring a perspective for a concept of Being on the basis of which both positions may become intelligible.

I. The Discussion of the Ancient Doctrines of ὄν (242c–245c)

§64. General characterization of the first ontological attempts[1] *(242c–243c). Sketch of the theses about* ὄν. Μῦθον διηγεῖσθαι. *Predelineation of Plato's procedure: elevation into the ontological dimension.*

The historical consideration begins with a general characterization of the ancients. This characterization bears a somewhat superior and ironic tone, which, however, should not seduce us into taking it as a mere game. We will see later that only this basis—insofar as we acquire the correct way of questioning for the interpretation—makes intelligible the entire path Greek ontological research had to traverse in order to arrive at the foundation Aristotle himself firmly established. Μῦθόν τινα ἕκαστος φαίνεταί μοι διηγεῖσθαι (242c8): "It seems that each of these ancients is telling us a story about beings," and indeed παισὶν ὡς οὖσιν (c8f.), "as if we were children." This says that the ancients, insofar as they dealt with *Being,* told stories about *beings,* said what happens to beings. Hence the ancients did not at all arrive at a position from which they could determine something about the Being of beings. If, e.g., they said τρία τὰ ὄντα, then they were selecting definite beings, ones which had an emphatic sense for them, and they explained beings out of beings. This is the sense of their "telling stories"; i.e., they moved naively in the dimension of beings and did not at all enter into the dimension of the *Being* of beings.

1.) ὁ μέν, the one, says: τρία τὰ ὄντα (242c9), beings are three. The historiographical attribution of these various conceptions to individual schools and movements is not wholly unanimous, at least where definite names are not mentioned. And so it is uncertain who this ὁ μέν is, the one who says beings are three. Zeller[2] conjectures it is Pherecydes, who, to be sure, proposed a characteristic threefold as the proper beings, namely Zeus or the heaven, Chronos or time, and Chthon, the earth. I cannot get involved here in a detailed characterization; the sources are meager as well. In his *Psyche,*[3] Rhode has dealt profusely with the very early speculative contexts. The three of this threefold, which exist in themselves, are not determined

1. Title based on Heidegger (see p. 304).
2. Eduard Zeller, *Die Philosophie der Griechen*. Erster Teil, Erste Hälfte, 7. Aufl., Leipzig, 1923, pp. 102–105.
3. Erwin Rohde, *Psyche: Seelenkult und Unsterblichkeitsglaube der Griechen*. Erste Hälfte, Freiburg i. Brsg., 1890; Zweite Hälfte, Freiburg i. Brsg, 1894. In particular, in the second edition of 1898, second half, Rohde treats the Orphians (pp. 103–136) and philosophy (pp. 137–192).

narrowly but are conceived in the sense of human comportments. That is precisely what makes this a myth. They wage war among themselves, at times they battle, and at times they even love each other; and there is also γάμος, τόκος, τροφή (cf. d1f.), marriage, birth, and child-rearing.

2.) ἕτερος εἰπών (d3), "another says," beings are not three but two, ὑγρὸν καὶ ξηρόν, "the wet and the dry" or θερμὸν καὶ ψυχρόν (d3), "the warm and the cold." You see here again that what is addressed as Being in the proper sense is something that shows itself in a naive consideration, in purely sensible perception, i.e., definite qualities of beings themselves.

3.) The Eleatics, Xenophanes and his disciples, say: ἓν ὂν τὰ πάντα (cf. d5f.), "everything that is is one."

4.) The Muses of Ionia and Sicily, i.e., Heraclitus of Ephesus and Empedocles of Agrigentum, say: τὸ ὂν πολλά τε καὶ ἕν ἐστιν (e1f.), "beings are many as well as one." They hence put together what the earlier philosophers said: many and one. The Ionic muses are more severe, insofar as they maintain διαφερόμενον ἀεὶ συμφέρεται (cf. e2f.), the whole is constantly in conflict and in a movement of transition from the ἕν to the πολλά and vice versa; in Heraclitus, τὸ πᾶν is constantly in flames. The others, the Sicilian muses, are gentler, insofar as they allow a periodic rest and say: τοτὲ μὲν ἓν εἶναι τὸ πᾶν καὶ φίλον (cf. e5), sometimes the whole dwells in friendship, under the power of Aphrodite, the power of love, but τοτὲ δὲ πολλὰ καὶ πολέμιον (243a1), soon again τὸ πᾶν is πολλά, dissolved into many and at war, διὰ νεῖκος (a1).

The ξένος claims it is difficult to decide whether or not these ancients have in fact hit the mark or not. But one thing is certain, they dealt with their theme in such a way that in a certain sense they spoke beyond our grasp, οὐδὲν γὰρ φροντίσαντες εἴτ' ἐπακολουθοῦμεν αὐτοῖς λέγουσιν εἴτε ἀπολειπόμεθα (a7f.): "They were not at all concerned whether what they said would be intelligible for us, whether we could follow it or would have to remain behind." Upon closer inspection, this means that the ancients did not take into account the necessity of a discussion to be demonstrable, that οἱ πολλοὶ ἡμεῖς (cf. a6), we or others, have to understand them, that therefore such speaking about beings must be placed in check. That is, it must be possible to speak with others about the matter, such that everyone sees the things themselves as they are and does not simply have to look for the things in isolation, in arbitrary wild speculation. Hence what they have overlooked is *logos*, the criterion of an objective and substantive demonstrability and communicability in their treatment of things. They were just "telling stories," without a proper *logos*. The ξένος concedes that earlier, as a young man, he himself had believed he would understand these ancient doctrines; now, however, he has come into great difficulty and no longer believes he can understand them. With this remark at 243b, the ξένος is referring to the thought expressed at 234d, that many in the school of the sophists at first believe they understand and know everything, but that when they come near the things and actually try to grasp them, their complete ignorance is exposed. These discussions of the ancients about Being are hence altogether problematic, so that we find ourselves in the same difficulty as much in relation to ὄν as in relation to μὴ ὄν. Therefore we are led περὶ δὲ τοῦ μεγίστου τε καὶ ἀρχηγοῦ πρώτου νῦν σκεπτέον (243d1), "to begin a consideration of what is the greatest and what is properly first," i.e., of ὄν, and to ask τί ἡγοῦνται τὸ ὄν, "what do they maintain about beings," οἱ λέγοντες δηλοῦν αὐτό (cf. d4f.), i.e., those "who say they can reveal and exhibit them."

Here the genuine critical consideration begins. It reverts back to the positions characterized only very roughly in the preceding account but does so now in such a way as to take these positions seriously for the first time. Initially, the consideration deals with that school which professes ὄν is manifold. In the course of the critical consideration, Plato shows that those who say beings are manifold, τὰ ὄντα πλέονα ἑνός (cf. 245b8f.), use, without knowing it, in their speaking of a manifold of beings, a ἕν, a determinate sense of Being, which they do not themselves investigate at all. The δύο λέγοντες are thus led back to a ἕν. In connection with this, Plato discusses the ἕν of the Eleatics and shows that this ἕν is again insufficient to determine ὄν; it requires a πλεῖον. This, however, is not a simple return to the first position. On the contrary, the first ones who spoke about beings spoke about them *ontically:* there are manifold *beings*. Versus this, the Eleatics say there is *one Being*. But Plato says no, there must be a *manifold Being*. Over and against the manifold beings it is now a question of a manifoldness in Being itself. And this indicates that the position of Parmenides was no longer by any means a naive and ontical one but rather was the very first decisive inception of ontology, even if the entire body of this ontology resides in the principle: beings are. Yet this principle, in its philosophical attitude, is essentially superior to all the positions which claim that beings consist of many beings or of one being, for these positions do not at all succeed in raising the question of Being. In this way, the passage through the Eleatic position at the same time provides the possibility of bringing the question into the properly ontological domain and of discussing, on this basis, the γιγαντομαχία περὶ τῆς οὐσίας.

§65. The discussion of the thesis of the multiplicity of ὄν (243d–44b). Uncovering of εἶναι as unfinished task. Critique of today's "ontological" attempts: the forgetting of the question of the meaning of Being. Toward the elaboration of this question on the ground of a hermeneutic of Dasein.

Plato carries out his critique of the earlier age under the guiding line of the λέγειν τὰ ὄντα. That is why he asks at 243d: τὸ ὂν τί ποθ' ἡγοῦνται, "what then do they maintain beings are," οἱ λέγοντες αὐτὸ δηλοῦν (d3f.), "those who say they can reveal them?" The ξένος and Theaetetus agree that they should proceed by interrogating the ancients as if they were themselves present. Φέρε . . . δύο . . . τὰ πάντ' εἶναί φατε (d8f.): "You say everything would have its Being from two things," from the warm and the cold, or the like; to put it in a better way, beings in the proper sense, you say, are two. Thus you say ἄμφω καὶ ἑκάτερον εἶναι (e1f.), "both and each of the two are, εἶναι"; λέγοντες—notice the λέγειν—"you address both, as well as the one and the other respectively, as being." And now the question: τί ποτε ἄρα τοῦτ' ἐπ' ἀμφοῖν φθέγγεσθε (d9f.), "what is and what do you mean by this that you attribute to both of these here?" τί τὸ εἶναι τοῦτο ὑπολάβωμεν ὑμῶν; (e2): "What should we actually understand by this εἶναι of yours?"

The ξένος suggests three possible positions:

1.) Either the εἶναι, of which you speak in relation to ἄμφω, is a "third," τρίτον (e2), beside both the proper ὄντα. Is it in accord with your meaning if we then say, not as you say, τὸ πᾶν δύο, but τὸ πᾶν τρία (cf. e3)?

2.) Or, on the other hand, τοῖν γε δυοῖν καλοῦντες θάτερον ὂν (e4f.), you call one of the two, the θερμόν or the ψυχρόν, the genuine being. But then: οὐ . . . ἀμφότερα ὁμοίως εἶναι λέγετε (e4f.). Whichever of the two you identify with ὄν, you always arrive at a one, ἕν, not a δύο (e6).

3.) You want to address both, τὰ ἄμφω, as ὄν (e8). But even then, there will reside in your λέγειν a ἓν λεγόμενον, namely ὄν itself (244a1f.).

Notice this threefold possibility the ξένος poses to the ancients: the question is always what is said in λέγειν δύο τὰ ὄντα, hence what is said in λόγος. Either this comes down to a three or a one. In every case, we are forced to co-posit ὄν, insofar as, in each case, the λέγειν of ὄν co-posits the εἶναι. What is decisive is the critique on the basis of λέγειν. Plato's aim is not at all, as commentators claim, to create a "monism" by emphasizing the ἕν. The ἕν is of no consequence to him. What does matter to him is the demonstration that ὄν resides in λέγειν implicitly yet constitutively. Plato thus does not want to argue his opponents to death, but he wants to open their eyes and show them that in λέγειν, in all speaking about beings, something else is co-said. And this "something else" is no less than Being itself. In other words, Plato shows thereby that the answer δύο εἶναι τὰ πάντα does not at all touch the question of Being. I said the traditional interpretation, of Zeller, Bonitz,[1] etc., misses the actual matter at issue. It is not at all necessary to analyze the rest of the substantive question here. For the proper theme of this investigation is made abundantly clear at 244a. Ἐπειδὴ τοίνυν ἡμεῖς ἠπορήκαμεν, ὑμεῖς αὐτὰ ἡμῖν ἐμφανίζετε ἱκανῶς, τί ποτε βούλεσθε σημαίνειν ὁπόταν ὂν φθέγγησθε (a4ff.). "Because we do not know any way out as regards what you are saying here, you yourself must clarify for us what you properly mean when you utter this word ὄν." *That is the genuinely central concern of this passage and of the whole dialogue.*

Today we witness an ostensible return to metaphysics and ontology. But the question Plato raises here and poses by means of the whole dialogue has, in all haste, been forgotten. This forgetting of the main question is easy for us today. For we can appeal, either explicitly or silently, to two things:

1.) The concept of Being is obvious; everyone uses it constantly and understands what he means by it.

2.) The concept of Being is the highest; therefore it cannot at all be defined.

As to the first, we must remark that apart from the question of whether the supposed universal obviousness of the meaning of Being may or may not be identified with the clarity of a philosophical concept, in any case it is precisely this obviousness, and nothing else, that is the theme of the fundamental science.

As to the second, we must remark that it has not been decided whether the conceptual elaboration of the fundamental concepts may be posed under the rules that determine a definition, which itself presents only one form of determination, the one originating in a certain propositional and assertorial "logic." The "logic" of the determination of beings may not be invoked as the criterion for the explication of Being. Therefore the usual talk about the indefinability of Being means nothing. It merely manifests the common misunderstanding of what is at issue.

With regard to the primary task of any possible ontology, it must be said positively that it resides precisely in the *preparation*, in the preparation of a ground to ask about the meaning of Being in general. The question of the meaning of Being—what Being means in general, in the sense of the proposition from Plato cited above—is not somehow the final question of ontology, and this question cannot be answered by a summation of ontological results. On the contrary, the question of the meaning of Being stands at the beginning, because it must provide guidance as to the possible meaning in any concrete

1. Eduard Zeller, *Die Philosophie der Griechen*. Zweiter Teil, Erste Abteilung, 5. Aufl., Leipzig, 1922, pp. 648–649.
Hermann Bonitz, *Platonische Studien*, 3. Aufl., Berlin, 1886, pp. 161–164.

question about the particular ontological structure of various beings. On the other hand, it is not sufficient to raise the question of Being formally, i.e., to intend to answer it just as formally. Instead, the task is to understand that this questioning, of the meaning of Being, itself requires an elaboration, an elaboration of the ground upon which the interrogation of beings as to their Being is at all possible. We need to uncover and elaborate the *milieu* in which ontological research can and has to move in general. Without the disclosure and rigorous elaboration of this milieu, ontology remains no better than the epistemological theory of the Neokantianism of the past. To raise the question of the meaning of Being does not mean anything else than to elaborate the questioning involved in philosophy in general.

We can now clarify this questioning only briefly and in formal traits, to the extent that it is necessary for an understanding of what will follow. All questioning *[Fragen]* is an interrogating *[Befragen]* of something in some respect. In ontology, beings are the interrogated. The questioning of beings is directed toward their Being. Being is hence that which is asked about *[das Erfragte]*. And what is asked for *[das Gefragte]* in ontological research are the ontological characters of this Being itself. The questioning itself is hence, in its very sense, already a determinate discovering and disclosing. Every question already has a particular disclosive character. There is no blind question, with the exception of the one that it is blindly expressed, bruited about, and repeated, and hence is no longer understood. The questioning is nothing other than the expressed and communicated question in which what is asked about, what is interrogated, and what is asked for are implicitly co-expressed, in such a way that they do not thereby become visible directly and without further ado. (A question can be understood roughly as a problem, without the necessity of having to appropriate its meaning.) This is hence what is involved in a question about the Being of beings. That implies it is decisive for such questioning that the beings to be interrogated are available. Thus it is a matter of gaining the correct original mode of access to the appropriate domain of Being and establishing, within this mode of access, the guiding respect, according to which the question of the Being of beings is to be posed. This guiding respect is, for the Greeks, for Plato and Aristotle, λόγος. And thus Plato's entire criticism of the traditional and contemporary doctrines of Being, as well as his positive discussion of Being, move in this λέγειν. Therefore ontology for Plato is διαλέγεσθαι and dialectic—which has nothing to do with the hocus pocus of contradictions in today's sense, or with dialectic in Hegel. So much, then, for a characterization of the question: what then do you mean when you say "Being"? (244a5f.).[2]

2. See the appendix.

The ξένος emphasizes once more at 244b: this question we are posing to the ancients, the question of the meaning of Being, in which we simply demand instruction from them as to what they meant, is obviously justified (b3f.). Possibly we will receive a response the soonest from those whose answer is most concentrated, namely those who say: ἓν εἶναι τὸ πᾶν (cf. 244b6). Thus the discussion turns to the thesis of Parmenides. The formulation of the thesis of Parmenides varies; even Aristotle (*Phys.*, A, chapters 2 and 3) does not express it consistently. The discussion of Parmenides is articulated into two parts:

1.) Discussion of ὄν as ἕν (244b9–244d13).

2.) Discussion of ὄν as ὅλον, which is here still identical with πᾶν (244d14–245e5).

§66. The discussion of the thesis of the unity of ὄν *(244b–245a).*

a) The discussion of ὄν as ἕν. The discrepancy between the meaning of the thesis and its linguistic expression. Ὑπόθεσις and "hypothesis."

We can formulate the principle of Parmenides briefly this way: ἓν ὂν τὸ πᾶν (ὅλον). Thus if we ask the Eleatics what they really mean, what their opinion is about beings, they will answer: ἓν ὂν τὸ πᾶν. But then, we will object, do they not also use the expression ὄν for "something," ὂν καλεῖτέ τι; (b12), namely for precisely the ὅπερ ἕν (c1), which they always mean by ἕν? What they mean at the very outset and constantly by ἕν is what they express at the same time as ὄν. ἐπὶ τῷ αὐτῷ προσχρώμενοι δυοῖν ὀνόμασιν (c1f.): "So you then use two expressions with regard to the same thing, ἐπὶ τῷ αὐτῷ." They address one and the same thing in the ὄνομα ἕν and in the ὄνομα ὄν. The ξένος concedes: τῷ ταύτην τὴν ὑπόθεσιν ὑποθεμένῳ πρὸς τὸ νῦν ἐρωτηθὲν καὶ πρὸς ἄλλο δὲ ὁτιοῦν οὐ πάντων ῥᾷστον ἀποκρίνασθαι (c4ff.). "He who begins this way—namely by saying: ἓν μόνον εἶναι—does not easily find an answer to the question now raised and also to something else." He who professes this thesis of Parmenides is constantly in perplexity as regards his answer. For whatever might be said or questioned in relation to the ἕν (which alone is) is something and, as such, is something other than the ἕν. And yet the thesis is ἓν εἶναι. The ξένος thus recognizes the fundamental difficulty residing in this ὑπόθεσις, ἓν ὂν τὸ πᾶν, for every discussion.

We may not translate or understand this ὑποτίθεσθαι ὑπόθεσιν in the sense of "making a hypothesis." A hypothesis, in our modern sense, is the assumption of a state of affairs so as to ask: if we assume the facts of the matter to be such and such, does this or that then become intelligible? The hypothetical remains, according to its very sense, precisely in suspense; it acquires its possible rest and genuine persistence only from the measure of its appropriateness to the explanation of given facts. A hypothesis persists only by the grace of what it explains and to the extent it does explain it; the failure of this explanatory function collapses the hypothesis. The Greek ὑπόθεσις, e.g. in Plato's sense, has the opposite meaning. That which is posited in the ὑπόθεσις is not posited by the grace of something else. The ὑπόθεσις does not persist depending on this other it is supposed to explain but, instead, on the basis of itself as that which from the very outset persists in itself. It is that which exclusively decides the possible Being or non-being of everything else. An example is Parmenides' didactic poem itself, i.e., the principle: beings are. This ὑπόθεσις is not ruled by the "if . . . then"; on the contrary, the ὑπό is to be taken in the sense of ὑποκείμενον and ὑπάρχον: that which is already there in itself at the very outset, what the ancients called φύσις. I emphasize this distinction between ὑπόθεσις and hypothesis precisely because recently attempts have been made to interpret Brentano and, in the usual connection with Brentano, phenomenology as philosophies of the as-if, as fictionalisms, as though Brentano had converted to Vaihinger.[1] Thus Kraus, e.g., says in the wretched new edition of the *Psychologie vom empirischen Standpunkt*, that Brentano and phenomenology are nothing else than fictionalism.[2] The philosophy of the as-if, to the extent there is anything to it at all, lives only on the confusion of the meaning of ontical hypothesis and ontological ὑπόθεσις. If phenomenological research has any relation to Plato at all, then that relation certainly resides in what we have exposed here as the sense of the Greek ὑπόθεσις. We may not transform phenomenology into epistemology and interpret it as concerned with the conditions of possible experience, although this interpretation is essentially closer to the matter itself than the one just mentioned.

If the Eleatics say ἓν ὄν τὸ πᾶν, they are using for one and the same thing the ὄνομα ἕν as well as the ὄνομα ὄν. Thereupon, however, the ξένος says, δύο ὀνόματα ὁμολογεῖν εἶναι μηδὲν θέμενον πλὴν ἕν (244c8f.), those who say: ἓν ὄν, everything that is is one, are thereby actually maintaining there are *two* names, namely ἕν and ὄν, for one thing. Furthermore, they face a still greater difficulty, insofar as we consider in general the fact that they *speak* about beings or Being. And we do not at all need to go back to λόγος, which indeed, as Plato later analyzes, is a συμπλοκή of ὄνομα and ῥῆμα.[3]

1. Hans Vaihinger, *Die Philosophie des Als-Ob*, Berlin, 1911.

2. Oskar Kraus, *Einleitung zu F. Brentano: Psychologie vom empirischen Standpunkt*, Hamburg, 1924, pp. liv–lv.

3. 261d–262e, especially 262c.

Already in the ὄνομα itself, which is but one component of λόγος, the trouble with this position is visible. The ὄνομα, precisely as ὄνομα, as expression, is supposed to be an expression *of* something; the ὄνομα signifies something, and indeed something the ὄνομα itself is not, a ἕτερον. Τιθείς τε τοὔνομα τοῦ πράγματος ἕτερον δύο λέγει (244d3f.); hence already in the ὄνομα of something, in a signification that means something, they are saying two ὄντα. If they wanted to identify the ὄνομα and the δηλούμενον, the expression and what is meant in it, made visible in it, then indeed the expression would be an expression of nothing. Or else, if the ὄνομα is still supposed to be an ὄνομα τινός, an expression of something, yet without thereby referring to something other than itself, then τὸ ὄνομα ὀνόματος ὄνομα μόνον, ἄλλου δὲ οὐδενὸς ὄν (244d8f.), "this ὄνομα could only be an ὀνόματος ὄνομα but not the ὄνομα of something else." Thus the difficulty of this position is already clear in a fundamental component of λόγος itself. We need to notice that Plato is here conceiving the ὄνομα in the sense of its meaning something. To be sure, he does not reflect further on the specific structure of the connection of the word with what it means. He is satisfied with the simple formal-ontological fact that to the word as word belongs that which is meant. He understands this fact purely ontically here: something is together with something. In an expression as such, there is thus already a συμπλοκή.

You need to see clearly that this consideration cannot be taken as mere sophistical shadow-boxing. On the contrary, it is a matter of taking the thesis ἓν ὂν τὸ πᾶν seriously. Plato is concerned to show that in this ὑπόθεσις there resides a moment which reaches beyond its own proper sense. To understand Plato's explication here and particularly in the following case, we must recognize that he has not yet elaborated an actually precise concept of Being versus beings, but that the whole consideration runs its course in an indifference between the ontical and the ontological. And this applies not only here but ultimately to the end of the dialogue, so that this unclarity, present in Plato himself, constitutes the proper difficulty in understanding the dialogue. The explications, at first view, give the impression of being simple imitations of sophistical arguments. Seen on top of the laborious definitions in the first part, they occasioned the view, popular until very recently, that this dialogue, together with some others, was apocryphal. But if we are clear about the intention residing in the idea of dialectic—as this became visible in connection with the *Phaedrus*—namely the intention to go by way of συναγωγή toward the ἕν, so that on the basis of the ἕν the further characteristics of beings become intelligible, then we will not find ourselves in the difficulty of understanding these arguments as purely ontical in the sophistical sense.

The result, i.e., the conclusion of the consideration of the ἕν as a determination of ὄν, is propounded at 244d11–12. The statement is a summary, in a certain sense, of the result of the entire preceding discussion. This passage is admittedly corrupt, obviously since it was difficult to understand from the very beginning. There is a whole literature concerning this passage. We can limit ourselves essentially to two versions, both of which—and in general all the others as well—come down to the same meaning. The first version derives from Schleiermacher, and Heindorf took it over.[4] The second version stems from a conjecture by Apelt, and Burnet assumed it into his English edition.

1.) Καὶ τὸ ἕν γε, ἑνὸς ἓν ὂν μόνον, καὶ τοῦτο τοῦ ὀνόματος αὐτὸ ἓν ὄν.

2.) Καὶ τὸ ἕν γε, ἑνὸς ὄνομα ὂν καὶ τοῦ ὀνόματος αὖ τὸ ἓν ὄν.

Where a passage is corrupt, and hence it is not certain what Plato himself wrote, we have free choice. To understand this passage, recall that the point of departure was the principle ἓν ὂν τὸ πᾶν and that ἕν and ὄν, as δύο ὀνόματα, are to be one and the same. The difficulty thus consists in this, that the utterance of the principle already implies more beings than the principle itself, in its very meaning, admits, even if we take the something that is meant in the ὄνομα as itself an ὄνομα, so that the ἕν would then only be an ὄνομα ὀνόματος. The sense of ὄνομα, however, is mutilated by taking what is meant in the ὄνομα as itself an ὄνομα. We could translate the two versions as follows:

1.) "And so the one is exclusively the one of the one, and this again is itself the one of the name, of the expression."

2.) "And the one, as expression of the one, is then also again the one of the expression."

In both cases, the meaning is clear. The ὑπόθεσις: ἓν ὂν τὸ πᾶν, is a λόγος about ὄν, and it means that this ὄν is ἕν. This ὑπόθεσις, by its very sense, requires us to take it seriously as a θέσις or as a λόγος. Now a λόγος is always a λέγειν τί. That is, this τί, which is meant in the λόγος, is as such a τὶ λεγόμενον, a something which is λεγόμενον, said. This structure of λόγος hence provides, specifically with regard to the Eleatic θέσις: 1.) a τί, which is the λεγόμενον, the said, the meant, namely: ὄν. 2.) this ὄν is λεγόμενον, addressed, as ἕν, and 3.) ὄν is uttered as λεγόμενον in the ὄνομα. The whole of this meant and uttered content of the θέσις: ἕν—ὄν—ὄνομα, these three basic parts, therefore must, following the sense of the θέσις itself, be one and the same. And only this one is, the thesis says. In other words, the proper sense of the θέσις conflicts with the phenomenal content of what it itself is and means.

4. *Platonis Dialogi Selecti, cura L. F. Heindorfii,* 4 vols., Berlin, 1802–1810.

b) The discussion of ὄν as ὅλον. The difference between the ἕν as ὅλον and the ἓν ἀληθῶς. Consequences for ὄν as ὅλον; its untenability.

The interlocutors now take up the same thesis of Parmenides, ἓν ὂν τὸ πᾶν, from a different point of view. They do not simply consider that ὄν is addressed as ἕν, but instead they take up the principle as a whole: ἓν ὂν τὸ πᾶν. What this thesis deals with, properly speaking, is ὄν. And this "what," precisely ὄν, is conceived in its "how" as πᾶν; ὄν, which is what is spoken about, is understood from the very outset as τὸ πᾶν. And of this "what," ὄν, in this "how," πᾶν, it is said: ἕν. Thus the ἕν is that which it is addressed as.

The question now is how ὄν can be understood as πᾶν. That is, since the expression ὅλον now applies to πᾶν, the question is: in what sense is ὄν in the thesis ὅλον? Ὄν is indeed supposed to be ἓν μόνον! Hence it is now no longer a matter of ἕν and ὄν as ὀνόματα but a matter of elucidating the ἕν, the one, unity, oneness, since indeed the ὅλον is a mode of the ἕν. Τί δέ; τὸ ὅλον ἕτερον τοῦ ὄντος ἑνὸς ἢ ταὐτὸν τούτῳ; (cf. 244d14f.). "Is the ὅλον, in which ὄν is meant—ὄν which for its part is addressed as ἕν—is this ὅλον, as a character of ὄν, something other than the ὂν ἕν or the same?" Answer: "How could they not say it is the same; they certainly say so in the thesis!" (e1). But what sort of concept of ὅλον is being used here? In this regard, reference is now made to a fragment of the didactic poem of Parmenides himself:

> Πάντοθεν εὐκύκλου σφαίρης ἐναλίγκιον ὄγκῳ,
> μεσσόθεν ἰσοπαλὲς πάντῃ· τὸ γὰρ οὔτε τι μεῖζον
> οὔτε τι βαιότερον πελέναι χρεόν ἐστι τῇ ἢ τῇ (244e3ff.).

From this it is clear that ὄν is understood in the sense of a σθαῖρα, a sphere, and indeed a well-rounded one, comparable thus to a well-rounded sphere, a whole (ὄγκῳ here means the same as ὅλῳ), which μεσσόθεν, "from the middle out," πάντῃ, "going in all directions," is equally strong; "it is indeed not possible for it to be in any sense greater or stronger here or there." τοιοῦτόν γε ὄν (e6), "something like that," is the meaning of ὅλον in Parmenides. As a τοιοῦτον ὅλον it has a μέσον and ἔσχατα (e6). From the middle out, in all directions, up to the outer limits of the sphere, ὄν is uniform. Now insofar as the ὅλον has a middle and extremities, it is something that has μέρη (e7), "parts." Thus it is a matter of an entirely particular wholeness, a whole which has parts, and this wholeness can be understood as unity in a special sense, Ἀλλὰ μὴν τό γε μεμερισμένον πάθος μὲν τοῦ ἑνὸς ἔχειν ἐπι τοῖς μέρεσι πᾶσιν οὐδὲν ἀποκωλύει, καὶ ταύτῃ δὴ πᾶν τε ὂν καὶ ὅλον ἓν εἶναι (245a1ff.). The ὅλον is thus a μεμερισμένον, or, as Aristotle will say later, a διαιρετόν,[5] "something that can be taken apart." What is vaguely seen in this notion of the ὅλον as μεμερισμένον Aristotle later understood rigorously in the concept of συνεχές.[6] Such a ὅλον, a ὅλον in the sense of the μεμερισμένον, can therefore have πάθος τοῦ ἑνός, i.e., it can have the determinateness of the one; in such a ὅλον as μεμερισμένον the ἕν is in some sense present. But this ἕν is quite particular; it is a ἕν that is understood ἐπὶ τοῖς μέρεσι πᾶσιν, on the basis of parts, with regard to parts: ἕν as συνεχές. Therefore, the ὅλον as ὅλον is indeed a ἕν, but this ὅλον, which as ὅλον is a particular ἕν, a one (we do not have terms for these distinctions, i.e., for the sense of the unity of a whole composed of parts)—this ὅλον or one is certainly not τὸ ἓν αὐτό (245a5f.), "the one in itself." For (though not said here, this is what is meant) unity in the sense of wholeness is as such always still something else, namely oneness. It is referred to a more original one. Prior to it there is a sense of ἕν by which it is itself determined as unity. This ἕν, which is prior to the ἓν ὅλον, is ἀμερὲς παντελῶς (cf. a8), "altogether without parts"; it is the ἀληθῶς ἕν (ibid.), what is ultimately disclosed of its class. Thus if we follow up the sense of ἕν, we ultimately find this ἓν ἀμερές, or, in Aristotle, the ἀδιαίρετον. Hence the ξένος can say that this ἕν, the ἕν as τοιοῦτον—hence not the ἓν ἀληθῶς but the ἕν as συνεχές—ἐκ πολλῶν μερῶν ὄν (b1), "is of many parts," and exists only on the basis of them and for them. But, as such, οὐ συμφωνήσει τῷ λόγῳ (b1f.), "this ἕν does not coincide with the genuine sense of ἕν—if I address it properly." And in this way a first distinction arises within the concept of ἕν: 1.) the ἓn ἀληθῶς and 2.) the ἕν as πάθος ἐπὶ τοῖς μέρεσι: the one as unity of parts.

Now the interlocutors again ask: in what sense is the ὄν πᾶν or ὅλον? Either it is ὅλον in the sense of πάθος τοῦ ἑνὸς ἔχον (cf. b4), or else it is μὴ ὅλον. Assuming that ὄν is a ἕν in the sense of a derived ἕν, as wholeness, ἕν πως (cf. b8), then the ἕν is a πάθος τοῦ ὄντος. But if so, then ὄν or ὅλον is not the same as the ἕν in the proper sense (b8). Accordingly, the ὅλον is a ἕτερον over and against ὄν, insofar as the latter is understood in the sense of the ἕν as ἓν ἀληθῶς. But if the ὅλον is something other than ὄν, the result is πλέονα τὰ πάντα ἑνός (cf. b8f.), there is something more than this ἕν, the ἕν posited in the θέσις, if the θέσις itself says: ἓν ὂν ὅλον. But if, accordingly, ὄν itself—by having the πάθος τοῦ ἑνός—is *not* itself the ὅλον (c1f.), and the ὅλον is therefore other than ὄν, then this ὅλον is something ὄν as ὄν is not. Consequently, there is something which ὄν is not, which falls outside of ὄν, but which nevertheless *is*. Therefore ὄν is ἐνδεὲς ἑαυτοῦ (cf. c2f.), it is in itself needful in relation to itself; something is lacking to it, something

5. *Met.* V, chapter 13, 1020a7ff.
6. Ibid., chapter 26, 1023b32ff.

is still outside of it, something which for its part it is not. It is then ἑαυτοῦ στερόμενον (c5), it itself, ὄν, thus undergoes deprivation from itself, namely by being distinct from the ὅλον, while the ὅλον *is* something, i.e., by standing opposed, as ὂν ἕν in the proper sense, to the ὅλον as ὄν τι, as being in some way or other. This entire consideration becomes (at least relatively) transparent, if we are clear at the very outset about the two meanings of ἕν: ἕν in the derived sense, the ἓν ὅλον, and ἕν in the proper sense, the ἓν ἀληθῶς, as this is ascribed to ὄν as its essential predicate. But if ὄν is στερόμενον ἑαυτοῦ, then the result is that οὐκ ὂν ἔσται τὸ ὄν (c6), ὄν itself is not ὄν, i.e., not all beings; it is not the ὅλον.

The consideration takes a further step. The best way to understand this final argument is to grasp it from behind. The ὅλον has now been posited as something that does not belong to ὄν as ὄν; it is indeed πάθος, it is a ἕτερον. τὸ ὅλον ἐν τοῖς οὖσι μὴ τιθέντα (d5f.). But if the ὅλον is not posited under that which is, then neither οὐσία nor γένεσις can be posited as being, then neither γένεσις nor οὐσία *are*. For τὸ γενόμενον ἀεὶ γέγονεν ὅλον (d4), "everything that becomes, and has become, has come to be a whole." Here "whole," ὅλον, means the same as "finished," a finished thing there, a complete thing there as one. Here the concept of ἕν as one coincides with the concept of ἕν as whole, unity. If, accordingly, the ὅλον stands outside of Being, is a ἕτερον over and against ὄν, and if therefore even γένεσις and οὐσία cannot be, then ὄν cannot be either. And in this way the μὴ εἶναι of ὄν (245d1) arises, and furthermore there is no becoming: οὔτε οὐσίαν οὔτε γένεσιν ὡς οὖσαν δεῖ προσαγορεύειν (d4f.). In connection with this discussion, the ξένος refers again to the ὅλον in the sense of ποσόν (d9), the quantity of beings, and says that infinitely many difficulties will now emerge.

c) Fundamental unclarities.

I have already emphasized that if these things are read unpreparedly and without the correct ontological basis they are completely confusing. In anticipation I want to note briefly that there are three essential unclarities in this whole consideration—unclarities understood not in a critical sense, as mistakes Plato made, but in the sense of difficulties residing in the matter itself and in the traditional way of conceiving these things:

1.) The unclarity in the concept of the "not": if ὄν is distinguished from ὅλον, then to say that the ὅλον is not ὄν is at the same time to say that ὄν is *not* something; there is something which is not included in ὄν. This is possible only on the basis of an essential unclarity in the "not."

2.) The unclarity with regard to the distinction between ὄν as Being and ὄν as beings. This difficulty is exacerbated in the course of the substantive discussion inasmuch as the interlocutors must speak of: a) the Being of beings and b) the Being of Being.

3.) The unclarity stemming from the fact that definite ontological characters, ones we have already come to know, ὄν, ἕν, τί, are not seen in their equiprimordiality but that already here—and later still much more strongly with the κοινωνία τῶν γενῶν—there occurs a definite tendency to submit the ontological characters to a certain derivation, to a γένεσις (to a "history of the provenance," as we said earlier) out of the ἕν.

These unclarities are as such visible only out of a univocal basis of ontological questioning, in which Greek ontology is included and hence can come alive. The fundamental clarifications were not successfully attained by Plato himself later nor even by Aristotle. Today they are just as much out of reach; indeed we no longer understand them as fundamental problems. The unclarities can be cleared up in no other way than through the prior elaboration of the ontological basis. Still it is precisely this dialogue which, in the forthcoming discussions, will, in one direction at least, bring a certain light into the confusion: the dialogue sets on foot an essentially more positive grasp of negation, which then became of far-reaching significance for Aristotle.

It is possible to clarify the unclarities contained in the analysis of the principle of Parmenides—i.e., make them clear *as* unclarities, not solve them—in such a way that we realize how this whole consideration adheres to the λόγος ἰσχυρός of Parmenides, in the sense of how the Greeks in general, when they discuss theoretical things, adhere to λόγος. This fact is to be understood in a quite extreme sense. We must consider that the Greeks always took λόγος itself as what is spoken, as what is made public, which is why they speak of φθέγγεσθαι. τί ποτε βούλεσθε σημαίνειν ὁπόταν ὄν φθέγγησθε; (244a5f.). "What do you properly understand by the meaning of Being when you utter ὄν?" In this fundamental question, the mode of saying is conceived not as λέγειν but as φθέγγεσθαι, "uttering," expressing oneself to others. The ὑπόθεσις, in the sense of the principle of Parmenides, can therefore be analyzed in four directions:

1.) the principle has a definite thematic "what"; this is its object, that about which it speaks: Being.

2.) the principle has a definite content: that which it says about Being.

3.) insofar as the principle is uttered or said, this peculiar moment of sayability itself co-includes definite characters which must be distinguished from the content of the principle and which we must conceive as the characters of the sayability, of the being-said—sayability understood here as that of λέγειν as disclosive.

4.) Versus this sayability we must differentiate what is spoken as such, the utterance.

For only on this basis, only if the utterance as such is differentiated, can we understand the whole argumentation which is carried out as regards the ὄνομα and which brings the Eleatics to concede that the ὄνομα is a ἕν, in the sense of their thesis, a ἕν which can no longer mean anything, unless that which is meant in the ὄνομα is itself taken as an ὄνομα. This kind of argumentation makes sense only if the ὄνομα as ὄνομα, as φθογγή, as "sound," as something spoken, is itself conceived as an ὄν. And that is in fact the case. And in this way λόγος too is conceived as an ὄν. Only if λόγος is conceived in such a way, only under this aspect, does the whole way of dealing with λόγος in the last parts of the dialogue become intelligible. Thus we need to distinguish: the thematic object, the content of the principle, the characters of the sayability, and the moments specific to the utterance as such. These four structural moments in the ὑπόθεσις all provide, insofar as they are *something*, opportunities to alternate, to substitute for each other reciprocally, within the use of ὄν. Through this intercrossing of various ὄντα, which are given purely in the ὑπόθεσις, the argumentation in regard to the ἓν ὄν is first possible. And it is not only possible, but for Plato it is even necessary, in order to show that in the ἓν ὄν, if it is merely understood as τί, there is already given a whole series of phenomena, a multiplicity of ontological characters.

The ξένος summarizes: Τοὺς μὲν τοίνυν διακριβολογουμένους ὄντος τε πέρι καὶ μή, πάντας μὲν οὐ διεληλύθαμεν (245e6f.). "We have not thoroughly discussed all those," whom he names διακριβολογούμενοι, "who deal with beings in such a way that they determine them precisely." This expression has generated a great deal of controversy. The difficulty results from the fact that here suddenly Parmenides and his predecessors are characterized as ones who determine ὄν precisely, whereas it was said earlier that they are actually only telling fairy tales. We cannot bring these two characteristics together. Nor may we grasp this expression διακριβολογούμενοι in a broader sense. Bonitz[7] has correctly seen that the term refers to number; they are precise insofar as they posit a definite number of ὄντα, whereas the others maintain the ἄπειρον. This "strictly and precisely" hence does not refer to the methodological treatment but to the fact that they determine the genuine ὄντα according to number. These who determine "precisely" are set in opposition to the ἄλλως λέγοντες (cf. 245e8), those who deal with beings in a different way. These others are now going to be considered. Bonitz proceeds to a still more detailed articulation of the dialogue, which I do not think necessary. The beginning of the ontological discussion indicated that those who deal with beings consider them in two

7. H. Bonitz, *Platonische Studien*, 3. Aufl., Berlin, 1886, p. 162f.

respects: πόσα τε καὶ ποῖά ἐστιν (242c6), with regard to πόσα, "how many," and with regard to ποῖα, "how they are constituted." Bonitz wants to take these two respects as signifying the articulation of the dialogue. He says the first group of thinkers (the ones we have discussed up to now) deals with πόσα, quantity, and the second group with ποῖα, "quality." This distinction is not necessary as far as the matter is concerned. For, in the critical discussion we have followed, what is at issue is not so much a question of maintaining the ἕν as ἕν over and against a plurality or, conversely, maintaining a plurality over and against a ἕν; what is essential is that Plato considers the ἕν a determination of ὄν in the sense of the dialectical συναγωγή, such that, as this one, it is constantly co-present in each of the πολλά. Hence the issue is not whether ὄν is only one or is more than one—as if the number of the principles were uniquely or primarily decisive—but instead it is a matter of ὄν or the ἕν being co-present in the πολλά in the sense of κοινωνία.

II. The Discussion of the Contemporary Doctrines of ὄν. The γιγαντομαχία περὶ τῆς οὐσίας[1] (246a–250e).

§67. General characterization of the contemporary doctrines of ὄν *(246a–250e). First thesis:* οὐσία = σῶμα. *Second thesis:* οὐσία = εἶδος. *The proper task of the* γιγαντομαχία περὶ τῆς οὐσίας*: the disclosure of the beings corresponding to the guiding sense of Being. Being = presence. How the beings are encountered: 1.)* σῶμα: αἴσθησις, *2.)* εἶδος: νοεῖν, λόγος.

Before Plato critically examines more precisely the two other positions, he gives a preview of the opponents in the γιγαντομαχία περὶ τῆς οὐσίας (246aff.). Two factions are in opposition. Οἱ μὲν εἰς γῆν ἐξ οὐρανοῦ καὶ τοῦ ἀοράτου πάντα ἕλκουσι, ταῖς χερσὶν ἀτεχνῶς πέτρας καὶ δρῦς περιλαμβάνοντες. τῶν γὰρ τοιούτων ἐφαπτόμενοι πάντων διισχυρίζονται τοῦτο εἶναι μόνον ὃ παρέχει προσβολὴν καὶ ἐπαφήν τινα, ταὐτὸν σῶμα καὶ οὐσίαν ὁριζόμενοι, τῶν δὲ ἄλλων εἴ τίς <τι> φήσει μὴ σῶμα ἔχον εἶναι, καταφρονοῦντες τὸ παράπαν καὶ οὐδὲν ἐθέλοντες ἄλλο ἀκούειν (246a7ff.). "The ones ἐξ οὐρανοῦ καὶ τοῦ ἀοράτου πάντα ἕλκουσι, drag down εἰς γῆν, to earth, everything from heaven and everything that cannot be seen with sensible eyes, and clumsily grasp with their hands for rocks and oaks." They say: τοῦτο εἶναι μόνον ὃ παρέχει προσβολὴν καὶ ἐπαφήν, "only that is which offers itself, and can be encountered, in such a way that it permits being pressed upon, προσβολή, being assaulted like a citadel or barricade, or being touched, ἐπαφή." Only what can be encountered in this way, can be grasped, and can, as it were, be assaulted and touched, genuinely is. We could say quite briefly that for this position what is is what announces itself through resistance. Therefore, according to the guiding line of this concept of οὐσία and Being, σῶμα καὶ οὐσίαν ταὐτὸν ὁριζόμενοι: "They delimit body, material thing, and genuine Being, presence, οὐσία, as the same." Οὐσία, presence, announces itself, and certifies itself, for them primarily and solely through bodily resistance. Anything that cannot be encountered by way of this resistance is not. That is how we are to understand this position. If we call these people materialists that could mean they are like Vogt,[2] Moleschott,[3] and Buchner.[4] That, however, has nothing to do with it.

1. Title based on Heidegger (see p. 304).
2. Karl Vogt (1817–1895), *Köhlerglaube und Wissenschaft*, Gießen, 1855.
3. Jakob Moleschott (1822–1893), *Der Kreislauf des Lebens*, Mainz, 1852.
4. Ludwig Büchner (1824–1899), *Kraft und Stoff*, Frankfurt, 1855.

The essential is that οὐσία, presence, is primarily and uniquely represented by this particular realm of beings. If therefore someone says: μὴ σῶμα ἔχον εἶναι, "something which is bodiless, which has no body, may be, καταφρονοῦντες, "they would despise" him and "will hear of nothing else." Ἦ δεινοὺς εἴρηκας ἄνδρας (246b4): "You are speaking here of dreadful people."

Τοιγαροῦν οἱ πρὸς αὐτοὺς ἀμφισβητοῦντες μάλα εὐλαβῶς ἄνωθεν ἐξ ἀοράτου ποθὲν ἀμύνονται, νοητὰ ἄττα καὶ ἀσώματα εἴδη βιαζόμενοι τὴν ἀληθινὴν οὐσίαν εἶναι· τὰ δὲ ἐκείνων σώματα καὶ τὴν λεγομένην ὑπ' αὐτῶν ἀλήθειαν κατὰ σμικρὰ διαθραύοντες ἐν τοῖς λόγοις γένεσιν ἀντ' οὐσίας φερομένην τινὰ προσαγορεύουσιν (246b6ff.). The opponents on the other side are "those who are in conflict with them and who draw their defense from above." "From above" means here precisely not by an appeal to what is below, namely to what is on earth, as constituting beings, but instead they attempt to interpret the meaning of Being differently, i.e., not from what is visible, from what can be seen with the eyes, but from what is invisible. They posit as existing, in the sense of unconcealed Being, the εἴδη, the εἶδος, the "outward look" of beings, as that can be seen in νοεῖν. Therefore what genuinely is is viewed in insightful discussion *[im hinsehenden Besprechen]* (insofar as νοῦς and λόγος are identified here). If, e.g., I say "table," I actually mean that which is there most properly, something present without having the character of resistance, something unassailable, as it were, by sense perception. And the ones who interpret the Being of beings from above, from the invisible, have at the same time a position enabling them to understand their opponents. They have the means of making intelligible their opponents' ontological interpretation, namely insofar as their λόγοι, their discussions, are capable of διαθραύειν, "breaking asunder," the λεγομένη ἀλήθεια, the "truth their opponents say," i.e., what they address as uncovered beings. This breaking asunder signifies that they are capable of resolving it in a certain sense into what has being in this ὄν, in the σῶμα. Their possibility of understanding their opponents already implies that the position of the ones who say οὐσία = εἶδος is an essentially higher one scientifically. That means it is no longer a purely ontical one—the same applies basically even to the first mentioned thesis—but already an explicitly ontological position. And if they attempt to understand the ontological interpretation of their opponents on the basis of the meaning they themselves give to Being, they will say that what the others maintain as Being is nothing else than γένεσις, "becoming," a γένεσις φερομένη, a becoming that possesses the character of φορά, of change of place, in the broadest sense of movement. Bodily Being is present, is there, in resistance, i.e., at the same time, in movement. Ἐν μέσῳ δὲ περὶ ταῦτα ἄπλετος ἀμφοτέρων μάχη (246c2): "Between these two a battle is raging," and, to keep up the image, we must think of Plato himself, in this discussion, as standing in the middle and undermining both sides from the middle.

What genuinely is at issue in this γιγαντομαχία περὶ τῆς οὐσίας? The issue is the disclosure of beings, the ones that genuinely satisfy the meaning of Being, and consequently the issue is the demonstration of the meaning of οὐσία itself. The way to demonstrate the meaning of οὐσία is to produce the beings which satisfy the meaning of Being. This latter task is not independent but is entirely included in the first. The question of the meaning of οὐσία itself is not alive for the Greeks as an ontological theme; instead they always ask only: which beings genuinely satisfy the meaning of Being and which ontological characters result thereby? The meaning of Being itself remains unquestioned. This does not imply, however, that the Greeks had no concept of Being. For without one the question of what satisfies the meaning of Being would be groundless and without direction. It is precisely the fact that the Greeks did not ask about the meaning of Being which testifies that this meaning of Being was obvious to them. It was something obvious and not further interrogated. This meaning of Being does not naturally lie in the light of the day but instead can be understood explicitly only by means of a subsequent interpretation. The meaning of Being implicitly guiding this ontology is Being = presence. The Greeks did not get this meaning of Being from just anywhere, they did not just invent it, but rather it is the one borne by life itself, by factual Dasein, insofar as all human Dasein is interpretative, interprets itself as well as everything that is a being in whatever sense. In this interpretation there is operative an implicit sense of Being. And indeed the Greeks drew their implicit sense of Being out of the natural immediate interpretation of Being by factual Dasein, where Being means to be there already at the very outset as possession, household, property *[Anwesen]*—put more sharply: as presence *[Anwesenheit]*. We will make use of this meaning of Being (which we ourselves first make visible, although of course we cannot discuss it further in this context), namely Being = presence, because it includes the whole problem of time and consequently the problem of the ontology of Dasein. We will simply make use of this meaning of Being if we can demonstrate, by the success of an actual interpretation of Plato's ensuing discussions, that this sense of Being in fact guided the ontological questioning of the Greeks—otherwise there is no way to demonstrate the function of this meaning of Being in Greek philosophy. And this will happen all the more easily to the extent that the following parts of the dialogue are precisely and thoroughly controversial, for that means people have not clearly inquired into what is at issue there.

The battle is first of all over what primarily and genuinely satisfies the meaning of Being, i.e., presence. That includes a battle over which mode of access to the genuine beings is the original one. For the two opponents, this is either αἴσθησις, ἁφή, touching, feeling, sense perception, or else νοεῖν, i.e., λόγος. This question of the mode of access to what most properly possesses Being is not one the Greeks themselves raise as such. But, *de facto*, they do raise it, insofar as they ask what else still belongs to the Being of beings, whether, i.e., νοῦς would also belong to beings. This remarkable question, which arises later,[5] means nothing else than this: if beings are that which always is, still the meaning of Being as presence can have legitimacy only if there is something in attendance on them. The meaning of Being is thus dependent on the possibility that beings can be encountered by a being which possesses something like the present in general. This does not at all mean, however, that beings as beings would in some sense be dependent on Dasein or on consciousness or the like. This is enough for an initial orientation. Later we will deal with the question in a more precise way.[6]

We will require both opponents to answer the question: ὑπὲρ ἧς τίθενται τῆς οὐσίας (246c6), "what do they respectively posit as Being?" The ones who interpret οὐσία as εἶδος are ἡμερώτεροι (c9), "tamer, more manageable," i.e., more reasonable, since they are not wedded to an extreme position, as are the others, with whom it is almost impossible to deal. It is hardly possible to have any dealings with the ones who say οὐσία = σῶμα, because they deny the existence of everything not sensible and visible, and because for them there is basically no λόγος, which indeed lies in principle beyond mere προσβολή and ἁφή. Thus it is actually impossible to speak with them at all. This is the thought implicitly lying at the foundation here. In order therefore to be able to deal with them at all, to take them seriously as opponents, Plato approaches them as if they were more reasonable and knew the matters at issue better than they actually do. He acquires thereby the advantage of now having, in a certain sense, a more serious opponent. That means a real opponent—the stronger his position, the better—in a scientific discussion can help one to get hold of the matter and attain truth. For we are not concerned with the opponent himself, ἀλλὰ τἀληθὲς ζητοῦμεν (246d8f.), but are concerned only with the matter at issue; that is all we seek. And so we assume the λέγοντες: οὐσία = σῶμα have become better than they really are and, in a certain sense, fit to be dealt with. We now want to ask them and have them tell us how they actually interpret the meaning of Being. The ξένος challenges Theaetetus to inform him what is said about each: τὸ λεχθὲν παρ' αὐτῶν ἀφερμήνευε (e3). Ἑρμηνεύειν means to inform in the sense of making intelligible, making possible an

5. 248eff.

6. AH: Cf. *Vom Wesen des Grundes;* note. Editor's annotation: i.e., "*Vom Wesen des Grundes*" (58), note 59, in *Wegmarken*, GA Bd. 9 (pp. 123–175), p. 162. [English translation by Terrence Malick, *The Essence of Reasons*, Evanston: Northwestern University Press, 1969, p. 97.—Trans.]

appropriation. Ἑρμηνεία is informing by expressing oneself, coming to an understanding with someone, communicating; and Aristotle, in the *De Anima*, Book II, chapter 8, 420b19, exposes this as an essential structure of the human soul.

§68. *The discussion of the thesis* οὐσία = σῶμα *(246e–248a).*

a) Exhibition of the two kinds of beings: ὁρατόν and ἀόρατον. Εἶναι as συμφυὲς γεγονός.

The critical consideration Plato carries out in regard to each opponent in the *gigantomachia* περὶ τοῦ ὄντος aims first of all at those who claim: οὐσία = σῶμα, Being is properly represented by the presence of bodies. It is remarkable what Plato puts into discussion in relation to beings in order to get the criticism underway. He offers these opponents an ὄν having the character of the θνητὸν ζῷον (e5), a being which lives and which, as living, can die. It is obvious that this refers to man, although it is not said so explicitly, because it will become a matter of showing that next to the σῶμα in a ζῷον as σῶμα ἔμψυχον there is present something like a ψυχή. Several times, at important passages, Plato again has recourse to this ὄν we ourselves are, though he does not bring to life an explicit questioning directed at the Being of man. It is only the factual state of the matters dealt with which requires this being to be made co-thematic. The λέγοντες: οὐσία = σῶμα—what will they then say of a θνητὸν ζῷον? If something like that is presented to them, a "living being that can die," will they then say εἶναί τι (e5), something like that is? Πῶς δ' οὔ (e6), why not! Will they not, like us, address that which is now at issue, namely the θνητὸν ζῷον, as a σῶμα ἔμψυχον (e7)? Σῶμα ἔμψυχον means "a corporeal being in which there is also a soul present." Will they then posit the soul, which is indeed also present in a ζῷον, as something like a being? Certainly. But what then? What will they say about the fact that the soul, the psychic, which is co-present in the σῶμα, can be "just, unjust, prudent, foolish" (247a2f.)? What about this? *Is* there then that which we are attributing to the soul: δικαιοσύνη, ἀδικία, φρόνησις? Here the ξένος raises quite a penetrating question and employs an essential expression: παρουσία, presence. Ἀλλ' οὐ δικαιοσύνης ἕξει καὶ παρουσίᾳ τοιαύτην αὐτῶν ἑκάστην γίγνεσθαι, καὶ τῶν ἐναντίων τὴν ἐναντίαν; (247a5f.). If they say that the soul is co-present in a living being, and that the soul is just, unjust, etc., then this certainly means that the soul is what it is, namely τοιαύτη, ἕξει καὶ παρουσίᾳ, "by co-possessing and by the presence" of justice, prudence, etc. Only by the presence of prudence and on its basis is the soul prudent. But what then will they say? Nothing else than: τὸ δυνατόν τῳ παραγίγνεσθαι καὶ ἀπογίγνεσθαι (cf. a8f.). They then will say—and we must consider this sentence very carefully—what is determined by the "can," τὸ δυνατόν, in the sense of παραγίγνεσθαι καὶ ἀπογίγνεσθαι, in the sense of "being able to become present and to become absent," τινί (τῳ), in relation to something else, is in every case something or other." It *is* something or other through the possibility of its presence in relation to something else that is. Being thus means here: to be capable of presence with something. What is determined by the ability to co-exist with something, i.e., what has this ability, is. In anticipation, let us point out here that this concept of Being already includes: 1.) presence, οὐσία, 2.) the "co-," συμπλοκή, κοινωνία, and 3.) ability, δύναμις.

If therefore δικαιοσύνη, φρόνησις, and the like, and thereby also the ψυχή in which they are present—if all these have Being, how will they then speak about them? Are these beings ὁρατὸν καὶ ἁπτόν τι (cf. 247b3)? "Can they be seen with the eyes and be touched?" Are they accessible to sense perception? Or is all this invisible but yet present? What then is the case concerning the presence of the soul and of the other things? Σχεδὸν οὐδὲν τούτων γε ὁρατόν (b5). "Surely none are visible with the sensible eyes," Theaetetus says. Will they then want to say μῶν σῶμά τι ἴσχειν (cf. b6), that these things have a body, because they indeed are? Theaetetus answers that they will not answer all the parts of this question κατὰ ταὐτὰ ἀποκρίνονται (b7), "in the same way." They will fight shy of τὸ τολμᾶν (c1), "the risk," of either taking all these, the soul, φρόνησις, and the like, as non-beings or maintaining that each is σῶμα. But if they hesitate to explain all this as non-being on the basis of their theory, hesitate to say, for example, that if something is, a body must necessarily be co-present with it, then they intimate in doing so that they are prudent in regard to these givens; they will not risk a decision. This restraint already makes them better. For that is the proper comportment to the matters, the proper respect for them, namely not to intrude upon them precipitously with fixed theories but to keep silent if one cannot say anything about them. In this silence the matter is in every case acknowledged as it is given. They will then be prudent, but at the same time they will not be able to determine anything about the other mode of givenness. What remains open here—which we must take up—is the Being of φρόνησις and the like. In a certain sense they concede ψυχή; it is. But they cannot say anything about the Being of φρόνησις. That is important, because the discussion of the opposite faction will later thematize this phenomenon again.[1] This makes it clear that the

1. *Sophist*, 248aff. Cf. p. 330ff.

whole discussion of these two opponents has an unequivocal background in the matters themselves. The better ones, therefore, restrain themselves when asked about the Being of φρόνησις, δικαιοσύνη, etc. With regard to the Being of these givens, φρόνησις, δικαιοσύνη, and the like, they hesitate to say anything at all. They are unwilling to explain them as non-beings, nor do they want to appeal to their theory of Being and in a certain sense force all this to be ultimately a σῶμα. On the other hand, the αὐτόχθονες (247c5), the original holders of this position, i.e., the ones who are genuinely infatuated, will not abandon their theory. They will continue to maintain that anything they cannot grasp with their hands is not. At the same time, the way Plato deals with these λέγοντες: οὐσία = σῶμα makes it clear that in the field of such fundamental considerations even the greatest display of scientificity, in the sense of proofs and arguments, fails. The only work to be performed here is that of opening the eyes of one's opponent or giving him eyes to see in the first place. The better ones are thus not distinguished from the infatuated by having better theories but only by keeping alive a tendency toward objectivity.

Insofar as they possess this tendency, πάλιν ἀνερωτῶμεν (cf. 247c9), we will continue to put our questions to them. For if they maintain this objectivity, it is possible that they will indeed finally see what actually resides in that about which they speak. εἰ γάρ τι καὶ σμικρὸν ἐθέλουσι τῶν ὄντων συγχωρεῖν ἀσώματον, ἐξαρκεῖ (247c9f.). "If they concede that there is something or other, even if a trifle, which we can characterize as ἀσώματον, then that is already enough." If they maintain this seriously and see it, then they must say: τὸ γὰρ ἐπί τε τούτοις ἅμα καὶ ἐπ' ἐκείνοις ὅσα ἔχει σῶμα συμφυὲς γεγονός, εἰς ὃ βλέποντες ἀμφότερα εἶναι λέγουσι (247d2f.). I will unravel this statement in such a way that you will understand the meaning immediately: τὸ συμφυὲς γεγονός, that which for both is already "at the same time," ἅμα, "co-present"—for "both": i.e., for the ὁρατόν as well as for the ἀόρατον—is that εἰς ὃ βλέποντες, "upon which they look" and on the basis of which ἀμφότερα εἶναι λέγουσι, "they address both as existing." Thus we find here once again the same sort of consideration based on λόγος: the ὁρατόν and ἀόρατον which are said in λέγειν are addressed as something which is, εἶναι. This εἶναι is characterized as συμφυὲς γεγονός. Φύσις is that which is already present at the very outset. Συμ- means for both together, for the visible and the invisible. Γεγονός (perfect tense) means it is already there, before them. This γεγονός is related to γένος: that out of which they have their ontological provenance. And the συμφυές is that which for both at the same time, for the one and the other, is already there, and it already includes the μέθεξις, i.e., the κοινωνία τῶν γενῶν. It is precisely here that we must see the whole structural connection of what Plato will later expose. I stress this explicitly, because it is customary to conceive the entire following consideration, in which Plato elaborates a definite concept of Being, simply as a provisional one, as one Plato did not take seriously, since he says he will take it up εἰς ὕστερον (247e7) quite differently. Yet we may not interpret this reference to what is coming later as if the elaboration of the determinate meaning of Being had the mere goal of refutation, to make the opponent utterly speechless, as it were. On the contrary, this consideration already points at the positive and is not provisional in the sense of something that is later to be renounced. It is provisional in the sense of preparatory; later it will indeed be understood quite differently, but that only means more originally.

b) The determination of εἶναι as δύναμις εἴτ' εἰς τὸ ποιεῖν εἴτ' εἰς τὸ παθεῖν.

Thus the initial result of the criticism of those who say οὐσία = σῶμα is that the ὁρατόν, σῶμα ἔμψυχον, i.e., the ψυχή, presents an ἀόρατον, and that both, the ὁρατόν and the ἀόρατον, already imply a συμφυὲς γεγονός: that which for both is already there and in relation to which we can say εἰς ὃ βλέποντες λέγοντες, ψυχή as well as σῶμα εἶναι—ψυχή *is*, just as much as σῶμα. What is prior to them, what we address as Being itself, must now be determined more precisely. And indeed Plato here offers the opponents, in a certain sense, a definition, though they do not completely understand it. Λέγω δὴ τὸ καὶ ὁποιανοῦν <τινα> κεκτημένον δύναμιν εἴτ' εἰς τὸ ποιεῖν ἕτερον ὁτιοῦν πεφυκὸς εἴτ' εἰς τὸ παθεῖν . . . τοῦτο ὄντως εἶναι· τίθεμαι γὰρ ὅρον <ὁρίζειν> τὰ ὄντα ὡς ἔστιν οὐκ ἄλλο τι πλὴν δύναμις (247d8). τὸ ὁποιανοῦν κεκτημένον δύναμιν, "what possesses possibility in some way or other," i.e., what is in itself determined in some way as possibility, εἴτ' εἰς τὸ ποιεῖν εἴτ' εἰς τὸ παθεῖν, such that from itself it can either "affect" something else or "be affected" by something—whatever is determined in this way, πᾶν τοῦτο ὄντως εἶναι, "all properly is," ὄντως, and "nothing could be more being"; τίθεμαι γὰρ ὅρον ὁρίζειν τὰ ὄντα, "for I posit as delimiting beings," ὡς ἔστιν, "insofar as they are," nothing else than δύναμις. This is a determination of ὄν, οὐσία, as δύναμις. And Plato says specifically, προτεινομένων ἡμῶν (d5), it is "proffered." That does not mean it is merely suggested tentatively, simply as a way out; on the contrary, it is "pre-offered" as something which εἰς ὕστερον ἕτερον ἂν φανείη (cf. 247e7f.), "which later will show itself as something else." Thus the determination proffered here of ὄν as δύναμις will be dealt with more thoroughly later. Yet it is in no sense an artifice Plato employs simply to give the two opponents a common denominator, as if he were not serious about this definition. If the traditional interpretation says Plato could not be serious about this definition, that is because δύναμις is translated as "power"; Bonitz even translates it as "creative power." He says the Ideas are being defined here as "creative powers," δυνάμεις.[2] The difficulty people have found in the proffering of this quite new definition derives from their conceiving δύναμις too massively from the very outset, almost in the sense of those who say οὐσία = σῶμα. Above all, it derives from the fact that people have not investigated how precisely this determination of ὄν as δύναμις bears the entire ensuing meditation and indeed how it was already prepared earlier in the discussion of προσγίγνεσθαι.[3] Being thus means, put briefly, *possibility*, whereby this expression δύναμις is still to be conceived in a wholly neutral sense. Δύναμις is related here εἰς τὸ ποιεῖν and εἰς τὸ παθεῖν. This could mean, if taken roughly: powers which effect something or which have properties, on the basis of their ontic constitution, by which they can suffer something. This is of course the literal meaning. But, as regards παθεῖν, we must remember it was not accidental that Plato said earlier that the ὅλον can be a πάθος of ὄν[4]—which has nothing to do with the fact that the ὅλον in a certain sense falls like a boulder on Being or vice versa. It only means that ὄν can be affected by the ὅλον; it can, as ὄν, be determined in its Being by the ὅλον. Πάσχειν means here simply: to be determined by an other. We already know ποιεῖν; it means ἄγειν εἰς οὐσίαν, to bring something into being, to help something into being, to genuinely arrange for the Being of a being.[5] What is capable of something like that, what has such a δύναμις, properly is. Ἀλλ' ἐπείπερ αὐτοί γε οὐκ ἔχουσιν ἐν τῷ παρόντι τούτου βέλτιον λέγειν, δέχονται τοῦτο (247e5f.). Because these people obviously do not for the moment have anything better at their disposal, with which to answer the question of what οὐσία is, they will possibly accept this determination. But perhaps, says the ξένος, what is given here in relation to Being will show itself afterwards, to us as well as to them, differently, ἕτερον ἂν φανείη (248a1). Plato discovers this ἕτερον precisely in the *Sophist*, in a certain sense for the first time, as a particular kind of non-being and precisely as the kind that does not express a total difference from the other, or from the one in relation to which it is the other, but instead expresses the fact that every being, insofar as it is, is itself *and* something other. The ἕτερον expresses what something, as itself, is additionally. Hence when Plato says the determination of ὄν as δύναμις will later be revealed as a ἕτερον, this cannot mean that it is to be abandoned but only that it should be grasped more originally, in order to acquire a more perfect determination. This becomes quite clear from the passage at 250a4f., where Plato, after the criticism of the two positions, or

2. H. Bonitz, *Platonische Studien*, 3. Aufl., Berlin 1886, p. 203: "living powers."
3. Cf. pp. 291f. and 297ff.
4. According to the sense of *Sophist* 245aff. Cf. p. 315f.
5. *Sophist* 219b4f. Cf. p. 186ff.

of the last position, proceeds to the decisive steps in the determination of ὄν, and does so specifically by returning to what he discussed earlier, all the way to the point at which he carried out the critique of the ancients. He says: we will not simply repeat what we discussed there, but instead we want to deal with it in such a way ἵνα ἅμα τι καὶ προΐωμεν (250a5f.), "that we thereby take a step forward at the same time." This is nothing else than the ὕστερον ἕτερον. Unless we see that clearly, the whole dialogue will be a great confusion.

Now the critique passes over to the opposite side. Pay attention once more to the results of the critique of the first faction: there is given not only the ὁρατόν but also the ἀόρατον and, prior to both of them, the συμφυὲς γεγονός, and that is interpreted as δύναμις.

§69. The discussion of the thesis: οὐσία = εἶδος *(248a–249b).*

a) The interpretation of the phenomenon of knowledge through the concept of the κοινωνία.

α) Knowledge as κοινωνία of the ψυχή with οὐσία (εἶδος).

The opposite side says: οὐσία = εἴδη. What is is what shows itself in λέγειν and νοεῖν, in pure discoursive insight *[im reinen besprechenden Hinsehen]*: namely, the outward look of beings which comes to presence in pure perceiving. "Pure" means here "non-sensible." Those who now say not that οὐσία = σῶμα or γένεσις, but that οὐσία = εἴδη, say this in such a way that they at the same time posit οὐσία "separately," χωρίς, and independently from γένεσις. Γένεσιν, τὴν δὲ οὐσίαν χωρίς που διελόμενοι λέγετε (248a7). This implies that what is characterized as γένεσις must be a μὴ ὄν; for the εἴδη, exclusively, are οὐσία. The way the criticism of this position begins is again telling. I emphasized with regard to the critique of the first position that it occurs in a return to the ζῷον ἔμψυχον, and the Being of φρόνησις remained problematic.[1] Now the criticism takes place in a return to the same phenomenological state of affairs of ψυχή and explicitly in relation to φρόνησις, i.e., γιγνώσκειν: ἡμᾶς γενέσει δι' αἰσθήσεως κοινωνεῖν, διὰ λογισμοῦ δὲ πρὸς τὴν οὐσίαν (cf. 248a10f.). This constatation is initially quite unexpected; but we must keep in mind the result of the earlier discussion. Here the expression κοινωνεῖν appears for the first time. Κοινωνεῖν means "to share in something" *[etwas mit-haben]*. "We, ἡμᾶς, as knowers, share in γένεσις, becoming, by way of αἴσθησις; we, ἡμᾶς, share in οὐσία

1. Cf. p. 327.

by way of λογισμός, λέγειν." This κοινωνεῖν, this "sharing," is specifically the indication of an objective phenomenal datum, but it may initially be understood, quite superficially only, in the phenomenological sense of having present. The meaning turns over immediately, however, to a wholly naively ontical one: we ourselves, through αἴσθησις, keep company with that which is caught up in becoming; through λογισμός, we keep company, in our Being, with the other, οὐσία. Κοινωνεῖν thus means to be related toward an other, to keep company with it, and, in relation to οὐσία, to keep company with the one. And indeed what γένεσις designates is characterized as ἄλλοτε ἄλλως (a12f.), it is "in each case different"; whereas οὐσία is characterized as ἀεὶ κατὰ ταὐτὰ ὡσαύτως ἔχει (cf. a12): genuine beings keep themselves constantly in a determinate self-sameness.

Now Plato takes up the expression κοινωνεῖν; it is the proper center of the consideration.

β) The explication of the concept of κοινωνία by means of the concept of the δύναμις τοῦ ποιεῖν καὶ τοῦ πάσχειν. Being = δύναμις κοινωνίας. Recapitulation of the previous formulations.

The expression κοινωνεῖν is, as we said, the proper center of the consideration; the way of speaking, the rather solemn tone, already indicates it: Τὸ δὲ δὴ κοινωνεῖν, ὦ πάντων ἄριστοι, τί τοῦθ' ὑμᾶς ἐπ' ἀμφοῖν λέγειν φῶμεν; (248b2f.). "What then is to be said in regard to these modes of κοινωνεῖν?" What is κοινωνεῖν in itself? Is it not precisely that which we have already said, namely in the determination of οὐσία as δύναμις? In fact the ξένος now gives each of the two modes of κοινωνεῖν, as κοινωνία, the same definition he had previously offered for οὐσία: Πάθημα ἢ ποίημα ἐκ δυνάμεώς τινος ἀπὸ τῶν πρὸς ἄλληλα συνιόντων γιγνόμενον (b5f.), "a being affected, πάθημα, or an affecting, ποίημα, that has γιγνόμενον ἐκ δυνάμεώς τινος, arisen on the basis of a certain 'can,' a certain possibility, and out of things that pass over into one another." Thus again we have the being with one another, the being related to one another, and the possibility for that. This possibility is nothing else than the meaning of Being. Κοινωνεῖν is simply another version of the πρὸς ἄλληλα, "to affect one another," in such a way that Being now means, if we insert κοινωνία: δύναμις κοινωνίας, the possibility of being with one another.

What now will the εἰδῶν φίλοι, "the friends of the Ideas," say about this interpretation of κοινωνεῖν? Plato, i.e., the ξένος, takes it upon himself to answer, because, as he says, he κατακούει διὰ συνήθειαν (cf. b7f.), "understands their position better, on account of his familiarity with them." These εἰδῶν φίλοι are the Megarians, followers of Euclid of Megara, whose school Plato attended when he was young. What position will they take up regarding this definition? Οὐ συγχωροῦσιν ἡμῖν (c1), "they will not agree" with our determination of οὐσία = δύναμις. And the ξένος repeats this definition once again—the fourth formulation, which is actually no reason to interpret this definition as an artifice: ἡ τοῦ πάσχειν ἢ δρᾶν δύναμις (cf. 248c5). Consequently, we now have the following formulations:

1.) δυνατόν τῳ παραγίγνεσθαι καὶ ἀπογίγνεσθαι (247a8).
2.) κεκτημένον δύναμιν εἴτ' εἰς τὸ ποιεῖν εἴτ' εἰς τὸ παθεῖν (cf. 247d8f.).
3.) δύναμις ἐξ ἧς πάθημα ἢ ποίημα γιγνόμενον (cf. 248b5f.).
4.) ἡ τοῦ πάσχειν ἢ δρᾶν δύναμις (cf. 248c5).

Why will the εἰδῶν φίλοι not agree with this interpretation of Being? They will say in opposition the following: ὅτι γενέσει μὲν μέτεστι τοῦ πάσχειν καὶ ποιεῖν δυνάμεως, πρὸς δὲ οὐσίαν τούτων οὐδετέρου τὴν δύναμιν ἁρμόττειν (248c7ff.). "Γένεσις indeed involves, μέτεστι, δύναμις"; where there is motion and change there can perhaps be something like potentiality, such that we can ultimately interpret in this way the Being we ourselves address as μὴ ὄν. "But there is no ἁρμόττειν πρὸς οὐσίαν, between οὐσία and δύναμις." Thus again we have προσ-αρμόττειν—just as earlier we had προσγίγνεσθαι τῷ ὄντι ἕτερον τῶν ὄντων, something comes to be attached to something else—and the other corresponding expressions.[2] To be related to each other, to be with each other—this is the one phenomenal state of affairs constantly dealt with here. Being means nothing else than to be able to be with each other, or formulated differently, in relation to Being as δύναμις, to be capable of presence with something.

But the εἰδῶν φίλοι resist this interpretation of Being. For this interpretation ultimately includes—as will be shown—the co-presence of movement in οὐσία.

b) The co-presence of movement in οὐσία.

α) Being-known as the πάθος of οὐσία.

If the εἰδῶν φίλοι resist the interpretation of Being as δύναμις κοινωνίας, and hence do not agree with it, then the question arises: Οὐκοῦν λέγουσί τι; (c10), "do they have good grounds for doing so?" To this extent, says the ξένος, that we must ask them for more precise information concerning εἰ προσομολογοῦσι τὴν μὲν ψυχὴν γιγνώσκειν, τὴν δ' οὐσίαν γιγνώσκεσθαι (248d1f.). Here there occurs again the state we left open earlier: φρόνησις.[3] "Do they agree that the soul can be familiar, or is familiar, with something, and that what it is familiar with in knowledge is οὐσία?" Will they concur with this? Yes. But what about this γιγνώσκειν? How must it be conceived?

2. Cf. p. 291ff.
3. Cf. p. 327.

Τί δέ; τὸ γιγνώσκειν ἢ τὸ γιγνώσκεσθαί φατε ποίημα ἢ πάθος ἢ ἀμφότερον; ἢ τὸ μὲν πάθημα, τὸ δὲ θάτερον; ἢ παντάπασιν οὐδέτερον οὐδετέρου τούτων μεταλαμβάνειν; (d4ff.). "Will they say that γιγνώσκειν, knowing, or γιγνώσκεσθαι, being known, is ποίημα or πάθος, or that the one is ποίημα and the other πάθος?" Or will they deny that these ontological determinations, ποιεῖν and πάσχειν, apply to this ὄν, γιγνώσκειν, φρόνησις? Obviously they will deny it. They will deny, in short, that γνῶσις μεταλαμβάνει δυνάμεως. And they must do so if they want to adhere to their position and do not want to speak against themselves. If they conceded that this κοινωνία of γιγνώσκειν can be interpreted as δύναμις, they would be saying the opposite of what they maintained previously. Why? They indeed say: οὐσία χωρὶς γενέσεως, what genuinely is has nothing to do with movement, is free of all change. If, however, as they indeed conceded above, ψυχὴ γιγνώσκει, οὐσία γιγνώσκεται, οὐσία is therefore "known," γιγνωσκομένη (cf. e2), as object, then that implies οὐσία is determined as πάθημα; it is in some way affected by knowledge itself. Insofar as οὐσία is known and thereby affected, it itself contains the moment of μεταβολή, κίνησις. But according to their own position, that is not possible. Something like that cannot be περὶ τὸ ἠρεμοῦν (e4f.), "in the field of what is at rest." This ἠρεμοῦν refers to what was indicated at the end of 248a: to remain constantly in a determinate self-sameness,[4] free of all change. To concede that οὐσία is known and knowable implies it is codetermined by πάθημα and consequently by δύναμις. Since, for them, κίνησις has no place in οὐσία, they must reject this position. Yet that is not tenable either; this has now been demonstrated in principle.

β) The παρουσία of φρόνησις, νοῦς, ζωή, and κίνησις in the παντελῶς ὄν.

The ξένος becomes excited: By Zeus, we can scarcely believe ὡς ἀληθῶς κίνησιν καὶ ζωὴν καὶ ψυχὴν καὶ φρόνησιν τῷ παντελῶς ὄντι μὴ παρεῖναι, μηδὲ ζῆν αὐτὸ μηδὲ φρονεῖν, ἀλλὰ σεμνὸν καὶ ἅγιον, νοῦν οὐκ ἔχον, ἀκίνητον ἑστὸς εἶναι; (cf. 248e6ff.). The passage is the center and is decisive for understanding the whole ontological discussion. We can scarcely believe "that in what is παντελῶς, in what completely, genuinely is, in beings in the most proper sense, there would not also be present movement, life, soul, knowledge." Note well that it is a matter of the παρεῖναι of something, the co-existence of something, namely of ζωή, ψυχή, in what genuinely is. We can therefore scarcely believe that life and knowledge do not pertain to beings in the most proper sense; we can scarcely believe that beings stand

4. 248a12: ἀεὶ κατὰ ταὐτὰ ὡσαύτως ἔχειν.

there, as it were, σεμνὸν καὶ ἅγιον (249a1f.), "solemn and sacred," "unmoved and changeless," so that, as beings, they are devoid of νοῦς: νοῦν οὐκ ἔχον (a2). Plato has been interpreted to be saying here that the genuine beings, the Ideas, would have understanding, life, and the like. This is sheer nonsense. What the passage says is that φρόνησις, νοῦς, and ζωή keep company with the genuine beings; in other words, the meaning of Being must be conceived in such a way that νοῦς, κίνησις, and ζωή can also be understood as beings.[5] Therefore the Ideas are not spirits of some sort, fluttering around, and they are not, on top of that, "creative powers"! If we denied being to νοῦς, κίνησις, and ζωή, then δεινὸν μέντ' ἄν λόγον συγχωροῖμεν, "we would be admitting a terrible proposition." This matter is now pursued more closely at 249a4ff.: if, conversely, we concede that νοῦς belongs to Being, and so does ζωή, then *a fortiori* we must address ψυχή as an ὄν. But that implies τὸ κινούμενον εἶναι (cf. 249b2f.). That is, it implies that what is moved and movement itself belong to beings and that the meaning of Being must be conceived on the basis of this constatation and in correspondence with these new facts. We can now ask whether or not, precisely for all these beings—not only for the εἴδη, but also for νοῦς and ζωή—whether or not for this whole as a whole the definition already given, namely ὄν = δύναμις, accomplishes a real clarification.

If we look closer at these factions and above all at the following passages, we can hardly avoid seeing the young Aristotle in the background of the discussions. A confrontation with him is already in play here.

c) The question of Plato's confrontation with the young Aristotle.

α) The Aristotelian moments in Plato's ontological research: the σώματα as ground; the inclusion of δύναμις.

I emphasize explicitly that this surmise—that behind the mentioned factions stands a confrontation with the young Aristotle—is simply my personal conviction. Siebeck had already expressed this surmise in 1896.[6] I differ from Siebeck, however, since I believe it cannot be *demonstrated* that Aristotle is at work here. It remains a conviction which as such has no scientific value. Yet, as a conviction, it must have its grounds, even if it cannot play a scientific role. And these grounds reside in the fact that this dialogue is the first to take into account positively, and with a special

5. AH: An understanding of Being pertains to Being.

6. H. Siebeck, "Platon als Kritiker aristotelischer Ansichten," in *Zeitschrift für Philosophie und philosophische Kritik, Neue Folge*, Bde. 107 and 108, Leipzig, 1896. On the passage at issue, cf. Bd. 108, pp. 5–9.

acuteness, the Being of the σώματα, and indeed it does so not in a vague sense but such that those who say οὐσία = σῶμα become in a certain way able to be dealt with. Plato hence concedes that even this may be the basis for a higher position. This is in fact the proper impetus of Aristotle's research, which he again and again repeats up to his latest works: that in the question of οὐσία one has to start with the αἰσθητά, i.e., the σώματα, and that the Being of beings must first be discussed in relation to them. This determination, that one must begin with the αἰσθητά, does not mean the interpretation of Being would be exhausted therein. Plato is obviously taking this determination into account, with the result that the σώματα in fact do provide a basis for a discussion of Being, but only in such a way that the research presses on from them to a further realm of Being. This hence is one moment which argues in favor of the conviction that the young Aristotle is in the background: the positive incorporation of the σώματα into the ontological discussion.

The second moment, which points to Aristotle even more strongly, is the incorporation of the concept of δύναμις into the discussion of οὐσία and ὄν. It could admittedly also be—although I personally do not believe it—that Plato by himself drew in this phenomenon of δύναμις for an interpretation of Being and that Aristotle derived his ontology from it. This possibility entails a great difficulty, however, namely this, that Aristotle does not develop his concept of δύναμις the way Plato does but instead develops δύναμις from the very outset as an ontological category in connection with ἐνέργεια. He does so because he sees the phenomenon of movement positively, which Plato never does. Thus Aristotle's treatment of δύναμις presupposes a much more radical ontological meditation than does the Platonic concept of δύναμις, so that it seems to me improbable Aristotle would have come, on the basis of the concept of δύναμις as it occurs in the *Sophist,* to his own basic ontological doctrine. Therefore it is more plausible that the beginnings of Aristotle's investigations, which indeed developed under the eyes of Plato, and in which these categories were already alive—that it was these Aristotelian rudiments which provided Plato the impetus to draw the notion of δύναμις into the ontological discussion in his own way and within his own position. Only in this sense can I make intelligible the interrelation of the two philosophers, and only in this way can the creative independence of each be saved. Siebeck has attempted to substantiate, as it were, their interrelation doxographically, by collecting all the passages in which Aristotle speaks about δύναμις and the αἰσθητόν, but this procedure can decide nothing at all. Such doxographic theses can contribute nothing to the substantive question standing behind the detached propositions. Because there is a fundamental difference in their ontological orientations, it is not probable that the ontological concept of δύναμις originated with Plato, but the reverse: Plato attempts to take it into account. With this aim, one could even, as is often done, appeal to the fact that in the ontological dialogue *Parmenides,* an Aristotle appears as one of the collocutors. But, as we said, these are only surmises and do not settle anything substantively. I only bring them up here to clarify the basic difference in the application of the ontological concept of δύναμις.

β) Plato's own solution. Presence as the basic meaning of Being in the two preceding positions. Plato's concept of Being: παρουσία δυνάμεως κοινωνίας.

We know that Plato presupposes two positions for his own ontological solution: the one says that what is is what manifests its permanence by means of resistance; the other says what is is what shows itself in λέγειν, i.e., in νοεῖν as pure perceiving. The first concept of Being, Being as resistance, gives rise to the substantive question of whether this meaning of Being can be understood detached from the moment of being-present, i.e., whether there is a resistance which is, according to its very sense, non-present, or whether every sense of resistance includes the moment of being-present. The second concept of Being, what exists is what is present in pure perceiving, engenders the corollary question of whether this Being in the sense of presence can be understood without the moment of resistance, i.e., whether there is an irresistant presence. These are the two substantive questions resulting from the two positions on the interpretation of Being. Being itself, then, will mean for Plato, if he is to make both these positions intelligible, δύναμις, as the possibility of co-presence with something, in short δύναμις κοινωνίας, or in a fuller determination, παρουσία δυνάμεως κοινωνίας, factual occurrence of the possibility of being with one another. In all these formulations, we say Being is *being*-present, but that may not be turned into an objection, in the sense that we might be accused of making use of the meaning of Being we are trying to clarify in the first place, with the result that we are presupposing that meaning. For "being" in the expression "being-present" has merely an entirely formal sense. This assertion about Being, in the sense of something formal that applies to everything uttered and said as such, does not signify anything as regards substantive content, in the sense of the structure of Being itself. This concept of δύναμις κοινωνίας, as the possibility of being with one another, is the focus of Plato's entire ensuing discussion.

III. The Discussion of the Summary of the Theses about ὄν (249b–251a).

§70. The summary of the theses about ὄν *with regard to the phenomenon of knowledge. The Being of* κίνησις *and* στάσις *as condition of the Being of knowledge.*

It is important to note how Plato proceeds from the two previously mentioned positions and which phenomenon he draws upon to make the two positions *unitarily* thematic. This phenomenon is γιγνώσκειν, knowledge, as a quite particular κοινωνία. Κοινωνεῖν in the sense of γιγνώσκειν is itself an ὄν, a something. This κοινωνεῖν includes, in the first place, a connection, a companionship, of the ψυχή, of νοῦς, with the εἴδη, i.e., a connection of γένεσις with the ἀεὶ ὄν. If there is a γιγνώσκειν, if it itself is an ὄν, then there exists a κοινωνία between γένεσις and ἀεὶ ὄν, between κίνησις and στάσις. We have here thus a grouping of phenomena that corresponds quite well to the case of ψεῦδος: there it was a matter of a συμπλοκή between Being and non-being, here it is a matter of a κοινωνία between κίνησις and στάσις. The question is hence whether ζωή, ψυχή, and φρόνησις belong to ὄν and whether, correspondingly, the determination of Being must take into account these beings, νοῦς, ζωή, etc. But when Plato says ζωή and νοῦς belong to ὄν, he is not claiming—let us repeat—that the Ideas themselves think and live. Plato now indirectly shows the necessity of the Being of this κοινωνία: Συμβαίνει δ' οὖν ἀκινήτων τε ὄντων νοῦν μηδενὶ περὶ μηδενὸς εἶναι μηδαμοῦ (cf. 249b5f.). Assuming everything was unmoved, assuming no movement existed, then νοῦς and ζωή, and thus every νοεῖν, would be impossible. Yet this is what follows if one says: οὐσία = εἴδη, and the εἴδη are determined as resting in themselves, and γένεσις is accordingly excluded from Being. If everything is at rest, then νοῦς cannot be; there is then also no νοεῖν, no knowledge of οὐσία, of the εἴδη.

Καὶ μὴν ἐὰν αὖ φερόμενα καὶ κινούμενα πάντ' εἶναι συγχωρῶμεν, καὶ τούτῳ τῷ λόγῳ ταὐτὸν τοῦτο ἐκ τῶν ὄντων ἐξαιρήσομεν (249b8ff.). "On the other hand, the proposition that everything is in motion also excludes from being ταὐτὸν τοῦτο, namely νοῦς." To claim everything is in motion is also to deprive νοῦς and ζωή of the possibility of being. This ἐξαιρήσομεν makes it clear that it is not at all a matter here of the εἴδη themselves possessing ζωή but is simply a matter of counting νοῦς and ζωή among beings. For if we say everything is in motion, then there does not exist that which was established at 248a12 as a possible object of νοεῖν: <τὸ> ἀεὶ κατὰ ταὐτὰ ὡσαύτως ἔχειν, (that which) maintains itself constantly in a determinate self-sameness. If everything is in motion, this self-sameness does not exist, i.e., the disclosability of beings in a pure νοεῖν is impossible.

Accordingly, there must be an ἀεὶ ὄν in order for νοῦς to be what it is supposed to be, and there must likewise be a κίνησις in order for νοῦς to be what it is: a living disclosure, the carrying out of the uncovering of beings themselves. We must therefore strive with all our means against the one who ἰσχυρίζηται περί τινος ὁπηοῦν (249c7f.), the one who wants to press ahead to something, to assert something, show something, exhibit something, about beings while νοῦν ἀφανίζων (c7), allowing νοῦς (ἀληθεύειν) and ζωή to disappear, i.e., considering them non-beings. For whoever says anything at all about an existing thing is thereby already asserting: it is movement and it is ἀεὶ ὄν. In this way the phenomenon of γιγνώσκειν, under the title of a determinate κοινωνεῖν, becomes the central phenomenon, in relation to which both these interpretations of Being themselves become visible and intelligible in their necessity. On the other hand, each interpretation, οὐσία = σῶμα, γένεσις, and οὐσία = εἴδη, ἀκίνητα, is, by itself, insufficient. Neither one, taken as an absolute theory, can make intelligible the Being of νοῦς, of γνῶσις, of γιγνώσκειν. If there is indeed to be something like φιλοσοφία, ἀνάγκη . . . συναμφότερα λέγειν (249c11ff.), we are compelled to count "both together," the moved and the unmoved, as beings, to address both of them as existing.

Thus the exemplary phenomenon of κοινωνία, which allows the κοινωνία to be introduced into the discussion at all, is γιγνώσκειν. Γιγνώσκειν is determined in its Being according to its two aspects: 1.) as accomplishing, disclosing: κίνησις; and 2.) with regard to what is known, something that, in the sense of the Greek conception of knowledge, must always be: στάσις. This γιγνώσκειν thus provides Plato with the two concepts of κίνησις and στάσις, both of which are related to a unitary phenomenon, γνῶσις, as one and the same ὄν. By setting in relief κίνησις and στάσις, Plato acquires the two basic concepts alive in the positions of the preceding ontologies, the στάσις of Parmenides and the κίνησις of Heraclitus, and he does so specifically in such a way that he can at the same time unite these positions in the phenomenon of γιγνώσκειν.[1]

1. See the appendix.

§71. *The discussion of the thesis:* κίνησις *and* στάσις = ὄν.

a) Characterization of the situation. Reversion to the position of the ancient thesis: ὄν = δύο. Ἄγνοια ἡ πλείστη.

The ξένος now asks: Τί οὖν; ἆρ' οὐκ ἐπιεικῶς ἤδη φαινόμεθα περιειληφέναι τῷ λόγῳ τὸ ὄν; (249d6f.). "Does it not seem we have now already in our discussion disclosed and grasped, in an adequate way, Being, the meaning of Being?" Πάνυ μὲν οὖν (d8). Theaetetus is already satisfied and believes they have in fact reached their goal. For now both γένεσις (or κίνησις) and εἴδη (or ἀεὶ ὄν) have been given their due. But the ξένος makes him wonder: ὅτι νῦν ἐσμεν ἐν ἀγνοίᾳ τῇ πλείστῃ περὶ αὐτοῦ (e2f.), "we precisely now find ourselves in the greatest ignorance," i.e., precisely now that we think we have understood something about Being. The ξένος asks him σκόπει σαφέστερον (cf. e76), to take a closer look, i.e., as always, to look to the λόγος, to what is said in λέγειν itself. Look to what we say when we say: Being consists in the unmoved and the moved. Does not "the same question now revert back" on us ourselves ἅπερ αὐτοὶ τότε ἠρωτῶμεν (250a1), which we at that time raised," τοὺς λέγοντας εἶναι τὸ πᾶν θερμὸν καὶ ψυχρόν (a1f.), "against those who say: all beings are warm and cold." For they also said δύο, two beings, properly constitute ὄν, just as we are now saying the ἀκίνητα and the κεκινημένα are together τὸ ὄν, beings, καὶ τὸ πᾶν (249d3f.). Hence with all our discussions we are in the end basically no more advanced than the position we already rejected.

The ξένος now tries to take up again the same question πειράσομαί γε δρᾶν τοῦτο . . . , ἵνα ἅμα τι καὶ προΐωμεν (250a4f.), specifically in such a way "that in doing so we make some progress," progress in the understanding of the ἕν, i.e., of ὄν, which is constantly the theme. And so the same consideration will be repeated at a higher level—hence we shall examine that which was already dealt with and about which it was said that we would treat it ὕστερον ἕτερον. We will see that ultimately this treatment again draws upon precisely the same concept of the δύναμις κοινωνίας which had already been claimed for the interpretation of the ἕν, and that accordingly this concept of δύναμις is for Plato not an auxiliary notion to be used against the opponents but is genuinely positive.

b) The solution of the difficulty by means of the concept of the δύναμις κοινωνίας.

α) The avoidance of the coincidence of κίνησις and στάσις by means of the τρίτον λέγειν of ὄν.

Therefore κίνησις and στάσις are ὄντα, and obviously ἐναντιώτατα ἀλλήλοις (cf. 250a8f.), "most opposed to one another." "And yet you say": ἀμφότερα αὐτὰ καὶ ἑκάτερον ὁμοίως εἶναι (cf. 250a11f.), "both in themselves and each for itself would be in the same way." Therefore both, and each for itself, are in the same way. This again makes it clear that Plato does not mean that those beings which possess στάσις in an eminent sense—seen from the standpoint of the opponents, the εἴδη—would themselves be determined by κίνησις in the sense of life and νοῦς, i.e., that the Ideas themselves would be alive and knowing, but that κίνησις and στάσις each, ἑκάτερον, *are*. Ἆρα κινεῖσθαι λέγων ἀμφότερα καὶ ἑκάτερον, ὅταν εἶναι συγχωρῇς; (b2f.). But if now both are, then are not both in motion? Or, ἑστάναι αὐτὰ ἀμφότερα εἶναι (cf. b5f.), if both are, "are then not both at rest?" These conclusions drawn in regard to κίνησις and στάσις can be made clear by means of something like a syllogism.

κίνησις ὄν
<u>στάσις ὄν</u>
Therefore κίνησις στάσις
Motion is at rest.

Or, conversely, στάσις is, κίνησις is, and therefore στάσις is in motion. What is characteristic of this kind of argumentation is that it always looks at κίνησις and στάσις in such a way that ὄν functions in a certain sense only as an auxiliary concept and is not at all dealt with thematically.

Therefore the question arises: Τρίτον ἄρα τι παρὰ ταῦτα τὸ ὂν ἐν τῇ ψυχῇ τιθείς (b7), or "do you then posit in the end something like a third thing, next to κίνησις and στάσις, namely ὄν?" This τιθείς ἐν τῇ ψυχῇ is only a paraphrase for λέγειν, in the sense I have already referred to: the soul's conversation with itself about something.[1] Thus the ξένος is asking: in the end, when you say κίνησις is and στάσις is, are you addressing this "is" as a third, and specifically ὡς ὑπ' ἐκείνου τήν τε στάσιν καὶ τὴν κίνησιν περιεχομένην (b8), "in such a way that thereby κίνησις and στάσις are addressed as encompassed in it," συλλαβὼν καὶ ἀπιδὼν αὐτῶν πρὸς τὴν τῆς οὐσίας κοινωνίαν, οὕτως εἶναι προσεῖπας ἀμφότερα; (b9f.). In this final clause, Plato provides a short, yet fundamental, analysis of the τρίτον λέγειν; i.e., he offers here for the first time the precise basic structure of συναγωγή and consequently of διαλέγεσθαι. Because Plato's theme is now specifically ontological, he can determine more precisely the structure of what earlier, in the *Phaedrus*, he could only characterize with a general orientation.

1. Cf. p. 283.

β) The more precise determination of the structure of συναγωγή. Συλλαβεῖν and ἀπιδεῖν as structural moments of συναγωγή. The κοινωνία of ὄν with κίνησις and στάσις.

The first moment of συναγωγή is συλλαβεῖν, "taking together," both κίνησις and στάσις. This taking together does not mean to perceive each, κίνησις and στάσις, for itself, to grasp each for itself thematically. On the contrary, it means to take together both—"both" again not in the sense of two objects simply grasped as two—in view of something which resides in them but which they, κίνησις and στάσις, as such are not. Thus in order to be able to take them together we must precisely look away from them, from them as such in their immediately given content—therefore: συλλαβὼν καὶ ἀπιδών. This ἀπιδεῖν, this looking away, is not simply an occluding of the gaze, a neglecting of the perception of both; thus, in brief, it is not a non-looking but is precisely a looking at both, but in view of what? The term ἀπ-ιδεῖν has the same structure as ἀποδιδόναι, ἀποφαίνεσθαι, ἀπομαντεύεσθαι (250c1); it signifies an extractive seeing *[Heraussehen]* of something out of what is seen. Thus ἀπιδεῖν does not mean to overlook something, and disregard it as illusory, but to extract something, in seeing, from what is seen and to pursue what is thus extracted in the extractive seeing. In such extractive seeing and pursuing, that from which something is extracted in seeing, the ἀφ᾽ οὗ, is in a certain sense always present. We have hence: 1.) the συλλαβεῖν, the taking together of both in view of something, 2.) καὶ ἀπιδών, and intrinsically with the former, the pursuing which extracts in seeing. In this formulation, "the pursuing which extracts in seeing" *[das heraussehende Nachgehen]*, I want to make clear the double meaning of ἀπό: ἀπό in the sense of taking away something and in the sense of pursuing what is taken away as such. Therefore, the συλλαβεῖν, the taking together, is a not-letting-become-thematic of each single pregiven thing, a taking together in view of something; and the ἀπιδεῖν, the extracting, is a pursuing in this direction of the "in view of something," namely: πρὸς τὴν τῆς οὐσίας κοινωνίαν <αὐτῶν> (b9), "in view of the being-with of it," κοινωνίαν αὐτῶν, in view of its being-with, namely "with Being itself." In this taking together and in the pursuing which extracts in seeing, οὐσία is taken into view not as something isolated but as *the* κοινωνία, *the* being-present-together of Being, of ὄν itself: κίνησις and στάσις as ὑπ᾽ ἐκείνου περιεχομένη (cf. 250b8f.). In the speaking and seeing which are structured in this way, εἶναι προσεῖπας ἀμφότερα, "you say that both are." Thus here the συναγωγή, characterized earlier as a συναγωγὴ εἰς ἕν, is now revealed in its structure in a phenomenologically more precise way, and the mode of carrying out διαλέγεσθαι becomes visible.

Thereby Plato has premised to the proper dialectical investigation a methodological meditation, precisely the clarification of the συναγωγή which bears the whole process of διαλέγεσθαι. Its main structural moments are συλλαβεῖν, taking together, and ἀπιδεῖν, extractive seeing. What is important, as we said, is to grasp the ἀπό- in the correct way as an extraction from something and a pursuit of what is thus extracted. In this pursuit, the ἀπιδεῖν comes together with the συλλαβεῖν, insofar as the taking together of κίνησις and στάσις precisely does not mean to grasp them simply as two but to look away from them, in a particular way, such that in this looking away they are yet still there as those pregivenesses for which the ἕν, which is supposed to be seen in this ἀπιδεῖν, is determinative.

It is a matter here of what today we would call an essential consideration or a cognition of the apriori.

γ) The cognition of the apriori (= essential cognition) in Plato. Critique of the Kantianizing misinterpretations. On the genesis of Neoplatonism: ὄν as τρίτον in the *Sophist* and the ἐπέκεινα of Neoplatonism.

This cognition of the apriori is not an occasion to find a so-called "aporia of the apriori" by asking how something can be seen by looking away from it. If "to look away" is taken in the sense of "not looking at," then for all eternity it could not be determined how something can be seen that way at all. But this ἀπιδεῖν does not mean to look away, but instead to extract, in seeing, from what is pregiven and to pursue what is extracted in the extractive seeing. The second difficulty that has been found in the cognition of the apriori is this: we say that the soul is speaking here; the soul, however, is, as consciousness, something immanent. How then can it, when it speaks unto itself, i.e., remains in "immanence," determine something about the transcendent apriori? This difficulty is not a whit more substantial than the first. It is ignorant of what this λέγειν means. The λέγειν of the soul does not mean speaking unto oneself as something psychic, immanent, subjective, but instead means precisely to let be seen what is there. The difficulty arises only from carrying the position of Kantianism over to the cognition of the apriori. But we should not see in this Greek elucidation of the cognition of the apriori the difficulties that would be introduced by the Kantian position, which places the phenomenon of the apriori in the closest connection with subjectivity. For that is precisely what is to be excluded. And if the ψυχή is present, in this context, that does not in the least indicate subjectivity but means, on the contrary, that the grasping of the apriori resides on the same level as the grasping of the ontical in general. Admittedly, this merely gives us a first beginning toward the elucidation of this peculiar cognition of the apriori as well as toward the clarification of what is cognized therein, the apriori itself. It has by no means settled the whole complex of questions attached to the cognition of the apriori or to the knowledge of the essence. Phenomenology today still faces the basic task of clarifying the methodological moment of eidetic knowledge, which has nothing whatsoever to do with the eidetic "type" in psychology. This eidetic knowledge is connected to the general problem of Being, to the question of how something in general can be prior to something else and what this peculiar order of priority means. The Greeks had no occasion to reflect on all this, because they let the whole context of beings and Being play out, from the very outset, in the present. And hence it was not difficult for Plato to extract, in seeing, from the pregiven, from κίνησις and στάσις, a third thing, and to posit it as ὄν for itself.

To be sure, it is not that Plato was unaware of the difficulties here, but instead he asked: how can something be which is neither at rest nor in motion, and yet nevertheless *is?* This question is, for Plato and the Greeks, a very weighty one, if we realize that beings—as before—are necessarily either moved or at rest. And now there is supposed to be something which resides beyond both and yet is, and indeed not only is but constitutes Being in the proper sense. This questioning, as it occurs here in the *Sophist,* later became for the Neoplatonists a *locus classicus.* They derived from it the idea of the ἐπέκεινα, of what resides beyond all concrete beings: the idea of the τί, of the ἕν, of ὄν. The Neoplatonic commentaries, above all the ones on the *Parmenides,* take their orientation precisely from this passage in the *Sophist.*

c) The heightening of the difficulty of the elucidation of ὄν through the positing of ὄν as τρίτον. The similarity of the difficulty in relation to ὄν and in relation to μὴ ὄν. On the question of the interpretation of the transition.

The first result is this: the orientation toward λόγος makes ὄν visible as a third thing beside κίνησις and στάσις. And συλλαβεῖν and ἀπιδεῖν are to be taken positively as the mode of execution in which, from what is pregiven, here from two pregivens, κίνησις and στάσις, a ἕν, namely ὄν, as encompassing both, is extracted in an extractive seeing. Κινδυνεύομεν ὡς ἀληθῶς τρίτον ἀπομαντεύεσθαί τι τὸ ὄν, ὅταν κίνησιν καὶ στάσιν εἶναι λέγωμεν (250c1f.). "In this way we have come into the situation," Theaetetus says, "of announcing Being as something like a third thing." Ἀπομαντεύεσθαι means to announce something as existing, to let something be known. The ξένος replies: accordingly, it is not as simple as you believed before (249d8), namely that we would already be at the end of our difficulties simply by conceding that the ἀκίνητον and the κεκινημένον both are. But precisely therein resides the difficulty, because the Being of both of these proves to be a third thing and accordingly is obviously a ἕτερόν τι τούτων (cf. 250c4), "something other than them." If this is the case, however, i.e., if ὄν is for itself something and is so in being other, over and against κίνησις and στάσις, then τὸ ὂν οὔτε ἕστηκεν οὔτε κινεῖται (c6f.), then "Being is neither at rest nor in motion," i.e., rest and motion are not possible "predicates" of Being, not possible determinations of ὄν. The concepts of rest and motion, therefore, do not make Being intelligible but only heighten the essential difficulty involved in asking about the meaning of Being. For now the question arises: Ποῖ δὴ χρὴ τὴν διάνοιαν ἔτι τρέπειν (c9), "whither should the discernful apprehension now turn," if it ἐναργές τι περὶ αὐτοῦ παρ' ἑαυτῷ βεβαιώσασθαι (c10), "if it wants to appropriate something transparent—i.e., something fully and genuinely seen—about ὄν unshakably and as a secure possession?" What moves and what is at rest may be presentified, but whither should the gaze proceed, if it is a matter of a sheer apprehension of ὄν beyond both? The ξένος replies; Οἶμαι μὲν οὐδαμόσε ἔτι ῥᾴδιον (c12), "no direction is easier than any other," i.e., it is everywhere equally difficult. If something is not in motion then it is indeed at rest, and if something is not at rest then it is in motion—how can there be a τρίτον, a third thing, ἐκτὸς τούτων ἀμφοτέρων (d2), standing "beyond" change and unchange? The problematic ὄν has now obviously revealed itself νῦν ἀναπέφανται (cf. d2f.), as such a thing. This τρίτον brings us to a πάντων ἀδυνατώτατον (cf. d4), to the "most impossible of all," to something entirely counter to what we can understand and clarify.

At this place, τόδε μνησθῆναι δίκαιον (cf. d5), we must recall something we have already dealt with: the question of what we could mean by μὴ ὄν had given us the same difficulty, and we did not know a way out. At that time, at 237c, the question of μὴ ὄν was formulated in quite the same way as the current question of ὄν: ποῖ χρὴ τοὔνομ' ἐπιφέρειν τοῦτο, τὸ μὴ ὄν (c1f.), "whither should we properly convey the expression 'non-being'?" What is the original content which non-being is supposed to make present to us, which will allow us to exhibit the meaning of this word, and which will give it its proper sense? There we read, corresponding to πάντων ἀδυνατώτατον (cf. 250d4), παντάπασιν ἄπορον (237c6), "altogether without a way out." Thus the difficulty regarding ὄν is obviously not less than the one relative to μὴ ὄν, indeed in the end it is still greater (250e1ff.). And yet νῦν ἐλπὶς ἤδη (e7), there exists "now the prospect," since both, ὄν and μὴ ὄν, ἐξ ἴσου (e6), are "equally" difficult, that if we succeed in bringing one of them to show itself in a more clear and precise way, then by that very token the other will also "become visible," ἀναφαίνηται (e8). This is an anticipatory indication that the following discussion of Being will genuinely apprehend μὴ ὄν first. καὶ ἐὰν αὖ μηδέτερον ἰδεῖν δυνώμεθα (251a1), "and even if we should bring into view neither of them," hence assuming we are not successful (Plato is not particularly convinced of the definitiveness of the discussion he is about to launch here in the *Sophist,* which is an important warning for anyone who would want to expound a system of Platonic philosophy!), and even if we shall not succeed in getting either of the two into view, τὸν λόγον εὐρεπέστατα διωσόμεθα (cf. a2f.), "we nevertheless want to attempt διωσόμεθα (from διωθεῖσθαι) "to carry out, pursue," τὸν λόγον, the investigation, in the most appropriate way. The word διωσόμεθα is controversial. Stallbaum has suggested διασωσόμεθα[2] (from διασῴζεσθαι) "to redeem thoroughly." But this cannot be reconciled with the word εὐρεπέστατα. The Renaissance translation of the passage runs: *Sermonem igitur quantum possumus decentissime circa utrunque pariter persequamur.*[3] But this Renaissance translation is unclear. It is excusable to try to impose on this passage a univocal sense. That would not be without interest, for the passage forms the transition to a new discussion. A possibility I have pondered founders on the linguistic makeup of the passage. But I might say that λόγος is to be understood here (251a2) in an explicit sense, not in the neutral sense of a treatise, but as a discussion of a matter, so that what is meant here is this: Even if we do not get ὄν and μὴ ὄν into view as such, we shall still try to submit our speaking about them, our mode of talking about them, to a concrete investigation. Interpreting and translating the passage this way would give us a substantive transition to what follows; otherwise there is none. We could also then understand how in what follows the προσαγορεύειν (cf. 251a6) becomes thematic, for it is itself a more precise expression for λέγειν. Yet, as I said, this is only an expedient; I myself resist imposing this positive meaning onto the passage. I propose it merely as a possibility.

The abrupt transition indicates the questioning is now passing over to something for which we are not prepared, at least not on the basis of what immediately preceded, where the issue was κίνησις and στάσις. But everything which preceded concerning the definition of the sophist has indeed prepared us for it. For there it was always shown forcefully that λόγος is the phenomenon in which the sophist, and thereby also μὴ ὄν, exist, such that we surmised the whole dialogue would finally focus on this phenomenon of λόγος. And that is here the case. Admittedly, the transition is somewhat abrupt, assuming the passage in question cannot be interpreted as I suggested.

2. *Platonis opera omnia. Recensuit et commentariis instruxit G. Stallbaum,* vol. III, sect. II, Gothae, 1840, p. 177.

3. *Omnia divini Platonis opera, tralatione M. Ficini, emendatione et ad Graecum codicem collatione S. Grynaei, in officina Frobeniana, Basileae,* 1546, p. 189. ["We will therefore pursue the argument, in the most appropriate way we can, about both of them equally."—Trans.]

Chapter Three

The Positive Resolution of the Problem by Means of the κοινωνία τῶν γενῶν[1] (251a–264c)

§72. The question of the unity of the many (κοινωνία) in λόγος (251a–251c).

The ξένος now broaches a question derived from an orientation toward contemporary tendencies and school controversies, i.e., from the position of the Megarians and Antisthenes and their doctrine of λόγος. He asks καθ' ὅντινα τρόπον πολλοῖς ὀνόμασι ταὐτὸν τοῦτο ἑκάστοτε προσαγορεύομεν (cf. 251a5f.), how is it possible that we can always address ταὐτὸν τοῦτο, one and the same thing, by many ὀνόματα? For every ὄνομα means some one thing. Therefore, if many names, many expressions, are uttered, then we are addressing many things. Accordingly, it is not understandable how many names can mean one single thing. What is for us today readily obvious presented at that time a difficulty; it is the entire question of the distinction between meaning and reference with respect to one and the same object. In this προσ-αγορεύειν, which now becomes the theme, i.e., in the guiding line of this whole question, in the πολλὰ ὀνόματα ἓν ταὐτόν, what is pointed up is the προσ-γίγνεσθαι, the συμπλοκή, the κοινωνία, the "connection with" and "connection to." The consideration thus remains with the same basic theme, the theme of the κοινωνία, but not in relation to ὄν and μὴ ὄν; instead, the issue is now the κοινωνία within λόγος itself. What is in question is the προσ-λέγειν as well as a definite form of this προσ-λέγειν, namely δια-λέγεσθαι; for even in dialectic a λόγος is given which by itself also requires the possibility of a κοινωνία for the sake of λέγειν. To begin, the interlocutors take up an example, one obviously much discussed at that time. Λέγομεν ἄνθρωπον δήπου πόλλ' ἄττα ἐπονομάζοντες, τά τε χρώματα ἐπιφέροντες αὐτῷ καὶ τὰ σχήματα καὶ μεγέθη καὶ κακίας καὶ ἀρετάς (251a8ff.). "We address a man, πόλλ' ἐπονομάζοντες, in such a way that we call him many things, ἐπιφέροντες, and attribute to him determinations such as color, shape, height, wickedness, virtue." What about all these determinations and a thousand others we attribute to a being? οὐ μόνον ἄνθρωπον αὐτὸν εἶναί φαμεν (251a10f.), in addressing him we do not merely say that the one addressed, the man,

1. Title based on Heidegger (see p. 161f., the articulation of the *Sophist*).

is, ἀλλὰ καὶ ἀγαθὸν καὶ ἕτερα ἄπειρα, but that he, this one ἕν, is at the same time something else and countless other things. The same holds for the other beings we speak about. The peculiar state of affairs in λέγειν is: ἓν ἕκαστον ὑποθέμενοι (b2f.), in every λόγος, from the very outset, we address something, and posit it, as one, which is then pregiven, ὑποθέμενοι, for all further discussion; πάλιν αὐτὸ πολλὰ καὶ πολλοῖς ὀνόμασι λέγομεν (b4f.), and at the same time "we call this one *many things* and name it in many significations," πολλοῖς ὀνόμασι. In this way, the difficulty of the κοινωνία is expressed here in the formula: ἓν ἕκαστον ὑποθέμενοι πάλιν αὐτὸ πολλὰ καὶ πολλοῖς ὀνόμασι λέγομεν. It must be noted that λόγος here, above all within the discussion of the schools under attack, has not yet attained the clarification it will receive in Plato or, more fully, in Aristotle. Λέγειν refers here to an addressing characterized preponderantly as calling by name. This calling does not merely mean giving a thing a name but also means bringing the thing to knowledge, δηλοῦν. The ξένος says: Ὅθεν γε οἶμαι τοῖς τε νέοις καὶ τῶν γερόντων τοῖς ὀψιμαθέσι θοίνην παρεσκευάκαμεν (b5f.), "I believe we have hereby (with this question of how a ἓν πάλιν αὐτὸ πολλὰ λεγόμενον can be) provided young people, and old people who have come late to knowledge, a feast, veritable fodder"—insofar as this question was at that time wildly disputed in all directions, without anyone ever asking what this λόγος genuinely says. The "old man who has come late to knowledge" is Antisthenes, who, remarkably, always receives from both Plato and Aristotle such derisive epithets. For ὀψιμαθής should not mean it is a reproach to still learn in one's old age; it is a reproach only if one attempts to do so with insufficient spiritual possibilities and yet puts on airs. These ὀψιμαθεῖς—Antisthenes and his followers—fancy they have discovered the most profound of whatever things there are to be discovered, when they maintain that we can, in one λόγος, only say what is addressed itself, i.e., we can, in speaking about ἄνθρωπος, e.g., only say, ἄνθρωπος ἄνθρωπός ἐστιν, but not ἄνθρωπος ἀγαθός.

Aristotle is the prime source, and Plato a derivative source, of our knowledge of the doctrine of the Antisthenians. Their doctrine is of particular significance for the development of Greek logic, because it indirectly gave an impetus to a more radical reflection on λόγος. Here I can only characterize the doctrine briefly, insofar as it is important for an understanding of the end of the dialogue, i.e., for an understanding of λόγος ψευδής.

§73. *Excursus: The "logic" of the Megarians and Antisthenes*[1] *(according to Aristotle).*

a) Antisthenes' interpretation of λόγος. Λόγος as simple φάσις; the denial of ἀντίλογος.

Aristotle speaks of Antisthenes in the *Topics*, A, chapter 11, 104b19ff., in the passage where he elucidates the term θέσις, "thesis." θέσις δέ ἐστιν ὑπόληψις παράδοξος τῶν γνωρίμων τινὸς κατὰ φιλοσοφίαν, οἷον ὅτι οὐκ ἔστιν ἀντιλέγειν, καθάπερ ἔφη Ἀντισθένης, ἢ ὅτι πάντα κινεῖται καθ' Ἡράκλειτον, ἢ ὅτι ἓν τὸ ὄν, καθάπερ Μέλισσός φησιν (104b19ff.). "A thesis is a ὑπόληψις, an opinion," and specifically a ὑπόληψις παράδοξος τῶν γνωρίμων τινός, "one whose content resides outside of what is known," outside of ordinary knowledge, κατὰ φιλοσοφίαν, and whose content concerns fundamental cognitions rather than some accidentally omitted idea. The content of the thesis must relate to φιλοσοφία. Aristotle cites examples: Οὐκ ἔστιν ἀντιλέγειν, "It is not possible, in speaking about something, to say something contradicting it"—the thesis of Antisthenes; or "Everything is in motion"—the thesis of Heraclitus. Thus Aristotle quotes Antisthenes as saying Οὐκ ἔστιν ἀντιλέγειν. That means, put positively, that all we can say of something is itself, i.e., a thing is only itself and nothing else. This implies it is not possible to speak of something "as" something opposed to what it is. Orienting ourselves more precisely from Aristotle, we can say that every ἀντιλέγειν is ἀντίφασις; but an ἀντίφασις is possible only in the form of κατάφασις or ἀπόφασις, affirmation or denial, i.e., in the form of the "as." Yet Antisthenes maintains: there is no κατάφασις at all and no ἀπόφασις; on the contrary, I can say of something only itself, i.e., there is only mere φάσις. Therefore since Antisthenes says (without clear consciousness) that there is only φάσις, he must necessarily say that there is also no ἀντίφασις, no ἀντιλέγειν, which would be founded on the κατάφασις and ἀπόφασις. In other words, there is contradiction, ἀντιλέγειν, only in a genuinely explicit speaking that is always an addressing of something *as* something. In mere φάσις there is no contradiction and accordingly, taken strictly, no falsehood either.

1. Title in Heidegger's manuscript.

b) Λόγος ψευδής in Aristotle. Λόγος ψευδής as "deception," "distortion." The distinction between two forms of λόγος in Aristotle: λόγος ὡς εἷς and λόγος ὡς πολλοί. The synthetic structure of λόγος as a condition of the possibility of λόγος ψευδής. Antisthenes' denial of λόγος ψευδής.

A further passage from Aristotle, where he again cites Antisthenes, namely *Metaphysics*, Book V, chapter 29, 1024b26–34, can help clarify this claim that there is no falsity in mere φάσις. This chapter 29 deals with ψεῦδος. λόγος δὲ ψευδὴς ὁ τῶν μὴ ὄντων, ᾗ ψευδής (b26f.): a λόγος, an addressing that discloses, a λέγειν in the proper sense, is "false," as we say for the most part, or, to put it a better way, it "deceives," ᾗ ψευδής, "to the extent that, precisely as deceptive, it lets something be seen as present, τῶν μὴ ὄντων, which is not present." This is the exact meaning of the short sentence just quoted (b26f.). Thus it does not mean that a false λόγος concerns that which is not at all, but rather it lets something not present be seen as present. διὸ πᾶς λόγος ψευδὴς ἑτέρου ἢ οὗ ἐστὶν ἀληθής (b27f.): "Therefore every deceptive addressing of something—and accordingly also every deceptive self-expression about something—is related to something other than that which is made visible in the genuine disclosure." οἷον ὁ τοῦ κύκλου ψευδὴς τριγώνου (b28), thus, e.g., to address a triangle as a circle, and to communicate by means of this addressing, signifies precisely not to have the circle present thematically, as that which is to be exhibited and about which I am actually speaking. This does not mean there is no circle, as if the circle were a μὴ ὄν pure and simple, but rather: it is not there; that about which I speak is not present. In my speech I shove, in a certain sense, in front of what is there something else, and I pass off what is there as something it is not, i.e., as something that is not present. This makes it clear that ψευδής is in fact to be translated here as "deceptive." Λόγος ψευδής is a deceptive addressing, a deceptive utterance. That which is uttered in this way, the content of such a deceptive addressing and uttering, the λεγόμενον, can then be designated a "false proposition," although the expression "false" or "falsity" does not capture what the Greeks mean. It would be better to call such an uttered, deceptive proposition a fraud. Λόγος, even as λεγόμενον, is, in the Greek sense, always oriented toward being communicated, expressed for another person, so that the other can participate in the seeing. Insofar as the other, in the case of a deceptive λόγος, cannot participate in the seeing, such a λόγος is not simply "false" but fraudulent. The term "falsity" therefore takes the edge off the phenomenon thematic for Aristotle in ψευδὴς λόγος. Hence it is an error to claim, as Scheler does in his "Analysis of the phenomenon of deception,"[2] that Aristotle reduced the phenomenon of deception to false judgment. That would be correct only on the assumption of the traditional interpretation of the Aristotelian doctrine of λόγος. As soon as we see, however, that ἀληθεύειν is not a matter of the agreement of an uttered proposition with some other being, but is instead a matter of letting be seen, then the counter-phenomenon is distortion, so that we could say precisely the reverse, namely that Aristotle pursued the phenomenon of deception all the way to λόγος and understood it as a basic possibility of λέγειν.

Λόγος for Aristotle has two possibilities: ἑκάστου δὲ λόγος ἔστι μὲν ὡς εἷς, ὁ τοῦ τί ἦν εἶναι, ἔστι δ' ὡς πολλοί (1024b29f.), "a λόγος, addressing, ἑκάστου, of any being, can be, first, ὡς εἷς, as the unique one," i.e., the one and only λόγος cut to the measure of the being in question. There is only one proper λόγος of a circle, and we call it the definition, the essential determination, so that λόγος is identical here with εἶδος. Thus, in the first place, there is this λόγος of a being "as that which it is:" ὁ τοῦ τί ἦν εἶναι. In the second place, however, there is also at the same time a λόγος ὡς πολλοί, a λέγειν in relation to any being which provides multiple determinations of the thing in manifold aspects. For in a certain sense every being coincides with itself as itself and with itself as it is qualified. Every something is itself and is itself as it is qualified: οἷον Σωκράτης καὶ Σωκράτης μουσικός (b30f.), e.g., "Socrates" in himself as Socrates and "the cultivated Socrates." Because there is a certain connection here, ἐπεὶ ταὐτό πως αὐτὸ καὶ αὐτὸ πεπονθός (b30), because the cultivated Socrates is the same ἕν, the one also meant in "Socrates as such," because in both a ταὐτό is meant, two forms of λόγος must be distinguished for every being: first, λόγος as ὁρισμός, which addresses something simply in itself, and, secondly, λόγος in the trivial sense, which addresses something in relation to something else, even if this is something wholly extrinsic. Every λόγος in the latter sense is determined by σύνθεσις; to the identical something, something else is attributed. ὁ δὲ ψευδὴς λόγος οὐδενός ἐστιν ἁπλῶς λόγος (1024b31f.), "the deceptive λόγος, however, is not in relation to any being a simple λόγος," i.e., a φάσις; on the contrary, every deceptive addressing is possible only as an addressing of something as something. The *De Anima* says the same: τὸ ψεῦδος ἐν συνθέσει ἀεί (chapter 6; 430b1f.). And therefore—because he did not make this distinction between ὁρισμός and λόγος in the trivial sense—διὸ 'Αντισθένης ᾤετο εὐήθως (*Met.* V, chapter 28, 1024b32f.), "therefore Antisthenes had a quite simple-minded view" of λόγος when he

2. Max Scheler, "Die Idole der Selbsterkenntnis," in *Abhandlungen und Aufsätze*, Leipzig, 1915, pp. 3–168. (2. Aufl.: *Vom Umsturz der Werte. Der Abhandlungen und Aufsätze zweite durchges. Aufl.*, Leipzig, 1919).

believed μηθὲν λέγεσθαι πλὴν τῷ οἰκείῳ λόγῳ, "nothing can be addressed except in the λόγος proper to it," i.e., in the λόγος just set forth as ὁρισμός, ἓν ἐφ' ἑνός (b33), the one self-same thing posited in relation to itself: ἄνθρωπος—ἄνθρωπος. Nothing else can be said at all—that is the doctrine of Antisthenes and the circle of his followers. The consequence he drew was: μὴ εἶναι ἀντιλέγειν (b34), "it is impossible to utter a contradiction," indeed more generally: μηδὲ ψεύδεσθαι (b34), "there is no deception whatsoever"; every λόγος, as λόγος, is true. This position is perfectly consistent. That is, if one says λόγος is pure φάσις of a ἓν ἐφ' ἑνός, if thus every possibility of a λέγειν κατὰ τινός, every "addressing of something as something," is excluded, then the very possibility of deception is undermined.

Thus you see that λόγος, which is now becoming thematic in Plato's *Sophist*, includes in itself the phenomenon of μὴ ὄν, of ψευδὴς λόγος, and hence includes the question of how in λέγειν itself such a συμπλοκή of ὄν and μὴ ὄν could be possible. At the same time there lurks in the background the still further question of how λόγος as λόγος can stand in a possible κοινωνία with the ὄν it is supposed to exhibit.

c) Prospect: the synthetic structure of λόγος in Plato. The double συμπλοκή.

In the interpretation of λόγος in Plato's *Sophist*, two questions, therefore, are at issue:

1.) To what extent is a συμπλοκή of ὄν and μὴ ὄν possible in the structure of λόγος as such?

2.) To what extent is a συμπλοκή or κοινωνία possible between λόγος and the ὄν it addresses?

These two questions were separated only later, by Aristotle; for Plato they are still tightly bound together. Put differently, and explicated further, Plato considers λόγος in two respects:

1.) insofar as there resides, in λόγος itself, a συμπλοκή: in addressing something, something is addressed *as* something. Although Plato did not yet have an explicit consciousness of the structure of this addressing, he is still aware of a composition, a συμπλοκή, of λόγος out of ὄνομα and ῥῆμα. This distinction is the origin of an articulation found in the later logic and above all in grammar: noun and verb.

2.) λόγος is considered with respect to the fact that as such, with this structure resident in it, it still has a relation to the ὄν, the being, about which it speaks. This is a second κοινωνία. Note that Plato does not conceive the relation between the saying and what is said in a phenomenological sense—with regard to the moment of grasping and uncovering—but purely *ontically*. His position is that speaking of something shows that all speaking possesses in its Being in general a κοινωνία toward some ὄν, it relates to something else. And Plato does not make a distinction within the κοινωνία between the κοινωνία of λόγος toward ὄν versus a κοινωνία of, e.g., κίνησις toward the determination of ἕν or ὄν. In this way it becomes clear that he classifies λόγος as an ὄν among many others in the universal realm of what is in general, and that the relation of speaking about something is by no means a privileged relation but instead ranks in the same order as the συμπλοκή residing within λόγος itself and as the relation in general of one thing to another. If we do not have this clear, the entire following explication of λόγος will be incomprehensible.

This consideration of λόγος marks an essential advance beyond the traditional one (traditional for Plato), insofar as Antisthenes and the Megarians, in their doctrine of λόγος, still had no explicit consciousness of the structure of the addressing of something as something but instead understood λέγειν in the sense of ὀνομάζειν, calling by name. In this calling by name, which has the character of a "single-rayed intention," as phenomenology would say, it is always that which is called as such, and only it, that can be intended. Therefore every λόγος is related to a ἕν, such that only this ἕν itself can be said about itself. Because Antisthenes did not see a richer structure in λόγος, in the sense of καταλέγειν and ἀπολέγειν, for him an ἀντιλέγειν, "contradiction," is structurally impossible. This is precisely what is expressed in the proposition handed down from Antisthenes: οὐκ ἔστιν ἀντιλέγειν (*Top.* I, chapter 11, 104b20f.), "there is no counter-locution," no contra-diction, no ψεῦδος, no deception (*Met.*, Book V, chapter 29, 1024b26–34).

d) The positive meaning of Antisthenes' doctrine of λόγος for Aristotle. Aristotle's discovery of the λόγος καθ' αὑτό. The discovery of the γένος and its presupposition.

A final passage we shall cite from Aristotle's *Metaphysics*, Book VIII, chapter 3, 1043b24–28, refers to the difficulty of the doctrine of λόγος in Antisthenes. Aristotle points out that the difficulty the Megarians, i.e., Antisthenes and his followers, found in λόγος—that there is no ἀντιλέγειν but only a mere calling by name—yet contains something significant. ὥστε ἡ ἀπορία, ἣν οἱ Ἀντισθένειοι καὶ οἱ οὕτως ἀπαίδευτοι ἠπόρουν, ἔχει τινὰ καιρόν (b24ff.): what the followers of Antisthenes and others like them with no idea about science dealt with ἔχει, has, τινὰ καιρόν. This is at first view a remarkable use of καιρός! The expression means nothing else than what we today would call "decisive," something decisive, something significant. Namely: ὅτι οὐκ ἔστι τὸ τί ἐστιν ὁρίσασθαι (τὸν γὰρ ὅρον λόγον εἶναι μακρόν), ἀλλὰ ποῖον μέν τί ἐστιν ἐνδέχεται διδάξαι, ὥσπερ ἄργυρον, τί μέν ἐστιν, οὐ, ὅτι δ' οἷον καττίτερος (cf. b25ff.), "that it is not possible to delimit, ὁρίσασθαι, what something is, the essence of a thing," i.e., to determine it in a λέγειν, and specifically not because the ὅρος would be a λόγος μακρός, a "long λόγος," i.e., a λόγος composed of several words and therefore in a certain sense a λόγος that claims to express several things about one matter. This delimitation is still impossible, according to the thesis of Antisthenians. They say: one cannot determine a τί ἐστι in λόγος; at most one can determine a ποῖον. For example, it is not possible to determine silver in its essence, in its "what," by means of λόγος; one can only say: it looks like tin. It is remarkable that Aristotle emphasizes here that the thesis of Antisthenes, οὐκ ἔστιν ἀντιλέγειν, although it interprets λόγος simply as calling by name, still contains something decisive. Aristotle means Antisthenes is proceeding consistently when he denies that there can be a definition. A ὅρος is precisely supposed to elucidate a thing according to its substantive content; i.e., it is supposed to offer something substantively relevant, something new, about the thing in question. On the other hand, this λόγος as ὅρος, as definition, must be such that it does not express something arbitrary about the being, e.g., how it is related to other beings, but instead must express determinations residing in the being itself. Aristotle was the first to see this problem of the addressing of something as itself, beyond the mere positing of its identity with itself, and he set it forth in his *Metaphysics*, Book Z, 4. Here he makes the fundamental discovery that there is a λέγειν as λέγειν τι καθ' αὑτό, "an addressing of something for what it itself is," and specifically such that this addressing is not simply an empty tautology, as is the calling by name of Antisthenes, but such that this λέγειν τι καθ' αὑτό at the same time discloses the thing addressed for what it is. This discovery of the genuine λόγος, the original λόγος, was possible only because Aristotle had prepared his doctrine of λόγος through a corresponding doctrine of beings and their possible determinability. For what this λόγος, which addresses something as that which it is, exposes about the being is its ontological provenance, namely that which already resides in it, what it itself in a certain sense is, although this is indeed prior to it itself. This theory of λόγος, which verifies in a positive sense precisely what Antisthenes maintained only in a rough way, thus presupposes the discovery of the γένος. And this discovery was itself made possible only by the fact that a Plato preceded Aristotle. It is precisely this connection that we will explore in the following lectures. The important point—the reason I referred to these passages about Antisthenes—is to see how the theory of λόγος cannot be separated from the question of Being.

Plato himself cites Antisthenes even more often, but I will not now elaborate these passages, since they do not add anything particularly substantial. The citations occur in the *Cratylus*, 429aff.; the *Euthydemus*, 283e,

285e; the *Theaetetus*, 210d; as well as in the *Sophist*, 251b6ff., which is the passage we have been dealing with. Natorp, in a valuable article in the *Realenzyklopädie* of Pauly-Wissowa[3] (where many important early works of Natorp are hidden), deals extensively with Antisthenes, from whom nothing has been handed down directly. Furthermore, at the same time or even earlier, Dümmler carried out research into Antisthenes in his *Antisthenica*. Dümmler was one of the most gifted young philologists of the '80s. He was reputed to be the hope of the school of Usener, but he died an untimely death in Basel.[4] Actually, these quite early works demonstrate an uncommon ability to see substantive content beyond the merely doxographical ordering of quotations.

This question of λόγος ushers in a new discussion, one which, however, remains to be sure within the more general question, i.e., within the question of the κοινωνία of beings: is there such a being with one another on the part of beings? How?

§74. The discussion of the fundamental possibilities of κοινωνία *within beings (251d–252e).*

a) Introductory remarks. The further articulation of the *Sophist*. Determination of the "pre-possession." The κοινωνία within beings as the foundation for dialectic. Exposition of the fundamental possibilities of κοινωνία.

The question of the κοινωνία of beings is clearly formulated at 251d: πῶς τὰ ὄντα ἐν τοῖς παρ' ἡμῖν λόγοις τιθῶμεν (cf. d6f.), "how should we posit the Being of beings in our λόγοι?" This way of questioning is clearly governed by the fact that ὄν is interrogated thematically here as λεγόμενον, as encountered in λόγος. But we must be careful not to say, on the basis of this connection, that the Greek theory of Being takes its orientation from logic. Λόγος in the sense mentioned is still very far removed from what was later called logic. The Greeks asked how ὄν is present in λόγος, or, more precisely, how there can be a κοινωνία in ὄντα.

The question of the κοινωνία can be unfolded in three respects. There are three possibilities Plato initially discusses at 251d–253a. Then, at 253a–254b, he shows how a definite τέχνη corresponds to this field of possible ontological research and that this τέχνη is nothing else than dialectic. At

3. P. Natorp, "Antisthenes," in *Paulys Real-Encyclopädie der classischen Altertumswissenschaft. Neue Bearbeitung*, hg. von Georg Wissowa. Erster Band, Stuttgart, 1894. Columns 2538–2545.

4. F. Dümmler, *Antisthenica*. Phil. Diss., Halle, 1822. On Hermann Usener, see p. 217, note 15.

254bff., he carries out a dialectical investigation, specifically with regard to the basic concepts of Being and λέγειν. Why he chooses precisely these concepts will become intelligible on the basis of the antecedent characterization of dialectic, which we are about to learn.

If, in what follows, Plato discusses the various possibilities of κοινωνία, he does so because the elaboration of the κοινωνία *within beings* is for him the foundation upon which he builds his idea of dialectic. We can designate this as the "pre-possession" that guides the following investigations.[1] To understand the dialectic, we must realize that the κοινωνία is the presupposition of its possibility and that therefore it is not dialectic which first demonstrates the κοινωνία. There is dialectic in general only if the possibility of the κοινωνεῖν exists in its own right. Therefore, as will be shown, the concept of the δύναμις ἐπικοινωνίας (cf. 252d2f.) is fundamental. Before carrying out a determinate dialectical consideration, Plato attempts to clarify the idea of dialectic on the basis of this κοινωνία and does so from quite different sides and from ever new starting points. Because it is this κοινωνία that sustains the dialectic itself, Plato must exhaustively discuss the possibilities involved in that idea.

There are three possible ways to interrogate the κοινωνία.

1.) We could maintain μηδενὶ μηδὲν μηδεμίαν δύναμιν ἔχειν κοινωνίας εἰς μηδέν (251e8), "that no being has the possibility of keeping company with another being." Pay close attention to the expression δύναμις in this formulation.

2.) πάντα εἰς ταὐτὸν συνάγειν (cf. 251d8), it is possible "to reduce everything to the same," such that all things whatsoever δυνατὰ ἐπικοινωνεῖν ἀλλήλοις (d9), "stand in the possibility of being with one another." Therefore: either no being at all with another (the first possibility), or "all things with one another," πάντα ἀλλήλοις (252d2), (the second possibility).

3.) τὰ μέν, τὰ δὲ μή (251d9), in part a κοινωνία, in part not.

These are the three possibilities of κοινωνία now to be discussed.

b) The carrying out of the discussion.

α) First thesis: the exclusion of every κοινωνία whatsoever. The untenability of this position. The self-refutation of the Antisthenians.

The first thesis is: μηδενὶ μηδὲν μηδεμίαν δύναμιν ἔχειν κοινωνίας εἰς μηδέν (251e8). Note how strikingly this intensifies the earlier expressions for κοινωνία: προσκοινωνεῖν (cf. 252a2f.) and ἐπικοινωνεῖν (251d9). If this thesis held, that no being, no "something," could ever keep company with

1. See the appendix.

another,[2] if, in general, every συμπλοκή were excluded, then πάντα ἀνάστατα γέγονεν (252a5f.), everything would be in turmoil. Every onto-*logy* would collapse. For even those who say πάντα κινούμενα or ἓν τὸ ὄν all co-say, in their λέγειν, Being; πάντες οὗτοι τό γε εἶναι προσάπτουσιν (cf. 252a8f.), they attach ὄν to everything they speak about. Even the theory of Being which reverts back to the στοιχεῖα (b3), the elements—whether these are conceived as limitless, ἄπειρα (b2), or as having limits πέρας ἔχοντα (b3)—even this ontological theory would be impossible, if it did not presuppose the possibility of a σύμμειξις (b6). And, finally, precisely those who, like Antisthenes, say that a being can be addressed exclusively and only as itself, free from every other being—precisely they become καταγελαστότατα (252b8), "the most laughable." They do not admit "that something can be grasped beyond itself as something else," μηδὲν ἐῶντες . . . θάτερον προσαγορεύειν (b9f.), which is possible only on the basis of a κοινωνία παθήματος ἑτέρου (cf. b9f.), "through a togetherness that derives from being affected by something else," through the possibility of a relation to the other. And why do these men, who do not admit such a κοινωνία, make themselves precisely the most laughable? Because in their λόγοι they always already speak about "εἶναι," "Being," "χωρίς," "separate from," "τῶν ἄλλων," "the others," "καθ' αὑτό," "in itself" (c2ff.). In their thesis about λόγος they express already a whole series of determinate ontological structures; their thesis already contains implicitly a whole theory of Being. They are in a certain sense ἀκρατεῖς (c4), they cannot avoid employing quite fundamental determinations of the Being of beings. These people do not at all need an opponent, who would refute them from the outside, for ἔχοντες οἴκοθεν τὸν πολέμιον (cf. c6f.), "they have the enemy in their own house," the ἐξελέγζων (cf. c6), "the one who exposes them to ridicule." They need only speak to make evident that all speaking, all addressing of something, co-intends determined structures in the very sayability. The result is that λόγος as such, by its very structure, already co-says determinate moments of beings, determinate formal-ontological configurations. The constitution of sayability as such is already many-layered. Thus this thesis is not tenable, if there is to be any discourse at all.

β) Second thesis: unrestricted κοινωνία. Its untenability. Κίνησις and στάσις as ἐναντιώτατα.

The second thesis is πάντα ἀλλήλοις δύναμιν ἔχειν ἐπικοινωνίας (cf. 252d2f.), "every being can be together with every other," it is possible for beings to combine without exception, unconditionally and unrestrictedly. Theaetetus is confident he can demonstrate the impossibility of this thesis

2. AH: no δύναμις of the πρός, ἐπί.

himself, even though throughout the whole dialogue he has not particularly accomplished very much. He says that this thesis would allow us even to take motion together with rest and rest together with motion; and that is certainly quite impossible, for motion is indeed, in relation to rest, the ἐναντιώτατον (cf. 250a7), the furthest opposed. Here the distinction is clear between the essentially still ontical treatment of motion and rest in Plato versus the ontological treatment in Aristotle. Although Plato later says (256b6ff.) that there is a certain κοινωνία between κίνησις and στάσις—i.e., insofar as they are different, determined by the ἕτερον—he does not yet see the genuine connection, the peculiar substantive κοινωνία between motion and rest. In order to understand that κοινωνία, we may not take motion, as Plato does, purely ontically. Only if we ask about the Being of being-in-motion and about the Being of being-at-rest will we be able to understand it. If we say that what is at rest is not what is in motion, then we can in fact say that what is in motion is excluded from what is at rest, and that, in a pure sense, what is at rest is not what is in motion. On the other hand, in the Being of rest, i.e., in the ontological meaning of rest, being-in-motion is precisely co-posited, insofar as only something that has the possibility of motion can be at rest. That is to say, rest is, as Aristotle discovered, not an ἐναντίον in relation to motion, something opposed to motion, but, on the contrary, precisely requires motion. Rest is nothing else than a determinate limit case of motion, an eminent possibility of what is in motion with regard to its possible Being. But this analysis of motion can be carried out only if the Being of motion is seen and explicated, something for which Plato had neither the means nor the potential.

γ) Third thesis: conditioned κοινωνία. Its recognition as the only tenable thesis. The preservation of knowledge.

Thus, in view of the impossibility of the first and second theses, only the third remains: τὰ μὲν ἔχειν δύναμιν κοινωνίας, τὰ δὲ μή (cf. 251d9), or, as will be said later: τὰ μὲν ἐθέλειν, τὰ δὲ μὴ συμμείγνυσθαι (252e2), "that the one ἐθέλει, is prepared for a κοινωνία, the other is not." Therefore the κοινωνία within beings is in general a conditioned one and is conditioned by the present ontological and substantive constitution of the beings that are to be combined. This κοινωνία is conditioned *["be-dingt"]* in a quite peculiar sense: it is grounded in the things *[Dingen]*, in the matters themselves, and is pre-delineated by them. Only this last possibility of κοινωνία can be sustained, whereas both the others subvert the possibility of knowledge.

§75. Further clarification of the conditioned κοινωνία *of beings (253a–253b).*

a) Illustration of the conditioned κοινωνία by means of letters. The special position of the vowels as an illustration of the special position of the fundamental determinations of beings: δεσμὸς διὰ πάντων.

This peculiar fact of a conditioned κοινωνία is now first illustrated by means of γράμματα (253a1), "letters," and φθόγγοι (cf. b16), "sounds." σχεδὸν οἷον τὰ γράμματα πεπονθότ' ἂν εἴη (252e9f.); this relation of a conditioned κοινωνία among ὄντα is almost exactly the same as the one within γράμματα. Plato often refers to letters or sounds to illustrate ontic-ontological relations: *Theaetetus,* 202eff.; *Statesman,* 277eff.; *Republic,* III, 402b; *Philebus,* 18bff. It is significant that letters are employed for the sake of illustration in these late dialogues at the properly scientific level. It is of course no accident that precisely γράμματα are introduced, it is no mere whim on Plato's part, but is grounded in the fact that every λόγος, every λέγειν, is a determinate manifold of sound-structures. In every λόγος, however, in every λέγειν, there is a λεγόμενον, something said. In λόγος, what is addressed is preserved; the being disclosed in it is, so to speak, invested. In this way, what is said and, in a further sense, the sounds are, as it were, the representatives of the beings themselves.

This manifold of sounds in the linguistic utterance is characterized by the fact that there is among them a special class: the vowels (253a4). Plato says of them that they διαφερόντως τῶν ἄλλων (a4), they are distinct in terms of their behavior in relation to the others, οἷον δεσμὸς διὰ πάντων κεχώρηκεν (a4f.), "as a bond they penetrate everywhere"; they are everywhere, in every concrete sound-structure, in every word, always already there, κεχώρηκεν (perfect tense!). ἄνευ τινὸς αὐτῶν ἀδύνατον ἁρμόττειν καὶ τῶν ἄλλων ἕτερον ἑτέρῳ (a5f.): "Without them it is completely impossible for the other sounds, the consonants, to keep company with each other." They are the "bond," δεσμός, throughout all the others. They function, to borrow an image from physics, like the nucleus in crystallization; around them a word, as a unitary sound-structure, precipitates. These φωνήεντα, the vowels, which are the bond in all words, are supposed to suggest that there may possibly also be with regard to ὄντα something which διὰ πάντων κεχώρηκεν, is always already present in all beings. These are nothing else than the original determinations of Being: ὄν, ἕν, ταὐτόν, ἕτερον. This analogy had them in mind all along. It implies there are among ὄντα, and in everything subject to a possible κοινωνία, privileged determinations which can be found everywhere.

b) Excursus: further clarification of the universal presence of the fundamental determinations of beings. The analogy of the dovecote in Plato's *Theaetetus.*

Plato treats this peculiar relation, between the manifold of beings and the pre-eminent beings among them, in a similar context in the *Theaetetus,* 197bff. There he attempts to clarify λόγος ψευδής and ψευδὴς δόξα and uses a double image: the soul first as ἐκμαγεῖον (191c96), as a "wax tablet," and secondly as a dovecote (197d6). The latter analogy leads to the same context we have here: sounds. Plato introduces the consideration with a distinction between κεκτῆσθαι and ἔχειν, i.e., with an attempt to expose a distinction between "owning" and "having." For the Greeks, the expression ἔχειν has a special, emphatic meaning and expresses, in opposition to κεκτῆσθαι (mere ownership), something pre-eminent. Οὐ τοίνυν μοι ταὐτὸν φαίνεται τῷ κεκτῆσθαι τὸ ἔχειν. οἷον ἱμάτιον πριάμενός τις καὶ ἐγκρατὴς ὢν μὴ φορῶν, ἔχειν μὲν οὐκ ἂν αὐτὸν αὐτό, κεκτῆσθαί γε μὴν φαῖμεν (197b8ff.). "If someone buys a coat for himself and keeps it at his disposal, though without wearing it, we do not say that he *has* the coat but that he merely owns it." Ἔχειν thus means to put on, to wear, to "have on." This indicates that ἔχειν includes the sense that the ἐχόμενον is present, being worn, visible,[1] and not that it is hanging at home in the closet. This sense of ἔχειν as explicitly being-present-there also resides in the Aristotelian concept of ἐντελέχεια, which has the privileged sense of self-showing in presence.

This distinction between κεκτῆσθαι and ἔχειν also exists with regard to ἐπιστήμη. In order to show this, Plato introduces the analogy of the doves. Someone can catch doves and put them away in a dovecote. τρόπον μὲν <γὰρ> ἄν πού τινα φαῖμεν αὐτὸν αὐτὰς ἀεὶ ἔχειν, ὅτι δὴ κέκτηται (197c4f.): "Then we say that in a certain sense he has them, because he obviously owns them." We say therefore he owns them; but we also say he has them. Τρόπον δέ γ' ἄλλον οὐδεμίαν ἔχειν (c7): "In another respect, however, he does not have them"; he only has a certain δύναμις (cf. c7), namely λαβεῖν καὶ σχεῖν ἐπειδὰν βούληται . . . καὶ πάλιν ἀφιέναι, καὶ τοῦτο ἐξεῖναι ποιεῖν ὁποσάκις ἂν δοκῇ αὐτῷ (c9ff.). He thus genuinely *has* them only when he makes use of a determinate possibility, namely "to grasp them or to let them fly again; and this he can do as often as he wants." The soul as well, in relation to the cognitions that can be found in it, in relation to what is known and what the soul has at its disposal, can also be understood in a certain way as a dovecote, and one can say that there is in the soul a manifold of birds (d6). This manifold is characterized in the following way:

1. AH: concerning ἔχειν: on oneself, in the self.

some of these many birds are κατ' ἀγέλας χωρὶς τῶν ἄλλων (cf. d7), "gathered together in flocks, apart from the others, separated"; others again are only κατ' ὀλίγας (d7f.), together "with few others in small groups"; ἐνίας δὲ μόνας (d8), "some, however, are alone," διὰ πασῶν ὅπῃ ἂν τύχωσι πετομένας (ibid.), "they fly, each for itself, among all the others, wherever these happen to be." Thus some of them can be encountered everywhere, they have no definite dwelling place, but are διὰ πασῶν, "present everywhere." What is intended here as regards ἐπιστήμη, as regards what is known, what is appropriated (whereby again the διὰ πασῶν is set in relief, corresponding to the διὰ πάντων in the *Sophist*), is the same connection: among the knowables, i.e., among beings, there are those which have the fundamental privilege of universal presence. The *Sophist* illustrates precisely these relations by means of γράμματα. What is essential to this analogy in the *Sophist* is that, as in the case of the manifold of γράμματα, so also, among beings, there are certain ὄντα which, as ὄντα, are pre-eminent in their Being. If Being is interpreted as presence, then that means that there are determinations which are always already, in advance, present in all beings. Thus these offer a pre-eminent presence. In the *Theaetetus,* this remarkable fact of a privileged rank of certain beings, and of certain ontological structures, is illustrated from another side: at issue there are not ὄντα as such but rather ὄντα insofar as they are known. For, presumably, this fact of a privileged rank of certain beings must also be relevant for the knowledge which discloses beings. The analogy shows this in that there are, among the multiplicity of birds dwelling in the dovecote of the soul, ones which can be found everywhere. I cannot here enter into a closer explication of ψευδὴς δόξα in connection with this image. But that is not necessary, because the interpretation of ψεῦδος, as Plato presents it in the *Sophist,* is far more advanced than the one in the *Theaetetus*. Consequently, the elucidation of μὴ ὄν and λόγος ψευδής in the *Sophist* settles the questions raised in the *Theaetetus*.

c) The κοινωνία of letters and sounds as "object" of a τέχνη. Reference to a corresponding τέχνη regarding the conditioned κοινωνία of beings.

Just as now with regard to γράμματα there is a τέχνη (*Sophist,* 253a8ff.), a know-how in relation to the possible combinations of letters, so there is also a τέχνη in relation to the combination of φθόγγοι, of tones, with respect to their height and depth. The relations and totality-structures of the manifolds of tones are not arbitrary. The one who has know-how with regard to them, with regard to their possible combinations, is μουσικός (b3), whereas the other, who μὴ συνιείς, is ἄμουσος (ibid.). In this way, presumably, also in relation to the manifold of beings, of which we ὡμολογήκαμεν (b9), "have conceded" that in part they have a κοινωνία, and in part not, a τέχνη must exist which has the task, and which preserves the possibility, of bringing to light the κοινωνία and connections among individual beings.

§76. The idea of dialectic (253b–254b).

a) First characterization of dialectic. Dialectic as πορεύεσθαι διὰ τῶν λόγων. Γένος and εἶδος. The disclosure of the history of the provenance of "concrete" beings as the task of dialectic. The five principal moments of dialectic. Συναγωγή and διαίρεσις. Dialectic as uniquely free science, i.e., as philosophy.

The idea of this τέχνη, the one that elucidates the κοινωνία of ὄντα, receives its first determination at 253b8–c3. The characterization is ushered in by an expression we have already met, at the beginning of the dialogue, and we called attention to it at that time:[1] τὰ γένη (b8), that from which beings originate in their Being. It is significant that this explication of the τέχνη related to the κοινωνία of ὄντα begins with the term τὰ γένη.

For the most part, especially in the earlier dialogues, Plato exclusively uses the expression εἴδη. Now, however, this term γένη appears, and it occurs in Plato only in the late dialogues: in the passages just mentioned, as well as in the *Parmenides* (135b), the *Philebus* (12e), and also in the *Laws* and the *Timaeus*. The use of γένος strengthens the conjecture that Aristotle is in the background here—as Campbell[2] also surmises—since within Plato's terminology the word does not otherwise have an emphatic function. "Whoever assumes the task," τὸν μέλλοντα ὀρθῶς δείξειν (cf. b10f.), "of showing, in accord with the matters themselves," ποῖα τῶν γενῶν ποίοις συμφωνεῖ (cf. b11), "which stems harmonize," καὶ ποῖα ἄλληλα οὐ δέχεται (b11f.), "and which do not"—notice in this δέχεσθαι again the idea of the δύναμις κοινωνίας!—and, furthermore, whoever wants to show εἰ συνέχοντ' ἄττα διὰ πάντων (cf. c1), "whether there are stems which hold together, and are present throughout, everything," ὥστε συμμείγνυσθαι δυνατὰ εἶναι (c2), such that they δυνατά—again δύναμις!—συμμείγνυσθαι, "stand within the possibility of an all-pervasive and unrestricted combination," thus whether there is one thing necessarily

1. Cf. pp. 167 and 171.
2. *The Sophistes and Politicus of Plato, with a revised text and English notes by Lewis Campbell*, Oxford, 1867, p. 144.

co-present in every possible something, as ὄν in general, καὶ πάλιν ἐν ταῖς διαιρέσεσιν (c2f.), "and, conversely, whoever wants to show in relation to the setting off" of one thing against another, εἰ δι' ὅλων ἕτερα τῆς διαιρέσεως αἴτια (c3), whether or not certain things set off δι' ὅλων, extend "throughout everything," and are present as such, in which all other distinctions are grounded—whoever wants to make this three-fold demonstration will find it "necessary," ἀναγκαῖον, μετ' ἐπιστήμης τινὸς διὰ τῶν λόγων πορεύεσθαι (cf. b9f.), "to run through the λόγοι with a certain know-how," namely in order to extract, on the basis of this ἐπιστήμη in addressing beings, the λόγοι, i.e., to extract the addressednesses *[Angesprochenheiten]* of what is addressed. In this ἐπιστήμη, therefore, λόγος becomes thematic; the λόγοι must be run through in terms of how what is addressed is present in them as addressed. Hence it is not a matter of simply addressing beings in the natural and immediate way of talking about them, but instead the λόγοι themselves become thematic, and specifically within an intention of showing, δεῖξειν, the constitution of what is encountered in them. In other words, dialectic has the task of making visible the Being of beings. For such a task, Theaetetus now says, obviously what is needed is a τέχνη, or ἐπιστήμη, μεγίστη (cf. c4f.), "the highest science."

Concerning this elucidation of dialectic (or of what it deals with), we must keep in mind that Plato does here employ the expression γένος, though not in explicit distinction to εἶδος. On the contrary, Plato uses γένος and εἶδος promiscuously; i.e., he does not yet possess a real understanding of the structure of the concept of the γένος, a structure that can be elucidated only on the basis of a more original insight into the meaning of Being. Γένος means stem, descent, lineage, that from which something originates; i.e., it refers to a being in its Being, thus that which a being, as this being, always already was. The horizon of this interpretation is, of course, Aristotelian, whereas the specifically Platonic term for beings in their Being is εἶδος. Εἶδος, in its structural sense, is not oriented toward the provenance of beings, toward the structure lying in them themselves, but instead concerns the way the Being of beings may be grasped. The εἶδος is relative to pure perceiving, νοεῖν; it is what is sighted in pure perceiving. Thus the terms γένος and εἶδος, in their conceptual sense, are oriented toward entirely different contexts. Γένος is a structural concept pertaining to Being itself; εἶδος is a concept referring to the givenness of the Being of beings.[3] Γένος already clarifies the founding ontological connections: that which is already there, the anterior, the apriori. It presupposes a sharpened ontological insight. Εἶδος, on the other hand, emphasizes a being's autonomous percep-

3. AH: Insufficient. γένος: pastness. εἶδος: outward look, presentness. 364. (= p. 369 below)

tual content and, precisely as such, is not a sufficient basis for gaining clarity concerning the Being of the Ideas themselves. Εἶδος, as a concept pertaining to the givenness of beings, basically says nothing about the Being of these beings, beyond expressing the one directive that beings are to be grasped primarily in their outward look, i.e., in their presence, and specifically in their presence to a straightforward looking upon them.[4] Since it is precisely this concept of εἶδος that guides Plato's ontological questioning, at the beginning and actually throughout its entire course, he does not rise above certain difficulties in ontological research.

From the passage quoted, which renders the task of dialectic in a very compressed way, we can now extract various moments of dialectic:

1.) What is fundamental is that ὄντα—beings—are grasped as λεγόμενα, i.e., as encountered in λόγος.[5]

2.) If we take γένη and εἴδη together as the determinations of beings following from the way beings are thematic in dialectic, then we have to say that dialectic grasps ὄντα—beings—in terms of what was always already there in them, and this shows itself only in pure perceiving. In a certain sense, this is tied to the first determination, insofar as νοῦς, νοεῖν, and λόγος, λέγειν, are often identified; even Aristotle still posits εἶδος = λόγος.

3.) These beings, encountered in λόγος and now to be grasped in their γένη, are interrogated regarding their δύναμις κοινωνίας, regarding their δέχεσθαι συμφωνεῖν, i.e., as δυνατὰ συμμείγνυσθαι.

4.) Within this κοινωνία, there are some, ἄττα, a few, which are present διὰ πάντων, everywhere, "pervading everything"; they are distinguished by universal presence.

5.) The mode of disclosing the κοινωνία of beings includes reducing the multiplicity of beings to one, συνάγειν, and also includes, at the same time, the opposite movement, taking them apart, διαίρεσις. Διαίρεσις in a certain sense runs through the history of the provenance of a being forward, up to its arrival at the presence of the concrete being, out of what is already there, i.e., out of the γένος. Even the grasping of the full concretion of a being, as Aristotle later made explicitly thematic, is a matter of a mode of encountering beings which is relative to λόγος. The abiding question is therefore: how is something present as λεγόμενον? Insofar as it is always a matter of an encounter in λέγειν, even as regards the concretion of the factually existing thing here and now, the concrete presence is always an εἶδος; and precisely this, in the full history of its provenance, makes intelligible the presence of the "this here," which is all that counts. That, however, is

4. AH: In *commerce* with them, broadly understood.
5. See the appendix.

Aristotle's later explicit questioning. Plato deliberately places διαίρεσις third in the enumeration of the various tasks of the dialectician, because διαίρεσις is grounded in συναγωγή. Hence it is not what is primary in dialectic. Accordingly, a fundamental mistake plagues even the investigations of Stenzel,[6] in that he believes dialectic can be made intelligible on the basis of διαίρεσις. That, however, is an extrinsic access, since διαίρεσις is founded on the συναγωγή in συλλαβεῖν and ἀπιδεῖν.

This is the idea of dialectic. It admittedly leaves much to be desired with regard to a real elucidation of both the structure of knowledge and the structure of what is known. This deficiency is betrayed precisely by the fact that, in what follows, Plato again and again attempts to understand dialectic more adequately. But we will see that, for us today at any rate, the determinations that follow are still more obscure than this first one.

πρὸς Διὸς ἐλάθομεν εἰς τὴν τῶν ἐλευθέρων ἐμπεσόντες ἐπιστήμην (253c7f.): "By Zeus, we have in the end, hidden to ourselves, come across the science of free men," and we have ζητοῦντες τὸν σοφιστὴν πρότερον ἀνηυρηκέναι τὸν φιλόσοφον (c8f.), "in seeking the sophist, found the philosopher first." This ἐπιστήμη, therefore, the one characterized as dialectic, is here designated as ἐπιστήμη τῶν ἐλευθέρων, "the science of free men," i.e., of those who, in their actions and commitments, are not in need of what the masses require in all their undertakings, namely an immediate, visible goal. Small and narrow-minded people are not capable of sustaining a labor in which they do not at the very outset know where it will carry them. But that is the pre-condition of the free man who would venture upon this science. This peculiar concept of freedom, as used here in connection with the highest philosophical science, can be found taken up again by Aristotle in the passages we discussed in our introduction. In the *Metaphysics*, Book I, chapter 2, Aristotle also characterizes σοφία, the first science, in those terms: δῆλον οὖν ὡς δι' οὐδεμίαν αὐτὴν ζητοῦμεν χρείαν ἑτέραν, ἀλλ' ὥσπερ ἄνθρωπος, φαμέν, ἐλεύθερος ὁ αὑτοῦ ἕνεκα καὶ μὴ ἄλλου ὤν, οὕτω καὶ αὐτὴν ὡς μόνην οὖσαν ἐλευθέραν τῶν ἐπιστημῶν· μόνη γὰρ αὕτη αὑτῆς ἕνεκέν ἐστιν (982b24ff.), it is unique among the modes of knowledge that are free in a real sense; all other knowledge is oriented toward an εἰς ὅ, whereas this mode of knowledge is there simply "for the sake of itself" and accordingly posits the knower purely upon himself.

6. J. Stenzel, *Studien zur Entwicklung der platonischen Dialektik von Sokrates zu Aristoteles*, Breslau, 1917.

b) The second and third characterizations of dialectic. Ἕτερον and ταὐτόν as guiding concepts of dialectic. The obscurity of the third characterization.

Now there follows, at 253d1–3, a renewed characterization of dialectic. The ξένος indicates that it is important κατὰ γένη διαιρεῖσθαι (d1), "to divide according to stems," and thereby μήτε ταὐτὸν εἶδος ἕτερον ἡγήσασθαι μήτε ἕτερον ὂν ταὐτόν (d1f.), "neither to take the same for an other nor the other for the same," hence to divide beings according to stems and thereby keep the regard open for what is same and what is other, i.e., for sameness and otherness. Plato emphasizes precisely these moments within the task of the dialectician, because, in what follows, that becomes the discovery enabling him in general to progress within dialectic. He actually understands sameness as sameness and otherness as otherness, and on the basis of insight into the ταὐτόν and the ἕτερον he is able to grasp the concept of μὴ ὄν. Accordingly, he explicitly emphasizes that the dialectician must attend to the sameness and otherness of any given being.

The next determination of dialectic follows at 253d5–e2. It is again explicitly formulated and comprises four tasks. I confess that I do not genuinely understand anything of this passage and that the individual propositions have in no way become clear to me, even after long study. I can thus give you only an approximate translation. Other people are of the opinion, to be sure, that it is all very clear, but I cannot convince myself of that and so do not want to waste time on their surmises. The passage says, <διαλεκτικὸς> τοῦτο δυνατὸς δρᾶν (d5):

1.) μίαν ἰδέαν διὰ πολλῶν . . . διαισθάνεται (d5ff.), the dialectician "sees *one* idea throughout many," one determinateness of beings in its presence in many, of which ἑνὸς ἑκάστου κειμένου χωρίς (d6), "each lies there detached from the others," such that this idea, which is seen throughout all the others, πάντῃ διατεταμένην (d6), is extended and ordered from all sides.

2.) The second task: καὶ πολλὰς ἑτέρας ἀλλήλων (d7), the dialectician sees many ideas, which are different from one another in substantive content—this is partially understandable—but then Plato adds: ὑπὸ μιᾶς ἔξωθεν περιεχομένας (d7f.), "they are encompassed by *one* idea from the outside."

3.) καὶ μίαν αὖ δι' ὅλων πολλῶν ἐν ἑνὶ συνημμένην (d8f.), the dialectician sees "that the *one* idea is again gathered together into *one* throughout many wholes."

4.) καὶ πολλὰς χωρὶς πάντῃ διωρισμένας (d9), the dialectician sees "that many ideas are completely detached from one another."

Of course, it is more or less clear that at issue here are the same questions we have already come to know in the preceding determinations of dialectic. But the formulations are related among themselves in such a way that it is difficult to work out real structural distinctions. The traditional interpretation has been eased by the introduction of a distinction between γένος and εἶδος, genus and species. This is an unjustifiable procedure, since Plato does precisely not make that distinction. And so in fact it remains completely obscure what is meant by this μίαν δι' ὅλων πολλῶν ἐν ἑνὶ συνημμένην, and furthermore by the ὑπὸ μιᾶς ἔξωθεν περιέχεσθαι, and above all by the κειμένου χωρίς within the unity of one idea. I shall completely leave this passage out of consideration here.

c) Λόγος as mode of access to beings. Distinctions in the meaning of "λόγος." Conclusion of the third characterization of dialectic.

From what has resulted thus far concerning dialectic, the following is clear: λόγος is the mode of access to beings, and λόγος uniquely delimits the possibilities within which something can be experienced about beings and their Being. It is therefore important, on material grounds, that we clarify the concept of λόγος. Within Plato's foundational task, the concept is of course used plurivocally, and we must clarify it so far that we can at least see the distinctions in meaning, which for Plato always interpenetrate, and which, correspondingly, also occur in the concept of ὄν.[7]

1.) Λόγος means λέγειν, to address something in speech.

2.) Λόγος means λεγόμενον, what is addressed, i.e., what is said, the content of a λέγειν.

3.) At the same time, λόγος means what is addressed in the sense of the beings which are addressed—i.e., in a certain sense what a thing that is addressed itself says of itself, how it, so to speak, answers our interrogation of it.

4.) Λόγος means the way of saying, the proposition, τὸ λέγεσθαι.

5.) Λόγος means addressedness, i.e., the structure of what is addressed insofar as it is addressed: τὸ ἐν λόγῳ λεγόμενον.

These five different meanings of λόγος must be kept in mind, and one or the other must be employed to understand any given case, depending on the context.

Furthermore, in the determination of λέγειν as an addressing of something as something, we must note that what a being is addressed *as* can mean:

7. AH: (in the margin of the following comments): 1. a reference to a later passage (p. 403 below), 2. the δηλοῦν, cf. later ἀποφαίνεσθαι, ἀληθεύειν.

1.) it is addressed *as a being*, i.e., with regard to a concrete ontological determination (addressing as the uncovering of a determinate objective content of a being).

2.) In the addressing of something as something, the "as something" can refer to a character of Being and not of beings.

The expression λέγειν is thus used for ontical as well as ontological discourse. That the latter one is in fact in view is shown by the formulation: διαπορεύεσθαι διὰ τῶν λόγων (cf. 253b10), to run through the λόγοι, whereby what is thematic is what is said in the "how" of its sayability.

Thus we can briefly determine dialectic in the Platonic sense, as it presents itself on this higher level of Plato's meditation—according to the conclusion (253e1–2) of the characterization given above—as the demonstration of the possibilities of co-presence in beings, insofar as beings are encountered in λόγος.

d) Dialectic as a matter for the philosopher. The dwelling place of the philosopher and that of the sophist: the clarity of Being and the obscurity of non-being. The precedence accorded the thematic clarification of the sophist.

This dialectical science is possible only to one who is capable καθαρῶς τε καὶ δικαίως (e5), of philosophizing "purely and appropriately," hence only to one who can dwell in νοεῖν, thus to one who sees the ἀόρατα, who sees precisely what sensible eyes cannot see. Only someone who has at his disposal pure seeing can carry out dialectic. ἐν τοιούτῳ τινὶ τόπῳ φιλόσοφον ἀνευρήσομεν (cf. 253e8f.); only in this place, i.e., where one looks upon beings in their Being by means of νοεῖν, "can the philosopher be found." Yet even here: ἰδεῖν μὲν χαλεπόν (e9), "he is difficult enough to see." The "difficulty," χαλεπότης (254a2), in seeing the philosopher and the difficulty in seeing the sophist are quite different, however. The sophist flees εἰς τὴν τοῦ μὴ ὄντος σκοτεινότητα (254a4f.), "into the darkness of non-beings," and he plies there his dark trade. διὰ τὸ σκοτεινὸν τοῦ τόπου κατανοῆσαι χαλεπός (a5f.): "He is difficult to see on account of the obscurity of his dwelling place." The philosopher, on the contrary, τῇ τοῦ ὄντος ἀεὶ προσκείμενος διὰ λογισμῶν ἰδέᾳ (cf. a8f.), is wholly given over to beings insofar as they are purely sighted. It is difficult to see him διὰ τὸ λαμπρὸν τῆς χώρας (cf. a9), "because of the brightness of the place" in which he has to dwell. For this brightness blinds, in such a way that in it no distinctions are visible to the unexercised and unworthy eye. The eyes of the multitude, Plato says, are incapable πρὸς τὸ θεῖον καρτερεῖν ἀφορῶντα (cf. b1), "of sustaining for long a regard cast upon the divine." Concerning the philosopher, τάχα ἐπισκεψόμεθα σαφέστερον, ἂν ἔτι βουλομένοις ἡμῖν ᾖ (b3f.), "we could indeed deal with him more closely if we wished." That means a further consideration of the philosopher is left to our option; it is not required by the matters at issue themselves. But περὶ τοῦ σοφιστοῦ δῆλον ὡς οὐκ ἀνετέον πρὶν ἂν ἱκανῶς αὐτὸν θεασώμεθα (cf. b4f.), "in the case of the sophist, we may not desist until we have got him in our sight in a wholly sufficient way."[8] Here it is clear that the investigation of the place in which the sophist dwells, and what he himself is, has precedence over the investigation into the philosopher. For—this is the unexpressed thought—the philosopher clarifies himself from himself and does so uniquely in philosophical work itself. The sophist, on the contrary, must from the very outset be made thematic, because, as long as he is not understood, he condemns all philosophical research to impossibility. As the incarnation of non-being, he must be disposed of first, so that the philosopher's gaze upon the Being of beings and their manifoldness can become free. Thus we may not infer from this passage that Plato had planned another dialogue, as a sequel to the *Sophist*, namely one about the philosopher. This is so little true that it is rather quite the reverse; i.e., the corresponding thematic explication of the philosopher clearly has less urgency than that of the sophist. This entirely accords with Plato's Socratic attitude, which provides the positive only in actually carrying it out and not by making it the direct theme of reflection. Hence it is important to keep in mind that in the midst of the discussion of dialectic—and there is about to come a renewed characterization—Plato again refers to the sophist and his clarification, so that it becomes clear enough that the definitions of the sophist are not at all an empty game but have the positive sense of demonstrating the factuality of μὴ ὄν as the obstruction blocking the path of every philosophical investigation.

Before proceeding to the proper dialectical investigation, let us consider once more the result of the previous characterization of dialectic.

e) The result of the previous characterization of dialectic. The essential moments and basic presupposition of dialectic.

For Plato, the task of mastering dialectic requires one μετ' ἐπιστήμης τινὸς διὰ τῶν λόγων πορεύεσθαι (cf. 253b9f.), "to run through the λόγοι—as λόγοι—with a certain know-how." The knowledge presupposed, in the sense of a παιδεία, i.e., a methodological disposition, concerns, first, an orientation toward the fact that this research is a matter of presentifying the λεγόμενον ὄν, as it is present in λόγος, and, secondly, an orientation

8. AH: to see through.

toward the fact that it is thereby a matter of interrogating this λεγόμενον ὄν as regards the δύναμις κοινωνίας, and specifically in such a way that the connections of the ontological structures, as they arise in this orientation, are not simply juxtaposed arbitrarily. On the contrary, the task is always to reduce them to one, εἰς ἓν συνάγειν, such that from this one the entire ontological history of a being can be pursued up to its concretion. These are the essential moments of the basic methodological structure of dialectic in Plato's sense.

The basic presupposition for this dialectical task and for its mastery is what Plato previously analyzed in the methodological discussions of the ontologies: that Being means nothing else than δύναμις, δύναμις *of* κοινωνεῖν; i.e., Being pertains to the possibility of being-together *[das Möglich-sein als Zusammen-sein]*.[9] This ontological concept of the δύναμις κοινωνίας is the genuine ὑπόθεσις, that which is already posited in advance and which must be understood if one wants to take even the smallest step within dialectic. This ontological concept is not something provisional but, on the contrary, is precisely for Plato the basic presupposition for the activity of dialectic. When Plato puts forth this notion of δύναμις as an interpretation of the genuine meaning of Being, he obviously has a clear consciousness of the presuppositional character of this ontological concept. That becomes clear in the dialectical investigation itself. To be sure, Plato does not further reflect on what is genuinely presupposed in the δύναμις κοινωνίας. An interrogation of it did not lie within the horizon of his ontology or of Greek ontology in general. What Plato exposed with the δύναμις κοινωνίας as ὑπόθεσις is, in a certain sense, the last matter at which Greek ontology can arrive while maintaining the ground of its research. That does not mean this δύναμις κοινωνίας would not itself allow and require a further clarification of its sense.[10]

§77. The fundamental consideration of dialectic[1] *(254b–257a). The dialectic of the* μέγιστα γένη.

a) Introductory remarks. The ground, theme, and intention of the ensuing dialectical analysis.

Above all, we must keep in mind, in the ensuing dialectical analysis, that, along with the substantive results of the individual steps, the ontological

9. Editor's note: This formulation occurs only in Moser's transcript.
10. AH: *Time*. Cf. εἴδη, γένη above 354 (= p. 362).
1. Title based on Heidegger (see p. 386).

concept of the δύναμις κοινωνίας is manifest everywhere as the ground of the discussion. That is why Plato once again briefly emphasizes, prior to the investigation proper, the meaning of this ὑπόθεσις and of all that it includes. In the idea of the δύναμις κοινωνίας there resides:

1.) τὰ μὲν τῶν γενῶν κοινωνεῖν ἐθέλειν ἀλλήλοις (cf. 254b7f.),

2.) τὰ δὲ μή (b8)

3.) τὰ μὲν ἐπ' ὀλίγον (b8)

4.) τὰ δ' ἐπὶ πολλά (b9). The third and fourth determinations underline a more or less far-reaching substantive kinship of the ontological structures.

5.) τὰ δὲ διὰ πάντων οὐδὲν κωλύειν τοῖς πᾶσι κεκοινωνηκέναι (cf. b9f.). There are ontological structures present "throughout everything," and "nothing prevents them from being already there (note again the perfect tense) common to everything." They are pre-eminently present and in the present, such that nothing else would exist if these structures were not already co-present διὰ πάντων.

For the consideration at hand, Plato says, it is important that we <σκοπεῖν> μὴ περὶ πάντων τῶν ειδῶν, "do not undertake to investigate all possible εἴδη," ἵνα μὴ ταραττώμεθα (c2f.), "lest we become confused" by the multiplicity of these structures. Instead, προελόμενοι τῶν μεγίστων λεγομένων ἄττα (c3f.), "we will extract some of the ones addressed in the highest degree," i.e., some of the ones that are always addressed in every λέγειν. Thus it is a matter of a certain selection, and indeed not an arbitrary one, but an extraction out of what is proper to every being as a being. Accordingly, what this discussion will expose, within the limits of the ensuing dialectical consideration, must obviously have the character of the διὰ πάντων. The structures and results that are to be exposed will have universal-ontological significance. These extracted μέγιστα γένη will be interrogated in two respects: 1.) ποῖα ἕκαστά ἐστιν (c4), how each in itself looks as λεγόμενον, and 2.) πῶς ἔχει δυνάμεως κοινωνίας ἀλλήλων (cf. c5), "how it stands with regard to the possibility of being together with others." It is hence a matter of considering the ontological characters in view of: 1.) ποῖα, how they look in themselves according to their proper categorial content, and 2.) which categorial function is possible for them within the κοινωνία of beings.

Plato emphasizes explicitly that this investigation does not aim at every possible transparency that a dialectical consideration could attain, but instead we desire only as much clarity as will make intelligible our genuine thematic interest: ὡς ἔστιν ὄντως μὴ ὄν (d1), "that in fact non-beings are." In this way Plato now returns, from the general ontological discussion and from the critique of the preceding ontologies, back to the question posed by the sophist. At the same time we can now see clearly the methodological horizon within which this question is to be raised: it must be resolved within a dialectical discussion of what is said most properly and primordially in every addressing of things as such. Accordingly, the resolution of the question of the Being of non-beings must also be understood in a corresponding universal sense.

Plato now begins the proper dialectical investigation (254d4ff.). In order to understand this consideration, we must realize that it may indeed be easily intelligible in a rough verbal sense and that it is not difficult to succeed in explaining the interconnection of the individual steps and arguments. But this does not at all guarantee that the proper phenomenal content of what is here at stake has been demonstrated. If you yourselves try to follow this discussion by carrying it out yourselves—which of course you must do if you are to understand it—you will realize that you do not always and without further ado see the connections with the same transparency. What is needed here is always a very keen disposition of the eyes, which we do not, as we might wish, constantly have at our disposal. Hence I explicitly bring to your attention the difficulty of this discussion, so that you will not delude yourself with a certain merely verbal understanding.

b) The five μέγιστα γένη: κίνησις—στάσις—ὄν—ταὐτόν—ἕτερον. Exposition of their autonomy.

α) The pregivenness of κίνησις—στάσις—ὄν. Their relationship.

The consideration begins by enumerating the μέγιστα of the γένη at stake here: τὸ ὂν αὐτό, Being itself, στάσις, and κίνησις. These three basic concepts, ὄν, κίνησις, and στάσις, are pregiven. They are the stems around which the preceding critical discussion of the ontologies was concentrated. With them is pregiven the total horizon at issue in this dialogue, insofar as κίνησις and στάσις determine γιγνώσκειν, i.e., the ἀληθές and ψεῦδος, and, in unity with them, the possible object of γιγνώσκειν, ἀεὶ ὄν. At the same time, they form those titles of the question of Being which preoccupy ancient Greek ontological research, such that the ancient discussions are superseded in this new dialectical consideration.

The ξένος initially emphasizes that the relation between στάσις and κίνησις is one of exclusion. Καὶ μὴν τώ γε δύο φαμὲν αὐτοῖν ἀμείκτω πρὸς ἀλλήλω (d7f.). He says, just as he said earlier (250a8f.), that κίνησις and στάσις are ἐναντιώτατα, the furthest opposed to one another.[2] Κίνησις and στάσις represent a total mutual exclusion, here formulated by calling them ἀμείκτω, "unmixable." Κίνησις and στάσις are thus excluded from one

2. Cf. p. 356f.

another. On the other hand, however, τὸ δέ γε ὂν μεικτὸν ἀμφοῖν (d10), "Being is mixed in with both of them," i.e., Being is present in both. For both indeed *are* in some way or other. And an earlier analysis clarified the Being of each of them by means of the phenomenon of γιγνώσκειν, which, insofar as it is, includes κίνησις and στάσις.[3] Thus three γένη are pregiven for the dialectical discussion, and specifically in a determinate nexus: κίνησις and στάσις in mutual exclusion, both, however, in association with ὄν.

β) Ταὐτόν and ἕτερον as themes of the further investigation. Determination of the task and anticipation of the result.

At the end of 254d, the ξένος raises the proper question and thereby broaches a new phenomenal connection within these ontological structures: Οὐκοῦν αὐτῶν ἕκαστον τοῖν μὲν δυοῖν ἕτερόν ἐστιν, αὐτὸ δ' ἑαυτῷ ταὐτόν (d14f.): "Each of them, ἕκαστον τοῖν μὲν δυοῖν, κίνησις and στάσις, is indeed, however, on the one hand, ἕτερον, an other, and, at the same time, αὐτὸ δ' ἑαυτῷ ταὐτόν, itself; each is for itself, something self-same." Τί ποτ' αὖ νῦν οὕτως εἰρήκαμεν τό τε ταὐτὸν καὶ θάτερον; (e2f.): "But what have we now in this way said when we utter 'same' and 'other'?" This question makes it clear how the πορεύεσθαι διὰ τῶν λόγων will now actually be carried out: there will be a questioning back to what was said in the preceding sentence—that each of the two is ἕτερον and ταὐτόν. This is the first genuinely dialectical step. And now what is actually said in this λέγειν ἕτερον, αὐτὸ δ'ἑαυτῷ ταὐτόν is to be made explicit, or, put differently, what was formulated in the preparation of the analysis only as δύο ἀμείκτω ("both are unmixed in relation to one another") is to be said more precisely and brought into view. Therefore, when we say that κίνησις and στάσις are different, we co-say in both, κίνησις and στάσις, with regard to their opposition, something previously hidden to us, namely ταὐτόν and θάτερον. The ξένος then questions whether what is now said on the basis of this more precise consideration of the λεγόμενον in λόγος, whether both of these, ταὐτόν and θάτερον, are themselves δύο γένη (e3), "two proper new stems," and, furthermore, whether they τῶν μὲν τριῶν ἄλλω (e3), "are each themselves something other in relation to the first three pregiven γένη," and also whether they συμμειγνυμένω ἐκείνοις ἐξ' ἀνάγκης ἀεί (cf. e4), "are constantly and necessarily present together with those," whether they are therefore γένη which deserve to be characterized as διὰ πάντων, or, speaking in an image, whether they have the character of vowels. This questioning is simply the concretization of what was formulated previously: each of the following γένη is to be interrogated ποῖα—here,

3. Cf. p. 337f.

whether both are proper γένη—and πῶς ἔχει δυνάμεως κοινωνίας—how they stand in relation to the possibility of being together—whether these new γένη, in case they indeed are such, are universally present in every being, in every possible something, or not. Thus what we have here exposed, in view of the λεγόμενον, in view of the things we have just now said, is to be confronted, at the same time, with the dialectical criterion, i.e., it is to be interrogated as to its δύναμις κοινωνίας. Should these three questions—are they proper γένη, are they different from the other three, and are they universal—need to be answered in the affirmative, the result would be πέντε (e4), "five" such γένη, instead of three. And indeed, as we now see, this would happen without anything substantively new, any new substantive objects, supervening; on the contrary, purely out of λόγος itself something previously hidden is now uncovered. We do not in any sense deduce it but only uncover and take notice of what is still, and was already, there.[4] I stress explicitly the wholly non-deductive character of this dialectical consideration. ἢ . . . λανθάνομεν ἡμᾶς αὐτούς (e5ff.), "or are we in the end hidden to ourselves" when προσαγορεύοντες, we address, ταὐτόν and θάτερον, the same and the other, basically ὡς ἐκείνων τι (255a1f.), "as something of them"? That means: are we in the end blind as regards these two phenomena, ταὐτόν and θάτερον, and do not see that they present something other in relation to the three? The earlier critique of the ancient ontologies carried on its arguments with the help of this blindness, i.e., by overlooking ταὐτόν and the ἕτερον. That must now cease. We must now uncover this λανθάνειν. We must see quite clearly that we have before us new ontological characters, ones which do not coincide with the other three. It is therefore a matter of explicitly making visible the autonomy of ταὐτόν and θάτερον, on the one hand, and, at the same time, their universal presence in every possible "something."

Understanding the definitive proper analysis of the ἕτερον is a matter of seeing that Plato is concerned with securing these five in advance, with demonstrating a determinate limited κοινωνία in relation to these five γένη. He needs to exhibit the autonomous character of ταὐτόν and the ἕτερον because that is important for the further elucidation of the ἕτερον and μὴ ὄν. He must show that ταὐτόν, as well as the ἕτερον, are different from the three pregiven ones and that accordingly each is to be grasped for itself as something; i.e., they must be counted in the Greek sense, so that the ἀριθμὸς πέντε must be held fast.

I want to anticipate the result of the consideration, in order to provide you with a certain orientation to guide your understanding. Ἀλλ' οὔ τι μὴν

4. AH: self-asserting, being in power: δύναμις.

κίνησις γε καὶ στάσις οὔθ' ἕτερον οὔτε ταὐτόν ἐστι (255a4f.). Κίνησις does certainly not mean ἕτερον, and neither does it mean ταὐτόν, just as little as στάσις means ἕτερον and ταὐτόν. The substantive content of each of these four γένη is different from that of the others. Ὅτιπερ ἂν κοινῇ προσείπωμεν κίνησιν καὶ στάσιν, τοῦτο οὐδέτερον αὐτοῖν οἷόν τε εἶναι (255a7f.). "What we address as co-present, κοινῇ, in both, in κίνησις and στάσις, cannot be one of the two themselves as such." What can be attributed to both in the same way, to κίνησις and to στάσις, is something that cannot be identified with κίνησις as such, and just as little can it be identified with στάσις, insofar as the ὑπόθεσις of their difference from one another remains standing. This impossibility is already clear regarding both phenomena, κίνησις and στάσις, themselves. If one of them, e.g., κίνησις, were the other, it would, so to speak, "force," ἀναγκάσει (a12), the other to turn into the opposite of its own φύσις. Thus if κίνησις were a ἕτερον—understood here as *the* other—then στάσις would have to become κίνησις and vice versa, ἅτε μετασχὸν τοῦ ἐναντίου (255b1), since indeed, insofar as κίνησις is the other, this other would indeed "participate in its opposite." It would then come down to this: κίνησις στήσεται καὶ στάσις αὖ κινηθήσεται (cf. a10). The question is thus whether κίνησις can in general be determined as ἕτερον, yet without becoming στάσις. If that is to be possible, then (this is the implicit thought guiding the consideration) the concept of exclusion, of non-being, must undergo a more precise determination, and a distinction must subsist between these two characterizations: that something is itself *the* other and that it is other*wise*, an other in relation to others. The formulation at the end of 255a is so difficult to make intelligible because the investigation is still purposely proceeding on the ground of unclarified concepts of ἕτερον and ταὐτόν. And it can proceed that way because this sort of formulation—that κίνησις is ἕτερον—corresponds precisely to Plato's earlier position, according to which something is addressed in its essence, and this addressing is interpreted to mean that in it the essence is present. For example, if I say this chair here is wood, that means, in terms of Plato's earlier position and also in a certain sense still in accord with the current new position: in this something, woodness is present. Analogously, to say that κίνησις is ἕτερον means nothing else than that κίνησις, movement, is otherness, and στάσις is sameness. It must therefore be made intelligible that sameness can be attributed to both without their being the same, and that difference can be attributed to both without each being the other. Here is the proper crux of the problem. It is a matter of uncovering this unclarity in λέγειν and elucidating, correlatively, the sense in which ταὐτόν and ἕτερον are to be attributed to κίνησις as well as to στάσις and also to ὄν.

γ) The autonomy of ταὐτόν and ἕτερον over and against κίνησις and στάσις.

It is indisputable, and must be held fast as the phenomenal point of departure, that μετέχετον μὴν ἄμφω ταὐτοῦ καὶ θατέρου (255b3). "Both obviously partake in ταὐτόν and θάτερον, the same and the other." μὴ τοίνυν λέγωμεν κίνησίν γ' εἶναι ταὐτὸν ἢ θάτερον μηδ' αὖ στάσιν (b5f.). But we do not want to say that motion, as one and the same, as something self-same, would be sameness, or that rest, as different-from, as different from motion, would be differentness. Thus sameness and differentness are neither κίνησις nor στάσις, and yet we say: κίνησις is ταὐτόν and ἕτερον. Thereby we gain this much, that ταὐτόν and ἕτερον are initially, over and against κίνησις and στάσις, χωρίς, something other.

But the question has not yet been carried through to its end, insofar as there now occurs the possibility that ταὐτόν and ἕτερον are perhaps identical with a third, ὄν.

δ) The autonomy of ταὐτόν and ἕτερον over and against ὄν. Ταὐτόν and ὄν. Ἕτερον and ὄν. The disparity between ὄν and ἕτερον. The πρός τι as founding character of the ἕτερον. Results and further task.

The question is thus whether ταὐτόν and ἕτερον are identical with ὄν. Ἀλλ' ἆρα τὸ ὂν καὶ τὸ ταὐτὸν ὥς ἕν τι διανοητέον ἡμῖν (255b8f.): "Perhaps in the end Being and sameness are to be understood ὥς ἕν τι, as one." This possibility, however, is easy to undermine. For if we identify sameness with Being and, on the basis of this assumption, say what we have said at the beginning, that κίνησις and στάσις *are*, that Being is in them, then we would have to say, assuming the identity of Being and sameness: κίνησις and στάσις are ταὐτόν. But that is impossible. Therefore even sameness, ταὐτόν, is different from ὄν. Ταὐτόν is therefore just as different from κίνησις as it is from στάσις and also from ὄν. Accordingly, it is a τέταρτον (c5), a "fourth," a fourth ontological determination, which possesses its own ontological character and cannot be dissolved in the pregiven three.

Τί δέ; τὸ θάτερον ἆρα ἡμῖν λεκτέον πεμπτον; (c8): "Are we perhaps, then, to take the ἕτερον as a fifth?" ἢ τοῦτο καὶ τὸ ὂν ὡς δύ' ἄττα ὀνόματα ἐφ' ἑνὶ γένει διανοεῖσθαι δεῖ; (c8ff.); or should we say in the end that differentness falls, with ὄν, into *one* γένος? Note that Plato is not simply deriving this in the sense of a result, a formal conclusion: that the ταὐτόν is other over and against the three pregiven and that accordingly the ἕτερον is autonomous and a fifth. On the contrary, it is again demonstrated in single steps. Plato displays a special energy in the delimitation of the ἕτερον over and against the four others, in such a way that he does not merely carry out this delimitation once but pursues it a second time on a higher level. What is essential in the whole consideration is precisely this demonstration of the difference between the ἕτερον and the now pregiven four. For through the demonstration of the difference between ἕτερον and ὄν, κίνησις, στάσις, and ταὐτόν, the concept of the ἕτερον will become transparent. This transparency provides a new concept of "against," of "againstness," and thereby lays the foundation for a new concept of negation. The whole analysis is oriented toward the ἕτερον and its possible, or not possible, κοινωνία with the others.

What then is the relation between the ἕτερον and the three or, including ταὐτόν, the four? Is it πέμπτον λεκτέον (cf. 255c8), to be addressed as a fifth? Or is it in one γένος together with ὄν? For an understanding of what follows, and also of the proper delimitation of the ἕτερον over and against the ἐναντίον, we must realize that ἕτερον is still ambiguous for Plato here and that it even retains a certain ambiguity throughout the whole dialogue. In the first place, ἕτερον means an other. Secondly, it means τὸ ἕτερον, being-other-than; hence it is the ontological determination of an other as other, as being precisely in the mode of being-other. And thirdly, it means ἑτερότης, otherness. Because it is a matter here for Plato of a γένος which is as it were quite empty, a highest γένος, which pertains, as will become clear later, to every possible something, the distinction is blurred from the very outset; i.e., he does not at all succeed in distinguishing the ἕτερον as "an other" from the ἕτερον as "being-other" or as "otherness." This ontological consideration is specifically Platonic in the intertwining of these three meanings.

Plato introduces the consideration of the ἕτερον in its delimitation over and against the four—which also means in its κοινωνία with the four—with a general observation he will later, in a certain sense, retract: τῶν ὄντων τὰ μὲν αὐτὰ καθ' αὑτά, τὰ δὲ πρὸς ἄλλα ἀεὶ λέγεσθαι (c12f.)—note here the word λέγεσθαι!—the λέγειν of ὄντα is such "that we always speak of τὰ μέν, certain beings, καθ' αὑτά, from themselves, τὰ δέ, others, however, πρὸς ἄλλα, in relation to something else." Insofar as this proposition concerns the ἀεί, it is a universal and applies universally to every being. Λόγος, therefore, is taken here quite generally, either as a simple addressing of something in itself or as an addressing of something in view of something else, determining something pregiven in relation to something else. This means that λέγειν, addressing beings, taken quite generally, discloses beings in two directions: first, as they themselves are in simple presence, and secondly in the mode of the πρός τι, in terms of a relation-to. Correlative to λόγος, beings can therefore be characterized in their possible presence either as simply there in themselves or as πρός τι, in-relation-to. In λέγειν a double presence of beings becomes graspable: "in themselves" and "in relation to."

On the basis of this general observation, Plato says: Τὸ δέ γ' ἕτερον ἀεὶ πρὸς ἕτερον (255d1), every ἕτερον is in itself πρός. Hence there resides in the structure of the ἕτερον itself a still more original character, one which Plato does not here establish firmly, the πρός τι. In every case, the other is possible only as other-than. In this other there resides precisely the πρός, the "relation to."[5]

It is remarkable, and is precisely one of the clear witnesses to the inner limitation of Greek ontology, that here in the analysis of the ἕτερον Plato encounters the phenomenon of the πρός, the phenomenon of the relation-to, but is not capable, precisely in view of his own dialectic and his dialectical task, of making visible this πρός τι as a universal structure, insofar as this πρός τι is also an apriori structural moment of the καθ' αὑτό. Even sameness, the "in-itself," includes the moment of the πρός τι; it is just that here the relation-to points back to itself. This therefore documents a state of affairs often observed in such investigations, that in a certain sense a phenomenon is already within reach and is to a certain degree explicit, but that the researcher is nevertheless incapable of explicitly raising the phenomenon itself to the conceptual level and assigning it its categorial function. For, Plato here, and in the later dialogues as well, does not allow the πρός τι to attain the fundamental and universal significance which should properly and substantively pertain to it in relation to ταὐτόν and ἕτερον. In the *Philebus,* e.g., it is clear that Plato is indeed aware of the πρός τι but does not genuinely see it in its categorial function and in its primary position *prior* to the ἕτερον. He says there: Ταῦτα γὰρ οὐκ εἶναι πρός τι καλά, ἀλλ' ἀεὶ καλὰ καθ' αὑτά (cf. *Philebus,* 51c6f.), "these beings are not beautiful relationally," i.e., beautiful in view of something else, "but are always beautiful, in themselves." Here, in the *Sophist,* Plato claims the πρός τι only for the ἕτερον itself, as a conceptual determination of it, and does not set the πρός τι off against the ἕτερον as an original apriori, prior to the ἕτερον itself.

On the basis of this distinction between beings in themselves and beings in the character of the πρός τι, Plato now attempts to delimit the ἕτερον over and against ὄν. If the ἕτερον is necessarily other-than, i.e., if the structure of the ἕτερον necessarily includes the πρός τι, then there resides between ὄν and θάτερον a διαφορά. For, εἴπερ θάτερον ἀμφοῖν μετεῖχε τοῖν εἰδοῖν ὥσπερ τὸ ὄν, ἦν ἄν ποτέ τι καὶ τῶν ἑτέρων ἕτερον οὐ πρὸς ἕτερον (255d4ff.). If there were otherness, in the sense of the πρός τι, in the field of ὄν, just as in the field of the ἕτερον, then there would be othernesses which are not what they are, namely ἕτερον πρός. That is to say, if ἕτερον

5. See the appendix.

and ὄν had the same field, and if there are ὄντα, nevertheless, as we have heard, καθ' αὑτά, then there would be othernesses which are not other in the character of the other-than. Now, however, the ξένος says, it is for us perfectly clear that what is characterized as other is necessarily what it is in relation to an other. ὅτιπερ ἂν ἕτερον ᾖ, συμβέβηκεν ἐξ' ἀνάγκης ἑτέρου τοῦτο ὅπερ ἐστὶν εἶναι (d6f.). Whatever is as ἕτερον is so as ἕτερον πρός. Thus ὄν and ἕτερον do not coincide, insofar as there are ὄντα which do not have the character of the πρός τι. There is otherness only in a limited field: where the ἕτερον dominates. The noncoincidence of ὄν and ἕτερον, Being and otherness, means Being is different from otherness. That in turn means the ἕτερον is itself, as otherness, something other than ὄν and is, accordingly, a fifth, next to ταὐτόν, κίνησις, στάσις, and ὄν. The idea here is that in every ἕτερον there is indeed an ὄν, but there is not in every ὄν a ἕτερον.

And so a distinction must be made between the φύσις of a γένος (that which it itself already is according to its proper categorial content: Being, otherness, sameness)—between this φύσις and the γένος insofar as it is μετασχόμενον ἄλλου, insofar as an other is co-present with it. At the same time, it must be noted for what follows that the distinction now brought out between Being and otherness—a distinction concerning the categorial content of both these γένη—does not exclude the possibility that precisely every being, as something, is an other. This is the remarkable unclarity we still find here in Plato: he indeed operates with this distinction but does not genuinely expose it. Here, at this point, Plato speaks of a noncoincidence of the categorial content of ὄν and ἕτερον; later, however, he tries to show precisely that every ὄν is ἕτερον. The noncoincidence of the categorial content does not contradict the coincidence of the realm of categorial presence, of that which is determined by these categories. Hence there is a distinction between the noncoincidence of the categorial content and the coincidence of the realm of the presence of the categories which are under discussion here and which as such are διὰ πάντων, present throughout everything. In every ὄν, there is thus also the ἕτερον.

In this way, Plato exposes five γένη as autonomous. Πέμπτον δὴ τὴν θατέρου φύσιν λεκτέον ἐν τοῖς εἴδεσιν οὖσαν (255d9f.). He designates them here as εἴδη. This clearly shows that Plato makes no distinction between γένος and εἶδος. Thus even in regard to the earlier passage we—or at least I—dismissed as inexplicable,[6] the interpretation may not enlist the later distinction between genus and species.

These five are now ἐν οἷς προαιρούμεθα (255e1), that "in which" we will move to carry out the ensuing investigation. People have attempted to

6. 253d5–e2. Cf. p. 365f.

simplify this ἐν οἷς προαιρούμεθα, since it is linguistically remarkable, into ἃ προαιρούμεθα. That corrupts the sense. The peculiar linguistic form, which is very rare, is quite appropriate to what is at stake here. Plato does not simply want to note that these five are the theme of what follows—it is not a matter of an announcement of the outline—but he wants to say rather that we are to hold fast to these five as exposed, ἐν οἷς—and precisely not ἅ—προαιρούμεθα, "in the circuit of which" the anticipation moves. That is, we must hold fast to these five as the *ground* of the further dialectical analysis; the προαιρούμεθα therefore has an emphatic sense.

In introducing the dialectical investigation, Plato had already characterized the two respects under which the εἴδη are to be considered: 1.) ποῖα, and 2.) as regards their δύναμις κοινωνίας. So now the question is: what is the δύναμις κοινωνίας of the ἕτερον? The whole ensuing consideration is concentrated on the ἕτερον. Is it such, such a φύσις, which διὰ πάντων διεληλυθυῖαν (cf. e3f.), is present as "permeating everything else"? This is now to be shown, initially as limited to these five. But these five are formally universal ontological characters in the Platonic sense. Therefore what is determined about them will later be seen as universally valid.

c) The δύναμις κοινωνίας of the ἕτερον.

α) The pervasive presence of the ἕτερον in the realm of the five μέγιστα γένη. Exemplified in κίνησις.

Plato takes up again the distinction used above to characterize ὄν and ἕτερον, and he emphasizes that every "something" οὐ διὰ τὴν αὐτοῦ φύσιν (255e4f.), is not by its own categorial content as such an other but διὰ τὸ μετέχειν τῆς ἰδέας τῆς θατέρου (e4f.), "by sharing in the idea of the other." That means: every something, every γένος, is ἕτερον "by the fact that it has in itself the ἰδέα, the visible-ness, of being other." This is a very precise formulation, provided we understand ἰδέα correctly: "visible-ness" of being other. Plato is trying to say here that every possible something, as something, possesses at the same time the possibility that its being other, over and against another, can be seen: δύναμις κοινωνίας. The φύσις does not exhaust what is; on the contrary, Being is to be understood more originally precisely on the basis of the δύναμις κοινωνίας. From here, Plato now attempts to pursue the ἕτερον systematically through all other γένη. I emphasize explicitly that the ἕτερον, not κίνησις, is the dialectical theme, although the latter is spoken of constantly in what follows. Κίνησις is only the guideline for showing the universal presence of the ἕτερον throughout all γένη. Ὧδε δὴ λέγωμεν ἐπὶ τῶν πέντε καθ' ἓν ἀναλαμβάνοντες (255e8f.). "So we want to discuss," λέγωμεν (not to be understood in the pallid sense of λέγειν but in the dialectical sense of setting in relief what is said in λέγειν), thus we want to set in relief, in this dialectical sense, what is said "in relation to these five, and specifically in such a way that we perceive each of the five singly for themselves." After having established the five in their differentness, the goal of the ensuing consideration is to demonstrate the pervasive presence of the ἕτερον in them.

αα) Point of departure: taking up again the relation between κίνησις—στάσις—ὄν—ταὐτόν.

At first Plato takes up something said earlier: Πρῶτον μὲν κίνησιν, ὡς ἔστι παντάπασιν ἕτερον στάσεως (255e11f.). Κίνησις was initially distinguished over and against στάσις; we said: if they are ἐναντιώτατα, then κίνησις is *not* στάσις, it is παντάπασιν ἕτερον. Furthermore, we already claimed: Ἔστι δέ γε διὰ τὸ μετέχειν τοῦ ὄντος (256a1), κίνησις *is*. Thus, in the first place, στάσις is not present in κίνησις, but on the contrary ὄν is. We said further: Αὖθις κίνησις ἕτερον ταὐτοῦ (cf. a3), κίνησις is also distinct from ταὐτόν. This is all nothing new; it is just that what had already been said is taken together for the following consideration. Note well that what is set in relief as regards κίνησις over and against στάσις is being-different, over and against ὄν co-existence, and over and against ταὐτόν again being-different.

The more precise explication begins at 256a7, and specifically in the following order: Plato treats 1.) ταὐτόν, 2.) στάσις, 3.) the ἕτερον, and 4.) ὄν, and does so specifically with the intention of showing that the ἕτερον is present in them as well as is ταὐτόν. Plato thereby adds an essential supplement to what was previously acquired regarding στάσις, ὄν, ταὐτόν. He demonstrates: 1.) over and against the complete difference of κίνησις in relation to στάσις, that a certain ταὐτόν of κίνησις and στάσις is indeed possible, 2.) over and against the co-existence of ὄν, that κίνησις is a μὴ ὄν, and 3.) over and against the difference in regard to ταὐτόν, that ταὐτόν is also co-present in κίνησις. In the fifth and sixth Enneads, Plotinus later took up this passage about the five γένη and set it into a general metaphysical system with the aid of Aristotelian categories.

ββ) First stage: κίνησις and ταὐτόν.[7]

The first question concerns the connection between κίνησις and ταὐτόν. Ἀλλὰ μὴν αὕτη γ' ἦν ταὐτὸν διὰ τὸ μετέχειν αὖ πάντ' αὐτοῦ (a7). It was established above that αὕτη, κίνησις, is ταὐτόν, "self-same with itself," διὰ τὸ μετέχειν πάντ' αὐτοῦ, "because everything indeed participates in ταὐτόν," because ταὐτόν is διὰ πάντων. Now, however, it must be stressed, versus the sameness of κίνησις and ταὐτόν, that they are different in terms

7. Title based on Heidegger's manuscript.

of their categorial content. Τὴν κίνησιν δὴ ταὐτόν τ' εἶναι καὶ μὴ ταὐτὸν ὁμολογητέον καὶ οὐ δυσχεραντέον (a10f.). "We must therefore likewise say and not be troubled about it," i.e., we must simply accept it as the way the matter stands: κίνησιν ταὐτὸν τ' εἶναι καὶ μὴ ταὐτόν. To be sure, in speaking thus: αὐτὴν ταὐτὸν καὶ μὴ ταὐτόν, οὐχ ὁμοίως εἰρήκαμεν (cf. a11f.), "we are not speaking about κίνησις in the same respect." Hence there is, as was already indicated, regarding the way something may be addressed in λέγειν, the possibility of differing respects: something pregiven as present can be addressed in speech as this or that, i.e., it can be taken in different respects. In the background again here is the δύναμις κοινωνίας: the differences in respect, and in general something like a respect at all, are based on the δύναμις κοινωνίας, on the possibility that the δύναμις κοινωνίας co-constitutes the Being of something and its presence in λέγειν. ἀλλ' ὁπόταν μὲν ταὐτόν, διὰ τὴν μέθεξιν ταὐτοῦ πρὸς ἑαυτὴν οὕτω λέγομεν (a12ff.); if we say κίνησις ταὐτόν, we are speaking about the μέθεξις ταὐτοῦ πρὸς ἑαυτὴν, "its participation, *with regard to itself,* in sameness." Insofar as it is κίνησις with this categorial content, as κίνησις, it is determined as the same. But if we say μὴ ταὐτόν (b2), "motion is not sameness," we say this διὰ τὴν κοινωνίαν αὖ θατέρου (b2), "in view of its κοινωνία with the ἕτερον"; we say it πρὸς ἕτερον, "in view of otherness." By the presence of otherness, i.e., δι' ἣν ἀποχωριζομένη ταὐτοῦ γέγονεν οὐκ ἐκεῖνο ἀλλ' ἕτερον (b2f.), by the presence of the ἕτερον in κίνησις, in a certain sense κίνησις is ἀποχωριζομένη, "removed," from sameness, so that it is then οὐκ ἐκεῖνο, not the same, not ταὐτόν, but ἕτερον. And thus we can also quite justifiably address κίνησις as οὐ ταὐτόν. Here in ταὐτόν there appears again the peculiar dual meaning: "sameness" and "the same." Κίνησις is indeed the same and hence ταὐτόν, but, according to its categorial content, it is not sameness itself and therefore is ἕτερον, different, from ταὐτόν, and thus is οὐ ταὐτόν. Hence this one γένος is, with regard to ταὐτόν, both ταὐτόν and, equally, not ταὐτόν. Κίνησις is ταὐτόν and οὐ ταὐτόν.

The same consideration, as has just been carried out with regard to the relation between κίνησις and ταὐτόν, is now repeated with regard to κίνησις and στάσις.

γγ) Second stage: κίνησις and στάσις.[8]

Up to now we have been speaking of κίνησις and στάσις as ἐναντιώτατα, two φύσεις which stand opposed to one another in their substantive content, which exclude one another. This way of speaking is justified, provided we limit ourselves to the λόγος Antisthenes established as the only possible

8. Title based on Heidegger's manuscript.

one: it is possible to speak of something only as regards its own self-sameness. Then κίνησις is precisely κίνησις, and στάσις στάσις. But now the question arises: Οὐκοῦν κἂν εἴ πῃ μετελάμβανεν αὐτὴ κίνησις στάσεως, οὐδὲν ἂν ἄτοπον ἦν στάσιμον αὐτὴν προσαγορεύειν (b6f.). "Is it then so wholly inappropriate to address αὐτήν, namely κίνησις, as rest, as στάσιμον, as standing still, in the sense of μεταλαμβάνειν στάσεως, thus in the sense of the concept of Being we are now laying at the foundation: δύναμις κοινωνίας? Then perhaps πῄ, in some way, στάσις is indeed co-present with κίνησις. And this μετεχόμενον, this παρουσία, this co-presence of στάσις in κίνησις would justify saying that κίνησις and στάσις are not sheer ἐναντία but are in a certain sense ταὐτόν. Indeed, says Plato, we have previously[9] already factually established ὡς ἔστι κατὰ φύσιν ταύτῃ (256c2f.), "that the Being of κίνησις is of itself like that," i.e., in it στάσις is co-present. There it was shown that the ontological possibility of the concrete phenomenon of γιγνώσκειν includes its being movement, and, as γιγνώσκειν τοῦ ὄντος, it is at the same time movement toward the things to be known. The ψυχή or the ζωή is κίνησις and, as κίνησις, in a certain sense κίνησις εἰς ἀεί. The soul is the being in which we can see that in fact στάσις is co-present with movement. The soul is movement in the sense of ὄρεξις, and, as Plato shows in the *Symposium*, the soul does not merely have desire as one among many other lived experiences, but instead the soul is desire and nothing else. The soul is the μεταξύ, the between, which is directed to the ἀεί, i.e., to στάσις. In the soul, as desire, the ἀεί is co-present. Accordingly, κίνησις is related to στάσις just as it is related to ταὐτόν. It is not utterly distinct from στάσις but is itself "in a certain sense," πῄ (b6), στάσις. "In a certain sense"—the sense of this "certain sense" is clarified by the κοινωνία. Ontologically co-present with what is moved, namely the ψυχή, is the ἀεί. This remarkable and yet objectively grounded demonstration of the κοινωνία of κίνησις and στάσις must not be confused with the Aristotelian analysis, which says that rest is itself motion, as the limit case of motion. For Plato is not at all concerned with making motion as such thematic. On the contrary, he is speaking of what is in motion or, more basically, of the relation between what is in motion and what is unmoved. This moved being in its relation to the unmoved is here simply grasped dialectically-eidetically in the sense of εἴδη. Thus Plato is not here investigating κίνησις as κίνησις but κίνησις as a γένος, as an ὄν among others, whereas Aristotle elucidates the thesis that rest is motion from the meaning of motion itself. Plato does not at all inquire into this meaning here. Thus

9. 228c and 248a–249c. Cf. p. 337f.

we have the second stage: κίνησις and στάσις. With regard to both it has been shown: they are ἕτερον as well as ταὐτόν.

Plato now takes up the same demonstration with regard to κίνησις and ἕτερον as the third stage.

δδ) Third stage: κίνησις and ἕτερον.[10]

Λέγωμεν δὴ πάλιν (256c5), λεγόμεν again has an emphatic sense here, the sense of διαλέγωμεν; πάλιν, "let us carry on the theme": ἡ κίνησίς ἐστιν ἕτερον τοῦ ἑτέρου, καθάπερ ταὐτοῦ τε ἦν ἄλλο καὶ τῆς στάσεως (c5f.). "As was shown above, κίνησις is other than sameness and rest, and hence motion is also something other than otherness." Here we have in one sentence the dual meaning of ἕτερον: movement is something other over and against the other in the sense of otherness. Thus κίνησις is on the one hand a ἕτερον versus otherness, but at the same time it is ταὐτόν; it is not otherness and yet is an other. That is precisely what we said previously in the proposition in which we established the otherness of κίνησις versus otherness itself. We can in general only say: ἡ κίνησίς ἐστιν ἕτερον τοῦ ἑτέρου, if κίνησις itself is ἕτερον. Precisely in the proposition in which I say: movement and otherness are other, I say that in κίνησις the ἕτερον is co-present and that κίνησις is therefore ταὐτόν along with the ἕτερον in the sense of the κοινωνία. Κίνησις is thus not other and is other. It is not other in the sense of otherness, we can say interpretatively; and it is other precisely insofar as it is ἕτερον, different, from otherness and στάσις.

εε) Fourth stage: κίνησις and ὄν.[11]
The being-other of κίνησις as non-being.

Τί οὖν δὴ τὸ μετὰ τοῦτο; (c11). "What then now after all that" we have exposed with regard to κίνησις: namely that in relation to the three, ταὐτόν, στάσις, and ἕτερον, it is them and is not them. Are we to leave it at that? ἀπ' αὖ τῶν μὲν τριῶν ἕτερον αὐτὴν φήσομεν εἶναι, τοῦ δὲ τετάρτου μὴ φῶμεν (c11f.). Are we indeed to say that κίνησις is different from ταὐτόν, στάσις, and ἕτερον, but not draw in also the fourth, the one still remaining? Hence are we not to go on to say, as a supplement to the previously established thesis (κίνησις is ὄν) that it is also ἕτερον from ὄν and hence μὴ ὄν?

Here we see the meaning of the expression: ἐν οἷς προαιρούμεθα (255e1).[12] ὁμολογήσαντες αὐτὰ εἶναι πέντε, περὶ ὧν καὶ ἐν οἷς προυθέμεθα σκοπεῖν (256d1f.). Προυθέμεθα is now what corresponds to προαιρούμεθα.

10. Title based on Heidegger's manuscript.
11. Title based on Heidegger's manuscript.
12. Cf. p. 378f.

We have from the very outset thematically delimited the κοινωνία throughout the five. The five, κίνησις, ταὐτόν, στάσις, ἕτερον, and ὄν, are the basis of the dialectical consideration, which aims at the ἕτερον and whose goal is the elaboration of its structure. These five were exhibited in advance as κεχωρισμένα, i.e., as autonomous εἴδη, and, as these five, they were διαιρετά, taken apart from one another and held fast as such. This basis alone makes possible the explication which aims at delimiting κίνησις not only in opposition to ταὐτόν, in opposition to στάσις, and in opposition to the ἕτερον, but even in opposition to ὄν.

We must clarify the relation of κίνησις to ὄν. Ἀδεῶς ἄρα . . . διαμαχόμενοι λέγωμεν (d5f.), "we must hence struggle through without fear or hesitation" to the proposition: τὴν κίνησιν ἕτερον εἶναι τοῦ ὄντος (d5), "that motion is also different from Being." And here Plato follows the same train of thought: motion *is;* we already saw that κίνησις μετέχει in ὄν insofar as it is at all.[13] In this respect, it is ταὐτόν with ὄν. The question is now whether it can also be ἕτερον τοῦ ὄντος. In the case of κίνησις, Plato already demonstrated the presence of the ἕτερον in relation to the three earlier γένη. Therefore insofar as motion in itself already has the ἕτερον present in it, and insofar as ὄν is for its part co-present as a fifth, thereby κίνησις is also ἕτερον τοῦ ὄντος. We must say here that motion, or, more precisely, movement, is different from Being, or, more exactly, from Beingness. Accordingly, κίνησις is ὄντως οὐκ ὄν καὶ ὄν (cf. d8f.), "it is, in its mode of Being, not ὄν, and it is ὄν."

Thereby we have shown: τὸ μὴ ὂν ἐπί τε κινήσεως εἶναι καὶ κατὰ πάντα τὰ γένη (d11f.), that in the case of κίνησις, τὸ μὴ ὂν εἶναι, that in all directions—in relation to the four others—κίνησις is not the others, i.e., it has in relation to all the others the character of the ἕτερον, insofar as the ἕτερον is διὰ πάντων. Hence on the basis of the universal presence of the ἕτερον, κίνησις is at the same time a μὴ ὄν. But that means μὴ ὄν is present in κίνησις with regard to the κοινωνία of κίνησις with all the others. This demonstrates, within in the circuit of the five, the οὐσία μὴ ὄντος, the presence of non-being, in the Being of κίνησις. Notice that this is not a matter of a conclusion from the three to the fourth but instead is a demonstration within the five themselves, with a thematic orientation toward κίνησις, in which the presence of the ἕτερον was already made clear. Insofar as the ἕτερον is already present in κίνησις, but also insofar as the κοινωνία of the five already exists, κίνησις is as such different from ὄν. Thus this consideration has not demonstrated something about κίνησις but instead

13. 256a1. Cf. p. 380.

has dialectically shown the pervasive presence of the ἕτερον in the κίνησις toward all other εἴδη.

Insofar as this consideration is a formal-universal one, insofar as the ἕτερον enjoys this pervasive presence, this result is valid without further ado κατὰ πάντα.

β) The universal presence of the ἕτερον in all ὄντα in general. The universal presence of non-being.

κατὰ πάντα γὰρ ἡ θατέρου φύσις ἕτερον ἀπεργαζομένη τοῦ ὄντος ἕκαστον οὐκ ὂν ποιεῖ (d12f.), the pervasive presence of the ἕτερον in all things constitutes their being different from ὄν; i.e., the presence of the ἕτερον constitutes the non-being of every being: ἕκαστον οὐκ ὂν ποιεῖ, "it makes everything into a non-being." Recall the expression ποιεῖν, which we have encountered earlier: ποιεῖν = ἄγειν εἰς οὐσίαν.[14] The presence of the ἕτερον thus in a certain sense brings the μὴ ὄν into being, into presence. σύμπαντα κατὰ ταὐτὰ οὐκ ὄντα ὀρθῶς ἐροῦμεν, καὶ πάλιν, ὅτι μετέχει τοῦ ὄντος, εἶναί τε καὶ ὄντα (cf. e2f.). Everything, therefore—insofar as we have carried out the demonstration on something that is διὰ πάντων—is οὐκ ὄντα καὶ πάλιν ὄντα; all beings are and, as beings, at the same time are not. Hence there remains in the background what later will be shown explicitly, that here non-being means ἕτερον. This ἕτερον not only provides the demonstration of the constitution of non-beings but at the same time also reveals the ground for understanding this proper "non," whose previous concealment was made possible in general by the thesis of Parmenides. Hence insofar as the ἕτερον has an all-pervasive presence, it turns every being into a non-being.

And indeed now the mode of Being of the other is different. Every εἶδος, Plato says, is many, πολύ (e5), i.e., every concrete being, taken in its essence, still contains a manifold of other objective determinations, which are there potentially and can be brought out. Every concrete being has a manifold of essential contents which the dialectical consideration can demonstrate in the λέγειν of this ὄν as they are co-present in pure νοεῖν; and precisely this co-presence determines the ὄν in its essence. This is at the same time the basis for what Aristotle later exhibited as the ὅρος, the λόγος κατ' ἐξοχήν. Hence every εἶδος is many and is at the same time ἄπειρον (e6), "limitless," in what it is not. καὶ τὸ ὂν αὐτό (257a1), "and the being itself" is what it is in such a way that it ὅσαπέρ ἐστι τὰ ἄλλα, κατὰ τοσαῦτα οὐκ ἔστιν (a4f.); "insofar as it *is* the others, to that extent it precisely *is not.*" That means being other is the non-being of ὄν, or, conversely, non-being is εἶναι

14. Cf. *Sophist* 219b4f. See p. 186ff.

τὰ ἄλλα, "*being* the others." This state of affairs within beings must simply be assumed, ἐπείπερ ἔχει κοινωνίαν ἀλλήλοις ἡ τῶν γενῶν φύσις (a8f.), since every proper content, every γένος, as a φύσις, has a κοινωνία with the others. Here it is quite clear that the Being of non-beings can be clarified only on the basis of the κοινωνία.

And so we have gone through the fundamental dialectical consideration in the *Sophist*, which is usually taken as the proper kernel of the dialogue, whereas the treatment of the sophist himself is regarded as the so-called shell. In this fundamental consideration, which analyzes the dialectical relations of ὄν, στάσις, κίνησις, ταὐτόν, and μὴ ὄν, or ἕτερον, it is κίνησις that guides the consideration. I want to emphasize explicitly once more, however, that κίνησις is not the primary and proper theme. What is properly supposed to be shown is that the ἕτερον, being-other, is there in each of the possible εἴδη, that it can be present with them, i.e., that it has a κοινωνία with them all. I emphasize that it is not in principle necessary for this dialectical consideration to be carried out upon κίνησις. Στάσις, or ὄν, or ταὐτόν, could just as well serve to guide the proper consideration. We will later see why nevertheless it is precisely κίνησις that is thematic and why the possible presence of the ἕτερον is demonstrated precisely in relation to κίνησις.

Just as the present dialectical consideration aims at the ἕτερον in order to delimit it over and against the ἐναντίον, so the new phenomenon of the ἕτερον makes visible the dialectical field of the ἕτερον; in other words, it conceptually elucidates the structure of the ἕτερον itself. The concept of μὴ ὄν then becomes determinable.

§78. The conceptual elucidation of the structure of the ἕτερον*. The determination of the concept of* μὴ ὄν *(257b–259d).*

a) The πρός τι as the fundamental structure of the ἕτερον. The character of the "not" as disclosing the matters themselves.

α) The distinction between two modes of "not": ἐναντίον and ἕτερον (empty "opposite" and substantive other).

Ὁπόταν τὸ μὴ ὂν λέγωμεν, ὡς ἔοικεν, οὐκ ἀναντίον τι λέγομεν τοῦ ὄντος ἀλλ' ἕτερον μόνον (257b3f.). "When we speak of μὴ ὄν we are not talking about something like an ἐναντίον, that which, in its opposition to beings, is simply excluded, but rather ἕτερον μόνον; we mean by μὴ ὄν only something other." This "only," ἕτερον μόνον, means that ὄν remains preserved. Putting it sharply, the Being of the "not" (the "non-"), the μή, is nothing else than the δύναμις of the πρός τι, the presence of the Being-in-relation-to. This is only a more precise formulation given to our interpretation of the idea of κοινωνία. The Being of the "not," the μή in the sense of the ἕτερον, is the δύναμις of the πρός τι. Plato does not exhibit this as such, but it is implicit in the idea of κοινωνία.

Οἷον ὅταν εἴπωμέν τι μὴ μέγα, τότε μᾶλλόν τί σοι φαινόμεθα τὸ σμικρὸν ἢ τὸ ἴσον δηλοῦν τῷ ῥήματι; (b6f.). Μὴ μέγα thus means not simply "small" in the sense of the minimum of μέγα, but instead it can mean "not bigger," "same." And so it is clear again that Plato did indeed not attain perfect clarity regarding the relations of opposition which play a role here. For him it is simply important that the ἕτερον is an ὄν, that therefore something still remains preserved in being, and that the ἕτερον does not entail an utter exclusion. Accordingly, ἀπόφασις may not be interpreted as if denial meant the "opposite," in the sense of exclusion, but instead denial only means that the prefixed οὐκ, or μή, τῶν ἄλλων τὶ μηνύει, shows something of the others, in relation to which the μή is said. Οὐκ ἄρ', ἐναντίον ὅταν ἀπόφασις λέγηται σημαίνειν, συγχωρησόμεθα, τοσοῦτον δὲ μόνον, ὅτι τῶν ἄλλων τὶ μηνύει τὸ μὴ καὶ τὸ οὔ προτιθέμενα τῶν ἐπιόντων ὀνομάτων, μᾶλλον δὲ τῶν πραγμάτων περὶ ἅττ' ἂν κέηται τὰ ἐπιφθεγγόμενα ὕστερον τῆς ἀποφάσεως ὀνόματα (b9ff.). This characterizes ἀπόφασις explicitly as τὶ μηνύει, as "showing something," and indeed τῶν πραγμάτων, "of the matters themselves."[1] The μηνύειν of ἀπόφασις is περὶ τὰ πράγματα; i.e., the μή has the character of δηλοῦν, it reveals, it lets something be seen. This denial is presentifying, it brings something into view: namely the otherness of the πράγματα, which as such are encountered in a pregiven horizon of substantive nexuses. Thus the ἐναντίον, as the empty "opposite," is different than the substantive "other."

β) The "not" in λόγος. Negation as letting be seen. The positive understanding of negation in phenomenology.

The distinction between the ἐναντίον, the empty "opposite," and the ἕτερον, the substantive other, already predelineates a more precise grasp of λόγος. Over and against a blind addressing of something in merely identifying it by name, there is a disclosive seeing of it in its co-presence with others. And in opposition to the mere blind exclusion that corresponds to this identification by name, there is, if our interpretation of ἀπόφασις is correct, a denial which discloses, which lets something be seen precisely in the matters denied. Hence Plato understands the "not" and negation as disclosive. The denying in λέγειν, the saying "no," is a letting be seen and

1. Editor's note: This interpretation occurs both in Heidegger's manuscript and in the various transcripts.

is not, as in the case of the mere exclusion corresponding to the pure calling by name, a letting disappear, a bringing of what is said to nothing.

If these connections are pursued further, it becomes clear that negation, understood in this way, as possessing a disclosive character, can have, within the concrete uncovering of beings, a purifying function, so that negation itself acquires a productive character. To understand this properly, in all its consequences, and above all in its significance for the structure of the concept, and for conceptuality in general, we must free ourselves from the traditional theory of knowledge and of judgment, from the traditional version of knowledge, judgment, the concept, and the like. Above all, the positive understanding of negation is important for the research that moves primarily and exclusively by exhibiting the matters at issue. Phenomenological research itself accords negation an eminent position: negation as something carried out after a prior acquisition and disclosure of some substantive content. This is what is peculiarly systematic in phenomenology, that, provided it is practiced authentically, phenomenology always involves an antecedent *seeing* of the matters themselves. What is systematic is not some sort of contrived nexus of concepts, taking its orientation from some construct or system. On the contrary, the systematic is grounded in the previous disclosure of the matters themselves,[2] on the basis of which negation then attains the positive accomplishment of making possible the conceptuality of what is seen.

Furthermore, it is only on the basis of this productive negation, which Plato has at least surmised here, even if he has not pursued it in its proper substantive consequences, that we can clarify a difficult problem of logic, a problem residing in the copula of the proposition or judgment: namely, the meaning of the "is" or the "is not" in the propositions "A is B," "A is not B." The meaning of this "not," in the context of judgments about beings, has long caused difficulties for logic, and it has not been properly clarified even now. In the last part of our lectures, about λόγος, following this discussion of the ἕτερον, we will have the opportunity to pursue it more closely. Hegelian logic, obviously in conjunction with Aristotle, gives the concept of negativity a positive significance, but only insofar as negativity is a transitional stage, because the total orientation of this dialectic is directed toward essentially other structures than is the simply disclosive dialectic of the Greeks.

The consideration of the five γένη aimed at the exposition of the ἕτερον and thereby at the possibility of making intelligible μὴ ὄν as ὄν. What now follows grasps this structure of the ἕτερον itself still more precisely, in the

2. AH: Sketch.

sense that it exhibits the ἕτερον as ἀντίθεσις. The clarification of ἀντίθεσις makes the οὐσία of μὴ ὄν quite clear for the first time. The clarification of the ἕτερον as ἀντίθεσις and of μὴ ὄν as οὐσία brings the stricter dialectical consideration of μὴ ὄν to a conclusion. What is then carried out concerning λόγος indeed introduces something substantively new about λόγος but not about dialectic. It is simply an application of the consideration carried out here with regard to κίνησις and the ἕτερον. We must keep in mind the connection of the preceding consideration with the ensuing one, which is to offer a more precise grasp of the ἕτερον, in order to understand the somewhat forced transition at 257c.

b) More precise grasp of the structure of the ἕτερον: the clarification of the ἕτερον as ἀντίθεσις. Μὴ ὄν as οὐσία.[3]

α) The concretion of the idea of the ἕτερον as πρός τι. Counter-part (μόριον) and opposite (ἀντίθεσις).[4]

The consideration begins suddenly with the assertion: Ἡ θατέρου μοι φύσις φαίνεται κατακεκερματίσθαι καθάπερ ἐπιστήμη (257c7f.); we see that the φύσις of the ἕτερον κατακεκερματίσθαι. Κατακερματίζειν means "to partition" and is mostly used in the sense of exchanging a larger denomination of money for smaller ones. This image can most readily clarify the meaning of the expression as used here and also in the following passage (258e1) as well as in the *Parmenides* (144b4f.). Κατακερματίζειν means to exchange a larger denomination of money for smaller ones, such that the smaller denominations themselves are still money. It is a changing, a particularization, of such a kind that the μέρη themselves are of the same character as the whole greater piece. The κατακεκερματισμένα are nothing else than what the *Phaedrus* calls the διεσπαρμένα (265d4): not just any particulars, which intermingle confusedly, but instead the smaller coins of a larger one, of the γένος. This exchange of the larger into the smaller is now to be clarified in regard to the ἕτερον.

With this aim in view, Plato refers to ἐπιστήμη: καθάπερ ἐπιστήμη (*Sophist*, 257c8). Even the idea of ἐπιστήμη can be exchanged in this way into smaller coins, as we saw earlier in the first part of the dialogue: πολλαὶ τέχναι εἰσίν (cf. d1), "there are many τέχναι," in all of which the character of τέχνη is present as such. Οὐκοῦν καὶ τὰ τῆς θατέρου φύσεως μόρια μιᾶς οὔσης ταὐτὸν πέπονθε τοῦτο (d4f.). Obviously the μόρια, the parts, of the φύσις of otherness will find themselves in the same situation as the ἐπιστῆμαι in their relation to ἐπιστήμη or as the τέχναι in their

3. Title based on Heidegger's manuscript.
4. Title based on Heidegger's manuscript.

relation to τέχνη. Here Plato uses the expression "μόρια"; the φύσις of the ἕτερον thus has μόρια. The question is: ὅπῃ δὴ λέγωμεν (d6), "how are we now to understand" that the φύσις of the ἕτερον can be exchanged into single parts? This particularization of the φύσις θατέρου must be grasped more precisely in the sense of a concretion of the initially empty idea of otherness. For Plato, this "particularization" is not a matter of making tangible as specific individuals, here and now, but instead is a matter of a simple concretion of the empty general ἕτερον. As regards this concretion, the question now arises as to how the μόρια, the parts, the small coins, are constituted. Ἔστι τῷ καλῷ τι θατέρου μόριον ἀντιτιθέμενον; (d7): "Is there for the καλόν μόριόν τι a part which is counter-posed?" This question makes it clear that Plato is using the expression μόριον here in a two-fold sense: in the first place, in the sense of a small coin, i.e., the concrete particularization of something formal, and, secondly, in the sense of an other over and against the one within otherness. This double meaning of μόριον is not possible with the image of τέχνη, i.e., in comparison with τέχνη. Therefore the comparison with τέχνη misses the mark as regards what is decisive. Τέχνη in itself does not possess the specific character of the ἕτερον, i.e., of the πρός τι, as that is under discussion here. By the fact that otherness is in itself characterized by the relation to something other, every concretion of otherness is as such and at the same time a specification of a determinate other. Along with the concretion, there is posited at the same time a concrete other of a determinate otherness, so that μόριον here means something two-fold: first, pure and simple concretion versus the γένος "otherness," and secondly, and especially, the concrete "other" versus the particularized "one."

Now it is to be shown that, just as the ἕτερον is present everywhere, so also there is posited along with the Being of the one the Being of the other. The expression ἀντίθεσις emerges here in place of ἕτερον. Θέσις is to be understood as positing, not in the sense of establishing or producing, but in the sense that something already there is posited *as* there, thus in the sense of "letting it present itself as there." This is the sense of θέσις in the term ἀντίθεσις. The question is whether the ἀντιτιθέμενον for the καλόν is a τί, something, an ὄν, or whether it is ἀνώνυμον, "nameless"—which is here equivalent to possessing no substantive content of its own and which therefore also ἔχει no ἐπωνυμίαν. Τοῦτ' οὖν ἀνώνυμον ἐροῦμεν ἤ τιν' ἔχον ἐπωνυμίαν; —Ἔχον (d9f.). "Does it have a possible name," i.e., does it provide of itself, on the basis of its own substantive content, a direction for a univocal naming of itself? "Indeed." ὃ γὰρ μὴ καλὸν οὐκ ἄλλου τινὸς ἕτερόν ἐστιν ἢ τῆς τοῦ καλοῦ φύσεως (cf. d10f.). For the μὴ καλόν, the ἀντιτιθέμενον to the καλόν, is nothing else than the ἕτερον ἄλλου τινός, it is opposed to an other.[5] That which is posited in the ἀντίθεσις, in the "not," is not understood in the empty field of an arbitrary nothingness but rather is the ἕτερον ἄλλου τινός, the "not" of an other. The saying "no," the denial, in the ἀντίθεσις is hence a bound one. What are the consequences?

β) The structure of μὴ ὄν as ἀντίθεσις. The substantive content of μὴ ὄν. Its full dignity of Being (οὐσία). Μὴ ὄν as autonomous εἶδος within the five μέγιστα γένη.

We have seen that the saying "no" in the ἀντίθεσις is not arbitrary but is bound. The question arises: what are the consequences? Ἄλλο τι τῶν ὄντων τινὸς ἑνὸς γένους ἀφορισθὲν καὶ πρός τι τῶν ὄντων αὖ πάλιν ἀντιτεθὲν οὕτω συμβέβηκεν εἶναι τὸ μὴ καλόν; (e2ff.). The consequences are that the μὴ καλόν is: 1.) ἄλλο τι; it is itself by itself "something other," "delimited on the basis of a determinate substantive stem, γένος, of beings"; the ἀντιτιθέμενον, as something other, has a determinate substantive provenance, which is present in it. 2.) It is set apart, precisely as this delimited one, αὖ πάλιν πρός τι τῶν ὄντων ἀντιτεθέν, "again back" on that from which it stems. It is not only determined in terms of its provenance, but as such, as originating from this γένος, it is posited in the character of the "over and against," of the "again back to that from which it originates." On the basis of its provenance and its reference back to its history, it makes visible, in a certain sense, its own substantive content.[6] Accordingly, the μὴ καλόν is ἀντίθεσις, and specifically ἀντίθεσις ὄντος δὴ πρὸς ὄν, ἀντίθεσις "of something present, factually existing, over and against something factually existing." Here we must understand ἀντίθεσις, just like λόγος, in a two-fold sense; here it means ἀντιτιθέμενον, just as λόγος very often means λεγόμενον. But if in this way the μὴ καλόν stems from the ἀντίθεσις out of a γένος (the καλόν), then is not in the end the καλόν, from which it stems, μᾶλλον τῶν ὄντων, more of Being, and is not the μὴ καλόν ἧττον (cf. e9f.)? Οὐδέν (e11). "By no means"; on the contrary, both are ὁμοίως (258a1); they have the same basic mode of presence. Καὶ τἆλλα δὴ ταύτῃ λέξομεν (a7), and thus we can also understand dialectically all other beings in which the ἕτερον is present, all other μόρια θατέρου, in such a way that the ἀντιτιθέμενον is an ὄν and specifically ὁμοίως, like that against which it is posited. This makes it clear that, just as in the sense of otherness as such, the other is present over and against the one through the πρός τι, so likewise also in every exchange of otherness into small othernesses, i.e., in the substantive concretions, the μὴ ὄν is an ὄν. Accordingly, ἡ τῆς θατέρου μορίου φύσεως καὶ τῆς τοῦ ὄντος πρὸς ἄλληλα

5. Thus in the transcripts of S. Moser and H. Weiß.
6. See the appendix.

ἀντικειμένων ἀντίθεσις οὐδὲν ἧττον, εἰ θέμις εἰπεῖν, αὐτοῦ τοῦ ὄντος οὐσία ἐστίν (a11f.). The concrete other in otherness is no less present than that against which it is posited: οὐσία.

Plato emphasizes once more that the ἀντίθεσις οὐκ ἐναντίον σημαίνουσα (cf. b3), does not mean the empty and pure "not," ἀλλὰ τοσοῦτον μόνον, ἕτερον ἐκείνου (b3), but "simply so much" of the "not" that therein it comes to appear precisely as "the other" of each single one. Δῆλον ὅτι τὸ μὴ ὄν, ὃ διὰ τὸν σοφιστὴν ἐξητοῦμεν, αὐτό ἐστι τοῦτο (b6f.). In this way it has become clear that non-beings, which we were led to seek on the basis of the undeniable factual existence of the sophist, are precisely, and nothing else than, what we have now exposed with the ἀντίθεσις, namely the ἀντιτιθέμενον or ἕτερον in λέγειν as necessary λεγόμενον.

Thereby Plato has made the ἕτερον itself conceptually transparent. He did so by showing that otherness as such, insofar as it is present in a specific concrete being, implies that in every case the concrete other of otherness, and thus the concretion, the μόριον ἑτέρου, is itself an ὄν, a being, and that consequently the opposite of ὄν, μὴ ὄν itself, is to be addressed as an ὄν, and specifically as an ὄν which, as the other over and against the one, is not at all ἧττον ὄν, less in regard to Being, but is ὁμοίως ὄν. In the field of this newly discovered ἕτερον, in opposition to the empty ἐναντίον, both, the one and the other, therefore have the full dignity of presence, of Being. This is a peculiar mode of demonstration; actually it is not a demonstration but an exhibition of the meaning of the concretion of otherness. Otherness implies, insofar as it encompasses the one and the other in the mode of difference, that both are. Thus Plato acquires μὴ ὄν as ὄν.

The considerations in the dialogue thereby reach their preliminary goal. Μὴ ὄν is ἀντίθεσις; ἀντίθεσις is the structure of the ἕτερον; and the ἕτερον is διὰ πάντων, it is pervasively present in everything: ἕκαστον οὐκ ὂν ποιεῖ (256e1f.). Accordingly, μὴ ὄν is οὐδενὸς τῶν ἄλλων οὐσίας ἐλλειπόμενον (258b8f.), "with regard to οὐσία, presence, it occupies no less a position than the others." ἐνάριθμον τῶν πολλῶν ὄντων εἶδος ἕν (c3), it is itself something properly "visible" among beings, it can be co-seen in all beings as such, and, as this autonomous εἶδος, it is ἐνάριθμον, "counted" among the manifold of εἴδη, and it occurs in the κοινωνία of beings. This ἐνάριθμον, "counted," relates explicitly to the "five" anticipated in the ὑπόθεσις above. Here number represents nothing else than the completeness and thoroughness of relations within a determinate, thematically posited κοινωνία, namely the κοινωνία of ὄν, κίνησις, στάσις, and ταὐτόν, under which the ἕτερον arose as εἶδος ἕν.

Thus we have μακροτέρως, "to a considerable extent," transcended the ἀπόρρησις (cf. c6f.), the "prohibition," of Parmenides (to keep away from the path of investigation into μὴ ὄν); we have in a certain sense denied it our trust. We have transcended the prohibition not only by daring in general to investigate μὴ ὄν, which Parmenides indeed prohibits, but εἰς τὸ πρόσθεν ἔτι ζητήσαντες ἀπεδείξαμεν αὐτῷ (c9f.), "we have gone further and have demonstrated something substantively new about it": we have made μὴ ὄν itself visible as an εἶδος.

γ) Plato's substantive advance over Parmenides' doctrine of μὴ ὄν. Ἀντίθεσις and ἐναντίωσις.

Plato now has an explicit consciousness of this new, fundamental discovery of μὴ ὄν. He clearly formulates what this discovery concerns when he says: οὐ μόνον τὰ μὴ ὄντα ὡς ἔστιν ἀπεδείξαμεν (d5f.), we have shown not only that μὴ ὄν is, but secondly, and above all, τὸ εἶδος ὃ τυγχάνει ὂν τοῦ μὴ ὄντος ἀπεφηνάμεθα (d6f.), "we have exhibited τὸ εἶδος, the outward look, of this μὴ ὄν itself." We have shown how μὴ ὄν itself looks. This exhibition encompasses two things: τὴν θατέρου φύσιν ἀποδείξαντες οὖσάν τε καὶ κατακεκερματισμένην ἐπὶ πάντα τὰ ὄντα πρὸς ἄλληλα (cf. d7f.). We have pursued what is properly visible in it itself and 1.) have exhibited τὴν θατέρου φύσιν as οὖσα, by making intelligible its structure as ἀντίθεσις: μὴ ὄν is something ἀφορισθέν (257e2), "delimited," first against an other, but as thus delimited it is at the same time πάλιν, "back again," πρός τι (e3), "connected to the other," in relation to which it is delimited, and belongs with it to the same γένος, to the same stem. 2.) We have thereby shown at the same time the possibility of the exchange of otherness throughout all beings: every concrete other is what it is in its descent out of a particular γένος, such that it is opposed as the other to the one. Thus μὴ ὄν is κατακεκερματισμένον ἐπὶ πάντα (cf. 258e1), "partitioned to all," in the sense of changing money; the large denomination of otherness as such has been broken down into the possible concretions of other beings. Now no one can say any longer that in speaking about μὴ ὄν, in maintaining the ὄν, the εἶναι, of μὴ ὄν, we are intending the nothing and are trying to prove the Being of the nothing. On the contrary, we have found for μὴ ὄν a determinate new concept, a structure, the ἀντίθεσις, which is different from ἐναντίωσις.

At 259a–b, Plato again repeats the result by summarizing it and placing it within the task of dialectic. For only now, on the basis of this disclosure of μὴ ὄν, will dialectic be visible in its possibility as fundamental research. Thus does Plato first bring it to the conceptual level.

c) Μὴ ὄν *qua* ἕτερον as ground of the possibility of dialectic. Fourth characterization of dialectic.

Μὴ ὄν as ἕτερον, as well as the possibility of the exchange of the ἕτερον itself into concrete beings, first make possible dialectical science. This science is not an idle game but something χαλεπὸν ἅμα καὶ καλόν (259c4f.), "difficult yet at the same time beautiful." It is difficult because dialectic is not the work of empty and blind conceptual hair-splitting. On the contrary, the genuine sense of διαλέγεσθαι is ἀποφαίνεσθαι, to let be seen what is properly visible, the εἴδη, of beings themselves. And this science is beautiful because dialectic as διαίρεσις, as taking apart beings in regard to what is most properly visible in them, exposes the limits of beings in their Being and thus first exhibits beings in their presence. Accordingly, the fundamental task and basic requirement of the διαλεκτικός is τοῖς λεγομένοις οἷόν τ' εἶναι καθ' ἕκαστον ἐλέγχοντα ἐπακολουθεῖν (c8f.), "to be capable," ἐπακολουθεῖν, of "pursuing," τοῖς λεγομένοις, "what is said," and specifically what is said in its sayability, i.e., pursuing what is co-said, in every λεγόμενον, about ὄντα, i.e., the εἴδη, and ἐλέγχειν, "exposing publicly," exhibiting, letting be seen, the εἴδη not in some arbitrary connection but ἐκείνῃ καὶ κατ' ἐκεῖνο (d1), in the present aspect in which they are spoken and in relation to that toward which the aspect leads. Only thus is this διαλεκτικὴ ἐπιστήμη an ἔλεγχος ἀληθινός (cf. d5f.). The genuine determinate idea of dialectic, as it arises here, would hence first be possible through the idea of the ἕτερον and through the determination of the ἕτερον as ἀντίθεσις over and against the ἐναντίωσις.

d) Excursus: the "theory" of the "not" in Plato and Aristotle.[7] The "not" in Parmenides, Antisthenes, and Plato *(Republic, Symposium, Sophist)*. The overcoming of Antisthenes' tautological logic. Dialectical logic. Aristotle's theory of opposition. Toward the further articulation of the *Sophist.*

Plato had already, long before the *Sophist*, perhaps from the very beginning of his genuine philosophizing, seen the distinction between ἐναντίωσις, empty negation, and ἀντίθεσις, the disclosive "not." But he actually mastered this distinction much later; i.e., he actually saw the concept of the ἕτερον very late. This distinction shows itself above all in the absurdities implicit in the claim that ἐναντίωσις is the one and only negation and that identification is the one and only κατάφασις, as Antisthenes held. The distinction is precisely meant to resolve these absurdities. Thus Plato says, e.g. in Book V of the *Republic:* ἡ φύσις φαλακρῶν καὶ κομητῶν ἐναντία (cf. 454c2f.), "the φύσις of the bald and the hairy is different." On the basis of the thesis of Antisthenian logic, namely that λόγος can only express identities, we could certainly draw the conclusion: ἐπειδὰν ὁμολογῶμεν

7. Title in Heidegger's manuscript: "Theory" of opposites in Plato and Aristotle.

ἐναντίαν εἶναι, ἐὰν φαλακροὶ σκυτοτομῶσιν, μὴ ἐᾶν κομήτας, ἐὰν δ' αὖ κομῆται, μὴ τοὺς ἑτέρους (c3ff.). "If the bald possess the τέχνη of shoemaking," if shoemaking befits them, then "those who have full heads of hair" cannot become shoemakers. Plato characterizes this procedure as follows: κατ' αὐτὸ τὸ ὄνομα διώκειν τοῦ λεχθέντος τὴν ἐναντίωσιν, ἔριδι, οὐ διαλέκτῳ πρὸς ἀλλήλους χρώμενοι (a7ff.), it is saying the contrary, i.e., saying "not," while adhering simply to utterances as such, to the extrinsic identity and uniqueness of the words, by reason of a concern with disputation alone and not with a discussion of some matter at issue. Thus Plato is here relating the διαλεκτικός, or διαλέγεσθαι, to the discussion of some matter at issue, and the ἀντιλογικός, i.e., the ἐριστικός and ἐρίζειν, to mere word-play. But one cannot object to the thesis above, so long as one has not made λόγος transparent as something other than a λέγειν of ταὐτόν. This apparently entirely formal logical task has a bearing that first makes possible dialectical science in general. Here for the first time the problem of negation is posed and pursued in its first steps.

Phenomenologically, this can be clarified very briefly. Every "not," in every saying of "not," whether explicitly expressed or implicit, has, as a speaking about something, the character of exhibition. Even the empty "not," the mere exclusion of something over and against something arbitrary, shows, but it simply shows that on which the negation is founded, thus what, in saying "not," is delimited against the nothing. This empty negation places discernment, λέγειν and νοεῖν, prior to the nothing; it lets the nothing be seen as founded by the negated. That is the meaning of negation in Parmenides. This negation, placed prior to the nothing and purely exclusionary, has thus been uncovered for the first time in the history of the development of our logic, in our grasp of λόγος. That should not seduce us into thinking that this negation, empty exclusion, is the most immediate one and the primary one carried out in λέγειν. On the contrary, the original negation is precisely the one Plato exposes as ἀντίθεσις and Aristotle then, in a remarkable reversal of terms, calls ἐναντίωσις. The empty negation, as it dominated the understanding of λέγειν up to Plato, did not spring from a primordial study of λόγος but from the ground of a particular and over-hasty (this is not meant as a reproach) theory of Being, namely the Parmenidean theory of Being. The universal character of presence, of εἶναι, which Parmenides was the first to see, became for him the substantive realm of beings in general. He thus identified the ontological meaning of Being with the ontical totality of beings. To that extent, for every saying "no," there remained left over only the nothing, since indeed it is nothing else than the ἕν as ὄν.[8] This makes it clear that the clarification

8. Thus in the Moser transcript.

of λόγος and logic leads back to the respective level of clarity concerning the meaning of Being. We may suppose that Plato acquired, on the basis of the new insight into the ὄν of μὴ ὄν, a new basis for the interpretation of λόγος and that therefore Plato's advance in the determination and clarification of beings corresponds to a new possibility of a radical conception of λόγος, as in fact occurred for the first time in the *Sophist*.

Thus Plato saw the ἕτερον very early—that is to be emphasized—but did not grasp it conceptually. For example, in the *Symposium* Diotima says: Μὴ τοίνυν ἀνάγκαζε ὃ μὴ καλόν ἐστιν αἰσχρὸν εἶναι, μηδὲ ὃ μὴ ἀγαθόν, κακόν. οὕτω δὲ καὶ τὸν Ἔρωτα ἐπειδὴ αὐτὸς ὁμολογεῖς μὴ εἶναι ἀγαθὸν μηδὲ καλόν, μηδέν τι μᾶλλον οἴου δεῖν αὐτὸν αἰσχρὸν καὶ κακὸν εἶναι, ἀλλά τι μεταξὺ τούτοιν (cf. 202b1ff.). Only later did Plato uncover the ἕτερον as a category and bring it into a concept, and even then he did so still on the basis of the essentially Parmenidean ontology which also held for Aristotle. Aristotle pressed ahead further in the disclosure of negation. He grasped more sharply the theory of opposition whose first steps were developed by Plato. I cannot present it here in its entirety but can only give you the bare essentials.

Aristotle includes under the formal term ἀντικείμενον all the various modes of opposition, the "against," the "not" in the widest sense. He distinguishes four modes of ἀντικείμενα: 1.) ἀντίφασις, contradiction, which he was the first to discover, although it was indeed latent already in Plato, for contra-*diction* can be seen only on the basis of insight into φάσις itself; 2.) the opposition between ἕξις and στέρησις; 3.) the ἐναντία; 4.) τὰ πρός τι.

Examples: 1.) of ἀντίφασις: A is B—A is not B; 2.) of ἕξις and στέρησις: the moved—the unmoved; 3.) of ἐναντία: beautiful—ugly; 4.) of πρός τι: double—half, before—after. Aristotle has then grasped the ἐναντίον, thus the Platonic ἕτερον, more sharply. Versus Plato, he has seen more clearly that a self-sameness is constitutive for the ἐναντίον and that it is with respect to this sameness that a διαφορά can first be given. He thus asks about the self-same aspect, with regard to which something can be said to be an other over and against the one. Insofar as this self-same aspect can be represented first through the γένος and secondly through the εἶδος, there arises here a distinction within the ἐναντίον itself. This context of the more precise grasp of the ἐναντίον, and, in general, of opposition, was what modified the purely ontological concepts of γένος, stem (lineage), and εἶδος, what is properly visible, into actual formal-logical categories, which then later play a role as genus and species. The entire question of the transformation of the ontological concepts into formal-logical ones is connected with the purely ontological doctrine of μὴ ὄν. Γένος and εἶδος in Plato must never be translated as "genus" and "species." Aristotle deals with the doctrine of opposition in Book X of the *Metaphysics*, chapters 3 and 5, summarizing Book V, chapter 10.[9,10]

Plato's characterization of dialectic on the basis of the newly discovered ἕτερον is linked at 259e to the interpretation of λόγος. Specifically, Plato shows at 259e–261c why λόγος must be clarified explicitly in connection with the theme of the *Sophist*. The analysis of λόγος occurs at 261c–263d, and the analysis of δόξα and φαντασία at 263d–264d. Notice that the latter is subsequent to the analysis of λόγος and is built upon it. What follows, from 264d to the end of the dialogue, is a clarification of the earlier interpretation of sophistical τέχνη as τέχνη ἀντιλογική, now on the basis of the new meaning of μὴ ὄν, λόγος, and δόξα. Precisely this transition, from the newly acquired idea of dialectic and of fundamental dialectical research to the analysis of λόγος, is important for an understanding of the dialogue as a whole. The constant theme of the dialogue is the clarification of the existence of the sophist in its possibility. I emphasize that precisely in this transition we can and must reflect fundamentally on what the basic dialectical consideration has gained, how the analysis of λόγος stands in regard to it, and how all this belongs to the theme of the dialogue itself. The basic dialectical consideration will thereby prove to be no sterile conceptual hair-splitting, nor a mere augmentation of the doctrinal content of the formal scholastic discipline called "logic," but the clarification of the basic structures which manifest themselves in regard to what is actually at issue here, namely human existence—that of the sophist and, indirectly, that of the philosopher.

§79. Transition from the fundamental dialectical consideration to the analysis of λόγος (259e–261c). The question of the meaning of the fundamental dialectical consideration.

a) Exhibition of the necessity of the analysis of λόγος. The problematic character of the συμπλοκή of ὄν and μὴ ὄν with respect to λόγος.

The existence of the sophist is a comportment within λέγειν or δοξάζειν. Thus we can characterize the τέχνη of the sophist as εἰδωλοποιική, and his λόγος as λόγος ψευδής. Plato presents a full portrayal of λόγος ψευδής at

9. AH: and ἕν ibid., chapter 6.
10. See the appendix.

240d: ψευδὴς δόξα ἔσται τἀναντία τοῖς οὖσι δοξάζουσα (cf. 240d6f.). The theme of the sophist's λέγειν is thus the ἐναντία. There is concretely, in sophistical comportment, an ontological unification of λέγειν with ψεῦδος, i.e., with μὴ ὄν. Thus to maintain that the sophist *is*, that there factually are sophists, is to admit a προσαρμόττειν τοῦ ὄντος, namely of λέγειν, πρὸς μὴ ὄν.[1] As I emphasized earlier, the sophist is the factual existence of μὴ ὄν itself. The sophist, however, will dispute this—on the basis of the principle of Parmenides, namely that μὴ ὄν does not exist. The sophist says there is no μὴ ὄν and therefore no possible conjunction of μὴ ὄν with λέγειν; i.e., there is no ψευδὴς λόγος. Thus the sophist claims he cannot at all be what we accuse him of being. On the other hand, the fundamental dialectical consideration has demonstrated the συμπλοκή of ὄν with μὴ ὄν. We have made visible the δύναμις κοινωνίας of ὄν with μὴ ὄν, i.e., with the ἕτερον. That means we have actually disclosed the possibility of the existence of the sophist. Thereby the bulwark behind which the sophist defends himself has apparently collapsed.

Yet Plato had already indicated that the sophists are a δυσθήρευτον γένος (cf. 261a5f.), a stem difficult to hunt down.[2] That is, this hunt requires proper know-how as regards that which is hunted. In fact, the sophist has still not let himself be captured. He will say: fine, let it be granted, there are non-beings. But at the same time he will remind us that we ourselves have indeed stressed that we cannot admit πάντα ἀλλήλοις δύναμιν ἔχειν ἐπικοινωνίας (cf. 252d2f.). We ourselves have repudiated the possibility of everything being able to be together with everything else without exception. The sophist will therefore say: φαίη (260d6), τῶν εἰδῶν, a few "of the things most properly visible" *[Sichtbarkeiten]* in beings will μετέχειν τοῦ μὴ ὄντος, τὰ δ' οὔ (d7). With many beings μὴ ὄν will be present, can be present, but with many not. And λόγος and δόξα belong to the latter (cf. d8). We have not shown, the sophist will say, that λόγος, as an ὄν, can possibly have a κοινωνία with μὴ ὄν and that there can therefore be something like a λόγος ψευδής or a τέχνη in the sense of φανταστική (cf. d9). As long as that has not been shown, the possibility of the existence of the sophist has not actually been proved. Thus we have to undertake anew our assault on the sophist.

In fact, if we look more closely, we will see that the fundamental dialectical consideration has moved not in the field of λόγος but within the five completely universal εἴδη: ὄν, κίνησις, στάσις, ταὐτόν, and ἕτερον. But now, because the theme of the dialogue is the sophist in regard to his existence, we have to exhibit the possible conjunction of λόγος with μὴ ὄν,

1. According to 238c5f. Cf. p. 292.
2. Cf. 218d3f. Cf. p. 178.

the co-presence of non-being in a particular being, namely λόγος. For this, two things are presupposed: 1.) that in general there is a conjunction possible between ὄν and μὴ ὄν, and 2.) that we see clearly what λόγος and δόξα themselves are. For only in that way, i.e., from the substantive content of λόγος and δόξα, can we make evident the possibility of their κοινωνία with μὴ ὄν. The first presupposition, that there is in general a conjunction possible between ὄν and μὴ ὄν, has been established by the fundamental dialectical consideration. τὸ . . . μέγιστον ἡμῖν τεῖχος ᾐρημένον ἂν εἴη, τὰ δ' ἄλλα ἤδη ῥᾴω καὶ σμικρότερα (261c2ff.): "The highest and greatest battlement of the bulwark should now be scaled, and the other will be smaller and easier."

b) Λόγος (or ψυχή) and λόγος ψευδής as central themes of the fundamental dialectical consideration. The κοινωνία of the εἴδη as condition of the possibility of λόγος in general. Κίνησις and στάσις as basic phenomena in the cognition of beings. The συμπλοκή between κίνησις and ἕτερον as predelineation of λόγος ψευδής. The Being of ψεῦδος as ontological foundation of the phenomena of falsity.[3]

The first essential on the way toward demonstrating a λόγος ψευδής, i.e., the κοινωνία of this ὄν with μὴ ὄν, is insight into the impossibility of πᾶν ἀπὸ παντὸς ἀποχωρίζειν (cf. 259d9), of "separating everything from everything else."[4] Whoever holds that everything can be absolutely detached from everything else is ἄμουσος and ἀφιλόσοφος (e2). Such a διαλύειν ἕκαστον ἀπὸ πάντων (e4f.) amounts to a τελεωτάτη πάντων λόγων ἀφάνισις (cf. e4), "a complete abolition of every addressing of things." If there is in general no κοινωνία, there is also no exhibition of anything and no access to what is properly visible, to the εἴδη, and then λέγειν and therefore human Dasein, ζῷον λόγον ἔχον, are blind. And insofar as κίνησις is determinative of this Dasein, the blind Dasein of man is delivered over to chaos. That is the proper tendency behind the energy Plato brings to the clarification of λόγος. If λόγος is ἡμῖν γέγονεν (cf. e6), already present in our Being itself, then it is so only διὰ τὴν τῶν εἰδῶν συμπλοκήν (cf. e5f.), only on the basis of the συμπλοκὴ τῶν εἰδῶν. Only if there is a possible conjunction of what is properly visible in beings,[5] only if beings themselves allow something like a disclosure of themselves in the character of the "as," is there a λέγειν;

3. Reading *Trug* for *Täuschung* ["deception"], since for Heidegger *Täuschung* = ψεῦδος.—Trans.
4. AH: λέγειν: to gather something, to collect.
5. AH: an interweaving that is in itself referential.

and only if there is a λέγειν is human existence possible. Therefore what must be fought for and wrested away, before anything else, is ἐᾶν ἕτερον ἑτέρῳ μείγνυσθαι (260a2f.), the possibility, "the admission, that the one can mix with the other" or, put differently, the presence of the ἕτερον in ὄν. Only thus can we at all save the possibility of λόγος as an ὄν, quite apart from what it itself is. <λόγου> στερηθέντες, τὸ μὲν μέγιστον, φιλοσοφίας ἂν στερηθεῖμεν (a6f.); if we were deprived of λέγειν, the highest constituent of our Being, then we would be bereaved of philosophy. Here the indirect positive aspect of the investigation into the sophist comes to light anew. It is therefore superfluous and a mistake to expect that Plato would have written another dialogue about the philosopher; on the contrary, he would have scoffed at that. For the fundamental question of Being and non-being centers equally in the question of the pre-eminent being, the philosopher, as well as in the question of the *negativum*, the sophist. These constitute, in the Greek sense, the question of the ζῷον πολιτικόν, the Being of man in the πόλις. If there is no philosophy, i.e., no λέγειν in the genuine sense, there is also no human existence. The anthropological question is thus ontological, and vice versa, and both questions center in the "logical" pure and simple, provided "logical" is understood as that which properly concerns λόγος, thus not understood in the sense of formal logic but in the Greek sense. The priority of λόγος both in the dialogue as a whole and also in the exhibition of the phenomenal structure of the sophist should thereby be clear. For only on that basis can we properly understand the fundamental dialectical consideration. It is neither something insulated, like a kernel within a shell, nor is it formal. For it is quite striking that within the five γένη, around which the dialectical consideration travels, movement and rest are called "something," "sameness," "otherness." Κίνησις and στάσις, however, are obviously, over and against ὄν, ταὐτόν, and ἕτερον, substantive εἴδη but not arbitrary ones which came to Plato accidentally. On the contrary, κίνησις and στάσις—as we recall—have been read off phenomenally from γιγνώσκειν, or, which amounts to the same, from νοεῖν and, which again is identical, from λέγειν.[6] Thus if κίνησις and στάσις belong to the fundamental consideration, then λόγος itself is already thematic in the dialectical analysis.

Furthermore, we explicitly emphasized that the five εἴδη within the dialectical consideration are at first all on the same level, none has a priority over another, but that the consideration is carried out under the guideline of κίνησις.[7] What is the significance of the fact that κίνησις guides the dialectical analysis? It means nothing else than that the dialectical consid-

6. Cf. p. 337ff.
7. Cf. p. 379.

eration properly focuses on the ψυχή, and specifically on the ψυχή in its basic comportment of λέγειν, and, further, on this λέγειν of the ψυχή *qua* κίνησις, i.e., precisely with regard to how the ἕτερον can be together with it. For the fundamental dialectical consideration indeed ends precisely with the demonstration that in κίνησις there is also μὴ ὄν, the ἕτερον. The fundamental dialectical consideration, which apparently has to do with something quite remote from the rest of the dialogue, thus actually deals with nothing else than the same single theme: the existence of the sophist himself. The fundamental dialectical consideration is nothing else than the predelineation of the παρουσία of μὴ ὄν in λόγος. The result of this investigation signifies that the ἕτερον can κοινωνεῖν with κίνησις, i.e., with the ψυχή, with λόγος. Κίνησις is nothing arbitrary here but is the apriori title for ψυχή and λόγος, specifically in the sense, even if unclarified, of the μεταξύ. Thus if κίνησις is the theme of the dialectical consideration, that means the theme is nothing else than human Dasein, life itself, insofar as it expresses itself and addresses the world in which it is. Presumably στάσις, too, is not an arbitrary concept, the mere formal counter-concept to κίνησις, but reveals itself upon closer inspection to be the apriori determinateness of beings themselves, and specifically the determinateness which makes possible their disclosability in λέγειν, i.e., which makes knowledge possible. For στάσις signifies nothing else than ἀεὶ ὄν, what perpetually is, the permanent, so that we will no longer translate στάσις as "rest," since we are actually interpreting, but as "permanence" *[Ständigkeit]*.[8] Thus you see that in this concept of permanence, of the perpetual, factually, although implicitly, yet in accord with the matter itself, for Plato the phenomenon of time emerges, as the phenomenon which determines beings in their Being: the present, παρουσία (which is often shortened simply to "οὐσία"). And λέγειν, the disclosure of beings in speech, is nothing else than the making present of what is most properly visible in beings themselves and thereby the making present of beings in their essence; as presentifying disclosure, λέγειν appropriates the present. Thus λόγος (and thereby man, the sophist, the philosopher, the highest possibility of existence) is the theme of this apparently scattered conceptual hair-splitting.

The phenomenon of λόγος is thus the kernel. To demonstrate the possible conjunction of λόγος with μὴ ὄν is to show that ψεῦδος is an ὄν. Ὄντος δέ γε ψεύδους ἔστιν ἀπάτη (260c6), "but if deception, ψεῦδος, exists, then there is also falsity, ἀπάτη." Thus my translation precisely reverses the usual terms: for ψεῦδος I say "deception," and for ἀπάτη "falsity." The reason is that ἀπάτη does not here refer to a person's deceptive comportment but to

8. AH: 1.) To have a standing *[Stand]*, to stand in itself. 2.) to endure in this standing, to remain.

a possibility pertaining to beings themselves, namely that they can be false, just as we speak of false appearances. Ἀπάτη is thus a determination of beings themselves. The possibility of ψεῦδος necessarily allows ἀπάτη. But if ἀπάτης οὔσης (c8), then εἰδώλων τε καὶ εἰκόνων ἤδη καὶ φαντασίας πάντα ἀνάγκη μεστὰ εἶναι (c8f.), then everything is necessarily full of εἴδωλα, εἰκόνες, φαντασίαι. Εἴδωλα are proper visibles which merely seem to be, but are not, what they present themselves as. Εἰκόνες are images, presentations of something which they themselves are not. Φαντασίαι, in Plato's sense, means the same as φαίνεται: that which shows itself as, merely appears as, something. Thus the proof of the ontological possibility of the conjunction of λόγος and ἕτερον, i.e., λόγος ψευδής, guides the possibility of understanding the peculiar phenomena of εἴδωλον, εἰκών, and φαντασία. It is mysterious that something should be what it at the same time is not. Plato has now come to understand this and has thereby at the same time taken a step in the ontological understanding of the αἰσθητόν itself. We must get unused to applying to Plato's philosophy the scholastic horizon, as if for Plato in one box were sensibility, and in another the supersensible. Plato saw the world exactly as elementally as we do, but much more originally.

§80. The analysis of λόγος *(261c–263d).*

a) Exposition of the problem. Articulation of the analysis of λόγος into three stages.

Λόγος now becomes thematic on the background of the fundamental dialectical investigation. This investigation allows Plato to grasp conceptually, for the first time, the basic structural elements of λόγος, namely ὄνομα and ῥῆμα. Plato had already employed these terms in earlier dialogues, e.g. in the *Cratylus*, but there he still had no genuine understanding of ὄνομα and ῥῆμα[1] and certainly not of their συμπλοκή. Thus the question is: how can λόγος enter into a possible κοινωνία with μὴ ὄν? This question can be decided only by exposing λόγος itself in its essence, hence by carrying out an analysis of λόγος or δόξα (which for Plato are identical), specifically guided by this concern, namely πότερον αὐτῶν ἅπτεται τὸ μὴ ὄν (261c7), "whether μὴ ὄν can be joined to them." I referred earlier to the various expressions for κοινωνία: προσάπτειν, προσλέγειν.[2] We have to show not only that in general μὴ ὄν can be joined to λόγος but that the phenomenal

1. AH: as titles for the word-form and meaning-accomplishments.
2. Cf. pp. 292 and 297.

structure of λόγος as such involves the possibility of a conjunction with μὴ ὄν, i.e., with the ἕτερον. The question can thus be formulated: πότερον αὐτῶν ἅπτεται τὸ μὴ ὂν ἢ παντάπασιν ἀληθῆ μέν ἐστιν ἀμφότερα ταῦτα (c7ff.), whether a conjunction is possible, or whether every λέγειν[3] *qua* λέγειν is already true and can only be true—as Antisthenes maintained—i.e., whether every λόγος can be joined only to ὄν in itself, which means, versus the ἕτερον, ταὐτόν. The question is now to be discussed in a much more sharp formulation, the question, that is, which was already alive in the reference to the position of Antisthenes: whether λέγειν, in its genuine function, is identification, or whether it is something else, and if it is identification, then whether it is so simply in the sense that what is addressed can be identified only with itself ("Man is man"), or whether there can also be an identification of beings with respect to their δύναμις κοινωνίας.

The analysis of λόγος can be articulated into three stages:

1.) The exhibition of the "onomatic" and "delotic" basic structure of λέγειν. I have to use these terms, because our language contains nothing comparable. "Onomatic" means "naming," λέγειν as linguistic expression. "Delotic," from δηλοῦν, denotes λέγειν as revealing, letting be seen. A unitary consideration will thus show discourse as: a) self-expression and b) a discussion that addresses the matter at issue and that has the sense of disclosure, δηλοῦν. It will be clear afterwards why precisely these two phenomena of discourse, expression (or utterance) and the function of disclosure, are taken together here.

2.) The second stage of the analysis is the elaboration of the structure of the λεγόμενον as λεγόμενον: in other words, the elaboration of the constitution of the disclosure of beings which resides in every λόγος as such. Every λεγόμενον is a δηλούμενον. What is the structure of the λεγόμενον as δηλούμενον?

3.) The third stage is the analysis of the disclosing itself in its possibility; i.e., Plato will ask ποῖος ὁ λόγος, of what sort is λόγος itself, with respect to its essence, with respect to δηλοῦν.

Formulated Platonically, the first stage deals with λόγος as πλέγμα, as an intertwining, and this term has a double sense. The second stage deals with λόγος as λόγος τινός; all discourse is discourse *about* something. The third stage deals with λόγος in terms of ποῖος, the manner of its Being, i.e., with regard to δηλοῦν. What is relevant for the first and third stages is, above all, what the fundamental consideration previously established regarding ὄν. In the second stage, Plato encounters a new phenomenal nexus, one already intimated in the first stage but not analyzed there genuinely and

3. Heidegger crossed out the word λέγειν in the Moser transcript and refers in the margin to p. 366 (as printed above).

thematically. Plato indeed saw the phenomenon of the λεγόμενον as λεγόμενον but did not grasp it conceptually. All the more must our interpretation, precisely here, secure the phenomenon in order to understand the third stage and therewith the goal of the whole consideration within the fundamental dialectical analysis.

b) First stage: the exhibition of the onomatic and delotic basic structure of λέγειν.[4]

α) The point of departure: ὀνόματα as the most immediate mode of encountering λέγειν. The phenomenal content of λέγειν in Plato: ὀνόματα—γράμματα—εἴδη—εἴδη *as* ἐπιστητά. The connection between ὀνόματα and εἴδη by means of δηλοῦν. The recourse to Being-in-the-world as the task of a "phenomenological" interpretation of Plato's analysis of λόγος.

The theme of the first stage of Plato's analysis of λόγος is thus the exhibition of discourse as self-expression (the onomatic, ὄνομα) and as disclosure (the delotic, δηλοῦν). The exhibition of these two structural moments, which phenomenally are one and the same, sets forth from the onomatic. The λέγειν in every discourse is present first of all in its being uttered, in its being spoken out loud, in its phonetic character. This sound presents itself, and is encountered by us, among the beings there in the world. The word is spoken, it is outside, on the streets, just as a wagon creaks on the pavement. Creaking and speaking thus present themselves openly; they are conspicuous. But even this first mode of encountering λέγειν in the sense of speaking out loud is not to be understood as implying that what is immediately apprehended phenomenally is some living being that produces noises with its mouth. On the contrary, already, in its very first aspect, λέγειν is understood as utterance and is genuinely and primarily understood as a speaking with others *about something*.[5] The phonetic character is not apprehended as noise—that is a purely theoretical construct—but primarily as a speaking with others about something. Without explicitly establishing this phenomenal ground of the primary givenness of speaking as a "speaking with others about something," Plato nevertheless sets out from this mundane immediate mode of encountering discourse as speaking.

What then shows itself in this phenomenal state of affairs, that discourse is first encountered as speaking? What is encountered in the saying of words

4. Title based on Heidegger (see the articulation of the analysis of λόγος, p. 403).
5. AH: more precisely: what is apprehended first is the "about which."

are first of all words,[6] many words, a sequence of words. Thus along with speaking there is given something that can be understood as a manifold of formations, a structural manifold, καθάπερ περὶ τῶν εἰδῶν καὶ τῶν γραμμάτων ἐλέγομεν (261d1f.), "as we have already exhibited with regard to εἴδη and γράμματα." And just as there we exposed a manifold of formations, περὶ τῶν ὀνομάτων πάλιν ὡσαύτως ἐπισκεψώμεθα (d2f.), "so now we want to direct our gaze, in the same way, to the structural manifold of locutions, words."[7] The structural manifold of εἴδη, thus the manifold of what is properly visible in beings, was characterized as a κοινωνία, and specifically as one in which there are εἴδη διὰ πάντων, proper visibles distinguished by their all-pervasive visibility; they are thoroughly present, in every possible something. At that time I supplemented the analysis with a reference to the comparison, in the *Theaetetus*,[8] of the soul with a dovecote, where the same phenomenon was shown, not with regard to ὄν or εἶδος, but with regard to ἐπιστήμη: there are certain doves which are everywhere. The second structural manifold—or the third, if we count the example of the doves—is that of letters, γράμματα, or sounds. Nor is this manifold arbitrary; also there we find something pre-eminent, the φωνήεντα, the vowels. They have the character of δεσμός and first make a conjunction of letters genuinely possible.

It is no accident that in the present context Plato refers to this double structural manifold, of εἴδη and of γράμματα. There resides between these two manifolds and that of ὀνόματα not only a formal correspondence, in the sense that there is to be exhibited also in the case of ὀνόματα a possible conjunction as well as pre-eminent connecting links, but, in addition, between these structural manifolds (εἴδη, ὀνόματα, γράμματα, and even the ἐπιστητόν, if we count that in) there exists a substantive, intrinsic connection.[9] In the ὀνόματα, in the λόγοι, εἴδη are visible through the κοινωνία of γιγνώσκειν, of δηλοῦν; and what is visible is the νοητόν, the ἐπιστητόν. The ὀνόματα themselves, in which the εἶδος is visible, are for their part a manifold of γράμματα.[10] The structural manifolds are therefore not juxtaposed, isolated realms but instead stand in an intrinsic substantive κοινωνία: the matters at issue, what is properly visible in them, word, word-sound—beings, world, disclosure of beings, discourse, manifestation. This is nothing else than the universal context of phenomena within which man, the ζῷον λόγον ἔχον, ever exists. This context is ultimately grounded in Being-in, in the antecedent uncoveredness of the world.

6. AH: Vocables?
7. AH: Vocables!
8. Cf. p. 359f.
9. AH: of intentional, hermeneutic! existence.
10. AH: the naive ontological levelling, which became for Hegel a conscious task!

We must see this context if we are to understand Plato's analysis. That is, the task of the interpretation is precisely to penetrate through to this foundational context of phenomena, one not explicitly investigated by Plato but still operative for him. Only in that way will we presentify the ground out of which his analyses are drawn; only in that way can we pursue which phenomena have the priority and how far Plato deals with them. That is why I showed earlier, not unadvisedly, with reference to the *Phaedrus*,[11] what Plato had already acquired by way of insight into the context of disclosure, discourse, language, and writing, and I added a discussion of the "Seventh Letter,"[12] where the problem of λόγος stands connected to the innermost existence of man. We need to remember that. In the *Sophist*, these contexts are there in fact but are not treated explicitly. They are drawn in only to provide a methodological guideline for the treatment of ὀνόματα. In this regard, Plato says: φαίνεται γάρ πῃ ταύτῃ τὸ νῦν ζητούμενον (261d3), "it shows itself"—φαίνεται is stressed here and we should actually translate as follows: "what is now sought (namely the κοινωνία of ὀνόματα) can be brought to show itself," ταύτῃ, "in the way" of inquiring we already employed regarding the structures and manifolds mentioned above. Φαίνεται does not here mean "to seem" but "to show itself," in a completely positive sense.

Today phenomenology uses the term "phenomenon" in this sense of φαίνεται, φαινόμενον. Phenomenology signifies nothing else than disclosing in speech, exhibiting beings, exhibiting the beings that show themselves, in their way of showing themselves, in the way they are "there." That is the formal idea of phenomenology, which to be sure includes a richly articulated and intricate methodology. This formal idea of phenomenology—which was emphatically an essential advance over the constructions of the tradition—is usually confused with the methodology of research, with genuine research and the concrete mode of carrying it out. Phenomenology then seems to be an easy science, where one, as it were, lies on a sofa smoking a pipe and intuiting essences. But things are not so simple; on the contrary, it is a question of *demonstrating* the matters at issue themselves. How the demonstration happens depends on the access, the content, and the ontological constitution of the realm under investigation. Even the Greeks, Plato and Aristotle, use φαίνεται in this sense, although, to be sure, it is often detached from this sense and means simply "it seems," "it merely appears to be so." The terms "phenomenon" and "phenomenology" were used with this latter sense for the first time in the rationalism of the school of Wolff.

11. Cf. p. 214ff., especially p. 235ff.
12. Cf. p. 239f.

β) The κοινωνία of the ὀνόματα in λόγος.

αα) Δηλοῦν as criterion of the κοινωνία of ὀνόματα in λόγος. Rejection of the interpretation of ὀνόματα as signs. The essence of ὀνόματα (in the general sense) as δηλώματα.

The question now concerns the manifold of ὀνόματα: Τὸ ποῖον οὖν δὴ περὶ τῶν ὀνομάτων ὑπακουστέον; (261d4). "What is the outward look of that which we properly have to perceive in the field of linguistic expression?" What actually is it that we must hearken to? It is striking—purely terminologically—that Plato here uses the expression ὑπακούειν, whereas he otherwise, as is usual among the Greeks, employs the term ἅπτεσθαι, or ὁρᾶν, for the direct grasp of things. But here it is a matter of a particular phenomenon, speaking, which is primarily perceivable only in hearing. Ἅπτεσθαι, ὁρᾶν, and ἀκούειν have the character of αἴσθησις, of perceiving, but not of grasping by way of λογίζεσθαι. The latter is a matter of the proper hearkening to the manifold of spoken words, in order thereby to see what is at stake in this manifold with respect to its κοινωνία. Ὑπακούειν[13] precisely does not mean simply to hear sounds but instead properly signifies genuine perception, understanding what is said. It is a matter of hearkening to this, εἴτε πάντα ἀλλήλοις συναρμόττει εἴτε μηδέν, εἴτε τὰ μὲν ἐθέλει, τὰ δὲ μή (d5f.). That is again the same question which emerged in the case of the two previous manifolds, the question of the three general possibilities of conjunction within a domain of manifoldness. Here, too, as in both previous cases, the third possibility will be maintained. The task is therefore to hearken to such structural manifolds, such sequences of words, that can be co-present with one another and those that cannot. More precisely, we are to hearken to what genuinely constitutes the being with one another in the sequence of words and distinguishes the genuine from the ungenuine being with one another. For the ungenuine, immediately given, being with one another of words is τὰ ἐφεξῆς or τὰ ἐφεξῆς λεγόμενα (cf. d8), the speaking of words one after another. But not every speaking of words one *after* the other is itself a genuine saying of words *with* one another.

What phenomenon then constitutes the being with one another? What phenomenal state of affairs in the speaking of words one after the other is the criterion for the presence of a genuine κοινωνία within the manifoldness of words? Τὸ τοιόνδε λέγεις ἴσως, ὅτι τὰ μὲν ἐφεξῆς λεγόμενα καὶ δηλοῦντά τι συναρμόττει, τὰ δὲ τῇ συνεχείᾳ μηδὲν σημαίνοντα ἀναρμοστεῖ (d8ff.). There is present a κοινωνία among ὀνόματα (words, taken in the broadest

13. AH: ὑπο-: in what sense?

sense) if the ἐφεξῆς λεγόμενα are δηλώματα, if the speaking, as a determinate sequence of words, reveals something, if the sequence of words in itself, just as it is, lets something be seen, shows something: σημαίνειν, σημεῖον, the Aristotelian σημαντικός. Σημεῖον must not be translated here in an arbitrary and empty sense as "sign." Instead, σημεῖον has already been interpreted here in this Platonic context as δηλοῦν, with which it is interchangeable terminologically. Thus it has the sense of revealing, letting be seen, or in Aristotle: ἀποφαίνεσθαι.[14] Consequently, it is, strictly speaking, not in accord with the matter itself to connect in any way the act of meaning or revealing something with the phenomenon of the sign. Even Husserl, who was the first in the contemporary age to take up again the phenomena of meaning, still placed, following John Stuart Mill, this idea of the sign at the foundation of his analysis of meaning and its relation to the word-sound. The criterion for the existence of words in the unity of a discourse is their disclosive character. Words have a genuine[15] δύναμις κοινωνίας as δηλώματα, as "revealing," i.e., revealing beings, as δηλώματα περὶ τὴν οὐσίαν (e5), "as showing something in the field of presence," in the field of what may possibly be exhibited as there, the field of what is present at hand, and specifically τῇ φωνῇ (e5), in passing "through the phonetic character." This is not to be interpreted as if the showing took place through the φωνή itself, as if the sound were a sign of the thing, but instead the φωνή is only a structural moment, which in the spoken communication, as a self-expression to another about something, is indeed invested but does not as such have the function of δηλοῦν. The manifold of ὀνόματα is thus determined on the basis of δηλοῦν, and thereby on the basis of the δηλούμενον, on the basis of the beings to be exhibited.

This direction, toward what can be exhibited pure and simple, now also provides the characterization of ὀνόματα. For Plato now acquires, on the basis of this orientation, a possible differentiation within ὀνόματα. Already earlier, in the *Cratylus* and in the *Theaetetus*, Plato had seen the ὀνόματα and the ῥήματα without actually and properly distinguishing them as categories. Now it is a matter of finding in the field of ὀνόματα the corresponding phenomena, which are, so to speak, διὰ πάντων, in every possible λέγειν, which belong in general to every possible discourse as discourse. The task is to find the δεσμός, the structural moments, which cannot be missing if there is at all to be a κοινωνία as exhibiting something.

14. AH: Not yet so far. Aristotle actually distinguishes σημαντικὸς λόγος versus ἀποφαντικός. Plato—the latter versus the former—as in general signifying something.

15. AH: i.e., ontologically unique, because existential-hermeneutical.

ββ) The basic distinction within ὀνόματα in general between ὄνομα (in the stricter sense) and ῥῆμα. The δηλούμενον as the point of departure for the acquisition of this distinction. Ὄνομα = δήλωμα of the πρᾶγμα; ῥῆμα = δήλωμα of πρᾶξις. Plato's determination of ὄνομα and ῥῆμα as preparation for Aristotle's determination of them. "Noun." "Verb."

ἔστι γὰρ ἡμῖν που τῶν τῇ φωνῇ περὶ τὴν οὐσίαν δηλωμάτων διττὸν γένος. Τὸ μὲν ὀνόματα, τὸ δὲ ῥήματα κληθέν (cf. e4ff.). The δηλώματα are "of two stems": ὄνομα and ῥῆμα. This distinction gives ὄνομα a stricter sense versus its broader use up to now. Previously, ὄνομα meant any word of the language, but now its sense is restricted to particular ὀνόματα, ones distinguished from other pre-eminent words, i.e., from ῥήματα. But even after this distinction, Plato still sometimes uses ὄνομα in the broader sense, e.g. at 262d6. The proper designations in this field are so difficult for the Greeks because they actually have no word for "language," which is quite a remarkable fact. They have only λόγος, "speech," and διάλογος, "conversation," on the one hand, as well as φωνή, "locution," on the other hand. That is significant and indicates that the Greek consideration of language, the Greek understanding of speaking, did not descend as far as does the consideration of language in the modern and contemporary ages, where the place of departure is the φωνή and where language is essentially seen from that point of view. It indicates that the Greeks understood language, from the very outset, as discourse and discussed "language" with reference to it.

The question is how ὀνόματα and ῥήματα can be distinguished from one another. What aspect will provide a criterion for the differentiation? We already intimated that Plato acquires this distinction from the λεγόμενον as δηλούμενον. Ὄνομα and ῥῆμα are the primary modes in which beings as such are sayable. Τὸ μὲν ἐπὶ ταῖς πράξεσιν ὂν δήλωμα ῥῆμά που λέγομεν. Τὸ δέ γ' ἐπ' αὐτοῖς τοῖς ἐκείνας πράττουσι σημεῖον τῆς φωνῆς ἐπιτεθὲν ὄνομα (cf. 262a3ff.). The ὄνομα is the δήλωμα of the πρᾶγμα; the ῥῆμα is the δήλωμα of πρᾶξις. The ὄνομα uncovers and shows that which[16] is dealt with, and the ῥῆμα discloses the dealing-with. We must leave these terms in this indeterminate sense. As Plato intends them here, they are very difficult to translate. At all events, we may not translate them as "noun" and "verb," because the distinction between noun and verb is precisely not to be found in Plato, although he is aware of it.[17] The concept of noun first

16. In the Moser transcript, Heidegger writes over this: concerning which. AH: that with which one has "to do" in all doings, whether practical or theoretical. ὄνομα: the "concerning which." ῥῆμα: the dealing-with, the "concern" of the "concerning which."

17. AH: the distinction which the terms mean fundamentally.

arose out of Aristotle's ὑποκείμενον; i.e., the grammatical category of noun goes back to the ontological category of the ὑποκείμενον.[18] Aristotle was the first to discover the ὑποκείμενον—in connection with his uncovering of κίνησις, i.e., on the basis of the new foundation he gave to the question of Being, a foundation in κίνησις. It is a matter here of a genuine grasp on Aristotle's part of something Plato already glimpsed: that there is something like a ὑποκείμενον in κίνησις, in the κινούμενον. It was Aristotle who uncovered the "categories" here as well. Aristotle was thus the first to see in regard to the κινούμενον that there is something in movement that remains, that has στάσις, that is already there from the very outset. Πρᾶγμα in Plato's sense also inclines in this direction, in the direction of that which is already there at the very outset and always remains, the permanent. But Plato did not extensively elucidate this sense, because he did not yet see the characteristic distinction for establishing it, as did Aristotle, who then determined the ὄνομα as ἄνευ χρόνου, and the ῥῆμα as προσσημαῖνον χρόνον.[19] The ὄνομα shows something without explicitly presentifying the mode of its presence. The ῥῆμα, however, which by itself signifies nothing, and always discloses only κατά,[20] has the peculiarity of establishing with respect to its temporality that which it shows as a being, and that means for the Greeks: with respect to its presence or non-presence. Therefore, in German, the term "tense-word" *[Zeitwort]* is much more appropriate than the synonym "verb" *[Verbum]*. Only on the basis of these phenomena can we see the proper categorial structure of ὄνομα and ῥῆμα. Plato's discussion itself tends in this direction. It would be going much too far—at any rate there is no motive in the text—to identify πρᾶγμα, hence that which the ὄνομα exhibits, with στάσις, and πρᾶξις, hence that which the ῥῆμα exhibits, with κίνησις.

γγ) The συμπλοκή of ὄνομα and ῥῆμα as an essential condition of the κοινωνία of ὀνόματα in λόγος. Δηλοῦν as the primary phenomenon within the structure of language and as the constitutive determination of Dasein: Being-in. Λόγος σμικρότατος (the "proposition"). Naming and saying. Summary of the first stage.

Thus only that sequence of words one after the other in which a ῥῆμα is present together with an ὄνομα, which therefore exhibits a συμπλοκή of πρᾶγμα and πρᾶξις, is a λέγειν. A mere sequence of ῥήματα one after the

18. AH: Phenomenologically considered, Plato's distinctions are actually more radical. The naive primitiveness does not see the state of affairs as such but instead approaches it from "feelings"—i.e., remains close to it.

19. *De Interpretatione*, chapter 2, 16a19ff., and chapter 3, 16b6.

20. Supplement by Heidegger: i.e., (ἀπό?).

other: "βαδίζει," "τρέχει," "καθεύδει," . . . λόγον οὐδέν . . . ἀπεργάζεται (262b5ff.), results in no λόγος, because this sequence does not make visible the unity of a present being. Just as little as does: ὅταν λέγηται "λέων" "ἔλαφος" "ἵππος" . . . κατὰ ταύτην δὴ τὴν συνέχειαν οὐδείς πω συνέστη λόγος (b9ff.). Here, too, with regard to this συνέχεια, no λόγος actually occurs. οὐδεμίαν οὔτε οὕτως οὔτ' ἐκείνως πρᾶξιν οὐδ' ἀπραξίαν οὐδὲ οὐσίαν ὄντος οὐδὲ μὴ ὄντος δηλοῖ τὰ φωνηθέντα, πρὶν ἄν τις τοῖς ὀνόμασι τὰ ῥήματα κεράσῃ (cf. c2ff). The essential is that, in a λόγος, τὰ φωνηθέντα, the utterance, the locution, δηλοῖ, "reveals" (and this formulation is important for what will come later) οὐσίαν ὄντος καὶ μὴ ὄντος, "the presence of beings or of non-beings."[21] Δηλοῦν therefore is a matter of presentifying beings or non-beings. Such a δηλοῦν, such a disclosive presentification, does not occur, however, until πρὶν ἄν τις τοῖς ὀνόμασι τὰ ῥήματα κεράσῃ, "ὀνόματα and ῥήματα mix together." Only then is there a λόγος, not before. This state of affairs, the necessity of a συμπλοκή of ὄνομα and ῥῆμα, must not be understood as if λόγος resulted in some sense from a summation of ὄνομα and ῥῆμα. On the contrary, the δηλοῦν itself, the revealing, is the primary phenomenon, prior to both of these. That is why they are δηλώματα. And only insofar as they are such, is the κοινωνία possible.

The order of the description, in which Plato begins with an isolated ὄνομα and ῥῆμα, is not identical with the structure of the phenomena in itself. It is not the case that words first flutter about in isolation and then are taken together, whence the δηλοῦν arises. On the contrary, the δηλοῦν is primary. It is the fundamental phenomenon. And only with reference to it does there exist the possibility, as a deficient mode, of isolated, merely recited words. The δηλοῦν, which harbors the possibility of discourse, is a constitutive determination of Dasein itself, a determination I am wont to designate as Being-in-the-world or Being-in. Plato says nothing about this, but we must avoid misunderstanding it as a matter of a conjunction of representations. That idea of an extrinsic shoving together still dominates the entire traditional categorial material of the grammar of the Indo-Germanic languages. This material is not reducible to logic and is not anchored in it but in Greek ontology. If we wanted to see the original and phenomenal connection between the phenomenon of language and the Being of man, we would have to get rid, at the very outset, of the proposition as the point of departure for our orientation toward language. This development, as it has come to be today, was perhaps not the intention of the Greeks, but it has for them a justifiable sense, since λόγος and speech were for them given initially in this character.[22]

21. AH: Presence. The *Being* of εἶναι, of the "copula"!
22. AH: Why?

Such a λόγος, which consists of ὄνομα and ῥῆμα, is the λόγος πρῶτός τε καὶ σμικρότατος (cf. 262c6f.), "the first, most original, and the smallest." That means there can be no λόγος composed of fewer elements than these; ὄνομα and ῥῆμα are constitutive for λέγειν. Λέγειν is thereby distinguished essentially from ὀνομάζειν μόνον (cf. d5), from mere naming, from the mere reciting of words, where nothing is made visible. Ὀνομάζειν as such is not disclosive of things;[23] it is only λόγος that τι περαίνει (cf. d4), "finishes something off." Only in λόγος does something come forth within speaking in the sense of discourse: something shows itself, the εἶδος of some being becomes present. And only τὸ πλέγμα τοῦτο (d6), "this intertwining" of ὄνομα and ῥῆμα, εφθεγξάμεθα λόγον (d6), "do we call λόγος."

The first stage of the consideration of λόγος sets out, as we have seen, from discourse as spoken expression. As so pregiven, discourse shows itself initially as a manifold of words. The consideration, however, from the very outset does not simply attempt to make understandable this manifold of words in itself, isolated, so to speak, as a manifold of sounds,[24] but instead the regard is directed from the very first toward the basic structure of λέγειν in the sense of δηλοῦν. From this phenomenon of δηλοῦν, the ὀνόματα are then grasped as δηλώματα, and, on that basis, the simultaneous orientation toward the possible themes of disclosure reveals a fundamental distinction within ὀνόματα. Thus the criterion for the Being of words in the unity of discourse is their disclosive character. And the objective criterion for distinguishing these δηλώματα is the unity of the possible object of the disclosure: πρᾶγμα-πρᾶξις. I emphasized that these terms are to be taken here in the widest sense. We have no corresponding expressions, either to capture the positive aspect of this discovery or to express that what is uncovered here is not already fixed appropriately by Aristotle's later attempt to do so in relation to the criterion of time. Δηλοῦν itself is now, within λόγος, insofar as λόγος is a συμπλοκή of δηλώματα, not the *result* of their composition, but, on the contrary, the κοινωνία of ὄνομα and ῥῆμα is possible at all only because λέγειν in itself is a δηλοῦν. On this basis, what grammar calls the categorial proposition can be designated the πρῶτος and σμικρότατος λόγος. Thereby Plato acquires, versus the *Cratylus* and *Theaetetus*, the possibility of delimiting λέγειν positively over and against the ὀνομάζειν μόνον (cf. d3). Naming, the addressing of beings by way of naming, makes visible nothing of the beings themselves. Calling by name can never determine what is named in its substantive content. Naming thus does not have the character of disclosure. Instead, if anything at all is visible in naming, it is simply the way the named object is, as it were, summoned:

23. AH: not even σημαντικόν, as in Aristotle?
24. AH: Not a manifold of vocables, but a word-totality.

its appellation. That is indeed a disclosure of something not known prior to the calling by name, but the disclosure of the appellation, the name, is not an uncovering of the substantive content of the thing itself.[25] Naming is thus indeed a disclosure, in the broadest sense of the term, but not a substantive disclosure in the stricter sense of a relation to the named thing itself.[26] Plato uses ὀνομάζειν in this double sense of naming, which he delimits against λόγος, and it is only the latter that properly brings something to an end and that can properly be a δηλοῦν.

This first stage of the analysis of λόγος provides at the same time an insight into a particular κοινωνία, namely the κοινωνία that occurs as πλέγμα of ὄνομα and ῥῆμα. This κοινωνία is viewed in terms of ὀνόματα, but at the same time it announces the delotic. The further analysis of λόγος shows that the full phenomenon of λόγος still includes three other structures of κοινωνία, all of which Plato grasps uniformly and without distinction as σύνθεσις and does not explicitly establish as such, though they are there latently. That is, the proper structure of λόγος remains for him essentially unclarified. Our interpretation must explicitly set in relief these further structures of κοινωνία.

c) Second stage: the elaboration of the structure of the λεγόμενον *qua* λεγόμενον (= *qua* δηλούμενον).[27]

α) The basic determination of λόγος: λόγος = λόγος τινός. Its rediscovery in Husserl: "intentionality."

The second stage in the analysis of λόγος has the task of exposing the structure of the λεγόμενον as such, i.e., the genuine constitution of the possible uncoveredness of something addressed, how it looks outwardly, what in general is said in a λέγειν as something said. For this analysis of the λεγόμενον in its structure, Plato draws upon a fundamental determination: λόγος is λόγος τινός (cf. e5), every addressing is an addressing *of something*. Λόγον ἀναγκαῖον, ὅτανπερ ᾖ, τινὸς εἶναι λόγον, μὴ δὲ τινὸς, μὴ δὲ τινὸς ἀδύνατον (e5f.). Whenever λόγος exists, it is λόγος τινός; μὴ δὲ τινὸς ἀδύνατον, there is no λόγος that would not be λόγος τινός. It pertains to the very Being of λόγος to be "of something." Here Plato expresses a fundamental insight into λόγος, even if he does not make full use of it

25. AH: This interpretation of ὀνομάζειν based too much on the completed λόγος. Ὀνομάζειν is not yet that! Otherwise if interrogated in terms of the origin of language. Then ὄνομα = ῥῆμα.

26. AH: What is the meaning of naming as an interpretation and a making present? To retain?—a first cognition? Possibility of the ideal structure of the proposition. That is such and such—its name. What is intended—as merely *first*, i.e., in a deficient mode, as merely intended. How do both these ends—first naming and ultimate idle talk—meet?

27. Title based on Heidegger (see the articulation of the analysis of λόγος, p. 403).

phenomenologically. Nevertheless, the phenomenon is important enough for Plato, and through him it became decisive for the entire further history of logic.

If a Plato does not blush to proclaim this triviality, that λόγος is λόγος τινός, then it must be a matter of consequence. It is only apparently self-evident.[28] The history of philosophy, above all that of modern and contemporary logic, shows that this insight, this triviality, has been forgotten long ago or is no longer used. We can express the nexuses as follows: there are word-sounds which enter into the psyche; to these are joined, by way of association, so-called general representations; and all these together play out in consciousness. Then the question arises as to how these associations within consciousness can have objective validity for the things outside. That is almost exactly the current position still, even among our best. For instance, even Cassirer has basically not transcended this position. Thus no one any longer makes use of the insight: λόγος is λόγος τινός. Husserl was the first to discover it again with his concept of intentionality. It is not at all so self-evident and not at all so simple a matter to see this phenomenon of intentionality and thus to see that only on its basis will the structures of λόγος again be intelligible.

It is thus not true that λόγος as speaking occurs initially in isolation and that an object then incidentally emerges, with which it can enter into alliance as the case may be, but not necessarily. On the contrary, all discourse, according to its most proper sense, is a disclosure of something. This establishes a new κοινωνία, the κοινωνία of every λόγος with ὄν. This κοινωνία is included in the very sense of λόγος itself. We will quite soon see the full bearing of this constatation that λόγος is λόγος τινός.

β) The moments of the articulation of the τί as the τινός of λέγειν: 1.) "about which" (περὶ οὗ), 2.) "as-which" (ὅτου), 3.) "of which." The structure of the τί as λεγόμενον: something as something. Distinction between three modes of κοινωνία in λόγος.

Let us first ask about the τί of this τινός. Our inquiring into it does not amount to asking about a concrete being, a particular accidental object which just happens to be spoken about. We are not even interrogating this or that particular *domain* of Being, out of which a definite being comes to be addressed. On the contrary, the question of the τί of this τινός is the question of the λεγόμενον. For the τινός is a τινός of λόγος. The structure of carrying out the δηλοῦν, the exhibiting, was characterized as determined

28. AH: That is, we must never take what is at issue here as trivial but always as problematic.

by the πλέγμα of the δηλώματα, of the ὄνομα with the ῥῆμα. The constitution of the τί as δηλούμενον, as λεγόμενον, is thus πρᾶγμα *in the mode of* πρᾶξις. Therefore the possible λεγόμενον, according to its very sense, is pregiven precisely as something to be dealt with. That properly means πρᾶξις-πρᾶγμα. The dealing with something is thus what is pregiven in every λόγος according to its most proper sense. Plato designates this by means of the term περὶ οὗ (263a4). There belongs to every λόγος the περὶ οὗ. The task is to understand this περὶ οὗ as a structural moment of the λεγόμενον and not to misunderstand it, led astray by the tradition. Λόγος, as addressing something, possesses, as pregiven from the very first, the unarticulated unitary being. There belongs to λόγος, as a determinate moment, the creaking wagon on the street, for example. I do not hear noises in an isolated way, as if I were a subject in an institute of experimental psychology, but I hear the wagon on the street. The ξένος sees Theaetetus sitting before him. Theaetetus, as a unitary pregiven whole, is the περὶ οὗ. We can call this the "about which" of the speaking. In the circuit of what is thus pregiven, λέγειν now sets something in relief. What is set in relief is the ὅτου (a4). In it, therefore, in the pregiven and still unarticulated being, λέγειν will set something in relief, specifically so as to make the being understood *as* something and thereby determine it. Thus the "about which," the whole of what is pregiven, e.g. the creaking wagon, is then grasped in terms of the creaking itself: the wagon passing by on the street is now experienced and determined *as* creaking. The περὶ οὗ therefore harbors a double structure:

1.) It means the "about which," as a whole, of the discourse in general, the whole, present, still unarticulated given being.

2.) Insofar as the setting in relief is carried out upon this περὶ οὗ, insofar as creaking is attributed to it *as* a special determination, the articulation of the wagon itself proves to be what is spoken about. The περὶ οὗ then means, more particularly, the specific "of which" of the discourse.

We therefore distinguish: 1.) the "about which" of the discourse, i.e., the unarticulated whole, and 2.) the "of which," i.e., what is thematically articulated and set in relief: what grammar calls the "subject" of the proposition.

Thus, clearly, the proper phenomenal carrying out of a setting in relief, by δηλοῦν or λέγειν, does not occur in such a way that two representations are linked with one another, but, instead, out of the presence of an unarticulated "about which," i.e., a determinate unarticulated state of affairs,[29] it happens, precisely through the setting in relief of the "as-which," of the creaking or the sitting, that at the same time the "of which," the wagon or

29. AH: Whence and how so? The "Being"-already-present!

Theaetetus, is first made prominent. The way runs precisely not from the subject, over the copula, to the predicate but, instead, from the pregiven whole to the setting in relief of what we afterwards call the predicate, and thereby for the first time to a genuine making prominent of the subject.

The analysis of the τινός, of the τί, in the phenomenon of λόγος τινός therefore shows this phenomenal structure in addressability as such: "something as something," in which a simply pregiven being is properly brought into presence. This "as," the as-character, is the properly logical category,[30] "logical" not in the traditional sense, but in the sense of that which is given in λόγος as constitutive, insofar as λόγος is an addressing *of* something: that which constitutes in the λεγόμενον the structure of the λεγόμενον as such.

This primary structural form of the "something as something" results in a new κοινωνία within the whole of λόγος itself. We had: 1.) the κοινωνία between ὄνομα and ῥῆμα within the possibility of expression, 2.) the κοινωνία between λόγος and ὄν: λόγος τινός, and now we have: 3.) within the τί, the κοινωνία as structural form of the "something as something." This last, therefore, which is determined through the character of the "as," we call the specifically *logical* κοινωνία in λόγος. The second one, on the basis of which λόγος is, according to its essence, λόγος τινός, we call, following phenomenological terminology, the *intentional* κοινωνία.[31] And the first, the one between ὄνομα and ῥῆμα, which pertains to the ὄνομα in the widest sense, we call the *onomatic* κοινωνία.

On this basis, it first becomes possible to make quite clear the third stage of the analysis of λόγος, which now has the task of determining λέγειν itself with regard to the possibilities residing in it, namely λόγος as ποιός (263a11ff.).

d) Third stage: the analysis of λόγος with respect to δηλοῦν.[32]

α) The basic determination of λόγος *qua* λόγος τινός as the fundamental condition of deceptive λόγος. The ποιόν (ἀληθές or ψεῦδος) as a necessary character of λόγος.

The third stage has, as we said, the task of determining λόγος as ποιός. Here it is important that *every* λέγειν is a λέγειν τί. There is no modification of λόγος which does not modify it as λέγειν τί; i.e., every modification of λέγειν is a modification of it in its character as revealing. Through such

30. AH: Not merely related or restricted here to the theoretical proposition.
31. AH: the delotic.
32. Title based on Heidegger (see the articulation of the analysis of λόγος, p. 403).

modification, the δηλοῦν does not somehow come to nothing, the λέγειν to a λέγειν μηδέν (which it cannot be, by its very sense), to a total lack of disclosure, but because the λέγειν τί, as a constitutive structure, is necessarily preserved in every modification of λόγος, λόγος can be modified into a non-disclosure only in the sense of concealing, distorting, obstructing, not letting be seen. Every λόγος, thus even the one modified in this way, is and presents itself as a λέγειν τί. Every self-expression, and every speaking about something, is taken quite naturally and primordially as a δηλοῦν. Thus we have, assuming that the δηλοῦν can undergo a modification, the following structures: 1.) A λέγειν presents itself, and is there, as a disclosure of something. 2.) This λέγειν, however, can in itself be distorting; it can pass something off as other than it is. Insofar as it presents itself, and always presents itself, as λέγειν τί, but factually, in a particular case, does not impart the being, this λέγειν is a deception. Deception is thus possible, and understandable in general, only in terms of λέγειν as λέγειν τί. Because it is λόγος τινός, λόγος in itself can be false. Just as we speak of "false money," which looks like genuine money but is not, so the λέγειν that distorts something presents itself as what it is not: the λέγειν distorts itself, it is in itself "false." Every λόγος is therefore, as λόγος, a λέγειν τί. But it need not show that about which it speaks; it can also distort it, in such a way, of course, that this "false" judgment pretends to be true. Deception, ψεῦδος, is thus founded, according to its very possibility, in the intentional constitution of λέγειν. It is λέγειν as λέγειν τί that can be a distortion.

Thus it is clear that every λόγος, on the basis of this constitution, always and necessarily occurs in a certain "mode." It discloses *in such and such a way:* it is either disclosive or distortive; i.e., every λόγος is ποιός. Ποιὸν δέ γέ τινά φαμεν ἀναγκαῖον ἕκαστον εἶναι τῶν λόγων (263a11f.). "We say that every λόγος is necessarily ποιός, in one mode or another," precisely because it is λέγειν τί. Likewise, ποιόν τινα αὐτὸν εἶναι δεῖ (262e8), "it is necessary that λόγος always be ποιός." In every λέγειν, therefore, just insofar as it is, a decision has always already been made regarding its δηλοῦν. ἀδύνατον λόγον ὄντα μηδενὸς εἶναι λόγον (cf. 263c10f.): "It is impossible that a λόγος could at all be what it is if it were λόγος of nothing." The possible ways for λόγος to be ποιός are none other than λόγος ἀληθές and λόγος ψευδής.

β) Plato's dialectical interpretation of ψεῦδος and ἀληθές. The κοινωνία of ὄν (*qua* λεγόμενον) with ταὐτόν and ἕτερον as ground of the possibility of λόγος ἀληθές or λόγος ψευδής. The fourth κοινωνία in λόγος.

The decisive question is now for us: how does Plato interpret ψεῦδος or ἀληθές? The answer in brief is: purely dialectically, which means: by way of exhibiting a κοινωνία, and specifically one such as we already know, but now this κοινωνία, which we are acquainted with from the fundamental consideration, includes λόγος itself, as an ὄν. It was shown earlier that every ὄν or τί stands in a κοινωνία with ταὐτόν and ἕτερον. Every "something," in the widest sense, is itself, and, as this "itself," it is the one and not the other. Now this ὄν, this τί, upon which the fundamental dialectical consideration was carried out, is grasped in a κοινωνία with λόγος; i.e., ὄν is now grasped as δηλούμενον through λόγος as λεγόμενον. In this new κοινωνία, ὄν remains ὄν, i.e., the possibility of its κοινωνία with ταὐτόν and ἕτερον is not taken away, since these were indeed positively shown to be διὰ πάντων, through everything, and thus also through the something that is the λεγόμενον. This is the place where the sophist's objection is pressed hard by saying: it has not been settled whether μὴ ὄν can also enter into a κοινωνία with λόγος.[33] This objection collapses under the weight of the exhibition of λόγος as λόγος τινός.

The λεγόμενον is a τί, an ὄν; as such, it stands in a δύναμις κοινωνίας with ταὐτόν and ἕτερον. If ταὐτόν is present in an ὄν, that means the ὄν is in itself, it is what it is. And that means, relative to δηλοῦν, relative to the ὄν as δηλούμενον, that the ὄν is *disclosed* just as it is in itself. If a being is disclosed just as it is in itself, then the disclosure is an ἀληθεύειν, an undistorted imparting of the being in itself; the λόγος is ἀληθής. Ἀληθεύειν is thus a λέγειν τινός in which the τί is distinguished through the presence of ταὐτόν—provided it makes visible a being in its self-sameness. But the ἕτερον too—as was shown dialectically—can stand in a possible κοινωνία with ὄν. Then, first of all, the ὄν is other than itself. If the ὄν is now grasped as a λεγόμενον τί, that means it is ἕτερον λεγόμενον, it is *exhibited* as other than itself. This exhibiting of something as other than it is is nothing else than concealing, distorting, distortive making visible. Such a λέγειν, therefore, in which the λεγόμενον as ὄν is distinguished by the presence of the ἕτερον, is λόγος ψευδής.

Λόγος ἀληθής and λόγος ψευδής are thus grasped as follows: Λέγει ὁ λόγος ἀληθὴς τὰ ὄντα ὡς ἔστιν (cf. 263b4f.) (the ὡς ἔστιν is simply a paraphrase of ταὐτόν), it exhibits beings *as* ταὐτά; the presence of ταὐτόν is constitutive. Ὁ δὲ δὴ ψευδὴς ἕτερα τῶν ὄντων (b7), it exhibits them *as* ἕτερα; the presence of the ἕτερον is constitutive, and the λεγόμενα are determined by the presence of the ἕτερον.

Earlier we demonstrated, quite generally, the possibility of the παρουσία of the ἕτερον and ταὐτόν in ὄν alone. Now, however, it has become clear that the same connection also applies to ὄν as λεγόμενον. Thus a new κοινωνία appears in λόγος as λόγος τινός, i.e., in the λεγόμενον as ὄν: the

33. *Sophist* 206a5–261c5. Cf. p. 398f.

κοινωνία with ταὐτόν or with the ἕτερον. This κοινωνία determines the possibility of λόγος as ποιός, i.e., the mode of its disclosure as true or false. We are calling this κοινωνία the delotic one, the κοινωνία pertaining to δηλοῦν. Note (here our interpretation goes beyond what is strictly speaking given and touches what is latent ontologically) that this ὂν λεγόμενον was already characterized in the second stage as περὶ οὗ and ὅτου: it was exposed as constituted by the "something as something." Thus ὄν, which is the possible "something" of a λέγειν, already possesses in itself a κοινωνία, namely the "something as something." And now there occurs the possibility of the new κοινωνία, of the presence of ταὐτόν and the ἕτερον in this ὄν. That is, the pregiven ὄν in the character of the "something as something" can for its part be disclosed as self-same or as other than it is. Thus we see a doubling of the character of the "as" in λόγος. Thereby the fundamental function of this peculiar category of the "as" in λέγειν first becomes clear. In the phenomenon of the "something as something," the "as" means: 1.) something in the substantive determinateness of something, and 2.) something thus pregiven in its determinateness as itself or as an other.

γ) Summary of the result of the analysis of λόγος. Λόγος as σύνθεσις. The fourfold κοινωνία in λόγος.

Plato summarizes the result of his analysis of λόγος at 263d1ff.: Περὶ δὴ σοῦ λεγόμενα μέντοι θάτερα ὡς τὰ αὐτὰ καὶ μὴ ὄντα ὡς ὄντα, παντάπασιν ἔοικεν ἡ τοιαύτη σύνθεσις ἔκ τε ῥημάτων γιγνομένη καὶ ὀνομάτων ὄντως τε καὶ ἀληθῶς γίγνεσθαι λόγος ψευδής. This summary clarifies λόγος as σύνθεσις and specifically as τοιαύτη σύνθεσις. This τοιαύτη pertains to the possible κοινωνία of the λεγόμενον with ταὐτόν or with the ἕτερον. Plato takes into account here only the possibility of a κοινωνία with the ἕτερον, because what is at stake is primarily the proof of the possibility of λόγος ψευδής. At the same time, the σύνθεσις is characterized as γιγνομένη ἔκ τε ῥημάτων καὶ ὀνομάτων; i.e., reference is made simultaneously to the κοινωνία we have designated as the onomatic. Thus there resides in the whole of the phenomenon of λόγος a fourfold κοινωνία:

1.) the onomatic: between ὄνομα and ῥῆμα as πλέγμα.

2.) the intentional: every λόγος is λόγος τινός; λόγος as ὄν is in a κοινωνία with ὄν as its object.

3.) the logical: every τί of λέγειν is addressed in the character of the "something as something."

4.) the delotic, the one that pertains to δηλοῦν: in every δηλοῦν, in every λέγειν τί, the λεγόμενον is either "identified," as we say, with itself, or an other than itself is placed before it and the λόγος thereby becomes deceptive and, in itself, false.

This exposition touches Plato's genuine aim, which consists in showing the possibility, founded in the Being of λόγος itself, of a conjunction with the ἕτερον, i.e., the possibility of λόγος to be ψευδής, as a possibility residing in λόγος itself. That, however, is a proof of the possibility of the existence of the sophist; this existence is thus made visible dialectically.[34]

§81. The analysis of δόξα *and* φαντασία[1] *(263d–264d). The clarification of the* τέχνη σοφιστική *as* τέχνη δοξαστική *and* τέχνη φανταστική *through the proof of the possible conjunction of* δόξα *and* φαντασία *with* ψεῦδος. Διάνοια, δόξα, *and* φαντασία *as modes of* λέγειν; *their possible conjunction with the* ἕτερον *(i.e.,* μὴ ὄν *or* ψεῦδος*).*

Plato has determined the τέχνη σοφιστική as ἀντιλογική, and also as δοξαστική and φανταστική, if you recall the fifth and seventh definitions. In order to carry out fully the exhibition of a possible conjunction of λέγειν, in the broadest sense, with μὴ ὄν, he must also show that δόξα and φαντασία can enter into a κοινωνία with μὴ ὄν and the ἕτερον, i.e., that there can be a δόξα ψευδής. In other words, Plato must prove in principle, for all the comportments which, by their every sense, can be true or false, a possible conjunction with the ἕτερον. These comportments are: δόξα, διάνοια, and φαντασία. Τί δὲ δή; διάνοιά τε καὶ δόξα καὶ φαντασία, μῶν οὐκ ἤδη δῆλον ὅτι ταῦτά γε ψευδῆ τε καὶ ἀληθῆ πάνθ' ἡμῶν ἐν ταῖς ψυχαῖς ἐγγίγνεται; (263d6ff.). The proof of the possible conjunction of these comportments with the ἕτερον is relatively brief (263d–264d6), because Plato builds these phenomena—δοξάζειν, διανοεῖν, φαντασία—upon the phenomenon of λόγος. Here again there appears unmistakably the priority of λόγος over all other possible modes of uncovering and disclosing. The proof of a connection of διάνοια with λόγος, and, further, of δόξα with διάνοια, as well as, finally, of φαντασία with δόξα, simultaneously shows the descent of φαντασία, διάνοια, and δόξα out of λόγος. These are all τῷ λόγῳ συγγενεῖς (cf. 264b2f.), they have the same ontological lineage as does λόγος. Plato thus interprets these phenomena as λέγειν.

Διάνοια is ἐντὸς τῆς ψυχῆς πρὸς αὑτὴν διάλογος ἄνευ φωνῆς γιγνόμενος (263e4ff.). Νοεῖν is a λέγειν; it is just that it is not proclaimed and communicated. It is a λέγειν of the soul to itself, not to others. That is the opposite of ἐντὸς τῆς ψυχῆς. It is not at all a matter here of the opposition between immanence and transcendence, as if the aim were to

34. See the appendix.
1. Title based on Heidegger (see p. 397).

determine διανοεῖν as a subjective speaking, with regard to which the famous problem would arise as to how it could come out of immanence and have so-called transcendent validity for objects. Ἐντὸς τῆς ψυχῆς means only that διανοεῖν is a speaking that is μετὰ σιγῆς (264a2), "not communicated." But precisely as this silent speaking, it is completely immersed in the matters at issue. Λόγος, as λόγος τινός, even if it is spoken silently, is a speaking about the matters themselves. It would be senseless to give ψυχή here the meaning of mere interiority, as if διανοεῖν were a subjective speaking, whose objective validity would be problematic. The identification of the ψυχή with consciousness and of consciousness with subjectivity injects into the interpretation of Plato's philosophy an ungodly confusion from which we will never extricate ourselves as long as we have not learned to disregard the worn-out categories of modern logic, i.e., as long as we have not learned that this disregard is the primary requirement for an objective understanding of historiographically pregiven phenomena. Διανοεῖν as a λέγειν is precisely a disclosure of beings, and Plato characterizes λέγειν explicitly as φάσις and ἀπόφασις (263e12), addressing in the sense of affirmation and denial. Aristotle later apprehended φάσις more sharply as κατάφασις and placed φάσις before both κατάφασις and ἀπόφασις.

Finally, a brief interpretation of the two other phenomena. Plato traces δόξα back to διάνοια and thereby to λόγος. Δόξα is the ἀποτελεύτησις διανοίας (cf. 264b1), the "consummation" of a διανοεῖν, of a λέγειν, of an addressing; i.e., it is the fully realized claim, the explicit taking of something for something. What is essential in δόξα is thus again, just as in διανοεῖν, to take something for something, i.e., the as-structure.

Λέγειν, now in the sense of διανοεῖν, is a presentifying of what is addressed καθ' αὑτό (264a4). The being in its essence, in its εἶδος, is there in διανοεῖν, πάρεστιν (cf. a4). Διανοεῖν is thus a seeing of something, but not with the sensible eyes. Insofar as it is characterized as a seeing, that means the seen is present as itself. Beings can also, however, δι' αἰσθήσεως παρεῖναι (cf. a4), "be present through sense perception." This presence of what is perceived in sense perception is determined as φαίνεται (b1). What shows itself in αἴσθησις is, in the stricter sense, φαντασία. Φαντασία does not here mean to fantasize, merely imagine, but refers to what is present in such mere imagining, such presentation. Φαντασία is thus equivalent to λόγος as λεγόμενον. The expression, however, even in Aristotle, has the characteristic double meaning of all these terms for the comportments of ἀληθεύειν, namely λόγος, δόξα, θέσις, ὑπόληψις. All these variations in meaning refer on the one hand to the carrying out of ἀληθεύειν and on the other to what is disclosed as such. Plato interprets φαντασία as δόξα, and specifically as σύμμειξις αἰσθήσεως καὶ δόξης (264b2), as δόξα *based on* αἴσθησις. Aristotle, as is well known, subjected this Platonic definition of φαντασία to a sharp and trenchant critique in the *De Anima,* Book III, chapter 3, 428a25–b9.[2] Insofar as φαντασία, according to Plato, is a δόξα based on αἴσθησις, it also possesses, as δόξα, the character of λόγος; i.e., it is determined through the phenomenon of the "taking something for something." Διάνοια, δόξα, and φαντασία are thus τῷ λόγῳ συγγενεῖς (cf. 264b2f.), they have the same ontological lineage λόγος has and can therefore also be ψευδεῖς (cf. b3).

In this way τέχνη σοφιστική is clarified as φανταστική, δοξαστική, and ἀντιλογική. The sophist has been made intelligible in his existence.

But thereby—and this is decisive—the *philosopher* has become transparent in himself, and that has happened uniquely by way of concrete philosophizing itself: i.e., not in relation to arbitrary matters but, as we heard at 254a8f., τῇ τοῦ ὄντος ἀεὶ διὰ λογισμῶν προσκείμενος ἰδέᾳ.

2. See the appendix.

APPENDIX

Supplements

From Heidegger's Manuscript
(Remarks, Additions, Annotations to the Lectures)

I. Supplements to the Introductory Part

1. (to page 16)

ἀληθεύειν

Possibility of Dasein—determined thereby in its Being. Ways—a highest one—σοφία. Φιλοσοφία—to decide in favor of this *truth*!
Plato—himself—to go along the way for a distance.
As *dialogue*—διαλέγεσθαι—the mode of research and mode of access to the matters at issue.

2. (to p. 40)

Striking: the *highest understanding*—together with τέχνη and this again with ἐπιστήμη.
Not surprising if τέχνη is held to be an ἀληθεύειν,—as such, a mode of comportment in which the possibility of *being carried out* can *withdraw*.

3. (to p. 44)

With regard to Plato's *Sophist*, which exposes what a philosopher is (σοφία), an explicit preliminary consideration of σοφία as ἀληθεύειν becomes necessary.
The philosopher: τῇ τοῦ ὄντος ἀεὶ διὰ λογισμῶν προσκείμενος ἰδέᾳ. (*Sophist*, 254a8f.). "He lies with, is occupied with, a looking upon beings, in such a way indeed that he carries out a speaking about them."

4. (to p. 86)

as regards 4.): the *full autonomy* of σοφία
1.) on the basis of the theme
2.) on the basis of the ontological tendency of the comportment of Dasein.

1.) The full autonomy characterizes recognizing and knowing, which is τοῦ μάλιστα ἐπιστητοῦ ἐπιστήμη (*Met.* I, 2, 982a31). μάλιστα ἐπιστητά: τὰ πρῶτα καὶ τὰ αἴτια.
διὰ γὰρ ταῦτα καὶ ἐκ τούτων τἆλλα γνωρίζεται, ἀλλ' οὐ ταῦτα διὰ τῶν ὑποκειμένων (b2) (through that which initially lies there already as point of departure).
The ἀρχικωτάτη ἐπιστήμη—καὶ μᾶλλον ἀρχική—ἡ γνωρίζουσα τίνος ἕνεκέν ἐστι πρακτέον ἕκαστον (cf. b4ff.).
A connection of products and modes of producing, a sequence of levels. Ἐπιστήμη as an average concept. Cf. *Nicomachean Ethics:* grasped more basically—with regard to every comportment and concern with something.
That which stands in πρᾶξις, determined from it—οὗ ἕνεκα—*for the sake of which* something is attended to with concern.
τοῦτο δ' ἐστὶ τἀγαθὸν ἐν ἑκάστοις (982b6)—this is for each "the good"—that means: that which constitutes its *com-pletion*—being finished—*that which brings the object of concern in* πρᾶξις—ποίησις—ἐπιστήμη—*to its proper Being.*
Knowing as the uncovering of πρᾶξις—which discloses beings in their ἀγαθόν.
Accordingly the μάλιστα ἐπιστητόν—the μάλιστα ἀγαθόν = ὅλως τὸ ἄριστον—the best, proper *Being*—ἐν τῇ φύσει πάσῃ (cf. 982b6f.). The proper τέλος and πέρας—that which constitutes beings as a whole in their existence. *Most proper* beings—most proper *Being*. The most proper beings exist properly as νοεῖν of themselves. Beings as Being—ἀρχαί. In this questioning "ontology" and "theology" predelineated. Cf. νοῦς—νοητόν / ἀρχή—ὂν ᾗ ὄν. Τὸ ζητούμενον ὄνομα (σοφία, σοφός) πίπτει ἐπὶ τὴν αὐτὴν ἐπιστήμην (cf. b8). If we investigate what the expression under discussion means—the expression in the speech of natural, immediate Dasein—then what is thereby found falls under the same ἐπιστήμη.

2.) τῶν πρώτων ἀρχῶν καὶ αἰτίων—although toward οὗ ἕνεκα and ἀγαθόν—yet not ποιητική (b9)—it has already upon closer inspection in the history of its origin in Dasein an ontological tendency of Dasein for itself. Whether or not it precisely liberates itself only slowly from

the ἐπιστῆμαι ποιητικαί, it is *not* simply a transformation of this but is at the very outset sustained by the tendency merely to see and know. (This liberating of itself)[1]—συμβεβηκός—concomitant appearance—of σοφία in its relation to the other modes of ἀληθεύειν. τοιαύτη φρόνησις (b24), insofar as οὗ ἕνεκα and ἀγαθόν also for *Dasein* itself—and not χρεία (b24)—παρά, but in itself it is the *Being of Dasein.*
The ἑαυτῆς ἕνεκα becomes visible at the same time therefore in that it—σοφία—is founded in an originally proper mode of Being of human Dasein.
ὅτι δ' οὐ ποιητική (b11)—although ἀγαθόν—Aristotle understood this precisely in its *ontological* function—δῆλον καὶ ἐκ τῶν πρώτων φιλοσοφησάντων (b11). Here to be understood positively that it at the very outset—next to ποίησις—constitutes an autonomous mode of Being of man.
Visible from two primary moments of carrying it out: 1.) θαυμάζειν 2.) διαπορεῖν (b12ff.).

5. (to p. 113)

νοῦς (perceiving) ἐπ' ἀμφότερα

αἴσθησις—uncovering of the present site, of the positionality toward the circumstances and the like.
ἀεὶ ἀληθές—Being in the having and as the having of world.
Being-in-the-world—the *basic modes*.
But Being means: being present (for what is alive: being present *to*), and this is something proper if the "whereby" itself is a proper being, i.e., everlasting.
At issue is Being itself—simply, καθ' αὑτό.

6. (to p. 128)

πᾶν τὸ διανοητὸν καὶ νοητὸν ἡ διάνοια ἢ κατάφησιν ἢ ἀπόφησιν—ὅταν μὲν ὡδὶ συνθῇ φᾶσα ἢ ἀποφᾶσα, ἀληθεύει, ὅταν δὲ ὡδί, ψεύδεται (cf. *Met.* Γ, 7, 1012a2ff.).
This passage brought up in order to confront a common error in logic and in the interpretation of Aristotle.

1. Editor's supplement.

It is held that affirming is σύνθεσις, connection; denial is διαίρεσις, separation.
But, instead, the passage above makes it clear: disclosure by way of affirmation and disclosure by way of denial are *both* σύνθεσις.
Or: ἐνδέχεται δὲ καὶ διαίρεσιν φάναι πάντα (*De An.* Γ, 6, 430b3f.). "Affirmation and denial are likewise to be interpreted as a taking apart." Taking apart is indeed the mode of carrying out *perception*, νοεῖν, i.e., of keeping the ἕν, the whole, in view. And taking apart is a preserving mode of letting the whole be seen, i.e., positing the one with the other.
Σύνθεσις and διαίρεσις constitute the full mode of the carrying out of νοεῖν; and this latter itself, insofar as the νοεῖν is that of the λόγον ἔχον, can be a κατάφασις and ἀπόφασις.
Cf.: *Met.* E, 4, 1027b2ff.
τὸ ἅμα ἢ τὸ χωρὶς νοεῖν—a mode of perceiving, encountering. Ἅμα and χωρίς—μὴ τὸ ἐφεξῆς (b24) "not discretely one after the other"—the standing next to each other of the νοήματα. But instead: ἕν τι γίγνεσθαι (b25) is the decisive feature of this νοεῖν.
ἅμα νοεῖν—τὸ συγκείμενον / χωρὶς νοεῖν—τὸ διῃρημένον. κεχωρισμένον: ἓν νοεῖν. ἓν νοεῖν: as σύνθεσις and as διαίρεσις too. For even ἅμα νοεῖν can be understood as διαίρεσις. *Constitutively,* in terms of intentional determination.
αἴτιον (b34) this mode of Being of beings—to be unconcealed or to be distorted in λόγος—is τῆς διανοίας τι πάθος (b34f.), "a being affected of the discerning." Insofar as the discernment encounters something, what is encountered is itself disclosed. ἀληθές and ψεῦδος: οὐκ ἔξω δηλοῦσιν οὖσάν τινα φύσιν τοῦ ὄντος (1028a2). They do not provide a determination of the Being of beings which pertains to them as beings in themselves but only insofar as they are encountered.
τὸ ἀληθὲς ὄν—πάθος ἐν τῇ διανοίᾳ (cf. *Met.* K, 8, 1065a21ff.). "The *unconcealedness* of beings is something that affects the discerning disclosure." *Disclosed* presence.
Ἐν διανοίᾳ does not mean: a process of thought—factual occurrence, but rather: to be discerned—to be encountered. For: disclosive having-there. Being—as *disclosed* presence—world of a living thing.

7. (to supplement 6)

τοῦ ὄντος αὐτοῦ—ᾗ ὄν—τὰς ἀρχὰς σκεπτέον (cf. *Met.* E, 4, 1028a3f.).
ἀληθές—ψεῦδος, disclosed—distorted: οὐκ ἐν τοῖς πράγμασιν, ἀλλ' ἐν διανοίᾳ (cf. *Met.* E, 4, 1027b26ff.). *No determination of content*—like ἀγαθόν—,

that constitutes the *being finished*, the presence at hand, but instead a character of the encountering—a *"how" of possible presence.*
Not: ᾗ ὄν—in itself, but ᾗ *unconcealed, liberated* or distorted.

ἐν διανοίᾳ γίγνεται the ἕν, in τὸ ἅμα and in τὸ χωρὶς νοεῖν, in νοεῖν (cf. b23f.). No ἐφεξῆς (b24)—*succeeding one another*. Τὸ ἅμα and τὸ χωρὶς νοεῖν: to admit proper Da-sein.

8. (First supplement to p. 129)

ἀληθές: beings as unconcealed—with regard to the way they are discerned and perceived and as such preserved.
The immediate mode of this preserving: λόγος as λεγόμενον. What is said in an ἀποφαντικὸς λόγος: beings as uncovered. The λεγόμενον is ἀληθές—λόγος ἀληθής.
ἀληθές: not ἐν τοῖς πράγμασιν (*Met.* E, 4, 1027b25f.) but instead ἐν διανοίᾳ (b27), and that means ἐπὶ τῶν πραγμάτων (*Met.* Θ, 10, 1051b2).

But yet in Θ 10 κυριώτατα ὄν (b1).
1.) the expression can only be understood on the basis of the correct interpretation of Being itself,
2.) on the basis of the genuine meaning of ἀληθεύειν.

Beings as appropriated. *Presence*, proper. Letting *be present* purely and simply!

"The main thing, of which one speaks the most"—Jaeger claims.[2]
Unaristotelean, if it is related to the / a[3] being itself!

Precisely here the real misunderstanding: that Jaeger and the usual tradition—already in *scholasticism*—maintain: it would be a matter of psychic Being—and of Being as validity.

Both meet in the "There."

It is beings themselves—only with regard to a character of Being which pertains to them insofar as they can be encountered and are there uncovered or covered over.
Beings in their *unconcealedness*. Unconcealedness in λόγος. λεγόμενον. There also the possibility of being distorted.

2. Werner Jaeger, *Studien zur Entstehungsgeschichte der Metaphysik des Aristoteles*, Berlin, 1912. According to the sense of p. 36f.
3. Heidegger crossed out the word "the."

Jaeger maintains:
1.) another being is the theme,
2.) the ἀληθές of the ἀδιαίρετον is a special case, indeed even contradicting the first truth of λόγος.[4]

The proper *unconcealedness.*

κυριώτατα ὄν are beings themselves as *proper*—ἀλήθεια; what dominates and decides—a.) in its ultimate ἀρχαί, b.) these simply—purely—perceived as uncovered. φιλοσοφήσανες περὶ ἀληθείας (*Met.* A, 3, 983b3).

ἀληθεύειν: ψυχή: Dasein—Being-in.
ἀληθές: 1.) beings—world—Dasein, 2.) λεγόμενον—λόγος—beginning of the ungenuine theory of truth and judgment.
ἀλήθεια: ὄν—ἀρχαί—αἴτιον (*Met.* α, 1, 993b23).

9. (to supplement 8)

Ἀληθές—ὄν ὡς ἀληθές. Ἀληθεύειν. Ἀλήθεια.

κυριώτατα ὄν in Θ.
"the main thing, of which one speaks the most."[5]
Unaristotelean, if it is placed in relation to beings themselves.
φιλοσοφήσαντες περὶ ἀληθείας. ἀλήθεια = ὄν, in the most proper sense of being uncovered.
Aristotle does not intend a special case of truth but what is radical and original in the ἀρχαί.

10. (to supplement 8)

Truth and assertion

Speaking out—the said. A certain understanding—*intending* of. To take what is intended as what is. "Out": from the average, its *being known* and the self-satisfaction with the familiar.
This *Being* is stamped, elevated, to a being. But the reverse is the case with experience. And what is hypostatized in this way—something in the rela-

4. Jaeger, op. cit., according to the sense of p. 18ff.
5. See supplement 8, p. 427, and note 1 there.

tion-to—should be in relation to real beings. Being-in-relation-to as between two different beings. *Which Being?*

What . . . [6] sense does the ὂν ὡς ἀληθές have, and what does it mean?

It "is true"—only a how—but a preeminent one.

11. (to supplement 8)

Why true (ἀληθές) = *actual being?*

Because Being = presence, not validity and the like, to be uncovered = *genuine* presence.
Or because "truth" is *uncoveredness* of *beings,* ἀληθές belongs to ὄν—"dialectics," "logic" in *ontology.*
The true is. Not idealistically and not realistically but Greekly. Being and truth. Truth and genuineness.
And therefore κυριώτατον. "Truth"—for perception—is an *affair of beings* (!)—although ἐν διανοίᾳ!

12. (to supplement 8)

Why ἀληθές, ὡς ἀληθές, as a character of Being?

Presence—uncoveredness—the *proper present*—oriented toward νοῦς. ἔστι πως πάντα! ἡ ψυχή,[7] in its highest possibility.

13. (to supplement 8)

ἀληθινόν

Sophist 240ff. / ibid. b3 = ὄντως ὄν. Here clearly: ἀληθινός—"ontological." ἀληθεύειν with ὄντως ὄν, ψεῦδος with μὴ ὄν. Transparent only if clear: 1.) ὄν, 2.) ἀληθεύειν, 3.) λόγος, i.e., existence, Dasein, ψυχή.
Why *"true"* as a preeminent character of beings?

6. Illegible.
7. Cf. *De An.* III, 8, 431b21.

14. (to supplement 8)

Cf. *Cratylus* 421b3f.: ἀλη-θεία, a divine roaming around, πλανᾶσθαι! hence precisely humorously transformed into the opposite. In opposition to having there as uncovered.

15. (second supplement to p. 129)

Σοφία—first of all as κτῆσις and ἕξις, according to *Nicomachean Ethics* K, 10. Not like ἰατρική but ὑγίεια, as Being.[8]
ἀληθεύειν—*truth:* μετὰ λόγου (διάνοια)—ἄνευ λόγου.

A. λόγος.

1.) in general not simply ἀποφαντικός.

2.) as ἀποφαντικός σύνθεσις. Corresponding: ἀληθεύειν already as something derived, passing through the possibility of being false. "As." *De An.* Γ, 6.

3.) λόγος—λεγόμενον—the said: a) as content, b) the being said, the repeated, having been said by "them." Proposition—assertion—connection of representations. (Subject—as *act of thinking*. Agreement!)

ἀληθές—uncovering. *To discuss what is uncovered in discourse,* in the *"as."* "As-structure"—that of λέγειν—encountering in this what is uncovered *in such a way.*

B. ἀληθεύειν—truth—as θιγεῖν.[9] Originally—truth.
On the contrary Jaeger.
ὂν ὡς ἀληθές. κυριώτατον. Cf. *Met.*, Jaeger.[10]
οὕτω καὶ τῷ ὄντι ᾗ ὂν ἔστι τινὰ <ἐπισκέψασθαι> ἴδια, καὶ ταῦτ' ἐστὶ περὶ ὧν τοῦ φιλοσόφου ἐπισκέψασθαι τἀληθές. *Met.* Γ, 2, 1004b15f.

ἀλήθεια—unconcealedness.
Transition: a.) *Unconcealedness of something* (in the mode of νοεῖν, διανοεῖν) b.) the *unconcealed itself*—what is most properly *unconcealed:* that which most of all is already there. Cf. *Met.* α, 2.[11]

C. λόγος—to press ahead in uncovering—dialogue.

To be true purely and properly, i.e., to uncover, and the *discursive—true—*discussing in the tendency toward the proper. What is first carried out: as λέγειν. But in this there already resides in general the Being of the θιγεῖν.

8. *Nic. Eth.* VI, 13, 1144a4f.
9. *Met.* IX, 10, 1051b24.
10. See p. 427, note 1.
11. *Met.* II, 1, 993b26ff.

This is not a special case, but conversely—that one improper mode (cf. νοῦς—διανοεῖν), yet in fact the closest of those. Αἴσθησις. To speak—*basically never*.

1.) Aristotle does not only not degrade dialectics;
2.) he cannot at all degrade it, because it must necessarily remain below,
3.) he first sees this, in the proper sense, in opposition to Plato.

16. (to supplement 15)

1.) ἀλήθεια pure and simple
2.) ὂν ὡς ἀληθές

1.) relates to beings in the unconcealedness of their Being—of the ἀρχαί. Thus: ἀληθές—κυριώτατον ὄν—τἀληθές in an emphatic sense.
2.) ὂν ὡς ἀληθές—ὂν *qua* λεγόμενον—διανοούμενον. As encountered and spoken of as such. The *true*—as it is initially and for the most part and is passed on.

17. (to supplement 15)

τἀληθές

Formally universal: ὂν ὡς ἀληθές.
From ἀληθεύειν *noematically to* ὂν ἀληθινόν. The *highest* ἀληθεύειν: σοφία. The most proper ὄν. κυριώτατον—why ἀληθές? Because Being: "There"—presence. *Being undistorted*—the encountered-character, noematically, not *psychical* Being. Not a realm next to others, but beings in the "how" of their Being. *Characters of Being different in their very characterization.*

18. (third supplement to p. 129)

ἀληθεύειν—in principle νοεῖν—αἴσθησις. Μετὰ λόγου—λόγος—*rhetoric!*—λόγος—διά.
ἀληθές—ὂν ὡς. ἀλήθεια—ὂν ᾗ ὄν / λεγόμενον.
λόγος—as the immediate form of ἀληθεύειν—above all: to conceal, to hold oneself properly in ignorance. As mode of carrying out and mode of uncovering, of *fundamental* significance! The "logical": that which is accessible in speech and in spoken discourse, constituting the Being of what is accessible in this way and present as such.

διαλέγεσθαι: interpretation—hermeneutical. Justification in Aristotle according to two directions. Example: μὴ ὄν (= ψεῦδος) as ὄν—unprecedented—new—i.e., spurning the usual prattle.
Dasein and Being.

19. (to supplement 18)

If ὄν—ἀλήθεια, then *discussion* of ὄν in passing through the discussion of ψεῦδος, *in case* μὴ ὄν *is discussed.*
Why ἀληθεύειν *relevant for the problematic of Being?*
1.) as ground in general—phenomenologically,
2.) for the Greeks, a character of beings themselves—ἀληθές.
Why *possible?* ἀλήθεια—the beings. Jaeger? Psychologism!

20. (to supplement 18)

μὴ ὄν—ὡς ψεῦδος: non-beings—that which something is not. That which as such is *distorted*—which, however, it should not be, because the ἀληθές should be; the ἀγαθόν of κατάφασις. What is, what it is not supposed to be.
ὂν ὡς ἀληθές: beings—which uncovers or is uncovered. "To be *true.*"
Beings—in the sense of the unconcealed—proper presence.
Non-beings—in the sense of the concealed—not present for themselves—*not being.*

II. Supplements to the Transition

21. (to p. 132)

The unfolding of the problematic of Being—*hermeneutically*—the concrete existentiell "whereby" of the encountering of beings—*phenomenology of the encounter and of discourse as the ground of the "ontology" of beings.* The *Sophist*—even if only a first pressing ahead—cf. Parmenides: νοεῖν—εἶναι—yet remarkable if we grasp it originally enough in what was not and could not at all be settled.

22. (to p. 134)

ἀλήθεια and the proper character of Being and as *Being of beings.* οὐσία—ἕν—ὑποκείμενον.
The uncovering of beings is something proper if it discloses them in their constitution as ἀρχή-τέλος (proper presence).
ἀρχή-τέλος—as characters of Being—the meaning of πέρας: whence and whereby beings in what they are—as *beings*—are finished. No "as something." Therefore the character of intended-ness and of uncovered-ness: ἀδιαίρετον—ἀσύνθετον—ἁπλῶς.

23. (to p. 137)

διαλέγεσθαι

To discuss thoroughly, to lead on more and more to the matters themselves, out of immediate everyday λέγειν, to the ἔσχατον, in order to see. πέρας!

Dialectics can only make an attempt, try, test. It can never come to a resolution, because it does not, according to the possibilities of its execution, arrive there. That is available only to pure θεωρεῖν as such.
But it does have the directedness, it already expresses itself on what is actually the theme of σοφία. ὑποκείμενον.

Tradition says that Aristotle degraded dialectic into a technique. That overlooks:

1.) τέχνη means know-how. δύναμις. Cf: *Rhetoric:* potentiality as *Being*. Its explicit establishment presupposes precisely the understanding of the carrying out of διαλέγεσθαι. *Possibility*—to understand—more radically: as uncovering. For: reality: to reproduce. *(Possibility:)*[1] What something can properly be, what *it already* is prior to every actualization.

2.) he has not thereby degraded dialectic but has discovered an original proper domain of the everyday possibility of speaking with one another: the pretheoretical discourse about something, which, as a determinate way of thorough discussion, presses ahead to θεωρεῖν—γνωρίζειν, γνωριστική—and claims to be an explicit mode of pressing ahead and of genuine questioning.

Aristotle was the first to be able to understand dialectic positively and to appropriate it. Superseding it in a properly disclosive original ontology. Cf. *Met.* Γ, 2.

Plato saw clearly neither the one (σοφία) nor the other (διαλέγεσθαι). His result corresponds. On the other hand, his was the unclarity of genius, and it stirred up things.[2] "Genius"—because this unclarity bears genuine roots of disclosure. Not a fantastic unclarity blind to the things.

The *Sophist:* διαλέγεσθαι—a mode of Dasein—and precisely a pretended highest one—which is: a being-with, cognizing and knowing beings.

To uncover a "Being-in" in the dialogue and thereby the entire phenomenal nexus residing therein: beings—Being— / Being-toward / the Being of the existing (sophist) itself.

Hence: in the transition: *Dasein*—ἀληθεύειν—*Being-in*. Phenomenological basis. Intentionality rightly understood.

1.) Hermeneutical meaning of the dialogue,
2.) what becomes thematic in it,
3.) how.

Intertwining of the *three* questions unclearly and yet wholly a matter of principle.

To verify this conception of the dialogue by means of Aristotle's directions of development: *Metaphysics* Γ and *Topics* (Rhetoric)

Not to look for intuition and thinking. Thinking is dialectic precisely only insofar as it is intuitive—this is not something.

1. Editor's supplement.
2. Reference by Heidegger to supplement 29 (supplement to p. 152).

24. (to p. 140)

λόγος

As speech—speaking, relating, something as something. ἀνάλογον—to correspond, here: *relation.*

That λόγος can be formalized this way is an indication that this phenomenon of something *as* something—the *there*—shows itself *primarily*. The "logical." And specifically λόγος as λεγόμενον, the "as-ness," "from-one-to-the-other-ness."

25. (to p. 142)

Aristotelian philosophy

That is, to understand the Greeks in their proper difficulties. The hidden movement: ὂν ᾗ ὄν—διαλεκτική—"Logic": ζωή—Dasein. λόγος.

26. (first supplement to p. 149)

Aristotle speaks of διαλεκτική

1.) in connection with the determination of the task of the fundamental philosophical science (σοφία),

2.) in the theory of λόγος.

Thus: in consideration of the phenomena of ἀληθεύειν: νοεῖν and λέγειν.

(. . .)

as regards 1.): *Metaphysics* Γ, 1 and 2.

(. . .)

as regards 2.): πειραστική—in relation to λέγειν—to discuss with one another—shared world thereby ἀγνοοῦντες,[3] but to speak with them κατὰ τὸ πρᾶγμα.[4] "Theory" of theoretical-practical dealing with one another. ἀπόδειξις. διαλεκτική, the further concept. It can be: 1.) πειραστική (*Top.* 171),[5] 2.) theory—δύναμις (*Top.* I, 101); also here ἔνδοξον, ἐρώτησις. Goal: ἀλήθεια.

3. *Sophistical Refutations* I, 11, 171b3ff.
4. Ibid. I, 8, 169b23.
5. Ibid. I, 11, 171b4.

Sophist: μὴ κατὰ τὸ πρᾶγμα ἐλέγχοντες.[6] But thereby οὐκ ἐν δυνάμει[7]—as rhetoric—as theory of speech—, but a βίος speaks factually—has resolved to this. But how? Formally—not concern with substantive content.

27. (second supplement to p. 149)

(Transition:)[8]

Clarification of dialectics. First characterization of sophistry.
Connected to it: ἀληθεύειν, ἀληθές. ὄν. The basic meaning of ontology. The logical. Second part of the transition in connection to the first.
a) τἀληθές (*Met.* Γ, 2, 1004b17) b) πρότερον ἡ οὐσία.[9] Ontology. 1.) Concrete research into Being: οὐσία—κατηγορίαι—δύναμις / ἐνέργεια.[10] Uncovering, positive, of λόγος. The logical.

28. (third supplement to p. 149)

Philosophy: ἀληθεύειν—ἀληθές. ἀλήθεια—ὄν. κυριώτατον ὄν. διαλέγεσθαι —σοφία—νοῦς—in a certain sense free of λόγος.
"The logical." The "proposition."

29. (to p. 152)

λέγειν—*Rhetoric and Sophistry.*

(Cf. Diels, *Fragmente der Vorsokratiker* II, p. 218ff.)[11]

Protagoras of Abdera. Rhetoric. *Basic grammatical concepts. Epideictic conception of rhetoric.*
Gorgias of Leontini.
Thrasymachus of Calcedon. (cf. *Gorgias*)
Prodikos of Keos. Cf. *Protagoras*. Rhetoric. *Semiaxiology. Moralizing in the choice of the material.*

6. Ibid. I, 8, 169b23f.
7. *Rhetoric* I, 1, 1355b17.
8. Editor's supplement: the articulation of the transition shows 1.) that Heidegger intended to include in the transition more than he actually presented and 2.) that the actual course of the lectures corresponded to the projected outline only in part.
9. *Met.* IV, 2, 1004b9.
10. Cf. *Met.* VI, 2, 1026a32ff., and *Met.* IX, 10, 1051a35ff.
11. *Die Fragmente der Vorsokratiker, griechisch and deutsch von Hermann Diels.* Zweiter Band, 4. Aufl., Berlin, 1922.

Hippias of Elis (cf. Prodikos): *Antiquarian scholarship.*
Antiphon of Athens (cf. Prodikos)
Anonymus Iamblichi (Protagoras)
Author of the *Dialexeis* (Protagoras). The development of the *Antilogica.*

Sophists: teachers of youth—paid. Orators. ταὐτόν (. . .) ἐστὶν σοφιστὴς καὶ ῥήτωρ, ἢ ἐγγύς τι καὶ παραπλήσιον. (*Gorgias* 520a6ff.).
Thucydides III 38.[12]
ἁπλῶς τε ἀκοῆς ἡδονῇ ἡσσώμενοι καὶ σοφιστῶν θεαταῖς ἐοικότες καθημένοις μᾶλλον ἢ περὶ πόλεως βουλευομένοις.
Sophists: orators—not philosophers or statesman or educators.
Taken as a whole: "You are wallowing in the delight of listening (correlative to speaking!) and are rather similar to the ones who are sitting there gaping at the sophists and who are supposed to decide about the destiny of the state."
Unconcern with substantive content is precisely nurtured by the sophists.

The formal goal of education. *Given thereby: unconcern with substantive content, lack of substantive content.* δεινότης of the εὖ λέγειν (παιδεία). a) the level of the sophists is different, b) the determinate concrete world in which they predominantly move.

A mistake of interpretation. Which was the occasion to arrive at positivity, but what did not correspond to it at the scientific level was retrospectively intensified by it in the historiographical consideration. Therefore press on to the scientific, philosophical possibilities.
Not skepticism, relativism, subjectivism, but the formal goal of education. παιδεία.
(. . .)
Plato condemned not only the sophists but at the same time the orators as well. The *Phaedrus:* attempt at a positive appreciation? *Aristotle,* because of his original insight into λόγος and ζωή, established for them positive, though limited, rights.

30. (to p. 154)

"Ontology"—"Theology." Aristotle.

In both cases: beginning with beings as a whole—ὅλον[13]—ἁπλῶς—simply

12. Thucydides, *History of the Peloponnesian War.*
13. Cf. *Met.* XII, 1, 1069a18ff.

for itself, as what is there. θεία. To understand the ὅλον in its ὅλον—as being. Beings—of the world—, but still a determinate μέρος: κινούμενον, not ἀριθμός. The heavens and everything under them. It corresponds, as to content, with the ancient problematic of Being and transposes it through the disclosure of κίνησις onto a new ground.
Disclosure of κίνησις provides: 1.) the possibility of seeing the φύσει ὄντα categorially. 2.) This concrete material-ontological research opens the eye for the sense of purely *ontological* research and genuinely allows for the correct appropriation of Plato. Both in *Physics* A! Critique of the *Eleatics*. *Categories*.
As κίνησις (ἀκίνητα—ἀχώριστα / ἀκίνητα—χωριστά / κινούμενα) guiding lines for a division of beings.
Κίνησις, ποίησις—being produced = 1.) being finished 2.) presence. Cf. *Met.* Θ. Discussion of δύναμις-ἐνέργεια beyond κίνησις.

Cf. *Met.* Γ, 2: κινούμενον—στερεόν explicitly *ontological* theme, or material? No, but by all means not ὂν ᾗ ὄν. This itself,—not in its connection with the others! πρὸς μίαν ἀρχήν?[14]

Not: how to change, or which is to yield to the other, how to improve, to "round out," a "satisfying picture of the world." Instead: how he was forced into these two paths. Why? Being—presence! Sheer presence; the highest and most proper coming to presence, the first, original presence.
Problem not in θεολογική but in πρώτη φιλοσοφία. *Universality* of the ὂν ᾗ ὄν.
The logical.

31. (to p. 155)

ὂν ᾗ ὄν. οὐσία—λόγος—ὑποκείμενον. "The logical." Present.

ὂν ᾗ ὄν: beings in their Being; beings as beings; anything that is, insofar as it is. The theme thus is *Being*. What every being *is* already from the very outset, *what is already there at the outset*, what properly constitutes presence, i.e., *proper Being*. The "already at the very outset"—condition of the possibility of the presence of something.

Unseparated: genus—general universality and apriori universality. Onti-

14. *Met.* IV, 2, 1003b6.

cally: "class," provenance of the essence. *Ontologically:* πρὸς μίαν ἀρχήν—φύσις—οὐσία, not κατά.

Not formal, not genus (this latter *explicitly rejected*), but instead: purely and simply *"ontological."* "Formally," however, with an emphasis on οὐσία: πρότερον ἡ οὐσία, in the temporality of the pure presence of beings. ὄν—what is spoken of—ὑποκείμενον—not *posited.* But instead: what is already there in the discerning disclosure of λέγειν. Here the irruption of λόγος into ontology. Cf. *Met.* Z, 4.

ὄν—as uncovered—in a broader sense: that which is spoken of.

a) To what extent the "already at the outset" in the λεγόμενον in the broader sense. οὐσία—sheer presence—that which is there at the very outset—in immediate everyday concerns. This, however, is λόγος!

b) Of what sort is the "logical"? = that which is already encountered in what is spoken of as such, co-constituting presence.

concerning a): For the Greeks νοῦς—λόγος; in speaking about—the world—something—beings—there—initially and for the most part. This "initially and for the most part" is and remains in principle μετὰ λόγου! λόγος: *the basic mode of Being-in as coming to presence.* That which primarily is encountered as already there: ὑποκείμενον. Speaking remains the primary mode of access and mode of appropriation of beings. The basic mode of disclosive Being-with—of life—with beings. Even the ἄνευ λόγου—is something—is still seen in terms of λόγος: but *not with* the "as."

καθ' αὑτό. But: by and in λόγος—as a mode of ἀληθεύειν—of the ὑποκείμενον

(. . .)

Concerning b): The "logical" is as such onto-logical! Precisely not: thinking and technique of thinking. But instead: that which is accessible in speaking (uncovering) and discourse. The Being of the beings encountered and spoken of in this way, what thus possibly comes to presence, already constituting its presence.

32. (to p. 155)

The indicated origin of the Greek concept of Being makes clear at the same time, however, that the *Being of beings is interpreted (on the basis of) time.* Why? Because every ontology, as an interpretation, is itself a mode of Being-in. Insofar as the world is to be determined in its Being, these beings must be *experienced,* and the interpreting must address these beings with regard to their Being. Experienceability and addressability of the world include in themselves: letting the interpreting Dasein along with the world itself, in which Dasein always already is, be encountered purely from themselves. The letting be encountered is based, in its possibilities, on the Being of Dasein. But the Being of Dasein is temporality. And the pure letting the world be encountered is a making present. As *such*, it is only temporally that it can express *itself* in the appropriate speaking about the world: the Being of the world is presence. The dominance of this notion of Being makes it clear why Aristotle interprets time itself on the basis of the present, the "now." What is present is genuine Being, and the Being *no longer* of the past, as well as Being not yet, can be determined on the basis of it . . . [15]

But if Dasein itself must be interpreted ontologically in its Being, i.e., even in its determinate non-genuine temporality of presentifying *[gegenwärtigen]*[16] presence, then temporality in its genuineness must be explicated. But that implies: the beings which emerge in the ontological interpretation of the Being of the world cannot determine the hermeneutic situation of the ontological research which is supposed to interpret the Being of Dasein itself. Rather, it is precisely on the basis of this that the mode of Being and the origin of the former is positively clarified ontologically, i.e., is given in the character of Being as conceived in terms of presence.—The immediate meaning of Being.

33. (to supplement 32)

Concept of Being—Concept of knowledge and idea

Being—what is always present on its own. Therefore *"is" properly* the "what"—"essence"—and it the genuine object of proper knowledge.

15. Illegible.
16. Editor's note: presumably Heidegger meant "anticipating" *[gewärtigenden]*.

III. Supplements to the Main Part

34. (to p. 191)

Care (historicality—temporality—discoveredness)

Τέχνη seen in terms of two basic comportments, both ones of immediate everyday Dasein: production—appropriation (tendency toward Being). In both, the basic phenomenon of *furnishing oneself* with something—as *concern over something*—in the sense of *making provisions*. Temporality . . . This concern—supplying oneself something in a broad sense—determinable as commerce with the immediately encountered world. The commerce-with founded on an already-being-in-it. For this Being-in—as concern—know-how.

Τέχνη—as ἀληθεύειν μετὰ λόγου—itself has the character of *appropriation*. In all operations—production, and in possession, a pre-eminent appropriation—of the world *as oriented*—in its "there" . . . concern as making present.

NB: These phenomenological nexuses never seen—taken for primitive and naive distinctions—no match for modern systematics. To be seen only when these phenomena are in advance already uncovered originally and their phenomenal nexus is understood as a primary one (Dasein—existence). Systematic work—not in order to construct a system and take history to task from there, but in order to let the phenomena become visible for this pressing ahead toward the ontological roots of our Dasein itself.

35. (to p. 195)

The phenomenological interpretation purposely too broad—versus the naive-ontic understanding—about the ἀσπαλιευτής.

This appurtenance not first arisen by way of a shoving together of previously isolated contents. It is an original one. The only firm directive at first. To see the phenomenon as a whole. If it (the appurtenance) is supposed to be original, then it must be made visible out of a new *unitary* fundamental content—out of the mode of Being of the phenomenal content itself *(Being-in)*, e.g., under the guideline of τέχνη as such. ἕξις—δύναμις—ψυχή—ἀλήθεια—discoveredness—the "there"—the possibility of every individual "Da"-sein—for the proper Being. Cf. above: concern—care.

Necessity of a fundamentally investigative, methodic appropriation of this field—more precisely—first laying it bare! because covered with debris—why?—something still not genuinely disclosed—(fallen into decay!)—only in pressing horizons—ontologically diverted in the direction of the world.

36. (to p. 268)

Anthropology as ontology

Not *a* new conception and mode of treatment, but *the* central ontology, in which all others first acquire their ground, and insofar as the traditional, only positive one up to now—of the Greeks—was basically mundane and formal-logical ontology, this one must be appropriated, taken up in a new intention, and set free. I.e., to pose radically and concretely the ontological problem as a whole for the first time. To open up and pose the questions in the treatise on time.

37. (to p. 284)

Definitions of the sophist

Double function. *Triple* function?

1. To make vivid the *factual existence* of μὴ ὄν. Concretion—"there."
2. Anticipation of the phenomena: "ποιεῖν"—οὐσία. λόγος.
3. Ontic διαλέγεσθαι—*co-presence:* γένος—ἕν—preparation for the ontological διαλέγεσθαι.

38. (to p. 298)

Now the first turning of the attention toward the τέχνη of the sophist (i.e., δόξα, λόγος): ποιεῖ εἴδωλα—he has to do with what only looks to be, i.e., with the immediate, ungenuine *outward look*—what merely poses immediately as something—mere semblance: περὶ τὸ φάντασμα (240d1). He calls this non-being! And specifically his ποιεῖν is an assumption of mere semblance, of the immediate mere outward look, and specifically in such a way that he passes off as something what he has thus taken up. He deceives, i.e., he moves in this passing off of mere semblance as Being. Insofar as we are duped by him in this way, it is called ψυχὴ ἡμῶν ψευδῆ δοξάζει (cf. 240d2f.).
He leads us astray. But there is a going astray (deluded opinion) only when

one is trying to get somewhere or other in the first place. *A missing of the mark only in a directedness toward the* ἀληθές, and indeed a missing of the mark such that the pretence is taken for the ἀληθές. Only within an intention toward seeing uncovered beings can distortion be possible. Distortion of this pretended sight.

ψευδὴς δόξα: deluded, believing the imposture; to be of an opinion, and specifically a false one. I.e., τὰ ἐναντία τοῖς οὖσι δοξάζειν (cf. d6f.): *to be of the opinion, to maintain, that something is uncovered when faced with the opposite of beings,* when faced with what stands there, with what has thrust itself forward. I.e., ψευδὴς δόξα = τὰ μὴ ὄντα δοξάζειν (d9): to *take* non-beings for beings.

Is this δοξάζειν of ψευδὴς δόξα or of μὴ ὄντα a maintaining that they are not, μὴ εἶναι (e1)? Here the stumbling block, the blank in the discourse (Greek). (. . .)

ἤ πως εἶναι τὰ μηδαμῶς ὄντα; (e1f.) Εἶναί πως τὰ μὴ ὄντα δεῖ (e3). Non-beings must themselves be in some way or other, for them to be taken as something (as being). I.e., δόξα ψευδής includes, *in its very structure,* taking non-beings themselves as being in some way, in order *then* first to become what it is. Passing them off—as beings.

Therefore: the condition of its possibility, that the φάντασμα can at all found a deception—pass *itself* off as—is: that it is in itself *taken as existing,* and only on this basis can *it* pose *as* some other being.

Wherever a deluded opinion, even if only briefly and to the smallest extent (cf. e3f.), always necessary:

1.) it itself as in some way there—present; the Being of *that which* itself brings about the opinion, founds the pretense, and
2.) that which it passes itself off as, as a being, the pretended; the Being of that which stands there as pretended.

39. (to supplement 38)

Deception

It deceives—it leads astray, defrauds, *imposture,* ψεῦδος. I deceive myself, *delusion*—ἀπάτη. 260c. I deceive *another*—in speaking, communicating. Imposture ontologically primary, i.e., visibility—γιγνώσκειν—κοινωνία with μὴ ὄν.

"It errs"? I *err*—I have led myself into error—it is *"false."*

Cf. WS 23–4.

Deception, error, falsity, incorrectness, lie—and the function and the meaning of the "not"—and λόγος and νοεῖν.

Deception—*Being-in*—1.) as what—prepossession, 2.) as something—to address, 3.) basic phenomenon of the "as." "Pre"-possession: To have from somewhere, not simply *there!* "As"—in the *Being-in*. Care—interpretation—*knownness*—pre-tense. Being-in—as which Being?

40. (to supplement 38)

Deception—error

Deception—upon *giving*—to address. Error? upon a formal conclusion? But if error on the ἀληθεύειν—giving of the things—χειροῦσθαι? I.e., ψεῦδος—also in λόγος. The latter (judgment) still entirely delotic.

41. (first supplement to p. 310)

To pose the question of the meaning of Being signifies nothing else than to elaborate the *questioning* of philosophy.
The phenomenological sense of the "questioning into the Being of beings"—what that means and what tasks it includes: *hermeneutic of Dasein.*
Questioning:
Interrogating something in some regard. The interrogated (beings), the asked about (Being), the asked for (the ontological characters of beings).

a) primary *attitude—Being-in of the question*:* questioning is discovering disclosure.
   *What is the mode of access to beings in ontological questioning? Plato and Aristotle: λόγος—and indeed with a certain explicitness, but only this far, that λόγος remains *the only one*. But that does *not* mean: *ontology is determined by logic*—or else one must say what *"logic"* signifies here. Not: λόγος—oriented toward *logic* and thereby still placing at the foundation a modern ontological concept, but instead: λόγος oriented toward νοεῖν—ἀληθεύειν—*Dasein.*
   On the lectures: if from the beginning, in the preparation as well as in the interpretation of the definition of the sophist, we were constantly referred to λόγος, it should have been clear from the outset along what paths ontology plays out. Only to experience at the end how Plato takes λόγος itself within the ontological problematic.

b) The *posing of the question* is the expressed, communicated question, in which the interrogated, the asked about, and the asked for are co-addressed implicitly, without the primary attitude of genuine questioning being simply given thereby. Content of the questioning; the *asked for in the broader sense*—about which, in what respect, how far the question relates.

Thus far on the characterization of the question: what do you mean when you say "Being."

42. (second supplement to p. 310)

Intention to clarity* in Greek ontology

Guideline: making present—as *what*. *To address*. To address *how?* to let it be encountered in itself—ὅλον—, or to make of it itself a *being*. Whence otherwise the explicate? How the "there" in λέγειν-νοεῖν?—As conclusion of Being and Time. Thus systematic and historiographical acquisition.
*Development of the situation of possible interpretation grows with clarity about λέγειν. To address beings as beings. No longer as beings but "Being." What Being means. No answer. But ontological characters *uncovered*. Unseparated: formal and material ontology.

43. (third supplement to p. 310)[1]

Saidness of ὄν

I. *The question of the saidness and sayability of* μὴ ὄν *is that of the* σημαίνειν *of* ὄν (244a5f.). τὸ ὂν οὐδὲν εὐπορώτερον εἰπεῖν τοῦ μὴ ὄντος (cf. 246a1). *Saidness:* genuine disclosure of the meaning!

Greek ontology, basically:
Orientation of *ontology* toward *"logic."* Is that surprising? But λόγος for the Greeks the *mode of access*—the immediate.
Greek ontology—not only world—*objectivity*—and what is encountered, the immediate, but also the how of reaching the immediate,—and both *in indifference!*
A making present—in *immediate availability*. A *neutral making present*.
Confirmation: λόγος—that in which everyday seeing and saying emerge—*place of sojourn of Being-in*.
In the discussion of ὄν, λόγος as mode of access is now so isolated that, with no regard to the *what*, that which is asked for is simply the saidness

1. Cf. also p. 142f. as well as supplements 25 and 32.

and the sayability.
244cff. therefore at the same time a *formal-logical,* yet, presumably a *material-ontological* (investigation),[2] i.e., both still unseparated. On the basis of λόγος.
Still the standpoint of Parmenides, only νοεῖν more sharply in λόγος.

II. Therefore: διαλεκτική delotic as *logical: absolute* priority—the fundamental science. Not on the basis of "logic" in our sense—but the genuine, investigating attitude precisely—genuine immediate access and disclosure.
Precisely Aristotle defends himself, with his clear grasp of λόγος, against "logic" (δύναμις—ἐνέργεια).

44. (to p. 338)

Ψυχή—life—Dasein. And anthropology. *Plato.*

Problem—in "Phaidon," chap. XIV, in the phenomenon of νοεῖν, i.e., of *Being-to,* Being-with. Whereby—as ἀεί—; *Being* as γένεσις. Soul as "in between"—simple because ontic—the phenomenon of Being-in—, whereby world is taken as ἀεί—elementally. νοεῖν—basic character of Dasein, a perception-of. And thus the entire later anthropology. (But not a *Being* in itself!—And the latter genuinely hermeneutical).
The soul *is* desire (*Care* is the Being of Dasein!). *Intentionality—Being-to—* ψυχή—in the horizon of κίνησις and στάσις, γένεσις—ἀεί, *Heraclitus—Parmenides.*

45. (to p. 355)

Prepossession: the κοινωνία bears everything, therefore to be clarified.
Into it the possible τέχνη διαλεκτική is built—and formulated in the following in repeated, ever new approaches.

2. Editor's supplement.

46. (to p. 363)

τὰ ὄντα as λεγόμενα

Limits of Greek ontology: In λόγος and its predominance. Compensated: Insofar as ἀποφαίνεσθαι. Not *"logic."*

47. (to p. 377)

In addressing beings, they are disclosed in two directions: 1.) in their *"there"*—present—*as themselves,* 2.) as πρός τι—*in relation to.* Selfsame—and the *"respectively."* In themselves—and the *relation-to.*
In λέγειν a *double tendency toward disclosure:* 1.) simple having-there of something, 2.) to take up in some respect. In λέγειν this double possibility of encountering beings.
Something possibly present (i.e., possible presence)[3] according to the original nexus of λέγειν: 1.) making present of the now here, 2.) making present out of and in the having of an anticipation—in *consequence* of it—*whence*—something possibly present is addressed. The *factual anticipation* in the present Being-out-for—from it—the *immediate.*

48. (to p. 391)

The opposition makes visible the genuine objectivity of the negated. The negation in the μή of the ἕτερον is not only one bound in the objective provenance but *at the same time one that is objectively exhibiting:* it exhibits something determinate.

49. (first supplement to p. 397)

concerning 3.): with regard to Plato.
ἐναντίον and ἐναντιότης at times even in Aristotle still an over-reaching formal treatment. *Categories,* chapter 6, a15: ἐοίκασι δὲ καὶ τὸν ἄλλων ἐναντίων ὁπισμὸν ἀπὸ τούτων ἐπιφέρειν· τὰ γὰρ πλεῖστον ἀλλήλων διεστηκότα (distance) τῶν ἐν τῷ αὐτῷ γένει ἐναντία ὁπίζονται. Thus paradigmatically: ἐναντίον κατὰ τὸν τόπον. This according to the *Physics,*

3. In Heidegger's manuscript: */heit* ["-ence"]. Expanded by the editor according to the sense.

E, chapter 3, 226b32f.: τὸ κατ' εὐθεῖαν ἀπέχον πλεῖστον—what keeps away if we go from one to the other in a straight direction, as the other farthest from the one.
How does Aristotle clarify this "distance"? Aristotle, unlike Plato, makes an immediate distinction between ἕτερον as formal otherness and ἐναντίον. He introduces the διάφορον, "non-being," in a *determinate concrete* respect. *Met.* I, chapter 3, 1054b25: τὸ δὲ διάφορον τινὸς τινὶ διάφορον, ὥστε ἀνάγκη ταὐτό τι εἶναι ᾧ διαφέρουσιν, τοῦτο δὲ τὸ ταὐτὸ ἢ γένος ἢ εἶδος. The selfsameness of the respect expressly grasped and various possibilities uncovered. Thereby γένος and εἶδος came to play the role of formal-logical categories, either as πλεῖον or πλεῖστον διεστάναι. Cf. *Met.* I, chapter 4, Δ, chapter 10.

50. (second supplement to p. 397)

Supplements and notes to the "not" and "non-Being"[4]

a.

"not"

not—"none"—mundane! The *immediate* "not" is the not-there—absence—simply and utterly the "not there." "Un-there." The "un" and "away"—within the "there." The "not" seen in the present—the corresponding delotic saying.
The *possibility of a revision up to* στέρησις—in face of which states of affairs—*in the world and* λέγειν? στέρησις clear: descent out of absence. Temporality and negation.

Cf. δύναμις (genuinely phenomenal: the *being* not!)
ἐναντίον is not μὴ ὄν but instead ἕτερον μόνον (257b3f.). Ibid. b9: τί σημαίνει ἀπόφασις? ἕτερον, not ἐναντίον.

b.

Non-being

The non-being of deception, error, self-evident. Everything μή is not. Sophist—Parmenides. Sophist: the factual existence, on which he (can)[5] maintain

4. Title supplied by the editor.
5. Editor's supplement.

it, demonstrates precisely "Being." Versus this, *to open the eyes for these phenomena.*—Dialectic: 1.) as ὁρᾶν of ἕν, 2.) as correct (?) λέγειν.

"Copula"—how understood?
I.e., λόγος, how seen? Delotically—or factically worldly, and still in some way apophantically! Guiding: meaning of *Being!* or not—otherwise, not as not there = "against . . . ". Aristotle, *Top.* 104b20f.: οὐκ ἔστιν ἀντιλέγειν, i.e., ἕτερον = ἐναντίον! Cf. not and negation!

Difference	διαφορά	
Distinction Otherness	ἑτερότης	
Opposite	the most extreme: ἐναντιότης	within the delotic λόγος or in ὄν itself
Conflict Contra*diction*	Disaccord (accord) ἀντίφασις	

Formal: The "not" as *saidness,* i.e., to *express* oneself, oneself: disclosive—being with; addressing that makes present.
Nexus of *self-sameness—(difference)*—otherness—as "formal"-ontic. Not: "not"—as formal-*logical.* From making present—from the "there"—*self-sameness* and otherness! The "already there" of the "logical."

c.

Non-being

Non-beings—for Plato—τὸ ἕτερον—as such not ἐναντίον. Specifically ἀντίθεσις, ἀντικείμενον, but precisely θέσις, κείμενον 257d–e. The ἀντί in this sense: differentiating, *delotically,* out of *making present!* (ἀντί:)[6] connection with "not." (ἀντί:)[7] therein a taking up of a respect—*"secundum quid"*—i.e., in all disclosing, to have there. The *pre- in the making present,* i.e., speaking and Being: a precisely full temporality.—Where the against which—the already—if this not explicitly?—because speaking, at first, as emergent and also a futural *making present.* The *"already* there" for—at the same time the in advance out of—anticipation. And everything in the making present.
Remarkable: in the ῥῆμα and in the principle of contradiction (ἅμα)—χρόνος *explicit.*

6. Editor's supplement.
7. Editor's supplement.

d.

negatio—negatum

Origin in absence—for Being-with—presentifying having of—. The *not there any longer*—the immediate "not"-phenomenon. The un-there—in change—alteration. The making present can only say "*not* there any more."

The hermeneutical possibility of the "not."

e.

Beings as beings in their Being—there for Being-with—in discernful speaking about them; an uttered—said—*a*—something—"*it.*" The *being-said of something*, of "nothing," is *something!*
Non-beings:
1.) the not something—nothing—"not,"
2.) beings not "thus"—but *in some way* otherwise—distinction—(alteration),
3.) beings not thus, but a determinate other, op-position.

51. (to p. 420)

Plato and λέγειν. "Language"[8]

a.

Cratylus

No word for "language"! φωνή: sound; διάλεκτος: conversation; λόγος: speech; ὄνομα: word.
Are the ὀνόματα φύσει or νόμῳ? The question concerns the δηλοῦν of the ὀνόματα.
φύσει—ὀρθῶς; τῇ ἀληθείᾳ, ἐτεῇ (Democritus). Do words (ὀνόματα) give the πράγματα in themselves? φύσει? Does the word as such, as factually extant, give the thing? In the word as such is the thing visible? Question of the role of λέγειν as ἀληθεύειν.
Or: ξυνθήκῃ—νόμῳ—ὁμολογίᾳ—ἔθει—, does it *signify*, does it give the thing only on the basis of, and after, mutual agreement? Without possessing the things—from mere δόξα about the πράγματα? so that one may not at all adhere to ὀνόματα in scientific research?

8. Title from Heidegger's manuscript.

φύσει—not: arisen from nature, but precisely: *founded* by the one who knows the things, ἀληθεύων, and founded as preserving the things, so that one can adhere to the ὀνόματα . . . [9]—
Theme: ὀρθότης τῶν ὀνομάτων, their mutually giving directedness toward the matters themselves!—Reflection on λέγειν also concerns its ἀποφαίνεσθαι οὐσίας.—*Cratylus:* interpretation of the word—the way toward the uncovering of the thing. Every ὄνομα—ὀρθόν. There is no falsity. Is there? Or not? I.e., ὄνομα φύσει? ὀρθότης: relation of the name to the thing.

λέγειν like τέμνειν: a having to do with, and all dealings must conform to the thing. ᾗ πέφυκεν—as everything already prior to our doing-with and taking-for *is*. ὀνομάζειν a πρᾶξις, and specifically a part of the πρᾶξις of λέγειν. ὀνόματα through νόμος—become νομοθέτης and the νόμοι φύσει; *drawing from the matters themselves!*
With ὀνόματα not the word-sounds, but the sounds having become a tool. ὄργανον. Tool, one which is to show, and which shows by *signifying*. (ὄνομα):[10] διδασκαλικόν τί ἐστιν ὄργανον καὶ διακριτικὸν τῆς οὐσίας (388b13f.). The meaning drawn from the εἶδος of the matter at issue. Every πρᾶγμα has its ὄνομα φύσει, i.e., its possible, disclosable proper visibility,—according to possibility, but not factually.

This interpretation of the meaning of ὄνομα is taken up again in a certain way in the second part. The δείξειν is νόμῳ, not stemming from the genuine διαλέγεσθαι but from δόξα. ἀληθεύειν not in the ὄνομα but in λόγος; and λέγειν is an addressing of something as something, uncovering of the κοινωνία: and the essential is not the sound—as copy, μίμημα, but the δηλοῦν of the meaning—δηλώματα! ὄνομα is δήλωσις ὧν διανοούμενοι λέγομεν (cf. 435b6)—disclosive manifestation *in* λέγειν. ὄνομα exposed from the isolated relation to πρᾶγμα—understood in terms of λόγος—in *this*, φύσει put into effect as demand. But λόγος not clarified.

ὀρθότης as at 434e6f.: ὅτι ἐγώ, ὅταν τοῦτο φθέγγωμαι, διανοοῦμαι ἐκεῖνο, σὺ δὲ γιγνώσκεις ὅτι ἐκεῖνο διανοοῦμαι: everything posited on communicating disclosure, bringing one another to the matters themselves.

Cf. Steinthal, *Geschichte der Sprachwissenschaft* I, 1890, pp 79–113.[11]

9. Illegible.
10. Editor's supplement.
11. Heymann Steinthal, *Geschichte der Sprachwissenschaft bei den Griechen und Römern mit besonderer Rücksicht auf die Logik.* Zwei Hälften, Berlin, 1862–1863. 2., verm. u. verb. Auflage, Berlin, 1890–1891.

b.

Theaetetus

Antisthenes.—λόγος: ὀνομάτων συμπλοκή (cf. *Theaetetus* 202b4f.), not only ὀνόματα, but also ῥήματα. ῥῆμα like λόγος—μῦθος—ῥῆσις—ῥήματα: sayings of the seven wise ones. ῥῆμα: "dictum," saying—in opposition to long discourse, λόγος, e.g., γνῶθι σεαυτόν. No ὄνομα therein! That in the manifold of words which is not λόγος and not ὄνομα. But not positive = predicate.

In the *Cratylus,* relation between ῥῆμα and ὄνομα unclear. Speaking does not say the things, but says the seen, uncovered, things, beings; is itself disclosive. *Theaetetus* 206d1f.: τὸ τὴν αὑτοῦ διάνοιαν ἐμφανῆ ποιεῖν διὰ φωνῆς μετὰ ῥημάτων τε καὶ ὀνομάτων. Also in the *Theaetetus,* still no clarification, first in the *Sophist*. And here the concepts of ὄνομα and ῥῆμα "logical," out of the saidness as such. πρᾶγμα—πρᾶξις. ὄν (στάσις)—κίνησις? here built into λόγος—as κοινωνεῖν τοῦ ὄντος, in its συμπλοκή. Only λόγος περαίνει, leads something in the field of speaking to an end, i.e., shows beings. Essentially again: the ontological foundation! Περὶ ὅτου—the substrate of the discourse, the about which unexplicit. Ὅτου—what is addressed thematically grasped therein and what is demonstrated by being addressed in discussion.

The ὀνόματα give and do not give, they are what they are only in the δηλοῦν of λέγειν. But the δηλοῦν can be carried out through δοξάζειν, i.e., ψευδής.

In the *Cratylus,* Plato still had no insight into λόγος. All the more positive is the significance of this dialogue. Here is the history of the rise of Greek logic, which for us today no longer possesses the compelling questionableness it had for Plato and Aristotle. For us it has become a so-called "possession," one which suppresses in its own field all living problems.

52. (to p. 422)

φαντασία

Aristotle, *De Anima,* Γ, 3

φαντασία γὰρ ἕτερον καὶ αἰσθήσεως καὶ διανοίας (3, 427b14), different from sense perception and thinking of something. It itself οὐ γίγνεται ἄνευ αἰσθήσεως (b15f.), without it itself no ὑπόληψις (b16), taking something for something (something as something), simple *non-binding* presentification of something in such a way. Thereby, however, ὑπόληψις distinct from νόησις. (φαντασία)[12]: ὅταν βουλώμεθα (b18), it remains with us. δοξάζειν δ' οὐκ (b20)—to be of an opinion about something, to take something for something—οὐκ ἐφ' ἡμῖν (b20), it is, by its very sense, the uncovering or distorting of beings. (Distinctions: ἐπιστήμη—δόξα—φρόνησις and: ἐναντία). In δοξάζειν—to be at beings themselves, in δόξα, belief, to take as being. κατὰ φαντασίαν (b23) on the contrary indeed something there, but beings factually canceled in their bodily "there." I let something show itself to me in such a way. Not *making present*—having there—, but only *presentification of something*. Not ὄντως ὄν, but ὥσπερ ἐν γραφῇ (b24)—it only appears that way. ἐφ' ἡμῖν (b18)—not letting beings be encountered from themselves, but instead the "there" *with me*.

Is φαντασία the δύναμις (ἕξις) of κρίνειν? (428a3f.)
αἴσθησις—ἀληθεύειν—beings present, ὑπάρχοντος (a7); likewise διανοεῖν—ἀληθεύειν—beings present, therein ὑπολαμβάνειν—formal structure. *Even* φαντασία has this—but thereby precisely not ἀληθεύειν. φαίνεται δέ τι (428a7)—φάντασμά τι ἡμῖν γίγνεται (a1f.)—καὶ μύουσιν ὁράματα (a16)—μηδετέρου ὑπάρχοντος τῶν αἰσθητῶν (a7f.)—αἴσθησις always there—we always adhere in some way to it—i.e., surrounding world there. Not so φαντασία. τῇ ἐνεργείᾳ not τὸ αὐτό (a9)—with regard to the mode of constantly and properly finished Dasein not the same.

φαντασία ψευδής (a18)—not ἀεὶ ἀληθεύουσα (a17), it is also what it is as ψευδής. On the contrary, there is no νοῦς ψευδής, ἐπιστήμη ψευδής (a17f.). But indeed δόξα—ἀληθὴς καὶ ψευδής (a19). In δόξα πίστις (a20)—taking as—to take as being—as *making present!!* φαντασία, however, not, and therefore also not δόξα μετ' αἰσθήσεως (a25). Neither one of these, nor out of them. οὔτε ἕν τι τούτων, οὔτε ἐκ τούτων ἡ φαντασία (428b9). The latter not: δόξα always on αἰσθητόν-οὐκ ἄλλου τινός (a27). Φαίνεσθαι would then be δοξάζειν ὅπερ αἰσθάνεται (428b1)—to have an opinion about something which precisely does show itself of itself.

φαντασία—κίνησις (428b11)—shift from perception, *modification* of the *having-there of something*. ὁμοῖα τῇ αἰσθήσει (cf. b14)—is just like αἴσθησις—*having-there* of the same content, but not *qua* ὑπάρχον. Αἴσθησις in the full sense can also be ψευδής (b17). And so the shift out of that—to—only presentification likewise. φαίν-, φά-, φῶς (429a3)—the light, by which one sees—it *is something* there. Also λόγον ἔχοντα derived from it, because νοῦς *obscures* (429a7).
"Shift"—neutralization of the proper presentifying.

12. Editor's supplement.

53. (to supplement 52)

δόξα *and* φαντασία
De Anima Γ, 3

In δόξα co-present the about which, so that in it something speaks for it. δοξάζειν—an agreeing with it—to be *in favor of,* to be of an opinion about something. The about which in some way pregiven—in itself there—οὐ καὶ ἡ αἴσθησις (428a28).

From the Notes of Simon Moser

1. (to p. 299)

Transition to the class of the 26th session (February 10, 1925)[1]

In the introductory considerations I constantly emphasized the essential importance of the fact that Plato ties the discussion of Being to the factual existence of the sophist. The sophist has been exposed as the actually extant μὴ ὄν. That implies: ψεῦδος exists along with the sophist; which implies that beings combine with non-beings, a συμπλοκή—so that the question of how the sophist can be is centered on the question of how a συμπλοκή of beings and non-beings is possible and how a συμπλοκή is possible at all. The exhibition of the κοινωνία τῶν γενῶν provides the answer. If Being can mix with non-Being, then it is possible that λόγος as an ὄν can combine with ψεῦδος as μὴ ὄν. If this combining is possible, then there is a λόγος ψευδής, then deception, ἀπάτη, is possible. And if there is deception, the existence of the sophist is possible in ἀπατητικὴ τέχνη. And if there is this possibility, it guarantees the possibility of the genuine positive λόγος, i.e., the possibility of philosophy as dialectic. Thus, in the dialogue as a whole, the question of the possibility of both the sophist and philosophy revolves around the question of Being. The συμπλοκή is the proper question, on which the consideration now centers under the title of the question of ὄν. The latter is taken up directly and explicitly at 251a5, a decisive passage in which Plato considers the προσαγορεύειν in λόγος. This transition from ὄν to λόγος as a determinate ὄν leads Plato into a confrontation with the ancients . . .

1. This transition is presented here separately because its summary character would disturb the continuity of the lectures.

Editor's Epilogue

This text reconstructs Martin Heidegger's lecture course at the University of Marburg during the winter semester 1924–25. It was announced as a four-hour-per-week course under the title *"Sophist."* The lectures began on Monday, November 3, 1924, and were at first held four times weekly (Monday, Tuesday, Thursday, Friday) in one-hour sessions, regularly until Friday, November 28, totaling sixteen sessions. Then in December the first six sessions were canceled, and in that month the course met only two times, on Thursday, the 11th, and Friday, the 12th, before the Christmas break, which at that time began on December 15. Heidegger's manuscript contains the remark: "Thursday, December 11, six sessions canceled, to be made up during the semester." According to a notice in the *Kant-Studien,* the cancellations were occasioned by a lecture trip.[1] After the Christmas break, the lecture course resumed on Thursday, January 8, 1925, and continued regularly five times per week (Wednesday was added) in one-hour sessions until February 27, with the exception of the week of February 1, in which there was no class on Friday and thus only four sessions. The course therefore included thirty-six sessions after the Christmas holidays and, in all, fifty-four sessions.

After some preliminary considerations, Heidegger devoted the meetings prior to Christmas to an interpretation of Aristotle. This first part, which Heidegger called "Introduction,"[2] deals, above all, with the *Nicomachean Ethics,* Book VI and Book X, chapters 6–7, as well as with the *Metaphysics,* Book I, chapters 1–2. To these, Heidegger related other parts of the Aristotelian corpus: in particular, passages from the *Metaphysics,* the *Topics,* the *Physics, De Interpretatione,* and the *Categories.* Only in the sessions after the Christmas break, i.e., in the second part, the actual main part, did Heidegger turn, after a "transition," to the interpretation of Plato. Specifically, he did not, as originally planned, interpret "two later dialogues,"[3] namely, the *Sophist* and *Philebus,* but instead only the *Sophist* (as well as the *Phaedrus,* in an excursus), and he also brought in other parts of Plato's writings, especially from the *Theaetetus* and the "Seventh Letter."

In preparing this volume I had available the following manuscripts:

1. According to the announcement in the *Kant-Studien,* Bd. 29, 1924, p. 626, Heidegger presented a lecture (previously worked out in the winter semester 1923–24) on "Existence and Truth after Aristotle (Interpretation of Book VI of the *Nicomachean Ethics*)" in six cities on the following days: Hagen, Dec. 1; Elberfeld, Dec. 2; Cologne, Dec. 3; Düsseldorf, Dec. 5; Essen, Dec. 6; and Dortmund, Dec. 8.

2. See p. 131, note 1.

3. See the text of the lectures, p. 7, and note 1 there, as well as p. 132, note 2, which is a marginal remark Heidegger made.

I. The Marbach photocopy of Heidegger's original handwritten manuscript. The photocopy consists of two bound files, the first of which bears on the binding the title: "Plato's *Sophist* (Introduction)," and the second: "Plato's *Sophist* (Interpretation)." In his manuscript, Heidegger did not work out the lectures sentence by sentence but for the most part only anticipated what he would say with notes consisting of key words and rough sketches, and he formulated them completely only in his oral delivery. The two files together contain 271 sheets of DIN A 4 size,[4] written partly in a very crabbed hand and partly more loosely, as well as a multitude of interspersed annotations. Heidegger wrote in very small German script across the long side of the page and saved the righthand margin for supplements and remarks of wider bearing. The first file includes Heidegger's lecture notes up to and including the "transition," thus above all the Aristotle part, and the second file begins with the actual interpretation of the *Sophist* and contains the main part of the course, devoted to Plato.

The first file consists of 100 sheets, loosely numbered by Heidegger partly with Arabic numerals, partly with Roman, and partly with other symbols, some sheets labeled as addenda and some—e.g., the annotations, but also other pages—not labeled at all. Thus this file presents at first view a marvelously confusing multiplicity. Upon closer inspection, the first file is composed in the following way:

1.) 3 sheets, numbered 1–3, on the "*In memoriam* Paul Natorp";[5]

2.) 51 sheets, in part numbered loosely 1–29, in part labeled as addenda, along with annotations containing notes on the "preliminary consideration," on the interpretation of *Nicomachean Ethics* VI, chapters 2–7 (first part), on *Metaphysics* I, chapters 1 and 2, and on the excursus on mathematics in Aristotle (according to *Physics* II, chapter 2, and *Physics* V, chapters 1–5);[6]

3.) 5 unlabeled sheets (pp. 55–59 of the Marbach photocopy) with notes on the interpretation of *Nicomachean Ethics* VI, chapters 7 (second part)–9;[7]

4.) 11 sheets loosely numbered i–x (pp. 60–71 of the photocopy) with notes on the interpretation of *Nicomachean Ethics* VI, chapters 10–13, and *Nicomachean Ethics* X, chapters 6–7;[8]

5.) 18 pages (pp. 72–89 of the photocopy) with sheets partly designated as "E.W." (= "Introduction, Recapitulation" *[Einleitung, Weiderholung]*), partly numbered loosely W1–W4, as well as mostly unlabeled addenda and annotations containing notes on the "transition";[9]

4. I.e., German letter-size paper (29.6 x 21 cm.).—Trans.
5. Pp. 1–4 as printed above.
6. §§1–18, pp. 5–93 as printed above.
7. §§19–21, pp. 93–99 as printed above.
8. §§22–25, pp. 99–123 as printed above.
9. §§27–32, pp. 131–155 as printed above.

6.) 11 pages (pp. 90–100 of the photocopy) with two further sheets labeled xi and xii (pp. 90 and 92 of the photocopy) as well as mostly unlabeled sheets, addenda, and many annotations with notes: a) on the truth (ἀλήθεια) of λόγος in Aristotle (according to *De Interpretatione*, chapter 4; *De Anima* II, chapter 8; and *Metaphysics* VI, chapters 2 and 4), which were expounded in the lecture course, *prior* to the "transition," in connection with *Nicomachean Ethics* X, chapter 7,[10] but which also coincide with passages from the "transition," and b) on the question of the place of truth (ἀλήθεια) according to *Metaphysics* VI, chapter 4, and *Metaphysics* IX, chapter 10, as well as on a critique of the theses of Werner Jaeger, which was not carried out in the lectures.[11]

The second file of the manuscript consists of 170 pages, organized as follows:

1.) 25 pages, with sheets loosely numbered So 1–So 16, as well as addenda and annotations, for the most part labeled, with notes on the Plato part, up to the fifth definition of the sophist, inclusive;[12]

2.) 14 pages (pp. 26–29 of the photocopy) along with sheets loosely numbered α–η, and partially labeled addenda and annotations containing notes on the *Phaedrus* excursus;[13]

3.) 94 pages (pp. 42–135 of the photocopy) along with sheets loosely numbered So 16–So 69 and partially labeled addenda with notes on the interpretation of the *Sophist*, up to the end of the lectures;[14]

4.) 35 pages (pp. 136–170 of the photocopy) along with a few disparate sheets labeled "So," containing notes on the interpretation of the *Sophist*, as well as an abundance of unlabeled addenda and annotations with notes especially on the Plato part but also on the Aristotle part and on the question of the lectures as a whole.

II. A typewritten transcription of Hartmut Tietjen's deciphering of Heidegger's handwritten manuscript.

III. The following notes taken down by students who attended the lectures:

1.) a typewritten transcript of the notes taken by Helene Weiß, which trace the entire lecture course. This transcript was produced by Tietjen and amounts to 497 pages.

10. §26, pp. 123–129 as printed above.
11. See the appendix, especially supplements 8 and 9.
12. §§33–49, pp. 157–213 as printed above.
13. §§50–55, pp. 214–244 as printed above.
14. §§56–81, pp. 245–422 as printed above.

2.) a typewritten transcript (447 pages) of the stenographic notes of Simon Moser. These begin only after the Christmas holidays and thus render the lectures from the "transition" on, i.e., the Plato part. Heidegger himself revised this transcript; he employed it as a working basis, supplied it with marginal remarks, and authorized it.

3.) the notes of Hans Jonas (6 notebooks), which trace the entire course and on only one occasion, the twenty-eighth session (January 21, 1925), display a handwriting that is not his own, and, finally, the notes of Fritz Schalk (5 notebooks), which, with the exception of the beginning of the ninth session (November 17, 1924), likewise cover the entire course. These two sets of notes progressively come to match one another until they finally correspond word for word.

Following Heidegger's directives for the publication of his lecture courses, it was my task as editor to prepare, from the philosopher's handwritten manuscript and from the various transcripts, an integrated, continuous text. To that end, I compared, word for word, Heidegger's handwritten manuscript with the typed transcript of Tietjen's deciphering of it, and I corrected the passages that were deciphered inaccurately. In a few cases of thorny problems with the reading, I had to consult the original manuscript. Furthermore, I compared Heidegger's manuscript with the students' notes. Thereby it appeared that Heidegger for the most part followed his manuscript while delivering the lectures, merely expanding the formulation, and enlarging, often rather broadly, upon the ideas already sketched out. Occasionally, however, he went entirely beyond his notes and added whole passages obviously *ex tempore*. Such passages, for which there are records only in the students' notes, are:

1.) the excursus on καθόλου and καθ'ἕκαστον as well as on the way of philosophy in Aristotle, according to *Metaphysics* V, 26; *Topics* V, 4; and *Physics* I, 1.[15]

2.) the interpretation of Aristotle's basic distinction within ποσόν (συνεχές and διωρισμένον), according to the *Categories*, chapter 6.[16]

3.) the interpretation of the priority of σοφία over φρόνησις, according to *Nicomachean Ethics* VI, 13, 1144a1–6.[17]

4.) the interpretation of πρώτη φιλοσοφία in Aristotle, according to *Metaphysics* IV, 1 and 2, in the "transition."[18]

In preparing the text of the lectures I took my guidance, following

15. §12a–c, pp. 54–62 as printed above.
16. §15b, γ, γγ; pp. 81–83 as printed above.
17. §24b, pp. 116–118 as printed above.
18. §30a, pp. 144–147 as printed above.

Heidegger's directive, especially from the idea of integrating Heidegger's own manuscript and the various transcripts in such a way that—as is said in the epilogue to the publication (which Heidegger saw to and approved) of his Marburg lecture course, "The Basic Problems of Phenomenology"—"no thought, whether already written down or conceived while delivering the lectures, would be lost."[19] Since for the first part of the lectures the authorized transcript of Moser's stenographic notes did not apply, Heidegger's own manuscript was basically the standard in preparing this part of the text. Yet the manuscript and the available transcriptions were incorporated in such a way that, in the case of conceptual unclarities in the former, the priority was accorded to the latter, provided they agreed among themselves and offered a clearer formulation. The notes of Weiß, due to their relative completeness as regards the text of the lectures and in terms of the Greek citations, were an indispensable aid, and, on the other hand, the concise, unerring formulations of the notes of Jonas and Schalk offered welcome assistance in the case of conceptual difficulty. Since for the second part of the course an authorized transcript of Moser's stenographic notes existed, it became the standard, yet in such a way that all the other textual sources (Heidegger's manuscript and the other transcripts) were still considered, and, in the case of conceptual unclarity, Heidegger's manuscript always received the priority, provided it was superior to the formulations in the transcripts. I deciphered and presented in footnotes Heidegger's marginalia (which obviously stemmed from various stages on his path of thinking) in the typewritten version of Moser's notes. As for the passages mentioned above, the ones Heidegger delivered extemporaneously, I prepared them in accord with Heidegger's directive—to the extent that this was possible—by carefully examining and comparing the students' notes. The class transitions, which for the most part Heidegger delivered extemporaneously at the beginning of each session, though he occasionally had prepared a few key words, were, in accord with the directives, worked into the continuous text of the lectures. The interjections peculiar to oral delivery were, again in accord with the directives, stricken, all the while preserving, however, the style of a lecture.

Heidegger's lectures, both in his writing and in his oral delivery, present, in large measure, a mixture of Greek citation and German commentary. Heidegger quoted the Greek text of Plato according to the first Oxford

19. Martin Heidegger, *Die Grundprobleme der Phänomenologie. Marburger Vorlesung Sommersemester 1927*. Gesamtausgabe, Bd. 24, edited by F.-W. von Herrmann, Frankfurt a.M., 1975, p. 472. [English translation by Albert Hofstadter, *The Basic Problems of Phenomenology*, Bloomington: Indiana University Press, 1982, p. 332.—Trans.]

Edition of Plato's Works, edited by I. Burnet[20] and the Greek text of Aristotle according to the edition published by Teubner in Leipzig with various editors.[21] The text I have presented here likewise cites Plato according to Burnet and Aristotle according to Heidegger's just-named copy. When Heidegger freely varied the Greek original for philosophical or pedagogical reasons, I retained his way of quoting and prefaced the corresponding reference with a "Cf." Rather long ellipses within the original Greek text were marked with suspension points (. . .). On account of the difference in the circumstances of the students' notes for the two parts of the course, I took over the Greek citations in the first part, where Heidegger's oral quotations cannot be reconstructed, either from Heidegger's manuscript or, most often, from the notes taken by Weiß, in which the Greek texts were interpolated, obviously later, in mostly complete sentences. For the second part, I retained Heidegger's oral quotations, as fixed in the transcript of Moser's notes, in order to preserve the lecture style. For the first part, it was not clear which citations Heidegger had translated in his oral delivery, and so I included either the translation occasionally found in Heidegger's manuscript or, in the case of difficult Greek passages, when there was neither a translation nor an interpretative paraphrase in the manuscript or the transcripts, my own translation, employing Heideggerian terms, as long as it did not disturb the flow of the text. In the second part, such translations could be dispensed with, since almost all of Heidegger's translations, paraphrases, and paraphrasing interpretations are present in Moser's stenographic notes and could be taken from them. For Heidegger's translations the boundary between literal translation and paraphrasing commentary is often fluid. I put in quotation marks only literal translations as well as paraphrases that were nearly translations.

The literary style of the text I am presenting must unavoidably vary between the first part and the second, since it was only Moser's stenographic notes of the latter which permitted an approximate reproduction of the idiosyncratic formulations of Heidegger's oral delivery.

I supplied the continuous text of the lectures, for which no table of

20. *Platonis Opera*. Recognovit brevique adnotatione critica instruxit Ioannes Burnet. Oxonii e typographeo Clarendoniano, 1899ff.

21. *Aristotelis Metaphysica*. Recognovit W. Christ. Lipsiae in aedibus B. G. Teubneri, 1886.

Aristotelis Physica. Recensuit Carolus Prantl. Lipsiae in aedibus B. G. Teubneri, 1879.

Aristotelis Ethica Nicomachea. Recognovit Franciscus Susemihl. Lipsiae in aedibus B. G. Teubneri, 1882.

Aristotelis De Anima Libri III. Recognovit Guilelmus Biehl. Editio altera curavit Otto Apelt. In aedibus B. G. Teubneri Lipsiae, 1911.

Aristotelis Ars Rhetorica. Iterum edidit Adolphus Roemer. Editio stereotypa. Lipsiae in aedibus B. G. Teubneri, 1914.

Aristotelis Topica cum libro de sophisticis elenchis. E schedis Ioannis Strache edidit Maximilianus Wallies. Lipsiae in aedibus B. G. Teubneri, 1923.

contents can be found in Heidegger, with a very detailed one, and I articulated the text itself by sections in a meaningful way. I did these things, in accord with Heidegger's directive, by considering Heidegger's own hints as to the articulation, ones found occasionally in his own manuscript or in the transcripts. I planned the table of contents to completely reproduce the course of thought in the lectures in its main points and in its continuity and thus to be able to substitute for the index Heidegger did not want. To the extent that there were, in the manuscript or in the transcripts, formulations concerning the articulation of the lectures, I took them over and in each case indicated in footnotes that they were titles deriving from Heidegger himself. Also, I was the one who, according to the sense, introduced all the italics within the text, since the directives say that the underlinings in the manuscript were determinative only of the oral delivery and were not binding for the publication. To be sure, I based myself on these underlinings and on those in the transcripts. Underlinings within Greek texts, however, could not be reproduced for technical reasons. In the appendix, which presents the annotations in Heidegger's manuscript, the italics correspond exactly to the underlinings there.

Since, for want of a stenographic record, Heidegger's manuscript was basically the standard for the first part of the lectures, I incorporated into the text—following the guiding idea of letting be lost "no thought whether already written down or conceived while delivering the lectures"—*all* the annotations in the manuscript, insofar as I could merge them into the sense of the lectures and they did not positively disturb the flow of the text. I relegated to the appendix, as supplements, those annotations which contained an essential thought or a clarification of a determinate passage but which were destructive of the continuity. This applies to only a few supplements.[22] Nevertheless I could not maintain the principle of incorporating as many annotations as possible into the text for the end of the first part.[23] On account of the cancellation of the six classes in December, Heidegger could not bring the course to a close before Christmas the way—according to his notes—he had planned. The lectures seem to break off abruptly before the Christmas holidays.[24] Heidegger's manuscript, however, contains, as was said above, eleven further pages, consisting mostly of key words, sketches, and notes, which obviously form the first foundation for a further continuous development of the course. In connection with the delimitation of the truth (ἀλήθεια) of λόγος, they revolve around the question of the place of truth (ἀλήθεια) according to *Metaphysics* VI, 4, and IX, 10, and hint

22. Appendix, supplements 1–5.
23. From §26b, p. 124ff.
24. P. 129.

at a critical confrontation with Jaeger's theses. I did not find it possible to formulate out these annotations and incorporate them into the main text. I relegated them to the appendix as supplements to the end of the first part.[25] The same applies to a series of annotations on the "transition," which to a certain extent intersect with those on the end of the first part. In the "transition," which Heidegger also labels "*W.E.*" (= "Recapitulation, Introduction"),[26] he takes up again the interrupted course of thought,[27] but in such a way that he incorporates it into a presentation of the overall perspective guiding the previous Aristotle part and its relation to the Plato part. In doing so, Heidegger obviously modified and abridged in oral delivery the course of thought he had planned for the transition. He left out the passage on ἀληθές.[28] Here, too, the manuscript contains annotations giving the key words on the relation of λόγος—ἀλήθεια—ὄν, and again it was not possible for me to fill them out and place them into the main text. I assigned them to the appendix as supplements.[29] During the winter semester 1925–26, in his lecture course at Marburg entitled "Logic: the Question of Truth," Heidegger took up again and expressly thematized this problematic which he only drafted sketchily within his lectures on the *Sophist*.[30]

In preparing the text of the Plato part of the course, I did not face these difficulties, thanks to the continuity of Heidegger's annotations and thanks to the authorized transcript of Moser's stenographic notes. Here, too—this time basing myself primarily on the authorized transcript—I integrated the manuscript and students' notes so that "no thought was lost." I placed in the appendix, as supplements, merely those annotations which contained auxiliary commentaries or which were difficult to incorporate and would have disturbed the flow of the lectures. Here belong also a series of annotations on the hermeneutic of Dasein, which forms the horizon for Heidegger's interpretation of Aristotle and Plato in the *Sophist* course.[31] To be sure, this hermeneutic does not found the interpretation in a dogmatic way but is won precisely through a confrontation with the central problems posed in the Greek texts, i.e., in productive mutual relation.

The all-encompassing basic theme of this course on the *Sophist* is the relation of truth (ἀλήθεια) and Being (ὄν). These lectures testify, as do the

25. Appendix, supplements 8–20.
26. See p. 131, note 1.
27. From §28a, p. 135ff.
28. See the sketch of the articulation of the "transition" in the appendix, supplement 27.
29. Appendix, supplements 25, 27, 28, 31 (end).
30. *Logik. Die Frage nach der Wahrheit*. Marburger Vorlesung Wintersemester 1925–26. Gesamtausgabe Bd. 21, edited by Walter Biemel. Frankfurt a.M., 1976. Especially pp. 162–174.
31. Appendix, especially supplements to the "transition," nos. 23 and 25.

other already published Marburg courses, that Heidegger acquired the question he posed in *Being and Time* on the meaning of Being, i.e., on the accessibility or the clearing of Being, in a confrontation with the philosophical tradition. The "introductory part" of the course, devoted to the interpretation of Aristotle (above all, *Nicomachean Ethics* VI and X, chapters 6–7, as well as *Metaphysics* I, chapters 1–2), is given over to the task of acquiring ἀληθεύειν as the ground for Plato's research into Being. The "transition" has the task of establishing, based on this ground, the thematic field of philosophy, namely ὄν *qua* ἀληθές or μὴ ὄν *qua* ψεῦδος. The main part, containing the interpretation of the *Sophist* as well as of the *Phaedrus,* takes up the task of carrying out, *in concreto,* the Platonic ontological research. Here the leading basic thought is that μὴ ὄν, viewed from the standpoint of ἀληθεύειν, or from ψεύδεσθαι, has its ontological possibility only on the basis of the new thought, opposed to Parmenides, of ὄν, previously clarified already in λόγος, as δύναμις κοινωνίας. The thought of the self-disclosure of Being, in its apriori relation to language, as δύναμις κοινωνίας anticipates not only the analysis of world in *Being and Time* but also the analyses of λόγος and world in the later Heidegger.

Heidegger personally entrusted to me the editing of the "Sophist" on the occasion of my visit to him in Freiburg on September 30, 1975. As a basis for this work, he presented me the Marbach photocopy of his handwritten original manuscript as well as a typewritten transcript of Moser's stenographic notes on the second part of the course. The following March, I received the typewritten transcript, prepared by Tietjen, of the lecture notes of Weiß. After I began my work by deciphering the first 50 pages of Heidegger's handwriting, Dr. Tietjen was kind enough to check the deciphering I had done and then to undertake, with the remaining 271 pages, the deciphering of the manuscript as a whole. In the summer of 1978, Prof. Fritz Schalk (University of Cologne) notified me that he had prepared a transcript of the lectures, now in the possession of Prof. Klaus Reich (University of Marburg), and he bid me to obtain it from him. Reich was so kind as to let me have this transcript, which he had critically revised, on the occasion of a visit to him in Marburg in November, 1978. After thoroughly familiarizing myself with the content of the lectures, I was able to begin, during the summer holidays of 1982, in Lausanne, my elaboration of the text destined for publication. In the summer of 1984, Dr. Hermann Heidegger discovered in the "Rötebuckspeicher"[32] the lecture notes of Prof. Hans Jonas (New School for Social Research, New York), and he delivered them to me that September. I incorporated them belatedly into the Aristotle

32. I.e., in the storeroom of Martin Heidegger's house on the Rötebuck Weg in Freiburg.—Trans.

part, which I had already prepared, and they proved a valuable help for my work on the Plato part.

My handwritten version of the text of the lecture course was typed by the *assistants diplômés* working under me in the philosophy department of the University of Lausanne, namely Alexandre Schild, Mireille Rosselet-Capt, and André Jeanmonod. With them, in a common reading, my handwriting was cross-checked against their transcription. Mrs. Rosselet-Capt, *lic. ès lettres* in Greek, undertook especially the verification of the Greek citations. Vivien Oeuvray, *assistant diplômé* in the philosophy department, supplied the Greek texts with accents, since the computer printer could not correctly reproduce them. Guido Albertelli, at that time working under me as an *assistant diplômé*, prepared the printed manuscript and completed the bibliographical data. Finally, Dr. Tietjen and Mark Michalski (Ph.D. candidate, University of Freiburg) reviewed the printed manuscript with great care, verified the Greek citations in Heidegger's copy of the texts, and added the final bibliographical details in accord with the editions available in Freiburg. They all deserve my sincere thanks for their efforts on the printed manuscript. I thank Dr. Christoph Frhr. von Wolzogen (Offenbach) for the confirmation of the solution of a questionable abbreviation, and for supplementary bibliographical details, regarding the "*In memoriam* Paul Natorp."

My special thanks are due to Dr. Tietjen for the typewritten transcript of the notes of Helene Weiß as well as for deciphering Heidegger's handwritten original manuscript, and, further, to Prof. Friedrich-Wilhelm von Herrmann for his friendly counsel, and, lastly, to Dr. Hermann Heidegger for his patience over my long-protracted editing of the "Sophist."

Ingeborg Schüßler
Lausanne, Switzerland, August 1990

Glossary of Greek Terms

This glossary is meant to provide no more than a general orientation. Heidegger's subtle and original understanding of the concepts of Greek philosophy can be gained only from the text of the lectures themselves and cannot be captured in a mere lexicon, even one that employs, as does the following, Heidegger's own terms as much as possible.

ἀγαθόν: good
ἀγαθός: good, good man
ἄγειν: to conduct, bring
ἄγειν εἰς οὐσίαν: to bring into being
ἄγειν εἰς φῶς: to bring to light
ἄγνοια: ignorance
ἄγνοια ἡ πλείστη: the greatest ignorance
ἀγόμενον: that which is brought (into being)
ἀγοραστική: occupying the marketplace
ἀγχί: close by
ἀγχίνοια: presence of mind
ἀγών: contest, competition
ἀγωνίζειν: to struggle, battle for
ἀγωνιστική: appropriating by means of battle
ἀδιαίρετον: indivisible
ἀδιανόητον: indiscernible
ἀδιορίστως: undelimited
ἀδολέσχης: babbler
ἀδολεσχικόν: pedantic babble
ἀδύνατον: incapable, impossible
ἀεί: always, forever
ἀεὶ ὄν: eternal being
ἀθανατίζειν: to make immortal
ἄθετος: not oriented
ἀΐδια: eternal beings
ἀΐδιον: eternal
αἱρεταί: to grasp
αἰσθάνεσθαι: perceiving
αἴσθησις: sense perception
αἰσθητόν: perceived thing
αἶσχος: ugliness
αἰσχρός: ugly
αἰτίας γνωρίζειν: to know the causes
αἴτιον: cause
αἰών: lifetime, epoch, aeon
ἀκέφαλον: headless
ἀκήκοα: something heard
ἀκίνητον: unmoved
ἀκοή: something heard, a legend
ἀκούειν: to hear, hearken
ἄκρατος: excessive
ἀκριβεστάτον: most rigorous
ἀκριβῶς: in a rigorous way
ἀκρότατον: highest
ἀλήθεια: unconcealedness
ἀληθεύειν: to disclose
ἀληθεύων: one who discloses
ἀληθής, -ές: unconcealed
ἀληθινόν: an unconcealed being
ἁλιευτική: fishing
ἀλλακτικόν: exchange
ἀλληγορία: allegory
οἱ ἄλλοι: the others
ἀλλότρια ἔργα: what others have produced
ἄλλως: otherwise
ἄλλως ἔχειν: to be otherwise
ἄλογον: not a possible object of any discourse
ἅμα: concurrent
ἀμαθία: ignorance, presumptive knowledge
ἁμαρτάνειν: to miss the mark, fail
ἁμαρτία: defect
ἀμελετησία μνήμης: unconcern with retention
ἀμετρία: inadequacy
ἀμιλλᾶσθαι: to contest, compete
ἄμουσος: uncultivated
ἀναγκαῖα: necessities
ἀνάλογον: analogy
ἀνάλυσις: analysis
ἀνάμνησις: recollection, re-seeing
ἀναφανδόν: openly, visibly
ἀνδρεῖος: manly, courageous
ἄνευ λόγου: without discourse

ἄνευ ὕλης: without matter
ἄνευ χρόνου: without time
ἀνθρώπινα ἀγαθά: human goods
ἀνομοιότης: dissimilarity
ἀντίθεσις: opposite
ἀντικείμενον: opposed
ἀντιλέγειν: to dispute, contradict
ἀντιλέγεσθαι: disputing
ἀντιλογική: contradictory
ἀντίλογος: contradiction
ἀντίσταθμον: counterpoised
ἀντίστροφος: counterpart
ἀντιτιθέμενον: what is opposed
ἄνω: up
ἀνώμυνον: nameless
ἀόρατον: invisible
ἅπαντα: all things
ἅπαντα αἰώνα: entire age
ἀπάτη: falsity, deception
ἄπειρος, -οι: inexperienced one(s)
ἄπειρος: limitless
ἀπεργάζεσθαι: to make, result in
ἀπιδεῖν: extractive seeing
ἁπλοῦν: utterly simple
ἁπλῶς: purely and simply
ἀποδεικτόν: something demonstrated
ἀπόδειξις: a showing forth
ἀποδιδόναι: to render, extract
ἀπολέγειν: to deny
ἀπομαντεύεσθαι: to announce, presage
ἀπορεῖν: to be unable to get through
ἀπορία: blocked passage
ἄπορος: without passage
ἀπορούμενον: blockage
ἀποτελεύτησις: consummation
ἀποφαίνεσθαι: to let be seen
ἀπόφανσις: manifestation, declaration
ἀποφαντικός: letting be seen
ἀπόφασις: denial
ἅπτεσθαι: to touch
ἁπτόμενον: that which touches
ἀρετή: excellence
ἀριθμεῖν: to calculate
ἀριθμητική: arithmetic
ἀριθμός: number
ἄριστον: the highest good
ἄριστον ἐν τῷ κόσμῳ: the highest good in the world
ἁρμόττειν: to attach
ἄρρητον: unutterable
ἀρχή: beginning, origin
ἀρχικωτάτη: supreme
ἀρχιτέκτων: architect
ἀσπαλιευτής: angler
ἄσχιστον: unseparated out
ἀσώματον: unembodied
ἄτεχνος: lacking know-how
ἄτομον εἶδος: the outward look that can be dissected no further
αὐτάρκεια: self-sufficiency
αὐτῆς ἕνεκεν: for its own sake
αὐτὸ ἀεί: always identical
αὐτόθεν: by itself
αὐτόθι: immediately
αὐτουργόν: made by oneself
αὐτόχθονες: originators
αὐτῷ ὠφέλιμον: self-advantageous
ἀφαίρεσις: separation, abstraction
ἀφή: touch
ἄφθεγκτον: unutterable
ἀφιλόσοφος: unphilosophical
ἀφορίζεσθαι: being set apart, extracted
ἄψυχον, -χα: soulless thing(s)

βαδίζει: walks
βέβαιον: the certain
βελτίστη ἕξις: highest disposition
βέλτιστον: best
βίαιος: by force
βίος: life
βουλευτικός: one who can deliberate well
βουλή: resolution, decision
βράττειν: to shake, winnow

γεγραμμένα: things written, articulated
γελοῖος: ridiculous
γένει γενναία: of noble ancestry
γένεσις: origin, descent, generation
γένη: plural of γένος, *q.v.*
γένος: stem, ancestry, lineage
γεωμετρία: geometry
γεωργία: agriculture
γιγαντομαχία περὶ τῆς οὐσίας: battle of the giants over Being
γίγνεται: it becomes
γιγνώσκειν: to know
γιγνώσκεσθαι: to be known
γνωρίζειν: to make known, become familiar with
γνωριμώτερον: more knowable
γνωριστικός: having knowledge
γνῶσις: knowledge
γνωστά: things known
γράμματα: letters
γραμμή: line

γυμναστική: gymnastics
γυμνόν: naked, denuded of Being

δεικνύναι: to show, exhibit
δεινότης: ability
δεσμός: bond
δεύτερον: second
δέχεσθαι: to be able
δῆλον: disclosed, seen
δηλούμενον: the manifest
δηλοῦν: to make visible, reveal
δήλωμα: manifestation, disclosure
δημηγορική: public speaking
δήμιον: public
δημιουργεῖν: to fabricate (something for public life)
δημιουργός: craftsman
διά: through
διαδοξάζειν: to go through opinions
διάγραμμα: diagram
διαγράφειν: to "write through"
διαγωγή: tarrying, leisure, amusement
διάθεσις: arrangement
διαιρεῖν: to cleave, divide, take apart
διαίρεσις: a taking apart
διαιρετόν: something taken apart
διακρίνειν: to set in relief, distinguish
διάκρισις: a setting off, distinguishing, discriminate
διακριτική: discriminating
διαλανθάνειν: to be hidden
διαλέγειν: to discuss, "speak through"
διαλέγεσθαι: discussing
διαλεκτική: dialectic
διανοεῖν: to think (through), intend, grasp
διανοητική: involving thought
διάνοια: thorough thinking, grasping, determining
διὰ πάντων: throughout all (masc.)
διὰ παραδειγμάτων: through examples
διὰ πασῶν: throughout all (fem.)
διαπονεῖσθαι: to be worked out
διαπορεῖν: to be unable to get through
διαπορεύεσθαι: to pass through
διαριθμεῖσθαι: to be reckoned up
διασήθειν: to shake, sift
διαστρέφειν: to distort
διατέμνειν: to cut through
διατέμνειν κατ' ἄρθρα: to cut through according to the joints
διὰ τί: from out of which
διὰ τὸ εἰδέναι: for the sake of seeing
διαττᾶν: to press through, strain
διαφθείρειν: to corrupt
διαφορά: difference
διδακτή: teachable
διδασκαλία: teaching
διδασκαλική: instructive
διδάσκειν: to teach
διεξέρχεσθαι: to go through
διερωτᾶν: to cross-question
διεσπαρμένα: things rent asunder, dispersed
δι' ἕτερα: because of something else
διηθεῖν: to strain through, filter
δίκαιον: just, right
δικαιοσύνη: justice
δικανική: speaking in courts
διωρισμένον: discrete
δοκεῖν: to show oneself, appear
δόξα: view, opinion
δοξάζειν: to have an opinion
δόξαντα πλήθει: the opinions of the many
δοξαστική: semblant, like opinions
δοξοπαιδευτική: seemingly educative
δυνάμει: potentially
δύναμις εἰς: potentiality for
δύναμις κοινωνίας: potential to associate, to be with another
δύνασθαι: to be able
δυσ-: mis-
δυσειδές: deformity

ἑαυτῆς ἕνεκα or -κεν: for the sake of itself
ἐγγύθεν: from near at hand
ἐθέλει: is prepared
εἰδέναι: to see
εἰδέναι ἀλήθειαν: to see what is unconcealed
εἴδη: plural of εἶδος, *q.v.*
εἶδος: outward look, what is properly visible
εἰδυῖα τὸ ἀληθές: sight of the unconcealed
εἴδωλον: image
εἰδωλοποιός, -ική: making mere appearances
εἰδῶν φίλοι: friends of the Ideas
εἰκαστική: making exact images
εἰκός: guise
εἰκών: image (an exact copy)
εἶναι: Being
εἴργειν: to enclose

εἷς, μία, ἕν: one
εἰς: toward, for
εἰς ἕν: to one
εἰς μίαν ἰδέαν: toward one aspect
εἰς ὅ: toward which
εἰς τὸ παθεῖν: toward being affected
εἰς τοῦτο: for this
εἰς ὕστερον: later
εἰς φῶς ἄγειν: to bring to light
ἕκαστον, -α: the particular(s)
ἕκαστον ἀγαθόν: the particular good
ἐκβάλλειν: to cast out
ἐκβολὴ τῆς κακίας: a casting out of the bad things
ἐκμαγεῖον: that which takes an impression
ἐκ πλειόνων: out of many
ἐκ προγιγνωσκομένων: out of what is known at the outset
ἐκ στιγμῶν: out of points
ἐκτρέπεσθαι: to diverge
ἔλαφος: deer
ἐλεγκτικός: refutational
ἔλεγχος: refutation, public exposure
ἐμπειρία: experience
ἔμπειρος: one who is experienced
ἐμποδίζοντα: obstacles
ἔμπορός τις: a kind of merchant
ἔμψυχον, -χα: besouled thing(s)
ἕν: one
ἐναντίον: over and against
ἐναντιώτατα: things most opposed
ἐνδεής: in need, deficient
ἐνδέχεσθαι ἄλλως ἔχειν: to be able to be otherwise
ἐνδέχεσθαι διαψεύδεσθαι: to be able to be deceived
ἐνδεχόμενον: something possible
ἔνδοξα: esteemed opinions
ἕνεκά τινος: for the sake of something
ἐνέργεια: presence, actualization
ἐνεργείᾳ: as actualized
ἐν ἰδίοις: between individuals, in private
ἐννοεῖσθαι: to understand
ἐν σμικροῖς: in small things
ἐντελέχεια: full presence
ἔντεχνον: within some field of know-how
ἐν τῇ ψυχῇ: in the soul
ἐν τῷ κόσμῳ: in the world
ἐν τῷ ποιοῦντι: in the producer
ἐνυγροθηρική: hunting aquatic animals
ἔνυδρον: living in water
ἐνυπάρχοντα: things there from the beginning
ἐξαιρεῖσθαι: to exclude
ἐξαιρήσομεν: we shall exclude
ἐξ ἐμπειρίας: out of (but not away from) experience
ἕξις: disposition
ἔξωθεν: from without
ἔξω τοῦ θεωρεῖν: outside of one's gaze
ἐπαγωγή: a leading toward
ἐπαΐειν: to perceive
ἐπαφή: being touched
ἐπέκεινα: beyond
ἐπί: unto
ἐπιθυμία: desire
ἐπικοινωνεῖν: to share with
ἐπίπεδον: surface
ἐπίστασθαι: knowing
ἐπιστήμη: science
ἐπιστημονικόν: developing knowledge
ἐπιστητόν: the knowable
ἐπ' ὄντι: about a being
ἐπ' ὄν τι: toward some being
ἔργον: finished work
ἐρίζειν: to wrangle
ἐριστική: disputatiousness
ἐριστικόν: disputation
ἕρκος: snare
ἑρμηνεία: comprehensibility
ἐσόμενον: that which becomes
ἔσχατον: outermost limit
ἕτερον: other
ἕτερον μόνον: merely other
ἔτι: furthermore
εὖ: well, rightly, the proper
εὐβουλία: prudence, good counsel
εὔγνωστον: well-known
εὐδαιμονία: man's proper Being
εὖ ζῆν: proper life
εὐηνίος: tractable
εὐθύ: directly, simply
εὖ λέγειν: to speak well
εὐπραξία: correct action
εὐστοχία: sureness of aim
ἐφεξῆς: successive
ἔχειν: to have, to hold oneself, to wear
ἔχεσθαι: self-having
ἐχόμενον: self-possessed, what is possessed
ἔχον, ἔχοντα: thing(s) having

ζητεῖν: to seek

ζήτημα πρῶτον: the first thing to be sought
ζητούμενον: the sought
ζῷα: living beings
ζωή: life
ζῳοθηρική: hunting after living beings
ζῷον ἔμψυχον: besouled living being
ζῷον λόγον ἔχον: the living being that has speech
ζῷον πολιτικόν: the being living a communal life in a city

ᾗ: as, *qua*
ἡγοῦμαι: to deem, regard
ἡδίστη: highest pleasure
ἡδονή: pleasure
ἡδυντική: giving pleasure
Ἠθικά: Ethics
ἦθος: comportment
ἥλιος: sun
ἡμεροθηρική: hunting tame animals
ἡμῖν: to us
ἦν: was
ἠρεμοῦν: at rest, quiet
ἧττον: less

θάτερον (= τὸ ἕτερον): the other
θαυμάζειν: to wonder
θέα: sight
θεῖα: gods
θεῖος: divine
θειότατον: the most divine
θειότερον: more divine
θεολογική: theology
θεός: god
θεὸς ἐλεγκτικός: the confuting god
θερμόν: the warm
θέσις: orientation, order, arrangement
θετός: oriented
θεωρεῖν: to see, behold
θεωρητικός: contemplative
θεωρία: pure seeing, onlooking
θεωρός: spectator
θήρα: hunting
θηρεύειν: to hunt down
θηρευτική: hunting
θηρίον: the hunted
θιγεῖν: to touch
θνητός: mortal
θυμός: spirit, temper

ἰατρική: healing
ἰατρός: physician
ἴδια αἰσθητά: specific objects of perception
ἴδιον: specific
ἰδιώτης: unlearned
ἱκανῶς δεδήλωται: it has been sufficiently disclosed
ἵππος: horse
ἱστορία: history
ἰσχυρός: strong, mighty

καθάπερ: just like
καθαρμός: purification
κάθαρσις: purification
καθ' αὑτό: for itself
καθ' ἕκαστον, -τα: the particular(s)
καθεύδει: sleeps
καθόλου: universal, universally
καθορᾶν: to look down
καιρός: decisive moment
κακόν: bad
κακῶς: badly
καλός: beautiful
καλούμενος: so-called
καλῶς: beautifully, appropriately
κάπηλος: shopkeeper
κατά: down, toward, according to, upon, beyond
κατάγειν: to spin
κατακερματίζειν: to change into small coin, cut up
καταλέγειν: to affirm
καταλείπειν: to leave behind
κατὰ λόγους: by words
κατὰ μέρος: according to a part
κατὰ πόλιν: in town
κατ' ἀρετὴν τελείαν: according to perfect excellence
κατὰ συμβεβηκός: from the outside, accidentally
κατὰ τελείωσιν τελείαν: according to perfect completion
κατάφασις: affirmation
κατ' ἔργα: by deeds
κατ' ἐξοχήν: most eminent
κατηγορεῖσθαι: to predicate
κάτω: down
οἱ κάτω: the ones down there
κεκινημένον: the moved
κεχωρισμένον: separate, autonomous
κινεῖν: to move, stir
κινεῖν κατὰ τόπον: to move with respect to place

κινήσεως μετασχόν: partaking in motion
κίνησις: motion
κινούμενον: the moved
κοινὰ αἰσθητά: common sensibles
κοιναὶ αἴσθησις: common perception
κοινόν: the common, general
κοινὸς ὅρος: common term
κοινωνεῖν: to share in, associate, keep company with
κοινωνία: association
κοινωνία τῶν γενῶν: association of the kinds
κρατίστη ἕξις: the most excellent disposition
κράτιστον: best, most excellent, mightiest
κρείττων: mightier one
κρίνειν: to discriminate, set in relief
κρίσις: setting off something against something
κρυφαῖον: hidden
κτῆσθαι: to appropriate
κτῆσις: appropriation, possession
κτητική: appropriative
κύριον: dominant

λανθάνειν: to be concealed
λανθάνον: something concealed
λέγειν: to speak
λέγειν τι κατά τινος: to address something as something
λέγεσθαι: speaking
λεγόμενον: the spoken
λειπόμενον: what remains
λευκόν: white
λέων: lion
λήθη: a forgetting
λογίζεσθαι: to discuss
λόγοις πρὸς λόγους: words against words
λόγον ἔχειν: to possess speech
λόγον ἔχον: that which has speech
λόγος: speech, discourse, discussion, sentence
λόγος μακρός: lengthy treatise
λόγος μικρός: brief speech
λόγος πρὸς ἄλλον: dialogue
λόγος πρὸς ἕτερον: dialogue
λόγος σημαντικός: meaningful speech
λόγος σμικρότατος: the briefest possible sentence
λόγος ψευδής: deceptive speech
λύπη: pain

μάθημα, -τα: cognition(s), knowledge
μαθηματική: mathematics
μαθηματικόν, -κά: object(s) of any learning, esp. of mathematics
μαθηματικός: mathematician
μαθηματοπωλική: selling cognitions
μάθησις: learning
μαθητόν: learnable
μάλιστα: most
μάλιστα ἀληθεύειν: most disclosing
μάλιστα ἐπιστητόν: most known
μάλιστα καθόλου: most universal
μᾶλλον: more
μανικοί: madmen
μανικός: mad, deranged
μάχεσθαι: to fight against someone
μέγεθος: extension
μέγιστος: greatest
μέθοδος: the way
μείζονα: the more important things
μεμερισμένον: composed of parts
μέρος,-ρη: moment(s), part, character, determination
μέσος ὅρος: middle term
μεσότης: the mean
μετά: after, over, according to, in common with
μεταβαίνειν: to pass over, run through
μεταβάλλειν: to exchange
μεταβλητική: exchange
μεταβλητικόν: exchanging
μεταβολή: change, alteration
μετάθεσις: reordering, transposition
μετὰ λόγου: carried out in discourse
μεταξύ: intermediate, medium
μετάστασις: displacement
μετέχειν: to participate
μετρεῖν: to measure
μή: not
μηδὲν δ'οὐκ ἔστιν: neither is it not being
μὴ ὄν: non-being
μὴ πρὸς χρῆσιν: apart from usefulness
μία: one
μιμεῖσθαι: to present, represent, imitate
μίμησις: imitation
μιμητική: imitative
μισθαρνητικόν: mercenary, getting paid
μνήμη: retention
μονάς, -άδες: unit(s)
μόνον: alone, only
μνήμη: retention

μόριον, -ια: piece(s), portion
μορφή: outward look, Gestalt
μουσικός: cultivated, educated
μῦθον διηγεῖσθαι: to tell a story

νευστικός: swimming
νοεῖν: to discern, perceive
νόημα, -ματα: the discerned, the perceived
νόησις: deliberation, discernment
νόησις νοήσεως: the thinking of thinking
νόμοι: laws
νόμῳ: by custom
νοούμενον: the discerned, the seen
νόσος: sickness
νουθετητική: admonishing
νοῦς: discernment, perception

ξένος: foreigner

οἰκοδομική: architecture
ὅλον: whole
ὅλον λεγόμενον: a whole in speech
ὅλως: wholly, altogether, in general
ὁμιλεῖν: to associate with
ὁμιλία: communion, company, being together
ὅμοιον ἀφ' ὁμοίου: like from like
ὁμοιότης: resemblance
ὁμοιοῦν: to assimilate
ὁμοίως: to the same degree
ὁμολογούμενον: harmonious
ὁμολόγως ὀρέξει: in harmony with desire
ὄν: Being, beings, a being
ὂν ἀληθινόν: beings as unconcealed
ὂν δυνάμει: Being as possibility
ὂν ἐνεργείᾳ: Being as actuality
ὂν ᾗ ὄν: beings as beings
ὄνομα: name
ὀνομάζειν: to call by name
ὄνομα ὀνόματος: name of a name
ὄντα: beings
ὂν ὡς ἀληθές: beings as unconcealed
ὅπερ: precisely, just as
ὅπως: in such a manner
ὁρᾶν: to see, to look upon
ὁρατόν: the visible
ὄρεξις: desire
ὀρθὸς λόγος: appropriate discourse
ὀρθότης: correctness, appropriateness
ὁρίζεσθαι: to determine, delimit
ὁρισμός: determination, definition
ὁρμή: urge, striving, orientation
ὅρος: term, delimitation
ὅτε: when
ὅτου: as which
οὐ, οὐκ: not
οὗ ἕνεκα: for the sake of which
οὗ δεῖ: what is needed
οὐδὲν δημιουργεῖ: produces nothing
οὐδὲν διαφέρει: it makes no difference, does not matter
οὐρανός: heavens
οὐσία: Being
ὀψιμαθής: late to learn

πάθεῖν: to be affected
πάθη: affects
παθήμα: what is experienced
πάθος: something undergone
παιδεία: formation, education
παιδεύδειν: to educate
παιδιά: sport, jest
πᾶν: all, the whole
πᾶν παντὶ ὁμοιοῦν: to liken anything to anything
πάντα: all things
παντάπασι μανικῶς: utterly deranged
παντελῶς: completely, genuinely
παρά: beside
παράδειγμα: example, model
παραφορά: a going awry
παραφροσύνη: misperception
παραφυές: offshoot
παρεῖναι: to be co-present
παρέχεσθαι: to show, display
παρουσία: presence, co-presence
πάσχειν: to be determined from without
πατραλοίας: parricide
πεζόν: on land
πείθειν: to persuade
πειθοῦς δημιουργός: producing persuasions
πειραστικός: endeavoring
πέρας: limit
περιέχειν: to encompass
περιέχον: that which encloses
περὶ οὗ: about which
περὶ πάντων: about everything
περὶ τὴν ψυχήν: concerning the soul
περὶ τὸ σῶμα: concerning the body
Περὶ φύσεως: About nature
πιθανόν: persuading
πιθανουργική: persuasive

πίστις: belief, conviction
πλανᾶσθαι: to drift about
πλαστόν: formed, fabricated
πλάττειν: to form, feign, fabricate
πλέγμα: a braid, intertwining
πλεῖον: something more
πλῆθος: a multitude, manifold
πληκτική: striking, wounding
ποιεῖν: to make, produce
ποιεῖν δοκεῖν: to make appear
ποιεῖν δοκεῖν λέγεσθαι: to make it appear to be said
ποιεῖν πάντα δοκεῖν: to make everything appear
ποιεῖσθαι: to produce
ποίημα: a work
ποίησις: production
ποιητική: making, producing
ποιητόν: what is to be produced
ποῖον, ποῖα: how qualified
ποιός, ποιόν: so qualified
ποιούμενον: product
πόλις: city
πολιτική: referring to communal life in the city
πολιτικός, -οί: politician(s)
πολλαχῇ: in many ways
οἱ πολλοί: the multitude, people as they are at first and for the most part
πονηρία: badness
πορεύεσθαι: to traverse
πόρρωθεν: from afar
ποσαχῶς: in how many ways
ποσόν, πόσα: quantity
πρᾶγμα, -τα: thing(s)
πραγματεία: task, labor
πρακτική: pertaining to action
πρακτικὴ ἕξις: disposition toward action
πρακτικώτερος: better able to act
πρακτόν: something to be done
πρᾶξις: action
πρέποντα ἀλλήλοις: things suited to one another
προαίρεσις: anticipation; choice in advance
προαιρετόν: the anticipated
προγιγνωσκόμενα: things known from the very outset
προιέναι: to proceed
πρός: toward, to
πρὸς ἄλλον: to an other
προσαγορεύειν: to address, speak to
προσαρμόττειν: to attach, bring into harmony
προσβολή: an assault
προσγένεσις: an adding on, accrual
προσγίγνεσθαι: to be appended to
πρὸς διαγωγήν: toward amusements
πρὸς ἕτερον: to an other
πρὸς ἡμᾶς: in relation to us
πρόσθεσις: an addition
προσκεῖσθαι: to lie beside, cling to, be devoted to
προσκοινωνεῖν: to give a share to
προσλέγειν: to speak to
προσομιλεῖν: to associate with
προσομιλητική: speaking privately to another
προσσημαῖνον χρόνον: co-signifying time
πρὸς τὰ ἀναγκαῖα: toward the necessities
πρός τι: in relation to something
προστιθέναι: to associate with
πρός τι καί τινος: for something and for someone
προσφέρειν: to carry over to
πρὸς χρῆσιν: toward use
πρότερον μὴ ὄν: previously was not
πρόχειρος: ready at hand
πρῶτα: first things
πρώτη φιλοσοφία: first philosophy
πρῶτοι ὅροι: the first demarcations
πτηνόν: feathered, winged
πῶς: how

ῥῆμα: verb
ῥητορική: rhetoric
ῥήτωρ: orator

σαφές: clear
σελήνη: moon
σημαίνειν: to signify, let be seen
σημαντικός: meaningful
σημεῖον: a manifestation, letting be seen
σκεῦος: implement
σκέψις: searching inquiry
σκοπόν τινα θέμενα: aiming at some posited mark
σκοπός: what is sighted, aim
σκοτεινόν: hidden in darkness
σμικρότατος: smallest
σοφία: understanding, wisdom
σοφίαι: wisdoms
σοφιστής, -ταί: sophist(s)

σοφιστική: sophistry
σοφός: wise, wise person
σοφώτερος: wiser
σπουδαιοτάτη: gravest, most serious
σπουδῆς χάριν: for the sake of seriousness
στάσις: rest, insurrection
στερεόν: the solid, solidity
στήσεσθαι: to stand still
στιγμή: point
στοιχεῖον, -α: element(s)
στοχαστικός: having a good aim
συγγενῆ: having the same provenance
συγκείμενον: composite
συγκεχυμένον: intermingled
συλλαβεῖν: to take together
συλλογίζεσθαι: to speak together, collect
συλλογισμός: conclusion
συμμείγνυσθαι: to combine together
συμμετρία: adequacy
σύμπαντα: everything whatsoever
συμπέρασμα: what emerges at the end
συμπλοκή: entwining
συμφέρον: usefulness
συμφιλοσοφεῖν: philosophizing together
συμφυές: emerging together
συμφυὲς γεγονός: what already emerged with both
συμφωνειν: to harmonize
συνάγειν: to gather
συναγωγή: a bringing together
συνάπτεσθαι: to be bound together
συνεστάναι: to hold together in itself
συνέχεια: continuity
συνεχές: continuous, holding together
συνεχεστάτη: most self-coherent
συνεχόμενον: what holds itself together
σύνθεσις: a positing together
σύνθετος: composite
συνομολογεῖσθαι: to agree
συνορᾶν: to see together
συνορᾶσθαι: seeing together
συχνός: many together, continuous
σχεδόν: nearly
σχῆμα: figure, form
σχολάζειν: to be at leisure
σῶμα: body, flesh
σῶμα φυσικόν: physical body
σώματι πρὸς σώματα: body-to-body
σωφροσύνη: prudence

ταὐτὸ καὶ ἕν: one and the same
ταὐτόν: the same
ταὐτὸν τοῦτο: this itself
ταχύ: swiftness
τέλειον: something complete
τελείωσις: fulfillment, perfection
τελειωτέρος: more perfect
τέλος: end
τέλος τεθέν: the posited end
τέμνειν: to cut, dissect
τέταρτον: fourth
τευκτικός: attainable
τεχνάζειν: to see in accord with know-how
τέχνη: know-how
τεχνικὸς λόγων: one proficient in speech
τεχνίτης: one possessing know-how
τεχνοπωλικόν: selling know-how
τί: this, this one
τιμιώτατα: the most honored things
τινα θεόν: something divine
τινέ: those two
τινές: those, those many
τοιοῦτος, -αύτη: so peculiar
τόπος: place
τρέφεσθαι: to be maintained, maintenance
τρέχει: runs
τρίγωνον: triangle
τρίτον: third
τύχη: the accidental

ὑγίεια: health
ὕλη: matter
ὑπακούειν: to hearken
ὑπάρχειν: to be there from the outset
ὑπάρχον: there from the outset so as to command
ὑπόθεσις: what is laid down underneath
ὑποκείμενον: what lies there underneath
ὑπολαμβάνειν: to grasp from the outset
ὑπόληψις: to deem
ὑπομένον: what remains there underneath
ὑπόμνησις: a reminding
ὑποτίθεσθαι: to lay underneath
ὕστερον: later
ὕστερον ἕτερον: later (it will be) different

φαίνεσθαι: to show itself
φαινομένη: apparent, semblant
φαινομένη μόνον: merely semblant

φαινόμενον: that which shows itself
φάναι: to speak
φάντασμα: immediate apparition
φάρμακον: charm, remedy
φάσις: affirmation
φθέγγεσθαι: to utter
φθογγή: a sound
φιλοσοφία: philosophy
φιλόσοφος, -οι: philosopher(s)
φορά: motion
φρόνησις: circumspection, conscience
φρόνιμος: the prudent one
φῦλον: lineage, strain
φύσει: by nature, by self-production
φύσει ὄντα: natural beings, ones that produce themselves
φυσικά: physical bodies
φυσικὰ ὄντα: physical beings
φυσική: physics
φυσικὸν σῶμα: physical body
φυσικός: physicist
φυσιολόγοι: philosophers of nature
φύσις: the self-emergent, nature
φύσις τις: presence in itself
φωνή: sound, vocalization
φωνήεντα: vowels
φωνηθέντα: utterances

χαλεπόν: difficult
χαλεπώτατα: the most difficult things
χάριν: for the sake of
χεῖρον: the worse
χειροτέχνης: laborer
χειροῦσθαι: to seize
χειρωσόμενος: will be taken in hand
χειρωτική: seizing
χειρωτικόν: seizure
χρῆμα: property
χρηματίζειν: to deal with, procure
χρήσεώς τινος ἕνεκεν: for the sake of some use
χρῆσις: use
χρόνος: time
χώρα: place
χωρίζειν: to separate
χωρίς: separate
χωρισμός: separation, extraction
χωριστὰ τῇ νοήσει: things extracted in thought

ψεύδεσθαι: distortion
ψευδής: deceptive, distortive
ψεῦδος: deception, falsity
ψόφος: noise
ψόφος σημαντικός: a noise that signifies
ψυχαγωγία: guiding the soul, persuasion
ψυχή: the soul
ψυχρόν: the cold

ὥς: thus
ὡς: as
ὡς εἷς: as one
ὥσπερ: just as
ὡς πολλοί: as many
ὡς τί: as what
ὠφέλιμον: advantageous